ISLAM AND THE ENGLISH ENLIGHTENMENT

THE UNTOLD STORY

ZULFIQAR ALI SHAH

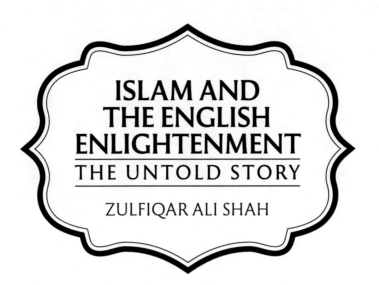

ISLAM AND
THE ENGLISH
ENLIGHTENMENT
THE UNTOLD STORY

ZULFIQAR ALI SHAH

CLARITAS
BOOKS

1 2 3 4 5 6 7 8 9 10

CLARITAS BOOKS

Bernard Street, Swansea, United Kingdom
Milpitas, California, United States

CLARITAS
BOOKS

© CLARITAS BOOKS 2022

First Published in May 2022

Typeset in Minion Pro 14/11

Islam and the English Enlightenment: The Untold Story
By Zulfiqar Ali Shah

Series Editor: Sharif H. Banna

A CIP catalogue record for this book is available from the British Library

ISBN: 978-1-80011-984-0

Dedicated to my teacher and mentor
Professor Anis Ahmad — with utmost
respect, appreciation and love

ZULFIQAR ALI SHAH received his B.A. and M.A. (Hons) in Comparative Religions from the International Islamic University in Islamabad, Pakistan and his Ph.D. in Theology and Religious Studies from the University of Wales, UK. He has taught at the International Islamic University in Islamabad, the University of Wales in the UK, the University of North Florida and Cardinal Stritch University in the US. He is former President of the Islamic Circle of North America and the Shariah Scholars Association of North America. Dr. Zulfiqar Shah is currently the Executive Director and Secretary General of the Fiqh Council of North America and Religious Director of the Islamic Society of Milwaukee, USA. He has authored many articles and books including *Anthropomorphic Depictions of God: The Concept of God in the Judaic, Christian and Islamic Traditions*, Islam's Reformation of Christianity and *St. Thomas Aquinas and Muslim Thought*. His forthcoming ground-breaking books include *Islam and the French Enlightenment* and *Islam and the Founding Fathers of America*.

Zulfiqar Ali Shah's *Islam and the English Enlightenment: The Untold Story* offers an important and hitherto underappreciated account of the impact of Islamic theology on the development of European and particularly English Enlightenment, tracing the path from the early Reformation through the development of Antitrinitarianism and the Enlightenment. This is a book that anyone interested in stepping outside a Eurocentric view of the rise of the West and of the modern age must read.

Michael A. Gillespie
Professor of Political Science and Philosophy
Duke University

Dr. Zulfiqar Ali Shah's *Islam and the English Enlightenment* is one of the most profoundly enlightening books I have read in years. Dr. Shah compellingly demonstrates that English Enlightenment thinkers were undeniably indebted to Islamic sciences and thought, and that the foundational principles of rationalist thought, scientific inquiry, and religious toleration were deeply anchored in the Islamic tradition. In my view, Dr. Shah's research soundly challenges the exclusionary and ahistorical idea of the West being a product of a Judeo-Christian tradition or civilization that exists in tension with the Islamic civilization. If the Western civilization is indebted to the Enlightenment then historians must come to terms with the fact that the Enlightenment is deeply indebted to the Islamic tradition. *Islam and the English Enlightenment* is a must read for every serious student of history, religion, or culture.

Khaled Abou El Fadl
Omar and Azmeralda Alfi Distinguished Professor of Law
UCLA School of Law

Students of European intellectual history are made to believe that the European renaissance has its roots in its liberation from church authority and rediscovering the Greek spirit of thought, the ideals of Liberal democracy, freedom of thought and critical thinking. The transformatory role of Muslim intellectual tradition in this process is confined to transfer of Greek thought through their Arabic translations. The scholarly work of Dr Zulfiqar, *Islam and the English Enlightenment: The Untold Story* is an evidence based exceptional and valuable contribution to the world of knowledge on the foundational role of the Muslim thought in the intellectual development of the so-called Western enlightenment

Anis Ahmad
Meritorious Professor and President/Vice Chancellor
Riphah International University, Islamabad

In this compelling and comprehensive study, Dr Zulfiqar Ali Shah responds with clarity and precision to those who continue to maintain that Islam is in need of some form of rational 'enlightenment.' Against such uninformed and Eurocentric accusations, Dr Shah convincingly demonstrates the central role that Islam – grounded in scientific enquiry, religious toleration and rationalist thought – played in shaping the values and ideas of the very Enlightenment reformers such as John Locke and Isaac Newton who helped to produce the modern world. While centrally focussed on examples from seventeenth- and eighteenth-century England, *Islam and the English Enlightenment* ranges widely, engaging global connections to Europe from the Renaissance that illustrate debts to the emergence and development of Islamic philosophy and science. This study provides an indispensible guide to how Islam and Muslim thinkers provided the principles and ways of thinking that challenged the superstitions of the medieval era and without which there would have been no Enlightenment.

Gerald MacLean
Emeritus Professor
University of Exeter

Although traditionally underexplored, the relation between Enlightenment and Islam is crucial to appreciating the complexity of the making of the modern world. With this book, Zulfiqar Ali Shah offers a significant contribution toward a better understanding of the role that Islamic religious, philosophical, scientific, legal, and political ideas played in the Age of Enlightenment. This impressively erudite book indeed shows that many important English thinkers of the seventeenth and eighteenth century, including religious enlighteners as well as radical Enlightenment philosophers, were deeply interested in Islamic concepts and, to a certain extent, were also influenced by Islamic views on scientific investigation, communal life, natural religion, and primitive Christianity. Thus, this book accomplishes a twofold purpose, as it sheds new light on the impact of Islamic intellectual traditions on Enlightenment culture and it provides a thought-provoking reassessment of Islam in itself, which Dr. Shah depicts as compatible with Enlightenment principles, values, and practices.

Diego Lucci
Professor of Philosophy and History
American University in Bulgaria

Contents

Foreword   19

Introduction   21

Weber's Eurocentrism   23

Critique of Eurocentrism   27

From Dark Ages to Medieval Renaissance   35

Islam and Latin Scholasticism   39

Italian Renaissance   44

Renaissance Art   47

Venice and Islamic World   50

Sixteenth-Century Protestant Reformation   53

Radical Reformation   61

CHAPTER 1 **Roman Christianity and Its Socio-Political Thought**   75

Augustinian and Cappadocian Models   78

The Divine Right Church and Salvation   81

The Divine Right State   82

Heresy and Divinely Sanctioned Terror   84

Augustine and Religious Coercion   86

CHAPTER 2 **Islam and the Southern Reformation of Christianity**   93

Islamic Anti-Trinitarianism and Its Natural, Republican Implications   95

Islam and Human Salvation   101

Unity of God and Unity of Creatures   105

Islam and Democracy   107

Islam and English Enlightenment   112

CHAPTER 3 **Seventeenth Century England, Overseas**
Trade and English Identity Formation 117

Anglican Church and State 121

Charles I and Archbishop Laud's Authoritarianism 123

Overseas Trade and Intellectual Transformation 126

Puritanism, Biblicism and Restorationism 131

Religious Roots of English Revolution 137

Economic Causes of English Revolution 140

Overseas Trade and English Revolution 144

Piracy and Barbary States 147

Capitulations and Muslim Soft Empire 149

The East India Company 152

Trade and Cultural Exchanges 157

Overseas Trading Companies and Domestic Politics 162

Travelogues and Acculturation Process 164

Islamic World and Scientific Revolution 168

Natural Philosophy and Natural Theology 180

Overseas Trade and Scientific Revolution 185

Arabic and Oriental Manuscripts 187

Overseas Trade and Royal Society 191

Royal Society, Westminster School and Oriental Languages 195

The Baconian John Beale and Islamophilia 197

Alchemy, Arabs and English Natural Philosophers 207

Spiritual Alchemy 210

Respublica Mosaica, Prisca Sapientia and Prisca Theologia 212

Near Eastern Knowledge and Biblical Hermeneutics 218

Overseas Trading Companies and Cross-cultural Diffusions 221

The Allure of Islamic World and English Identity Formation 224

Commonwealth Radicalism 229

Restoration of Monarchy and Dialectical Struggles 236

The Glorious Revolution, Anglican Monarchy and Church 241

Turkish Coffeehouses 245

Levant Trade and Coffee 246

The Centers of Dissent 249

Coffeehouses and Stuart Monarchy 255

CHAPTER 4 **Enlightenment: A Religious Revolution**   259

Enlightenment and Destruction of Old Regime   260

The Anthropomorphic Shift   264

Anti-Trinitarianism and Enlightenment   268

Anti-Trinitarianism and Islam   269

CHAPTER 5 **English Enlightenment and Unitarian Islamic Syncretism**   281

Muhammad, the Prophet of Enlightenment   285

Overseas Trade, Piracy and Turning Turk   287

CHAPTER 6 **Islam and the Early English Enlightenment**   299

Henry Stubbe and John Locke: The Pococke
and Shaftesbury Pedigrees   303

CHAPTER 7 **Henry Stubbe and Muhammadan Christianity**   307

Stubbe, the Father of Muhammadan Christianity   309

Muhammad, the Protestant Prophet   313

Muhammadan Christianity and Natural Law   320

Muhammad, the Machiavellian Prince   323

Stubbe and English Deism   323

Stubbe and English Civil Religion   325

CHAPTER 8 **John Toland and Muhammadan Christianity**   331

Toland and New Testament Criticism   335

Toland and Primitive Christianity   336

Toland and Gospel of Barnabas   337

Toland and Mahometan Christianity   341

CHAPTER 9 **John Locke: The Unitarian Heretic**   345

Locke and Travel Literature   347

Muslims in Locke's Horizons   350

Locke and Islamic Minimalism   354

Locke and Christ's Pre-existence: Some Discussions   358

Locke's Messianic Christology   366

Locke's Islamic Christology   373

Locke's Popular Sovereignty   380

Locke and Religious Tolerance   383

CHAPTER 10 **Socinianism: The Muslim Bridge** 389

 The Racovian Alcoran 390

 Miguel Servet: The Martyr of Liberty 393

 Servetus and the Quran 394

CHAPTER 11 **John Milton: The Pious Muslim?** 399

 Milton's Christology 400

 Milton's Scripturalism 404

 Milton and Middle Eastern Culture 406

CHAPTER 12 **Isaac Newton: The Enraged Anti-Trinitarian** 411

 Newton's Biblicism 412

 Newton and Primitive Christianity 414

 Newton and Early Christian Apologists 416

 Newton and Unitarian Theology 422

 Newton and Nicaean Christology 428

 Newton's Heterodoxy 435

CHAPTER 13 **English Unitarians: Pinnacle of Islamic Hybrid** 441

 Stephen Nye: The Roaring Unitarian 443

 Arthur Bury's Naked Gospel 446

 William Freke: The Mystic Unitarian 448

 Epistle Dedicatory: The Culmination of Unitarian Islamic Imagination 452

 Unitarian's Turkish Faith 459

 The English Abdulla Mahumed Omar and "Mahomet No Imposter" 464

 Historica Monotheistica and Islamic Republicanism 469

ENDNOTES 475

BILBIOGRAPHY 627

INDEX 671

Foreword

Robert F. Shedinger, Ph.D.
Luther College

Over the past twenty years I have had the great privilege to introduce scores of students to the Islamic tradition. The most meaningful assignment I give them is to research an area of medieval Islamic culture to present to the class. Some groups report on advancements made in mathematics by Muslim scholars like al-Khwarizmi. Others report on areas like biology and medicine, physics and engineering, art and architecture, astronomy and more. Students never fail to be amazed by the great cultural achievements of the medieval Islamic world, especially when they encounter achievements they thought (and were taught) resulted from the work of European Enlightenment thinkers like Leonardo da Vinci or Nicolaus Copernicus. Could Ibn Khaldun really have developed a theory of evolution centuries before Charles Darwin? Could Muslim astronomers really have calculated the circumference of a round earth before Columbus discovered that the earth was not flat? Could Muslim physicians really have been removing cataracts so many centuries before modern Western medicine?

Nothing impresses on my students the bias inherent in Western education more than this assignment. How is it possible, they want to know, that they never learned any of this before. They soon come to realize how important it has been for the West to deny its cultural roots in the Muslim world in order to maintain an image of Islam as a primitive force in the world. The primitive nature of Islam then becomes a mirror in which the West sees its own cultural superiority reflected back. With the ongoing rise of Islamophobia in the West, breaking down this stereotype has never been more important, and Dr. Zulfiqar Ali Shah with his new book *Islam and the English Enlightenment* makes a major contribution to doing just that.

Dr. Shah has produced perhaps the most comprehensive and deep analysis of the Islamic influence on the English Enlightenment ever produced. While Western scholarship presents figures like Isaac Newton and John Locke in cultural isolation, as if they developed their ideas in a complete cultural vacuum, Dr. Shah documents the deep and abiding influence of Islamic ideas on these and many other English Enlightenment figures. Far from being a primitive force, Dr. Shah demonstrates how Islamic ideas provided an important foundation for English Enlightenment thinkers as they broke away from the mysterious theology and authoritarian structure of medieval Christendom. If you think the English Enlightenment was a positive thing, then you just might have Muslims to thank!

Never before to my knowledge has the cross-fertilization of Western and Islamic ideas been so encyclopedically documented as it is here. In reading *Islam and the English Enlightenment*, you will never see the relationship between Islam and the West the same way again.

Introduction

Islam, Muslims and Islamic civilisation are under siege in the West. Subsequent to the tragic incidents of France and President Macron's misplaced reaction to it, Islam as a religion and community has witnessed some of the worst attacks upon its heritage and legacy. To President Macron, Islam is in crisis all over the globe and in dire need of enlightenment. The President is perhaps unaware of the historical fact that Islam played an important role in the French, English and American Enlightenments of the seventeenth and eighteenth centuries. It is the Muslim world, and not Islam as a faith, which needs enlightenment and revival.

Islam-bashing has become a lucrative profession; Islamophobes portray Islam as a barbaric faith that breeds nothing but violence, ignorance and superstitions. It is a set of irrational dogmas which promote theodicy, theocracy, barbarism, totalitarianism and terrorism. As such Islam is antithetical to rationalism, progress, modernity, liberty, freedom, democracy, enlightenment, republicanism and constitutionalism. Islamic civilisation is depicted as an alien culture with no or minimal contributions to human civilisation and progress, especially in the Western context. Islamophobes forget that sixteenth- and seventeenth-century Europe was marred with internal strife, religious wars, instability, insecurity, economic stagnation, irrationality, absolutism and persecutions. Europe's transition from its medieval absolutist *Old Regime* to enlightened republicanism passed through the Islamic world - its religion, wealth, sciences, institutions, ideas and practices. The Islamically inspired Unitarian, rational, theological, radical reformation of Michael Servetus, Socinians, Unitarians, Deists and seventeenth- and eighteenth-century overseas trade with the Muslim East (both Atlantic and Mediterranean) played a fundamental role in such a transition. The Whiggish Eurocentric historians tend to ignore these historical facts.

On the other hand, Western civilisation is presented as the superior mother of all civilisations, the true blessing to mankind. The West has achieved this climax on its own without any external non-Western help. Eric Wolf observes: "We have been taught, inside the classroom and outside of it, that there exists an entity called the West, and that one can think of this West as a society and civilisation independent of and in opposition to other societies and civilisations. Many of us even grew up believing that this West has a genealogy, according to which ancient Greece begat Rome, Rome begat Christian Europe, Christian Europe begat the Renaissance, the Renaissance the Enlightenment, the Enlightenment political democracy and the industrial revolution. Industry, crossed with democracy, in turn yielded the United States, embodying the rights to life, liberty, and the pursuit of happiness."[1] Colonial Europe and its institutions are directly linked to ancient Rome without any intermediaries or interlocutors. According to Anthony Pagden, "the theoretical roots of the modern European overseas empires reached back into the empires of the Ancient World. It was, above all, Rome which provided the ideologues of the colonial systems of Spain, Britain, and France with the language and political models they required."[2]

The superiority of Western civilisation, Judeo-Christian traditions and European manifest destiny are some of the underlying ethos of Euro-centrism and American specialism. It is argued that the West in general, and Europe in particular, is the cradle of democracy, modern science and civilisation while the East in general, and the Muslim world in particular, are the sources of ignorance, barbarism, paganism, irrationalism, economic stagnation, despotic feudalism and institutionalised patrimonial and parochial value system that impedes modernity in all its forms and expressions. Europe's so-called unique restless, rationalism,[3] liberal individualism, democratic value system, capitalism, moral ethos and manifest destiny are depicted as fundamental roots of the rise of Europe and regression of non-Europeans including the Muslims who lack the above-mentioned special traits and cannot keep up with the pace of European progress.[4] The process of modernisation and intellectualisation is unilateral and unilineal. It started with the Antiquity, moved through European Feudalism, crossed over to Enlightenment through medieval Renaissance humanism and resulted in Western Capitalism and Scientific/Industrial Revolution. Therefore modernity, science, mercantilism and capitalism all are the products of European rationalism, intellectualism and exceptionalism, and unique to Western mind and conditions; in fact, it is in European DNA. It is hereditary and an integral element of Europe's manifest destiny, imperialism and superiority.

Weber's Eurocentrism

The renowned sociologist Max Weber (1864-1920) specified "a number of fundamental socio-economic and religious factors which distinguished the European experience from that of the Muslim world, India and China, and which were of crucial importance to the emergence of modern capitalism."[5] He emphasised the Protestant, Calvinist, Puritan ideological foundations for North European capitalism, democracy and modernity. The critical point in Weber's argument was that seventeenth-century "dogmatic-predestinarian Calvinism confronted the believer with a crisis of proof on his prospects for salvation. Yet so deeply felt was the need for redemptive assurance by the doubt-stricken soul that the pastoral literature of Puritan divines responded to this cry by inserting good works in a mundane calling as a sign of grace. Private profit is hereby the recipient of Weber's 'psychological sanction' and is equated with eternal bliss, creating an 'ideal' stimulus for capitalist acquisition."[6] To Weber, capitalism was an unintended, indirect and psychological consequence of Calvinistic, Puritan ethos and not their theology. There was dogmatic uncertainty about salvation due to strict divine predestination, a crisis of proof which was met out not by Calvin or Calvinist theology but by English Calvinist pastoral literature such as that of Richard Baxter, which emphasised a psychological sanction for worldly calling, resulting in a capitalistic lifestyle. "This entrepreneur was filled with the conviction that Providence had shown him the road to profit not without particular intention. He walked it for the greater glory of God, whose blessing was unequivocally revealed in the multiplication of his profit and possessions. Above all, he could measure his worth not only before men but also before God by success in his occupation as long as it was realised by legal means."[7] This psychological premium for labour was a religious, transcendental cause for eternal perfection and felicity. It was not meant for worldy power or pomp, but for ethico-religious reasons, supplemented by other socio-economic factors. Weber emphasised the "separation of the productive enterprise from the household which, prior to the development of industrial capitalism, was much more advanced in the West than it ever became elsewhere."[8] He highlighted the "development of the Western city. In postmediaeval Europe, urban communities reached a high level of political autonomy, thus setting off 'bourgeois' society from agrarian feudalism. In the Eastern civilisations, however, partly because of the influence of kinship connections that cut across the urban-rural differentiation, cities remained more embedded in the local agrarian economy."[9] Weber pinpointed the "existence, in Europe, of an inherited tradition of Roman law, providing a more integrated and developed rationalisation of juridical practice than came into being elsewhere."[10] This tradition of rational Roman law was the main factor in "making possible the development of the nation-state, administered by full-time bureaucratic officials, beyond anything achieved in the Eastern civilisations. The rational-legal system of the Western state was in some degree adapted within business organisations themselves, as well as providing an overall framework for the co-ordination of the capitalist economy."[11] He also identified the "development of double-entry bookkeeping in Europe."[12] In Weber's view "this was a phenomenon of major importance in opening the way for the regularising of capitalistic enterprise."[13] The above sketched characteristics were "genetically the special peculiarity of Occidental rationalism."[14] They produced a unique tradition of European rationalism, which was genetically absent from all other non-European civilisations. This unique rationalism resulted in the superior European civilisation. This civilisational superiority was the manifest destiny of West, due to its unique humanitarian and geographical circumstances, and could not have been achieved anywhere other than Europe.

This unique sense of superiority was then roundly connected with Judeo-Christian traditions, with the exclusion of any possibility of Islamic, Hindu or Buddhist contributions to modernity or European civilisation. "For though the development of economic rationalism is partly dependent on rational technique and law, it is at the same time determined by the ability and disposition of men to adopt certain types of practical rational conduct. When these types have been obstructed by spiritual obstacles, the development of rational economic conduct has also met serious inner resistance. The magical and religious forces, and the ethical ideas of duty based upon them, have in the past always been among the most important formative influences on conduct."[15] In fact Weberian sociology excluded even the European Catholic Church from this unique rational tradition. "In this case we are dealing with the connection of the spirit of modern economic life with the rational ethics of ascetic Protestantism."[16] Weber pinpointed Protestantism as the main source of vibrant capitalism and specified the Puritans as the heralds of modern global capitalism. "Taken together, these represent a mixture of necessary and precipitating conditions which, in conjunction with the moral energy of the Puritans, brought about the rise of modern Western capitalism."[17] Democracy, science and modernity were the outcome of this Puritan, Calvinist and Protestant ethical lifestyle.

This narrow, idealist, teleological and moral interpretation of history and civilisation is too simplistic, dubious, sketchy, arbitrary, fictitious, fanciful and Whiggish. There was a time when Europe and Christendom including Protestant churches were marred with irrationalism, internal wars, religious intolerance, persecutions, trade restrictions, absolutism and superstitions. Christendom, from the Dark Ages to the premodern times, was a persecutory society while the Muslim world promoted relative religious freedom, republican ethos, free trade, limited monarchy and rational discourse. Muslim theology overly emphasised simple Unitarianism and good works as the foundation of eternal salvation and divine grace - Christianity was orthodoxy while Islam was more orthopraxy. The Prophet of Islam, Muhammad, was himself a merchant and sanctified trade, profit and wealth accumulation by lawful means. Richness, profit and wealth were not condemned the way Christianity, including Puritanism, Calvinism, Lutheranism and Protestantism as a whole, berated Mammonism over the centuries. Islam brought God and Mammon together within the moral confines, and moral worldly pursuits were sanctified as foundational spiritual acts. Man was not arbitrarily destined to Paradise or Hellfire based upon divine whims, but depending upon his good or bad actions in this worldly life. Christianity in all its forms, Catholics and Protestant included, insisted upon absolute predestination, selection and grace. The relative Catholic encouragement of good works was negated by insistence upon the atoning death of Christ, sacramental efficacy, confessions and indulgences. Both Luther and Calvin utterly demolished the need for good works, insisting upon absolute predestination, selection and grace; good works were useless, and divine grace through the atoning death was considered supreme. The Anglican Church's Calvinist theology was not much different from Calvin's diatribes against orthopraxy, and total dependence upon orthodoxy and right beliefs were highly emphasized by Anglican leaders. A long quote from M. H. Mackinnon is due here. Calvinist Synodal "doctrine is one of utter gloom and despair, complete with an omniscient and vengeful deity who has decreed for eternity the fortunate few for election, whereas the unfortunate majority has been doomed to perdition. Weber thus sees dogma in much the same way as Calvin, reporting that one's standing before God is made impossible by Calvin's system, of which Anglo-dogma is a complete reflection. Calvinism is unable to incorporate knowledge of assurance because of the complete transcendentality of its God and the inability to fathom His secret decrees. By Weber's account, unadulterated predestinarianism of this sort spurns the use of means (works): Man is the passive recipient of salvation. In Weber's mind the 'pure doctrine of predestined grace' was never entirely eliminated from Calvinism, inasmuch as acts of the individual could in no way influence God's election. By extension, the devout can never know their calling, which is 'both impossible to pierce and presumptuous to question'; personal salvation always; remains 'above the threshold of consciousness,' forever shrouded in 'divine mystery.' The elect are and remain God's invisible church."[18] Additionally, capitalism, science and modernity did not flourish in many areas where Calvinism was in the helms of affairs. Even the aesthetic Puritanism of Richard Baxter was far less insistent upon good deeds than Islam's positive reinforcement. Baxter's indirect, negative and foggy *The Aphorismes of Justification* (1649) was more directed towards free-spirited antinomians and their justification by grace alone reformed theology than positive insistence upon good works and profit accumulation. Baxter's emphasis upon human depravity, Christ's atoning death, grace-based salvation scheme and condemnation of Mammonisn was no less emphatic than the Calvinist Anglican Church. His emphasis upon good works was relative, and did not fully reject the essential principles of Anglican predestinarian theology and grace-based salvation. He promoted "a modified 'neonomian' version of Calvinism."[19] Weber confessed overall Christian (including Puritan) exhortations against usury, riches and wealth accumulation, but still concluded that modern capitalism somehow originated with Puritans.[20] He somehow ignored the fact that Catholics, Jews, Muslims and Hindus were into private profit and money-making as anybody else. Many took it as their religious calling and profession to make money and be generous, charitable and kind to those in need. "It is a grim twist of irony that Weber would choose such a spiritually worthless vehicle to realise his causal ambitions."[21]

Due to a multitude of theological and socio-economic reasons scholars such as Mackinnon, F. Rachfahl,[22] L. Brentano,[23] W. Sombart,[24] G. Simmel,[25] H. M. Robertson,[26] K. Samuelson,[27] A. Hyma,[28] R. H. Tawney,[29] Trevor-Roper,[30] H. Luthy[31] and many others have rejected Weberian Eurocentric, Puritan theories of modern capitalism, democracy, science and modernity.[32] Mackinnon, after a long discussion of various rebuttals of Weber's theory concluded that Weber's "thesis is ultimately wrong."[33] Samir Amin has amply demonstrated the absurdity of Weberian "Christianophilia of Eurocentrism."[34] He noted that the "arguments Weber advances, in this respect, are confused, despite their apparent precision."[35] But Weber's thesis has its own life and followers.

Following Weber's lead, many contemporary Eurocentric historians do not hesitate to put Europe and Christianity at the centre of global prosperity and influence.[36] For instance David Landes argues that "as the historical record shows, for the last thousand years, Europe (the West) has been the prime mover of development and modernity."[37] Trevor-Roper maintains that Christendom had "in itself the springs of a new and enormous vitality."[38] To a certain extent the same Eurocentrism and exceptionalism is reflected in the otherwise very objective works of Joseph Needham[39], M. Elvin[40] and F. Braudel.[41] They see European exceptionalism in the highly institutionalised forms of European democracy, freedom, capitalism and individualism. They also see a specifically European historical developmental scheme, from Renaissance to Reformation to Enlightenment to Scientific Revolution to modernity.

Critique of Eurocentrism

To Eric Wolf such "a developmental scheme is misleading. It is misleading, first, because it turns history into a moral success story, a race in time in which each runner of the race passes on the torch of liberty to the next relay. History is thus converted into a tale about the furtherance of virtue, about how the virtuous win out over the bad guys. Frequently, this turns into a story of how the winners prove that they are virtuous and good by winning. If history is the working out of a moral purpose in time, then those who lay claim to that purpose are by that fact the predilect agents of history."[42] He argues that "the world of humankind constitutes a manifold, a totality of interconnected processes, and inquiries that disassemble this totality into bits and then fail to reassemble it falsify reality. Concepts like 'nation,' 'society,' and 'culture' name bits and threaten to turn names into things. Only by understanding these names as bundles of relationships, and by placing them back into the field from which they were abstracted, can we hope to avoid misleading inferences and increase our share of understanding."[43] Daron Acemoglu, Simon Johnson and James Robinson, Saumitra Jha[44] and many other contemporary historians, economists and political scientists reject Weberian Eurocentric postulates and emphasise the significance of overseas trade and its impact on religio-political, socio-economic and scientific institutions of Europe in general and England in particular. For instance, Daron Acemoglu, Simon Johnson and James Robinson state: "The evidence presented [...] has established a significant relationship between the potential for Atlantic trade and post-1500 economic development, and suggests that the opportunities to trade via the Atlantic, and the associated profits from colonialism and slavery, played an important role in the rise of Europe. This evidence weighs against theories linking the rise of Western Europe to the continuation of pre-1500 trends driven by certain distinctive characteristics of European nations or cultures, such as Roman heritage or religion."[45] The overseas trade transformed English economy, society, politics and religion. Initially it contributed to deformation of the *Old Regime's* absolutist religio-political theology by questioning its scholastic, supernatural and authoritarian underpinnings and instead emphasizing the rational, natural, utilitarian, pragmatic, sort of republican reformation in conformity with simple and minimalistic message of Jesus and his early disciples. The overall Puritan frustration with the existing institutions and millenarian eschatology rooted in the books of *Daniel* and *Revelation* was initially fueled by the ruins, destructions and social dislocations of the Thirty Years' War and later on aggravated by the English Civil War. The unprecedented devastation was taken as a Biblical prediction that the golden age of Saints would be preceded by terrible destruction.

Charles I and Archbishop Laud's persecuting religious and restrictive trade policies were used to portray them as agents of anti-Christ, overseas trade with its voyages, discoveries, explorations and profits reflected Daniel 12:4's promises of golden age of social justice and scientific progress, "many shall run to and fro, and knowledge shall be increased", Puritan theocentrism, mercantilism, utilitarianism, pragmatism, work ethics and humanitarianism were all elemental to the Puritan and overseas traders' Holy War against the anti-Christ monarchical powers of Charles I and ecclesiastical debacles of Archbishop Laud. This utopian, idealistic and chiliastic Puritanism coupled with virtues of mutual help, justification by works and terrestrial gains as the bases of celestial prosperity translated into overseas explorations, discoveries and profits and played a fundamental role in the English Civil War and the subsequent Revolution, Restoration and Glorious Revolution giving urgency to socio economic, religio political and epistemic reforms. In the long process, the overall Puritan sense of disgrace at home and chiliastic zeal coupled with overseas trade reformed English religio-political theology on broader radical, natural, utilitarian, rational, republican, Unitarian, Deistic lines. The Trinitarian religio-political theology was absolutist, divine right, hierarchical and persecutory, and overseas trade helped in fomenting an alternative worldview and a new middle class of merchants which resisted the hierarchical, absolutist Church and monarchy, gradually transforming it into a limited monarchy and stifled episcopacy. Later democracy, religious tolerance, Scientific Revolution and modernity were all products of this multifaceted, multipronged seventeenth century dialectical struggles against the *Old Regime*. The English trade with the Muslim world, the global Muslim bridge to other civilations and alternative worldview was just one, but instrumental, factor in this transformation of the *Old Regime*. The frustrations, aspirations and urgencies were homegrown but some of the intellectual solutions and thought patterns were stimulated and influenced by outside ideas, appropriations and assimilations. This is the nature of dialectical struggles and Europe was no exception.

Civilisations do not crop up in vacuums;[46] they build upon other's achievements, though very often the credit is not given to the rightful contributors. This is exactly the case with Muslim contributions to the Western civilisation. For long medieval centuries Islam remained a dominant culture while Europe was experiencing regression. Muslims greatly borrowed from other civilisations such as the Greeks, Persians, Indians and Chinese but then in turn created a dynamic synthesis of philosophical thought, cultures and sciences. Europe during the medieval centuries was surrounded by mighty Muslim empires and prone to appropriate itself to their theological-philosophical thought, cultures and policies. The dominant European narrative tends to downplay and mostly obliterate any sense of Islamic contributions to the European civilisation; Europe is always portrayed as the lender while the Islamic East is always the borrower. Such a narrative was consciously constructed in post-medieval centuries and reflected the old European insecurities. Jack Goody observes that "the tendency to reject the eastern connection goes back to more general problems of 'roots' and of ethnocentrism, aggravated by the expansion of Islam from the seventh century and the defeats involved in the Crusades and the Christian loss of Byzantium. At that time the opposition between Europe and Asia took the form of one between Christian Europe and Islamic Asia which inherited the earlier stereotypes of 'democratic' and 'despotic' respectively. Islam was conceived as a threat to Europe, not only militarily, which it became early on in the Mediterranean, but also morally and ethically; Muhammad is consigned by Dante to the eighth circle of the Inferno. At the broadest level, ethnocentrism divides all of us from the others and so helps to define our identity. But it is a bad guide to history, especially to world history."[47] This is nothing short of theft of history. The same theft was committed by the Whiggish eighteenth- and nineteenth-century European historians[48] when they intentionally ignored Eastern contributions in the making of modern Europe. They portrayed the past in light of the progressive present[49] while they should have attempted to understand the past in terms of the past.[50] The theft of history "refers to the take-over of history by the west. That is, the past is conceptualised and presented according to what happened on the provincial scale of Europe, often western Europe, and then imposed upon the rest of the world. That continent makes many claims to having invented a range of value-laden institutions such as 'democracy', mercantile 'capitalism', freedom, individualism. However, these institutions are found over a much more widespread range of human societies."[51]

This imperial usurpation of history has serious consequences for inter-civilisational relationships.[52] The unique sense of Europe's call-

ing is one of the main sources of old and modern colonial mentality, hegemonic agendas and discrimination in the modern world. The
resultant resentment and radical blowback are equally disturbing.
Non-Europeans, especially Muslims, feel that their history has been
hijacked by some of the European historians, as their lands and resources were - and currently are - colonised by European masters. This
sense of intellectual and physical imperialism breeds hatred, and has
dire consequences for the future relations. "Europe has not simply neglected or underplayed the history of the rest of the world, as a consequence of which it has misinterpreted its own history, but also how it
has imposed historical concepts and periods that have aggravated our
understanding of Asia in a way that is significant for the future as well
as for the past."[53] China's current assertive foreign policy, grievances
and rhetoric well illustrate the situation.

Like Asia, negative sentiments towards Muslims are overwhelming due to the distortion of Islamic history and usurpation of Muslim
resources and lands. Euro-centrist Islamophobes and neo-cons forget
that Islam was a power to be reckoned with from 634 to 1800 AD, and
at the pinnacle of human civilisation and global economy for almost
1000 years from the eighth to the eighteenth century, having its own
systems of limited monarchy, republicanism, constitutionalism, capitalism, humanism, freedom of conscience and religion, tolerance for
dissent whether temporal or religious, well-developed and crafted socio-economic, politico-religious and scientifico-cultural institutions.

From the medieval to early modern ages Christendom was marred
with internal strife and civilisational backwardness while passing
through long centuries of the so-called Dark Ages. It clearly lacked
a rational discourse too deeply delving itself into irrational, superstitious and theoretical Church dogmas and divine right monarchical
fists. It obviously practiced collectivism at the expense of individualism and in reality, discouraged and punished individual liberty in
so many ways and forms. There was no sign of democracy or even
limited monarchy in medieval Europe, as the divine right absolute
monarchy was the norm, all the way to the eighteenth century. Catholic and Protestant blocks practiced absolutism and suffered from same
civilisational and economic stagnation. The dogmatic, authoritarian,
supernatural, superstitious, traditionalist, persecutory and interventionist Church controlled all avenues of knowledge making and al-

lowed no rival, competing, alternative epistemologies, ideologies, theories and knowledge mechanisms.

The medieval ecclesiasts purged Christian world of the so-called pagan Greco-Roman sciences, philosophies and ideas. Since Justinian times Aristotle and Plato became the pagan enemies; their philosophical thought was considered antithetical to divine revelation and morality. Only those aspects of their philosophy were incorporated which supported the Trinitarian, supernatural, hierarchical theology. Theology was the queen of all sciences, and all philosophy and natural science was subordinated to theology.[54] The Church leaders centered their life, culture and sciences upon their specific understandings of Biblical teachings and cosmology, shielding themselves from every possible foreign or non-Christian influence. The Greek philosophical, rational and scientific treatises were publicly burned, and the dissenting Arians and Nestorians were excommunicated and exiled into the Near East. That resulted in a philosophical, intellectual and scientific conundrum paralyzing civilisational growth in the Christendom. The Europe's Dark Ages were the outcome of such an intellectual stagnation. Christendom was not heir to Greco Roman rational, philosophical and utilitarian heritage but mostly to its paganistic, supernatural and mysterious theology.

The traditional, authority based medieval Church Christianity mostly barred Europe from independent scientific discoveries, philosophical and intellectual rationalism, universal humanism, political, social and economic liberalism. Its supernatural Trinitarian religious and political theology long preserved an awe-inspiring absolutist religious and political system, which curtailed individual freedoms, liberty and agency. Peace, security, dignity and the lives of many Christians were violated in the name of the Prince of peace. Individual and collective dissent were harshly punished, total obedience was required and uniformity was imposed by civic and ecclesiastical means. The Trinitarian hierarchical theology was equally imposed upon nature, natural philosophy and sciences. The medieval hierarchies in Church and state were reflections of Trinitarian hierarchy in the heavens.[55] The seven heavens were hierarchical, and the natural phenomenon was governed by hierarchical angelic beings as the Bible stated. Heavens were higher and superior than the earth while the highest heavens were superior to lower heavens. This concept of hierarchy was "rooted in the idea that the world was peopled by a graded chain of beings, stretching down from the Deity in the Empyrean heaven at the periphery of the universe, through the hierarchies of angelic beings inhabiting the nine heavenly spheres concentric with the earth, to the ranks of men, animals, and plants, of the base terrestrial sphere at the centre of the cosmic system."[56] A given creature enjoyed hierarchical dominion over the lower creatures while it served those above it in the scale of beings.[57]

In spite of all claims against it, God was Triune, and the Holy Trinity was hierarchical. God the Father had begotten God the Son and God the Holy Spirit proceeded from God the Father and God the Son.[58] God the Father neither proceeded from the Son or Holy Spirit nor was begotten by them. There was a time when the Son was begotten of the Father. The Son's eternity was relative to the eternity of the Father. Also, God the Father did not create the material world directly but through His Word, Jesus Christ who was Lord over everything. The Holy Trinity was supreme and at the head of the heavenly pyramid. The Earth reflected the heavenly hierarchy and the Church, the earthly representative of Jesus Christ, was Lord over earthly pyramid. Lower beings were subordinated to higher realms; submission to monarchs, civil magistrates and clergy was integral to the Trinitarian theological model. The social order of Christendom was hierarchical.

St. Thomas Aquinas synthesised Aristotle's principles inherent in nature as divine powers, installed by God to cooperate and assist him in the works of providence. "God *cooperated* with natural powers in a way that respected their integrity while accomplishing his purposes."[59] The concerns that such cooperation with natural phenomena and man would make God dependent upon them, and jeopardise his absolute sovereignty, were mitigated by the interpretation that nature and man were under God and served divine purposes. God participated in nature intrinsically through participating beings and not extrinsically as Supreme Lawgiver impressing natural laws on matter.[60] The nature was sacramentally expressing higher being of God as man was expressing God's providence through obedience to Church sacrements.[61] Nature and man were immanently divine sharing in the incarnation of Christ, the man God. S. F. Mason well summarised the medieval Trinitarian hierarchical world view. "Such a scheme was a particular manifestation of the general medieval view that the hierarchy of natural things was ordered triadically at every level - classes, orders, genera, species, and individuals within those species. All of the beings of the universe fell into one or other of three general classes - those that were wholly material, such as minerals, plants, and animals, those that were wholly spiritual, such as the angelic beings, and those that were mixed, namely human beings. Each group and sub-group divided triadically. Thus there were animals of the land, the sea, and the air, men of labour, men of prayer, and men of war, according to early medieval versions, or labourers, burghers, and nobles, with a separate ecclesiastical triadic hierarchy, according to late medieval versions, whilst above mankind were three triadic orders of angelic beings, and at the head of the scale of all beings in the universe was the supreme Trinity."[62]

Unitarian ideology, whether religio-political or scientific, was severely punished. The divinity, nature, cosmos, social order, human body and Church were all hierarchical. Even the human body was Triadic and Trinitarian, with natural, vital and animal spirits in it. It had three physiological fluids (two kinds of bloods and a nervous fluid); Liver was the source of dark red blood, heart of whitish red blood and brain the seat of nervous fluid.[63] Any discussions of divine simplicity, human equality, natural or body unity were banned and persecuted. Medieval Christendom was a persecutory society, persecuting Unitarianism in matters of social order, natural cosmos and human body. Independent scientific research, republican political ideology and Unitarian theology were taboos.

The long medieval centuries witnessed the absolute iron fists of the Church and monarchical abusive powers in matters of religion, politics, society and science. The Catholic Church, the only religious power during these long centuries, became the largest land owner, employer and power house of the European continent. Popes and bishops' power struggles within the Church (as well as outside the Church with local princes), their moral decadence and worldly pomp made many believers distrustful of both the spiritual and temporal authorities. Christendom was marred with internal strife, mistrust, scepticism and lack of direction. The Italians, Germans and French vied for papal offices and promoted their monarchical and national interests through spiritual means. Papacy moved between Rome and France and represented the interests and designs of its French, Norman or German sponsors.[64] The eleventh-century Crusades were used to bring about a European unity by pitching them against the Muslim East.[65]

Meanwhile, the Muslim Baghdad and Cordoba[66] were bustling with street lights, religious tolerance, rational inquiry and scientific pursuits while Geneva, Paris and London were sunk in darkness, religious persecutions, magic, witchcraft and irrational mysteries.[67] The Islamic simple, Unitarian theology, cosmology, anthropology and republican ethos emphasised upon God's simplicity, transcendence, incorporeality, direct sovereignty over everything as the First Cause, creator, nourisher and lawgiver, universal human dignity, equality and rights based on human soul, human dignity, rational discourse, natural inquiries, economic prosperity, competition and profit, social justice and human accountability. Medieval Christendom was exposed to some of these diverging traits due to its close proximity, warfare and interactions with Muslims. The thirteenth-century Muslim Spain and Sicily served as Europe's global bridge to science, technology and trade,[68] "at the turn of the second millennium. The reader might be surprised to learn that the only region in sustained direct contact with all the others at this time was the Islamic World, then undergoing its "Golden Age" under the Abbasid, Fatimid, and Umayyad caliphates based in Baghdad, Cairo, and Cordoba, while the one with the least contact with the others was Western Europe."[69] Europe was able to break away from its persecutions and intellectual stagnation, with the help of external resource portfolios and tributaries. The global Muslim bridge to other civilisations was a key element in this historical breakthrough.

From Dark Ages to Medieval Renaissance

The transition from Dark Ages to Medieval Renaissance began in the twelfth century, partly due to the translation of countless philosophical and scientific Arabic manuscripts to Latin. Charles Homer Haskins, the Harvard historian of the Middle Ages, and advisor to U.S. President Woodrow Wilson, noted that in Europe "a library of ca. 1100 would have little beyond the Bible and the Latin Fathers, with their Carolingian commentators, the service books of the church and various lives of saints, the textbooks of Boethius and some others, bits of local history, and perhaps certain of the Latin classics, too often covered with dust."[70] But the twelfth century witnessed a Latin campaign to translate books of "philosophy, mathematics, and astronomy unknown to the earlier mediaeval tradition and recovered from the Greeks and Arabs in the course of the twelfth century" ushering in the "Twelfth Century Renaissance".[71] Haskins stated that the "Renaissance of the twelfth century, like its Italian successor three hundred years later, drew its life from two principal sources. Each was based in part upon the knowledge and ideas already present in the Latin West, in part upon an influx of new learning and literature from the East. But whereas the Renaissance of the fifteenth century was concerned primarily with literature, that of the twelfth century was concerned even more with philosophy and science. And while in the Quattrocento the foreign source was wholly Greek, in the twelfth century it was also Arabic, derived from Spain and Sicily and Syria and Africa as well as from Constantinople."[72]

Early Muslims were heir to Greek scientific and philosophical traditions, long lost in the Western world. They also absorbed the Egyptian, Persian, Chinese and Indian traditions of knowledge and created an Islamic synthesis in conformity with the fundamental principles of their faith. Steven P. Marrone stated that "taken in its entirety, the evolution of speculative thought in the Muslim world marked a considerable enrichment of the philosophical heritage of late Antiquity. And Arabic achievements in mathematics and natural philosophy, especially astronomy, laid the foundations for later medieval science in the West and ultimately set the stage for the Scientific Revolution of the seventeenth century."[73] E. J. Holymard observed that "During the twelfth and thirteenth centuries there was a scientific renaissance in Europe, and scholars from Christian countries journeyed to Muslim universities in Spain, Egypt, Syria and even Morocco in order to acquire knowledge from their foes in religion but friends in learning. Arabic science soon began to filter through, and by the middle of the thirteenth century the trickle had become a river."[74] England's 'first scientist', Adelard of Bath, explained what he had learned from his Arab masters in these words: "From the Arab masters I have learned one thing, led by reason, while you are caught by the image of authority, and led by another halter. For what is an authority to be called, but a halter? As the brute beasts, indeed, are led anywhere by the halter, and have no idea by what they are led or why, but only follow the rope that holds them, so the authority of writers leads not a few of you into danger, tied and bound by brutish credulity."[75] Haskins observed that the Muslims "with no native philosophy and science of their own, but with a marvellous power of assimilating the culture of others, quickly absorbed whatever they found in Western Asia, while in course of time they added much from their own observation and from the peoples farther to the East. Arabic translations were made directly from the Greek, as in the case of Ptolemy's Almagest (A.D. 827), as well as from Syriac and Hebrew. Certain of the caliphs especially favoured learning, while the universal diffusion of the Arabic language made communication easy and spread a common culture throughout Islam, regardless of political divisions. The most vigourous scientific and philosophical activity of the early Middle Ages lay in the lands of the Prophet, whether in the fields of medicine and mathematics or in those of astronomy, astrology, and alchemy. To their Greek inheritance the Arabs added something of their own: observation of disease sufficiently accurate to permit of identification; large advances in arithmetic, algebra, and trigonometry, where we must also take account of Hindu contributions; and the standard astronomical tables of the Middle Ages. The reception of this science in Western Europe marks a turning-point in the history of European intelligence. Until the twelfth century the intellectual contacts between Christian Europe and the Arab world were few and unimportant."[76]

Muslim Spain played a major role in this transmission process.[77] "Spain's part was to serve as the chief link with the learning of the Mohammedan world; the very names of the translators who worked there illustrate the European character of the new search for learning: John of Seville, Hugh of Santalla, Plato of Tivoli, Gerard of Cremona, Hermann of Carinthia, Rudolf of Bruges, Robert of Chester, and the rest. Christian Spain was merely a transmitter to the North."[78] Haskins further observed that "when, in the twelfth century, the Latin world began to absorb this Oriental lore, the pioneers of the new learning turned chiefly to Spain, where one after another sought the key to knowledge in the mathematics and astronomy, the astrology and medicine and philosophy which were there stored up; and throughout the twelfth and thirteenth centuries Spain remained the land of mystery, of the unknown yet knowable, for inquiring minds beyond the Pyrenees.[79]

The European pursuit of the Arabic and Islamic knowledge continued for the next few centuries, culminating in an insatiable philosophical and scientific curiosity in France, Italy and many other areas of Northern Europe.[80] Haskins notes that "this Spanish tide flowed over the Pyrenees into Southern France, to centres like Narbonne, Beziers, Toulouse, Montpellier, and Marseilles, where the new astronomy appears as early as 1139 and traces can also be found of the astrology, philosophy, and medicine of the Arabs on into the fourteenth century."[81]

In Italy, the cultural and philosophical revival first started in the South. Sicily had been under Muslim rule from 902 to 1091.[82] Additionally, Italian City States such as Amalfi, Venice, Milan, Genoa and Florence were in constant close relations with the Muslim Spain, Sicily, North Africa, Syria and Egypt. Their lucrative international trade with the Middle East was on going long before the Crusades, and flourished during the two centuries of Crusader's presence in the Holy Land and continued afterwards. The Italian merchants transmitted a host of skills, sciences, arts and values to the Italian Peninsula. For instance, "Leonard of Pisa, son of a Pisan customs official in North Africa, acquired there a familiarity with Arabic mathematics which made him the leading European mathematician of the thirteenth century."[83]

The Sicilian contributions to the translation and transmission movement were far greater than any other Italian state. The process was not impeded by the Norman conquest of Sicily; it was the other way around, as it greatly enhanced and facilitated the transmission process. Huskins states that there was "one Italian land which took more direct part in the movement, namely Sicily. Midway between Europe and Africa, Sicily had been under Arab rule from 902 to 1091, and under the Normans who followed it retained a large Mohammedan element in its population. Moreover, it had many commercial relations with Mohammedan countries, while King Roger conducted campaigns in Northern Africa and Frederick II made an expedition to Palestine. Arabian physicians and astrologers were employed at the Sicilian court, and one of the great works of Arabic learning, the Geography of Edrisi, was composed at King Roger's command. A contemporary scholar, Eugene the Emir, translated the Optics of Ptolemy, while under Frederick II Michael Scot and Theodore of Antioch made versions of Arabic works on zoology for the Emperor's use. Frederick also maintained a correspondence on scientific topics with many sovereigns and scholars of Mohammedan lands, and the work of translation went on under his son and successor Manfred, while we should probably refer to this Sicilian centre some of the versions by unknown authors."[84]

Western Europe learned, understood and digested many Greco-Roman sciences through the Muslim medium. It does not make sense that Europe, which for centuries had no or minimal contact with Greco-Roman sciences and philosophy, suddenly woke up to understand, digest, master and apply these sophisticated philosophical concept and scientific precincts. The Europeans needed a continuous philosophical and scientific tradition with relevant contemporary vocabulary, concepts, explanations and understandings to make sense of an old philosophical legacy and scientific heritage. This legacy was well-preserved, explained, adapted and synthesised by the Muslim culture and tradition, as George Saliba very well demonstrated.[85] Latin Europe received a well-preserved and cooked scientific tradition from the East, initially absorbing it as it was and then expanding upon it with the passage of time. The assimilation and expansion process left its indelible imprint upon the ultimate outcome. Haskins noted that the "indebtedness of the Western world to the Arabs is well illustrated in the scientific and commercial terms which its various languages have borrowed untranslated from the Arabic. Words like algebra, zero, cipher tell their own tale, as do 'Arabic' numerals and the word algorism which long distinguished their use as taught by al-Khwarizmi. In astronomy the same process is exemplified in almanac, zenith, nadir, and azimuth. From the Arabic we get alchemy, and perhaps chemistry, as well as alcohol, alkali, elixir, alembic, not to mention pharmaceutical terms like syrup and gum arabic. In the field of trade and navigation we have hazar and tariff, admiral and arsenal, and products of Mohammedan lands such as sugar and cotton, the muslin of Mosul and the damask of Damascus, the leather of Cordova and Morocco. Such fossils of our vocabulary reveal whole chapters of human intercourse in the Mediterranean. If Arabic learning reached Latin Christendom at many points, direct translation from the Greek was in the twelfth century almost wholly confined to Italy, where the most important meeting-point of Greek and Latin culture was the Norman kingdom of Southern Italy and Sicily."[86]

Islam and Latin Scholasticism

Islam was also a vital part of Latin Scholasticism, Italian Humanism and Renaissance,[87] the three intellectual medieval movements which were the tributaries of the sixteenth century Reformation. The scholastics were original schoolmen who themselves engaged with dialectics to systematised Christian theology with the help of philosophy. Additional studies such as logic, grammar and rhetoric equipped them with extra skills. That is why scholastics mostly filled important theological positions at the universities. That is also the reason that unlike humanism scholasticism was mostly popular at the universities.[88]

Kraye observed that the "centres of scholasticism were the universities, where philosophy teaching was based on the Aristotelian corpus, in particular the works of logic and natural philosophy."[89] George Makdisi argued that the scholastic method had already been used in the Islamic East, a century or so previously.[90] The Muslim orthodoxy used this scholastic method to establish their authenticity, vitality and relevance. Islam had its scholastic renaissance in the eighth and ninth centuries. The Muslim influenced Jewish interlocutors, philosophers, theologians and intelligentsia such as Moses Maimonides played an important role in transmitting the Muslim philosophical and scholastic culture to the Latin Christendom.

St. Thomas Aquinas, the most known medieval philosopher-theologian and the stalwart of scholasticism, was greatly influenced by Muslim synthetic thought.[91] He widely quoted from Muslim philosophers and theologians such as Ibn Rushd, Ibn Sina, al-Farabi, al-Ghazali and acted and reacted to them in a number of ways.[92] In the estimation of E. Renan "St. Thomas owes practically everything to Averroes."[93] E. Gilson, Majid Fakhry and Edward Booth totally agreed. A. M. Giochon, David Burrell, John Wippel, Jon McGinnis held that Aquinas and his teacher Albert the Great were highly indebted to Ibn Sina. A. M. Giochon noted that "There is not one thesis on one of our medieval philosophers which does not examine his relations with Avicennan philosophy. And the deeper these examinations go, the more clearly one sees that Avicenna was not only a source from which they all drew librerally, but one of the principal formative influences on their thought."[94] Robert Hammond maintained that Thomas's metaphysics were totally Farabian. Herbert Davidson, Alfred Guillaume, Frank Griffel and others showed close affinities between St. Thomas, al-Ghazali, al-Razi and al-Shahrastani. St. Thomas was clearly indebted to Muslim thought; he read Latin translations of their works and incorporated many of their ideas, thoughts and arguments into his synthetic projects. He was a professional theologian who used philosophy to support his theology assimilating many philosophical ideas in the process of reconciling theology with philosophy. Muslim philosophers and theologians had undertaken the same project centuries before St. Thomas; consequently, he found a model in them to emulate and benefit from. He mostly preferred Aristotelianism against the Platonism of St. Augustine and other Church Fathers and ventured to reconcile Christian theology with it.[95]

He initially studied Aristotle's philosophy at the University of Naples which was part of Norman Sicily. Sicily was ruled by Muslims for close to three centuries (831-1072) and countless Muslims stayed behind even after the Norman conquest of it. The Norman rulers especially Frederick II had patronised Muslim sciences and encouraged translation of scientific works from Arabic to Latin. Transmission of Aristotelian philosophy constituted a major bulk of these inter-cultural endeavours. Muslim philosophers such as Abu Nasr al-Farabi, Abu Ali Sina and Abu al-Walid Ibn Rushd had long studied Aristotle and extensively commented on his philosophy. The Muslim Aristotelian tradition was well established before the times of St. Thomas, and the twelfth century witnessed the peak of translation and transmission of this tradition from Arabic to Latin as seen above. St. Thomas was very close to the epicenter of this movement as Southern Italy in general and Naples in particular was exposed to the Muslim philosophical ideas. The Muslim philosophy and scholasticism trickled to the Christendom from thirteenth century onward through interactions of giants like Aquinas.

Islam also experienced its phase of humanism long before the Latin West.[96] Human dignity, equality, freedom of will and choice, salvation through moral actions, freedom of expression and dissent, government through selective consent, limited monarchy, rhetoric and eloquence were all important parts of Islamic civilisation. Islam was not another worldly religion; it allowed enough room for material pursuits and accumulation of wealth. There were no restrictions on public displays of wealth, as long as wealth was shared with less fortunate members of the society through obligatory alms-giving. Trade was considered a prophetic profession; Prophet Muhammad was the model businessman who engaged in local, national and international trade. Cultural expressions of individuality, prosperity and power were not prohibited as long as they did not encroach upon others' dignity by exhibiting arrogance. Additionally, there were no ecclesiastical establishments, clerical impositions, papal political ambitions and corruptions, irrational mysteries, medieval filters to original scriptures, multiple layers of Church traditions, decrees, councils and sacraments. There was not much of a gap between the classical sciences (including the Arabic language) and contemporary Islamic discourse. There was no absolute divine right monarchy having the right to make or break laws; Islamic Shari'ah was to be followed by the clergy and laity, the elites and commoners. Knowledge and wisdom were thought to be the lost commodities of all believers; Muslims were encouraged to seek knowledge, even if they had to travel to far distant areas such as China - and indeed, they did. Muslims were trading with China and Western Europe by the middle of ninth century. There were cross-cultural transmissions of sciences and technologies from an early period of Islamic caliphate. Indian, Persian, Chinese and Greek sciences were all sought after. Muslims had already assimilated the so-called pagan Greek sciences and philosophy into their religious narrative Islamising them wherever needed. Jack Goody observed that "Islam itself experienced humanistic phases in the Magreb during which non-theological studies were developed, and scientific and secular knowledge was allowed a freer hand. After all Islam was a culture that sometimes reluctantly, sometimes enthusiastically, transmitted 'pagan' Greek ideas as well as Islamic ones, by means of schools of higher education, madrasas and academies."[97]

Islam as a dominant medieval culture, with its developed scholastic and humanist approaches, was the model emulated by the Latin West. George Makdisi in his *The Rise of Humanism in Classical Islam and the Christian West: With Special Reference to Scholasticism* has amply demonstrated that the medieval scholastic tradition, Italian Humanism and Renaissance had vital Islamic origins. Makdisi, after an exhaustive study of the Italian Humanism, stated that "I have come to the conclusion that classical Islam appears to have provided the model for Italian Renaissance humanism."[98] Jack Goody noted that in "Europe the process of liberation had its tentative roots in the humanist activity of the twelfth to fifteenth centuries, much influenced by Islam."[99] Michael G. Carter noted that although "at first sight the terms humanism and Islam might seem incompatible, there is good evidence that they are not. The highly developed urbanism of Islam, its elaborate bureaucracy, wealthy courts and associated patronage, and a universal respect for learning all combined to provide a fertile environment for the emergence of a kind of humanism analogous to that which arose in the West. The supreme importance of Arabic on the religious, cultural, administrative, and commercial levels made it inevitable that whatever kind of humanism appeared, it would have to give a special place to language."[100] Carter then identified the five distinct kinds of Islamic classical humanism namely the philosophical, religious, intellectual, legal and literary.[101]

In addition to demonstrating the historical fact that the medieval scholasticism and humanism had its origins in the Classical Islam, Makdisi showed that a major part of the Western intellectual culture owed its origins to Arabo-Islamic contributions, including the medieval universities and centers of learning. The Latin West borrowed many of its educational institutions from the Muslim Spain and Sicily. This fact is well presented in his book *The Rise of Colleges*.[102] Jack Goody argued that nobody should "neglect the fact that the rise of the universities was accompanied by a revival of learning between 1100 and 1200 when an influx of knowledge arrived from what had been Muslim Sicily (until 1091) but mainly through Arab Spain. Moreover, although the universities were said to be different from the madrasas which had been established throughout the Muslim world in the tenth and eleventh centuries, there were significant parallels between the system of education in Islam and that of the Christian West."[103] He further noted that "the college 'as an eleemosynary, charitable foundation was quite definitely native to Islam', based on the Islamic waqf. Paris was the first western city where a college was established in 1138 by a pilgrim returning from Jerusalem; it was founded, probably copying a madrasa, as a house of scholars, created by an individual without a royal charter. So too was Balliol in Oxford before it became a corporation."[104] Goody maintained that "Clearly Islam did have important institutions of higher learning for religious and legal education from an early period. Whether or not these stimulated Western Europe is a moot question but there were clear parallels as there were in other advanced written cultures. But perhaps more importantly, in Islam these institutions were more or less exclusively devoted to religious studies, whereas in Europe, although religion initially dominated, other subjects were allowed to grow up within the university domain. Gradually forms of secular knowledge became increasingly important. In Islam such forms of learning had to take place elsewhere."[105] In conclusion, he stated: "let us look not at origins so much as parallels of which there are many between Islam and Christian learning. Indeed in many ways it may have been Islamic methods that preceded the founding of the first European University at Bologna, teaching law, as did the Badras school in Byzantium. The *sic et non* (central to the work of the scholastics like Aquinas), the *questiones disputatae*, the *reportio*, and the legal dialectic could have their earlier Islamic parallels."[106] There is sufficient historical proof then, to conclude with J. Riberea, that "the medieval university owed much to the collegiate institution of Arab education."[107]

Italian Renaissance

The Renaissance, or rebirth, of classical antiquity's lifestyle and learning in many ways went through the Arab and Muslim medium. Renaissance leaders looked back at antiquity, through many Arabic books and sciences. Muslim philosophers, natural scientists, astronomers and physicians such as Ibn Sina, al Farabi, Ibn Rushd, Ibn Shatir, al Razi were read, analysed and well assimilated.[108] The Renaissance also involved more than just the intellectual stimulations; it needed financial means, intellectual tools and a change in the overall outlook.

Later Renaissance scholarship and interpretations mostly highlighted the intellectual, philosophical, liberal, individualistic, political and rational elements in the Renaissance. They were more Eurocentric than historical, and "rather than offering an accurate historical account of what took place from the 15th century onwards" they looked more like "an ideal of 19th-century European society. These critics celebrated limited democracy, scepticism towards the church, the power of art and literature, and the triumph of European civilisation over all others. These values underpinned 19th-century European imperialism."[109] This Whiggish interpretation of Renaissance ignored the fact that European society as a whole - including the Italian Peninsula - was a collective, persecutory and suffocating society where Church and state severely censored and persecuted dissent, individualism and freedoms. The projection of nineteenth-century democrated values and freedoms on an undemocratic and suffocating society of the sixteenth century is nothing short of bigotry. The Muslim East was far more prosperous, free and tolerant than the Italian city states or European Empires.

Jerry Brotton, while rejecting European hijacking of the Renaissance, argued that the "trade, finance, commodities, patronage, imperial conflict, and the exchange with different cultures were all key elements of the Renaissance. Focusing on these issues offers a different understanding of what shaped the Renaissance. It also leads us to think of the creativity of the Renaissance as not confined to painting, writing, sculpture, and architecture. Other artefacts such as ceramics, textiles, metalwork, and furniture also shaped people's beliefs and attitudes, even though many of these objects have since been neglected, destroyed, or lost."[110] The medieval Renaissance was a cross-cultural phenomenon, even though multicultural aspects of it are quite often ignored by the Eurocentric narratives. Islam was an important part of the medieval Europe's Renaissance.

It is commonly agreed that the Renaissance first occurred in Southern Italy, Florence being the centre of it, and then traveled to the rest of Europe. The Italian Renaissance was no doubt the birthplace of the broader European Renaissance. Jacob Burckhardt, in his famous book, *The Civilisation of the Renaissance in Italy*[111] has shown Italy as the birthplace of the Renaissance. He has maintained that the Italian states were the originating point of European Renaissance.[112] The Italian Renaissance followed the Greeks and Arabs;[113] there were Renaissances in Greek and Arab lands before the Italian Renaissance, and the latter took its cue from the formers. Brotton maintained that "the Renaissance was a remarkably international, fluid, and mobile phenomenon."[114]

Why would Renaissance and Humanism originate and flourish in Italy? Why was Renaissance developed in Southern Italy long before Northern Italy and why was Florence the epicenter? The answer lay in the region's geographical affinity, trade and cultural exchanges with the dominant and vibrant Muslim culture and civilisation. John Hobson put the point in the nutshell: "for behind Italy lay the more advanced East."[115]

The sixteenth-century Renaissance was the result of intercontinental trade and interactions, "trade, finance, commodities, patronage, imperial conflict, and the exchange with different cultures were all key elements of the Renaissance."[116] The Italian trade with Muslim East played a major role in the opulence and prosperity connected with the Italian Renaissance. A small fragmented Italian Peninsula with its small city states could not have pioneered the global economy, art and Renaissance on its own. To Hobson "the image of 'Italian pioneer' is but a myth."[117] Italy found itself in a strategic geographical position, and located itself in an already well-defined culture, civilisation and economy to transform itself. "It was not that Italy found the world and then transformed it; rather that the more advanced Eastern world found Italy and enabled its rise and development [...] virtually all the major innovations that lay behind the development of Italian capitalism were derived from the more advanced East, especially the Middle East and China, and diffused across the Islamic Bridge of the World through Oriental globalisation. Moreover, Italy indeed led the inferior or backward European subcontinent it was none the less a mere bit-player in the larger global arena, at all times playing second fiddle to the more advanced Islamic polities and merchants of the Middle East and especially North Africa."[118]

In addition to Italy's geographical proximity to Muslim Spain and Sicily, Italy's Mediterranean contacts played an important part in its' role as the birth place of European Renaissance. The Renaissance was dependent upon economic prosperity, which in turn was dependent upon the Muslim world. Janet Abu-Lughod observed that "this direct entrée to the riches of the East changed the role of the Italian merchant mariner cities from passive to active. The revival of the Champagne Fairs in the twelfth century can be explained convincingly by both the enhanced demand for Eastern goods stimulated by the crusades and, because of the strategic position of the Italians in coastal enclaves of the Levant, the increased supplies of such goods they could now deliver."[119] The Southern, Central and Northern city states were mostly reliant upon trade with and through the Muslim world. Abu-Lughod showed that the trade success of Venice, Milan, Genoa and Florence was contingent upon Anatolia, Fertile Crescent, Egypt and North Africa.[120] Up until the second half of the thirteenth century, the Italian merchants from Venice and Genoa used the gold coins of Ottoman Constantinople and Egypt's Cairo showing "their semi-peripheral status in world trade."[121] It was Italy's access to Muslim ports that saved them financial constraints and agonies of the Dark Ages of Europe.[122]

It is often argued that the discovery of the New World, and the treasures of Americas, stimulated the European economy and made it independent of the Muslim East and its resources. It is also argued that the resultant economic growth and prosperity ushered in the era of the Renaissance, independently of Eastern influences. Gerald MacLean argues against such a line of thinking. He instead maintains that the gold and silver "from the New World both fuelled and accelerated the rates of cultural exchange. The question is not whether, despite differences and disagreements, there was commercial and cross-cultural exchange between Muslim and Christian, or whether Renaissance artists and intellectuals engaged with eastern aesthetics and Islamic ideas. The question is rather how to describe and assess those widespread cultural exchanges that were taking place."[123]

Renaissance Art

Renaissance art is given considerable significance by modern students of that period. The art was reflective of Renaissance humanistic philosophy. The paintings, sculptures and other modes of decorative art made a transition from classical tradition to incorporate contemporary humanistic and philosophical ideas. These paintings reflected the inner thoughts and thinking processes of the artists, and gave important clues to their worldviews and outlooks. Renaissance art facilitated Europe's transition from Antiquity and the Middle Ages to modern times. There are significant and visible clues of Eastern and Islamic influences upon both the Southern and Northern Renaissance art. It places Europe in the centre of the globe, and then looks towards the Islamic East and its luxuries to model Italian and European society accordingly.

Hans Holbein (1460–1524) was a German painter who, along with his son Hans Holbein the Younger (1497 1543), represented the Northern Renaissance. Holbein the Younger was a friend of Erasmus of Rotterdam, and also helped in propagating sixteenth-century Reformation ideas through his paintings. On Erasmus's recommendation Holbein the Younger travelled to England and worked with many English humanists. He became the King's Painter for King Henry VIII and in 1536 produced the famous portrait of King Henry VIII. He also helped the King and his confidant Thomas Cromwell in their struggle against the clerical establishment. The English Reformation was well-propagated by Holbein's paintings.

Holbein's famous masterpiece *The Ambassadors*[124] portrayed Jean de Dinteville, an ambassador of Francis I of France in 1533, and Georges de Selve, Bishop of Lavaur, who visited London in the same year.[125] Francis I was badly defeated by the Hapsburg King Charles V in the Battle of Pavia on February 24, 1525 and was forced to give up Duchy of Burgundy[126] and the Charolais to Charles V, reluctantly signing the humiliating Treaty of Madrid, relinquishing his honours to Constable de Bourbon who actually betrayed him. Francis was imprisoned in Madrid and his mother Louise de Savoie started sending envoys to Sultan Suleiman the Magnificent[127] for help. The first envoy was lost in the Balkans or killed.[128] A second mission, under the leadership of John Frangipani, managed to reach Istanbul on December of 1525. Frangipani was able to secure the Sultan's positive response to Francis I and his mother's desperate appeals for help.[129]

On the incentives of Francis I, the Ottomans defeated the Hungarian King Louis II of Hungary and Bohemia in the Battle of Mohac in 1526, killed the King,[130] divided Hungary and put direct pressure on the Hapsburg Monarchy by appointing King Zapolaya as an Ottoman Hungarian vessel. The battle of Mohac was "related to the Habsburg-Valois rivalry between Charles V and Francis I. When Charles V defeated and captured Francis I at the Battle of Pavia in northern Italy (1525), the French king sought Suleyman's help. Suleyman chose to inflict harm on the Habsburgs [...] through Hungary, whose king Louis II was the brother-in-law of Habsburg Ferdinand and Charles V."[131] Francis I later admitted to a Venetian ambassador that the Ottoman Empire was the only factor that prevented Charles V from creating a Europe-wide empire under Habsburg authority.[132] Francis I formed a Franco-Hungarian Alliance in 1528 with King Zapolaya.[133] In 1529, Sultan Suleiman besieged Vienna with the help of many Protestants and Catholics, exerting direct pressure upon the Hapsburg Empire. Consequently, the first non–ideological[134] modern Ottoman-French alliance was formally signed in 1536 leading to 300 years of French Ottoman commerce, diplomacy, religio scientific and cultural exchanges, Orientalism, Turkism, Turquerie (lit. "Turkish stuff") and Eastern obsession. In 1533, Ambassador Dinteville was in London to convince Henry VIII to become part of the Franco-Ottoman alliance.

Jerry Brotton observes that Dinteville and de Selve were in "London to broker a new political alliance between Henry, Francis, and the Ottoman Sultan Suleyman the Magnificent, the other great power in European politics of the time. The rug on the upper shelf of the table in Holbein's painting is of Ottoman design and manufacture, suggesting that the Ottomans and their territories to the east were also part of the cultural, commercial, and political landscape of the Renaissance. Selve and Dinteville's attempt to draw Henry VIII into an alliance with Francis and Suleyman was motivated by their fear of the growing strength of that other great Renaissance imperial power, the Habsburg empire of Charles V. By comparison, England and France were minor imperial players: the terrestrial globe in the painting says as much."[135] In fact the "Oriental Rugs" along with Kufic script were commonly used in the Renaissance paintings to depict Muslim luxurious lifestyle.[136] The Venetian paintings in particular were known for their incorporation of Eastern styles, themes and carpets.

The Ottoman Muslim Empire, along with strong Muslim Moghul Empire of India and Safvid Empire of Persia, constituted the dominant Muslim civilisation that surrounded Europe. The small European powers such as France, England and Netherland were recipients of many elements of that glorious civilisation. Islamic concepts, symbols and arts were heavily deployed during the early Renaissance period; even Christian religious art and paintings incorporated Islamic prayer mats, *mihrab* (Mosque arch) and known symbols like *Ka'aba*.[137] Such incorporations dissipated after 1550 as a result of knowledge about their close connections with Islamic religion.

Islamic influences upon Renaissance art are well demonstrated by *The Ambassadors*, which reflects many Islamic symbols and themes. Brotton observes that many of "the objects in Holbein's painting have an eastern origin, from the silk and velvet worn by its subjects to the textiles and designs that decorate the room. The objects in the bottom section of Holbein's painting reveal various facets of the Renaissance – humanism, religion, printing, trade, exploration, politics and empire, and the enduring presence of the wealth and knowledge of the east."[138] The objects on the upper shelf "deal with much more abstract and philosophical issues. The celestial globe is an astronomical instrument used to measure the stars and the nature of the universe. Next to the globe is a collection of dials, used to tell the time with the aid of the sun's rays. The two larger objects are a quadrant and a torquetum, navigational instruments used to work out a ship's position in both time and space. Most of these instruments were invented by Arab and Jewish astronomers and came westwards as European travellers required navigational expertise for long-distance voyages."[139] In short, the Northern Renaissance paintings were equally influenced by Islamic symbols and themes.

Gentile Bellini (1429-1507) was a renowned Renaissance painter who belonged to a well-known family of Venetian painters. Venice was Europe's gateway to the Muslim Africa and Asia, and Venetian merchants enjoyed close business ties to Egyptian Muslim community, with separate Venetian quarters both in Alexandria and Cairo. St. Mark, the patron Saint of Venice, was born in Alexandria; The Venetians built a magnificent basilica of San Marco to honour St. Mark. Bellini's famous painting "St. Mark Preaching at Alexandria" is considered a masterpiece of the Renaissance art. This piece is also an embodiment of Islamic influences.

Bellini was known for his affinity with the Eastern Islamic art. That was perhaps the reason that he was selected by the Venetian senate in 1479 to be the ambassador of Venice to Muslim Istanbul. Bellini saw the results of peace settlement between the Ottomans and Venice, lived in Istanbul and polished his Islamic art skills. Sultan Mehmed II was a patron of Italian art, and happily asked Bellini to paint his portrait. The historical portrait of Mehmed II is now in the National Gallery of London. Bellini, the official painter of Sultan Mehmed II, incorporated a host of Islamic symbols, icons and ideas into his *St. Mark Preaching at Alexandria*. The painting was completed by his brother Giovanni at Gentile's death.

The San Marco painting portrays St. Mark preaching to a group of audience including women wearing white Islamic veil, featuring minarets, *mihrabs* and domes as well as Egyptian Mamluks, North African Moors, Ottomans, Persians, Ethiopians, and Tartars. Brotton observes that the "drama of the action takes place in the bottom third of the painting; the rest of the canvas is dominated by the dramatic landscape of Alexandria. A domed Byzantine basilica, an imaginative recreation of St Mark's Alexandrian church, dominates the backdrop. In the piazza Oriental figures converse, some on horseback, others leading camels and a giraffe. The houses that face onto the square are adorned with Egyptian grilles and tiles. Islamic carpets and rugs hang from the windows. The minarets, columns, and pillars that make up the skyline are a mixture of Alexandrian landmarks and the Bellinis' own invention. The basilica is an eclectic mixture of elements of the Church of San Marco in Venice and Hagia Sophia in Constantinople, while the towers and columns in the distance correspond to some of Alexandria's most famous landmarks, many of which had already been emulated in the architecture of Venice itself."[140]

Venice and Islamic World

Venice was surrounded by the vast Ottoman Empire, and enjoyed strong business ties with the Ottomans and Mamluk Egyptians. The mighty Muslim empires were far greater and powerful than a small city state such as Venice; therefore, the Venetians considered Muslims as an intrinsic part of their economy and civilisation. They were truly fascinated with the Muslim civilisation, and the Bellini family presented that fascination with Islamic culture very well through their Renaissance paintings. Brotton explains that the "Bellinis were fascinated by both the myths and the reality of the world to the east of what is today seen as Renaissance Europe. Their painting is concerned with the specific nature of the eastern world, and in particular the customs, architecture, and culture of Arabic Alexandria, one of Venice's long-standing trading partners. The Bellinis did not dismiss the Mamluks of Egypt, the Ottomans, or the Persians as barbaric. Instead, they were acutely aware that these cultures possessed many things that the city states of Europe desired. These included precious commodities, technical, scientific, and artistic knowledge, and ways of doing business that came from the east. The painting of St Mark in Alexandria shows how the European Renaissance began to define itself not in opposition to the east, but through an extensive and complex exchange of ideas and materials."[141]

Venetian prosperity was dependent upon their trade with the Muslims; their merchants were able to access business from China to North Africa and from Balkans to Persia through the permission and security of the Muslim empires. They also monopolised the European market due to the same privileged position. The Bellinis and their comrades did not hide their appreciation of the Muslim East. "The Bellinis' Venetian contemporaries were explicit about their reliance upon such transactions. Venice was perfectly situated as a commercial intermediary, able to receive commodities from these eastern bazaars, and then transport them to the markets of northern Europe. Writing at the same time as the Bellinis worked on their painting of St Mark, Canon Pietro Casola reported with amazement the impact that this flow of goods from the east had upon Venice itself."[142] The Islamic goods and exports' "impact upon the culture and consumption of communities from Venice to London was gradual but profound. Every sphere of life was affected, from eating to painting. As the domestic economy changed with this influx of exotic goods, so did art and culture. The palette of painters like the Bellinis was also expanded by the addition of pigments like lapis lazuli, vermilion, and cinnabar, all of which were imported from the east via Venice, and provided Renaissance paintings with their characteristic brilliant blues and reds. The loving detail with which the Bellini painting of St Mark reproduces silk, velvet, muslin, cotton, tiling, carpets, even livestock, reflected the Bellinis' awareness of how these exchanges with the east were transforming the sights, smells, and tastes of the world, and the ability of the artist to reproduce them."[143]

W. Montgomery Watt, in his *The Influence of Islam on Medieval Europe,* has elaborated the point that by the thirteenth and fourteenth centuries, the trade and political presence in Spain and Sicily had made the superior culture of the Arabs gradually known throughout Western Europe. Watt's conclusion, that "the influence of Islam on western Christendom is greater than is usually realised" is being realised by many contemporary scholars.[144] Montgomery Watt also noticed that "because Europe was reacting against Islam, it belittled the influence of the Saracens and exaggerated its dependence on its Greek and Roman heritage. So today, an important task for our Western Europeans, as we move into the era of the one world, is to correct this false emphasis and to acknowledge fully our debt to the Arab and Islam world."[145] Even the so-called Greco-Roman heritage was transmitted to Europe through the Ottoman inheritors of the Byzantium Empire, its institutions and policies. Constantinople was the true heir to Roman Empire, and the Ottomans were the true heirs to Constantinople.

The overpowering Ottoman Empire ransacked Constantinople in 1453 and besieged Otranto and Rhodes Island by 1480, not far from Rome. Pope Julius II (1503–1513) issued a bull on July 18, 1511, calling for a Church Council meeting at the Lateran Palace in April of 1512. The Archbishop of Spalato, while addressing the first session, warned about the Turkish threat in the following words: "Within the confines of Europe they have usurped no mean dominion with the effusion of much Christian blood. They could easily transport themselves to the gates of Rome in the space of one night from their domain in Dalmatia."[146] By 1529 the Muslims were knocking at the gates of Vienna, under the leadership of Sultan Suleiman the Magnificent; the German princes felt the brunt through Alpine Turkish raids. Hungarian Protestant Christians, along with a host of continental Christians, supported the Ottomans against their oppressive Hapsburg Catholic opponents. The real Rome (Constantinople) of the early modern times controlled one third of the European Continent and all the ins and outs of the Eastern Mediterranean. Western Europe was too divided and instable to be a threat to the mighty Ottoman Empire of the sixteenth century; its main Christian rival was the Habsburg monarchy and its Catholic Church, and both were battling against regional princes, monarchs and dissenting religious sects. Both the Church and monarchy were absolutists, persecuting, corrupt and self-serving, using the medieval

Crusade rhetoric and corrupt religious practices to fill their coffers. In spite of Scholasticism, Humanism and Renaissance the Church and monarchy barred Europe from true freedom, liberty, republicanism and individualism. By the late Renaissance and early modern period, the two contending worldviews were waring for universal hegemony. The Catholic Habsburg's absolutist monarchy employed Christian religion, divine right theology, uniformity, persecutions and crusades to usher a new millennium of Catholic universal monarchy and world dominion and the Ottoman Ghazis used Islam, religious diversity, tolerance, freedom and reformation to realize their hopes of millennial prosperity and world dominion. The East European princes and their contact zone Western neighbors were caught up between these two rival religio political ideologies. Both the Ottomans and Habsburg dynasties were missionaries, using religious propagation to expand the empire, though their missionary methodology and style diverged from each other. While the Habsburg used Roman Christianity to unify the Christendom and crusade against the Ottoman infidels by imposition of religio political uniformity, the Ottomans used claims of Catholic corruptions of the original Christianity, Islam's true representation and reformation of Christianity, multiculturalism, tolerance, liberties and mercantilism to divide the Christendom and to avoid the possibility of a Europe wide crusade. The Protestant Christian's rapprochement to Islam and affinities with Ottoman tolerant religio political structures through trade and military alliances were two cornerstones of the Ottoman foreign policy. Highlighting Christian internal strife, Church and state's persecutions, corruptions, impositions, abuse of religion for political gains and the possibility of Ottoman millennial reformation of the Catholic Christianity were elemental to the Ottoman foreign policy. The spiritual and physical conquest of Rome was a real goal and possibility during Sultan Sulieman's reign. He wanted to conquer Western Europe to liberate Christians from the oppressing yoke of Catholicism.[147]

Sixteenth-Century Protestant Reformation

Such was the socio-political situation which led many Christian reformers of the sixteenth century such as Martin Luther, Huldrych Zwingli and John Calvin to look inward as well as outward, to identify Christian problems and their possible remedies. Islamic theology, rituals and history were quite known to these reformers, especially Martin Luther due to close travel and trade connections between Europe and the Muslim East, specifically due to Central Europe's proximity to the Ottoman Transylvania.[148] The Christian Holy Lands, the Classical lands of Egypt and Greek and the Oriental treasures were all controlled by the Muslim Empires; Christian Europe had essential knowledge of the Muslim East through their classical and biblical knowledge. Pilgrimage to the Holy Lands and recent history of Crusade states were handy tools for Western Europeans to know about Islam, its teachings, culture, history and threat.

Additionally, many Christians, especially in Transylvania, had converted to Islam and the flow was just one way. They were fascinated with Ottoman minimalism, rationalism, scripturalism, religious diversity and tolerance. Islam's simple creed, rational doctrines, piety, morality, simplicity and tolerance of dissent were among the main reasons for such a widespread Christian conversion. Of course, the economic prosperity and political allure of the Ottoman Empire were no less attractive but theological rationality, moral purity, religious tolerance, pluralism and republicanism were perhaps among the leading factors of this one-way conversion traffic. These converts or renegades enthusiastically defended their conversions, highlighted superiority of Islam over Christianity, reached out to their friends and foes and publically preached Islamic doctrines, institutions and practices. The Ottoman imperial machine encouraged and supported such a missionary zeal with Muslim millennial prophecies and impending Ottoman hope for a universal, rational, republican and tolerant monarchy. The new converts' missionary overtures, Ottoman ideology of Ghazis (the propagaters and defenders of Islam against Christianity), religio intellectual and military warfare with Christendom and messianic mantles of Sultans such as Suleiman the Magnificent made the Turko Islamic threat urgent and imminent. The threat was accompanied by countless theological discussions and tropes. Tijana Krstic noted that interest in "the original Christian and Jewish scriptures, as well as the nature of spiritual authority, the possibility of spiritual renewal, and the proper role of the emperor and pope in religious and political life, was not confined to early modern European Christian humanists. On the contrary, the Ottoman and other Muslim polemical narratives testify to a much more significant interest and involvement of Muslim literati and politicians in the religious debates among sixteenth-century Christians as a consequence of the Ottoman emperor's aspirations to unite the world under the banner of Islam and arbitrate on matters of religion in his role as world ruler. Converts to Islam were particularly important participants in these debates. In their writings many discuss the veracity of religious scriptures, salvation, spiritual renovation, and the Day of Judgment as well as the Ottoman sultan's role in these matters."[149] The resonance of such debates and polemic were felt all over Europe especially the Mediterranean basin. The reformers including Luther, Calvin and Erasmus were forced to address Turkish military, religious and intellectual threats. As their expertise and abilities lay mostly in the theological and intellectual spheres, they thoroughly engaged themselves with Islamic theological heritage, acted upon and reacted to it with varying degrees and purposes and in the process absorbed, wittingly or unwittingly, a great deal of Islamic ideas and concepts. Theirs was the second, alternative Christian voice on the Continent which established its independent identity in opposition to the Catholic Church but also in conjunction with the Ottoman anti-Catholic rhetoric. The common enemy somehow led to some common agendas, ethos and tropes. For instance the German Baroque poet and mystic Quirinus Kuhlmann (1651-1689) supported unification of Protestants and Turks, attempted audience with Sultan Mehmed IV, encouraged religious union between Muslims and Protestants against Catholics and a Utopian Kingdom of Jesus. The distinguished Moravian Hungarian philosopher, theologian and pansophic pedagogue Johann Amos Comenius (1592-1670), whose ideas were extremely influential all around the Protestant Europe including England and America, was an ardent enemy of social inequality and persecutions. He appreciated Ottoman justice and toleration and encouraged unified fight against the persecutory Catholic Habsburgs. He prophesied divine help for anyone willing to destroy the hegemonic Habsburg dynasty including the Muslim Turks. The Transylvanian and English Protestants' participation in Ottoman anti-Catholic wars are well documented.[150]

The sixteenth-century magisterial reductionist Reformation produced a metamorphosis of Islamic and Christian theologies. The reformed churches and theology were closer to Islam than to the Catholic Christianity in many ways.[151] Luther was accused especially by the Catholics of being a "Muhammadan" who replaced Christianity with

Muhammadan faith. In fact, Luther's anti-clerical, anti-saints and images, anti-church hierarchy, anti-tradition, anti-sacraments, anti-iconoclasm and solo scripture Christianity more resembled Turkish[152] faith than Papal faith, and so it was branded by the Pope.[153] Ottoman Muslims felt special affinity with Luther's struggles against the Catholic Church; special prayers for Luther's success were offered in mosques across the Ottoman Empire. Islam and Protestantism were considered allies. The Ottomans militarily pressurised the Habsburg monarchy to release pressure from the Protestants. "Ottoman intervention was thus not only a decisive factor in the rise of national monarchies, as in France, but also in the rise of Protestantism in Europe."[154] The Romanian American historian Stephan A. Fischer-Galati noted that in 1530 "Charles with the support of Ferdinand and the Catholics, pronounced a death sentence on Protestantism at the Diet of Augsburg [...] But the Protestants won a reprieve, primarily because of a powerful Ottoman offensive against Hungary and the Empire. Charles and Ferdinand could interdict Lutheranism at Speyer and Augsburg but could not dispense with its assistance when their secular interests in Eastern Europe and the very security of the Empire itself appeared in grave danger. In return for support against the Turks the Emperor was prepared to guarantee the existence of Lutheranism until the meeting of a council."[155] The Ottoman activities in Hungary and the Mediterranean, and their ally the French Emperor Francis I's aggression in Italy, forced Charles to renew and extend the guarantees which the Lutherans had received from him in the 1530s.

It is pertinent to note that there had been numerous efforts before Luther to reform the Christian tradition from within.[156] The eleventh- to thirteenth-century Catharism, Peter Waldo's Waldensians, the French Albigenses and John Huss and Hussites were almost all annihilated by Papal orders. There were numerous crusades directed at the dissenting Christians throughout the Middle Ages; the history of the Inquisitions is well known, and there were thousands of Christians who were burned at the stake as a result of mere doubt about their orthodoxy. Luther and his Reformation would not have succeeded without sympathy of the Muslim Turks and their unrelenting pressure on the Holy Roman Empire. Kenneth Setton in *Europe and Levant in the Middle Ages and the Renaissance* observes that "It is often said that the Reformation aided the Turks; certainly the Turks aided the Reformation;

without them Protestantism might conceivably have gone the way of Albigensianism."[157] Emperors Charles, and Ferdinand of the Habsburg family inheritance, were threatened by Ottoman pressure; they gave priority to defending their inheritance over Protestant affairs in Germany. They also gave recognition to Lutheranism in 1555, because they needed German support against the dreaded Ottomans. The Lutherans very much appreciated the indirect Ottoman help, as their fortunes were directly linked with the military pressure and successes of the otherwise-despised Ottomans. Fischer-Galati concluded that the "consolidation, expansion, and legitimisation of Lutheranism in Germany by 1555 should be attributed to Ottoman imperialism more than to any other single factor."[158] Ottomans, to Fischer-Galati, were the "saviour of Protestantism in Germany and the ultimate guarantor of Protestant interests in Hungary and Transylvania."[159] Jae Jerkins, in *Islam in the Early Modern Protestant Imagination,* observed that "European commercial relations with the Ottomans flourished across Europe as different nations saw the advantage that could be gained from Ottoman support. France and England independently sought alliances with the Ottomans against Catholic Spain. With Suleiman's siege of Vienna in 1529, the Lutherans were placed in a favourable position to force concessions from the Habsburg Holy Roman Emperor Charles V. Feeling pressure from the Lutherans within, the French to the west, and the Ottomans to the east, Charles V sought a truce with the Ottomans in 1539. This indirect relation of power between the Lutheran Protestants and the Ottoman Muslims is typical of the Islamicate–Christian relations of the period. Typically, it was Catholic forces and funds that resisted the advance of the Ottoman Empire. Despite the anti–Islamic and anti–Muhammad rhetoric of theologians like Luther and Calvin, Islam was the best thing to happen to the Protestant cause, qua Catholic hegemony. Luther's struggle with Charles V could have gone very differently had Suleiman's armies not been knocking at Germany's door."[160]

The Ottoman and early Protestant alliances were not confined to mere political and economic spheres; in fact, they extended to theological and religious affinities. This is how the reformed leaders, politicians and masses described it. The very Christian and Protestant English Queen Elizabeth 1 of England wrote a personal letter to Ottoman Sultan Murad III in an effort to forge an alliance against the so-called idolater Habsburg Catholic Emperor Charles V of Spain.[161] In the letter she tried to show more affinity with Muslim Unitarianism than the so-perceived Catholic polytheism. To J. Goody, Elizabeth was daring enough to send her ambassador William Harbourne to Constantinople to bargain with Sultan Murad III to charter the Levant Company.[162] She wrote: "Elizabeth, by the grace of the most mighty God, the three part and yet singular Creator of Heaven and Earth, Queen of England, France and Ireland, the most invincible and most mighty defender of the Christian faith against all the idolatry of those unworthy ones that live amongst Christians, and falsely profess the name of Christ"[163] Jerkins notes that Queen Elizabeth "framed her hopes of political alliance as being a partnership between the pious monotheists of England and Turkey against the idolatrous Spanish Habsburgs."[164] Brotton noted that Elizabeth wrote from a "position of subjection"[165] to establish commercial relationships and political alliance with the mighty Ottomans. She wanted the Sultan to intervene against the aggressions of Habsburg Spain on the English coast.[166] She emphasised the theological and devotional similarities between Islam and Protestantism to forge an effective alliance between the Ottoman and Tudor dynasties. Her trade and military alliances of 1600 with the Morrocan King Abd el-Ouahed ben Messaoud and other Barbary States greatly annoyed Spain.[167] The Catholic Christendom (including Pope Sixtus V) viewed her and her subjects as "New Turks", as Matthew Dimmock's book *New Turkes: Dramatizing Islam and the Ottomans in Early Modern England* demonstrates. To the Catholic commentator, publisher and antiquarian Richard Verstagen (1548-1636), England was involved not only in dividing Christendom and undermining its long crusade against the Ottoman Muslims but actively engaged in the counter crusade of Ottomans to establish universal Muslim monarchy in Europe. The English would soon exchange their Geneva Bible for the Turkish Alcoran. The charge was so damning that the English government commissioned the philosopher-stateman Francis Bacon to refute Verstagen's polemics. Bacon's response, entitled "Certain Observations Upon a Libel" was written in 1592, presumably within months of Verstegan's "A declaration". Elizabeth effectively used the religious affinity between Islam and Protestantism to leverage her interests in the Muslim World, following Martin Luther in this respect. The shared iconoclasm between Protestants and Muslims can be traced back to Luther's 1528 tract, where he speaks of the "Turk's holiness, that they tolerate no images or pic-

tures," commending Muslims as being "even holier than our destroy-
ers of images" who still tolerate images on rings and ornaments, while
"the Turk tolerates none of them and stamps nothing but letters on his
coins".[168] In the 1580s, Queen Elizabeth utilised this shared iconoclast
ideology when she reminded Murad in her diplomatic correspondence
that both Protestants and Muslims shared a religious rejection of icons.
With Elizabeth, the Protestant religio political accommodation of Islam began in England. Sultan Murad III was to exploit that accommodation and affinity in his correspondence with other Protestants such
as in Flanders and Spain. Her successor, King James I, originally a Tur-
co-phobe and champion of Christian unity, under the influence of his
Levant and East India Company friend Sir Thomas Smyth, his dire financial needs to support his Protestant son in Law Frederick, the Elector of the Rhineland Palatinate and leader of the German Protestant
Union in the Thirty Year's War (1618- 1648), his loans from the Levant
Company, his diplomatic efforts to prevent the truce between Ottomans and Habsburg to avert mounting military pressure from Frederick and multiple other factors caused him to continue Ottoman-Islam-
ic accommodations like Elizabeth. Additionally, he had to devise an
ideological strategy to ward off unrelenting Habsburg polemics against
English-Protestant heresy, illegitimacy and treason. He wittingly or
unwittingly, incorporated Ottoman anti Catholic tropes of Catholic
corruptions, interpolations and manipulations into his scheme of refuting the Catholic Habsburg propaganda of Protestant treason and
Anglican betrayal of true Catholic Christian faith. His insistence upon
Erastian Church Settlement, scripturalism, bypassing the Catholic traditions, Church Councils, Settlements, absolutist claims and instead
direct appeal to Antiquity, pre-Catholic first three century's original,
pristine Christianity and Erastian church somehow reflected the long
Ottoman reformative propaganda against Roman Christianity and so
it was branded by the Catholic Habsburg propaganda machine. His
purer English Bible spurred biblical criticism. To the Catholic leadership, Anglican King and Church were playing the Muslim cards to
establish their independent Protestant English identity and monarchy.
King James' publication of a purer English Bible in conjunction with
Eastern manuscripts, promises of equal treatment and support of Eastern Orthodox Church based in Istanbul and plans for a unifying ecumenical council without authorization of Pope were no less dangerous

than Sultan Suleiman the Magnificant's plans for Catholic reformation and an ecumenical council to bring the warring Catholics and Protestants under Suleiman's leadership to resolve the ongoing Christian strife and bloodshed. Suleiman "saw a role for himself in the religious turmoil that ripped Europe: as his grand vizier Ibrahim Pasha told the Habsburg envoy to Istanbul in 1534, Suleyman planned on convoking and presiding over an ecumenical council where the pope and Martin Luther would come together to resolve their conflict. Like Constantine, from whose city he aspired to rule the world, Suleyman was going to bring about the unification of religions under imperial and presumably Islamic auspices. Active involvement in religious issues was from Suleyman's perspective central to his role as emperor-a concept that he would insist upon even more rigorously later in his reign."[169]

England's close diplomatic relations with and overseas trade especially to the warring Ottoman Empire was a proof of Ottoman support of English subversive agenda. To the Catholics, England had somehow become a prey to the Ottoman designs of a universal Muslim empire at the expense of Habsburg Christian universal monarchy. The raw Protestant England's identity was formed in opposition to the Catholic Church while appropriating the useful ingredients from the lesser enemy, the Ottomans, due to their support and trade.

The Hungarian Protestants perhaps were the biggest beneficiaries of the Ottoman support and interference.[170] The Hungarian academic historian Bela K. Kiraly, in *Tolerance and Movements of Religious Dissent in Eastern Europe*,[171] stated that "the simultaneity of Luther's rupture with Rome and Ottoman penetration of Hungary's underbelly prefigured one of the most striking characteristics of the spread of Protestantism through Hungary: the interdependence of the Ottoman conquest in central Hungary and the dissemination of the new faith."[172] The Ottoman Empire conquered the Hungarian heartland during the sixteenth century. Consequently, Protestantism also grew rapidly, and during the second half of the century Catholic Hungary became a Protestant land. To Kiraly, the Protestant successes in Hungary and Transylvania were dependent on the Ottoman conquest of these lands and their favourable treatment of the Protestants.[173] The Ottoman Muslims did not burn, kill and maim Protestant Christians as the Catholic Church did in the Habsburg areas. The Ottoman allowed them religious freedom, financial support and political stability, supported reformed churches against their Catholic foes and greatly helped them in developing their political and religious identity.[174] Islam and Muslims were an integral part of this identification and differentiation process, and left a subtle but visible impact upon the outcome.[175]

Radical Reformation

The radical reformation of Michael Servetus (1509-1553), Socinians and Unitarians were shaped by this Muslim support and experience. Their radical Unitarian reformation was the second and parallel Protestant reformation, along with the moderate, magisterial reformation of Luther and Calvin.[176] The overall reformed Christian identity, outlook and orientation, especially of the radical Unitarians, were more Muhammadan than the medieval Church Christianity. The later European anti-Trinitarians, Unitarians and Socinians would all emerge from Transylvania and play an extremely important role in disseminating the Islamic anti-Trinitarian rational theology and republican political outlook all across the European Continent. Socinians and Unitarians would play an important role in early seventeenth century Holland and English religious debates, engage both clerical and lay theologians and shape the anti-Trinitarian, rational and republican trends in Holland, as well as pre–Civil War and post-Revolution England.[177] Sarah Mortimer observed that "Scholars from every confessional and political background read and engaged with Socinian writing, developing their own thoughts and programmes in the process. Socinianism was a central part of early modern political and religious debates and ... those debates can look very different when the Socinian dimension is restored to them."[178] Italian and Heidelberg anti-Trinitarian rationalists would seek refuge and flourish in Transylvania and German Unitarian theologians, and clergy such as Adam Neuser would go to Constantinople through Hungary to convert to Islam.[179] The first Protestant edict of religious tolerance would be enacted here in Hungry.[180] The Ottoman support, tolerance and empowerment of Protestantism had long religious and political consequences.

The Italian anti-Trinitarian Giordano Bruno (1548-1600), the Hermetic occultist, mathematician, philosopher, cosmologist and Dominican friar, also struggled to rid Catholic Christianity of its supernatural extravagances such as the Trinity, incarnation, Christ's divinity, Consubstantiation and triadic cosmology.[181] Inspired by Servetus' heterodoxy and courage,[182] alchemy tradition of Hermeticism,[183] Arabic astrology, theology especially Averroes' philosophy[184] Bruno considered Christianity as a human fabrication to be discarded or totally reformed. The famous Renaissance philosopher, religionist and historian Alfonso Ingegno put the point in a nutshell. "Bruno's reform, therefore, is not only philosophically significant but also has religious consequences. It challenges the developments of the Reformation, calls into question the truth-value of the whole of Christianity, and claims that Christ perpetrated a deceit on mankind."[185] Bruno, like Servetus, argued that the Trinitarian supernatural philosophy had tremendous negative impacts on religion, society, man and cosmos. His Unitarian, Arian revision of the Christian theology, atomist materialistic revision of old philosophy and cosmology and Hermetic experimental alchemy would usher in a new reformative scheme which would radically change the world. "The consequences of this new philosophy are wide-ranging and radical because this new vision of the cosmos changes our relationship with the divinity, and this, in Bruno's eyes, transforms the very meaning of human life. He claims that this new vision will reconcile us with the divine law which governs nature, and free us from the fear of imaginary divinities, cruel and unfathomable, who look down from heavenly heights, controlling the sublunary world in a mysterious way."[186] Bruno was burned on the stake by the Catholic authorities as Servetus was burned by Calvin before him. Both the Catholic and Protestant Churches were hell-bent against radical, rational reformation of theology, politics, society and nature; they did not want to relinquish their absolute powers and divine right authority.

Sixteenth-century Trinitarian reformers focused more upon the Church structure, politics and abuses and less upon religio-political theology and natural cosmology. They kept intact some fundamental Christian dogmas such as the Trinity, Jesus' divinity, original sin, no salvation outside the Church, infant baptism,[187] predestination and justification through faith, along with their cosmological and political implications. "The Reformation was not even the most radical form of the ideological rupture with the European past and its "feudal" ideologies, among others its earlier interpretation of Christianity. It was, on the contrary, its primitive and confused form."[188] This continuity was perhaps necessary though for the sake of historical continuity and to ward off Catholic allegations of Luther Muhammadanism. Consequently, the triadic hierarchical worldview, divine right king and Church with their absolutist persecutory policies remained intact. The newly-established Protestant Churches, such as Lutheran, Calvinist and Anglican, struggled to establish their orthodox beliefs and curtail heterodox doctrines.[189] They resorted to civil authorities for imposition of their orthodoxies and persecution of heterodoxies.[190] In reality the Catholic Inquisitions and persecutions multiplied after the Protestant Reformation, and were copied by the Protestant national Churches. Some radical reformers, such as Michael Servetus, Bruno, Transylvanian Unitarians and Socinians, felt that the Reformation needed further theologico-political and scientific reformation, but they were rebuffed and persecuted by the Catholic and Protestant Churches. They pushed the Reformation ideas to their logical conclusions; if the Catholic Church was the perpetrator of the ecclesiastical fraud and corruption, then what was the guarantee that it did not corrupt the Christian theology, natural philosophy and political thought? "The spirit of scepticism, which at the Reformation extended only to the authority of particular Churches or to the justice of particular interpretations of Scripture, had gradually expanded till it included the whole domain of theology, and had produced a series of violent attacks upon the miracles."[191] The radicals did not find Original Sin, Trinity, Jesus' divinity, atoning sacrificial death, authoritative Church and absolute monarchy expressly delineated in the scriptures the way Church traditions had laid them down. They did not see the triadic hierarchy in divinity, cosmos, social order and human body; they instead experienced simplicity, unity and harmony in the natural phenomena, equality among the humans and unity in the physiological system. For instance, Servetus in his book *The Restoration of Christianity* (1553) emphasised the Unitarian reformation of Christianity in theology, social order and natural realms. He rejected the Trinity in theology as well as physiology. "Just as he denied the supreme Trinity, so Servetus denied the general concept of triadic hierarchy. In particular, having had a medical training, Servetus criticised the application of the concept to physiological theory, claiming that the natural, vital, and animal spirits in a human body were one and the same, as 'In all of these there is the energy of the one spirit and of the light of God'. Thus there were not two kinds of blood, the venous and the arterial, differentiated by the natural and the vital spirits, but only one blood containing a single spirit, since 'The vital is that which is communicated by the joins from the arteries to the veins in which it is called the natural'. This single spirit of the blood was the soul, or rather 'The soul itself is the blood', a view which Servetus supported with texts from the Old Testament."[192] Servetus' theological and physiological Unitarianism was punished by Calvin and Servetus was burned alive on the stake.

The Muslim contacts, cultural exchanges and debates in Spain, Eastern Europe and Italy had highlighted the disparities between the Trinitarian and Unitarian worldview, and radical reformers had aspired for a radical Unitarian reformation. But the demands of these reformers were too radical for the Protestant clergy and princes whose authorities were dependent upon the traditional, supernatural, Trinitarian theology and political outlooks. Consequently, they suppressed theological radicalism of Unitarians and Socinians with united zeal and enthusiasm. The political structures were equally threatened by Unitarian political and rational theology, and supported Trinitarian theologians in their persecution of Unitarians.

The partial doctrinal continuity of Protestants, without the long traditional foundations of Catholicism, led to countless confessional wars between the Protestants and to a myriad of diverging doctrinal interpretations. The Reformers were willing to grant individual access to the scriptures, but not individual liberty to understand or interpret the scriptures. They stifled unrestrained rational inquiry, logical inferences and demonstrations from the nature of things. They instead continued the old Catholic doctrinal tradition with metaphorical - and at times allegorical - interpretations of scripture, which appeared artificial and arbitrary to many rationally-oriented radical reformers such as the Unitarians and Socinians.[193] The sixteenth-century Reformation replaced the absolute and persecutory Catholic Habsburg monarchy with equally absolute and persecutory national states, and churches which merged confessional uniformity with political fidelity. Religious tolerance and liberty of conscience were considered as anarchic and evil as in the Catholic block; religious and political uniformity was imposed with iron fist and persecutory zeal.

The inter-Protestant scuffles, in addition to the long Catholic Protestant wars, had debilitating effects upon Europe and forced the seventeenth- and eighteenth-century reformers to face the dividing dogmas head on. They felt that the sixteenth-century Reformation required further reformation. "Whereas magisterial Protestants had (in the words of Lancelot Andrewes) embraced 'one Canon. . .two Testaments, three Creeds, the first four Councils, five centuries', radical Protestants were dismissive of creeds, councils, and patristic authorities, especially after the watershed of Constantine's conversion in 312 and the Council of Nicaea in 325."[194] While the Reformers appealed to the Patristic Church of the first five centuries, the radicals appealed only to the Apostolic Church of the first century because, to them, the Church was compromised soon after the initial generations. Religious persecutions were the inventions of compromised church. The Reformation did not resolve the problems connected with Church and state abuses. The supernatural, Trinitarian, Augustinian political theology, with its absolutist tones, suffocated the European society by hampering religious freedom, curtailing rational discourse and combating republican empowerment of masses. That Trinitarian belief system needed to be dismantled or reformed for its hierarchical and persecutory policies to subside. The overseas trade, mid-century English Revolution, abolition of Anglican Church and monarchy, subsequent religious proliferation, relative tolerance, restoration of a weaker monarchy, dialectical struggles between various segments of English society especially between monarchy and parliament, and the Trinitarian controversy of the late seventeenth and early eighteenth century proved to be turning points in the history of Europe in general and England in particular. Islam, Muslims, Turks, Persians and Mughals were constant fixtures through all these crises. Muslims were used and abused but never ignored or discarded, as Nabil Matar, Gerald MacLean, Matthew Birchwood, Humberto Garcia, James Mather and others have shown. Islam featured prominently in the intense battle of early seventeenth century English intellectual warfare and later Enlightenment ideas becoming the voice of religious freedom, tolerance and inclusivism in so many ways and forms.

Through trade, diplomacy, drama, stage and press England encountered Islam, its theology, culture, civilization, history, empires, people and institutions and constructed its identity, aspirations, directions, institutions and policies in conjunction with as well as in opposition to it. The news from Istanbul, Isfahan and Agra were well circulated and digested in London. As the Ottoman and Mughal Empires were experiencing the climax of their civilizational heights, the nascent British aspirations for an empire were being laid in the constitutional transformations, religious reformations and socio cultural and scientific regeneration. The Ottoman, Mughal and Persian Muslims were elemental in shaping the English nation which emerged from the late seventeenth century "Glorious Revolution", limited monarchy, relative religious toleration and diversity. Throughout the long seventeenth century, the English ties with the old Catholic foundations and its religio political theology were gradually weakened and preoccupations with, representations and appropriations of things Islamic were increasingly accelerated. They permeated almost all aspects of the English society from political, religious, commercial, diplomatic and social discourses in limitless ways and forms. Islam was requisitioned in countless discussions about religious dogmas such as the Trinity, Christ's divinity, original sin, satisfaction through Crucifixion, predestination, free will, divine revelation, miracles, Church governance and structure, monarchical sovereignty, tyranny, persecution, liberty of conscience, religious toleration, rights of the rulers and subjects, natural religion, human rights and trade policies. Islam was repeatedly summoned to analyze, evaluate, criticize and reform many English ideologies, policies, emergencies and challenges. The level of engagement with Islam and Muslims depended upon the level of English anxieties. The more the uncertainties such as the English Civil War, Regicide, Interregnum, Restoration, Exclusion Crises, Trinitarian Controversy, Glorious Revolution, the more the eruptions of things Islamic along the ideological fault lines. Through multitudes of actors, networks and mechanisms the ideas of Islam were transmitted to almost every stratum of English society. The English fascination with Islam and Muslims to the extent of obsession was a long-lasting phenomenon throughout the turbulent seventeenth century. It had its religio political and cultural impacts as the encounter with Muslims took a central stage in English identity formation process both positively and negatively. By the end of the seventeenth century, many Islamic ideas, debates, ideals and institutions were totally domesticated, assimilated, appropriated and Anglicized. Through these processes of cultural diffusion, assimilation, appropriation and mirroring, the radical reformation of Servetus, Bruno, Socinians and Unitarians became relevant, palatable and was gradually appropriated by the English intelligentsia.[195]

The mid-century Puritan Revolution was the watershed moment. J. Scott noted that "England's troubles began … as a struggle for reformation, first on the European and then on the local stage. With the collapse of religious and then civil magistracy, civil war radicalism emerged as the radicalisation of that cause. In England, unlike in Germany, the radical army was on the winning side. Consequently the English revolution unleashed in the 1640s became the last and greatest triumph of the European radical reformation."[196] John Coffey has well demonstrated this fact in his chapter "The Last and Greatest Triumph of the European Radical Reformation'? Anabaptism, Spiritualism, and Anti-Trinitarianism in the English Revolution."[197] The rejection of Trinity was the first step towards denying the clergy and kings' claims to absolute power and triadic hierarchical cosmology. The anti-Trinitarian man Christology brought Jesus from the supernatural realms to the terrestrial moral realms. The Church and monarchy and their triadic natural interpretations came crumbling down, along with eradication of supernatural Trinitarian foundations. The anti-Trinitarians insisted upon the human nature of ecclesiastical and monarchical authority, interpretations and institutions. Purging Christianity of its Trinitarian and incarnational supernaturalism meant the demolition of supernatural foundations of clerical/monarchical authority and old educational systems, structures and hierarchy. Divine sovereignty, simplicity, unity and Unitarianism were emphasised; man and nature were directly connected with the One and Only God, bypassing the intermediary beings and institutions. The invisible magical powers and miracles of priests and kings were scrutinised, while miraculous divine and angelic interventions in the natural world were analysed and rejected. Fixed, universal natural laws were hailed and rational, mathematical, empirical, experimental and scientific discourse was encouraged.[198] Man was released of the torturous guilt of original sin, tainted nature, absolute predestination, arbitrary grace-based salvation scheme and ensuing Church and King's absolute prerogatives. Man was dignified, exalted, empowered and incentivised to engage in good works and work towards his felicity.

The gradual socio-economic, religious, scientific and political changes were extensions of the same revolutionary zeal which overtook England during the 1640s. Reason was pitched against Christian mysteries, natural law and religion against supernatural, unintelligible, miraculous, dogmatic Christianity, universal faith against localised particular Christian tradition and moral against ritualistic way of life. To Barbara J. Shapiro, the seventeenth century was the century of "culture of fact" and natural investigation against the medieval culture of mere meditative, contemplative, imaginative, supernatural and miraculous discourse.[199] The nature of Church and King's authority was theological, so the problems of power and authority were resolved by theological alternates. This transition was made possible by the overseas Atlantic and Mediteranean trade with Muslim East, and its drastic impact on religious and political theology and institutions. The rise of an increasingly wealthy merchant middle class diminished the investigative and persecutory powers of Church and state and allowed spread of heterodox doctrines and views. The Muslim world of the sixteenth and seventeenth century was not the marginalized but the dominant other. The overseas trade forced England to adapt itself to the Muslim world. The overseas trade with Muslim empires dictated the terms, conditions and relations and the trade became a central mechanism of cultural exchange between East and England. In Izmir, Aleppo and Istanbul the English engaged in a complex web of cultural negotiations and interactions not only with Eastern Muslims but also with Eastern Christians, Jews and Hindus and rival Western Christians. The outsiders were English merchants and not the Ottomans or Mughals. This experiential inventory and international exposure were instrumental in cross cultural diffusions and cultural hybridity. The English religio political and cultural identity was formulated through these complex webs of encounters, experiences, negotiations and assimilations. I am not referring here to Edward Said's *Orientalism* thesis which emphasizes the role played by the "Orient" in Western ideology, politics and logic of power albeit negatively but to S. C. Chew, Nabil Matar, Gerald MacLean, Daniel Vitkus, Linda McJannet, Matthew Dimmock, Matthew Birchwood, Jonathan Burton and others thesis of "Ottomania", "Turkophilia" and "Islamophilia" which showcases the positive, emulative, apish, mimic and grudging effects Islam and Muslims had upon the English trade, politics, religion, culture and society, as will be elaborated throughout this book. The English identity was formulated both in opposition to and in conjunction with this fascinating Muslim "Other". Mark Greengrass has extended the same hybridization and Levantinization to the entire Continent of Europe.[200] The overseas traders, factors, chaplains, councilors and travelers infused the English public sphere with discussions, arguments and precedents of religious tolerance, diversity, freedom of conscience, social cohesion, wall between Church and state,

Unitarian rational theology, moral anthology, ensuing peace, stability and prosperity effecting overall English identity, culture, race, and religion. The internal English response, both negative and positive, to things Islamic was tremendous to the extent of obsession. From the Elizabethan Settlement to the Glorious Revolution discussions about Turkism, Islamism and Ottoman Empire were the vehicles as well as conceptual field of the English national debates. The Ottoman Sultan spoke various dialects and the English listened with full care and attention, as Linda McJannet has shown. The evolving Anglo Protestant identity and character was both directly and discursively shaped as a result of these encounters. Robert J. Topinka stated that "as England increasingly interacted with Islam, Islam increasingly played a role in shaping English identity."[201] The post Reformation anti-Catholic enthusiasm of the English Crown, parliament, intelligentsia, natural philosophers and dissenters to return to the pristine, primitive Christianity, to certain extents, passed through the Islamic sciences, institutions, religion, history, theology, languages and regions.

Seventeenth and eighteenth-century reformers like John Locke, Isaac Newton, Henry Stubbe, John Toland and Deists were influenced by the radical Unitarian strain of reformation championed by Servetus, Bruno and Socinians. John Coffey noted that "by the late seventeenth century the most intellectually distinguished anti-Trinitarians were Isaac Newton and John Locke, closeted within the establishment and afraid to broadcast their manuscript heterodoxies in print."[202] They dissimulated their heterodox beliefs to avoid persecutions. The seventeenth century was the century of Nicodemism as Perez Zagorin has amply demonstrated. He further stated that "anti-Trinitarianism that had flourished among certain radical Puritans would in due course exercise its greatest appeal among members of the established church, including John Locke, Isaac Newton, and Samuel Clarke (though the most radical speculations of Locke and Newton remained unpublished). In the eighteenth-century Church of England, Arianism and Socinianism would provoke fierce controversy. Radical Reformation had entered the bloodstream of English Protestantism."[203] English and French Unitarians and Deists such as Henri Boulainvilliers, d'Argenson, Du Marsais, jean-Baptiste de Mirabaud, Nicolas Boindin, jean Levesque de Burigny, Louis de Brehant, comte de Plelo (1699-1734), the Chevalier de Ramsay and other known French deists[204] purged Christianity of the remaining incarnational reservoirs, the remnants of ancient Christian Platonic grafting, and brought it in line with the pristine moral Christianity of Jesus Christ and his original followers, the *Nasara* or Nazarenes.[205] Moral Christianity required the clergy and royalty to showcase moral leadership instead of claiming supernatural God-given rights and privileges based on direct communication with God. This moral, anti-Trinitarian Christianity was in total opposition to the supernatural, Trinitarian, Incarnational, miraculous and abnormal Christianity. There was no room in it for Trinity, original sin, justification through faith and grace, predestination, ecclesiastical hierarchy and clerical abuses. It replaced the miraculous abnormality with normal, natural and moral laws.[206] This Christianity was nothing but a moral tradition in line with the universal monotheistic prophetic tradition. In other words, it was a Muhammadan Christianity, as Henry Stubbe and John Toland termed it, in direct opposition to the traditional Church Christianity. The seventeenth-century reformation of Roman Christianity was made possible by the century-long cross-cultural exchanges, experiences and interactions between countless Levant and East India Company's overseas traders and Muslims, causing a commercial consumer culture, a paradigm shift from supernatural to natural, from authority based miraculous knowledge to experimental, empirical knowledge leading to a scientific revolution, as well as the creation of a public sphere and egalitarian public places such as Turkish coffeehouses, which contributed to British internal instability. It was politically facilitated by English merchants, overseas trading companies' stake holders all across Britian, including gentry and members of parliament, who curtailed and balanced the Crown's authority. Intellectually, natural philosophers such as the fellows of Royal Society provided an alternate natural, rational, impartial, universal and empirical method of certitude through data collection and experimentation. The authority based Aristotelian scholasticism and old Ptolemaic cosmology was challenged and corrected by experience, experiments and overseas explorations especially to the Near East. Their rational discourse was a welcome addition to a culture of religious scepticism, anxiety and uncertainty created by radicals such as Socinians, Unitarians and Deists. The scientific rational discourse and data-driven experimentation supplanted the Church claims of Christian mysteries over and beyond reason. The theological discursive rationalism of Unitarians and Socinions was supplemented by the scientific and philosophical rational certitude of Boyle, Newton and Locke and Anglican Latitudinarians;[207] they were two sides of the same coin in matters of theology. The main difference between the radical secretaries, Unitarian, Socinian and Deist radicals and moderate reformers such as Locke, Newton, Royal Society fellows and Latitudinarians was that the radical reformers aspired and intended to abolish hierarchical social order, absolutist church and monarchy and replace it with republican, voluntarist and egalitarian religio-political and social institutions. The moderates, on the other hand, did not intend to abolish Church and monarchy in an effort to preserve social order, stability, peace and hierarchy. The socio-economic and political upheavals caused by the mid-century English revolution were appalling enough to be avoided at all costs. The moderates vouched for an internal reformation which struggled to rationalise theology, curtail and constitutionalise monarchy, empower parliament and support a commercial, mercantile and capitalist market economy with social hierarchy and stratification.[208] The moderates were more calculated, catious and systematic than the radical reformers and their subversive strategies, but their moderate internal reformation was quite radical in its ambitions and ultimate goals, in addition to being Unitarian and republican. This way, the reformation of Reformation, aspired by Michael Servetus, Bruno and their intellectual disciples such as Socinians, Unitarians and Deists with the help of Oriental manuscripts and exposure and their absorption by the English natural philosophers, brought about the early English Enlightenment (1650-1720) and a limited monarchy which led to High Enlightenment and later democratic systems. The late Renaissance period and seventeenth century were crucial landmarks and flash points of this radical reformation and transition. Throughout this crucial period both Muslims and their legacy were integral to English identity and self-definition. From trade to fashion, theology to politics, domestic to foreign affairs, preachers to renegades, churches to coffeehouses, soldiers to sailors, international merchants to local weavers, the Ottoman, Mughal and Persian Empires, their people, cultures, policies and affairs were hotly debated, analyzed, discussed, described, accepted and rejected. The Briton's engagement with things Islamic especially from 1558 to 1685 was unprecedented. No other single non-Christian civilization left such a mark on England as the Muslim civilization did during this long and crucial period of English identity formation. Therefore, the English Renaissance and Enlightenment were inter-Mediterranean and inter-religious affairs. Islam, Muslims, Muslim thought patterns were useful both in religio political theology. England did not engage Islam and Muslims for the love of them but because they were too relevant to be ignored. They were "useful enemies" as Sir Noel Malcolm's recent book *Useful Enemies* amply demonstrates. "The East was not only too important to be ignored; it was too interesting—and, most of all, too useful."[209]

To truly grasp the scope and depth of this transformation we need to delineate the nature of divine right monarchy and Church, its theological foundations and its long medieval history. The absolutist Church and monarchy were integral parts of the socio-religious consciousness and imagery of Christendom from the fourth to the eighteenth century. Its roots were very deep, its branches were widespread and its overwhelming religious power and political reach did not allow any serious internal intellectual or political challenge. It was only due to the Protestant Reformation that the constituent elements of such an absolutist supernatural ideology were indirectly weakened, allowing the possibility of penetration through its porous borders. The Protestant slogan *Sola Scriptura* posed serious challenges to the Church traditions. The new emerging national states and churches did not have enough time and tradition to construct a full-fledged or well thought-out doctrinal system and political theology. Their existence was hinging on opposition to Catholicism, and they could not afford to transport Catholic doctrines and ideas into the new system. The ensuing doctrinal instability, fluidity and uncertainty allowed the emergence of radical interpretations and unorthodox understandings, and the individual approach to the Scriptures opened a floodgate of new interpretations and directions.[210] The absence of overwhelming ecclesiastical and overpowering state establishments exasperated the situation. The inter Catholic and Protestant and intra Protestant wars additionally drained resources and increased instability, insecurity and radicalism. The foreign Muslim ideas of religious tolerance, pluralism, limited monarchy and rationalism appropriated and propagated by the Levant and East India Company influential merchants added fuel to the fire. The extra ordinary geo-political and religious circumstances of seventeenth-century Western Europe facilitated the intellectual and theological revolution, which eroded the foundations of the *Old Regime* absolutism and allowed further reformation of Protestantism on Islamic rational, natural and republican lines. The outcome was the Muhammadan Christianity of Henry Stubbe, John Toland, John Locke and others.

We need to understand the process of Islamic reformation of Church Christianity to fully grapple the contours and long-term impacts of this Muhammadan Christianity upon the Roman Christianity.

Chapter 1

Roman Christianity and Its Socio-Political Thought

The Christian faith is very unique and complex; it revolves around a historical person Jesus Christ who is simultaneously considered God and man.[211] Its Trinitarian metaphysics and faith-based salvation scheme is very distinctive. Its incarnational theology is supernatural, top-down, hierarchical, absolutist, paradoxical and mysterious. Its concept of human nature, society and human destiny is amazingly arbitrary, puzzling and complex.[212] It is a faith which is neither fully Semitic nor fully Hellenistic, but a metamorphosis of Jewish and Roman traditions. The historical Christian faith system is supernatural where God, heavens, cosmic threats, sacrifices, atonements and salvation are emphasised often at the expense of man, nature, society, terrestrial realms and utilitarian sphere of now and here. Man is a small pawn in the cosmic scheme of things. This celestial, supernatural Christian faith system is antithetical to the terrestrial, natural, moral, ethical, monotheistic Semitic consciousness.[213]

Historical Jesus lived among the Jews and inherited the Semitic monotheistic consciousness.[214] The occupying Roman Empire was ruled by pagan emperors. The egalitarian Jesus and his early followers were at a loss to fight the overpowering absolutist Roman authorities and were severely persecuted by the Roman officials. The moral, natural and simple monotheistic faith of Jesus was pitched against supernatural, complex, polytheistic and mystery religions of the Roman elites.

The Greco-Roman world was filled with mystery religions and cults which preached mystical cleansing of sins through sacrificial death of a saviour. The tragedy and sacrificial ritual narratives were central to Greco-Roman culture, drama and religious landscape. The Early Christian Church had difficulties in winning over the Roman pagans to Semitic monotheism. Its long conflict with mystery religions left an indelible impact upon the Church theology. It is impossible to deny such a long-lasting influence.[215] Consequently, the Church developed a number of dogmas, using biblical vocabulary but Greco-Roman imagery and concepts, to win over the Roman masses; the result was a Roman Christianity, at odds with the original Semitic monotheistic consciousness of Jesus and his surroundings.

The central Christian dogmas such as the cosmic threat to man due to inherent human depravity (fallen nature, original sin), need for a cosmic saviour and substitutionary sacrifice, incarnation, belief in the saving acts of the saviour, initiation in the cult and salvation through the atoning death were reflections of the dominant Greco-Roman culture. Once incorporated they rendered human participation in the Christian scheme of salvation insignificant, while emphasising divine incentive and grace; outward moral virtue, good actions and righteousness played second fiddle to inward belief and knowledge. Faith in the mystery of Trinity, incarnation and atoning death was required over and beyond knowledge, reason and human actions. Faith and salvation were dependent upon true knowledge of supernatural realities and doctrines; that knowledge was not earned but a gift given to a selected few due to divine selection and predestination. The Church stood at the top of pyramid as the repository of divine knowledge, the revelation. True faith and knowledge were reflected through the interpretations given to divine revelation by the Church Fathers. These understandings made up the "tradition" of the Church, the lens through which the Christian faith and salvation were to be mirrored. The Church was central to human salvation as the dispenser of divine knowledge and grace; there was no salvation outside the Church and there was no authentic knowledge outside the Scriptures and Church tradition. The Church enjoyed sole interpretive authority, due to its supposed direct link with the Holy Spirit. Theology was the queen of sciences and all sciences, including natural sciences, were to submit to it. Any deviation from the Church dogmas and interpretations was heretical and punished by God. The Church was hierarchical and its clerical establishment enjoyed absolute authority, privileges and honours due to its transcendental dimensions.

The Christian religion was distinctive in the sense that it diminished human dignity, ethico spiritual capacities and self-esteem. The Christian dogma of original sin and depraved human nature downplayed human autonomy, freedom and dignity. Man was too evil, childish and wretched to be left on his own, and needed God via the Church and rulers to keep himself in line. It diminished larger human participation in salvation, socio-political and civic arena. The social order was hierarchical, top-down and absolutist. The Christian notion of God was equally beyond the comprehension of man due to his tainted fallen nature. The Trinitarian Godhead was mysterious, complex and paradoxical, and only the Church could fully grasp it. It was to be believed and obeyed, in conformity with the Church interpretations, without asking questions or delving deep into its mysteries.

The Christian dogmas about creation, human nature, virtues, salvation, justice and love were equally arbitrary; they were solely God's incentives mostly beyond human logic and comprehension. Man was to believe in these lofty, mysterious and unintelligible dogmas to attain his eternal salvation. The supernatural completely dominated and absorbed the natural, logical and rational realms. Man was truly depraved and deprived. Additionally, the central dogmas of Christianity were understood and interpreted divergently, even within the Church tradition. The diversity of opinions, interpretations and implications was mind-boggling. The authentic, sanctioned and genuine was to be determined by the Church without much participation from believers who were supposed to blindly follow the Church teachings under spectacles of dire punishments. The Church Christianity was an absolutely top-down system of submission, conformity and obedience.

God created Adam and Eve with omniscience to live in the Garden of Eden and commanded them to abstain from eating fruits of the forbidden tree. The Serpent deceivingly persuaded them to eat the forbidden apple, with the promise that they would live for eternity. Eve, the weaker partner, succumbed to the plot and not only ate the forbidden fruit but also gave it to Adam. God expelled them both from the Paradise. This was called the original "Fall" due to original sin. Man was destined by God to live for eternity, but Adam's sin brought upon man death, ignorance and perdition. Consequently, all children of Adam were born with that original sin and fallen nature. Man, as a result of that fallen nature, was depraved, wretched and destined to hellfire; his human nature was tainted, and man was born as sinful, lustful and wretched. He did not have the capacity to differentiate between right and wrong, between good and bad and was always inclined towards evil, if left to himself. There was no exception to this rule. All mankind, all children of Adam inherited the original sin and tainted nature and were liable to its evil consequences and eternal punishments. In short, all were condemned to hellfire.

The Merciful God could not see that happening. He thought of forgiving Adam and his progeny, but his sense of justice did not allow him to forgive mankind without exacting punishment. His boundless love on the other hand demanded forgiveness. God could not see countless children of Adam eternally condemned to hellfire. Therefore, he came up with a plan to save humanity of its original sin and its eternal evil consequences. As the sin was against God and of cosmic nature it needed a cosmic solution. No man could be part of that solution as all men were equally tainted, depraved and wretched. Consequently, God decided to sacrifice his only begotten Son for the sake of mankind. Jesus Christ, the Son of God and the Second Person of the Holy Trinity took on the flesh to understand the human conditions, to unite with humanity in everything other than sin and to die on the Cross for their sins as satisfaction of human debt to God. This way both God's love and justice were satisfied. God could justly forgive human sins out of his love by accepting the sacrificial death of his only begotten, sinless, cosmic Son of cosmic significance.

Consequently, anybody who believed in the Trinity, divinity of Jesus Christ, his Lordship, atoning death and resurrection was saved and those who denied Christ's divinity, Lordship, Incarnation or Crucifixion were condemned.

The Christian tradition was a Trinitarian faith where monotheism was reflected through the prism of a triune God. God the Holy Father, Son and Holy Spirit made up the Godhead.[216] They were considered equal in Godhead, from the same divine substance, having three different persons, identities and consciousness. They were three in one and one in three.

Augustinian and Cappadocian Models

The Trinity meant different things to different schools of Christian thought.[217] The Cappadocian Trinitarian paradigm was considerably different from the Augustinian model. The Cappadocian model emphasised distinction of persons, a sort of diversity within divine unity, while the Augustinian model underscored unity of persons, will and substance. The Cappadocian social unity leaned more towards three independent, self-conscious persons while the Augustinian Trinity gravitated more towards Unity of Father, Son and Holy Spirit, differing only in modes. The Cappadocian model was accused of tri-theism while the Augustinian model was blamed for Modalism, a blurring of the difference between the Father, Son and Holy Spirit. Both parties accused each other of compromising the spirit of true doctrine, but there were countless unresolved issues inherent in both of the classical models. Was the internal unity of three persons a social unity of independent persons, wills, actions or a unity of substance? Were the three persons of the Trinity the three individual modes of existence of the one and same God, consisting in their mutual relationship, or did it refer to three distinct individuals, separate centers of consciousness, three self-conscious personal beings? In both scenarios the question remained the same. On the Cross (Matt. 27:46), was God calling upon Himself for help or was one independent person of Godhead calling upon another independent person of Godhead for help? In the first scenario it was "Modalism" or "Docetism", a total absurdity. Why would God call upon his own self for help? In the other scenario it was a "vulgar tritheism", to use Karl Rahner's term,[218] or at least "Subordinationism" i.e., a lesser god was seeking a higher God's help. Centuries of Church Councils, controversies and solutions could not resolve this puzzle and finally it was declared a mystery. This Trinitarian, supernatural mystery was too complicated, mysterious and unintelligible to many believers; it needed civic power to impose it. That became the herald of a long-lasting intolerant, persecutory, inquisitorial, abusive, supernatural, hierarchical and offensive system of Christian Church and state.

The supernatural incarnational theology and Bible were used as the foundational stones for the absolute political theology and hierarchical social order. A divinely appointed political order was made essential to direct man and his world. The world was divided into sacred and profane; the sacred was the realm of spirituality supervised by the priests and clerics, while the profane was directed by the kings and magistrates. The depraved man needed constant supervision otherwise evil, anarchy and oppression would prevail. Man, his rights, freedoms, participation in the affairs of society, culture and government were all trampled in the name of depraved fallen nature, evil disposition and uncivilised manners. The democratic and republican political models of Greco-Roman world were replaced with the absolute Church and state. Man was merely a recipient of divine grace facilitated through the good offices of the Church and monitored by the monarchy. It was an absolutely top-down system of religious and political theology. God, cosmos, salvation and redemption were too complicated and mysterious for a common person to understand; therefore, blind imitation of the Church was the only way out. Society was organised based upon this supernatural worldview.

It was hierarchical, just like the natural order and universe. The Church as the sole dispenser of divine knowledge and grace stood at the top of the spiritual pyramid. Monarch and nobility followed the clergy. Everybody else was the laity, the commoners and the followers. This way human participation, in both the spiritual and political realms, was limited mostly to submission and obedience. The limited elites, including the ecclesiastical and monarchical establishments, ruled the society with iron hands and absolute laws. They ruled in the name of God, and were responsible only to Him. Christendom became an authoritarian, close and suffocating society for long medieval centuries. The Church dogmas, especially the Trinitarian incarnational theology with its absolutist political theology, were directly responsible for this mystery filled, anti-intellectual, anti-republican persecutory culture.

The supernatural faith system completely devoured the natural realms. The revelation dominated reason, faith suppressed intellectual inquiries and divine right monarchy inhibited democratic and republican values. Demand for religious and political uniformity curbed diversity, creativity, freedoms, rights and tolerance. Politico-religious intolerance led to persecution of dissent, diversity and individualism. All paths to individual liberty, independent thinking, initiatives, creativity, competition and growth were systematically, religiously and transcendentally closed. The Christian belief system emphasised success in the hereafter mostly at the expense of this worldly life. The Church was the sole proprietor of eternal salvation, and hence submission to Church dogmas was central to salvation.

The Divine Right Church and Salvation

Success in the life to come was far more significant than success in this life. Eternal salvation was not attained via morality, good actions or human incentives; it was a gift of God. The original sin of Adam and Eve was transmitted to their progeny and humanity shared that tainted, depraved and wretched nature. Man was unable to achieve salvation, perfection and happiness by his finite knowledge, capacities and incentives. It needed divine intervention of cosmic level. God incarnated in the material world to save humanity of its wretchedness.

The salvation began with belief in the saving acts of Lord Jesus Christ and the act of human cleansing ensued. Self-purification, moral reformation and righteous acts were not the foundations of Christian salvation. Rather, moral reformation was an automatic consequence of faith in Christ. The gift of eternal life was also not the result of human efforts but of divine grace. Therefore, salvation was selective, predestined and in a sense arbitrary; it was as mysterious and foggy as the Holy Trinity. It was God who bestowed the gift of salvation upon the sinful by forgiving them (Acts 13:26, 46; 28:28; Eph 4:32; Col 2:13) and reconciling them to Himself (Rom 5:10; 2 Cor 5:18-19; Eph. 2:8-10; Luke 15:11-32; 19:10)

In spite of multiple controversies and divergent interpretations, the official Christianity, remained faithful to the dogma of original sin and man's depravity. St. Augustine theorised[219] it further and entrenched it in the Christian faith.[220] The sixteenth-century Reformation stayed close to these understandings of original sin,[221] redemptive crucifixion of Christ and predestination.[222] The Catholics and Protestants (Lutherans, Calvinists, Anglicans and Evangelicals) insisted upon the grace, at the expense of good works and human efforts. The whole Trinitarian, incarnational and substitutionary sacrificial scheme was promoted to atone for the so-called "Original Sin" or later human inequities. The end result was a total sense of guilt consciousness, lack of confidence in human abilities and sheer dependence upon Church and polity for success and salvation.[223]

The Trinity, incarnation and resurrection were mysteries and could not be grasped by limited human reason; they needed faith and grace, and the only source of true faith was the revelation. God had spoken to us through His Word, Jesus Christ, and the spoken word of God was preserved in the Bible. Therefore, the only thing one needed to attain salvation was the Bible; there was no need for additional thinking, sciences and knowledge. All truth, wisdom, morality and common sense were contained in the revelation. In short, to succeed, one needed to understand the divine revelation, digest its precepts and live one's life accordingly. Nobody had understood the revelation more than the Early Church Fathers, as they were closest to the times of Christ. The Catholic Church, or the Church, was the repository of their teachings. Therefore, obeying the Church was tantamount to obeying the Church Fathers and obeying them was tantamount to obeying Christ, the God. Therefore, instead of wasting time in studying the pagan Greek philosophical writings, one was required to study the Church traditions and willingly submit to the Church. There was no salvation outside the Church.[224] The Church, according to the favourite image of the Fathers, "was a solitary ark floating upon a boundless sea of ruin. Within its pale there was salvation; without it salvation was impossible. 'If any one out of Noah's ark could escape the deluge,' wrote St Cyprian, 'he who is out of the Church may also escape.' 'Without this house,' said Origen, 'that is without the Church, no one is saved.' 'No one,' said St. Augustine, cometh to salvation and eternal life except he who hath Christ for his head; but no one can have Christ for his head except he that is in His body the Church.' 'Hold most firmly,' added St. Fulgentius,' and doubt not that not only all pagans, but also all Jews, heretics, and schismatics who depart from this present life outside the Catholic Church, are about to go into eternal fire, prepared for the devil and his angels.' So prominent and so unquestionable was this doctrine deemed, that the Council of Carthage, in the fourth century, made it one of the test questions put to every bishop before ordination."[225]

The Divine Right State

In addition to ecclesiastic authority, God also established the civic authority to manage affairs of the world. Unqualified submission to worldly authorities was as essential as submission to the Church. The smooth, secure, peaceful and stable society was the prelude to spiritual stability and that depended upon unqualified submission to worldly laws and authorities.

The New Testament books in general (for instance 1 Peter 2:13-17) and the Pauline corpus in particular were the most precise, pinpointed and unequivocal proponents of such a submission.[226] Paul was highly interested in peace and order and provided religious undergirding for a stable society. In Roman 13:1-7 Paul clearly equated obedience to higher authorities with divine submission. The political, social, moral and legal authorities were not manmade but God-made, and hence absolute submission to them was divinely ordained. The Epistle of Paul to Romans 13:1-7 clearly laid down the fundamentals of Paul's exousiology. This passage had the contours of divine right monarchy and absolutism cherished by later Christian communities; it was crystal-clear in its aims and implications.[227] God was the sole authority in the world, and nothing happened without his permission and plans; Paul's doctrine of absolute predestination was at full play here. The kings, monarchs and magistrates were voluntarily appointed by God and did not have the capacity to usurp the authority from him. This was in conformity with overall theology of the Bible.[228] Obeying the rulers was equal to obeying God, and resisting them was tantamount to resisting God. Christianity was no politics.[229] This was the duty of each soul. Civil and political revolt or unrest was divinely proscribed and punished.[230] The civil authorities had a religious role in implementing God's plan for peace, order and security. God was the creator of an orderly cosmos. The political and civil authorities were a prototype of the divine realms in creating order in the temporal society.

The Pauline passage was generic, universal and unqualified; it did not differentiate between good and bad, Christian or non-Christian, monarchical or democratic, consultative or dictatorial power structures. It demanded an absolute submission to the higher authorities whosoever they were.[231] Any relativity, qualification or restriction on their power was superfluous.[232] Paul insisted that the existing power structures embodied the will of God by rewarding goodness and punishing evil.[233] This was an extension of Jesus' command of rendering unto Caesar what was due to Caesar.[234] (Mk. 12:17; Matt. 20:21) Jesus' trial and crucifixion were interpreted as a voluntary submission to the temporal authorities; Jesus presented himself to the Roman court and accepted the crucifixion as a token of submission to their authority. Jesus also told the persecuting Pilate that his authority was from God. The idea of unqualified submission to human authorities even at time of persecution was augmented by the Pauline treatment of the subject. Paul in reality Hellenised Christianity. The idea of an absolute submission even to the persecuting evil dictators was equal to paganisation of Christianity.

The early Church from Constantine's times onward and both the Catholic and Protestants down the centuries all had accepted this interpretation of the New Testament as official. Therefore, the doctrine of absolute submission to the worldly authorities was considered religious, official and orthodox. In short, historical Church Christianity was totally imperial, absolutist and top-down. There was no room in it for Greco-Roman rationalism, individualism, self-pride, pagan, anarchist democratic institutions, republican values, rights and freedoms. Church Christianity was antithetical to individualism and republicanism. The divinely-sanctioned Church and state had the right of disciplining the sinful, depraved and wretched masses to the extent of physical torture, maiming, killing and other kinds of persecutions.[235] The Christian Church became known for its persecution of heretics.

Heresy and Divinely Sanctioned Terror

The idea of heresy was found in the New Testament, but no concept of punishment, coercion or silencing was attached to it; coercion against heretics was the creation of later orthodoxy.[236] There was no heresy in Christianity of the first century as there was no established orthodoxy, New Testament Canon, Catholic or Orthodox hierarchical Church, Pope or a set of orthodox doctrine. The Roman Empire pretty much tolerated all sorts of religious sects, and early Christianity was quite diversified.

The efforts to unite Christians upon a unitary Christian doctrine concerning Jesus and his relationship with God had to wait till 325 AD when Emperor Constantine struggled to rein in the warring bishops in the Council of Nicaea. Initially, Constantine was not inclined towards coercion or persecution of heretics; he encouraged dialogue and toleration for the sake of unity. Constantine turned the previously persecuted Christian church into an imperial Church, and the wealth and power brought envy, jealousy and rivalries. The processes of identification and differentiation were intensified.[237] In spite of his efforts to restore peace and unite Christians on a unitary doctrine, Constantine did not use torture or physical coercion to rein in the so-called heretics. The theological controversies continued after his death. The West was mostly Nicene and the East mostly Arian, and Constantine's son emperor Constantius II (emperor from 337-361) was pro-Arian. He, through a number of councils, rehabilitated the heretic Arians at the cost of the Nicene party, rendering them virtually powerless. His successor Julian ruled by dividing the warring Christian factions further. The Christological controversies had rocked the entire Roman Empire by the time of Theodosius, Roman Emperor from AD 379 to AD 395. Constantinople was a city where everyone was a theologian. Gregory of Nyssa observed that "this is a city where every slave and artisan is a profound theologian. Ask one of them to change some silver and he explains instead how the Son differs from the Father. Ask another the price of a loaf of bread and he replies that the Son is inferior to the Father. Ask a third if your bath is ready and he tells you that the Son was created out of nothingness."[238]

Theodosius was a different kind of emperor. He was a child of the Mother Church, seeing everything through the prism of his eternal salvation. As a staunch believer in the Nicene Creed, he allowed the Church to use the political arm of the state to impose the Nicene Christology. Under the influence of Ambrose of Milan, he prohibited all sorts of heresies and enacted laws to punish them. In Salonica, in February of 380, Theodosius issued as decree establishing the Apostolic Creed and religion of Peter as the sole authority in his empire.[239] He further ordered that "we command that those persons who follow this rule shall embrace the name of Catholic Christians. The rest, however, whom we adjudge demented and insane, shall sustain the infamy of heretical dogmas, their meeting places shall not receive the name of churches, and they shall be smitten first by divine vengeance and secondly by the retribution of our own initiative, which we shall assume in accordance with divine judgement."[240]

This edict transformed the concept of heresy in Christianity requiring punishment both spiritual and temporal.[241] Such a strict and abusive concept of heresy was a Christian invention not found in Judaism or the early Roman laws. Arians and other anti-Nicene Christian sects were persecuted.[242] Previously the dissenting actions and practices were proscribed, but Theodosius extended it to intent and belief. Harbouring wrong belief was detrimental to the soul and its salvation. Saving the soul was a Christian duty. The emperor as the chief Christian was supposed to help the Church in saving the lost souls to ensure divine pleasure and grace for the empire. Therefore, submission to the orthodox Nicene Christology and Creed was in reality a submission to the state and rebellion against the established official Church was tantamount to rebellion against the state.[243] The resultant hierarchical, absolutist social order well suited the divine right Church and monarchy.

Theodosius created a new religious order, uniting the Roman imperial power closely with the Catholic Church. The Bishop of Rome was also exalted as the supreme religious authority in the empire.[244] Persecution of heretics entailed mostly economic and social sanctions until the fourth century; the theological formulations for the use of physical coercion were a later development. It was St. Augustine (354–430) who provided the theological foundations for religious persecution and coercion.[245]

Augustine and Religious Coercion

St. Augustine initially believed in religious freedom and shunned religious persecution. Later on, he changed his mind after seeing a great number of Donatist heretics returning to the Catholic Church as a result of imperial laws. He felt that civil coercion was a useful tool in maintaining religious orthodoxy and uniformity. The history changed along with the change of Augustine's mind.[246]

Augustine around 400 A. D. seemed to accept and encourage religious coercion. In a letter to the Donatist bishop Parmenian, he justified use of imperial power to coerce Donatists into Catholicism. Quoting Romans 13:1-7, Augustine established the God-given right of the emperor to persecute those responsible for schism. He used Matthew 13:24-30 (parable of weeds) to authorise physical coercion against the heretics. The parable was usually interpreted as permitting religious pluralism and differing opinions leaving the judgement to God on the Day of Judgment. Augustine, however, drew from it a very different lesson, "if the bad seed is known, it should be uprooted."[247] Augustine argued that the Lord Jesus Christ used physical coercion and compulsion to make Paul submit and believe.[248] To Augustine, fear was a category of love, and absolutely permitted to save the soul from eternal condemnation.[249] The Catholic Church as mother must coerce its children to follow its creeds and practices, and the fear of flogging might keep the sheep together.[250] He insisted that "Paul was compelled by Christ; therefore the Church, in trying to compel the Donatists, is following the example of her Lord."[251] These pastoral metaphors "allowed Augustine and like-minded colleagues to rationalise policies that forced people, willing or not, toward the good. Charity—the Christian duty to love one's neighbour—demanded no less."[252] Augustine and the Catholic Church demanded the charity of submission and reconciliation on its own terms without any regard to the neighbour and his needs of charity and reconciliation. To reinforce his view, he quoted the parable of the feast in the Gospel of Luke (Luke 14:21-23); in the parable of the feast Jesus is reported to have asked the disciples to compel people to come in. Augustine required forcing heretics and others to join the fold of orthodoxy.[253]

Augustine combined the spiritual reasons with the needs of the empire to construct a comprehensive doctrine of religious coercion and persecution. The emperors had always considered peace as the foundation of imperial prosperity and dissention as the source of divine wrath. The Catholic Church was doing nothing short of realising peace by dint of religious coercion.[254]

The Saint seems to have a bad legacy. The world might have not witnessed the killing, maiming, burning and torturing of countless Christians and non-Christians throughout the late antiquity and medieval world had Augustine not provided the scriptural basis for religious coercion. The medieval Inquisitions[255] took their lead from the Saint and did the most unholy crimes in the name of the Most Holy. The Saint might not have thought of this legacy, but the outcome of his theorising has been barbaric.[256] The historian Peter Brown, who has extensively studied and written about St. Augustine, noted that Augustine was the only Church Father who had discussed the subject of religious coercion with such precision and length.[257] Brown argued that Augustine's prophetic interpretation of human history, close interactions with the harsh theology of the Old Testament and peculiar concepts of grace and predestination played a role in his attitude towards religious coercion.[258] The Saint had a totalitarian vision; unqualified imperial support for the Church, continuous retreat of paganism and scathing pursuit of the Jews and heretics by the state substantiated his dream that the kingdom of God was at hand, and a new era of absolute and universal submission to the gospel was about to commence. All people and nations must praise the Lord, and any deviations from the Catholic Church and its creeds were nothing short of belligerence that needed to be uprooted. The Saint intended to expedite the kingdom by his attitude of religious coercion and reformation. This was an expression of his ultimate love for the heretics as he wanted to compel them to enter the kingdom. Unfortunately for the heretics, he was nothing short of the Antichrist. They lost their personal properties, churches, jobs, businesses and at times their lives due to Augustine's attitude and doctrine.[259] Unfortunately religious coercion and persecution were Augustine's horrible legacies for future generations. Both the state and Church adopted them as official policies without many changes or modifications. The emperors initiated the persecuting laws and the bishops made their implementation certain.[260]

Religious persecution - especially those of pagans and Christian heretics - had become an intrinsic part of the emperor's responsibilities by the time of Justinian.[261] Inward and outward conformity to the Catholic Church and its creeds was required of all citizens, and outsiders were persecuted.[262] Jews, pagans and Christian heretics were "barred from schools, court jobs, public offices, inheritance and even charity. They were really despised as pestilence. The traitors of the Church and Lord were the traitors of the empire. Justinian would personally oversee the execution, burning and drowning of many heretics. One orthodox observer would exclaim that "the *dux* has lately become a Christian by zeal of the Christ-loving emperor."[263] The following Christian centuries were well-known for their persecution of heretics and dissenters, and the medieval Inquisitions well-illustrated the persecuting impulses of the medieval Church. Religious persecution continued in the Christendom all the way to the eighteenth century.

Over the centuries, the Roman Christianity manifested itself into antinomianism, irrationalism, monarchism, absolutism and religious intolerance.[264] These tendencies were to become the legacy of Roman Christianity to the medieval world all the way to the eighteenth century. The Habsburg Monarchy of the sixteenth century (in the person of Charles V) represented this post Constantinian Roman ideology of universal monarchy of "one king, one law and one religion", supplemented by the sixteenth century apocalyptic, messianic prophecies and imperial millennial propaganda based on astrological prognostications. This hegemonic ideology was enhanced by profound changes and upheavals in the world. The Church schisms, spectacular Ottoman rise to the power, vast and countless opportunities in the New World, inter-cultural and inter-continental navigations, communications, outbreak of plagues, wars, destructions and expulsion of Jews from Spain all fueled the fans of apocalyptic, messianic millennium. A missionary zeal, craze for uniformity, divine right monarchy and church, doctrinal purity, unity, obedience and second coming of Jesus accompanied the imperial millennial propaganda.

Both the Catholic and Protestant Churches inherited the above sketched historical Christianity and equally believed in its central dogmas, thought patterns, worldview and political theology.[265] The main difference was the Church settlement. The Catholic Habsburg settlement was non-Erastian and the Church and Pope were autonomous, independent and supreme in ecclesiastical matters while the Protestant world tended towards an Erastian Church settlement where the king or prince consolidated both religious and civic powers and the state was supreme in ecclesiastical matters. The Christendom of the sixteenth and seventeenth centuries, in spite of Catholic and Protestant divide, was pretty much unified on the central Christian dogmas such as the original sin, divinity of Jesus, the Trinity, Crucifixion, atoning death of Jesus, predestination, grace-based salvation scheme, ecclesiastical and monarchical absolutism. Jonathan Israel notes that "admittedly the Reformation had earlier engendered a deep split in western Christendom. But throughout the Sixteenth century and the first half of the Seventeenth, there was still much, intellectually and spiritually, that the western segments of Christendom shared. Mid-seventeenth- century Europe was still, not just predominantly but overwhelmingly, a culture in which all debates about man, God, and the World which penetrated into the public sphere revolved around 'confessional'-that is Catholic, Lutheran, Reformed (Calvinist), or Anglican issues, and scholars fought above all to establish which confessional bloc possessed a monopoly of truth and a God-given title to authority. It was a civilisation in which almost no one challenged the essentials of Christianity or the basic premises of what was taken to be a divinely ordained system of aristocracy, monarchy, land-ownership, and ecclesiastical authority."[266]

The seventeenth- and eighteenth-century Enlightenment reformers felt that "the 'corrupted' religion prevailing in both Catholic and Protestant Europe had been thoroughly muddled and muddied by 'superstition', bogus doctrines, and false 'miracles', as well as superfluous notions of ecclesiastical authority; and while the chief offender in all respects was the Catholic Church, and especially the papacy, all the other major and minor churches, including the Calvinists, Lutherans, Anglicans, and Greek Orthodox, were in varying degrees likewise at fault."[267] The countless lives lost during the Wars of religion, Inquisitions, witch hunts, continuous instability, insecurity and destruction led many elites to think that Christianity in all its forms and institutions was a problem, which needed to be replaced with something minimalistic, rational, republican and civic. Social peace, harmony, human betterment, prosperity and improvement were the fundamental goals and concerns of the Enlightenment and its leaders.[268] John Robertson placed "the commitment to understanding, and hence to advancing, the causes and conditions of human betterment in this world"[269] as the core of the Enlightenment. The early Enlightenment was predominantly theologico-political, mostly aimed at the authoritarian Church and monarchy.[270] It was Antichristian, anti-clerical and anti-dogmatic but not anti-faith as such.[271] The Enlightenment leaders targeted reformation of both the Catholic and Protestant forms of Christianity because the Christian politico-religious theology was equally fundamental to the Catholic Habsburg monarchy of the Seventeenth and Eighteenth century as it was to the Protestant Anglican Church and its patron, the British Crown. The eighteenth-century Enlightenment was intrinsically against this version of absolute religious and political authority and institutions. The Scientific Revolution, natural theology and cosmology were an outcome of such a sea change of mindset. The seventeenth-century political upheavals in England were the results of overseas trading companies, their stake holders and increasing middle class' struggle for protection of capital, distribution of power and previleges. As the Crown enjoyed executive powers over state and Church properties, courts and institutions and used absolute powers in the name of God, the opposition to divine right church and monarchy also took a religious garb.

The Enlightenment war against *Old Regime* and structures of authority was fought on the religious turf. In 1690s "there began in England a concerted attack both on the central doctrines and on the external proofs of orthodox Christianity. From one quarter, the divine inspiration of the Bible was questioned. Thereby the historic context and cosmological significance of Christ's mission were made to tremble. From another, the doctrine of the Trinity, which had become the badge of orthodoxy in the fourth century, and had been defended by fire and faggot ever since, was openly challenged. With it, not only the authority of the Fathers who had invented and imposed it, but the divinity of Christ himself, was put in doubt. These challenges were not indeed new, but they were now delivered far more forcefully than before, from inside as well as outside the established

Church; and they aroused a forceful response. In that last decade of the Seventeenth century, 'Arian'–that is, anti-Trinitarian–works were ritually condemned in both universities; new Blasphemy Acts were passed by Parliament in a vain attempt to stay the infection; and the alarm of the establishment was increased by the appearance of an alternative religion only loosely connected with traditional Christianity and quite incompatible with Trinitarian doctrines: 'the religion of Nature', or 'deism.'"[272] This transition to a more rationalistic, natural and minimalistic, civic religion was facilitated by Europe's encounter with Islam in general, and British encounters with Islam in particular. These encounters served as a catalyst to resolve the ongoing confessional disputes and dogmatic controversies with some sense of serenity, to increase internal stability and external commerce.[273] The Enlightenment was the result of these transitions, appropriations and accommodations. It was a reformation of the sixteenth-century Reformation, especially in Britain where Christianity was reformed but not discarded. Both the French and American Enlightenments were a sort of extension of the early British Enlightenment.[274] The Continental religious Enlightenment transformed the religious landscape and thought patterns of Europe and America on the way to a total transformation of political system and economy. The Islamic reformative scheme was handy and well-placed to be appropriated by the reformers. The Christian dogmas of original sin, Trinity, grace-based salvific scheme, incarnation, Jesus' divinity, atoning death, mediatorial role of Jesus, Church and Monarchs and hence divine right Church and Monarchy all were analysed, dissected and finally rejected. The Enlightenment was a total reformation of the Church Christianity on Unitarian, moral, rational and republican lines.

Chapter 2

Islam and the Southern Reformation of Christianity

Islam, as the rival faith, had long ago dealt with the same Christian supernaturalism, absolutism, blind dogmatism, antinomianism, Trinitarianism and grace-based salvationism which the Enlightenment leaders were handling in the seventeenth and eighteenth centuries. Unlike Roman Christianity, Islam insisted upon good human nature, human rational capabilities, reformation, training and growth through sense experience, experimentation, practice, moral discourse and education. It also warned against mythical traditions, authority-based knowledge, unintelligible dogmas and emphasized upon rationality and common sense in matters of faith and action. John William Draper has noticed that Islam was the "first or Southern Reformation"[275] of Christianity long before the Northern Reformation in sixteenth-century Europe.[276] To Lecky, Islam resolved the Christian problems of idolatry and was a total break with previous civilisational patterns. "It must, however, be acknowledged that there is one example of a great religion, reigning for the most part over men who had not yet emerged from the twilight of an early civilisation, which has nevertheless succeeded in restraining its votaries from idolatry. This phenomenon, which is the preëminent glory of Mahometanism, and the most remarkable evidence of the genius of its founder, appears so much at variance with the general laws of historic development [...] one of the great characteristics of the Koran is the extreme care and skill with which it labours to assist men in realising the unseen.[277] Islam rectified the Church excesses in areas of monotheism,[278] rationalism, nomianism, monarchism, clericalism and religious intolerance. Islam introduced the rule of many instead of a few, and incorporated the largest possible numbers of people in matters of religious knowledge, socio-political and civil affairs. It was a commoner's revolution against the religious and political elites. Martin Pugh notes that "Islam appeared as a purified and simplified form that superseded Christianity. This was felt to be necessary, because Muslims believed that Christians had introduced into the practice of the religion all kinds of dubious notions, elaborations and misunderstandings that had not been part of the original. Islam provided a clarification and a return to a truer, simpler, stricter form. This was a view that many Christians themselves were to welcome, especially during the Protestant Reformation in the Sixteenth and Seventeenth centuries (although it was to overlook the central disagreement about the divinity of Christ)."[279]

Islam brought its rival, simple, rational, natural and ethical monotheism; human, prophetic, anti-Trinitarian Christology; natural cosmology with direct divine sovereignty without any intermediaries, cooperating natural forces or quasi-divinities; ethical anthropology, teleology and soteriology; rational epistemology and republican exousiology (political thought). The ethical monotheism, rational Unitarianism, divinely ordained natural order and design, divinely installed natural laws and divinely inspired moral laws, human, prophetic Christology, virtue-based salvation, human reformation, participation and initiative and final reward and punishment were so emphasised and simplified by Islam that a cursory reader of its Scripture, the Quran, would not have missed it. Islam replaced the Christian supernatural, interventionist, overly miraculous, changing, irregular, abnormal and mutable cosmos with natural, regular, harmonious, immutable, orderly and hinged cosmos with fixed, unbroken and explorable laws.

The rival Islamic theology, cosmology, anthropology, sociology, political thought and soteriology were too relevant to the seventeenth- and eighteenth-century European society and its religious, political and scientific challenges that they could not be overlooked or ignored by the Enlightenment leaders. Overseas trading companies' exposure and close dealings with Muslim East were to play the central role in cross-cultural fertilization.

Islamic Anti-Trinitarianism and Its Natural, Republican Implications

Islam especially reformed Trinitarianism by restoring the pristine transcendental ethical monotheism of the Semitic consciousness. It also rejected original sin, atoning death of Christ and all its incarnational antecedents from intermediary role of Jesus, Church, state and natural forces. Divine absolute sovereignty with direct authority over man, nature and salvation was categorically established, beyond any sense of compromise. In this way, doors were opened for greater human participation in matters of religion, politics, science and society. Human dignity, self esteem and moral agency were restored and the pillars of *Old Regime* (divine right Church, monarchy and triadic natural hierarchy) were all shaken.

Islam contended that the Christian incarnational and redemptive scheme was arbitrary, unjust and mythological. It compromised God's unity, sovereignty, self-sufficiency, omnipotence, omnipresence, omniscience and cosmos' unity and integrity, and led humanity to an idolatry of persons and dogmas. Anthropomorphism, corporealism, fetishism, frequent miraculous interventionanism, abnormalism, supernaturalism and divine incarnation made God (the Father) and his natural laws obsolete.[280] Jesus and nature's intermediary cooperative roles made God too transcendent, aloof and irrelevant. It also made man too evil, depraved, ignorant and dependent on Church, state, natural phenomena and random grace.

God was too loving and just to eternally taint the human nature due to a single mistake of one man, Adam.[281] The hereditary guilt and collective punishment was inappropriate, unjustified and unwarranted.[282] God was too just to punish all children of Adam for a sin they did not commit or had no control over. He was too merciful and just to crucify Jesus as expiation for the sins that he had not committed; God did not need to shed blood to forgive human beings. Islam found too many loopholes in the Christian scheme of incarnation and salvation. Adam committed the mistake and got punished by expulsion from the heavens. That was sufficient of a punishment. The incarnational scheme instead made God continue harbouring grudges against Adam and eternally punish not only him but billions of his innocent children for the little bite of an apple. It tied God too tightly to arbitrary understandings of justice and love and in the end, God could not maintain either of them. The sin was against God and he could have easily forgiven that without any demand of bloodshed, especially after Adam's expulsion from the heavens and his ensuing repentance. Otherwise, he could have sent his supposed sinless Son, Jesus Christ, at the very beginning of humanity if it was essential for God to shed the blood for forgiveness, but he did not. Why would he wait for centuries and let many people suffer in perdition, including the beloved patriarchs like Abraham, Moses, David and many other righteous men and women, before sending his only begotten Son as a sacrificial lamb? If the animal sacrifice practiced by the Jews was sufficient for protection of billions of men from perdition, as the Church Christianity claimed, then that could have been the way out for the rest of humanity. There was no need for crucifying a sinless man - Jesus Christ - to accomplish a goal which was already achieved by animal bloodshed. If God's intention was to cleans the evil effects of original sin and let humanity live a moral life through the atoning death of Jesus, then he should have sent his Son at the very beginning of humanity to spare humanity of countless horrible crimes. The time selection for Jesus' inauguration and cosmic intervention was odd and arbitrary; why during the Roman era and why not during the earlier oppressive eras of Pharaoh, for example? Additionally, the cosmic intervention and bloodshed did not make much difference in regards to humanity's sinful nature and crimes. Humanity, including Christian believers, continued the same moral infractions as their predecessors, even after the atoning death of Jesus. What did God accomplish by such a merciless crucifixion? It was not just to crucify the sinless Jesus for the sins he had not committed any way, and it was no love either to crucify his only Son for the supposed love of his enemies; the forced crucifixion was no spiritual expiation. Jesus' recorded anguish on the Cross and desperate cries for help highlighted the fact that his crucifixion was not voluntary or consensual. How could the involuntary crucifixion be accepted as a spiritual, universal, cosmic expiation for universal sins? Surprisingly enough the atoning death and its antecedent, the salvific scheme, did neither diminish immorality nor connect salvation with virtue but with divine grace and mere attestation of it. In reality, such an arbitrary salvation scheme in certain ways increased and encouraged moral infractions; instead of emphasising the need for moral reformation it emphasised belief in a set of dogmas about divine nature, crucifixion and resurrection. It made God as erratic in his choice of forgiving the sinners as in his original condemnation of entire humanity due the sin of one man, Adam. The grace-based predetermined and selective salvific scheme in fact boosted moral infractions by the guarantees of eternal success, due to faith in the Trinity, incarnation and redemptive death of Jesus. It neither reformed the tainted human nature nor curbed its evil consequences, but gave a wrong hope of felicity in spite of it. It diminished the need for human moral incentive and agency to heighten the scope of divine grace and sacrificial acts. It was too supernatural, metaphysical and arbitrary, and made man solely dependent upon the divine initiative, selective grace and upon Church, the sole dispenser of that grace and knowledge. It also fogged human mind and blurred human clarity due to its supernatural, mysterious and illogical premises. Such a supernatural salvific scheme had no precedent in the Jewish faith, or in the long prophetic tradition enumerated in the Jewish scriptures; it was a total break with the established monotheistic, moral and logical principles. Additionally, it was not fully supported by the Christian scriptures. The idea of God incarnating in a feeble historical man and dying on the Cross in a state of helplessness was too novel for the Semitic consciousness of Jesus and his Jewish culture. The Triune notion of Godhead was a construct too foreign to the Jewish milieu of Jesus and his early disciples. The Trinitarian theology, with its triadic divine, natural and social order hierarchy, diversity of persons, roles and natures, was too drastic for Semitic Unitarian consciousness and sensibilities; it was anti reason, experimental science and republican political thought. It was totally mysterious, paradoxical and circular. The end result was mental confusion, intellectual bewilderment, scientific stagnation, moral numbness and human paralysis. God, priests, kings and magistrates ruled the masses in the name of God, Trinity, grace and salvation and Christendom was marred with absolutism both in the spiritual and material realms. Divine arbitrariness was translated into arbitrary, dogmatic religious and political theology.

Islam rejected the original sin, the depraved human nature, the Triune conception of God, the Trinity, the divinity of Jesus, divine incarnation, atoning death and predetermined, selective salvific scheme to usher an era of human individual freedom, moral agency, initiatives and capacities, mental and rational clarity and human participation in the spiritual as well as material realms. The mediatorial role of Jesus, church and state in the saga of salvation was strictly banned to connect man directly with God through moral laws, conduct, virtue, reflection, research and experimentation. God connected with man directly through his revelation and creation, and the book of revelation and the book of creation embodied divine revelation. The fixed natural and moral laws were two sides of the same coin; no church, intermediaries or spiritual entities were allowed to meddle in these laws. Both books supplemented each other and led man to God, as the source of both books was God Almighty. Hence natural study and exploration were equally meritorious and encouraged. Man was to explore, study and master the nature, as he was not intrinsically subservient to it. The triadic hierarchy in theology, political science, sociology and cosmology were all rejected; God's direct and absolute sovereignty over man and nature was pinpontedly established, and God was extrinsically and transcendently established as the supreme lawgiver, both natural and moral but ontologically different to man and cosmos. The sacramental and intermediary role of Jesus, nature, angels, saints, heavenly hierarchical beings and the earthly Church and state structures were all obliterated, to connect man and cosmos directly with the Sovereign God. Man was completely freed from all intermediary hierarchical shackles to explore the natural phenomena, master it and also master his own destiny by moral initiatives. The comprehensive Islamic reformative scheme insisted upon anti-Trinitarianism, anti-rationalism, anti-nomianism, anti-clericalism and anti-republicanism by emphasising ethical monotheism, absolute and direct divine sovereignty, moralism, rationalism and constitutional republicanism whether in the shape of limited monarchy, parliamentarian monarchy or popular sovereignty.

Islam from the outset claimed to be a reformation of the Church Christianity and its absolutist religious and political theology. Islam did not consider itself to be a new religion, but a restorer of the universal monotheistic prophetic tradition of Abraham, Moses and Jesus. It believed in the successive reformative prophetic histories and claimed to be an heir to this moral, reformative tradition. Islam was the submission to the moral commandments of God and peace with one's neighbour. All those who engaged in such a submission were muslims with small "Ms." The universal Islamic tradition of all the prophets was a moral scheme of human virtue, empowerment, participation, initiative, rights and duties. It was simplistic, minimalistic, rational, moral and republican, highlighting human equality in front of God and moral commandment, equal opportunities of salvation, understanding, participation, happiness and rewards. There were no ecclesiastical, monarchical or cosmological hierarchies in it. All humans were created in the image of God, and were equally capable of comprehending his essential moral message. Nature was the embodiment of divine laws, like moral laws. Both laws of nature and laws of moral were explorable, malleable and workable. Islam was a bottom-up revolution against the top-down Christian religious, political and cosmological theology. Man and God were directly connected ushering infinite human freedoms, incentives, explorations and possibilities.

The Islamic moral, rational and natural revolution was refreshing for many Christians, as they welcomed the needed correction. Martin Pugh notes that Islam "looked askance at the Christian idea of the Holy Trinity, because it suggested a deviation from the key principle of monotheism. This, too, was a criticism accepted by many Christians. Similarly, the majority of Muslims rejected the idea of saints as being inconsistent with monotheism, and saw the worship of saints as superstition. Although Muslims, like Christians and Jews, recognised Adam as the first human being, they rejected the claim that he passed on his original sin to the rest of humanity: their view was that Adam and Eve repented and God forgave them. For Muslims, the notion of original sin was a 'doctrine of despair', as an individual could achieve salvation through genuine repentance, without any need for confession to a religious intermediary."[283] Islam presented a simple, straightforward and logical concept of the One and Unique God. It absolutely rejected the incarnational jargon and established strict parameters to safeguard God's proper relationship with Jesus, Mary and cosmos. Muhammad, notes William Draper, was "horrorstricken at the doctrine of the divinity of Jesus, the worship of Mary as the mother of God, the adoration of images and paintings, in his eyes a base idolatry. He absolutely rejects the Trinity, of which he seems to have entertained the idea that it could not be interpreted otherwise than as presenting three distinct Gods. His first and ruling idea was simply religious reform—to overthrow Arabian idolatry, and put an end to the wild sectarianism of Christianity. That he proposed to set up a new religion was a calumny invented against him in Constantinople, where he was looked upon with detestation, like that with which in after ages Luther was regarded in Rome."[284] Muhammad was a "Protestant

Prophet"[285] long before Martin Luther; unlike Luther, his reformation of the Church Christianity was exhaustive and complete.

The Muslim Scripture insisted that one of its main purposes was to rectify the Trinitarian, Incarnational and redemptive Christian theology.[286] All problems connected to divine incarnation, diffusion or confusion were eliminated by Islamic concept of divine otherness. Draper observes that Islam was "the first or Southern Reformation. The point in dispute had respect to the nature of God. It involved the rise of Mohammedanism. Its result was, that much of Asia and Africa, with the historic cities Jerusalem, Alexandria, and Carthage, were wrenched from Christendom, and the doctrine of the Unity of God established in the larger portion of what had been the Roman Empire."[287] Islam released man of his alleged wretchedness, depravity and total dependence upon divine mercy and initiative. It liberated man of his metaphysical, supernatural and dogmatic shackles, and allowed him freedom, empowerment and moral capacities. Man, once freed of centuries' suffocation, unleashed his rational, natural and moral capacities and reached the pinnacles of human progress, dignity and civilisation. Draper states that "this political event was followed by the restoration of science, the establishment of colleges, schools, libraries, throughout the dominions of the Arabians. Those conquerors, pressing forward rapidly in their intellectual development, rejected the anthropomorphic ideas of the nature of God remaining in their popular belief, and accepted other more philosophical ones."[288]

This reasoned approach to religion was made possible by reformation of Christian incarnational salvation scheme. The Christian faith, by its supernatural Trinitarian interpretations, had rendered Jesus so lofty, unique and transcendent that he became really irrelevant to humanity except in spiritual realms of submission and repentance. He, in his divinity, was unapproachable and inimitable. Human beings had to rise to titanic moral heights to equal his co-eternal, co-equal, sinless Godhead. In view of this unsurmountable challenge, Jesus and his moral message became irrelevant to humanity. It was so ideal, angelic and lofty that only an angelic, divine person could rise up to it or realise it. Moreover, the Christian dogma of original sin and fallen nature weakened human self-confidence and self-belief in human abilities, killing all possibilities of human initiatives and hard work. Islam by attacking the Trinity as well as the original sin restored human self-esteem and provided them with a human model of excellence in man, Jesus, to pursue their moral and intellectual capacities without restraint. Islam made Christianity a rational, simplistic, moral and universal faith by removing its local, artificial, supernatural scaffolding and by connecting it with the universal, moral, monotheistic prophetic tradition of Abraham, Noah, Moses and Muhammad. This humanisation of Jesus resulted in moral, rational and intellectual empowerment of humanity. Islam's total rejection of Trinity, original sin and redemptive crucifixion was vital to this transformation. Islam demolished the Christian need for divine incarnation and crucifixion by denial of original sin and its antecedents. It was replaced with the concept of original love and forgiveness. (Quran 2:37; 7:23) Islam remedied the problems related to the notion of human depravity by launching a concept of pristine, pure human nature. (30:30) Islamic God was not the wrathful, unjust, arbitrary, condescending, irrational, conniving and impotent deity but the Most Merciful, Loving, Compassionate and Benevolent God. He did not taint the entire humanity for the bite of Adam but taught them repentance, forgiveness and morality through that original experience of expulsion from the heavens. Man was born pure, innocent and dignified. Izutsu states: "In fact, the Quran offers an entirely different picture of the human condition. All of a sudden, the sky clears up, the darkness is dissipated, and in place of the tragic sense of life there appears a new bright vista of the eternal life. The difference between the two worldviews on this problem is exactly like the difference between Night and Day."[289]

Islam and Human Salvation

Human salvation was directly connected with human endeavours. Human capacities, hard work and participation in the saga of salvation were highlighted. Righteous acts, morality, good intentions were mixed with divine grace to realise the salvation. (2:82) This way, man was at once relieved of the shackles of supposed cosmic threats, divine wrath, redemptive death and arbitrary predestination. Man was granted independence, innocence, freedom of choice and dignity, and made the crown of God's creation and God's representative and vicegerent on earth. Man was empowered to self-govern, self-discipline, self-reform and self-determination. They were invited to fully participate in the rough and tumble of this life, and to equally share the responsibilities of his reformation and felicity. Franz Rosenthal accurately captured the essential feature of Islam when he stated that "man was seen by Islam as the center of action in this world."[290] Lawrence Rosen showed the level of trust Islam placed in the rational and moral capacities of man so that man can control his passions and destiny.[291] Instead of being left to the mumbo-jumbo of cosmic threats, divine incarnation and the redemptive death of Jesus, man was enabled to take charge of his own life and surroundings; He was to work through the ups and downs of this earthly life with a rational outlook and moral bent to master his own destiny. The mediational agencies of Christ and priests were absolutely abolished; there was no inherent human wretchedness that needed cosmic interventions, divine redemptions, clerical intercessions or monarchical supervision. Spiritual realms were equally open and available to all through good works, righteousness and piety. God was not far off from man to necessitate priestly interventions; Islam put man in direct contact with God and nature through the moral examples of prophets such as Noah, Abraham, Moses, Jesus and Muhammad, all coming from the same God with the same universal message of ethical monotheism and human equality. Abraham's struggles against Nimrud, Moses' fight against Pharaoh, Jesus' challenge to the Roman authoritarianism and Muhammad's fight against the Byzantium and Persian totalitarianism were the one and same struggle for human equality, empowerment and justice. Islam like the early Christianity and original Judaism was an egalitarian ideology of human dignity, equality and moral agency.

The salvation scheme of Islam was homocentric. It revolved around human potentials, capacities and participation in the moral reformation here and now. Salvation was personal, moral and spiritual but its fruits were collective, a just moral system. The same human confidence, freedom[292] and empowerment were to be reflected in human society and state. Man was given the equal opportunities of doing good or bad, with human will and choice determining the outcome. Prophets, scriptures, religious and political institutions were meant to educate, civilise and empower man to make the right moral choices, and these inner civilisational and educational aspects contributed to the wellbeing of society. The church and state were equal participants in educating, civilising and encouraging man to behave morally and to contribute to a public, civil sphere of virtuous sociability. The church and state were not allowed to impose dogmas, inner beliefs or outward holiness but to inculcate a minimal public moral sensibility so that all citizens could equally enjoy the fruits of their labour, without discrimination, injustice or inequality. The rulers were not ordained by God to punish human depravity; rather, they were to preserve human dignity, equality and fair dealing. Justice was the fundamental religio-political responsibility. Patricia Crone states that "contrary to what medieval Christians said, coercive government did not develop among humans as a result of the Fall. All God's created beings were subject to His government, directly or through Intermediaries, whether they sinned or not [...] Disobedience, *ma'siya*, is the Muslim word for what the Christians call sin, and the archetypal act of disobedience is Iblis' refusal to bow down to Adam, not Adam and Eve's eating of the forbidden fruit, which only plays a limited role in the Muslim explanation of the human condition and none at all in the Muslim account of the origin of states."[293] She further observes that to Islam "government was the inseparable companion of monotheism, and since humans had originated in a monotheist polity, the problem was not how they had come to live in states but rather why government had so often been corrupted thereafter, or disappeared altogether. The answer was that human disobedience repeatedly caused things to go wrong so that God had to send messengers to set things right again."[294] The pristine good nature of man was often veiled by the dust of lust and sin. The divine guidance was a reminder, a proof and a cleansing agent that dusted off the effects of lust and sin rendering man and his heart to God, morality and spirituality. Revelation, Prophets and even belief in God and his goodness would not bring salvation until and unless man responded to them and acted upon their incentives; man was not to get anything except the fruits of his efforts. (53:39) God's mercy, grace and assurance were the outcome of these efforts and not a prelude to them. The Quranic dictum that "But he will prosper, Who purifies himself," (87:14) well summarised the above discussion. This scheme of salvation was the total opposite of what the Church Christianity preached.

The Islamic salvific scheme was founded on God's grace of revelation, human response to that through hard work, morality and reformation and God's ultimate grace to infinitely multiply the rewards. God guided whosoever he wanted and misled whomsoever he wanted based upon human response to his incentives of revelation, and not on arbitrary selection or predestination. The divine will was ultimate while the human efforts were relative but not insignificant. Righteousness and morality were directly connected with good deeds within the framework of Islamic devotional[295] and doctrinal systems.[296] Good intention, sincerity, humility, true spirituality and God consciousness were cherished to reduce the harms of dry legalism and ritualism. All systems of Islamic life, such as socio-economic and political, were directly connected with Islamic soteriology and human salvation, heightening the sense of human accountability before God rather than just the immediate human agencies such as police and judiciary.[297] The mediational agency of bishops, priests and kings was abolished and man was directly connected with the Omnipresent and Omniscient Loving God. (2: 186; 50:16) Equality before law and God and a strong sense of *Taqwa* (God's presence) was universally preached. Intercessions, indulgences and shortcuts were proscribed.

In spite of its strict ethical monotheism and moralistic salvific scheme, Islam was not an exclusivist religion; it was an inclusive faith with universal appeal and implications. It included the simple, monotheistic faith of all previous prophets and generations, relegated beliefs to the personal realms and did not permit religious coercion in any way or form. Faith was a very private and personal phenomenon; nobody could be forced to believe in something contradictory to one's reason, logic, feelings and understandings. The Quran used scriptural and rational arguments to substantiate its core tenets. Man could use his reason and logical inferences to look at the content, language, concepts, compilation, preservation, historical authenticity and continuity of the Quran and reach to the conclusion that it was an authentic revelation of God or could use demonstrative, data-driven, empirical knowledge, reason and knowledge to look at the Quranic belief system, law and morality to guage its authenticity and moral efficacy. There was nothing beyond human comprehension, mysterious or unintelligible in Islamic doctrinal or moral system. It was simple, Unitarian, natural, rational and universal. Man was encouraged to contemplate, understand and comprehend God's will through the Book of *Revelation* as well as the Book of *Creation*. Faith was substantiated by reason and not threatened by it. As reason was the common denominator in humanity, discursive analytical reason was a universal tool to elucidate and strengthen the true faith. A manipulated, unintelligible, forced or distorted faith was no faith at all. True faith was tantamount to one's totality of inner being and deep held convictions. That was why it could not be imposed from outside. Rather, it was the other way around; it traveled from the inside outward. External factors could influence faith in a number of ways, but could not create its facts or realities. That was why the Quran vehemently prohibited any compulsion in the matter of faith and religion.

Unity of God and Unity of Creatures

Al-Tawḥīd, the Unity of God, also meant unity of God's creatures in the ultimate sense. All humans were dignified creatures of God irrespective of their religion, colour or creed. Pugh observes that "despite the common origins of Islam and Christianity, Islam has long been misunderstood and misrepresented in Western societies, particularly over such matters as women, polygamy, sex, sexuality, slavery and jihad. Westerners today are largely unaware that Islam is a relatively egalitarian religion which does not endorse differences of birth, caste, wealth or race. In fact, it denounces privilege as un-Islamic, though this has not prevented the emergence of elites and aristocracies over time. Converts often find the egalitarianism a refreshing change. In this spirit, a number of Muslim states have, in modern times, adopted policies of socialist Islamism. And while Islam has always recognised differences between men and women, believers and unbelievers, and slaves and freeborn, historically the differences were significantly less under Islam than in other societies, especially as regards women and slaves."[298] Islam insisted that all human beings were created in God's moral image and were recipients of divine gift of soul. This universal divine gift entitled them to God-given universal human rights irrespective of their race, colour and creed. Respecting these inalienable rights of man was tantamount to loving man, and loving man was equal to loving God. The contemporary Muslim human rights violations, top-down state systems, religious and political absolutism, hierarchical society, discriminations and strict censoring of opinions are an aberration to the original Islam, and not a reflection of it. The ideal, Quranic Islam was and is a champion of human liberty, dignity and rights.

The fundamental human rights emanated from the dual Islamic concepts of transcendental monotheism and human dignity. All humans were created by the same God with equal dignity. The divine law was prescribed to preserve and guarantee ensuing human equality. The objectives of Islamic Law (Shari'ah) (preservation of life, faith, property, family, reason/honour)[299] were a reflection of God-given inalienable human rights. Amina Wadud noted that "The purpose of the Quran [...] is to establish social justice. In the eleventh century, Ibn Jawziyyah agreed with this notion when he described *shari'a* [...] He asserts that the *maqasid* of *shari'a*, the goal, or ultimate intent, is justice. Justice is both a social and moral term, as well as a principle, a virtue. It is not an abstraction. It is woven throughout the entire Quran and as such becomes the basis for establishing the idea in Islam of the five freedoms or rights: life, religion, intellect, family (or genealogy) and property."[300] Therefore the role of Islamic religion in the worldly reformation, improvement and betterment of man was as important as his felicity in the life to come. Worldly happiness preceded happiness in the life to come. The secular and material realms were integral to the spiritual realms; both realms belonged to God. as God was nothing short of justice and fair dealing. In reality He was the other name of justice. (Quran 4:135; 5:8) Consequently, religion was not mere holiness but morality and virtuous sociability.

Islam insisted upon human equality, universal human dignity, rights of life, property, privacy, family, religious, socio-economic and personal freedoms as God-given rights.[301] These fundamental rights were independent of both Church and state. Democratic values such as mutual consultation (*Shura*),[302] social contract (*Bay'ah*),[303] rulers' accountability (*Muhasabah*)[304] and service-based authority were introduced and practiced.[305] "The political system in Islam can be understood as a consultative rule, that is, rule by *shurah* (consultation). Consultation is a basic principle in all spheres of Islamic political and social systems. It is also essential for the proper function of the organs of the state, its overall activity and Islamic identity. The Quran commands Muslims to take their decisions after consultation in both public and other matters. This makes consultation mandatory, by virtue of it being the subject of a direct Quranic command as specific as those requiring obligatory prayers and tax (*zakat*)."[306]

The field and scope of mutual consultation was wide open, as the Shari'ah included only a small number of fixed commandments and detailed prescriptions. Its generic prescriptions, as well as the non-prescribed areas, allowed a wide range of human interpretations and legislation. Even the form and method of consultation was not fixed by the Quran: "The deliberate silence of the *shariʿah* about the form of consultation is suggestive of the need for continuous temporal legislation. This legislation would relate to administration and other affairs not touched upon by the *shariʿah*, as well as the affairs for which the *shariʿah* has provided only broad basic principles with no detailed laws."[307] The flexible and generic Islamic principles of governance necessitated a great deal of human participation, intellectualisation and appropriation in the form, method and direction of the state and government. "It would thus appear that the form of government, the form of consultation, the kind of legislature, and the procedures to be used all could have some alteration and adjustment from time to time without any compromise to their Islamic nature. In the view of this context, many scholars view the Islamic system of government as similar to a democratic system."[308]

Islam and Democracy

It is often argued that Islam and democracy are antithetical, that the democratic system assigns sovereignty to people, while Islam reserves that for God only. That is not true. The sovereign God does not descend to the earth to rule people; he sends laws to facilitate justice and equality, and the laws are understood, interpreted and implemented by people in conformity with their times, situations and cultures. The divine sovereignty means the sovereignty of laws, "'sovereignty' is not 'God', but it is vested in the law by God. An Islamic state is limited both by and to the law. It follows that the sovereignty of an Islamic state is practically the sovereignty of the law, and that the law limits the governmental power and regulates its functions. Limiting governmental power to the law does not imply autocracy, but implies democracy in its widest sense because the law requires consultation. In this way, the idea that 'sovereignty belongs to God' does not make the political theory in Islam differ from that in democracy but increases the elements of similarity and compatibility between the two systems."[309]

The humans share in that sovereignty in their role as interpreters, facilitators and administrators of the divine laws. Islam encourages the full-fledged human participation in matters of state and authority, but within the established parameters of the divine law and its spirit. Khatab and Bouma state "the claim that 'God is the only legislator' does not make the Islamic system against democracy where the 'people legislate' for themselves. This is because of the fact that the *shari'ah* did not give detail on everything in this life, but kept silent on some issues, including the method of consultation and other matters at the heart of the structures and functions of state, and between state and its subjects, between the subjects themselves, and between state and other states in the world community. The silence of the *shari'ah* about these affairs is suggestive of the need for continuous temporal legislation. Muslims are allowed to legislate for affairs not touched upon by the *shari'ah*, as well as the affairs for which the *shari'ah* has provided only broad basic principles with no detailed laws. This means, first of all that all, human legislation is temporal and interpretive and not absolute. Second, in Islam, people legislate to people, as people legislate to people in a democracy. In either case, human beings will use their talent and expertise to legislate in ways suited to their situation."[310]

The head of an Islamic state is its chief executive, bound by the laws like any of his subjects. The Islamic state is a constitutional form of governance rather than a divine right monarchy. J. Wellhausen calls it a theocracy founded upon the notion of justice. "The theocracy may be defined as the commonwealth, at the head of which stands, not the king and the usurped or inherited power, but the Prophet and the Law of God. In the idea of God justice, and not holiness, predominated. His rule was the rule of justice."[311] This was the fundamental difference between Christianity and Islam - that the notion of divinity in Islam was justice, while in Christianity it was holiness. Christianity was anti-nomian, while Islam insisted upon actions and moral law. This aspect of Islamic polity was most attractive to seventeenth-century English reformers such as Henry Stubbe, John Toland and John Locke who wanted to limit the divine right monarchy and Anglican Church.

The absolute divine right monarchy of Church Christianity was totally abolished and the Quran/Shari'ah/law was established as the ultimate constitutional authority, over and beyond human reach. The Quranic constitutional powers reserved the sovereignty and dominion for God while giving the Caliphs derivative and secondary powers within the established parameters of Quranic law.[312] The Muslim masses were thus empowered with the election and oversight process. The Christian clerical establishment and elitism was replaced with socio-religious egalitarianism. The Quran was the constitutional authority over and beyond the rulers, and all Muslims were required to understand and implement Quranic teachings. The constitution of Islamic state, the Quran, was understood and applied by the masses, just like the head of state and ministers. The authorities' executive and legislative powers were extremely limited by the constitutional powers of the Quran, and made conditional to their conformity with the universal egalitarian principles of the Quran. The Muslim obedience to the state authorities was qualified; (4:59) there was no obedience to the state in the matters of disobedience to God and morality. The moral, duty-bound and voluntary submission to the Islamic state with religious intent and zeal was highly encouraged; it was a social contract founded on bilateral commitments. But rebellion and revolt were encouraged if the authorities did not fulfill their part of the commitment and crossed the limits by persistently going overboard. Mass participation in the matters of state was aspired, and a communal sense of belonging to the new religious order, and commitment to its missionary zeal, was inculcated. The masses were charged with a new sense of mission and enthusiasm to galvanise the largest possible participation in the historical reformative scheme of Islam. Imperialism, clericalism and elitism, the hall marks of Christendom, were fought against with utmost vigour and courage.

The Prophet did not allow hereditary kingship or appoint a successor; he left it to the Muslim community to choose their leader. None of the first four rightly guided caliphs appointed their successor from among the ruling families.[313] Four different methods of election were exercised by the Rightly Guided Caliphs, making the election process flexible. The presidential, parliamentarian and other possible democratic forms of government could easily be deduced from the early models. Two main characteristics, non-hereditary and public contractual allegiance, were the hallmarks of these state models. The *Khilafah* or Caliphate was vicegerency and not a divine right monarchy.[314] The Caliph represented God's laws as understood and interpreted by the Prophet of Islam for the wellbeing of the Muslim community. Therefore, the Caliph represented God, his Prophet and people at the same time. Some members of the Muslim community revolted against the third Caliph Othman when they alleged nepotism, killing him in spite of his magnificent past and close ties to the Prophet. The early Muslim community was truly egalitarian, with active vigilance over their rulers. The transition to the hereditary form of government was an Islamic aberration and very much contested by the Muslim community of the first Islamic century. Imam Hussian, the grandson of Prophet Muhammad, resisted the transition to a limited monarchy and paid with the lives and blood of his entire family in the battle of Karbala.[315]

In spite of secularisation of the Islamic state, the Umayyad and later Muslim dynasties were not considered divine right monarchies. The caliphs were not divinely ordained, but usurpers of state power through force and corruption; they were true perverters of divine wisdom due to their wrong use of freedom and power. The Ulema (religious scholars) often opposed the political authorities, dubbing them un-Islamic dictators. The strong Muslim opposition to - and persistent struggles against - the monarchies resulted in a unique power-sharing Muslim paradigm where the executive and legislative powers of the Caliph and state were limited by the Quranic laws and scholarly engagement. The Ulema, or religious bodies, were granted the powers to interpret and legislate laws as well as oversee their implementation. The Caliph's legislative authority was especially limited through Islamic laws, norms and practices and relegated mostly to the areas where Islamic law was silent. He headed the executive branch of the government, while relegating the legislative and judiciary to the religious circles. The three branches of the government were required to work within the framework of Islamic Shari'ah and Shura (mutual consultation), curtailing and balancing their executive, legislative and judiciary powers. Therefore, the Islamic caliphate was neither a divine right monarchy nor a theocracy, but a limited constitutional monarchy where the powers of the caliph, *shura* or parliament and judiciary were thoroughly restricted by Qura'nic laws and juristic principles. The Caliph derived his political authority from the fact that he was to be the chief guarantor of the Islamic law's thorough implementation. He was *Amir al-Mu'mineen*, the chief of believers. His leadership was dependent upon him following the moral path delineated by the Islamic teachings and in no way or form God-given permanent privileges.

The authority of the Islamic state never extended to faith, intentions, inner convictions or private practices, as was the case in the Roman and Byzantine Christian empires. There was a wall between the Church and state in Islam. The Quran separated and differentiated between religion as institution and religion as a system of beliefs. The Islamic state's authority was limited to the outward public practices of the subjects.[316] The relative outward civil, socio-moral conformity rather than doctrinal unity was the aspired goal. Religious diversity and pluralism were generally tolerated. The state was governed by the Muslim rulers but their politics was not Islamic. All religions were allowed free practice and semi-independence. Atheists, agnostics and sceptics were not persecuted but allowed debates and public conversations. The People of the Book enjoyed special status among the minorities; they paid the state tax (*Jizya*) like all other religious minorities, but enjoyed greater freedom and privileges. They had their own independent courts, communities, business entities, temples, Churches and hierarchical clerical establishments. Had the politics of the Islamic state been Islamic they would have never enjoyed such independence and freedoms. Christendom did not allow religious diversity or pluralism, because its politics were merged with religion. The public discourse and decorum of the Islamic state was a sort of agreed-upon policy between the Islamic state and its religious minorities. Public consumption of wine, gambling and other un-Islamic activities were prohibited, while the same were allowed within non-Islamic settings and private places. There was a sort of minimal, agreed-upon civic religion practiced in the public square, while the full expression of faith was relegated to specific religious settings such as mosques, temples and churches. Such pluralism, religious tolerance, civic religion and religious autonomy were extremely attractive to the seventeenth-century English reformers, including Thomas Hobbes, Henry Stubbe, John Toland, John Locke, Unitarians, Socinians and Deists. John L. Esposito observes that "theologically and historically Islam has a long record of tolerance."[317] The Quran embraces pluralism on the level of salvation but inclusivism at the level of theology. He further states that "Muslims regard Jews and Christians as "People of the Book," people who have also received a revelation and a scripture from God (the Torah for Jews and the Gospels for Christians). The Quran and Islam recognise that followers of the three great Abrahamic religions, the children of Abraham, share a common belief in the one God, in biblical prophets such as Moses and Jesus, in human accountability, and in a Final Judgment followed by eternal reward or punishment. All share the common hope and promise of eternal reward: "Surely the believers and the Jews, Christians and Sabians [Middle East groups traditionally recognised by

Islam as having a monotheistic orientation], whoever believes in God and the Last Day, and whoever does right, shall have his reward with his Lord and will neither have fear nor regret" (2:62)."[318]

In brief, Islamic Unitarian theology, cosmology and republican pluralistic outlook was the exact opposite of the Christian religious, political and natural theology. Islam claimed to have come to reform Christian religious, political and cosmological accesses. The seventeenth-century English reformers found Islam handy in their reformative scheme of the *Old Regime*. Their appropriations of anti-Catholic (uniformity) and pro-diversity Ottoman themes facilitated their reformation of Reformation.

Islam and English Enlightenment

Islam rose in the seventh-century Arabian Desert, achieving territorial expansion with unprecedented speed, and overrunning much of the Middle East Christian world as well as crucial parts of the Church of North Africa within a few short years, following the death of its founder. This brilliant success was enormously threatening to the Christian Church and state. As a result, the initial seeds of hostility were sown as opposition to and propaganda against Islam and the Prophet mushroomed, becoming harsh and vociferous. Islam was depicted as Antichristian, heathenistic, idolatrous and superstitious while Muhammad was nothing short of the Antichrist prophesied in the Book of *Revelation*. And, from the time of Rudolph de Ludheim (620) through the medieval centuries, this antipathy had remained. For example, Nichlas de Cuse (1401-1464), German philosopher and bishop, Joan Lluís Vives (1493-1540), Theodore Bibliander (1506-1564), Valencian Spanish scholar and humanist, Louis Maracci (1612-1700), Johann Jakob Hottinger (1652–1735), and many other reputed figures down the centuries presented the Prophet as an impostor, Islam as a cluster of all heresies, the Muslims as brutes, and the Quran as a tissue of absurdities.[319] Christendom was totally closed to Islamic anti-Trinitarian theology and republican political thought. Both the monarchs and Church severely punished any discussion against the Trinity or divine rights of monarchs. Islam was Antichrist and needed to be confronted and eliminated. Those elements of Islamic philosophy, theology and political thought that could be utilised to support Christian Trinitarian Orthodoxy were allowed, but any and all discussion against the supernatural Trinitarian Church theology and its Augustinian political theology and cosmology were made totally off-limits.

Late medieval Christian encounters with the Islamic world were mostly concentrated in Eastern Europe and Italian city states such as Venice, Genoa and Amalfi. Scholars of Mediterranean interactions and intersections have emphasized a shared history of widespread cross-cultural diffusions, religious syncretism and cultural hybridization between Christians, Muslims and Jews on both sides of the Mediterranean which helped in shaping religious identities, renovated religious traditions, and patterned religious cultures of the Mediterranean. The impact of relatively tolerant, diverse and open Muslim World upon the intolerant, insular, uniform and persecutory Latin Christendom and its gradual but slow transformation is well documented by this group of scholars. Filomena Viviana Tagliaferri in her "Tolerance Re-Shaped in the Early-Modern Mediterranean Borderlands: Travellers, Missionaries and Proto-Journalists (1683–1724)" has underscored the process of multi-culturalism, hybridization and Levantinization by which the Muslim Ottoman ideas such as religious tolerance had impacted the Italian Catholics. The Ottoman tolerance of diversity and encouragement of conversions to Islam were processes of "syncretism", "latitudinarianism", "politicized differences" and "contact and reconciliation". The Transylvanian encounters led to some consequential syncretism, hybridization and Levantization leading to significant changes in Protestant theology, cosmology and political outlook. Many Hungarians, East and West European converts, renegades and Turkophiles enthusiastically engaged in Muslim missionary activities, polemics, interfaith debates, pamphleteering, Ottoman apocalyptic, messianic and millennial propaganda. The Ottoman war machine utilized the socio-economic allure, military might, intellectual warfare, state policies and Christian internal debacles to promote their version of a tolerant, diverse, prosperous, rational, civil and flexible world order. They also attempted to make contacts and forge alliances with persecuted, marginalized Christian minorities and oppressed sects within rapidly disintegrating Christendom to foment disunity, conflict, strife, internal disturbance, disruption and chaos among the Christian states. The Sultans, grand viziers, ministers, religious leaders and local officials all propagated "soft world empire" through state policies, rituals and ceremonies. The Ottoman state was not solely engaged in territorial expansions, acquisitions, occupations, taxations and revenue collections but also heavily invested in religious ideology, missionary zeal, economic allure, communicative strategies, power plays and social expressions of magnanimity, altruism and charity. The sixteenth and seventeenth century Ottoman Sultans showcased widespread conversions to Islam as proofs of their millennial hopes and geo political efficacies. The conversion ceremonies, gifts and resultant cultural transitions such as circumcisions and official turbans were publicaly orchestrated to convey a strong millennial message to European ambassadors, councils and merchants. The capitulation privileges, rituals and ceremonies were also brilliantly orchestrated to divide, contain and impress European diplomatic missions, merchants, consuls and to expand Ottoman "soft world empire" based not on territorial expansion, but instead on overtures of trade, mutuality, communication and religious ideology. The converts' softer agenda combined with hard Ottoman imperial strategies ushered an environment and public space of Muslim Christian polemics, debates, dialogues and exchanges which was quite effective. The millennial date of 1591 and hopes of a new world order under Ottoman universal monarchy made the interfaith debates more urgent and imminent. The Ottoman claims that the Catholic Church had corrupted the original, simple, Unitarian message of Jesus and Gospel with the help of Constantinian Roman state and Church Councils and introduced pagan Trinitarian incarnational theology, absolutist Roman divine right monarchy and Church along with their persecutions, miraculous, supernatural, interventionist and incarnational cosmology, antinomianism, monasticism, hierarchical clericalism, burdensome ceremonies, mythologies and mysteries, all these anti-Catholic tropes got a great deal of traction both in Eastern Europe and Western Protestant areas. The widespread propaganda detailed that Islam purged Roman Christianity of its Roman superstitions by restoring the pristine, simple, Unitarian, rational, moral, diverse, tolerant and republican message of Prophet Isa (Jesus) and was not a new religion but an extension of the original message of Jesus and his disciples. Islam was the reformed version of Christianity and not an anti-Christian faith. The implicit message was that Muslims were in reality true Christians. During the sixteenth century millennial fervor and Ottoman military expansions, the imminent revival of the original Unitarian Christianity under the auspices of Ottoman Empire and the demise of Catholic Habsburg dynasty were given a great deal of push and credence.

The Hungarian anti-Trinitarians, Unitarians and Socinians gravitated towards Ottoman scripturalism, moralism, rationalism, Unitarianism, religious pluralism, man Christology and constitutional, limited monarchy. Their persecutions by later Polish Catholic authorities forced them to migrate to Holland, England and other Protestant areas. Likewise, the Italian (mostly Venetian) anti-Trinitarians were too close to Rome to avoid persecution. They flourished like their counterparts when they migrated to Transylvania. They also migrated to various Protestant cities after the Reformation and established Italian anti-Trinitarian clusters in Geneva, Basil, Heidelberg and later on in Amsterdam and London.[320] Their anti-Trinitarian, pluralistic and republican ideology was suppressed due to the persecutory policies of the Protestant national states and churches. The situation became a little favourable when the Levant and East India Company merchants, workers and officers traveled to the Ottoman, Safvid and Mughal Empires and personally interacted with tolerant Muslims. Once out of the suffocating, persecutory and supernatural Trinitarian environment, some converted to Islam while many others became anti-Trinitarian, tolerant, republican, independent Congregationalists.[321] The seventeenth-century English inner instability, Civil War and religious dissent were the results of such an exposure and transition. The Crown's abuse, manipulation, customs, taxations, demands for loans, gifts, and briberies caused alarm to overseas trading companies and their stake holders including gentry all over Britain. The struggle between merchant and gentry supported parliament and absolutist abusive monarchy heralded the Civil War and English Revolution.[322] The overseas traders made enough fortunes to withstand the pressures of monarchy and to challenge the divine right king and church through the parliament. Their demands for civil and religious liberties and balance of power between the Crown and parliament safeguarded merchant's financial interests and further progress. The initial radical Interregnum period facilitated relative tolerance of religious dissent, better fiscal policies and allowed radical views to flourish. The continuous cross-cultural reinforcement from the Muslim world, radical missionary zeal of dissenters, consumerism and commercialism of Levant and East India merchants and religious and political instability of England created an atmosphere within the public sphere, congenial to religious and political dissent. The English Civil War and Revolution initially abolished the persecutory

Anglican Church and monarchy, allowed qualified dissent and liberty of conscience but at a later stage tried to impose a sort of Puritan, Presbyterian national church in its palce. Oliver Cromwell curtailed republican civil liberties just like an authoritarian monarch, leading nonconformists, Protestants and dissenters alike to accept Charles II for stability's sake as an enlightened replacement with hopes of religious tolerance, liberty of conscience and constitutional monarchy. Charles II and James II's failed attempts at religious tolerance of nonconformists and Catholics, their gradual support for an absolutist Anglican Church, persecutory policies and divine rights of king politics thoroughly disappointed the republican dissenters, merchants and Whig idealogues. They threw their support behind James II's Protestant daughter Mary and her Dutch husband William III, and brought about the so-called bloodless Glorious Revolution of 1689. The Revolution was the climax of the century's republican, dissenters, traders and Whig efforts to curtail the Church and monarchical powers, abuses and privileges. The Islamic Unitarian republicanism and religious pluralism, along with its political and economic allure, was initially adopted by the Unitarians and Socininas and then promoted by a sizeable influential Levant and East India related merchant community, garnering great political clout and transforming the English community from within by the end of the seventeenth century. Let us discuss seventeenth-century England, its geo-political landscape and overseas trading companies to properly understand the discussed transformation.

Chapter 3

Seventeenth Century England, Overseas Trade and English Identity Formation

Early seventeenth-century England was a small country with a population of around 3 million (by the middle of the century around 5 million) while just one of the three Muslim Empires, the Indian Mughal Empire had a population of 150 million in 1608. England was known for its bad weather, monotonous foods, dietary deficiencies, agrarian impoverished economy,[323] under-nourished ignorant population, limited natural resources, premature deaths,[324] bubonic plagues,[325] primitive living conditions,[326] instable society, dull politics, drunkenness,[327] gambling, and absolutist Church and state.[328] It was highly stratified, divided, instable, insecure, persecutory and an upside-down society.[329] The difference between rich and poor was conspicuous; wealth was concentrated in the upper five percent of the population.[330] Tensions between the Crown, gentry, nobility and merchants were the norm. This continuous tug of war was the main source of English instability and anxiety. There was not much state building, science, medical facilities, trained physicians, industrialisation, secular colleges, universities or other educational outlets. England was a medieval, under-developed and isolated isle. The English religio political identity was fluid, broadly based upon anti-Catholic sentiments and ethos.

Religious tensions were as high as the socio-economic disparities. The Elizabethan Settlement had identified religious conformity with political allegiance, and from 1559 onwards "subjects in England had to subscribe to the two Acts of Supremacy and Uniformity, the first declaring the monarch as head of the state and the second determining worship under the monarch as head of the Church."[331] The monarch's sovereignty extended to the Church, doctrine and practice. This placed state and Church properties under the authority of the Crown.

Freedom of worship and liberty of conscience were proscribed, and all sorts of political and religious dissent were persecuted. The imposed religious faith and uniformity were no solutions to natural inquiries and inner anxieties caused by the Reformation. The Protestants in general lacked confidence in Church teachings, rituals, traditions and harboured doubts about the way Christianity was developed by Catholic Church under the corrupting influences of the Roman Empire. The top-down imposition of religious, political and cosmological uniformity, and the resultant persecutions, were considered extensions of the same Catholic corruptions highlighted by the Reformation leaders. Elizabeth's successor James I pretty much continued her religious policies, Near Eastern affinities due to political reasons and divine right ideology to bolster his monarchical authority and appeal. His carefully crafted religio political ideology of "Antiquity", claims of direct inheritance of the original Christian institutions, bypassing the Catholic corruptions in scripture, dogma, and church settlements and directly connecting with the pre-Catholic simple Church of the first three Christian centuries through original Middle Eastern languages, Near Eastern Churches, manuscripts and Bibles but concurrent insistence upon the divine rights of King like Catholics accelerated English suspicions about their Christian heritage and boosted longing for further reformation of Roman Christianity. Many thinking Protestants believed that the Reformation needed further reformation based upon the pre-Catholic original Christianity of Jesus and his early disciples. The late Reniassance attitude of looking back to antiquity for purer forms of theology, ecclesiology, political systems, sciences, wisdom and knowledge was prevalent among the English intelligentsia of the late sixteenth and early seventeenth centuries. The Puritan ideology of exploring pristine, original and simple Christianity was pitched against the medieval scholasticism of the absolute Church and monarchy. Puritanism was a multifaceted movement with many variants and sects. Scepticism about, and distrust of, existing religio-political structures and restoration of original forms, doctrines and institutions were the common denominators. The longing for civil and religious liberties and the problems of authority were at the core of this constant puritanical struggle. Seventeenth-century England was a God-driven society, so all disputes and controversies were couched in religious language. The whole seventeenth century was marred with religious disputes, persecutions and wars. England, like the Europe of the seventeenth century, was a divided, upside-down and persecutory society.

From the perspective of the then pluralistic and opulent Muslim East, China and Japan, Britain was considered a third world country.[332] The English historian William Dalrymple observed that "At that time England was a relatively impoverished, largely agricultural country, which had spent almost a century at war with itself over the most divisive subject of the time: religion. In the course of this, in what seemed to many of its wisest minds an act of wilful self-harm, the English had unilaterally cut themselves off from the most powerful institution in Europe, so turning themselves in the eyes of many Europeans into something of a pariah nation. As a result, isolated from their baffled neighbours, the English were forced to scour the globe for new markets and commercial openings further afield. This they did with a piratical enthusiasm."[333] It was the "drabness and boredom at home [...] the monotony"[334] which forced them out of Europe to Asia, Africa and Americas. The transition was facilitated by Elizabeth's Protestant politics and aggressive trade policies, as briefly discussed above.

Queen Elizabeth's Protestant outlook caused alarm to the Pope and French neighbours. Her Anglican Church was a hybrid of Protestant theology and Catholic worship, reformed in doctrine, traditionalist and hierarchical in government and discipline, and a mixture of Catholic and Protestant ceremonies and forms of worship.[335] It was "crypto papist" neither fully Catholic nor fully Protestant. It was elastic, fluid, malleable and Erastian. For Puritans, it was only half reformed. Her trade overtures to Ottoman Sultan and expressions of religious affinities with Muslim Unitarianism were sufficient enough to outrage the Pope who had banned any trade with Ottoman Muslims. A number of plots by the Catholics to kill Elizabeth were foiled and the plotters were publicly hanged, drawn and quartered.[336] Elizabeth never married and had no heir,[337] so the Protestant Stuart King James of Scotland took over the throne. His strict divine right Church and monarchy caused growing discontent and brushed away many of his religious and cultural achievements, such as publication of the King James Bible (1611), efforts of Christian reconciliation and establishment of Jamestown colony in Virginia (1607). The Catholic Gunpowder Plot of 1605 to blow up the parliament and King only made him more authoritarian and persecutory.[338] Discontent with persecutory Church of England and monarchy spilled over to the reign of Charles I who was more radical in his divine right prerogatives, primitivism, antiquarianism, Near Eastern languages, knowledge, manuscripts and ancient wisdom than his father James I and resulted in the English Civil War between the royalists Cavaliers and parliamentary forces called the Roundheads. Consequently the "middle decades of the seventeenth century saw the greatest upheaval that has yet occurred in Britain."[339] Sir Robert Walpole, the renowned early eighteenth-century British Prime Minister, observed that "in the seventeenth century men killed, tortured and executed each other for political beliefs; they sacked towns and brutalised the countryside. They were subjected to conspiracy, plot and invasion. This uncertain political world lasted until 1715, and then began rapidly to vanish."[340] The early seventeenth-century England was chaotic, disoriented and in all sorts of crisis. Jonathan Scott noted that "during the seventeenth century every serious political disorder that could befall a kingdom did befall England and its Stuart-governed neighbours. Parliamentary crises immobilised English politics in the 1620s, 1640s, 1670s and 1680s. There were successful foreign invasions in 1640 and 1688, and other ineffectively opposed incursions in 1659, 1667 and 1685. There was civil war which, during the period 1640–51, resulted in casualties the extent of which are only now beginning to be understood. If England lost 3.7 per cent of its population between 1640 and 1660 (190,000 people), a greater percentage than in either of the twentieth century's world wars, Scotland may have lost 6 per cent (60,000) and Ireland a chilling 41 per cent (660,000)."[341] Countless people were killed, maimed and burnt due to their religious and political beliefs. Neither the state nor the Church was stable, secure and mature.[342] The English philosopher John Locke lamented that in his times religion had served as "a perpetual foundation of war and contention: all those flames that have made such havoc and desolation in Europe, and have not been quenched but with the blood of so many millions, have been at first kindled with coals from the altar."[343] Locke complained living in a whirlpool of storm for his entire life due to internal English anarchy and chaos.[344] The English, like their European counterparts, killed each other with religious zeal and passion. Political and religious authority was the main bone of contention.

Anglican Church and State

Severed from the long tradition of Catholic Church and united Christendom, the seventeenth-century English monarchy and Anglican Church
struggled to define its scope, authority, institutions and directions. The
monarchs tried to impose Catholic versions of rituals, sacraments, hierarchical ecclesiastical structure and divine right monarchy upon mostly
Protestant, Calvinist and a sort of reformed Arminian English society
which hated Catholicism, its rituals and structures with passion. Historians have even suggested that "with respect to these two supposedly
all-important issues of religious persecution and ecclesiology, there were
fundamental, revealing likenesses between the 'sacerdotalist' religious
ideology of conformist Anglicans and the Catholic clerical leadership
in France"[345] For instance, Andrew Marvell (1621 – 1678), the English
metaphysical poet, argued that most conformist Anglicans were in fact
agents of popish tyranny and Counter-Reformation.[346] But such a formally elaborate church was extremely important to Charles I due to its
political functions. "'Religion is the only firm foundation of all power,'
Charles I had said. The church and state do mutually support and give
assistance to each other,' wrote Bishop Goodman. The state pays them
[the clergy], and thus they have dependence upon the state,' as Hugh
Peter more brutally put it. The function of a state church was not merely to guide men to heaven: it was also to keep them in subordination
here on earth. Different societies, different churches: but to want no
state church at all seemed to traditionalists a denial of all good order."[347]
Charles I was convinced that Bishops were the foundational stones of
monarchy; no bishop, no king. The Anglican Church and monarchy
wanted Protestant Englishmen to obey the Church and monarch with
a Catholic religious zeal, while the Englismen had already lost confidence in the religious authenticity and validity of the Catholic religious
and political theology. King James I and Charles I's efforts to legitimize
their absolute divine right prerogatives through direct appeal to the Old
Testament Temple theology and Kingdom of David via original Near
Eastern Bibles, manuscripts, churches and cultures were unsuccessful.
This was a tough nut to crack.

England had neither the resources of the Habsburg monarchy nor the
socio-political grip of the Bourbon French dynasty, but English monarchs intended to rule like their Catholic models. The English monarchs
did not have a standing army or coercive state power, and their militias

were no matches to the standing armies of Spain and France. Even in 1661, when Charles II decided to have a standing army, it was minimal due to lack of resources and parliament's resistance. In 1685 there were fewer than 9000 soldiers in the English Army, in addition to low-funded disorganised Scottish and Irish troops. During William III's reign, especially from 1695-1697, the paper numbers rose to about 100,000 men but the parliament reduced the cadre to 7000 in 1697 while in 1608 the Indian Mughals kept a staggering 4 million men under arms[348] and the Ottomans in the 1670s kept over 225,000 men in arm.[349]

The English monarchs mostly depended upon the Church and religious sense of obligation to preserve unity, order and king's divine right prerogatives. Conrad Russell observed that "a government with overwhelming military force may survive without a generally accepted theory of obligation, though few have wished to make the attempt. But Tudor and Stuart governments were conscious of their lack of coercive and investigatory powers, and correspondingly felt the greater need for a theory of obligation. The standard point that fear was not enough to rely on was true: if obedience were not of conscience, it was unreliable [...] Charles I was quite right in maintaining that 'if the pulpits teach not obedience, the king will have but small comfort of the militia.'"[350] Archbishop William Laud absolutely subscribed to this maxim of religious conformity and national unity. The Augustinian theory of obligation in household and state, as discussed above, was preached from the pulpit and implemented through the parish courts. Anglican Church was an important arm of the English state. "The simplest theory of obligation in use was that of Romans xiii, 'the powers that be are ordained of God'. The subject, wife, child or servant obeys the immediate superior because in doing so he or she is obeying God, whom all are bound to obey. In the words of Ponet's gloss, 'neither is that power and authority which kings, princes, and other ministers of justice exercise only called a power; but also the authority that parents have over their children, and masters over their servants, is also called a power: and neither be the parents and masters the power itself, but they be the ministers and executors of the power, being given unto them by God."[351] This was the religious and moral conscience ingrained in every believing Christian. The innate idea of God was invoked to propagate the innatism of divine rights of kings and bishops. Submission to Christ was in reality submission to the monarch and bishop, the vanguards of Christian faith.

Charles I and Archbishop Laud's Authoritarianism

Charles I and Archbishop Laud felt that Reformation, with its anti-clerical overtones and individualistic *sola scriptura* doctrine, had compromised the Christian conscience and theory of obligations. To remedy the problem, Laud imposed a uniform Church with elaborate rituals, ceremonies and prayer books on Protestant England which hated Catholic Church, its cumbersome ceremonies, elaborate sacraments and authoritative ecclesiastical structure.[352] Charles I and William Laud were hell-bent on imposing uniformity, unity, order, manners and obedience.[353] Laud played the role of an Anglican Pope for Charles I's divine right pretensions, over-meddled in state affairs and consequently caused divisions within the Anglican Church - and frustrations to Charles I.[354] Laud's efforts of connecting his episcopal authority and King's divine right prerogatives directly to the ancient patristic foundations circumventing the long Catholic centuries was unsuccessful but unintentionally substantiated the puritan impulses of going back to the pre-Catholic, pre-Romanised pristine Church and original apostolic Christianity.[355] It played well into the general puritan rhetoric that the historical Church and monarchy were corrupted due to Catholic innovations; persecutions and religious strife were the consequences of that corruption, that religious wars and destructions were prophesised in the Scriptures, that Europe and England were passing through the Apocalyptic period delineated by the Bible and that the Second Coming of Jesus - as well as the ushering in of a new millennial- were at hand. The resistance to the corrupted ecclesiastical structures, teachings and rituals and its replacement with simple, original, pristine and egalitarian message of Jesus (the new temple and new Jerusalem) were necessary to realise the messianic and millenarian hopes. Two different Christian ideologies were undercutting each other with religious zeal and playing further havoc to an already disoriented English society. The King and Church were persecuting dissenters with absolutist religious convictions, imposing uniformity, good manners, piety and obedience to usher the expected millennial Protestant Stuart universal monarchy and the dissenters were fighting back with millennial religious enthusiasm. Two different schemes of eternal salvation were at war with each other.

Charles I (1600-1649) was absolutely convinced of his divine gifts, intellectual, spiritual and political acumen. He imprisoned, tortured and killed opponents with religious zeal and certitude.[356] He lacked flexibility, alliance building and financial resources. He was "a king so insecure, incompetent and malevolent as to constitute a complete monarchical self-destruction package."[357] In spite of not having any dynastic rivalry, "far greater security of title to the throne and an end to disputed successions,"[358] a quiverful of children for succession, a unified and imposing Anglican Church, a rebellion free England,[359] a supportive parliament, stable prices, surplus supply of grain and no immediate threat from the Habsburg military machine,[360] Charles I felt insecure because of the erosion of traditional religious foundations of monarchy due to Reformation's anti-clericalism and anti-traditionalism. He was paranoid about the Reformation's negative effects upon the English monarchy, and instead of state-building, focused more upon public obedience and manners. He was trying to impose the divine right monarchy and Church on a Protestant intelligentsia who had mostly lost trust in the religious foundations of such a medieval ideology.[361] The same arguments of corruption used by the Protestant Reformation leaders against Catholic Church and Habsburg monarchy were being used by the English dissenters against the Anglican Church and English monarchy. Charles I and Archbishop Laud were heretical Christians persecuting the dissenters while Jesus and his disciples never persecuted anybody but were themselves persecuted. Jesus never had this worldly kingdom; therefore, the persecuted dissenters were in reality following the original message of Jesus while Charles I and Bishop Laud were reflections of Roman corruptions. No obedience to Church and monarchy was required if it violated the commnadments of God. Charles I's persecutory policies and absolutism was heretical. Within the first fifteen years of his reign the King alienated almost all segments of his population due to his eratic authoritarianism.[362] The imposition of religious unity and manners was too much for an already anti-Catholic English society which was now additionally exposed to Eastern Muslim anti-Catholic rhetoric, subtle missionary overtures, millennial propaganda, pluralism, religious tolerance, freedom of conscience and bottom-up Presbyterian like mosque structures since the 1580s, through overseas trade. Both King James I and Charles I's antiquarian enthusiasm for Near Eastern theology, languages and wisdom added to English anxieties about Christian heritage, biblical authenticity and King's divine right prerogatives. Charles I and Archbishop Laud's craze for Near Eastern languages including Arabic, Eastern wisdom, manuscripts, sciences, philosophy, Bibles, coins and Churches was meant to consolidate their religio political powers as true inheritors of the original ancient Church of Near East and its primordial theology and philosophy. Assisted by a circle of theologians, the King stressed that the Anglican Church was a direct continuation of the "Primitive Church" that took shape in the first four centuries of the Christian church in the Near East. That pre-Catholic pristine Church was the original source of authentic theology, thought patterns and languages. That is why research of, speculation on and mastery of the Near Eastern languages, Bibles and manuscripts were essential to ward off Christian religio political differences and interpretive controversies. The King felt that the Old Testament Temple theology and political model of Davidic Kingdom were more congenial to his intended consolidation of powers, Erastian Church and absolutist Monarchy. He tried to superimpose such an ancient power structure on the Anglican Church and society. His enthusiasm for Near Eastern languages, texts, manuscripts, Bibles, coins and edifices was geared towards construction of such a consolidated power structure. That need was met by the Levant Company, its merchants and chaplains, as will be detailed in the coming pages. But the paradigm shift backfired as the appeal to primordial Eastern theology, scriptures, dogmas and structures opened the pandora box of scriptural corruptions, theological manipulations, Church and state's abuses and supernatural impositions. This played well into the long Ottoman religio political rhetoric, reformative claims and millennial prophecies. The Ottomans ruled the significant historical, sacred and political Christian landmarks such as Jerusalem, Constantinople, Nazareth, Mount Sinai and were patrons of ancient Christian Churches. Their claims of being the true heirs to pre-Catholic tolerant Roman Empire and pristine theology of Jesus seemed relatively genuine and plausible. Their material prosperity, military successes, multicultural allure, freedoms, diversity and reformative claims mesmerized some disgruntled English merchants and their persecuted friends at home. A gradual theological transformation accompanied English explorations to the Near East, overseas trade and subsequent material revolution.

Overseas Trade and Intellectual Transformation

The Levant and East India Company trading complex had transformed English material culture. The decade of the 1630s was the time of Indian cotton, calico and colourful textile's revolution in England. The Oriental obsession, in so many ways and forms, was quite visible in various segments and dimensions of the English material culture. Charles I himself was fond of Oriental fashions; the foreign material culture eroded the bricks and mortar of the old socio-economic hierarchical system. The Earls of Bedford, Warwick, and Essex, John Pym, overseas merchants and religious dissenters actively sought to transform England into a limited monarchy like the Mughals, Ottomans and Persians, a sort of aristocratic, quasi-republican oligarchy - like the Venetian monarchy - in which parliament occupied a prominent role, but the balance of power effectively laid with the nobility and merchants.[363] This was too radical for Charles I, as well as for many Englishmen.

The ideology of religious tolerance, freedom of conscience, separation of Church and state and rebellion against the immoral, corrupt and unruly kings was imported along with the Oriental material culture. Such ideology of religious diversity and tolerance had been totally absent from Christendom. Medieval and pre modern Christianity, in all its forms, imposed uniformity, persecuted heretics and punished dissent. The Dutch reformer D. Erasmus was no less punishing of heresies than Luther and Calvin. He considered killing of heretics necessary for the maintenance of state. The so called seventeenth century tolerant Dutch Republic and Church persecuted many Christian sects and were not open to other religious faiths, as John Marshall, Perez Zagorin and others have demonstrated. In the Mughal, Ottoman and Persian Empires on the other hand, Muslims, Jews, Christians, Hindus, Buddhists, Zoroastrians and athiests all lived together, engaged in business and contributed to prosperity and social cohesiveness. The state neither imposed its Islamic theology upon the non-Muslim subjects nor demanded uniformity from its Muslim populace. The interfaith and intra-faith diversity and toleration were the norms. The Church and state, civil and religious authorities were separated. The English also learned that religious tolerance and liberty of conscience were not antithetical to social peace, order and unity, and political allegiance did not require religious conformity. The civil realms were quite different from the spiritual realms. Additionally, the Sultan was neither divinely ordained nor permanently appointed. The Ottoman Sultan Mustafa I was deposed in 1618 and again in 1639, his nephew Sultan Osman II was deposed and murdered by the janissaries in 1622 and Sultan Ibrahim was publicly strangled in 1648 as a result of the Grand Mufti's fatwa. The news of these regicides was widely circulated in England through newsletters, newspapers and gossips not only in London and other big cities but also in small towns and villages. The Englishmen and women learned from Turks that revolt against a corrupt and authoritarian ruler was not only possible but required in certain situations. The single event continually remembered and rehearsed by English writers was the regicide of Sultan Osman II. These political shocks left a unique and indelible print on the imagination of seventeenth-century Englishmen. The royalists completely identified Cromwell with the rabble rouser "Muhammad" and the Model Army with Janissaries. Such an uprising or regicide was unheard of in England or in Europe. The same lessons of and discussions about political resistance were repeated in 1680's, 1690's and 1700's when Sultan Mehmed IV was deposed in 1687 after the defeat at the Second Battle of Mohac and Sultan Mustafa II was deposed in 1703. Some persecuted dissenters, nonconformists and Whigs insisted that rebellion and even regicide was permitted if the ruler acted contrary to the law while the High Churchmen, royalists and Tories argued that this Turkish ideology of rebellion and regicide was totally un-Christian. Many overseas European and English merchants, factors and visitors were witness to these realities. The Augsburg physician and traveller Leonhard Rauwolf (1535?-1596) who lived in Levant from 1573 to 1576 as an employee of the Augsburg merchant firm of Melchior Manlich and his associates, and visited the Syrian and Mesopotamian provinces of the Ottoman Empire, wrote extensively about it.[364] His "remarkable parable on religious toleration and the coexistence of various nations in one realm reads like an early precursor of seventeenth and 18th-century writings that pointed to religious diversity in extra-European empires in order to confront European readers with their own intolerance. Indeed the variety of religious beliefs in 16th and seventeenth-century western and central European monarchies was much more restricted than in the contemporary empires of the Ottoman sultans or the Indian moguls. European rulers typically sought to impose confessional conformity on their subjects, and where conformity proved impossible to enforce, granted only a grudging tolerance to certain Christian minorities. Jews were still banned from many European countries, and where they were accepted they often faced severe legal, political and economic restrictions."[365] William Biddulph, the English Levant Company chaplain from 1600-1608, noted that "the Turks give liberty of conscience to all men, and like well of every man that is forward and zealous in his own language" hence making them better trading partners than the "Papists". He added that Muhammad declared that excepting apostates, "every man shall be saved by his own religion."[366] In the early 1620s, the Levant Chaplain Charles Robson was struck by the religious diversity in Ottoman Empire.[367] Levant chaplains such as Dr. Edward Pococke, ambassadors such as John Finch and English visitors such as Henry Blount conspicuously highlighted Ottoman pluralism and loathed Europe for its religious persecutions.

Radical Protestants, who harboured hatred towards the Catholic Church due to its long historical corruptions, ecclesiastical and theological dissipations, came to the conclusion that religious persecutions in the name of unity, peace and prosperity were also Church's interploations into the primitive, original and peaceful faith of Jesus and his earliest disciples. Jesus and his disciples were persecuted but never persecuted others.[368] The Constantinian politics and Augustinian theology of persecution, loving torture and merciful punishment were rejected and long medieval inquisitions and persecutions were all viewed as anti-Gospel, Church inventions to instill fear and exact obedience.

The puritan religious zeal was supplemented by overseas trading companies' complaints against the Crown's fitful authoritarianism and erratic extortions.[369] Their charters, custom duty, taxation and privileges all depended upon the Crown and "unlike domestic property rights that were governed by common law precedent, foreign trade was governed by civil law, administered by the Crown in the Admiralty courts [...] English rulers also could grant and revoke charters to companies overseas, impose customs, and create monopolies of newly introduced goods, as commerce and innovation was believed to be protected by the king's foreign policy."[370] The Crown extorted overseas merchants through taxes, forced loans,[371] interlopers,[372] gifts and bribes. The King and Levant Company continuously fought over the strangers' consulage fees from the 1630's to the early 1640's and the King had the upper hand. The Levant Company took the matter to the Ottoman court and Charles appointed his loyal ambassador Sir Sackville Crowe to replace the Company's ambassador Sir Peter Wyche and to seek help and secure loans from the Ottoman Sultan Ibrahim (r. 1640-1648) against his parliamentarian enemies, a pattern, of rival ambassadors, loan requests and seeking Ottoman intervention in English affairs, followed by his son Charles II. This was a microcosm of Charles I's manipulative and extorting attitude towards his subjects in general. The Levant Company was £20,000 in debt as a result of the seizure of the strangers' consulage. S. Jha noted that "prior to the Civil War, even those joint stock companies that enjoyed initial profits faced not only foreign predation but also Crown expropriation through rising customs charges or the revocation of their charters. These setbacks eventually led to a decline in enthusiasm for investment in the 1630s. In contrast, the contribution of overseas customs to total Crown revenues rose from 5.2 percent in 1552 to 52.5 percent on the eve of the Civil War in 1642."[373] Charles I's exaction of overseas trading companies diminished his dependence upon the parliament, but disgruntled the trading companies and their countless gentry and parliamentarian stake holders.[374]

The troubles for Levant or East India Comapy meant troubles for England. Philip Lawson noted that "when the EIC experienced its worst troubles, there was matching instability in national politics."[375] The overseas trading companies and their parliamentarian allies pushed back and carved a special niche for them through the parliament. "Not surprisingly then, attempts to bargain over the control over rights over customs and foreign policy played a pivotal role in parliamentary debates from 1603 to 1625, with joint stock investors playing prominent roles."[376] Parliament wanted control over customs, but the King was not to surrender "the fairest flowers for profit and command in all his garland."[377] Traders and parliamentarians joined hands with puritan and religious dissenters against the Crown and its religious arm, the Anglican Church. "In November 1641, investor-reformers penned the Grand Remonstrance, a manifesto aimed at instituting parliamentary authority over remaining Crown rights, including over foreign policy, finance, and the armed forces. This led the king to illegally enter the House of Commons to arrest the Five Members considered the ringleaders of the parliamentary opposition in January 1642. Parliament summoned London's citizen militia in its defense. The king abandoned the city and, in June 1642, raised his war banner, threatening to use force in defense of Crown rights."[378] This was the beginning of the English Civil War. The Anglican Church was Charles' influential religious arm and an integral part of his military campaign while the overseas trading companies were elemental to the parliament's rebellion. The overseas traders praised Ottoman Sultan's charity and fairness against the unjust extractions of Charles I. In spite of Ottoman internal fiasco of 1640's and financial troubles, and unlike the English King, the Sultans did not extort English merchants. Subsequently, the parliamentary struggles against the Crown, Charles' regicide and subsequent publication of Turkish Alcoran were depicted as English extensions of Ottoman religious, intellectual and military invasion. To the Royalists, the new republic was anti-Christian. The Parliamentarians gave a millenarian slant to Charles' defeat at the battle of Naseby and Catholic defeat at Crete. Ottoman military victories and cultural accomplishments were accommodated and appropriated by the parliamentarians for domestic consumption.

The new English Commonwealth protected overseas trader's interests at home and abroad, increased English Navy's armament, made necessary administrative adjustments to protect and enhance Levant trade, added forty five vessels to the fleet and not only defended Levant trade against the foreign invaders such as Spain, Portugal, pro Stuart French Navy and pirates but also against the slain King's nephew, the Duke of Ormonde and Prince Rupert who was harassing Commonwealth ships and Levant Company vessels. The Commonwealth's aggressive trade policy well suited the Levant Company and they opened their wallets and supported it with customs, donations and loans. The English Revolution was a watershed moment for the Levant trade and the Levant merchants' support of the Commonwealth was depicted as Ottoman intervention in and invasion of England. Cromwell was a rabble-rouser Muhammad. The Revolution had turned England upside down.

Some Puritan radicals felt the need to sieze the opportunity "to realise a more godly reformation (that is to create church structures and patterns of worship and discipline more wholeheartedly based on a Protestant understanding of the commands of the Bible). This meant the repeal of the Elizabethan statutes setting up the Church of England; the abolition of Bishops and the system of church courts which had survived from pre-Reformation days; the abolition of the Book of *Common Prayer*, which was full of ceremonies and prayers which were Catholic in origin; and a ban on the celebration of Jesus' birth (Christmas), and of his death and resurrection (the Easter Triduum) as of all Saints' Days and 'superstitious' observances (with a contrasting emphasis on a more solemn and austere observance of the Sabbath day [Sunday]). This 'puritan' drive was not common to all parliamentarians, but it was characteristic of most parliamentarian activists."[379] The puritans were divided between conservative and radical tolerationists.[380]

Puritanism, Biblicism and Restorationism

Puritanism in a sense was primitivism, Biblicism and restorationism, meaning elimination of Catholic scaffolding to go back to the original, peaceful and otherworldly biblical faith of Jesus and his persecuted disciples. The term "Puritan" applied to a varying multitude of sects, ideologies and people. The General Baptists, Levellers, Presbyterians, Unitarians and Independents all were primitive restorationists, in one sense or the other. They were united in their appraisal of Catholic corruptions of the pristine Christian faith and the tarnished nature of Church and monarchy, but divergent in their restoration schemes. The Presbyterians focused upon ecclesiastical structure,[381] the Levellers on socio-economic order, constitutional reforms and popular sovereignty, the Fifth Monarchists on the judicial laws of Moses,[382] the General Baptists on Godly rule and millennial holism,[383] the Unitarians on Trinitarian theology, rational discourse and religious tolerance and the Independents on constitutional republicanism and limited monarchy. The language of socio-political change was religious, and the idiom was biblical. Puritanism was multifaceted and multi-pronged primitivism, Biblicism and restorationism. "Primitivism - the desire to restore an original pattern that has been lost - had always been one of the most powerful impulses of the puritan movement. Puritans were devoted to restoring the purity of the primitive church, a purity corrupted during the great popish apostasy, and now being recovered in a latter-day restoration.'! Cartwright and the Presbyterians, for example, were convinced that they were restoring the true pattern of church government laid down for posterity in the Acts and the epistles."[384] The Puritan theologian and American colonist Roger William argued that "Christianity fell asleep in the bosom of Constantine." The mission of Williams and other radical puritans was to wake the church up, to call it back to the patterns of the New

Testament."[385] Paul Best and John Biddle insisted that Trinitarian incarnational theology was a Roman invention, and antithetical to the Unitarianism of Jesus and his disciples. The Apocalyptic upheavals of sixteenth- and seventeenthcentury Europe were the final stages of the corrupted Church and theology and the harbingers of a new Millennium founded upon the original, Unitarian, simple and moral message of Jesus. The aspired primitive godly order and saintly community of Puritans was void of Church pomps, traditions, rituals, ceremonies, tithes, prerogatives, fines, courts and persecutions. It consisted of religious freedom, liberty of worship and conscience and a pluralistic civil order accommodating Jews, Turks, multiple Christian sects, heretics and even athiests just like in the pluralist Muslim East.

The General Baptists and Levellers originaly led the way for this radical toleration tradition. For example, Thomas Helwys, who established the first English Baptist church, published his pluralistic views in *A short declaration of the mistery of iniquity* (1612). He emphasised that the king's power extended to all the goods and bodies of his servants but not to their spirits. Helwys extended toleration to all peaceable religions: "Let them be heretikes, Turcks, Jewes, or whatsoever it appertynes not to the earthly power to punish them in the least measure."[386] In 1620 John Murton's *An humble supplication to the kings majesty* argued that the king was lord and lawgiver to the bodies of his subjects, but that Christ alone was lord over conscience, so that "no man ought to be compelled to a worship by persecution, even were he to `walk in falsehood."[387] Roger William stated that "it is the will and command of God that, since the coming of his Son the Lord Jesus, a permission of the most Paganish, Jewish, Turkish, or anti-Christian consciences and worships be granted to all men in all nations and countries: and that they are only to be fought against with that sword which is only, in soul matters, able to conquer: to wit, the sword of God's Spirit, the word of God."[388] He further argued that "God requires not a uniformity of religion to be enacted and enforced in any civil state; which enforced uniformity, sooner or later, is the greatest occasion of civil war, ravishing of conscience, persecution of Christ Jesus in his servants, and of the hypocrisy and destruction of millions of souls [...] An enforced uniformity of religion throughout a nation or civil state confounds the civil and religious, denies the principles of Christianity and civility, and that Jesus Christ is come in the flesh."[389] His friend John Milton could tolerate the Turks and Jews but not the Catholics whom he called "a mixed rabble, part papists, part fugitives, and part savages, guilty in the highest degree of all these crimes."[390] Toleration of Catholics was a perversion of true religion. "He [...] who makes peace with this grand enemy and persecutor of the true church, he who joins with him, strengthens him, gives him root to grow up and spread his poison, removing all opposition against him, granting him schools, abbeys, and revenues, garrisons, towns, fortresses [...] he of all true protestants may be called most justly the subverter of true religion."[391] Contrary to that, Charles I and the Stuart monarchy were fond of the Catholic Church and its absolutism.

The Quaker Samuel Fisher, in *Christianismus redivivus* (1655), deplored the fact that Protestants would exclude people of other faiths from citizenship and was convinced that heretics and Papists, "'heathens, Jews, Turks or Pagans', should be 'lawfully licensed to live in civil states, or in any Commonwealth under the Sun'. The magistrate should 'leave all men to worship God according to their severall ways', and concentrate on his real business-running the civil affairs of the state."[392] Levellers such as John Lilburne, Richard Overton and William Walwyn presented arguments in favour of toleration of all religions, notions of self proprietorship, social contract, annual elections, office term limits, free trade and severe restraints on the powers of parliament as well as monarchy. These religio-political ideas of the 1630s were to influence the thinking of later Whig leaders, such as Shaftesbury and John Locke. Richard Ashcraft noted merchants, traders, Green Ribbon Club members and Levellers connections and influences on John Locke and Shaftesbury's political views.[393] Ashcraft showed that Leveller Major John Wildman and Locke simultaneously worked for Earl of Shaftesbury.[394]

Lilburne wrote that God alone was Lord over conscience, and that "no Parliament, Councell, Synod, Emperor, King, nor Majestrate hath any spiritual authority or jurisdiction over this Kingdome."[395] Leveller pamphleteer and writer William Walwyn was a silk man who highly praised Islam and Turks for piety and tolerance. In his *Just Defence* (1649) Walwyn stated: "Compare but our manners unto a Turk, or a Pagan, and we must needs yeild unto them: whereas in respect of our religious superiority, we ought by much, yea, by an incomparable distance out-shine them in excellency, And well might a man say. *Are they so just, so charitable, and so good, then must they be Christians.*"[396] In 1641 he called for toleration of all professions whatsoever, including

Socinians and papists, whilst he later declared that even those "so far mis-informed as to deny a Deity, or the Scriptures" [397] should be tolerated. Don M. Wolfe noted that "fellow-Leveller with Overton and Lilburne, William Walwyn occupies a unique place among the tolerationists […] Walwyn anticipated by several years the extreme tolerationist views of *The Bloudy Tenent of Persecution*. Lover of Montaigne, Seneca, and Plutarch, urbane critic of Puritan theological excesses, Walwyn approached the toleration controversy with a sincere secular faith in the appeal of understanding and the efficacy of love. Alone with Lord Brooke among the tolerationists, he pamphleteered for the cause without bitterness or rancour, projecting into his tactics the principles of his creed. 'God onely perswades the heart,' he writes to Edwards: 'compulsion and enforcement may make a confused mass of dissembling hypocrites, not a Congregation of beleevers.'"[398] Overton, in *The arraignement of Mr Persecution* (1645), presented the same case arguing that "Turckes, Jewes, Pagans, and Infidels' should all be allowed to live together in society."[399] Within a few years, "the conviction that false religion should be tolerated had moved from being an eccentric opinion held by a handful of General Baptists to a genuine theological option embraced by a substantial minority within English puritanism."[400]

The mainstream Puritan leadership such as John Tombes and John Owen wanted toleration limited only to the godly, the saints,[401] the people of God[402] and not the unregenerate like Quakers, Unitarians and Socinians, but a vocal minority extended it to all loyal and peaceful citizens. There was "a minority of radical puritans who broke decisively with the mainstream puritan view and maintained that religious toleration should be extended to all who did not endanger the civil peace and safety of the commonwealth. This view first emerged among the godly in the reign of James I, and its earliest proponents were General (or Arminian) Baptists."[403]

The pluralistic knowledge transmitted by the overseas traders, and the examples of East India and Levant companies, were often on the minds of some Puritans. Roger William insisted that the state had no right to interfere in the matters of religion, conscience and worship and that church was a voluntary organisation like East India and Turkey companies. The Church was "like unto a Body or College of Physitians in a Citie; like unto a Corporation, Society or Company of East Indie or Turkie merchants, or any other societie or company in London."[404]

Independent Congregationalism was espoused.[405] The independent Quakers, Unitarians and Socinians all vouched for such a voluntary and tolerationist church and society where faith, religion and worship were left to individual conscience, and church organisations were consensual and voluntary. They extended tolerance, even to rejection of central Christian doctrines such as the Trinity and incarnation. "This revolutionary vision of a multi-faith society united around amoral code discerned by natural reason ensured a very wide degree of toleration indeed. Disbelief in the Trinity and the Incarnation of Christ, for example, could not be punished since they were by no means obvious to the conscience by the light of nature."[406] The Quakers, influenced by Muslim philosopher Ibn Tufayl's philosophical novel *Hayy bin Yaqzan* as translated by Levant Company chaplain Edward Pococke, emphasised a great deal upon the inner light, even at the expense of Bible and its exegetical traditions. The individualistic, tolerationist and republican ideology received traction during the 1630s.

A purer form of Christianity, void of Catholic excesses and centered around Gospal morality, was pitched against Laudian regime and Catholic looking episcopacy. This struggle for reformation of historical Christianity on primitive lines, messianic millenerianism, along with overseas trading companies' complaints against the Crown, were among the main causes of the English Civil War. There was "a genuine conviction that the civil war was a religious crusade to drive out old corruptions, and to establish new patterns of evangelism. In 1642, there was a self-confidence and energizing faith in religious renewal for which there is no secular equivalent."[407] The Presbyterians mostly focused upon the Church structure and services and insisted upon a new national church with Presbyterian leadership. The Quakers, following Muslim philosopher Ibn Tufyl's philosophical novel *Hayy bin Yaqzan*,[408] insisted upon the inner light and conscience at the expense of organised Church, liturgy and religion. The Unitarians, such as Paul Best and John Biddle, blasted the whole Trinitarian, incarnational supernatural theology and demanded its replacement with Unitarianism. The Socinians emphasised upon rational discourse, man Christology, religious tolerance, morality and scripturalism. The Levellers extended religious equality to social inequities and oppressions of the social order, insisting upon a sort of social contract between the rulers and the ruled.[409] The merchants and parliament struggled to curtail

monarchical and Church powers. The divergent religio-political ideologies converged upon the fact that the historical Christianity was
corrupted, religious and civil persecutions, abuses and manipulations
were anti-Christian, return to pristine Christianity of Jesus would usher a new era of peace, stability and prosperity prophesised in the Bible.
The end result will be *Parousia,* or the Second Coming of Jesus. Their
deconstructive outlook at the past was unitary, but their constructive
forward-looking schemes were incoherent. The ensuing anarchy, competition, religious pluralism and social levellism generated an alarm
and fear in the minds of English elites.

Unfortunately, the religious and social reformists, who were united
on the destruction of authoritative church and state, were divided on
the construction of potential alternates. Freedom of conscience and religious tolerance (both civil and religious liberties) and limited monarchy were the main points which glued them together.[410] Even freedom
of conscience, religious liberty and constitutional monarchy meant
different things to various Protestant radical sects.[411] The proto-dem-
ocrat or 'quixotic' libertarian[412], "free born Englishman,"[413] nascent,
evolving, unspecified and simmering Unitarian republican ideology[414]
- which stemmed neither from the persecuting Catholic nor from suffocating Protestant Churches, but mostly from the pre-Christian ancient Roman model prompted by the sixteenth- and seventeenth-century English exposure to Oriental pluralistic model - was too nascent
to be cooked properly. Its foreign outlook, Oriental connections, Muslim ingredients and rebellious aspirations were easily highlighted as
Antichristian, anti-Church and anti-monarchy by the royalists and severely crushed by Laud's Church and Charles I's state unifying policies.

Archbishop Laud's[415] Anglican Church resembled the Catholic ec-
celesiastical structure and rituals moreso than the reformed churches, and was accused of returning to persecutory Catholicism. Laud
struggled to elevate the Church over and beyond the civil authorities,
including the monarchy, resulting in an era of constant tensions. He
created an ecclesiastical state within a state. Charles I's failed efforts to
marry the Catholic Habsburg Princess Maria Anna (instead marrying
the Catholic Bourbon princess Henrietta Maria of France), his failure
to aid the Continental Protestant forces during the Thirty Years Religious Wars, Catholic-leaning insistence upon the divine rights of kings,
demands of absolute submission to the state and Church, support for

High Church Anglo-Catholic formalism and popular ritualism, reformation of manners (to bolster public obedience and uniformity) to the extent of intrusion of privacy, severe persecution of dissent and quarrels with merchants and English Parliament caused the Scottish Wars of Bishops and then the English Civil War.[416] The Protestant Puritans, Scottish Covenanters and emerging nonconformist sects, as well as English gentry and merchants, mistrusted, feared and disdained Charles I's religious, financial and political moves. Consequently, he was executed by parliament in 1649 along with his Archbishop Laud (1645). The monarchy, House of Lords, Parliament and Church of England were all abolished in one shot and the English Commonwealth Republic was ushered in, under the military leadership of Oliver Cromwell. "The years following the regicide saw the publication of an English translation of the Koran in 1649, the 'blasphemous' pamphlets of the Ranters, Thomas Hobbes'ss *Leviathan* (1651), John Goodwin's full-scale defence of Arminianism, *Redemption Redeemed* (1651), and the anti-Trinitarian Racovian Catechism."[417] The dissenting voices were finally given some room to breathe.

Religious Roots of English Revolution

The English Revolution was a religious revolution, promoted in part by the overseas trading companies; it abolished the corrupted absolutist Christianity along with its medieval power structures. It struggled to restore the puritan, primitive and egalitarian Christianity of Jesus and his early disciples. The parliament and Crown's battle for power and balance was fought on religious turf. Thomas Hobbes noted that the cause of the civil war was "nothing other than the quarrelling about theological issues."[418] John Coffey stated that "the English Revolution was a theological crisis, a struggle over the identity of British Protestantism."[419] Many traders, politicians and common folks engaged in religious debates, theology and ecclesiastical discussions. "Theology in the 1640s and 50s was far too important to leave to the ordained ministry. This was the great age of lay theologians. In 1644, one of them – the Londoner John Milton – imagined many 'pens and heads' in 'this vast city', 'sitting by their studious lamps, musing, searching, revolving new notions and ideas wherewith to present, as with their homage and their fealty the approaching Reformation.'"[420] The constructive phase of restoration was far more complex, difficult and bloody than the destructive phase of abolition of corrupted forms. The overseas trading companies and their local allies were instrumental in the destructive phase but they could not create a consensus about the exact religio-political alternates.

The English Civil War - and ensuing Commonwealth Revolution - was made possible by "the specific connections between economic developments and the momentous political overturning of the 1640s. Contemporary commentators writing before, or at the time of the Civil War were in no doubt that a great socio-economic transition had taken place in England. It was generally observed that there had been a transfer of property power from the king and the high nobility to 'the people,' or the middle ranks. This thesis was propounded most notably by James Harrington in the 1650s, but similarly held by all 'the best thinkers among his predecessors and contemporaries'—including Walter Raleigh, Sir Francis Bacon, James I, John Selden, Sir Henry Wotton, Sir Thomas Wilson, Spelman Bishop, Francis Quarles, Godfrey Goodman, Henry Parker, Henry Ireton, Gerrard Winstanley and Thomas Hobbes. Many of them believed that the change in the balance of landowning and wealth created a platform for the parliamentary challenge to the crown."[421] The overseas trade especially with the Muslim East and the resultant Oriental material and cultural revolution of 1630s was one of the main contributing factors. The domestic financial transformations and overseas personal experiences were the catalysts of English socio political and religious transfigurations.

Islam and Muslims were well known to 1630's England. The preoccupations with Turks, allusions to Islam, the Quran and Muhammad were proportionated to English anxieties at home. The more the tension the more Englishmen turned to Muslim texts, histories, models and precedents. The Muslim (Turkish) examples were frequently quoted to analyze, criticize and reform English religio political institutions. The rhetoric of the "Turk" was an important element of contemporary discussions, negotiations and navigations. For instance, the English Essayist Francis Osborne (1593 –1659) deployed the Turks as a barometer of Christian – and specifically English – failings such as ambition, selfishness, corruption and cruelty. He used Islam and Turks as a mean of warning and transforming the chaotic English society of 1640's and 1650's. Islam, Muslims, their ideologies and institutions were used as godly instruments in catalyzing reformation of English Reformation.

In his "Political Reflections upon the Government of the Turks" of 1656, the parliamentary sympathizer Francis Osborne criticized English customs, ideas and institution by using Ottomans as a whip. His pointed, piercing and critical social commentary loathed English society, religio political institutions and overall outlook with corruption, greed, ritualism, enthusiastic extremism and lack of directions while praising Prophet Muhammad, Islam and the Ottoman Empire for its balanced spiritual, moral, doctrinal and political approach. Influenced by the positive commentary of Henry Blount's popular travelogue, Osborn's "Political Reflections" was one of the most remarkable texts on Islam and the Ottoman Empire of the early seventeenth century. He preferred Muhammad's political ideas, institutions and policies over Alexander the Great and declared them the foundations of praise-worthy Muslim unity, fellowship, rationalism and empire building. Islamic devotional activities were celebrated as the most significant socio-political cohesive forces and Islamic governing model was highly appreciated as an ideal. Osborne hailed Islamic principles and their socio-political ramifications while lamenting the unceasing Christian internal strife, blood shedding and persecutions. He also highlighted the Muslim unity in diversity and toleration of dissent. Muslim separation of Church and state, civil liberties, religio political arrangements, rationalism, minimalism, tolerance and spirituality were the secrets of Ottoman civility, unity, morality, prosperity, good governance and expansions, "once you accept the premises of this way of looking at politics and religion, you will not be able to deny the advantages, in those terms, of the Ottoman system, and this will force you to think in a new way about the disadvantages of your own."[422] Islam could serve English interests very well and solve its problems of religious schisms, political anarchy, extremism and supernatural dogmatism. This shame-praising was widespread among English Protestant moderates as well as radicals.[423] The parliament was mostly supported by the religious radicals, independents, merchants, shopkeepers and gentry.[424] The parliament's struggle for limiting church and monarch's powers was not a mere teleological, constitutional development for its own sake, a solemn fight for civil liberty as the Whig historians portray it, but a reflection of socio-economic and religious upheavals on the ground which caused a communal longing for transfer of power from the monarch and bishops to the parliament and people. The mid-century English Revolution was the culmination of such a widespread longing and things Islamic intensified by Levant trade were integral to this transition. The revolution marked the highpoint of such an Islamic appraisal, fascination and collaboration. The early seventeenth century enthusiasm for Middle Eastern manuscripts, middle century cross cultural exchanges and late seventeenth century outbursts of "reasonableness of Christianity", church and monarchy were reflections of the same fascination, mirroring, appropriation, emulation and collaboration. The actors varied but the agenda was pretty much the same.

Economic Causes of English Revolution

Contemporary economists have focused on three key explanations of the English Revolution. D. C. North and Weingast's groundbreaking work argues that "a coalition formed to defend property rights in response to a political shock in the form of excessive executive greed by the Stuart monarchs led to the Revolution." The "successful removal of kings yielded a credible threat that enabled future rulers to commit not to expropriate property, leading to dramatic financial and fiscal development in England."[425] Others suggest that the overseas trading related economic shocks created new commercial middle classes that then sought to protect their newly acquired wealth from executive predation. For Karl Marx, England's Civil War was the "First Bourgeois Revolution." "Marx and Engels were the first to suggest that the English Civil War of the seventeenth century marked a stage in the shift from feudalism to capitalism. There were three semi-independent parts to the argument. The first was that the opposing forces represented two different attitudes towards labour and property. The second was that the Parliamentarians consciously willed the resulting destruction of feudalism. And the third was that the outcome was a distinctively bourgeois society characterised by the ideal of possessive individualism."[426] Acemoglu, Johnson, and Robinson, Brenner, Rajan and Zingales[427] suggested that this wealth was acquired by new merchants involved in trade across the Atlantic with Asia and America which gave them the financial capabilities to withstand the Crown's onslaught and demand religio-political reforms.[428] B. Moore[429] and R. H. Tawney[430] propose, in contrast, that the revolution was led by newly commercialised gentry that acquired land due to the dissolution of monasteries from 1536–1541.

The overseas traders increased in number and wealth, and purchased land and nobility with their financial fortunes. Religious liberties, freedom of worship and conscience were propelled to the forefront by the socio-economic changes produced by the overseas trade and ensuing economic imbalances. The relative economic empowerment of the middle classes resulted in their longings for religious and civil empowerment. Fights for combined civil and religious liberties were prompted by socio-economic and religious changes; the medium of change was religious. Even Sir Henry Vane Jr., the most emphatic constitutional republican and heterodox Christian[431] who paid with his life during Restoration, fought against the Anglican Church's excesses and used biblical language to convince others of his pronounced republicanism.[432] Civil liberties and constitutional developments were exacted through religious idioms and terminologies. A different, alternative, anthropomorphic and republican Christian narrative vied against the traditional supernatural Christian dogmatism.

This was the beginning of anthropomorphic transition from supernatural theology, divine right monarchy and Church, hereditary privileges and hierarchical social stratification to empowerment of man, people, natural theology and natural social order. This was what the republican ideologue James Harrington (1611–1677) meant when he said that "the economic rise of the people and the weakening of the force of the nobility undermined the position of the crown, to the effect that "the dissolution of this government caused the war, not the war the dissolution of this government."[433] This was the beginning of Harrintonian republicanism. It sparked a fire for communal empowerment, freedom of conscience and religious liberties, even though it did not realise it fully, during the Commonwealth Revolution. The Commonwealthism was a bit different than the aspired republicanism; it allowed rule of an individual ruler or a government, with the approval and consent of the community. Republicanism was more radical than Commonwealthism as it assigned sovereignty to people rather than a wise godly ruler. Cromwell's Commonwealth did allow restrictions upon the ruler's authority, highlighting a public sense of accountability and rights.[434] Cromwell was accepted as a sort of limited monarch and a wise Machiavellian prince, a Muhammad.[435] The period witnessed the birth of Islamic republicanism in England, as will be demonstrated in the coming sections.

The regicide of Charles I dissipated the religio-political sanctity and allure of both the monarchy and Church and enlightened people to the possibilities of a limited, constitutional monarchy and ultimately the popular sovereignty. The Islamic republicanism of the Ottoman Empire, where the Sultan's executive powers were limited by the Islamic Shari'ah laws, Muslim scholars' legislative, interpretive and judiciary powers and Islamic commands of no coercion in the matters of religion, served as the initial model of the limited monarchy and republicanism in England. The republican ideology was more pervasive among the religious radicals, nonconformists, independents, merchants, shopkeepers and some enlightened gentry, but not quite popular among the rural areas, where religious uniformity and monarchy carried the day. The country was equally divided between the Royalists and the Commonwealth supporters.

The struggle for limited monarchy was also successful in Protestant areas with close Muslim connections, such as England and Holland, where the Catholic Church was despised due to its absolutist religious and political theology, and the local Church did not have unlimited financial and political means like those of the Catholic Church. Here the Crown and Church were not as entrenched, solidified and absolutist as in the Catholic Spain, Portugal and France. The Spanish and French overseas trade profits filled the coffers of monarchs and gave them capital and means to instill fear and further their absolutism, while in Holland and Britain the overseas initiatives were privately-owned. The huge overseas trading profits went to individual merchants, mostly outside the Crown's circle, enabling them to demand religio-political reformation and institution-building. "The critical political institutions were those that constrained the power of the monarchy and allied groups. Checks on royal power and prerogatives emerged only when groups that favoured them, that is commercial interests outside the royal circle, became sufficiently powerful politically. From 1500, and especially from 1600, onward, in countries with nonabsolutist initial institutions and easy access to the Atlantic, the rise in Atlantic trade enriched and strengthened commercial interests outside the royal circle and enabled them to demand and obtain the institutional changes necessary for economic growth. Although profits from Atlantic trade were small relative to GDP, they were still substantial, and much larger than previous trading profits [...] The recipients of these profits became very rich by the standards of seventeenth- and eighteenth-century Europe, and typically politically and socially very powerful."[436] The struggle between the Crown, its Church and loyals and the overseas traders, along with their religious and parliamentarian allies, caused havoc to England.

The first half of the seventeenth century, including the Interregnum, was full of turmoil, uncertainty and chaos. Contrary to that, the sixteenth century was relatively calm. "The sixteenth century can look remarkably unradical. Strongly bound by hierarchy and an emphasis on order and social degree, successive regimes seem to have had an unlimited capacity to preach the virtues of obedience to established authority."[437] How can we explain a sudden outburst of religious and political radicalism in a society that valued unity, order, tradition, conformity and obedience conceptualised by Robert Filmer (1588–1653), preached and implemented by Archbishop Laud and James I?[438] How could we explain a sudden gushing of republican language, a language of popular sovereignty, commonwealth, limited monarchy and rights instead of long traditional language of absolute, true, pure, complete and unlimited divine right monarchy? How could we explain a sudden regicide, the demise and execution of a well settled, un-opposed, un-disputed, un-challenged King Charles I ruling over a united England?[439] "The act of 1649 was so uniquely shocking that on hearing of it, we are told, 'women miscarried, men fell into melancholy, some with consternations expired'. Men, that is to say, do not break lightly with the past: if they are to challenge conventionally accepted standards they must have an alternative body of ideas to support them."[440] Christopher Hill wonders about such a sudden revolutionary atmosphere. "The thinking of all Englishmen had been dominated by the Established Church. Yet, within less than a decade, successful war was levied against the King; bishops and the House of Lords were abolished; and Charles I was executed in the name of his people. How did men get the nerve to do such unheard-of things?"[441]

These are complex questions and the answers could vary. Any monocausal explanation for the English Revolution and later economic growth and great divergence will leave out many socio-political aspects. One possible answer could be the English exposure to the Muslim East and its material and intellectual implications. English overseas trade with the alluring, prosperous and pluralistic Muslim East could have served as a catalyst to stir pluralistic, rational, natural and republican impulses during the first half of the seventeenth century, as it certainly did during the second half of the century.

Overseas Trade and English Revolution

Inspired by the Spanish and Potuguese overseas routes to Asia and America, the English merchants started the Russia Company in 1552. The explicit purpose of this Company was to find the shortest sea route to the East Indies. This venture languished until September of 1580, when Francis Drake was able to break Spanish and Portuguese monopolies over India trade and returned with fortunes, which made him a national hero and triggered an Eastern trade mania in England. "Indeed, mentions of trade, Indies, and the Americas in published tracts in English experienced particularly large boosts in 1580 and 1585, thereafter achieving levels comparable to and often exceeding written mentions of Pope, Catholic, papist, and bishop and of rights, privileges, liberties, and freedoms in the years preceding the Civil War."[442] Starting in the 1580s Oriental trade increased to peak by the1630s, affecting a material revolution in England often termed as the "Oriental Obsession."[443] "Enthusiasm for shares in these companies spread beyond merchants to encompass a broad spectrum of political elites. The more than 6,366 investors between 1575 and 1630 included 23 percent of all members of Parliament seated in that period."[444] Almost 23.5% of members of Long Parliament (125 members) were overseas shareholders. They came from all over Britain.[445] The shareholder MPs supported the parliament against the Crown, gave loans to the parliament, defended its foreign policies and their own overseas investments. This way a broad, formidable and lasting coalition against the Crown and Church came into being.[446] A strong and politically engaged middle class, with capital and resources, drove the movement for religio-political reform and aggressive trade policies.[447] These politico-economic reforms, coupled with religious reformation, propelled Britian to its later imperial heights.

Multiple Puritan sects' misgivings about the Church's theological foundations, scriptural corruptions, anti-traditionalism, zeal for original message of Jesus via Oriental traditions - coupled with socio-economic utilitarian changes caused by overseas trade - and millennial hopes could have very well brought about this sudden revolutionary change. Merchants, shopkeepers and artisans - "the middling sort" people - were crucial to this change.[448] "Freeholders and tradesmen are the support of religion and civility in the land," Richard Baxter wrote."[449] The expansion of this middle class in numbers and wealth was the obvious new social factor. The merchants' free schools provided an alternative to the Church-dominated education and ideology. Individualism, utilitarianism, pragmatism, liberty of conscience and an urban way of republican life were stressed and traditional ideas of King, Church and nobility were in retreat. The supernatural ideology was giving way to natural, egalitarian and pragmatic outlook. "The vision of reality that had supported the rational consciousness of man for a thousand years was fading."[450]

Individual merchants and explorers initiated global projects while the Crown and Church were busy extorting and persecuting citizens. Corruption, adultery, sodomy and incest were rampant at the Court; national and international "disgrace caused or at least accompanied the change."[451] Merchants and Puritans glorified Queen Elizabeth for her Protestant ideology, aggressive trade and foreign policies while criticising James I and Charles I's betrayal of Protestant cause and squeezing of traders through custom and taxes. Overseas trade with Muslim East and its ripple economic effects in England, including the consolidation of middle class, cross-cultural exchanges of ideas, Eastern manuscripts, puritan distrust of the Church Christianity and a longing for return to the original Christianity of Jesus with the help of Middle Eastern languages, imagery, philology, theology, Oriental allure, national disgrace and millennial hopes, were some of the main factors of the sudden radical upheavals in England.

Overseas trade with the Muslim East was perhaps the main difference and the success story of the late sixteenth and early seventeenth century. Prosperity breeds independence, autonomy and a sort of moral laxity. Opulence (especially in the absence of a policing Church and state as happened during the Civil War) was a recipe for religious divergences and free-thinking. English exposure to pluralistic Ottoman, Mughal and Persian society and its egalitarian mosque environment and organisational structures added fuel to the fire. Interregnum resulted in religious diversity, free-thinking and a sort of tolerance often connected with material success, culture and Oriental influences. It could not have been the result of the sixteenth-century Reformation or the resultant Protestant Churches, as these Churches were equally persecutory and uniform. It could not have been instigated by American colonisation, as the Native Americans lacked any such ideology or the modeling capacity. The early American adventures and colonisations were unsuccessful due to local resistance. For instance, the original London Company and Virginia Company of London were bankrupted due to warring with native Americans and corruption,[452] and the Crown revoked the Virginia Company Charter in 1624.[453] The American colonisation experience was totally different to trade arrangements in the Muslim world, as the colonisation process was marred with inter-European warfare and jealousy. The Spanish, French, Dutch and English cutthroat competition cost countless lives, colonies and resources, instilling mutual fear, anxiety, instability and uncertainty. The American experience was different than the Orient, even when successful colonies were established. The Native Americans were not prosperous, civilised and mighty like the Ottomans, Mughals, Persians or Chinese. Sir Thomas Roe, the first English ambassador to the Mughal court (1615), made this clear to East India Company directors in London.[454] Unlike the American experience, the experience in the Orient was not imperial. It was alluring, exciting, profiting, gratifying and challenging. The sixteenth- and seventeenth-century Oriental experience of a superior, sophisticated and prosperous civilisation definitely impacted the English mind and imagination.

The early English merchants in the Muslim world were nothing but subdued traders, focused on profit and learning rather than colonisation. They left England between the age of fifteen and eighteen, and their Eastern experiences were formative. They learned the languages, business, communicative and social skills and acculturated themselves with a global, diversified and pluralistic society. They made fortunes in the Muslim world. Early sixteenth-century English voyages were not successful, but later voyages initiated a long chain of overseas opportunities. "Although the English had initiated direct trade to the Levant as early as 1511, a final English voyage in 1552 in the wake of clear Ottoman ascendancy had signaled the end of English commercial aspirations at least for a while."[455] It was in 1581 and 1592, when England received the permission (capitulations) to trade in the Ottoman Empire, that the Levant Company was initiated. The Company brought England to the Levant and the Levant to England. The English Crown did not have the desire or the means to fund an English Ambassador in Istanbul; the Levant Company merchants had to bear the burden.

The superior Islamic world certainly changed the English perceptions of Islam, Muhammad and Muslims, contributing to religious anxieties at home. "Expanding commercial engagement with the Ottomans, Morocco and Persia pressed their representatives (and their faith) to an increasing cultural prominence in the later sixteenth century, particularly following the official codification of those relationships that began with the Anglo-Ottoman 'capitulations' in 1580. Large numbers of Christian converts to Mahometanism in the sixteenth and seventeenth centuries only made the refutation of Mahomet more urgent."[456] The premodern allure of the Islamic East is often diminished by the modern historians but it was real, as will be discussed further in the coming pages. It suffices here to quote Allison P. Coudert who states that "the Eurocentric nature of most European history writing minimises or obscures altogether the fact that Europe was not a dominant power in the early modern period, just as it obscures the role that Islam played in shaping European identities. Few people realise how terrifying and threatening, but at the same time how awe-inspiring, Islam appeared to early modern Europeans."[457] Early modern Europe's mystique of Islam was real;[458] it was Europeans who went to the Orient for business and not the other way around. Had Europe been prosperous and superior, as it became in the nineteenth century onward, the sixteenth- to eighteenth-century Europeans would not have been flocking to the East. The journey to the Muslim East was infinitely dangerous, treacherous and perilous; the mortality rate was extremely high. The conditions on the sea and land were exceedingly unfriendly, especially after the Spanish expulsion of Moriscos in 1492. The conditions at home must not have been congenial to prosperity or profitability as compared to the Muslim East. The long-distance trade voyages, along with their perilous conditions and potentials, testify to this fact.

Piracy and Barbary States

In addition to inter-European piracy, the Barbary pirates played havoc to Europe. Over 3,000,000 Muslims were expelled from Spain between 1492 and 1610 and many of them joined Barbary pirates to avenge the wrongs done to them by Catholic monarchs. These pirates were truly menacing for the Europeans, as the Europeans were menacing for West Africans. Millions of Spanish, Italian, Dutch and English were enslaved by Muslim pirates, English being the least among them. To give an example from the British Isles alone, "between 1600 and 1640 Muslim corsairs captured more than 800 English, Scottish, Welsh, and Irish trading vessels in the Mediterranean and Atlantic, enslaving some 12,000 English subjects. The attacks were not confined to the sea but extended to port towns and inland villages. In August 1625, for example, Muslim pirates stormed the church in Monts' Bay, Cornwall, capturing 60 men, women, and children. In 1631 they captured 140 people in Baltimore, County Cork, which means they had become brazen enough to enter the waters of the Irish Sea. Even more brazen were the raiders who roamed the English Channel and traveled up the Thames estuary. According to the minutes of Parliament the fishermen are 'afraid to put to sea, and we are forced to keep continual watches on all our coasts.' The powerlessness felt by the English was summed up by the Vice Admiral of Devon Sir John Eliot, who lamented that the seas around Britain 'seem'd theirs.' Between 1660 and the 1730s another 6,000 men, women, and children were captured. Hence some 20,000 or more British were enslaved in North Africa and the Ottoman Empire during the seventeenth and first third of the eighteenth centuries, but this was only a fraction of the total number of Europeans who found themselves in the same predicament."[459] Nabil Matar and Matthew Birchwood have shown that problems related to the captives and renegades were major contributors to the English Civil War.

Robert C. Davis claims that by 1570, "enslaving Christians had been elevated to something approaching state policy in North Africa and Ottoman Empire."[460] European coastal areas, and islands all across the Mediterranean, were devastated. "Enormous flotillas attacked Christian shipping and devastated coastal areas of Spain, Italy, France, England, and the Mediterranean islands. On occasion the size of the fleets consisted of over 100 galleys and 10,000 soldiers, enabling the Ottomans to blockade major ports such as Genoa and Naples, threaten Rome, and sack coastal cities. In a diary kept between 1679 and 1685 Thomas Barker, the English Consul in Tripoli, frequently noted galleys setting off to go 'a Christian stealing' or 'a men-stealing.' In one entry he noted that the corsairs had set off 'Westward to Fish for Dutchmen, whom [...] they hope to meet in Great Schools.' Some corsair attacks became legendary like the 7,000 captives the Algerians took in the Bay of Naples in 1544; the 6,000 taken when the Algerians sacked Vieste in Calabria in 1554; the 4,000 men, women, and children seized in Granada in 1566; the 1,200 men and women captured in Madeira in 1617; the 400 seized in Iceland in 1627; the 700 taken in Calabria in 1636, followed by another 1,000 in 1636 and still another 4,000 in 1644. Between 1570 and 1606 Sicily was attacked at least 136 times, with some raids penetrating inland as far as 10 to 20 miles."[461] The Turks were a ruining, destructive and dreaded power in Europe.[462] The Muslim world presented a challenge as well as allure to the emerging but instable English state. The challenges were not worth the extreme dangers if the allure of profit had not outweighed it.

Capitulations and Muslim Soft Empire

The overseas trade with Ottomans was initiated by the capitulations or permission to trade in the Ottoman territories. The capitulations were gifts granted to evolving weaker Protestant states after several repeated requests and valuable gifts to the Sultan and his establishment;[463] they were neither reciprocal nor negotiables.[464] The Sultan even paid token salaries to the European ambassadors as his guests. The capitulations were integral to the grand Ottoman strategy of expanding influences, extending religio political ideology and millennial hopes of universal Ottoman monarchy. They were part of Ottoman strategy of dividing and containing Christendom and avoiding a united crusade. The Sultans effectively played competing European missions and merchants against each other and instilled strife between contending parties by wisely negotiating privileges and preferring some over others. They carefully orchestrated capitulation rituals and ceremonies to play one European nation against others. They also played the "religious card" by playing Protestants and Eastern Christians against the Catholics and persecuted Christian minorities against both Catholic and Protestant religious and political power structures. For instance the Moriscos, Flanders and other Protestants were sheltered and supported against Catholic Habsburg dynasty, Protestant Huguenots against French Catholic King and Socinian, Unitarians, Quakers and other minorities were encouraged to demand rights from their Dutch and English power structures. The Ottomans could afford to do so as they had the upper hand.

The early seventeenth-century Western Europe or England were in no position to demand or impose terms on the mighty, dreaded Ottoman Empire. The first English ambassador to the Ottoman court, William Harbourne (1542-1617), went through many humiliating protocols to gain the Sultan's approval to trade in the Ottoman Empire.[465] The humiliations of the first English ambassador to Mughal court, Sir Thomas Roe - who was known for his diplomatic experience and credentials - were no less. He had to wait for three years in perilous conditions to obtain a few limited, minor and ungratifying privileges from Jahangir, the Mughal Emperor.[466]

Until the nineteenth century all "European ambassadors were introduced formally to the Ottoman Sultan as "naked and hungry barbarians", who had ventured "to rub the brow of the Sublime Porte."[467] The Ottoman Sultan dictated the trade and diplomatic policies. The Europeans were there to follow rules, not to dictate. In Aleppo for example, every night European merchants were locked down in a Khan, a walled enclave with security and janissaries. Other cities allowed more freedom, but there was no sense of superiority or pretension. They knew that they were subdued, there to make profit and obey the law. The merchants, consuls and ambassadors were arrested and molested by the Ottoman authorities if found guilty of capitulation violations or Ottoman laws. The Dutch ambassador De Keyser was imprisoned in 1617 for months in Algiers.[468] The Dutch Republic could not get him released except through the efforts of a Dutch convert to Islam and a corsair pirate. In 1860, the well-connected high end English ambassador Sir John Finch[469] whose family was in the helms of affairs in England was tried in Ottoman court for bribery charges and threatened many times with imprisonment without much diplomatic influence or recourse.

The Turks, for their part, disdained and belittled the Europeans. "While the blond European may have appeared as a God to native Americans, for Muslims their reddish skin recalled the unclean pig. James Irving, who was held captive in Morocco for a year, noticed how the local inhabitants 'would never use any vessel that had touched our lips: so great was their detestation and contempt for us.' When Sir Daniel Harvey arrived in Istanbul in 1668 as ambassador to the Ottoman Empire, he had to wait a full year for an audience with the Sultan, so little did the Sultan think of him or the country from which he came. Muslims considered European dress with its tight waists for women and tight trousers for men obscene, if not immoral. Elizabeth Marsh describes a Moroccan woman who was extremely 'curious in examining my dress and person, and [...] highly entertained at the appearance I made.'"[470] Nabil Matar notes that "no Muslim fell on his knees before a Briton: rather he humiliated the "Goure" (Kafir, infidel) who could not but submit to the indignity. The Muslim not only did not fear the Englishman: he did not even recognise him [...] From whichever angle a Briton reflected on the Muslim perception of the Christians, he realised that Muslims saw themselves in power and certitude."[471] The Grand Vizier Kara Mustafa laid plain the Sublime Porte's most cynical view regarding Europeans, stating to English Ambassador Sir John Finch that all ambassadors were "sent hither by your representative princes to answer for the lives and estates of all Muslims all over the world that are damaged or suffer by your respective subjects, and you are here a hostage to answer for all damage done by English all over the world."[472]

In the Indian Mughal court, England was also considered small and unworthy. James I was painted even below the feet of Jahangir in the paintings of Mughal artist Bichitr.[473] In 1636, an English factory in Surat was seized, and all factors were imprisoned and threated with torture, because some English ships - not even East India Company vessels - had plundered some merchantmen of Surat in the Arabian Sea. The English were released only when the full compensation was paid.[474]

The Ottoman influence, power and might were well recognised[475] until 1774, when Europe in general - and England in particular - asserted itself, and the Ottoman Empire's shortfall became evident. Even then, the Ottomans were not to be fooled around; even a smaller independent Muslim state such as Morocco was considered mighty. "Only in the nineteenth century did the separation between West and East become clearer as a result of the establishment of supposedly scientific racial ideologies and the scientific and technological advances made in the West. Before 1750 what characterised advanced and powerful societies was the state of their towns and trade, both of which flourished in Islamic societies. Travellers to North Africa were stunned by the vastness and magnificence of Muslim architecture. The palace built by the Sultan Moulay Ismaïly was, according to one British traveller, the 'largest he had ever seen', and the stables, which were some three quarters of a mile long 'the noblest of the kind perhaps in the world.' In size this Muslim palace did indeed dwarf Hampton Court and even Versailles. Because of his reputation as a fierce warrior and his love of grandeur Moulay Ismaïly was compared to Louis XIV, but in actual fact he was far grander."[476]

The seasoned diplomate Sir Thomas Roe, who had experienced the Spanish, Dutch and English courts, was dazzled by the Mughal opulence and grandeur. Writing about the Emperor's birthday celebrations in 1616 Roe noted that "Here attended the Nobilitie all sitting about it on Carpets until the King came; who at least appeared clothed, or rather laden with Diamonds, Rubies, Pearles, and other precious vanities, so great, so glorious! His head, necke, breast, armes, above the elbowes, at the wrists, his fingers each one with at least two or three Rings, are fettered with chaines of dyamonds, Rubies as great as Walnuts – some greater – and Pearles such as mine eyes were amazed at […] in jewells, which is one of his felicityes, hee is the treasury of the world, buyeing all that comes, and heaping rich stones as if hee would rather build [with them] than wear them."[477] Roe was vexed to discover that the Mughals regarded relations with the English as a very low priority. On arrival he was shoved into a substandard accommodation: only four caravanserai rooms allotted for the entire embassy and even they were "no bigger than ovens, and in that shape, round at the top, no light but the door, and so little that the goods of two carts would fill them all."[478] More humiliatingly still, his slightly shop-soiled presents were soon completely outshone by those of a rival Portuguese embassy who gave Jahangir "jewels, Ballests [balas spinels] and Pearles with much disgrace to our English commoditie.'"[479]

Contrary to Roe's fascination, the local Indians' contempt, derision and low estimation of the English was an open secret. The later rowdy, uncivilised and immoral Englishmen were openly derided by the locals. William Dalrymple well depicted the contemptuous environment of eighteenth-century India: "Their private whorings, drunkenesse and such like ryotts […] breaking open whorehouses and rackehowses [i.e., arrack bars] have hardened the hearts of the inhabitants against our very names,' wrote one weary EIC official. Little wonder that the British were soon being reviled in the Surat streets 'with the names of Ban-chude and Betty-chude which my modest language will not interpret.'"[480] The Dutch, Potugues and French were equally despised and kept to their limits.[481]

The East India Company

While the East India Company directors were controlling the English Crown and parliament with their loans, briberies and corporate lobbying,[482] a company officer wrote in 1681 to his superiors that "'here every petty Officer makes a pray of us, abuscing us at pleasure to Screw what they can out of us.' We are, he wrote, 'despised and trampled upon' by Mughal officials."[483] They were considered low, base, quarrelling and fool dealers in India, while in London they were making fortunes for the company. The EIC was taught a humiliating lesson when its haughty and monied governor Sir Josiah Child (1630-1699),[484] a confidant of King James II, with the permission of the King and London company directors, tried to assert himself. In spite of a considerable English Royal naval fleet which sailed from London to teach a lesson to the Mughals of Bengal, the English were crushed beyond imagination. "The Mughal war machine swept away the English landing parties as easily as if it were swatting flies; soon the EIC factories at Hughli, Patna, Kasimbazar, Masulipatnam and Vizagapatam had all been seized and plundered, and the English had been expelled completely from Bengal. The Surat factory was closed and Bombay was blockaded."[485] EIC, the most powerful English corporation "had no option but to sue for peace and beg for the return of its factories and hard-earned trading privileges. They also had to petition for the release of its captured factors, many of whom were being paraded in chains through the streets or kept fettered in the Surat castle and the Dhaka Red Fort 'in insufferable and tattered conditions [...] like thiefs and murders.' When Aurangzeb heard that the EIC had 'repented of their irregular proceedings' and submitted to Mughal authority, the Emperor left the factors to lick their wounds for a while, then in 1690 graciously agreed to forgive them."[486] In 1757, when EIC Calcutta Governor Roger Drake showed hesitation in demolishing an un-authorised fortification to Company's fort, the Bengal Nawb Siraj ud Daula came thundering on Calcutta with 30,000 troops and inflicted an exacting punishment on 200 English factors and soldiers. The cowardly Drake escaped from the backdoor, leaving all the English factors at the mercy of Nawab. The chief English factor William Watt, who later became the *de facto* East India Company ruler of Bengal and had notable descendants including a British Prime Minister, had to kneel in front of the Nawab to seek his forgiveness. An English eyewitness report stated that "Upon Mr Watts' going before the Nabob, with his hands across and a handkerchief wrapt round his wrists, signifying himself his slave and prisoner, he [Siraj] abused him very much." Watts was made to hug the Nawab's feet, and cry: "Tomar ghulam, tomar Ghulam" – "I am your slave, your slave."[487] The Fort was opened, and the English were imprisoned.

"Upon opening the Factory gates, the enemy immediately entered in great numbers, and demanded the keys of the godowns [warehouses] both publick and private; they no sooner took possession of the arms and ammunition, but they behaved in a most insolent manner, threatening the gentlemen to cut off their ears, slit their noses and chabuck [whip] them, with other punishments, in order to extort compliance from them [...] Then he [Siraj] ordered all the Europeans out of the Factory, and put them under a strong guard. All the prisoners were sent to Murshidabad Cutcherry [gaol], and put in irons, where they remained."[488] The story of the English dying in the Black Hole of the fortress is too graphic to be narrated here.[489] "William Lindsay wrote to the future historian of the Company, Robert Orme, that it was 'a scene of destruction and dissolution [...] and makes me tremble when I think of the consequences that it will be attended with, not only to every private Gentlemen in India but to the English nation in General. I hardly think all the force we have in India will be sufficient to resettle us here into any footing of security, we now being almost as much in want of everything as when we first settled here."[490] Colin Newbury has noted that "it is abundantly clear that initial contact through maritime trade left the East India Company in a condition of dependency on Indian rulers, brokers, and financiers until the last decades of the eighteenth century."[491] It was not London, but the Muslim Agra and Instanbul, which dictated the terms.[492]

It was for the first time in 1758, and mostly in the later part of the eighteenth century, when the English, due to the central Mughal government's collapse, provincial autonomies, English bribes, mercenary activities and superior military technology,[493] were able to create anarchy and finally divide and rule India. By that time, the early and high Enlightenment was already complete. The English from the 1580s to the 1760s, while very successful in America and Siberia, were mostly tamed, subdued - and at times, humiliated - traders in the Muslim East.[494] The Mughal and Safvid Empires[495] were more welcoming than Ottomans of the merchants, but in no way under any political or diplomatic pressure to grant them concessions.[496] The subdued English traders mainly focused on trade and profit, without many imperial designs.[497] The English throughout the early (1680-1720) and high Enlightenment period (1750s) were mostly at the receiving end. The later British Empire was the outcome of the high Enlightenment, and not the source of it.

The Dutch, French and British merchants and diplomates competed with one another to earn the favours of Sultan.[498] Their entry into the world economic systems was late and dependent upon the Muslim world. "The north European countries entered into regular relations with the world overseas only after 1600."[499] Before that England was a tiny, isolated,[500] marginal kingdom.[501] The Protestant Western Europe in general, and Britain in particular, got connected with the world through its Muslim neighbours.[502] The Early Turkey Company (1581),[503] Levant Company (1592-1825)[504] and East India Company (1600-1874)[505] merchants lived and traded in the Muslim East, assimilated ideas, expertise, wealth[506] and utilised it to launch the Virginia Company[507] and American colonisation.[508] For instance, Sir Thomas Smythe (Smith, 1558 – 1625) the governor of Levant and East India Companies in 1600 was also the founding governor of the Virginia Company chartered in 1609, deputy governor of Somers Isles or Bermuda and original supporter, promoter and financiar of North-West Passage in North America. Alison Games noted: "It was in the Mediterranean that the English acquired their first significant experience with large-scale, long-distance trade in an alien and inhospitable environment. The crucial skills learned there anchored and shaped subsequent English enterprises around the world."[509]

The Levant and East India company governors were extremely influential in London, but relatively powerless players in the Muslim World of the seventeenth and early eighteenth centuries. For instance Sir Thomas Lowe, Sir Hugh Hammersley and Sir Henry Garraway were all Lord Mayors of London, and others went on to become the Sheriffs and members of the parliament. Its ambassadors came from influential English families and went on to become members of House of Lords, parliament and foreign office. Its merchants were from rich and influential business families. Its chaplains were highly educated graduates of Oxford and Cambridge. They played a significant role in cross-cultural cultivations, collection of countless manuscripts, their translations and disseminations. Their long exposure to the Muslim East was extremely helpful to English evolution into a commercial, political and imperial giant.[510]

The Levant English traders, consuls and ambassadors lived in Istanbul, Izmir,[511] Aleppo, Cairo, Cyprus and many other Ottoman cities for over 244 years.[512] The long overseas interactions with powerful Unitarian Muslims exacerbated the already heterodox impulses of the rich, opulent and relatively liberal cosmopolitan London traders. "Business in the seventeenth century was often equated with heresy or irreligion. Traders were suspect because they had both the opportunity and the means to challenge dogma and credulity; they were mobile, self-employed, literate, individualist, competitive and less wedded to the communal traditions of an agrarian society. Heresy did spread through commerce; although few notable businessmen had been prominent among the Lollards and Protestant martyrs, they may have found it easier to avoid prosecution."[513] A great majority of London and other city merchants were already Presbyterians, independent Congregationalist and Arian or Unitarian-leaning Arminian Calvinists, who doubted the Trinity and insisted on human free will.[514] Their further exposure to simple Islamic Unitarian theology added fuel to the fire. Young traders were more susceptible to Islam and Turkish influences; they brought back pluralistic religious ideas, arts, architecture, poetry, stories, expertise, ideas, observations and feelings along with silk, pepper and cotton. The dissenters were well represented in the London merchant community and city politics, as Richard Grassby has demonstrated.[515] The Levant and East India companies were equated with Independent churches.[516] "Merchants took risks by distributing seditious and heretical books; several suffered for their faith or went into exile whether under Mary Tudor or James."[517] We will later see that Thomas Firmin, a known London merchant, was pressurised and persecuted by Charles II and James II. Firmin supported the Father of English Unitarianism John Biddle during Cromwell Republic and helped in Unitarian and Socinian publications during the 1690s until his death in 1697. He was known to London merchants for his philonthrophic works and was a close friend and patron of John Locke and many other Unitarians. Likewise Mercer's Company merchant Henry Robinson (1604-1664) wrote about religious tolerance, freedom of trade, freedom of conscience and dissent and suffered due to his heterodox views. Robinson sponsored John Milton's publications. John Locke and Henry Stubbe's close relations with Bristol merchants are well-documented.

Trade and Cultural Exchanges

The intensity of trade, interactions and cultural exchanges can be gauged from the English activities in a relatively small Ottoman city like Aleppo. "Surprise is the usual reaction when people hear that 24 Church of England priests served as chaplains to the English Levant Company factory in Aleppo from 1597 to 1782. For two centuries this succession of Church of England clergy lived and worked in this most cosmopolitan of cities in the Arabic-speaking world that had a foreign community of around 5,000. These Anglican clerics included the greatest English Arabist of the seventeenth century, as well as a number who were to take high office as bishops and royal chaplains, fellows of the Royal Society and friends of notables such as Samuel Johnson and Robert Boyle."[518] They were there along with Dutch and French merchants and chaplains. The sophisticated and highly educated Anglican chaplains were sent to stop conversion of Levant merchants to Islam or Islamising effects, gather information, spy, collect manuscripts and write diaries about Ottoman religion, culture and government.[519] They were also integral to King James I and Charles I's antiquarianism, search for Eastern prisca theologia and prisca sapientia, Near Eastern manuscripts, languages, coins, measurements, histories, Bibles, apocalyptic prophecies and union with the Eastern Churches. The Early Stuart kings, with the help of English theologians, formulated an English Protestant Erastian political theology where the king and state ruled supreme over the Church and subjects and which projected them as the heralds of a new Protestant millennial prosperity, dominion and world dominance in apposition to Habsburg Catholic and Ottoman Muslim millennial claims. Many Levant Company learned chaplains enjoyed patronship of Archbishop Laud and King Charles and researched for Eastern manuscripts, correct measurements of sacred time, spaces, longitudes and latitudes to properly understand the biblical chronology, space-time and millennial prophecies. Using Aristotelian scholasticism and Ptolemaic geographical astronomy, the chaplains like John Greaves compiled data and manuscripts to construct and expand the Stuart millennial theology and hopes for Anglican universal monarchy. The appeal of the "Near East" was not primarily for the love of Muslims or to learn about the "Near East," but was part of a search for the original sources required to resolve various contemporary religious and political controversies. Some chaplains did far more than that. They collected manuscripts of all sorts, learned multiple languages, gathered religio scientific knowledge, histories and intelligence. This quest for Arabic manuscripts began almost simultaneously with the beginning of an English trading presence in Ottoman lands.

For instance, the erudite, learned and highly qualified Dr. Edward Pococke learnt Arabic, Syriac and Hebrew, read the Quran, its commentaries,[520] Hadith (Prophetic sayings, actions and approvals), Islamic history, biographies and languages, collected manuscripts on religion, medicine, astronomy, mathematics, geometry, chemistry, philosophy, philology, geography, literature and engaged with Muslim, Hebrew and Christian scholarship.[521] His local Arab friends supplied him manuscripts and information even after his return to England. On his return to England, he translated many of these manuscripts to Latin and English and became an international luminary whose scholarship was well recognised all across Europe. As the Arabic Chair at Oxford, he taught and interacted with high caliber Continental intelligentsia. His rational, anti-Trinitarian tendencies, objective Islamic sympathies and acknowledgements of Muslim contributions to science and human civilisation were translated to his Oxford students and colleagues such as Henry Stubbe, John Locke, Robert Boyle and others. His close coordination with Archbishop Laud and collection of Oriental manuscripts supplemented the Oxford Bodleian Library.[522] In 1692 the Library purchased four hundred Oriental volumes from Pococke's library.[523] He purchased a variety of manuscripts for the Royal Society of London's fellows and helped in translation of many into Latin. He also collected manuscripts for Archbishop Laud, who between 1635 and 1640 donated over a thousand Oriental manuscripts to the Bodleian Library.[524] Laud had obtained a royal letter to the Levant Company requiring that each of their returning ship must bring one Arabic or Persian manuscript. Laud's collection was second only to John Selden, who donated eight thousand volumes of manuscripts to the Library in addition to donating medical manuscripts to the College of Physicians. Pococke, along with John Greaves, mostly coordinated purchase of these manuscripts from Aleppo and Istanbul.[525] England had no scientific tradition, chairs in mathematics, astronomy or chemistry as both Oxford and Cambridge shunned these sciences as useless. Pococke and Greavas' translations were helpful resources for Oxford, Cambridge, Gresham College and especially for the Royal Society fellows.

Other Chaplains such as Charles Robson, Nathaniel Hill, Robert Frampton, Robert Huntington[526] and others were actively engaged in manuscript collections, cultural exchange and research. They learned Arabic language, interacted with local scholarship and purchased manuscripts of all sorts. For instance, in 1692 Robert Huntington sold six hundred Oriental manuscripts to Bodleian Library with a record sum of over 1000 pounds.[527] He also gave manuscripts to Oxford College, Royal Society and other bodies. His was the best collection on Islamic philosophy, history, lexigraphy, law, astronomy, mathematics, minerology, art, warfare and Eastern Christianity.

Robert Frampton became well-versed in Arabic language and an expert in manuscript collection. "In the 1650s Frampton studied Arabic in Aleppo. Frampton's biographer provides telling glimpses of Frampton using the language for different ends. He apparently progressed so far in both reading and speaking that he was able to compile a collection of Arabic proverbs, to intercede with local officials in Aleppo, and to ward off a band of thieves on the road to Istanbul."[528] He became an Anglican Bishop. "On his final return to England, Frampton had a steady rise in career. In 1670, two months after disembarking he was appointed preacher at the Rolls, and chaplain to the Lord Keeper. In 1671 he was made prebendary of Gloucester cathedral, and shortly afterwards of Salisbury cathedral. In 1673 he was made Dean of Gloucester and on 27 March 1681 was consecrated Bishop of Gloucester by Archbishop Sancroft in the chapel of All Souls' College, Oxford."[529]

Dr. John Covel travelled extensively in the Ottoman Empire, collected scientific manuscripts of all sorts, exchanged ideas with religious and political leaders and wrote extensive diaries.[530] He extensively corresponded with Locke, Newton and others while in Turkey. On his return to England, he became Chaplain to the Princess of Orange in Hague and finally the Vice Chancellor of Cambridge University. He was fully engaged with Isaac Newton and Cambridge Neoplatonists such as Joseph Mede and Henry More on multiple levels and capacities. Covel developed his heterodox views while in Turkey and was critical of "Whiflers" understandings of the Christian religion.[531] Covel regularly corresponded with John Locke and Isaac Newton from Istanbul, and was a close friend of these later luminaries and many other Royal Society fellows.[532]

The Levant, East India and Barbary Company ambassadors and consuls also played an important role in manuscript collection, cultural and religious exchanges. Throughout the seventeenth and eighteenth centuries, the Levant Consuls showed thorough knowledge of Islamic languages, customs, culture and religion. "The Englishman George Sandys, who visited the Levant in the early 1610s, thought the consul in Aleppo, Bartholemew Haggatt, 'expert in their language'. The French traveller the Abbe Carre noted that Benjamin Lannoy, the English consul in Aleppo for over a decade during the 1660s and 1670s, was 'well versed in all languages.' Writing in the late 1720s, Daniel Defoe mentioned 'a Turkey merchant' of his acquaintance who 'had liv'd at Aleppo, at Constantinople, and at Grand Cairo' and who 'spoke the Arabic in all its several dialects as spoken by the Turks at all those places.'"[533] Izmir factory Consul and famous Ottoman historian Sir Paul Rycaut was indistinguishable from the Turks. "Jezreel Jones, who served as British envoy to Morocco from 1704, was well known for his fluency in Arabic, and later served as translator to the Moroccan ambassador."[534] Later on Warren Hastings, the scholar and linguist who was the first Governor of the Presidency of Fort William, the head of the Supreme Council of Bengal and the de facto first Governor General of India from 1773 to 1785, became a noted Indophile.[535] He learned Urdu, Bengali, Persian and other oriental languages,[536] religion and cultures and commissioned Oriental dictionaries, manuscripts, books and university chairs.[537]

Levant merchants were equally enthusiastic; they learned Arabic, Turkisk, Persian and other Oriental languages to increase their sociability, business know-how, profitability and assimilation.[538] Many of them resided in Aleppo, Izmir and Istanbul for decades, spoke Arabic, Turkish and Persian and dressed in Oriental clothes. For instance, Roland Sherman lived close to sixty years in Aleppo, spoke perfect Arabic and fully adopted the local fashion, habits and culture.[539] Sir Dudley North, a merchant who spent over 20 years in Istanbul, Izmir and other cities of the Ottoman Empire and totally engrossed himself in Turkish life, habits and culture was elected as the Sheriff of London[540] on his return to England.[541] His family was well-connected with the Crown and Tory parliament and also to the closest friends of John Locke. He was elected to the parliament twice, knighted in 1683, appointed a commissioner of customs, and later of the treasury, and then again of the customs. He took the place of manager for the crown in all matters of revenue. He played an active role during the Restoration period faithfully executing the financial and political policies of Charles II and James II. He was the London Sheriff during the famous trial of Whig leaders involved in Rye House Plot and their executions.[542] He continued to trade in the Levant after his return to England and collected a great number of manuscripts.[543]

Likewise, the English ambassador and merchant Sir John Finch was from a noble English family which filled the highest offices in England.[544] Sir John Baines was also well connected with movers and shakers of his time. Their detailed reports of and correspondence with high officials at home about Islam, Ottoman government and culture steered many changes in English state and society. Finch's detailed accounts of Islam were the main sources of his philosopher sister Anne Conway's anti-Trinitarian tendencies, open sympathies with Islamic Unitarianism, rationalism and universalism and her conversion to rational and spiritual theology of Quakers.[545]

The East India Company's merchants, workers, chaplains and ambassadors equally played important inter-cultural roles.[546] The East India Company brought England to India, but also brought India to London and Manchester. Indian textiles, colours and patterns changed English fashion, culture and society, while Turkish coffee and Indian tea became national novelties. Other colonies such as Tangier also contributed to the intercultural exchanges. For instance, Lancelot Addison[547] (1632–1703) was English Chaplain in Tangier. He spent seven years in North Barbary States and wrote detailed accounts of history, customs, culture and Religion of West Barbary in his *West Barbary, or a Short Narrative of the Revolutions of the Kingdoms of Fez and Morocco,* (1671) and his *Life and Death of Muhamed* (1679). On his return to England he was appointed royal chaplain, or Chaplain in Ordinary to the King.[548] In 1683 he became Dean of Lichfield, and in 1684 Archdeacon of Coventry. His son Gulston Addison became EIC Governor of Madras, in India.

In addition to English ambassaders, consuls and merchants there were physicians and other supporting staff. For instance, two brothers Alexander and Patrick Russell served overlapping terms as physicians in Aleppo (from 1740 to 1772), learned Arabic, spoke regional dialects to be able to treat local Arabic speaking patients and collected medical and literary manuscripts.[549]

Overseas Trading Companies and Domestic Politics

Both the Levant Company and its offshoot East India Company merchants yielded great influence in the City of London, other provincial cities[550] and in national politics.[551] The cash-depleted and war-driven English Crown[552] - and later on confrontational parliament - was highly dependent upon merchants' custom duty, taxes, financial support and loans.[553] "In 1693, less than a century after its foundation, the Company was discovered to be using its own shares for buying the favours of parliamentarians, as it annually shelled out £1,200 a year to prominent MPs and ministers. The bribery, it turned out, went as high as the Solicitor General, who received £218, and the Attorney General, who received £545. The parliamentary investigation into this, the world's first corporate lobbying scandal, found the EIC guilty of bribery and insider trading and led to the impeachment of the Lord President of the Council and the imprisonment of the Company's Governor."[554] The loans and donations came with strings attached, and influenced policies.

The Levant Company traders intermarried among themselves and maintained close family connections with East India as well as Virginia Company owners and director.[555] These overseas traders played major roles in almost all political and economic events of the seventeenth century[556], "although they could be portrayed as an urban elite motivated by the all-consuming eagerness for private gain, overseas traders were at the heart of complex networks of mutually-dependent associates, the dimensions of which stretched far beyond the mercantile profession. By dint of their economic calling, merchants were middlemen in commercial, social, and political terms, and thus can provide an excellent insight into the workings of the late Stuart state."[557] They were actively involved in the English Civil War, Cromwell's Commonwealth, Restoration of Charles II and the Glorious Revolution in various capacities and with different parties. The vocal, republican, dissenter group was more active in soliciting donations and giving loans to the Crown and parliament to influence policy.[558] "It is unsurprising, then, that City political authority rested on wealth and overseas merchants. Having gained advantage due to the booming growth of trade during the 1660s and 1670s, Levant merchants felt a need to protect their new position, engaging in politics in hitherto unseen levels. Consequently, of those active in City politics, Levantine traders made up one-fifth of the whole. Only these elite rich, whether ennobled for their commercial efforts or the cream of merchant society, could afford the costs of political office. For example, they could satisfy the property qualifications for a sheriff in London set at £10,000 in 1631. Or, the qualifications for an alderman at the same amount, rising to £15,000 for the same positions in 1711. With the advent of party politics by the end of the seventeenth century, many of these political traders identified as Whigs rather than Tories."[559] The East India trading complex was even more influential in the city and national politics. Through them the Eastern trade, money and ideas entered seventeenth-century English society and changed it from within. They served as England's bridge to the Islamic world and its markets, cultures, sciences, religion and habits. Their influential role in the socio-economic and political life of the seventeenth century English society is well-documented[560] and will be discussed further in the coming pages.

Ralph Davis observed that three "things were commonly said of Levant merchants by their fellow-citizens of mid-eighteenth-century London: that they were, in the main, very rich men; that the trade they carried on was an exceptionally lucrative one; and that their wealth and large incomes were the result of their exercise of monopolistic rights over the English trade with the Levant."[561] These highly influential, rich and well-connected English individuals, like countless other Levant and East India Company traders, workers and ambassadors, were well aware of the Muslim religion, culture and customs. Their lucrative trade opportunities depended upon their knowledge of Islamic laws, religious and cultural sensibilities. They had no choice but to understand the Islamic business laws, socio-religious sensitivities and cultural norms. Many of them completely acculturated themselves in the Islamic mold to guarantee business success; Sir Dudley North and Sir Paul Rycaut were undistinguishable from the local Turks. The centuries-long close business associations, cultural interactions and religious intersections in the Islamic world were instrumental in the transfer of Eastern ideas, habits and norms to the British society.[562]

The Levant and East India company governors in London were equally engaged with the Islamic world, and their wealth and clout were directly connected with that. They studied the sea maps, weather patterns, Muslim ports, cities, pirates, corsairs, politics, princes, pashas and sultans to ascertain the success of company voyages, businesses, traders, ambassadors and workforce. They selected the imported commodities, maintained contacts with overseas traders and their Eastern suppliers, negotiated deals, maintained credit lines, loans and advance payments. They decided about new projects, new ports, amount and nature of gifts to local rulers, taxes and interest rates. London was fully engaged with Istanbul, Isfahan, Bombay, Bengal and Calcutta.

Till the 1800s, the Levant and East India companies strictly resisted the English missionaries or demands for proselytising Muslims. They focused on profit, financial expansion and good relations with the Muslim community and rulers. The majority of them shed their Englishness and engrossed themselves into local cultures and habits and were more Turkish, Persian and Mughals than some of the locals. The London merchants and company governors dressed in Oriental clothes, drank tea and coffee and invited their friends and families to their Oriental parties to launch, advertise and sell their Oriental projects or to solicit funds. England's seventeenth- and eighteenth-century "Oriental Obsessions" are well-documented.

Travelogues and Acculturation Process

Travelogues were also popular during this period; regular English travellers and their travelogues supplemented the acculturation process.[563] These texts "bear witness to new forms of knowledge and to an emergent identity-formation that was shaped by the religious, political, and economic conditions of the time."[564] The Turkish Empire was too mighty for the Western Europeans to conquer or overcome, so the Christian rulers sought friendly relations instead of mounting crusades; they sought emulation, profit and strategic advantages rather than confrontation. English writers followed the same strategy, by befriending and emulating the powerful Muslims they encountered. Thomas Palmer, in *How To Make Our Travailes Profitable* (1606), well represented this attitude of travelling "intelligencers." "[T]he very point which every Travailer ought to lay his wittes about [is] To get knowledge for the bettering of himselfe and his Countrie: This, being the object of their Countries defects and the subject of Travailers."[565]

The Royals,[566] elites, intelligentsia, Royal Society fellows,[567] Enlightenment luminaries and reformers used travel literature and Oriental manuscripts in different capacities and for varying agendas to better themselves, their knowledge and country. The Royal Society Secretary, Henry Oldenburg, translated Francois Bernier's four volumes of descriptions of India and the Grand Mogul from German to English. Michael Hunter has well demonstrated the fact that the Royal Society fellows extensively devoted themselves to studying travel literature.[568] Oldenburg identified Linschoten's travels as his main source of information on Surat and East Indies. Daniel Carey noted that these "examples alone suggest that travel literature constituted an invaluable resource and mine of information, assisting in the campaign for a comprehensive history of nature."[569] The travel of merchants, chaplains, consuls, ambassadors, staff and missionary and leisure travellers was incorporated by natural philosophers into their study and accounts of natural phenomena becoming its fundamental testimony and supplementing documentation of nature and its workings. The travelogues became accepted sources of information, queries, cross references, elimination of errors and advancement of knowledge. The travellers and Royal Society fellows closely followed Francis Bacon and Samuel Hartlib's instructions regarding useful travel, collections of man's histories, trades, customs and habits.[570] The early travels to the Muslim East greatly contributed to English scholarship at home.[571] "The production of knowledge about Islam, Turks, Moors, and Arabs was accelerated and dispersed to various sites of cultural production and consumption, including popular ballads, the visual arts, public pageants, court entertainments, public theater, as well as printed materials such as travel narratives or ethnographies."[572] The material fascination and envy of the Muslim East was conspicuous, but often marred with religious contempt. "The wealth, order, and discipline of the Ottomans was frequently admired and praised by writers who, at the same time, expressed contempt. The contradiction between condemnation and emulation is strongly apparent when these early modern travellers write about Jerusalem and Constantinople, two sites of great ideological significance for Christianity."[573] Quite frequently though the material allure, pluralistic fascination and republican appreciations overrode the religious zeal, enthusiasm and contempt.

For instance, the wealthy English traveller Henry Blount's 1634 influential travel account *Voyage into the Levant* popularised Turkey in the following words: "He who would behold these times in their greatest glory could not find a better scene than Turkey [...] Turks are the only modern people, great in action [...] whose Empire hath so suddenly invaded the world."[574] Blount was amazed by the Ottoman tolerance for religious diversity, and greatly admired Ottoman military for its might, discipline and reach, "yet I wondered to see such a multitude so clear of confusion, violence, want, sicknesse, or any other disorder."[575] While traveling through the Danube River valley Blount was asked by the local Pasha whether or not he would fight with Ottoman Muslims against Habsburg Christians. Blount's response was startling. "I humbly thanked him, for his favour, and told him that to an Englishman it was lawful to serve under any who were in League with our King, and that our King had not only a League with the Gran Signor, but continually held an embassadour at his Court, esteeming him the greatest Monarch in the World: so that my service there [...] would be exceedingly well-received in England; and the Polacke, though in name a Christian, [was] yet of a Sect, which for Idolatry, and many other points, I much abhorred."[576] This anti-Catholic and pro-Ottoman stance was a standard attitude of almost all English travellers to Ottoman Empire throughout the seventeenth century. Blount went on to extol "the Turkes, whom we not only honoured for their glorious actions in the world; but also loved, for the kinde Commerce of Trade which we find amongst them."[577] Earlier Richard Hakluyt expressed the same sentiments in his *Principall Navigations* (1589, one volume) and *Principall Navigations, Voyages, Traffiques and Discoveries* (1598-1600, three volumes). C. F. Beckingham pointed out that "the establishment of commercial relations with the Ottoman empire was, for [Hakluyt's] purpose, the most important event in the recent history of the Near East and much of his material is relevant to it."[578]

English visiters were captivated by the Ottoman might, prosperity, opulence, luxury and pluralism.[579] D. J. Vitkus well summarised the impact of travelling intelligencers upon English knowledge and identity formation. "Early modern representations of the Islamic "Other" helped to construct an identity for Protestant England when English identity was developing a proto-imperialist formation. Imperial envy, accompanied by anxiety about religious difference, is often expressed in English texts describing the Turks. Turkish power was a difficult reality to confront at a time when English authors and readers sought to construct a self-image of metropolitan masculinity. Fear and admiration of Turkish culture, and of 'the Great Turk' or 'Grand Seigneur' as the Ottoman sultan was called, were often mixed with condemnation and loathing. And yet English Protestant animosity for Spanish or Roman Catholic 'superstition' was usually stronger than feelings of hostility toward the more distant Ottoman Muslims. Some English narrators describing Turkish society are captivated by the sophistication, order, and strength that they observe, a unified power that they saw as a foil to a divided and corrupted Christendom. In any case, it was commercial exchange, not imperialist confrontation or conflict, which dominated Anglo-Islamic relations during the late sixteenth and seventeenth centuries."[580]

The unity, prosperity, plurality, religious freedom and limited monarchy[581] of the Ottoman Empire was constantly used by the majority of English travellers to highlight English disunity, relative impoverishment, religious persecutions, political corruptions and absolutism. These were the areas where emulation was highly encouraged, throughout the sixteenth to the eighteenth century.[582] This ideology of "Ottomanism" preceded the nineteenth-century "Orientalism," as Gerald MacLean has very well demonstrated.[583] Ottomanism reflected "the tropes, structures, and fantasies by means of which Europeans sought to make knowable the imperial Ottoman other: both the imperial dynasty and the vast maritime and territorial areas that they governed. Ottomanism will be found to be both strategic and interested. Like all systems of knowledge production, Ottomanism arises from both lack and desire, and in this sense tells us perhaps rather more about the desiring subject than about the object of knowledge."[584] Daniel Goffman noted that "as more and more northern Europeans visited the Ottoman domains, they also gained more profound insight into that world. The personal experiences of such sojourners as John Sanderson, George Sandys, Robert Bargrave, Thomas Bendysh, the Chevalier de la Croix, Jean de Thevenot, and Paul Rycaut, distributed across northern Europe through their writings, helped not only to diminish irrational fears of the Ottomans as a civilisation of the 'other,' but also to integrate that empire more securely into an emerging Europe."[585] He further observed that "The Europe of Louis XIV and Charles II, however, considered the Ottomans – as friend or foe – along with the other states of Europe in their diplomatic, commercial, and military policies. This was an Ottoman Europe almost as much as it was a Venetian or Habsburg one."[586]

The Ottomans ruled one third of the European Continent; they were heir to the Byzantium Empire and its institutions. Consequently, they directly inherited the Roman Byzantium institutions, taxations and governing policies far more than any other single European state. The pre-modern Europe reached to the Byzantium and Roman legacy through the Ottomans.[587] Europe enormously benefited from the Muslim world institutionally, financially and intellectually. For instance, at the height of its trade the East India Company controlled almost 50% of English imports. Both the Levant and East India Company provided the needed capital, knowledge and expertise for the later expansions of the British Empire. In a sense, the British Empire, Enlightenment and expansion were all facilitated by the Muslim world and in the end, it became the victim of British colonial designs.

Islamic World and Scientific Revolution

Muslim sciences, philosophical works and geographical tools were equally employed by English natural philosophers, astronomers, explorers and scientists to restore the *Prisca theologia* and *Prisca sapientia*. The Muslim world was central to English movement towards the restoration of pristine theology and science. Quantitative mathematical sciences were integral to overseas trade, and hence readily employed by the traders. The Oriental manuscripts on quantitative, natural, alchemical and medical subjects were transferred from the East to the West especially to England by overseas traders and well absorbed by the English mathematicians, physicians and natural scentists. Natural science was constructed in the British metropolis as a result of English overseas exposure to the Orient, Oriental commerce, knowledge, expertise and incentives. The authority based Aristotelian scholasticism, biblical interpretations of nature, Ptolemaic geography and astronomy were replaced with experimental geography, empirical natural philosophy and quantitive mathematical sciences with the help of Eastern mathematical sciences, overseas trade related exploration voyages, observations and subsequent corrections to the old Ptolemiac system. The European pursuit for prisca sapientia was supplemented by things Eastern and the Muslim world stood at the center stage of such a quest. Manuscripts, recipes, plants, instruments and countless other objects of knowledge were transferred to English centers of knowledge and digested, appropriated and incorporated by the English natural philosophers and scientists as Kapil Raj, Pamela H. Smith and many others have amply demonstrated.[588] The local, regional and national protoscience of the early modern era was supplemented by global knowledge.

The Scientific Revolution was a consequence of the global encouters, cross-cultural diffusions, assimmilations and constructions.

The historians of philosophy, intellectual history and discrete histories of science are divided about the complex origins and causes of modern science. The Marxists locate them in socio-economic ideas and realms, while the Weberians connect them with religion and capitalism. A great deal of scholarly effort has been spent to show the antagonism between religion and science in general, and Christian Church and science in particular. There has been an explosion of interest in early modern science since the 1930s, leading to multiple appraisals and theories regarding its origin, causes and expansion. Many historians apply the post-modern narrow categories of the twenty-first century on the protoscientific phase of early modern science to construct a teleological, genealogical, evolutionist, local and internal progression of science from Greeks to modern science.[589] The devil is in the details though. Some argue that science started in High Middle Ages (1277), others suggest that it began in the fourteenth century with "*via moderna*," while others see its origin in the Italian renaissance. The time period between Copernicus and Newton is then pinpointed as the main era of scientific flourishing. Some maintain that the seventeenth century was the century of Scientific Revolution, while others contend that there was no Scientific Revolution[590] in the seventeenth century but an explosion of theoretical and practical natural philosophy. Sometime a second Scientific Revolution is considered to have taken place in the first quarter of the twentieth century.[591] The field is quite saturated with divergent theories of rise of modern science.

This Eurocentric, heuristic, heroic and genius-based interpretation of science has its loopholes and drawbacks. It must be recognised that there was a huge gap between the Greek science and that of the Middle Ages, and between the seventeenth century onward and the Middle Ages. The Aristotelian atomistic, organistic science and deductive syllogistic rationalism was originally lost in the Latin Christendom and then refound with the help of Arab, Muslim medium in the twelfth and thirteenth centuries. The Aristotelian epistemology was quite different from the Newtonian mechanistic science, inductive, mathematical and experimental epistemology.[592] That was perhaps the reason that the revisionists held that the seventeenth-century natural philosophy was a radical break with previous centuries,[593] and must be contextualised in its proper socio-economic and cultural settings. The revisionists also have their differences.

The evolutionists argue that the Scientific Revolution of the seventeenth century was a natural evolution from previous centuries of scientific endeavours. The internists contend that the universe changing paradigm shift was the outcome of local, internal natural and scientific explorations, experiments and precise, controlled methods without much help from external world.[594] H. Butterfield's classic work is still popular among historians of science. He observed that "the so-called 'scientific revolution,' popularly associated with the sixteenth and seventeenth centuries, but reaching back in an unmistakably continuous line to a period much earlier still. Since that revolution overturned the authority in science not only of the middle ages but of the ancient world—since it ended not only in the eclipse of scholastic philosophy but in the destruction of Aristotelian physics—it outshines everything since the rise of Christianity and reduces the Renaissance and Reformation to the rank of mere episodes, mere internal displacements, within the system of medieval Christendom."[595] The conflict theorists argue that there was a constant warfare between religion and science, and the Scientific Revolution was made possible only when religion and theology were defeated and secularised.[596] Some revisionists claim that religion was among the fundamental influences which provided the necessary ideological tools and social legitimation for modern science.[597] The majority among this group of historians emphasise Protestant origins of modern science like modern capitalism.[598] A minority includes the Catholic Church and its counter reformation in the dialectical struggles, which finally led to the Scientific Revolution in the seventeenth century.[599] Those who vouch for Protestant origins are further divided into various camps. Some maintain that it was the general religious outlook of Reformation, but not its supernatural theology, which steered the Scientific Revolution.[600] Others insist that Calvinist theology and work ethics were particularly important factors.[601] Some emphasise the role of Anglican Church,[602] others pinpoint the Puritans[603] or Latitudinarian influences[604] while others emphasise apocalyptic millenarianism.[605] The field is uneven, bumpy, complex, saturated and sort of messy.[606]

These local, internal and Eurocentric theories have been challenged and refuted by the globalist historians, who argue that the British or

European Scientific Revolution was inconceivable except in a broader global context. Britain was a small, impoverished and isolated isle before its participation in the world trade circles through its overseas adventures. Its capitalism, commercialism, natural philosophy, educational systems, and religio-political theology were all shaped by and constructed through encounter and dialogue with the superior Eastern civilisations of early modern era. That era belonged to the dominant Ottoman, Mughal, Persian and Ming dynasties and not to European national states. The later British mechanical and industrial revolutions were facilitated and propelled by the demands and needs of overseas trade, its global corporations and their power and profit. The East served as the catalyst and springboard for the West's reformation, reconstruction, purification and propulsion to the global leadership. Therefore, the developed world of the sixteenth and seventeenth centuries (Islamic World and China) cannot be excluded from the Scientific Revolution.[607]

Contemporary historian of science Kapil Raj refutes the Eurocentric interpretations of science in the following strong words: "Recent scholarship tends to belie these commonly considered articles of faith. Indeed, in the past two decades the claimed unity of modern knowledge practices across European space has been convincingly demolished. In place of a unique 'modern science', it is now accepted that there are many national and local knowledge traditions and dynamics spread across most of North and West Europe, with diverse, and at times contradictory, intellectual agendas and influences throughout the early-modern and modern periods."[608] He further rejects the Whiggish narrative of history and notes that "a number of prominent imperial historians, although focusing primarily on the British empire, have called into question the concept of a simple diffusion to the rest of the world of the fundamental values of modernity—values such as democracy, justice, and the welfare state. They have argued that modernity and its institutions are not simple emanations from a pre-existing centre, but are rather the result of 'a complex saga of the collisions, compromises, and comings together' of England with the many countries it came to dominate, including Ireland, Scotland, and India. By focusing on the processes of construction, they thus imply that Great Britain, its modern institutions, and its empire were co-constituted."[609]

Modern science was no exception to this global cross-cultural diffusion. The English natural philosophers and scientists, such as the fellows of Royal Society, were closely connected with the overseas trading companies, their navy and military complexes,[610] and guided English sailors, captains, merchants and company officials to collect specific manuscripts, recipes, plants, herbs, instruments, data, habits and statistics, building their lab and research works with the help of that information.[611] R. K. Merton has amply demonstrated that "the needs generated by military technology influenced the foci of scientific interests to an appreciable degree."[612] The external socio-economic and political factors played a fundamental role in the rise of modern science.[613] Bacon, Boyle, Newton, Halley, Locke, Shaftesbury and many other natural scientists, philosophers and politicians emphasised the utilitarian aspect of science.[614] It was the commercial, utilitarian and market economy and resultant capitalism created by the English overseas trading companies which shaped and facilitated the English political, religious and scientific revolutions.[615] The Royal Society was the social microcosm of the greater macrocosm, struggling to unite the politically and religiously disunited English society by means of empirical experimentation, creating private profit opportunities through science and trade to increase public good, freedoms and autonomy. The Royal Society fellows tacitly argued that unlike their Catholic, Spanish absolutist counterparts, the British monarchy and Church should be more tolerant, rational and inclusive. There should be a balance between the powers of king, bishop, lords, commons, gentry and merchants. Such a balance would increase the trade, bring more revenues to the monarch, strengthen the empire and further the Protestant Reformation. The Church and Monarchical absolutism and exclusivism were detrimental to the state, monarchy and social cohesion. Intellectual exchange and competition of ideas in the market-place, within the established bounds, was the road to progress. Such was the Protestant way in contrast to the Catholic authoritarian model.

Therefore the Scientific Revolution was not an isolated, internal, controlled and teleological phenomena but an expression of the overall cultural milieu of seventeenth-century England. The "historians, sociologists, and philosophers of science have in the past decades radically undermined the traditional understanding that modern science has its own logic of development based on rigorous, immutable, explicit, and empirically tested rules and methods which lie beyond the pale of social and historical analysis. Moving away from a conception of science as a system of formal propositions or discoveries, these recent studies seek to understand the making, maintenance, extension, and reconfiguration of scientific knowledge by focusing equally on the material, instrumental, corporeal, practical, social, political, and cognitive aspects of knowledge."[616]

It is quite a task to categorically pinpoint or identify one cause, sect, denomination, ideology, region or church as the sole cause of the Scientific Revolution in the seventeenth and eighteenth centuries. There are pros and cons in every historical theory; these partial truths can be combined in a socio-cultural and global interpretation of the Scientific Revolution. There is no doubt that the natural philosophy, proto-science and inductive reasoning progressed leaps and bounds during the seventeenth and eighteenth-century Europe and especially Britain. This so-called Scientific Revolution was the outcome of revolution in religious and political theology, the main crisis of the Old Regime.[617] Modern historian of science Steven Shapin observed that "Some markers of that continuing crisis include the breakdown of the feudal order and attendant rise of strong nation-states from the thirteenth century onward, the discovery of the New World and both the cultural and the economic shocks emanating from that expansion of horizon; the invention of printing and consequent change in the boundaries of cultural participation; and the fragmentation of a unified Western European religious order that followed from the Protestant Reformation of the sixteenth century."[618] The religio-political crises shattered the medieval institutions of authority and knowledge-making. The Protestant reformers eroded the Catholic Church and Habsburg's absolutist authority. The subsequent nation states especially the English monarchy furthered that erosion by bypassing the whole Catholic tradition and directly connecting itself with ancient pre-Catholic Church of Near East, its simple theology and church structure, and the English dissenters, radicals, Latitudinarians and natural scientists weakened the Stuart grip on authority and knowledge making by including merchants, natural scientists, dissenters, gentry and parliament in the overall process of knowledge making with the help of Eastern theology and wisdom. The Reformation wittingly or unwittingly heralded a new era of scepticism. It "eroded the authority and the effective scope of institutions that had regulated human conduct for preceding centuries. The Roman Catholic papal authority that had-formally at least- unified

Western Europe under a single Christian conception of authority gave way to split sources of authority: clashes first between divine and secular notions of political authority, then between different versions of Christianity and their proper relation to secular political authority. The wars of religion between Catholics and Protestants that raged across Europe from the Reformation onward, but particularly the Thirty Years' War of 1618-48, were the immediate occasion for changed view of knowledge and its role in ensuring or subverting order."[619] The ensuing mistrust resulted in general scepticism in religious and political power structures and their efficacies. Natural philosophy and science of the seventeenth century was a reflection, extension and outcome of the socio-political, economic and religious upheavals. The same instability, disorder and revolution which destabilised, challenged and transformed the Old Regime in theology, politics and society transformed the Aristotelian, supernatural, scriptural, traditional and miraculous natural philosophy into natural, rational and mechanistic science. "The permanent crisis of European order was then the general backdrop to debates over natural knowledge and its relation to state power and social order."[620]

The seventeenth-century reformation of the sixteenth-century Reformation was the backdrop of sudden, radical explosion in the field of natural philosophy and protoscience. The Scientific Revolution was an unintended consequence of Reformation ethos and not Reformation theology or political ideology.[621] The Reformation leaders rejected the old Church authority and tradition and insisted instead on *sola scriptura*. The radical reformers took the trend to its logical conclusion by rejecting the authority and tradition of Protestant Reformation wherever and whenever it contradicted natural, rational, logical and utilitarian discourse. As there were radical reformers among the political and religious theorists, there were also radicals in natural philosophy and science. For instance, Newton, Boyle and Locke were as radicals in their religious and political theology as revolutionary in their natural philosophy. The reformation of Reformation, universal reformation of Old Regime in theology, politics, social order and cosmology, was the common denominator in multitudes of revolutionary groups, ideologies and systems which demolished the Old Regime of Catholic and Protestant Churches along with their absolutist supernatural power structures. The mid seventeenth-century English Civil War and Revolution was the culmination and violent outburst of such a simmering fire, which eventually engulfed and abolished the Anglican Church and monarchy. The Puritans, overseas traders, some nobles, middle class, parliament and natural philosophers were all part of that revolutionary reformative scheme. The Puritan, Protestant, Calvinist, Presbyterian theology was not fully in line with and supportive of radical, rational, natural theology and philosophy, but their desire to topple the Old Regime political theology and social order was radical enough to give them the leadership role in the revolutionary era. R. K. Merton, Christopher Hill and many other sociologists and historians who insisted on puritan origins of modern science have amply demonstrated and documented this fact. For instance, Merton noted that "it is thus to the religious ethos, not the theology, that we must turn if we are to understand the integration of science and religion in seventeenth century England."[622] Puritanism did not cause science; rather, it provided a cultural and social support for a not yet institutionalised science.

Puritanism was a multifaceted, multi-sectional, multi-dimensional and multi-pronged revolutionary movement which incorporated multitudes disgruntled with the Old Regime. Thomas Edwards enumerated 180 sects.[623] The subsequent gradual reformation of Anglican religious and political theology and power structures led to Latitudinarian moderate, rational, natural, accommodative and broader theology which facilitated, legitimised and propagated natural theology, philosophy and morality at the expense of old supernatural dogmatic theology and cosmology.[624] Latitudinarianism, in a sense, was an indictment of the High Church dogmatic Christianity and supernatural, absolutist religious and political theology of Reformation.[625] It extended reasonable doubt and scepticism to central Christian dogmas and even to the scriptures. It exalted morality, pious living and human reason beyond and over the dogmatic faith and traditional scriptural interpretations. It was a tacit confession of relevance of the parallel rational reformative scheme of Michael Servetus, which was vehemently censored and persecuted by Protestant churches. The parallel rational and natural reformative scheme of Servetus, Bruno, Socinians, Deists and Unitarians gradually permeated the knowledge-making structures and reformed them from within without destroying their outer skeleton and facade. The seventeenth-century Royal Society historian and fellow Bishop Thomas Sprat highlighted this reformative nature of natural science and Anglican Church. "They both have taken a like course to bring this about; each of them passing by the corrupt copies, and referring themselves to the perfect Originals for their instruction; the one to the Scripture, the other to the huge Volume of Creatures. They are both accused unjustly by their enemies of the same crimes, of having forsaken the Ancient Traditions, and ventured on Novelties. They both suppose alike that their Ancestors might err; and yet retain a sufficient reverence for them. They both follow the great Precept of the Apostle of trying all things. Such is the harmony between their interests and tempers."[626] The modern British historian H. F. Kearney underscores the significant role played by this parallel reformation in the rise of modern science. While concluding that there was no simple connection between Puritanism and science Kearney noted: "But this need not rule out alternative theories of a relationship between religious radicalism and scientific discovery... a more critical attitude towards religious authority created a climate of opinion which predisposed some men to be equally critical of dogma in science...To this movement, scientists such as Galileo and Kepler maybe said to have belonged, and even Francis Bacon. The religious views of the Cambridge Platonists, of Robert Boyle and Isaac Newton may also be traced back to the same tradition. If we are seeking a connection between the Reformation and the Scientific Revolution, this 'Major Reformation' seems likely to provide it."[627]

The natural reformative scheme was more successful in Protestant Holland and England because, unlike their Catholic counterparts, the newly established national Protestant Churches and traditions were not historically and intellectually entrenched enough to withstand the intellectual, theological and cosmological challenges caused by overseas trade and cross-cultural infusions. The power struggles between the Crown, Anglican Church, parliament, nobility, merchants, religious sects and other contending parties effectively weakened the institutions of authority and knowledge. Alternative mechanisms of patronage, knowledge-making and dissemination diminished the need and authority of the Old Regime, and gradually allowed alternative ideologies, theologies and cosmologies to flourish. Natural philosophy, theology and social order were the outcomes of this dialectical struggle, and this transition was mainly facilitated by the overseas commerce to the Muslim world. "Indeed, corporate commerce was quick to recognise that the continued existence and expansion of European overseas trade was largely dependent on scientific expertise and associated material practices. Thus, right from their inception, the trading companies supported and even employed mathematicians, practical astronomers, and hydrographers for navigation, and medics for treating crews and identifying commercially viable plants or derived products overseas. They were thus key actors in the early modern enterprise of knowledge-making and use."[628] The natural philosophers, scientists and astronomers were fully engaged in the commercial adventures financially, intellectually and socially. "Men of science invested substantial sums of money in international commerce [...] a number of eminent Fellows of the Royal Society, like Robert Boyle, Isaac Newton, and Joseph Banks, to name but some of the most well known, counted among the directors or major shareholders of the likes of the English East India Company [...] the longest lasting and most powerful of the British trading groups—or the South Sea Company. Initially enticed by the attractive dividends, reaching up to 20 per cent, offered by these investments, such men also found in it a sure means of raising their credit."[629] Their prestige was connected with the prestige and influence of these overseas companies.

Additionally, the information and data collectors such as the English merchants, sailors and company officials were not experts in the scientific fields. They learned, polished and expanded their natural and commercial knowledge through their Eastern interlocutors, intermediaries and partners.[630] "It is important to stress that most of these men left Europe between the ages of fourteen and eighteen, and their years spent in distant lands were crucially formative. As they moved across seas and continents and encountered different skilled practitioners, their own interests, ambitions, and skills were transformed. As representatives of commercial, and later colonial, institutions, the skills they embodied were also incorporated into these institutions, and, in that sense, their expertise did not impact on metropolitan science alone, but simultaneously produced effects on a global scale."[631] The British merchants and business elites learned a great deal from their Muslim, Hindu and Eastern Christian teachers, facilitators and interlocutors.[632] These historical facts impel us to take the "early-modern science as part of the market economy that partakes of the larger political economies of burgeoning nation-states, of early-modern mercantilism, and of nascent European colonialism."[633] Knowledge and science moved in the commercial, economic and utilitarian trajectories. "In the early modern period, knowledge of nature moved not just geographically, but also epistemically, as knowledge systems of different social and cultural groups intersected."[634]

The Columbia University contemporary historian of science, Pamela H. Smith, has amply noted that "the commercial and territorial expansion of Europe and the Ottoman Empire and the formation of long-distance trading networks in East and Southeast Asia led to an unprecedented movement of people and of knowledge. European merchants, backed by territorial powers, expanded into the Atlantic, down the coast of Africa, and to the Americas, as well as entered into well-established trading networks in South and Southeast Asia. Knowledge moved along with trade: with individuals as they migrated, or were resettled in new territories, and with sailors, soldiers, and merchants as they pursued trade and war. Knowledge traveled in objects, instruments, manuscripts, and printed books as trade routes opened up and collectors avidly sought rare and beautiful things, and it moved as factors and agents sent back information to the metropolis. Economic historians and art historians have begun to articulate just how much the period depended upon the flow of goods, ideas, and people from outside Europe."[635]

The European Renaissance in general, and the English epoch in particular, did not happen in a vaccum; it was facilitated by the Muslim East. The "flow and interaction of goods and ideas between Eurasian societies was masked until recently by the subsequent period of European dominance that began in the nineteenth century. This realisation about the impact of global commerce on the European Renaissance makes clear that changes in the period we call the Renaissance did not develop in isolation and cannot be viewed as the start of a distinctively European modernity."[636]

The early modern English exposure to the Muslim East set later English science, modernity and global empire in motion. "Just as British historians have begun to understand the ways that Britain and its empire were co-constituted, these historians of science argue that the material and social practices of science did not simply move outward from a metropolitan center, but rather, that science emerged through a complex process of negotiation, assimilation, and coproduction between coloniser and colonised, set in motion by the global encounters of the early modern period."[637] Modernity, science and modern institutions were a global, well coordinated and well connected production of countless global contributors. "The construction of new modes of knowledge-making about nature was a distributed, collective process, often involving large numbers of anonymous people: medical practitioners in the Americas, Southeast Asian informants, European herb women, artisans, and many others."[638] The story of science and Scientific Revolution is not the sole property of Copernicus, Newton and some other individual geniuses, but a narrative of global history, economy, natural sciences, arts, religio-political theologies and epistemologies. The "history of science must be integrated with social history, economic history, art history, and the history of technology and medicine. Moreover, while changes in theories of the cosmos are, of course, exceedingly important in the long run, in the period from about 1400 to at least 1650, I believe the real story lies in changing attitudes to nature, to natural knowledge, and to knowledge-making. The centrality of alchemy, astrology, and medicine; the technical engagement with nature, commerce, and the movements and intersections of knowledge; as well as the interaction with new environments and new knowledge systems that global movement engendered, have all displaced the account of the changing disciplinary content of astronomy at the heart of the story of science in the early modern period."[639] The English science - and Scientific Revolution - was an integral part of and extension of the overall English revolution in religio-political theology[640] which was shaped by overseas trade and experiences. T. K. Rabb "one of the sharpest critics of the Puritan-science thesis, has stated that the encouragement of science was the result of the revolution, not of Puritanism."[641] The revolutionary ferment as an important factor in the rise of science was confessedly recognised by Bishop Sprat in the seventeenth century itself. In his *History of the Royal Society* he wrote: "The late times of Civil War, and confusion, to make recompense for their infinite calamities, brought this advantage with them, that they stirr'd up mens minds from long ease, and a lazy rest, and made them active, industrious and inquisitive: it being the usual benefit that follows upon Tempests, and Thunders in the State, as well as in the Skie, that they purifie, and deer the Air, which they disturb."[642] Thomas S. Kuhn has amply demonstrated the parallelism between political and scientific revolutions.[643]

Natural Philosophy and Natural Theology

Science, natural philosophy, theology and politics were all enmeshed and intertwined in seventeenth-century England for the purposes of divinity and divine providence.[644] The seventeenth century was a God-driven society; restoration of true natural philosophy and true religion were two sides of the same coin.[645] They represented a move away from the supernatural, miraculous, unintelligible theology of the Church to natural philosophy, natural theology and reasonable Christianity. Stephen Gaukroger noted that a "good part of the distinctive success at the level of legitimation and consolidation of the scientific enterprise in the early-modern West, derives not from any separation of religion and natural philosophy, but rather from the fact that natural philosophy could be accommodated to projects in natural theology: what made natural philosophy attractive to so many in the seventeenth and eighteenth centuries were the prospects it offered for the renewal of natural theology. Far from science breaking free from religion in the early modern era, its consolidation depended on religion being in the driving seat."[646] The natural, rational and scientific reformation was closely linked with the natural, rational and moral reformation of Christian theology. The interventionist Trinitarian theology and unpredictable, uncertain and abnormal hierarchical cosmology was gradually replaced with normal, natural and predictable cosmology and anti-dogmatic rational and moral theology. There was no conflict between faith and science as such.[647] The universal religious concepts such as the divinity, unity of truth, simplicity of divinity and cosmos, divine providence, sovereignty, creationism, morality, human accountability, reward and punishment were all confirmed and reinforced, but supernatural Trinitarian theology, the hall mark of Christianity over the centuries, was avoided, shunned and finally rejected. Peter Harrison observed that "in the seventeenth century 'divinity' and 'theology' did not mean the same thing as 'religion' in general. The kinds of topics, regarded as off-limits to fellows of the Royal Society, were those dispute-engendering doctrines which, in the wake of the Reformation, had divided Europe and, closer to home, England itself."[648] The seventeenth-century natural philosophy and science was antithetical to overarching, supernatural, Church theology but not against God, theology and faith as such. Theological disputations, complexties and red herrings rather than theology per se were the perceived problems. Phrases such as "meddling with Divinity" expressed "a desire to avoid becoming entangled in unnecessary doctrinal disputation, without necessarily implying a desire to avoid making more broad religious claims."[649] The simplistic, Unitarian, rational and natural theology of Michael Servetus, Socinians and Unitarians was implicitly or tacitly appreciated and incorporated by individuals such as Locke and Newton. The Royal Society fellows and natural philosophers retained the outer theological skeleton, phrases and terms but transformed their meanings, conceptual parameters and implications. This was a paradigm shift from the supernatural to immutable natural laws and natural theology.

The English intelligentsia and many early Enlightenment leaders considered England a relatively under-developed, divided country due to its medieval, supernatural Church educational system and its suppressive policies. They had their cues in the sixteenth-century natural philosophers' misgivings about the church authorities. The Church's triadic hierarchical cosmology, biblical interpretations of natural phenomena, theological supremacy over other sciences and persecution of dissent were all suspected by astronomers, alchemists and natural philosophers such as Nicolas Copernicus, Johannes Kepler, Galileo Galilei, Tycho Brahe, John Baptist van Helmont and many others.[650] Both Catholic and Protestant Church were suspicious of natural sciences. "The findings of science conflicted with early Lutheran theology, and with that of Calvin too."[651] Impelled by the growing discrepencies between their astronomical experimentations and scholastic Aristotelian philosophical thought of both Catholic and Protestant churches,[652] they promulgated new scientific axioms, methods and research models at odd with Church theology. This way theology was dethroned. Immanuel Kant observed that "There was time when metaphysics was called the 'queen' of all the sciences, and if the will be taken for the deed, it deserved this title of honour, on account of the preeminent importance of its subject. Now, in accordance with the fashion of the age, the queen proves despised on all side; and the matron, outcast and forsaken, mourns like Hecuba: *'Greatest of all by race and birth, I now am cast out, powerless'* (Ovid, Metamorphoses, 13:508–510)."[653]

The natural philosopher's argument, that theology dealt with salvation while science treated mundane nature, was an effort to release science from the tutelage of Christian supernatural theology. The alchemists contended that God was as much manifested in the material natural phenomena as much in the heavens; discovering nature through alchemical experimention was in reality as meritorious as studying the Bible.[654] They exalted experimental mechanical philosophy over authority-based theological cosmology.[655] Kepler contended that "I have just one thing to say: while in theology it is authority that carries the most weight, in [natural] philosophy it is reason."[656] Copernicus argued that literal meanings of the Bible, and distortions of its passages, could not discount or denounce rational facts.[657] Galileo insisted that no theologian "will say that geometry, astronomy, and medicine are much more excellently contained in the Bible than they are in the books of Archimedes, Ptolemy, Boethius and Galen."[658] The Church geocentric system was replaced by astronomers' heliocentric system. The new sciences and philosophies were threatening to the Church authorities arrogating "to themselves an authority in interpreting Scripture that belonged properly only to the Church, speaking through its bishops and theologians."[659] The Church persecuted such rational, mechanical and experimental tendencies. The sixteenth-century Continental conflict between the Church and natural philosophers was transferred to seventeenth-century England.

Many seventeenth-century English religious radicals, nonconformists, independently thinking Puritans such as Samuel Hartlib, Cambridge Paltonist theologians such as Joseph Mede, Henry More, and natural philosophers such as Robert Boyle, John Locke and Isaac Newton were heirs to the experimental mechanical cosmology. They were thoroughly influenced by Ibn Tufayl's philosophical novel Hayy bin Yaqzan's emphasise upon autodidictism, natural discourse and antidogmatism. They believed that God had revealed the book of revelation and the book of creation to supplement each other,[660] and that the original revelation included knowledge of natural phenomena and its workings. Newton stated that "so then twas one designe of the first institution of the true religion to propose to mankind by the frame of the ancient Temples, the study of the frame of the world as the true Temple of the great God they worshipped. And thence it was that the Priests anciently were above other men well skilled in the knowledge of the true frame of Nature & accounted it a great part of their Theology."[661] The knowledge of natural philosophy and correct interpretations of scriptures were interrelated. "The most important thing to be discovered in the Biblical records is that God has laid down the plan of human history, as well as the plan of natural history. The latter is to be studied primarily in the Book of *Nature*, through scientific researches. The former is to be studied in the central prophetic statement about the course of human history, the books of *Daniel* and *Revelation*.["662] That knowledge was originally compromised due to Adam's fall, restored by Noah's prophetic agency but lost again during the Flood due to human sins.[663] Moses restored that divine wisdom and Jesus replenished it, but the Catholic Church and Roman emperors corrupted, compromised and misdirected that bulk of knowledge to create a tarnished absolutist Christianity which emphasised supernatural incarnational elements and suppressed natural theology, trial and error based innovatory experimentalism and sciences.[664] So the restoration of natural philosophy was in reality a restoration of true religion; alchemy, science and theology were intertwined.[665] The natural scientists insisted upon the experimental natural data, explorations and observations instead of authority based Aristotelian scholasticism, Church and monarchical authoritarian interpretations and divine magical prerogatives. Natural science was an extension of the religio political natural ideology which moved away from the divine right Church and monarchy towards natural rights, rationality and intelligibility. Return to the original, pre-Catholic universals, (puritanism) in science, theology, politics and piety constituted the essence of such a movement.

Puritanism and restoration required returning to the original message of Jesus and Moses through Middle Eastern (pagan, Jewish, Zoroastrian and Muslim) theology and sciences; the internal religious reformation and external natural transformation were one and the same idea. Both were directed against the supernatural and persecuting Church and state structures, and both wanted to purge Christianity of its intermediary arbitrators, forces and beings to assert direct divine sovereignty in nature and religion. It was a Unitarian revolution in metaphysics, physics and social order. The same One and Only God was supreme in the heavens, in the cosmos by dint of his natural laws and in humanity by his moral laws. Man could directly reach him through his moral laws, explore and master his cosmos by natural laws without any intercessors, in betweens or intermediaries. They just needed to bypass the Church and state authoritarianism to rediscover and realise the pristine, simple and Unitarian message.

Isaac Newton and his fellow natural philosophers subscribed to "the

Renaissance view of history as a declination from an original golden age, a time in which there had existed an original pure knowledge of things both natural and supernatural, a *prisca sapientia* subsequently lost or garbled through human sin and error and through temporal decay."[666] That natural theology and sciences, the *prisca sapientia* tradition (knowledge of God and nature), was preserved by the Egyptians, Jews - and later on by the Middle Eastern priests and scholars - in a mostly symbolic language.[667] Orient was the origin of Occident. "Certainly, the seventeenth century saw some crucial moments in the way scholarly Europeans have thought about the oriental, and in particular about the oriental as a category that should shape their understanding of their own religions."[668] Therefore Middle Eastern manuscripts, knowledge, wisdom, languages, symbols and sciences were essential to return to the original prophetic wisdom, the revival of *prisca sapientia*. Rabbinic and Middle Eastern knowledge and wisdom was required to understand the pre-Catholic pristine Biblical teachings and early Christianity. The quests for Middle Eastern alchemy, medicine/anatomy, mathematics, algebra, geometry, astronomy, physics, astrology, entomology, meteorology, mineralogy, theology, law and politics were all parts of the same search for *prisca sapientia* and *prisca theologia*.[669]

Samuel Hartlib (1600–1662),[670] a Polish grandson of a famous English merchant, a friend of anti-Habsburg, pro Ottoman Hungarian Johann Amos Comenius, who was born in Poland where the Ottoman, Unitarian and Socinian influences were quite visible, migrated to England in 1628, married and settled there. His European intellectual connections, anti-monarchy (anti-Charles I), anti-Church (anti-Archbishop Laud), anti-scholastic and anti-Aristotelian, Puritan, republican tendencies, close associations with Commonwealth leaders such as Lord Brooke, Francis Rous, John Pym, the revolutionary republican leader whose arrest started the English Civil War, the Commonwealth leader Oliver Cromwell and other parliamentarian affiliations propelled him to overcome English supernatural, supra rational, doctrinal differences, internal strife and civil war by means of natural, rational, utilitarian, vocational, mechanical, technical, mystical, scientific, and pedagogical training,[671] Baconian empiricism, utopian, boundless enthusiasm for natural history, history of philosophy, utilitarianism, Protestant unification, scientific progress, universal reformation and political renewal.[672] His Chichester Academy, "Invisible College", Utopian

Universal Reformation,[673] Solomon's House, Universal Padagogical Language,[674] Philanthropic, idealistic, chiliastic Puritanism, quest for *prisca sapientia* and *prisca theologia* took him to Arabic language as the language in which ancient *prisca sapientia* and *prisca theologia* were preserved.[675] His correspondence indicated that he was somehow connected with some English efforts to translate the Quran into English language. His frantic, radical, grandiose projects in reform, social regeneration, education, political economy, agriculture, husbandry, coinage, communications, mining, medicine, experimental philosophy, humanism, hermeticism, ethics and religion connected him with people and cultures of all sorts including the Eastern wisdom, sciences and cultures. The Gresham professors, Royal Society Fellows and many other English intelligencers were closely connected with Hartlib and his quest for Middle Eastern knowledge, wisdom and languages. Almost all founding members of the Royal Society were Hartlib's associates and carried the same quest forward.[676] Robert Boyle was his "chemical son"[677] and Boyle's radical and heterodox sister Katherine Boyle, Viscountess Ranelagh (1614–91) was fully engaged in his circle[678] which played an instrumental role in the later Scientific Revolution. Hartlib circle's thirst for the Eastern wisdom was quenched with the help of Levant and East India companies, their chaplains, merchants and directors.

Overseas Trade and Scientific Revolution

England was scientifically backward during most of the sixteenth century,[679] except the last quarter when overseas trade began with the Muslim Levant in thr early 1580s. R. K. Merton, the father of modern sociology, observed: "It is hardly an historical accident that the last year of the sixteenth century saw not only the publication of GILBERT'S *De Magnete*, the first important scientific work produced in England and the augury of the new era of science, but also the chartering of the East India Company, the first English joint-stock company of importance and herald of the forthcoming bourgeois age."[680] He further observed that the "relation between a problem raised by economic development and technologic endeavour is clear-cut and definite. It represents a connection which has frequently been observed in contemporary society as well."[681] The transportation, communication and navigational needs of Levant, East India and other overseas trading companies were met by the scientists of the late sixteenth and early seventeenth centuries. Boris Hessen, the Soviet physicist, philosopher and historian of science, noted that the merchants' need for efficient transportation and resolution of problems related to it set the modern science in motion. Initially it looked at four main problems:

1. To increase the tonnage capacity of vessels and their speed,
2. To improve the floating qualities of ships,
3. To develop means for better navigation,
4. To improve the construction of canals and docks.[682]

The practical problems and challenges related to the overseas trade were at the forefront of English scientific inquiries and research, and English scientific progress was proportionate to its foreign trade and expansion. Within the next sixty years, by 1640, England became one of the most scientifically-advanced countries in Europe. Christopher Hill pinpointed that "The science of Elizabeth's reign was the work of merchants and craftsmen, not of dons; carried on in London, not in Oxford and Cambridge; in the vernacular, not in Latin."[683] It was the allure of East Indies gold that took Columbus to the newland, America, still insisting that he was in India and that the Native Americans were Red Indians. The same allure of the prosperous Mughal India was the main cause of English navigational adventures, which served as the foundations for later Scientific Revolution in England.

The first English mathematician who popularised mathematics and science was Thomas Hood (1556-1611). He was the son of a merchant, and his 1598 lectures on mathematics and navigational technology were sponsored by Sir Thomas Smythe, the first Governor of the East India Company, Governor of the Muscovy Company, and Treasurer of the Virginia Company. Sir Thomas Gresham (1518–79), merchant and financier, as well as the son and nephew of Lord Mayors of London, "built the Royal Exchange and left the revenue from shops there jointly to the City of London and the Mercers' Company to endow a college. Despite pleas from Cambridge that the money might more appropriately be left to the university, Gresham followed the example set by many merchants who endowed grammar schools in the sixteenth century, and was careful to put control of his college in the hands not of clerics but of merchants like himself. He endowed seven professorships: in Divinity, Law, Rhetoric, Music, Physic, Geometry, and Astronomy, with higher stipends than Henry VIII had given the Regius Professors of Divinity at Oxford and Cambridge. Gresham College, like the Bodleian Library, was founded to combat popery."[684]

Anglican Church and its popish, supernatural and theoretical educational system were considered antithetical to practical technology and sciences. The natural, utilitarian and pragmatic nature of vocational sciences supplanted the supernatural teachings of the Church and provided an alternate system of education, especially to adults. Gresham College took the lead in vocational mechanics and technologies.[685] The College taught basic geometry, astronomy, geography and mathematics to adult mariners to enhance their navigational capabilities. It was a vocational college meant solely to train adult overseas traders in matters of trade and related technology. "The College brought together many groups of scientists. Raphe Handson, a pupil of Briggs's, was persuaded by Hakluyt in 1600 to publish the first English textbook on *Trigonometrie*, a translation with additions of his own. It greatly simplified the calculations necessary for mathematical navigation. It was dedicated to the two Governors of the East India Company who had founded Wright's lecture on navigation."[686]

Arabic and Oriental Manuscripts

Arabic and other Oriental languages, manuscripts and sciences were among the most valued commodities of the Hartlibian circle, Gresham College professors and natural scientists, not for the love of Islam or Muslims but because of their cultural and scientific value. The English mathematician and diplomat John Pell mastered Arabic language in the 1630s under the influence of Hartlib.[687] William Bedwell[688] and John Greaves[689] learned Arabic due to Gresham influences. Later on, Oxford and Cambridge imitated Gresham curriculum and established Arabic chairs. The importance of Arabic and Arabic sciences can be gauged from the fact that the Oxford Laudian Arabic Chair was established in 1636 when the Levant chaplain Dr. Pococke[690] was appointed the first professor of Arabic soon after his return from the Muslim Levant (Syria). Cambridge Adam Professor of Arabic was established in 1632 and Abraham Wheelock[691] was appointed the first professor. It is pertinent to mention that Cambridge established the Lucasian Chair of mathematics in 1663, some 31 years after the Arabic chair, while Oxford established the chemistry chair in the 1690s, appointing Robert

Plot as the first professor. These historical facts are sufficient to underscore the significance attached to Arabic language and Arabic sciences in early seventeenth-century England.

William Bedwell (1561-1632), the known European Arabist, an expert in Oriental languages, mathematics and geometry was the conduit, translator and connector of Greshamites. He was the enabler of Richard Hakluyt and Sir Walter Raleigh, the initial American colonisers, having insisted upon Arabic language as the vehicle of Arabic sciences. Bedwell was "a distinguished Arabic scholar, translator of the Authorised Version and of Ramus's *Geometry* (1636), who wrote popular science manuals for the use of carpenters and produced almanacs. Bedwell is said to have been a friend and admirer of Thomas Hood. So close was Bedwell's association with the Gresham group that Aubrey thought he had been a professor at the College. Bedwell, who dabbled in astrology, forms another link with Raleigh's circle, since he helped with the chronology of the *History of the World.*"[692] Sir Walter Raleigh, the first American coloniser's *History of the World* was the first global history book written in England. It was published in 1614 and was the most influential prose book of the seventeenth century. The book was too saucy for the monarch, as it criticised the King's ineptitude. It was used by British explorers and read by English politicians; it was the only book recommended by Oliver Cromwell to his son Richard. John Milton dedicated his collections of sayings about liberty, *The Cabinet Council,* to Raleigh, and the American revolutionary leaders named one of their navy ships after him. The Arabist Bedwell helped in the books' compilation and chronology, based on his readings of Arabic history and geography. John Greaves (1602-1652), the famous English mathematician, astronomer and antiquarian learnt Arabic and Persian, travelled to Turkey, Syria and Egypt (1636-1640) along with Edward Pococke, collected manuscripts for Archbishop Laud and was appointed professor of Geometry at Gresham College and Savilian professor of Astronomy at Oxford in 1643. He reformed the Gregorian calendar, and his astronomical tools greatly enhanced Oxford's nascent astronomical lab and observatory. Gresham College was central to advance sciences and adult education, and John Greaves and William Bedwell were central to Gresham College due to their knowledge of Arabic language and sciences.[693]

For forty years Gresham College, not Oxford or Cambridge, was the hub of technical and navigational expertise, assisting overseas trading companies Royal Navy and Trinity House. It was the allure of Muslim India, Turkey and Persia, and the search for the shortest route to India, which served as the springboard for English science and technology. The existence and search of the North-West Passage to India was the top priority of English explorers. "Its historical importance is that it led to scientific, nautical, and commercial enterprises, which linked John Dee with Sir Humphrey Gilbert and George Gascoigne, Gresham College (Briggs, Gunter) with practical explorers like Foxe and James, with Hakluyt, with the Virginia Company, with big City financiers like Sir Thomas Smith and Sir John Wolstenholme, and with Parliamentarians like Sir Dudley Digges. The discovery of a North-West Passage, John Davis argued in 1595, by offering the speediest route for the import of Indian commodities, would make England 'the storehouse of Europe.'"[694] The early seventeenth-century English merchants, natural philosophers and politicians were obsessed with Mughal India and Ottoman Levant due to their global economic glamour. The Royal Society of London was an extension of the same allure and the Greshamites were the foundational group who met in Gresham College and Oxford since 1645 to transition into the Royal Society in 1660. For the first twenty years of Gresham existence, no astronomy, geometry or developed mathematics were taught either at Oxford or Cambridge or taught badly and initially both universities resisted Islamisation and Greshamization of knowledge. They emulated Gresham College only when the gentry and Crown got mesmerised with the prospects of overseas trade.[695]

The Crown and Anglican Church seized the opportunity in the late 1620s and embarked upon Oriental manuscript collection and translation after seeing their importance in the technical revolutions of East India, Levant and other related overseas companies. The Crown also used ancient Near Eastern languages, manuscripts and cultures to strengthen its claims of divine right monarchy and hopes of millennial regeneration, as discussed above. The Anglican chaplains of the Levant and East India companies were specifically directed by Archbishop Laud and King Charles I to focus on securing Oriental knowledge, manuscripts and languages. The Irish Archbishop James Ussher (1581–1656) was also very enthusiastic about Arabic learning and manuscripts. The German orientalist Christian Ravis (also Ravius) during the 1640s, had travelled extensively in the East to collect manuscripts for him and in 1648 published "A Discourse of the Oriental Tongues in London." Hungarian Protestant chemists such as Hans Hunneades were connected with the Greshamite group by the 1630s and assisted in many projects partly due to their knowledge of Ottoman languages and sciences.

John Woodward, Gresham Professor of Physic, 1693–1728, writing probably in the late 1720s, was lyrical about his College: "The fame of it went over the whole world. The most important discoveries of those times took their rise from Gresham College..." [...][696] The East India Levant trading complex, Muslim sciences, manuscripts and languages were an integral part of this scientific transformation. The quantitative, empirically sound, and predictive laws of motion and later Scientific Revolutions caused by Newtonian Cosmology and synthesis were initiated, facilitated and mostly financed by the overseas trading companies with the help and knowledge of the Muslim East. The later speculative science (1625 onward) was an extension of this earlier practical science when the rich virtuosi (nobility and gentry) joined the bandwagon of science due to its socio-economic esteem and reputation.[697] Christopher Hill, Boris Hessen, George N. Clark, P. M. Rattansi, G. R. Tylor and Robert K. Merton all have highlighted the socio-economic roots of seventeenth-century science and the role played by East India Levant trading complex, its capital and patronage in the emergence, development and flourishing of both practical and speculative sciences in England.[698]

Foster Watson singled out navigational commerce for special emphasis, observing that England "owed the development of seventeenth-century experimental study of science to the successors of the mighty merchants and men of commerce who made possible the wealth and leisure for nobles, gentlemen and scholars. Thus it was those navigational interests, through whose needs English mathematics had been revived and directed into practical matters, that produced the wealth that made possible not only virtuosity but also the revolution in speculative mathematical science."[699] Oxford and Cambridge, the original seminaries, became interested in speculative science only when the gentry and nobility got fully engaged in them. Charles II established the Lucasian professorship in mathematics at Cambridge in 1663 with the financial help of Henry Lucas. Its first chair was Isaac Barrow, the teacher and mentor of Isaac Newton who had extensively travelled in Turkey, learned Arabic and other Oriental languages and collected many manuscripts. He was followed by Newton as the Lucasian Chair in 1669. The Royal Society combined the Gresham College, Oxford and Cambridge groups of Orientalists in one body.[700] The number of its members was restricted to fifty-five, but "any baron, Fellow of the Royal College of Physicians, and public professors of mathematics, physics, and natural philosophy could join."[701] The majority were not scientists. A minority, around twenty or so original fellows, was committed to science and controlled experimentations. Many clergy, gentry and virtuosi joined the Royal Society when King Charles II took up its fellowship. Many Anglican bishops were children of merchants and brought their broad, rational, natural, Latitudinarian impulses to the Society and promoted, legitimised and popularised the works of their fellow scientists.

Overseas Trade and Royal Society

The Royal Society merged practical and speculative science together. Boris Hessen has effectively demonstrated that "the technical problems experienced by the merchant capitalists, in dealing with transport, industry and war, led to the development of two particular sciences, mechanics and astronomy, that were united into a whole by the Newtonian synthesis."[702] Stephen F. Mason, the renowned British chemist, substantiated Hessen's thesis in the following words: "Thus the association between merchant capital and the more mathematical sciences, astronomy and mechanics, illustrated by Hessen, is substantiated both by the fact that scientific activity sprang up in the geographical areas of mercantile prosperity during the sixteenth and seventeenth centuries, and by the actual convergence and interpénétration of mercantile and scientific-mathematical activities, as exemplified in these men. Moreover, interest in science burgeoned in England during the Revolution and in the period immediately preceding and subsequent to it, as R. K. Merton's statistical analysis of the English élite testifies, and it was during this period that the English merchant capitalists came into their own. They included such men as John Pym, treasurer of a company trying to extend English trade in Central and South America, and the City Fathers who had been deprived of their charter to settle Londonderry by Charles I."[703]

Science became an instrument and agent of the merchant community. "Thus merchant capital as it developed and came to penetrate into production from above, found in science an agent to serve its material interests and to give content to a new world view. Science was freed from its subordination to the theological picture of nature that had accompanied religious ideals and values in earlier times, and finding first a harmony with the new Protestant attitude, came to dominate over theological ideas of nature."[704] Anne Winterbottom has demonstrated close intellectual, scientific, administrative and financial ties between the East India Company and the Royal Society. "In London, the EIC connected with the Royal Society both formally and informally, through overlapping membership and friendships and rivalries that spanned the organisations. From 1682, members of the Royal Society held stocks in the EIC, as well as the Royal African Company, on behalf of the Society. Many prominent members of the Royal Society, including the diarists John Evelyn and Samuel Pepys, also held their own stocks in the Company. Members such as John Fryer, Isaac Pyke, and Joseph Collet were elected to the Royal Society on the basis of their positions in the EIC. The personnel of both the EIC and the Royal Society also overlapped with members of the English parliament, court, and navy: prominent examples include Samuel Pepys, Sir Joseph Williamson, and William Petty."[705] The Royal Society became a prototype of the East India Company.[706] The Levant and East India finances, manuscript collections, classifications, descriptions, translations and assimilation of knowledge were as central to the Scientific Revolution as the experimentations of the natural philosophers.[707] Orient was equal partner with Occident in matters of scienctific discoveries, political thought and religious progress.

Both trade and science developed when the merchant middle class increased in wealth and numbers and was able to withstand the pressures of clergy, landed nobility and Crown. The overseas trade with Muslim East facilitated that transition financially and intellectually. It was the drastic socio-economic disruption of the 1630s, caused mainly by overseas trade, which translated into religio-political mayhem of 1640s. The sudden demise of *Old Regime* with its supernatural religious and political theology paved the way for an alternative natural, rational and scientific worldview. Islamic worldview, religio-political theology and business knowhow were the catalysts of early seventeenth-century English socio-economic and religious commotions.

Steven Shapin has emphasised upon the change of religious, political and economic patterns which occurred during the early seventeenth century as the main root causes of scientific change.[708] Richard Ross concluded that: "In the half-century, 1550-1600, overseas navigational interests revived the mathematical sciences in England and directed them into practical and, above all, navigational concerns... In the succeeding half-century, 1600-1650, the overseas navigational interests, and the conditions of mathematical activity that they had brought about, generated a new set of conditions that favoured speculative mathematical science."[709] He further observed that "a complementary development was the flow of wealth into England through expansionist enterprise. This wealth made possible increased opportunity and support for speculative mathematical science, and also made possible virtuosity, under whose auspices speculative science received further encouragement. As a result of these developments, Gresham College, Oxford, and, later, Cambridge became centers for speculative science. The Greshamites and Oxford's experimental science club stamped their character on the Royal Society, which was to be the platform for the scientific revolution."[710]

It is evident that there was no developed, specialised scientific body in seventeenth-century England except the Royal Society of London, which was founded in 1660 as a result of encounter with Oriental scientific knowledge and mostly to enhance overseas trade with the Muslim East. It was preceded by the accumulation of Islamic Oriental manuscripts, establishment of Arabic chairs at Oxford and Cambridge and a network of natural philosophers and Arabists to translate, study and discuss the so accumulated knowledge. Like its French counterpart Academy of Science, the Royal Society was heavily engaged with the Oriental knowledge. "The creation of the Academy of Sciences in France in 1666 was closely tied to previous contacts with Asia, as the study of travel and geography were at its inception. More than a century after the royal chairs were established by Francis I, all secular knowledge in France continued to be shaped and influenced by Orientalism."[711] The situation in England was no different; England started later in the game than France, but picked up the pace soon after that.

The Royal Society fellows studied everything[712] from Turkish coffee, Indian tea, crops, fruits, exotic herbs,[713] Persian silk, Chinese porcelain, varnishes, masonry, paper, leather, tapestry, parchment, enamels, engravings, red glass, the medical use of herbs in Aleppo, the method of inoculation against smallpox in Aleppo, the manner of hatching eggs in ovens in Cairo to Indian textile, colours and dyes.[714] Since its inception they discussed, analysed, interacted with and benefitted from countless Eastern ideas and concepts. The world's oldest, continuous scientific body, the Royal Society, greatly benefited from Oriental manuscripts on a variety of scientific and natural subjects. Its natural philosophers and founding members - such as Robert Boyle (1627-1691), Robert Hooke (1635-1703), Edward Bernard (1638-1697), John Wallis (1617-1703), Henry Oldenberg (1617-1677), Edmund Castell (1606-1685) and others - read and digested Arabic, Turkish and Persian Oriental manuscripts purchased by Edward Pococke (1604-1691), Thomas Hyde (1636-1703),[715] Edmond Halley (1656-1742), John Greaves (1602-1652) and many other chaplains, consuls and merchants[716], and applied the extracted ideas in their socio-scientific observations, experiments and researches.[717] The close global networks demonstrated "the ways in which specific global connections forged by natural philosophers, merchants, and political renegades to further projects of knowledge creation, profit making, and liberation from oppression transformed the worlds within which they were constructed."[718] England did not do it all by itself. It was helped and facilitated by Oriental knowledge, wealth and wisdom.

Robert Boyle, the Anglo-Irish natural philosopher, chemist, inventor, the richest man in England, a director and investor of the East India Company,[719] was influenced by the famous Irish Orientalist and Archbishop of Armagh James Ussher (1581-1656)[720] and Samuel Hartlib. He learned Arabic at the age of 50 to understand the Arabic manuscripts and sought the help of Arabists such as Edward Pococke, John Greaves and Thomas Hyde in translation.[721] Boyle's antidogmatic, natural, experimental and empirical proto scientific approach was developed in conjunction with Eastern manuscripts, ideas, sciences and cultures. The mathematician and astronomer Edward Bernard learned Arabic and used Arabic observations heavily in his astronomical research. John Wallis, the founding fellow of Royal Society, the Savilian Professor of Geometry at Oxford who taught John Locke as an undergraduate[722] translated Arabic manuscripts and often quoted Arabic mathematicians in his lectures. "He included Nasir Eddin Al Tusi's five-page proof to Euclid's fifth postulate in his book, *Opera Mathematica*."[723] Victor J. Katz observed that "by the seventeenth century, European mathematics had in many areas reached, and in some areas surpassed, the level of its Greek and Arabic sources. Nevertheless, given the continuous contact of Europe with Islamic countries, a steady stream of Arabic manuscripts, including mathematical ones, began to arrive in Europe. Leading universities appointed professors of Arabic, and among the sources they read were mathematical works. For example, the work of Sadr al-Tusi (the son of Nasir al-Din al-Tusi) on the parallel postulate, written originally in 1298, was published in Rome in 1594 with a Latin title page. This work was studied by John Wallis in England, who then wrote about its ideas as he developed his own thoughts on the postulate. Still later, Newton's friend, Edmond Halley, translated into Latin Apollonius's Cutting-off of a Ratio, a work that had been lost in Greek but had been preserved via an Arabic translation."[724] Edmond Castell[725] spent eighteen years developing extensive dictionaries of Oriental languages, including Arabic.[726] Edmond Halley (1656–1742), who gave his name to Halley's comet, also learned Arabic at the age of 50 to translate and digest the works of Muslim astronomers such as al-Battani as well as Apollonius's Conics, the advanced mathematics in antiquity.[727] Halley's close scientific coordinations with and funding of Newton's works and astronomical expertise are well-documented.[728] In a paper published in the Philosophical Transactions of the Royal Society in 1695 he wrote, "And if any curious Traveller or Merchant residing there, would please to observe, with due care, the Phases of the Moon's Eclipse at Bagdad, Aleppo and Alexandria, thereby to determine their longitude, they could not do the Science of Astronomy a greater service."[729]

Royal Society, Westminster School and Oriental Languages

Many fellows of the Royal Society came from the Westminster School of London where Arabic was taught as a language. Westminster, a highly reputable school, was frequented by both Royalists and Puritans. "In the library of Westminster School is a first edition of the *History of the Royal Society*. The copy epitomises the vitality and the central position of the institution that was Westminster in the latter part of the seventeenth century."[730] Richard Busby (1606-1695) was its Head Master for over 55 years. He was a graduate of Christ Church Oxford where he studied Arabic with Matthias Paser (1598-1658). Paser like Edward Pococke and other Orientalists hailed Arabic as the language of natural sciences, medicine, mathematics, astronomy, geography, philosophy and Oriental wisdom. In addition to other Oriental languages, the Arabic program at Westminster was initiated with great enthusiasm probably by the 1650s when Pococke's Polyglot Bible was published. Busby himself compiled Arabic grammar resource books and taught many of his students, even after hours, mostly at the school library as well as at his home. Henry Stubbe, Robert Hooke, Christorpher Wren and John Locke's Arabic interests all began at Westminster, which they further pursued in Christ Church Oxford under Dr. Pococke. John Evelyn, the famous diarist reported "that Arabic too is taught: 'I heard and saw such exercises at the election of scholars at Westminster School to be sent to the University in Latin, Greek, Hebrew, and Arabic, in themes and extemporary verses, as wonderfully astonished me in such youths, with such readiness and wit, some of them not above twelve, or thirteen years of age."[731] Dr. Busby believed in widening the availability of education; this led him to an interest in the wider social context. He was engaged in a School at Lutton in Lincolnshire and in the Green Coat Hospital in nearby Tothill Fields. He founded readerships in Hebrew and Mathematics at Christ Church, and took his love of Oriental languages with him wherever he went.

Busby was a dynamic academic figure who was well-connected and respected within the academic and scientific world of seventeenth-century England. His close connections with Oxford, Cambridge and Royal Society are well-documented. He was a go-between for many natural scientists, mathematicians and astronomers; his friendships with John Pell, Dr. Isaac Barrow, Isaac Newton's teacher and predecessor at Cambridge, Isaac Newton and Walter Needham are well known.[732] In spite of his royal loyalty and respect for Anglican leadership, he espoused unorthodox, mostly Arminian theological views which were tolerated by the Church hierarchy due to Busby's hardwork, academic stature and reputation. "The biographer of the Non-Conformist divine and diarist, Philip Henry writes: 'I have heard him tell how much he surprised the Doctor, the first time he waited upon him after he was turn'd out by the Act of Uniformity: For when the Doctor asked him, Pr'ythee (Child) what made thee a Nonconformist? Truly Sir, saith Mr Henry, you made me one; for you taught me those things that hindered me from conforming.'"[733] The early eighteenth-century essayist Sir Richard Steele was to say: "I must confess that I am of the opinion Busby's Genius for education had as great an Effect upon the age he lived in, as that of any ancient Philosopher, without excepting one, had on his Contemporaries."[734] Busby was the conduit through which several collections of books and papers passed to the Royal Society. For instance, John Pell's collection of Oriental manuscripts and writings went to the Royal Society through Busby.

The Royal Society had a huge collection of Muslim manuscripts and elected three Muslim fellows in the late seventeenth and early eighteenth century. They were Muhammad ibn Haddu, the Moroccan ambassador to Charles II's court who himself was son of an English woman and also married to an English lady,[735] Mohammed ibn Ali Abgali and Cassem Alqiada Aga of Tripoli. M. B. Hall notes that "at first thought, it seems unlikely that the Fellows of the Royal Society founded by the 'new philosophy' in England in 1660 'for the promotion of natural knowledge,' self-confessedly forward looking modernists, should have concerned themselves with Islamic learning. That they did so throws further light upon the complexities of the scientific revolution."[736] In short, the English Scientific Revolution in many ways was facilitated by Muslim knowledge, sciences and manuscripts. There was a widespreas fascination with Muslim sciences, culture, empires and even faith among members of Hartlibian circle, many fellows of Royal Society and some Latitudinarian clergymen. John Beale, one of those responsible for the original ideology of the Royal Society, well represents this widespread fascination with things Islamic as he was an active member of all three above mentioned circles.

The Baconian John Beale and Islamophilia

John Beale (1608-1683)[737] was an English clergyman, horticulturist, scientific writer, and early Fellow of the Royal Society.[738] He was a utopian, Baconian reformer instrumental in Samuel Hartlib's circle and closely connected with Robert Boyle, his sister Lady Ranelagh, John Evelyn, Henry Oldenburg and other influential fellows of the Royal Society and Anglican establishment. His fundamental role in the Royal Society's agriculture and trade policies is well documented. His enthusiastic engagement in multiple scientific fields, experimentation, data collection, communication, socio economic and religious reformation place him among the early models of Puritan, Baconian, Latitudinarianism who combined scientific and religious reform for social regeneration with millenarian zeal. His earnest search for *Prisca Theologia* and *Prisca Sapientia* and his closet Unitarian radicalism exemplifies the overall directions and sentiments of the early Hartlibian circle, Royal Society members and Latitudinarian segment of the Anglican Church establishment, the early and mid-seventeenth century "culture of fact" and "dissimulation". He also epitomizes the secret love affair which many Hartlibian, Royal Society members and Latitudinarians had for the "Eastern Wisdom" in general and Muslim civilization in particular. He symbolizes the overall English Oriental obsession of 1630's onward. Beale was a typical closet Islamophile, dissatisfied with Church Christianity's supernatural, unintelligible dogmas, magisterial Reformation, Continental and English sectarianism, internal strife, instability, backwardness; religio political persecutions and overly hierarchical society. He believed that the sixteenth century Protestant Reformation required further radical, rational reformation on Islamic Unitarian, moral and rational lines. Unlike the other radical Islamophiles such as Henry Stubbe, Beale kept his Islamic fascinations to his close circles of Hartlibian, Royal Society and Latitudinarian confidants such as Hartlib, Evelyne, Oldenburg, Boyle, Lady Ranelagh and others. Beale also typifies the overall pattern of secret oriental conversion which usually started with Renaissance humanism, Socinianism and was further fueled by exposure to Eastern wisdom, manuscripts, languages, sciences, alchemy, theology, philosophy and cultural achievements.

Beale was a typical young staunch Calvinist Anglican who got exposed to his Eton mentor Sir Henry Wotton's international diplomatic experience and preeminent humanist scholarship and heterodox theology of John Hales, the "theological mentor of Chillingworth and-other eirenicists who gathered at the Great Tew (Oxfordshire) estate of Lord Falkland. By his espousal of a rational, tolerant and simplified Christianity in emulation of the early Fathers, Hales reaffirmed the Erasmian tradition of Christian humanism which Beale had studied at Worcester."[739] Members of the 1630's Tew Circle such as Lucius Cary (1610 –1643), Second Viscount Falkland and King's Secretary of State, the playwright Ben Jonson (1572–1637), poets such as Edmund Waller (1606–1687), Abraham Cowley (1618-1667), and the divines Henry Hammond (1605–1660); Gilbert Sheldon (1598–1677), George Morley (1598–1684), William Chillingworth (1602–1644), Edward Hyde, later the first earl of Clarendon (1609-1674) and traveler George Sandys (1644-1578) were influenced by Renaissance humanism especially through the writings of Desiderius Erasmus and Hugo Grotius and leaned towards Socinian rationalism, minimalism, biblicism, anti-clericalism and toleration. Lord Falkland was considered the first Socinian in England. George Sandys, whose father Archbishop Edwin Sandys (1519-1588) was known for his hatred of dissent and enthusiasm for uniformity, had traveled to the Ottoman Empire and got inspired by its diversity. In spite of misgivings about Islam and its Prophet, Sandys admired Islamic rationalism, minimalism, religious diversity and toleration. John Hales reinforced George Sandys' overseas experiences with Renaissance humanism. His rationalism, minimalism and heterodoxy were transmitted to his brilliant student John Beale. Beale's Worcester Erasmian radicalism was augmented by his Cambridge mentor Abraham Wheelock, the distinguished orientalist and the first Sir Thomas Adams Professor of Arabic at Cambridge,[740] who gave Beale open access to Cambridge University's recently acquired oriental manuscripts, a rarity in England of 1630's.[741] Beale's thirst for Eastern wisdom, *Prisca Sapientia* and Muslim sciences lead him to Arabic language, alchemy, alchemical experiments, scientific pursuits, Baconian utopian universal reformation, Hartlib circle's frantic, grandiose projects, Royal Society, husbandry, overseas trade, discussion of Levant and East India Company trade policies, radical Unitarian reformation of Christianity on rational Islamic theological lines and aspirations of replacing the persecuting English politico religious systems with Muslim Turkish models and government. He did all this without losing his clerical status, high chaplaincy appointments, lifelong Royal Society membership and public calls for revival and spread of Gospel Christianity. His Christianity was anti-Trinitarian, anti-dogmatic, natural, rational, simplistic, minimalistic, moral, tolerant and illuministic but he masterfully disguised it in Trinitarian, dogmatic, Anglican garbs, like many other Latitudinarians, to the extent that Charles II appointed him as chaplain extraordinary to his court. To Dmitri Levitin he resembled the sixteenth and seventeenth century "Islamophile antritrinitarians such as Adam Neuser (who ultimately converted to Islam) and Henry Stubbe"[742] but to Charles II he was an exceptional chaplain. His Islamophile heterodoxy was an open secret to his close confidants in Hartlib Circle, Royal Society and Church establishment but it did not cause them alarm as many of them shared his sentiments in part or in toto. To grapple the intense appeal of this peculiar early seventeenth century English phenomenon let us look at Beale's celebrated Anglican and Royal Society career.

Beale was born in 1608, educated at Worcester Cathedral School and Eton, matriculate at King's College, Cambridge, in 1629 and travelled the Continent between 1636 and 1638. In spite of harboring some deviant theological opinions, he stayed on as a fellow of Cambridge until 1640. He was master of St. Catherine's Hospital, Ledbury (1649-early 1650s), and vicar of Stretton Grandison from 1656 onward. At the Restoration, he became a vicar of Yeovil and rector at Sock Denis; in 1663 he was elected Fellow of the Royal Society, and in 1665 he was appointed chaplain extraordinary to Charles II.

Beale's radical vision of religious history, reformation and Islamism was primarily outlined in his 1650's personal letters written to Samuel Hartlib and through him to John Evelyn, Lady Ranelagh and Henry Oldenburg.[743] Beale believed that the original Christianity of Jesus and his early disciples was simple, minimalistic and tolerant of diversity. "The first three centuries of Christianity saw very little in the way of doctrinal orthodoxy. The true primitive faith was even more doctrinally minimal than the Apostles' Creed."[744] According to Beale "when men dare reade the Historyes & chiefe writings of the Ages of first Martyrdomes impartially', they will find that 'twas best, when Symboles & Confessions were as short, or shorter, than the Apostles Creede, as it is called."[745] The Apostles' Creed was in fact a later invention "not finished as now we have it, till Austins dayes'; in any case, if one was to assess modern Christianity by its standards, one would find that 'Rome will get much ground against vs ... Our Apostles Creede in our sense is as young as our Reformation; & more defective, than the Romane Apostles Creede; & indeede not a symbole of faith, but a symbole of Heresie."[746] The Christian heresy was fabricated by the Roman Church of the fourth century with the help of pagan theology and for the sake of pagan accommodations, "in the first plantacion of the gospell Christianity took some alloy & was sullied partly by the intrusion of halfe converted Philosophers & partly by the compliance of Christians to Gentile <Rites> lawes & Customes."[747] This way the original Christianity of Jesus was compromised and corrupted by the Roman Trinitarian Paganism, "yea for 300 yeares together, are undoubtedly the purest times of the Gospell that have yet appeared, we find them [to] differ very much at least very far from all nationall confessions, in the high points of the holy trinity, of the state of the Soul after death, of Praedestination. Freewill & (to omit from particulers) from the maine body of our positive Theologie. Some were wholy for inspiracions as Tertullian & Origen, some were for Platonicall Ideas & raptures as Sinesius, & other semi-christian Philosophers, some soared aloft in the high straines of eloquence as Chrisostome & Nazianzene, some stood more strictly to close reasonings as Iustine ye Martyr, & Clemens of Alexandria, yet in their severall ways & <with> severall opinions they held firmer to bonds of unity & to the substance of Sanctitie then wee doe."[748] The corrupted Christian Orthodoxy and Canon Law were founded on the pagan foundations,[749] supported and imposed by the mighty arms of the pagan state.[750] Therefore it was impossible to derive a patristically grounded Christian Orthodoxy. "And for those primitiue Fathers whose authority is soe much claymed & boasted, this I have many yeares agoe undertaken & demonstrated, that all our authenticall confessions as well of Protestants as of Papists, are spun of such a fine thread of new distinctions as will utterly exclude all these old fathers, soe that if they must be called fathers, the fathers & children are very much unlike each other."[751] Dmitri Levitin observed that "the details of his history were more 'radical' than anything developed by virtually any other person in seventeenth-century England, if not Europe. On the other, the broader religio-political vision that informed this historical vision was far more complex than the 'Erasmian label usually signifies…Beale was particularly fascinated by the interaction between Christianity and paganism during the earliest growth of the new faith, and that this led him to posit that the earliest church fathers were already wrong about many matters of doctrine."[752] Beale towed the lines of radical reformers such as Servetus, Socinians and Unitarians. His was a standard Socinian, Unitarian and Islamic stance widespread among the early seventeenth century English radicals including the Hartlib and Tew circles.[753] Sarah Mortimer noted that "Indeed, the Socinians played a central role in Beale's religious journey…"[754] and that "the Socinians did begin to find interested, even sympathetic, readers in the 1630s. These were men who objected to several aspects of both Reformed and Catholic theology and found in the Socinians useful material with which to make their own religious choices."[755] Beale like the Socinians insisted that "The most Judicious & most Learned, that I have read, of Papists, Prelates & Zealous Protestants, (such as are called

Sectaries) doe affirme & undertake that our Saviour gave noe expresse command concerning water-babtisme nor brought in any other rituall precept concerning the breaking of bread the Cup or Supper of ye Lord or any other elementary point of discipline."[756] He attributed his theologico historical radicalism to his intense studies of "Eastern Wisdom" including alchemy, astrology, mysticism, dreams and hermeticism. He contended that Eastern asceticism, mysticism and self-discipline could prepare a seeker for spiritual illuminations and divine revelations/intuitions. The history of the 'eastern wisdom' had shown that "one could condition oneself both to receive such revelations, and to interpret them, through a 'certaine preparation of the minde & spirite, by humiliation of the flesh, & serene attention, & humble reguard, & many other meanes & methods w=" may bee layd downe … to obtaine this intercourse of Heaven."[757] He like Cambridge Platonist Joseph Mede and his successor Isaac Newton used Achmet the Arabian's famous text "*Oneirocriticon*" to decipher and interpret dreams, pristine scriptural teachings and prophecies. [758] Beale, like the hermit and mystics of his time Henry Hereford, believed in *Prisca Theologia*, the pristine Unitarian, universal, cyclical theology and prophetic tradition corrupted by pagan Christianity but preserved by the Middle Eastern wisdom, the Islamic faith. Levitin noted that for Beale, "the figure who everyone else would have agreed was the greatest enemy of early Christianity turned out to be a better communicant with God than the early Christians themselves. It is difficult to imagine an equally 'radical' historical claim in seventeenth-century Europe. And yet, Beale managed to provide one, in his comments about Islam."[759] The Islamic faith was the true heir to pristine, original Christianity of Jesus. He "wish[ed] that wee had either more or lesse of Mahometanisme".[760] He further stated: "I confesse their Doctrine more rationable, & their lives generally more righteous, than many of the succeeding sects, that have rolld over one another in pretence of confounding idoll Priests".[761] To Beale, Islam was not ideal but "morally and theologically superior to modern, confessionalised Christianity."[762] Islam bore resemblance to Beale's ideal of early pristine, rational, natural and Unitarian Christianity, the faith which will be restored by Turkish conquest of the Trinitarian, pagan Christendom. "I doe really expect, that wee shall bee renderd vnder the feete of Turkes, both for our juste chastisement & triall, & for their instruction & conversion. And in the meane time

I am resolvd to disowne any man to bee a Christian, or of our sect, till hee bee an honest man mercifull, & [*catchword:* better]."[763]

Such sentiments were not confined to Beale but were widespread among the English radicals. Many English were appreciative of Muslim morality, rational discourse and devotions. "As for positive statements about the morality and devotion of Muslims, these were relatively widespread, not least among those associated with the Hartlib circle."[764] Many English radicals accepted Muslims as the real inheritors of Patriarchal wisdom and asceticism who rejected the supernatural, ceremonial Church Christianity due to its pagan dogmas, cumbersome ceremonies and theoretical practices. "Muslims, Beale contended, were to be considered Abrahamites', who had understandably revolted from Christianity, given the idolatry that had infected it by the end of the sixth century, but who nonetheless 'had yet more of light by owr Lord Christ concerning the resurrection & future state of felicity & hell, than was comon to all Abrahamites of old'. There was thus a direct continuity between Islam and the ancient patriarchs whom Beale so venerated. This idea, he told Hartlib, had been instilled in him by Henry Hereford, the hermit of Buckberry Hill."[765] To many English Protestants "Alcoran" proved Christianity.

Beale, the Anglican Chaplain of Charles II, was a closet Islamophile and a radical Unitarian in 1650's long before the radical Islamism of Henry Stubbe (1670's) and John Toland (1690's). Levitin observed that "I am not familiar with any other seventeenth-century thinker drawing such a direct (and positive) relationship between the religion of the patriarchs and Islam."[766] He further noted that "It is difficult to imagine a more 'radical' historical position in mid-seventeenth century Western Europe than one which suggests that… Muslims had partially inherited true patriarchal religion and that their conquest of European Christendom was both imminent and, ultimately, positive. At this point, one might think that Beale fits nicely into a standard definition of 'radical' Protestant: illuminationist, individualist, tolerationist, and anti-clerical."[767] Beale wanted Unitarian and Socinian reformation of both Catholic and Protestant Churches because of their religio political affinity with Islam and with the original moral Christianity of Jesus. "And this I have generally found, that such as are touch'd with a dose of Socinianisme, (if scholars & studious) doe soone become serious students & admirers of the first, & best Monuments of Antiquity, I meane

Christian. And since some Liberty must be indulged, tis much safer yt wee take a relish of yt more authenticall Liberty, than addict to ye wildnesse of novel phansy. And in this wee may with more reputation keepe a safe distance from Rome ... then by bowing to Calvine, who hath subverted the wholy body of old Religion, & utterly defaced the purity & simplicity of Christianity. For hee it is, who hath corrupted all Power of Evangelicall precepts, polluted & interrupted all streames of divine Love, weakened all the promises, & disturbed all reasonableness of faith."[768] These mid-century radical traits were laid bare by the radical Islamophiles such as Henry Stubbe and John Toland, as will be seen in coming pages, and were permanently assimilated by John Locke and Isaac Newton into the bloodstream of Anglican religio political theology, as John Coffey has illustrated.[769]

Islam was part of English socio-political and religious revolutions. Paul Hazard, the famous French historian of intellectual thought, summarised the impact of Islam on the seventeenth century Europe very well. "They studied the original texts and the result was that the Arab emerged in a completely new light. They pointed out, these learned men, that so vast a section of the human race would never have followed in the footsteps of Mohammed if he had been no more than a dreamer and an epileptic. Never would a religion, so crude and childish as his was reputed to be, have exhibited such vitality and have made such progress. If, instead of giving currency to the falsest and most misleading stories, people would go to the Arabs themselves for information, they would perceive that Mohammed and his followers were endowed with qualities of heart and mind that rendered them not a whit inferior to the most illustrious heroes of the other races of the world. Look at the evil things the Gentiles had reported of the Christian religion! Look at the absurdities that were promulgated concerning it! So it is always when things are judged solely from the outside. Doctrines which the Mohammedans never professed were triumphantly refuted, errors they never committed were exposed and condemned. But this sort of victory was too facile by half. In point of fact, their religion was as coherent as it was lofty and full of beauty. Nay more, their whole civilisation was admirable. When the tide of barbarism swept over the face of the earth, who was it that had championed the cause of the mind and its culture? The Arabs [...] The change-over from repulsion to sympathy was the work of but a few years. By 1708, the process was complete."[770] Hazard continued: "Then it was that Simon Ockley gave utterance to an opinion [...] Ockley denied that the West was to be regarded as superior to the East. The East has witnessed the birth of as many men of genius as the West; conditions of life are better in the East. "So far as the fear of God is concerned, the control of the appetites, prudence and sobriety in the conduct of life, decency and moderation in all circumstances—in regard to all these things (and, after all, they yield to none in importance) I declare that if the West has added one single *iota* to the accumulated wisdom of the East, my powers of perception have been strangely in abeyance." This sort of thing gained ground. The Comte de Boulainvilliers, with due acknowledgements to Herbelot, Pococke, Reland and Ockley, compiled a Life of Mahomet in which the change of attitude is seen to be complete. "Every nation," he says, "has its own peculiar type of wisdom. Mahomet symbolises the wisdom of the Arabs. Christ symbolises the wisdom of the Jews."[771] Such was the difference which Eastern wisdom and knowledge had made in Europe during the long seventeenth century. The personal experiences of countless merchants and Eastern manuscripts radically changed European perceptions of Islam and Muslims.

The Church and state officials also greatly encouraged Arabic language for missionary reasons, and Muslim scientific knowledge and manuscripts due to their commercial and scientific value. Arabic study was also a Christian theological affair. Arabic was considered indispensable for study of Old Testament, philology and theology. Oxford Lord Chancellor - and later Archbishop of Canterbury William Laud - spent his own money to purchase Oriental manuscripts[772], donated them to Oxford Bodleian Library and established an Arabic press at Oxford.[773] Even his enemy Oliver Cromwell, and the parliament who hanged him, supported such a scholarly endeavour under the influence of John Selden and Samuel Hartlib.[774] "Cromwell's parliament voted to give Cambridge University 500 pounds to purchase a collection of Oriental books and another 40–50 pounds for printing Arabic books. The heterodox puritan reformer and Oriental manuscript collecter and distributer Samuel Hartlib was involved in these purchases. One of his correspondents, Thomas Smith, wrote to thank him: "not myself only but the whole Commonwealth of learning are eternally obliged to you for your earnest & happy endeavours for the promotion of all kind of learning especially Oriental." At the time Hartlib was trying to obtain Arabic and Syriac type faces for Cambridge, and a Marconite to read difficult oriental manuscripts. Hartlib studied the Oriental books purchased by Cambridge, along with ancient alchemical treatises as part of his attempt to promote learning and restore the Garden of Eden, the goal of many of his contemporaries. He was joined in these endeavours by Robert Boyle, John Locke, and Isaac Newton, and a host of other early modern natural philosophers, whose work contributed to the Scientific Revolution."[775]

Hartlib was a close friend of John Milton who dedicated his tractate *On Education* in 1644 to Hartlib.[776] Both were students of Cambridge Platonist theologian Joseph Mede. Hartlib was regarded as a "conduit-pipe" of knowledge, the "hub of the axletree of knowledge" and as the "great intelligencer of Europe."[777] He was a puritan reformer and a mystic, interested in setting up egalitarian communities and schools of science. His heterodox, pluralistic religious and political theology and republicanism was suspected by the Crown. He was harassed and arrested in 1639 as a puritan rogue plotting against the Church and Crown. In 1645 Hartlib was a witness against Archbishop Laud for high treason. His anti-royalist role in the English Civil War and Interregnum and extensive puritan circle was appreciated and rewarded during the Commonwealth Republic.[778] He founded "the Office of Address in England through the financial support of Parliament. The objective of this state-sponsored organisation was, ideally, to arrange a system of intellectual correspondences with international scholars and scientists who could supply rare books and manuscripts from remote libraries. In this context, the aim of the Office of Address was, according to Hartlib, to increase information on "matters of Religion, learning, and all Ingenuities."[779] He was a close friend of Robert Boyle, Sir Kenelm Digby, Seth Ward, John Wallis, Isaac Barrow, Henry More, John Locke, Henry Stubbe, Isaac Newton and George Starkey.[780] All were enthusiastic about authentic ancient knowledge, uncorrupted revelation, Eastern philosophy, theology and alchemy, universal *Mana*, mythical gold making philosopher's stone,[781] a vegetative principle operating in the natural world,[782] magic and alchemy.[783]

Alchemy, Arabs and English Natural Philosophers

Alchemy of the seventeenth century was different than later scientific chemistry;[784] it was more occult than chemical and more Eastern than Western. Alchemy was recognized in England as a science that had been mastered by the Arabs. The allure of Eastern scientific knowledge, especially of alchemy, was shared by the above sketched circle of natural philosophers. The Hartlibian circle was the precursor and enabler of the later Royal Society which continued alchemical pursuits.[785] Francis Bacon,[786] Robert Boyle,[787] Locke[788] and Newton all shared this allure of Eastern alchemy; in reality Boyle, Locke, Newton and some other Royal Society fellows were obsessed with Eastern alchemy and knowledge. F. Sherwood Taylor who, speaking about Newton's alchemical attitude, remarked that he was "in the fullest sense an alchemist. He conducted alchemical experiments, he read widely and universally in alchemical treatises of all types, and he wrote alchemy, not like Newton, but like an alchemist."[789] William R. Shea noted that "R. S. Westfall offers striking evidence that "Newton's interest in alchemy continued unabated between 1670 and 1696, the year he left Cambridge to become Warden of the Mint." However, Newton "devoted merely two years, 1664-1665, to mathematics and from that time on would only turn to it when solicited. He concerned himself with optics for a brief period around 1670 but he never returned seriously to it again. Mechanics and dynamics held his attention for a short while in the 1660s and then only in the two and a half years that produced the Principia. It is hard to escape the conclusion that this great work, which we see as the culmination of Newton's career, may have seemed to him as an interruption or no more than a partial fulfilment of a much more grandiose plan. Newton was convinced that there was an underlying unity to alchemy and that a comprehension of the alchemical 'work' could be achieved both by comparing the various symbols they used and by making experiments."[790] Dobbs has shown that Newton's interests in alchemy continued until the last decade of his life. The philosopher's stone, transmutation of metals into gold, search for the animating vegetative principle and control of natural phenomena through alchemical experimentation were among the top priorities of these natural philosophers; Middle Eastern, Arabic knowledge was considered central to these pursuits.

Newton believed that Egyptian pyramids held the keys to profound secrets; in the 1680s, he studied their units of measurement to unlock their cubit in an effort to measure the circumference of the earth. Newton supposed that the ancient Egyptions were experts in mathematics and were able to measure the earth. He also believed that Solomon's Temple carried multiple secrets and symbolism for the future political events. Alchemy was Newton's gateway to occult ancient knowledge and wisdom. Other Royal Society fellows followed suit. Sir Hans Sloane, who succeeded Newton as President of the Royal Society, collected scores of alchemical books just like Newton. Their printed works on alchemy were "but the tip of a very large iceberg."[791]

The Arabic books such as the *Secret of Hermes*[792], also known as *Emerald Tablet, as Smaragdine Table, Tabula Smaragdina* and the medieval best seller *Secretum secretorum* - which was translated into English in 1528 by Robert Copland - were very popular with the Royal Society's natural philosophers.[793] They thought that "everything knowable was contained in ancient sources. It appealed equally to Renaissance thinkers, who searched for a *prisca theologica* (or *prisca magia*) as an alternative to what they regarded as a bankrupt scholastic tradition. Moreover, books of secrets promised to give readers access to secrets of nature and the arts which might be exploited for material gain or for the betterment of the human condition. Underlying them was the assumption that nature was repository of occult forces that might be manipulated by using the right techniques. The utilitarian character of books of secrets gave concrete substance to this claim: unlike many of the recondite treatises on the philosophical foundations of magic, alchemy, and the occult arts, which barely touched base with the real world, books of secrets were grounded on a down-to-earth, experimental outlook, and hence they held forth a real, accessible promise of power."[794] This study of secrets of nature, alchemical experimentation and occult magical powers led to later scientific revolution.

Medieval Muslim philosophers, natural scientists and medicinal experts were models of merging theoretical sciences with practical endeavours.[795] William Eamon noted that "Arab civilisation was itself the product of older cultures, Syrian, Persian, and Greek, which in the course of imperial expansion the indigenous culture assimilated through translation and transformed by the dominating force of its official religion, Islam. Science assumed a prestigious role in Islamic civilisation. Affirming the importance of philosophy and natural knowledge in the hierarchy of knowledge, the Arabs gave science a new legitimacy.

By broadening its scope to include practical disciplines that had not generally interested the ancients, they reoriented science to serve new purposes. Mathematics aided commerce, alchemy contributed to the development of chemical technology, and medical theory forged a new alliance with pharmacy and public health. Scientific method also changed. By incorporating the work of artisans and instrument-makers, Arab natural philosophers enhanced their powers of observation and measurement, applied mathematics to new problems, and used experimentation as a methodological tool."[796] Francis Bacon, Newton, Locke and others imitated the Muslim natural philosophers and scientists in their utilitarian merger of natural philosophy with works of artisans, methematicians and instrument makers. The early seventeen-century scientific endeavours of London merchants, Greshamites and trademen were closely identical to the Eastern patterns; the later science emerged out of these alchemical and mundane experiments and efforts. Some of Newton's scientific discoveries, such as gravitational force, optics and calculus were probably accidental consequences of his alchemical natural and religious pursuits.[797] Both Westfall and Dobbs have argued that "Newton came to view gravity as an active principle by analogy with the active alchemical agent."[798] The same is true about Boyle's lifelong love with alchemical experiments and their impact upon his scientific discoveries and chemical procedures.

Boyle, using an old metaphor, "saw nature as a rare book of hieroglyphs, containing many "veil'd truths" which might be read if we could decipher the language; Robert Hooke spoke of peeping in at nature's windows; while Joseph Glanvill envisioned the opening up of an "America of secrets and an unknown Peru of Nature."[799] The Baconian experimental science developed out of occult natural and alchemical experimentation.[800] The seventeenth-century natural philosophers were not as precise, rational and scientific as their later biographers have made them to be. They studied magical healing, stroking, astrology, witchcraft, divination, sorcery, spirits, ghosts, fairies and old prophecies as possible realities to be dealt with.[801] Ann Talbot observed that "it was by no means clear to natural philosophers of the seventeenth century where the line lay between the natural and the supernatural. Vast areas of the natural world such as biology, medicine and even chemistry remained mysterious to them. Locke, Newton and Boyle all engaged in alchemical experiments. From the perspective of the twenty-first century their efforts may seem to have been at odds with their professed aims as natural philosophers. If Newton was prepared to spend more time at his alchemy than he did developing a theory of gravity then it might seem that the scientific revolution owed more to mysticism and irrationalism than it did to observation and investigation, and more to Neo-Platonism than to classical atomistic theories."[802] The esoteric was integral to exoteric knowledge, as B. J. T. Dobbs has well demostrated.[803] Newton's strong belief in astrology finally led to his astronomy, and his alchemical experiments were at the heart of his chemistry. The natural philosophers of seventeenth-century England were products of their society which was inundated with magic, sorcery, spirits and witchcraft.[804] Boyle, Locke and Newton believed in these invisible, irrational and misguided powers.[805] To the English virtuosity and natural philosophers nature was inundated with occult forces; understanding such forces could enable them to control natural phenomena. It was part of their religious curiosity as nature was not independent of God but a manifestation of God's signs and glory. The nature hunt and curiosity became the hobby of the English virtuosity.[806]

Spiritual Alchemy

There was another side to alchemy. The Muslim philosophers, theologians and natural scientists contended that alchemy had a spiritual dimension as well. Spiritual alchemy purified and transmuted the human soul as natural alchemy purified the metals and transmuted the base metals into gold. Ibn Sina, al Farabi and al Ghazali used alchemical vocabulary to construct a fully-fledged spiritual program of self purification; Al Ghazali's famous book *The Alchemy of Eternal Happiness* is a good example of such a trend. Medieval Christendom also witnessed the same tendency regarding alchemy. Martin Luther's famous identification of alchemy with religious pursuits and Biblical eschatological exegesis is telling.[807] Francis Bacon's Utopia - Salomon's House, Samuel Hartlib's "Invisible College," Newton and natural philosophers' alchemical pursuits were all geared towards divine providence, religious felicity, self purification, eternal salvation and religious reformation through experimentation, reason, revelation, mathematics and ancient wisdom. They were doubtful about the spiritual efficacy of Anglican Church's supernatural, Trinitarian and incarnational salvific scheme and elaborate system of rituals and ceremonies. They did not see a Trinitarian, Triune God with three distinctive persons, wills and consciousness in the unified nature; rather, they witnessed the hands of One and Only God in all patterns and laws of nature and that One and Only God they pursued through their alchemical and scientific experimentations. Simplicity and unity, rather than Trinitarian multiplicity and confusion, were their guiding principles. Dobbs has emphasised such a unitary, linear and overarching purpose in all scientific and alchemical designs of Newton and his fellows. "His goal was the knowledge of God, and for achieving that goal he marshalled the evidence from every source available to him: mathematics, experiment, observation, reason, revelation, historical record, myth, the tattered remnants of ancient wisdom."[808]

Alchemy went through such mystical and spiritual transformation during the sixteenth and seventeenth century.[809] E. J. Holmyard remarked that during the late Renaissance period alchemical esotericism slowly developed into alchemical praxis, into "a devotional system where the mundane transmutation of metals became merely symbolic of the transformation of sinful man into a perfect being through prayer and submission to the will of God. The two kinds of alchemy were often inextricably mixed; however, in some of the mystical treatises it is clear that the authors are not concerned with material substances but are employing the language of exoteric alchemy for the sole purpose of expressing theological, philosophical, or mystical beliefs and aspirations."[810] The external natural and the internal spiritual regeneration were one and the same truth sought by natural philosophers, though natural regeneration was more pronounced at times.

Newton's obsession with alchemy can be gauged from the fact that he secretly obtained alchemical papers from the estate of Robert Boyle, who was significantly invested in alchemy. Locke was executor of the Boyle's estate and provided Newton with the secret "loan" of these papers. Newton was not the first of the age of reason but he was the last of the magicians.[811] The occult alchemy was Newton's *chymistry*. He was obsessed with alchemy spending over 30 years of his life on alchemy related observations and experimentalisation, far more than the time he spent on mathematics or physics. He wrote over a million words on alchemy with his own hands, and had perhaps the largest alchemy collection in England. He shared Hartlib's enthusiasm for occult hermeic and alchemical writings, and engaged in secret alchemy fraternities and experimentation[812], secretly violating the laws against alchemy enacted by himself as the *Master of Royal Mint*.[813]

Richard Popkin well explained what "Newton was doing in his most puzzling papers on alchemy, astrology, theology, and various religious subjects into the context of the mix of disciplines that existed and co-existed all during the seventeenth century. In the period often interpreted as the scientific 'revolution' when, according to long hallowed tradition, rational science 'rose' and replaced medieval superstitions, we must remember some facts. This was also the period when Johannes Kepler could be one of the makers of modern astronomy as well as a leading astrologer; when the prophetic interpreter, John Dury, could discuss how best to discover a basis for certainty with Rene Descartes, whether in mathematics or in the discovery of the proper method for interpreting Scriptural prophecies; when Isaac Newton and Henry More could have had a monumental falling out over how to interpret the vials and the trumpets in the Book of *Revelation*; when Newton could undertake a trip to visit John Locke just to present him a chart for interpreting the symbols in Revelation and the chronological consequences thereof; and when Newton's chosen successor as Lucasian Professor of Mathematics at Cambridge, William Whiston, could deliver the Boyle Lectures on The Accomplishment of Scripture Prophecy, using the best modern mathematical techniques to estimate the probabilities as to when the remaining unfulfilled prophecies would be fulfilled. All of these events probably seemed normal to the seventeenth century participants though we today, now brainwashed by Whiggish interpretations of the Enlightenment, may find it difficult to fathom how our intellectual heroes of the past could have been so misguided."[814]

Respublica Mosaica, Prisca Sapientia and Prisca Theologia

Natural sciences, magic and religion were all lumped together. Avner Ben-Zaken has demonstrated that Islamic Hermetical and magical manuscripts, books and sources played a fundamental role in transforming discussions about alchemy and magic into new concepts of rising inductive and experimental philosophy. Johannes Kepler, Francis Bacon, Robert Boyle and Isaac Newton built on medieval Muslim literature and theories. The philosophical foundations of modern science were laid down with the help of Islamic civilization and concepts.[815]

Frances Yates argued that modem science "rose" out of occultism. Yates had claimed that it was revived Hermeticism which launched the modem scientific world.[816] Her student A. P. Coudert offered a different interpretation; she argued that "it was not Hermeticism but rather a revived Gnosticism in combination with ancient science which launched the outlook of Bacon, Comenius, Hartlib, and, later, Newton. According to this revived synthesis of Gnosticism and science, man was able to comprehend the universe by returning to a *prisca theologia* or *prisca sapientia* uncorrupted by the centuries of pagan metaphysics, kabbalah, etc."[817] Royal Society fellows such as Locke, Newton, Dury and the Hartlibian circle's misgivings about Biblical corruptions and historical inauthenticity were at the core of this search for authentic *prisca sapientia*.[818] Their inductive philosophy and experimental natural science was facilitated by the medieval Muslim alchemical and magical occult literature.

Newton like Hartlib believed in a hidden *prisca sapientia*,[819] a vast body of pristine ancient knowledge in the occult Eastern philosophy, somehow lost and forgotten during the centuries that came to be called the "dark ages" of western civilisation and to be rediscovered with a scientific approach and scriptural hermeneutics.[820] They also believed in *prisca theologia*, a doctrine about single, true, simple Unitarian ancient theology which was also last during the Hellenisation and Romanisation of Christianity.[821] The famous Cambridge neo-Platonistic Joseph Mede, Henry More, Newton's Cambridge teacher Isaac Barrow, Newton and Hartlib believed that "ancient knowledge from Egypt and Arabia was crucial in an era of scientific discoveries and political changes; More, in other words, was devoted to the alchemical tradition of the *prisca sapientia* supposedly buried in eastern texts that predate the Mosaic account of creation. For More and other Cambridge neo-Platonists, these mystical, non-Christian sources, mostly hermetic and Arabic works from the twelve and thirteenth centuries, can be reconciled with the basic monotheistic tenants of the true apostolic Christianity."[822] Mede, More and Hartlib-like radical Henry Stubbe were equally engaged in "a theological-political agenda in which the eastern sciences were the key to restoring Christianity to its primitive egalitarian condition, that of the *Respublica Mosaica*."[823] Hartlib laid the foundations of Henry Stubbe and John Toland's later quest for Muhammadan Christianity, in collaboration with many Levant and

East India Company merchants during the 1640s. He was punished and isolated during Restoration by Charles II due to his anti-royalist, Eastern republican agenda and Cromwell connections. Robert Boyle dropped him from the Royal Society under royalist pressure, because Hartlib was the ring leader of anti-clerical natural scientists and reformers who believed that Trinitarian Christianity was a corrupted form of the original Unitarian Christianity of Jesus and that divine right monarchy and persecuting church was Roman invention far from Jesus' other worldly moral theology. Hartlibians wanted to reform Christian Church and monarchy by rational education, pragmatic tools and republican outlook; Eastern wisdom and knowledge were some of their main reformative tools. They wanted to return to Moses' Republic through the uncorrupted Eastern wisdom embodied by Muhammad and his followers. Religious radicals, natural scientists and Deistic looking puritans were all part of this reformative scheme, with varying degrees and interests. The 1670s obsession with Islamic monotheistic republicanism and 1690s anti-Trinitarian controversies were extensions of 1630s and 1640s religio-political radicalism. The Glorious Revolution of 1689 was in reality a culmination of the 1640s English Revolution's quest for limited monarchy.

The *Respublica Mosaica, prisca sapientia, prisca theologia* and *Historia Monotheistica* were two sides of the same coin which promoted Islamic monotheism, sciences and republicanism as the true reflection of that lost body of knowledge and universal monotheistic prophetic tradition. This radical ideology culminated in the works of Henry Stubbe and John Toland's Muhammadan Christianity, as will be discussed in detail in the coming sections. John Locke and Isaac Newton were the silent partners in this reformative scheme; to them all, Ottoman Islamic republicanism was the reflection of *Respublica Mosaica*.[824] Islamic Unitarian republicanism was considered a solution to the European doctrinal disputes, ensuing religious wars, supernaturalism, Church and state persecutions.

The Swiss-born, German-speaking physician-alchemist Theophrastus von Hohenheim, better known as Paracelsus (ca. 1493–1541), the English alchemist's ideal, once characterised Luther and the Pope as two whores discussing chastity.[825] European intelligentsia was weary of Christian dogmatic supernatural theology as absolutist, divisive, irrational and irrelevant. Alchemy, with its soteriological and natural functions, was considered a viable alternate since the times of astronomers Johannes Kepler and Tycho Brahe. English naturalists and natural philosophers found religious solace in searching and demonstrating God's wisdom in plants, animals and countless other creatures of God as a movement away from corrupted dogmatic, ritualistic and formal Church Christianity. Peter Harrison aptly summarised that when "Thomas Sprat announced that the members of the Society 'meddle no otherwise with divine things', he immediately qualifies this by excepting from his prohibition considerations to do with 'the Power, Wisdom, and Goodness of the Creator [as] display'd in the admirable order, and workman-ship of the Creatures'. For Sprat, the exclusion of discussions of 'divinity' was not motivated by a belief in the irrelevance to experimental science of general religious concerns, but by the desire to avoid unnecessary and pointless debates about technical and indifferent points of theology and ritual. This stance, then, is entirely in keeping with the Charter's declaration that the Society's endeavours would promote 'the Glory of God.'"[826]

The English alchemists collected and studied the alchemical works of Ibn Sina (Avicenna), al-Razi (Rhazes), Albertus Magnus, Thomas Aquinas, Roger Bacon and other alchemists instead of Church Fathers and their slippery slope Trinitarian theology. This trend climaxed in the early members of Royal Society such as Boyle, John Dee, John Dury, Locke and Newton. The occult nature of alchemical experiments granted them a sense of freedom to pursue and develop their ideas away from the persecutions of confused Church. Through alchemy they envisioned a universal reformation, a spiritual enlightenment and a mystical revolution.

Individuals like Francis Bacon (1561-1626), John Comenius (1592-1670), Samuel Hartlib (1600-1662) and Newton spent most of their time exploring natural phenomena and conducting experiments at their laboratories. They believed in a universal natural life force and energy such as *"Mana," "Light of nature,"* the vegetative force that permeated the universe and could facilitate medical cure and maturation of metals into gold.[827] It was a "search for a unitary vision of the forces acting in the macrocosm and in the microcosm, the belief on a hidden *prisca sapientia* in the occult philosophy to be rediscovered with a scientific approach and the dispute with materialistic philosophy."[828] Isaac Newton, in a letter of his *Correspondences,* stated: "For alchemy does not trade with metals as ignorant vulgars think, which error has made them distress that noble science; but she has also material veins of whose nature God created handmaidens to conceive and bring forth its creatures [...] This philosophy is not of that kind which tends to vanity and deceit but rather to profit and to edification inducing first the knowledge of God and secondly the way to find out true medicines in the creatures [...] the scope is to glorify God in his wonderful works, to teach a man how to live well [...] This philosophy both speculative and active is not only to be found in the volume of nature but also in the sacred scriptures, as in Genesis, Job, Psalms, Isaiah and others. In the knowledge of this philosophy God made Solomon the greatest philosopher in the world."[829]

The Hartlibian circle, including Hartlib, John Dury, his son in law Henry Oldenburg (Secretary of Royal Society), John Dee, John Evlyn, Robert Boyle, Starkey, Locke and Newton, was actively engaged in alchemical experimentation since the early 1660s. Arabic alchemical works and theories were among the most discussed, analysed and practiced among this elite group of natural philosophers. In reality alchemical pursuits and its vocabulary were part and parcel of seventeenth-century English religion, natural sciences and politics.[830] The occult alchemical philosophy was well employed by the radicals[831] during the Civil War and Interregnum period, but coopted by Charles II after the Restoration for different reasons. The King initially wanted to portray himself as an enlightened figure and a unifying force. He, like many other European princes, was heavily invested in alchemy; he had his own chemist, laboratory and alchemical pursuits of philosopher's stone and tincture.[832] He patronised Royal Society's alchemical-chemical experimentations due to several political and cultural reasons.[833] Alchemical pursuits, with their strong Eastern connections, were royalist and radical priorities, but with different ends in mind. Charles II, a secret Catholic, purportedly employed alchemy to intellectually and financially support the Protestant Anglican Church and monarchy by turning metals into gold, while the secret heterodox natural philosophers used it to undermine the Anglican Church and Catholic-leaning Stuart monarchy.

Boyle and Newton worked on mechanical explanations of alchemical transmutations. Frustrated with Church's theological squabbling, disputed paths to eternal salvation and unintelligible doctrines, the natural philosophers at times exaggerated the mystical and eschatolocial significance of alchemy. Reform of natural knowledge, ideas about reform of religion, man and society, collection of authentic knowledge through experimentation and its proper dissemination became the aspired goals of this enthusiastic group of natural philosophers. This new pattern of socialisation and social cooperation gradually supplanted that of Church socialisation and community.[834] Natural scientists and reformists emerged as the learned alternates for the confused, squabbling and irrational theologians, the superstitious but absolute Church leaders. Christopher Hill has noted that the scientists favoured the puritan, parliamentarian and republican causes.[835] John Brooke and Ian Maclean have demonstrated the overwhelming religious heterodoxy, rational discourse and creative attitude of the sixteenth- and seventeenth-century natural philosophers, scientists and medical practitioners.[836] This rationalisation trend led to purging of alchemy from medieval quasi-religious aspects to more grounded objective chemistry, even though the giants such as Newton and Boyle never even hoped to transmute other metals to gold.[837] Frances Yates noted that "As a deeply religious man [...] Newton was profoundly occupied by the search for One, for the One God, and for the divine Unity in nature. Newton's marvellous physical and mathematical exploration of nature had not entirely satisfied him. Perhaps he entertained, or half-entertained, a hope that the 'Rosicrucian' alchemical way through nature might led him even higher."[838] The serach for *prisca sapientia* was truly a search for *prisca theologia*. S. D. Snobelen and Rob Iliffe[839] have amply demonstrated that such a religious reformative scheme run through all of Isaac Newton's scientific works. "The General Scholium serves as public testament to Newton's agendas for natural philosophy and theology, even though these agendas are accessible only to the highly adept reader. Not only is Newton at pains to champion an inductive natural philosophy and to stress that 'to treat God from phenomena is certainly part of natural philosophy', but he implies that a correct understanding of God will jettison Trinitological formulations. Ultimately for him, hypotheses in natural philosophy and religion lead to corruption. Newton's natural philosophy and his heretical theology are also linked by this methodology. Just as a humble and inductive reading of the Book of *Nature* leads one to the Creator, so a humble and inductive reading of the Book of *Scripture* leads one to the One True God of the Bible. The two reformations come together in the General Scholium."[840]

The anti-royalist and anti-clerical republican ideology maintained that the original knowledge of a universal matter, the common substance to all bodies and forms, was revealed to Moses along with authentic monotheistic revelation.[841] The same universal knowledge was given to Jesus and his disciples, but was corrupted by the Roman Church and Constantinian politics. The knowledge was transmitted in parables, secret metaphors, stories and tales and was preserved by the Arabs, especially from the ninth century to the thirteenth century, in a figurative symbolic language. Therefore, comprehension of Arabic neoplatonic and hermetical manuscripts such as those of Jabir bin Hayyan were essential to decipher the occult knowledge of alchemy.[842] The mystical knowledge of Kabbalah, Arabic Neoplatonism and hermetic corpus were essential to access the original *Respublica Mosaica* and *Historia Monotheistica*. Deborah E. Harkness observed that "Newton believed that such knowledge could be increased by consulting ancient authorities who lived and worked when human understanding had been less corrupted by the consequences of Adam's Fall. Newton hoped that his search through ancient texts would yield a true religion and a true natural philosophy, both of which would help to increase human understanding of the natural world as well as the divine."[843]

Near Eastern Knowledge and Biblical Hermeneutics

Newton, following his Cambridge predecessors and colleagues, did just that. "In 1632, the English theologian Joseph Mede proposed a new avenue for interpreting a text whose importance, for him and others, was literally worldhistorical. The biblical Apocalypse, Mede announced, should be read with the help of a Near Eastern book of ancient dream interpretations attributed to 'an Arab' called Achmet. Once it was understood that John's prophecies were, on one level, an accurate prediction of the course of world political history, Achmet's book of symbols allowed the attentive reader to cut with confidence through the Apocalypse's morass of bloody seas, horned beasts, and astronomical prodigies to determine exactly what part of John's prophecy was past and what was yet to come."[844] Achmet's book and interpretations reflected the authentic *prisca sapientia*.[845] "Achmet's Egyptians, Persians, and Indians should carry the same exegetical weight as the Greek-speaking Jews who translated the Septuagint, the Aramaic speakers who made the Targums, or even the Arabic speakers of Maimonides' Spain."[846] Mede equated Arabian Achmet's works with Prophet Joseph's dream interpretation expertise, explained the Hebrew Bible through Achmet's works and interpreted the Apocalypes with Achmet's symbolism. "If the Hebrew Bible could form a footnote for Achmet, Mede was quite ready to turn Joseph and Achmet together into a footnote for the Apocalypse."[847] Achmet became the established authority throughout the seventeenth and eighteenth centuries. "Indeed, Achmet's rapid rise to canonical stature – in the writings of Henry More, Isaac Newton, Charles Daubuz, William Warburton, and others – suggests that he answered a keenly felt discursive need for contemporary English Protestants who would explain the meanings of Biblical prophecy."[848] Henry More, Newton and other English theologian's techniques of dealing with Biblical prophecies were completely shaped by Joseph Mede, and their dependence upon Achmet was confessedly visible.[849] Richard Popkin and others have amply demonstrated this fact.[850] Newton considered himself a heir to Mede in millenaristic knowledge and biblical interpretations.[851] His sole dependence upon Achmet can be gauged from the following statement: "Now although these interpretations by their analogy with one another & resemblance to the things signified, may seem plain enough, yet that nothing be wanting to establish them, I shall further show their consent with the scriptures, & also with the translation of the Chalde Paraphrast & with the ancient doctrin of the Eastern interpreters (of Dreams) as it is recorded by Achmet an Arabian out of the ancient monuments of Ægypt Persia & India. For since these nations anciently bordering upon the Hebrews had great affinity with them both in Language & manners, & therefore wee scruple not to learn from them the use of words & phrases in the scripture, much less need we scruple to learn from them the use of figurative expressions wherin their severall nations were much better agreed than in the language of the common people. For the Prophets without doubt spake in a dialect then commonly known to the more understanding sort of men, & many of their types & figures which are unusuall & difficult to us appear by these records of Achmet to have been very familiar to those Eastern nations; at least among the interpreters. And therefore esteeming it pertinent to show the consent of our interpretations with the doctrin of these interpreters next after their consent with the scriptures: I proceed."[852]

The "Chalde Paraphrast" refers to the Aramaic Targums, paraphrases of the Hebrew Pentatuech (Five Books of Moses) into Aramaic. Achmet the Arabian refers to Achmet, son of Seirem, whose *Oneirocriticon* was a compendium of dream-symbols and their various meanings to aid in the prognostic interpretation of a ruler or official's dreams.[853] It was actually a Christian Greek work based on Arabic dream books, as Maria Mavroudi showed,[854] but was wrongly attributed to and printed in the name of Ahmad bin Sirien, the famous dream interpreter of Abbasid Caliph Mamun. Mede, More and Newton knew it as the original work of Achmet bin Siriem. They used the work as their gateway to unpacking the symbolic, figurative biblical language and prophecies. Achmet and Middle Eastern language, wisdom and knowledge were authoritative, established and authentic to Newton.[855] Paul T. Greenham observed that" For Newton, this symbolic prophetic language, the 'Prophetic dialect' was the key to understanding the prophetic texts of Scripture, which were themselves keys to the rest of Scripture. In his later discussion of the 'Prophetick ffigures,' in Keynes Ms. 5 (1680s), Newton stated that 'John did not write in one language, Daniel in another, Isaiah in third, & the rest in others peculiar to them selves; but they all wrote in one & the same mystical language as well known without doubt to the sons of the Prophets as the Hieroglyphic language of the Egyptians to their Priests.' Thus, 'He that would understand a book written in a strange language must first learn the language & if he would understand it well he must learn the language perfectly.'"[856] That language of both *prisca sapientia and prisca theologia* was consolidated in the Middle Eastern manuscripts like Achmet's. Decoding that language and proper understanding of the scriptures, natural sciences and Apocalypes would usher the prosperous millennium increasing human knowledge, opulence and spirituality. Middle Eastern alchemy, sciences, language, wisdom and theology were central to such a universal reformation of decayed Christendom. In short, Newton's natural sciences were as much shaped by the Middle Eastern wisdom and alchemy as was his Biblical hermeneutics and theology.[857]

This reformative scheme of knowledge was a reaction to the unintelligible, absolutist, persecutory dogmatic theology of both Catholic and Protestant Churches and its replacement with mystical, tolerant, alchemical, rational and observational natural knowledge.[858] The simple Unitarian republicanism of Islam was the true heir to *Respublica*

Mosaica and *Historia Monotheistica*[859] and it was facilitated by the Oriental manuscripts solicited and transported by the Levant Company chaplains, consuls and merchants. The Levant and East India Companies enabled economic, intellectual, mystical and religious enlightenment by transmitting Oriental knowledge, ideas, culture and wisdom.[860] They were integral part of "global early modernity,"[861] "connected histories"[862] and Enlightenment.[863] The British Atlantic world was a "kaleidoscope movement of people, goods, and ideas."[864]

Overseas Trading Companies and Cross-cultural Diffusions

The Levant and East India Company facilitated such a trans-cultural diffusion of Eastern knowledge and the travellers supplemented it with their travelogues. Foreign travellers to the Muslim Orient were given fellowship of the English Royal Society because of their knowledge and experience of Orient. For instance, the French Huguenote traveller Jean Chardin[865] settled in England in 1681 as a result of Protestant persecutions by Louis XIV. He was immediately appointed court jewller by Charles II because of his knowledge of Oriental jewllery, knighted at Whitehall, married the daughter of a famous merchant and elected a fellow of the Royal Society. "Upon his arrival in London, Jean Chardin immediately became part of the most prestigious scientific society formed in Europe. He received a visit from John Evelyn, Christopher Wren, and John Hoskins, who asked him to become a member of the Royal Society formed in 1660. The first written trace of Chardin's presence in London is his name, which is first recorded in the minutes of the July 8 (or 18), 1680 meetings, in the Council Minutes of the Royal Society of London for Improving of natural Knowledge. It is within this learned society, devoted to science, that Chardin started his writing project on Persia in the seventeenth-century scientific tradition."[866] He was involved in East India Company business, was sent to Holland as Charles II's envoy and became an authority in London on a number of scientific fields. "His knowledge of exotic drugs, of Asian markets, and of the flora and fauna of the East Indies was unsurpassed in England."[867] He closely interacted with John Locke, Isaac Newton and other fellows of the Royal Society, and was closest to Robert Boyle and John Evelyn. "He discussed his thoughts on Persia with other fellows such as Isaac Newton and Samuel Pepys, and it is documented that he participated in the new scientific tradition that was being elaborated on by the fellows of the recently founded Royal Society. Even if he did not frequent the Royal Society very assiduously, he was in close contact with its intellectual production."[868] This shows how valuable knowledge of Muslim Orient was to the King, bishops, intellectuals and merchants. England was not yet a power to be reckoned with and Orientalism was a prized subject. It was very different type of Orientalism[869] than the later nineteenth-century Orientalism analysed and criticised by Edward Said in his famous 1978 book *Orientalism*.[870] The England of the seventeenth century was importing Eastern knowledge and wisdom along with silk, pepper and cotton. The Orient was a source of Occident's rise to power and global expansion, and the Levant and East India Companies played a vital role in this revolutionary transition.

The Levant Company greatly profited from the silk and spice trade; the profit was worth the perilous treacherous trip from London to far distant Muslim cities for these very young wealthy English merchants. The journey was long, dangerous and full of risks; it took them months and years, and countless hurdles, to make it to the Muslim East.[871] Many died on the way. Richard Grassby noted that "itinerant and overseas merchants were particularly exposed to infectious diseases, like cholera, typhus, yellow fever, malaria, dysentery and tuberculosis. Two-thirds of the factors in Persia died within two years and in India, as Ovington put it, two monsoons were the age of man [...] It was merchant shipping which carried the pandemic diseases; the cemeteries in commercial outposts all over the world bore silent witness to careers cut short. Approximately 20 per cent of merchants whose wills were proved at Canterbury died abroad or at sea, though many of these would have lived a normal span."[872] The relative despair and disgrace at home, the allure of the prosperous Muslim East, and prospects of transformation and destiny propelled these rich Londoners into long and perilous journies.

Foreign lands with strange people, culture, climate and religion were quite risky. "Merchants who lived as resident aliens [...] faced political coups, rebellions, confiscation and requisition, interrogation as heretics and massacre by lynch mobs. When travelling, they could be poisoned by foreign competitors, captured by pirates and murdered or enslaved, kidnapped by mutineers, imprisoned, often under harsh conditions, by foreign governments as spies or hostages. Even in self-governing settlements overseas, they lived behind fortifications;

factors were expected to defend their ships and goods and some died in the attempt."[873] Shipwrecks, piracy and captivity did not subside but increased by the middle of the seventeenth century. The financial losses were cataclysmic. "Some 390 ships were lost, 1625-30, 700, 1672-3, 4,000, 1688-97 and some 3,250 during the War of the Spanish Succession; the *Johannah* went down with £70,000 in specie and the loss of the Levant fleet in 1693 was catastrophic."[874] The financial situation in London must have been dire, and the prospects of overseas profit must have been tantalising, for these rich Englishmen to go through these perfidious ordeals. The present-day Muslim world's migration crises and the allure of the West are a sort of rehearsal of the early modern European endeavours. The dangers involved in the journey were worthwhile due to the prospect of profit.

The Levant Company "quickly became the richest and most powerful of the London-based companies with the resources and authority to appoint and fund the English ambassador to the Sublime Porte."[875] These traders were as much involved in the business community of London as they were engaged with the merchants of Aleppo and Istanbul. For instance, "The merchants who engaged in the Aleppo trade represented some of the wealthiest and most influential families in London and the same names keep cropping up in the annals of the Company as directors, consuls and factors. For a century the Levant trade was immensely profitable with English woollen cloth and tin being traded initially for pepper and later for cotton and silk. Aleppo was the source of raw silk, which was then processed in England. In 1600 three hundred people were employed in London in manufacturing silk cloth. By 1640 this number had grown to ten thousand. However, as English trade with India and the Far East increased so the Levant trade waned and petered out by the late 1700s. Throughout its 244 year history the English Levant Company had strong connections with the Church of England."[876] Its merchants supported the Church establishment and its chaplains supplied the Church leadership and English intelligentsia with information about Ottomans, Islam, Eastern churches, culture and trade. Quite a few of the overseas merchants' children went on to become bishops in the Church of England, and maintained close relations with the merchant community. Some of the known Latitudinarian bishops' close relations with known dissenting merchants are well-documented. For instance, Anglican Archbishop John Tillotson (1630-1694) was son of a puritan clothier and a tutor of Edmond Prideaux's son. Prideaux was Oliver Cromwell's attorney general, the Commonwealth leader who abolished the Church of England. Tillotson was a fellow of the Royal Society and a Latitudinarian with rational, heterodox, Arminian tendeniec.[877] Due to his associations with Unitarian merchant Thomas Firmin, Stephen Nye, John Locke and others Tillotson was accused of Socinianism, the charge he denied in 1693.[878]

Many of the overseas merchants developed heterodox beliefs especially anti-Trinitarian republican and pluralist thoughts as a result of their interactions and discussions with their Eastern colleagues. Even the most conservatives among them harboured anti-clerical and anti-persecutory ideas, and strongly supported the reformation of Anglican Church and monarchy.[879] Their wealth, opulence and long international exposure to Eastern Christians, Hindus, Buddhists and Muslims convinced them of universally common moral elements in world religions, particularities of regional religious traditions - including Christianity - and the overall goodness of humanity. The Church claims of universality, monopoly of truth and salvation and specific role in the salvation through Christ were all analysed, debated and dissected. The Muslim interfaith and intrafaith tolerance, acceptance and mutual appreciation were especially noted, appreciated and propagated by these traders on their return to England. This pluralistic republicanism was Islam's gift to the persecutory Europe in general, and England in particular. The same Islamic republicanism became the subject of public outcry in England throughout the turbulent seventeenth century. The radical as well as moderate religious, intellectual and political leaders adopted it as their life mission and aspired goal, as Humberto Garcia has well demonstrated.[880]

The Allure of Islamic World and English Identity Formation

The Muslim Empires of the sixteenth and seventeenth centuries served as models of relative prosperity, diversity, mercantilism, cosmopolitanism and republicanism. The Mughal Empire was the richest empire on earth when Sir Thomas Roe, the first English ambassador arrived there. "It was certainly responsible for a much larger share of world trade than any comparable zone and the weight of its economic power even reached Mexico, whose textile manufacture suffered a crisis of 'de-industrialisation' due to Indian cloth imports. In comparison, England then had just 5 per cent of India's population and was producing just under 3 per cent of the world's manufactured goods. A good proportion of the profits on this found its way to the Mughal exchequer in Agra, making the Mughal Emperor, with an income of around £100 million, by far the richest monarch in the world."[881] The Mughal capital was perhaps the largest city on Earth, with a population of 2 million. Jesuit Fr Antonio Monserrate noted that with regards either to size, population, or wealth it was second to none. "'Their cities are crowded with merchants, who gather from all over Asia. There is no art or craft which is not practised there.' Between 1586 and 1605, European silver flowed into the Mughal heartland at the astonishing rate of 18 metric tons a year, for as William Hawkins observed, 'all nations bring coyne and carry away commodities for the same'. For their grubby contemporaries in the West, stumbling around in their codpieces, the silk-clad Mughals, dripping in jewels, were the living embodiment of wealth and power – a meaning that has remained impregnated in the word 'mogul' ever since."[882] The Ottoman Empire was no less splendid and imposing. "Istanbul, described by Fernand Braudel as an 'urban monster', had a population of 700,000 at the end of the sixteenth century. Naples reached 280,000 by 1595. Henry Blount said of Cairo that it was "populous beyond all proportion." In 1600, London's population was approximately 200,000 (and growing fast, thanks to immigration from other parts of the kingdom). But other English ports from which these Mediterranean-bound travellers sailed were tiny in comparison; Bristol's population hovered around 12,000 at the turn of the century."[883] English, French and Dutch merchants were stunned by the diversity, prosperity and breadth of the Ottoman, Mughal and Persian Empires. To the English travellers the Ottoman Empire was "the greatest that is, or perhaps that ever was from the beginning."[884] Rationalism, commercialism, cosmopolitanism, capitalism and pluralism, which Max Weber and others have identified as the bedrocks of modernity, were all practiced by the Mughals, Ottomans and Persians before the seventeenth-century European national states as Jack Goody has amply demonstrated.[885]

Islam and Muslims played an important role in the rise of the modern West, especially Great Britain. The Britain of the early sixteenth century, as seen above, was an isolated Isle with limited economic reach, systems and resources. Its constant warfare with its Catholic neighbour France and Protestant neighbour Dutch Republic in addition to Habsburg monarchy's hostilities had further drained its resources and potentials. Britain's opening to the Muslim world released that pressure and opened the doors of prosperity and success. The accumulated wealth, cross-cultural experiences, ideas, institutions and practices helped in stabilising Britain and propelled it to its later imperial heights. The overseas traders played the role of an intermediary and reaped the fruits of their hard work at home.

By 1650s, the overseas traders, especially the Levant-East India trading complex, had risen to the highest leadership of the London merchant community. Making their fortunes from the Ottoman, Safvid and Mughal Empires for over the past seventy years, by the 1650s they had become greatly rich and influential. They had encountered a Muslim world which was far freer, open and pluralistic than the closed, uniform and persecutory England. They tried to incorporate Muslim religious tolerance, commercialism and egalitarianism to English society, playing an important role in the civil war as well as in the Cromwell Commonwealth.[886] John J. Schroeder noted that "it is clearly evident that London was of paramount importance in the financing of the First Civil War. London was not only a wealthy city, but a city that had a ward organisation that could be used for assessment and collection and which the authorities were willing to use. London also controlled the surrounding suburbs and countryside, the wealthiest area in the kingdom. Loans, willing or not, could be extracted here on a large scale, and significant contributions could be obtained from the livery companies. London was the administrative center for and the richest source of assessments, sequestrations, and compounding. It furnished trained administrators for the excise and the customs, and although these men used their offices for their personal profit, they also furnished money when Parliament needed it. Although it was the New Model Army that finally brought the war to a close at Marston Moor and Naseby, there never would have been a New Model Army without the gold of London."[887] For instance, the anti-Royalist Lord Mayor, Isaac Penington, the Levant Company Governer and a Puritan, raised a huge amount of £130,000 in a short span of time (September of 1642) at the request of the Model Army. "A further £100,000 was raised in London through loans in 1644, but by 1645, harassed by taxes and assessments, Londoners were advancing money only for very

special projects - for undertakings that would contribute to an immediate ending of the war."[888] Alderman John Langham, a Levant and East
India Company man who lived and traded in Turkey, was assigned
treasureship of the Common Council and collected huge amounts in
taxes for the Army. "The customs, like the excise, were put into private hands; Aldermen Thomas Andrews, John Fowke, and Richard
Chambers, and five London merchants were named as collectors of
all customs in England."[889] Thomas Andrews was deputy governor of
the East India Company (1657), John Fowke had adventures with East
India Company and Richard Chamber was a Turkophile who admired
and appreciated Turkish business ethics and severely criticised English business practices. Chamber's seditious assertations that 'the merchants are in no part of the world so screwed and wrung as in England;
that in Turkey they have more encouragement" were noted and punished by King Charles I.[890] After the Revolution he was elected Alderman in 1642 and London Sheriff in 1644. The Levant and East India
Company merchants played a leadership role during the Civil War and
Commonwealth Republic. The famous historian Robert Brenner noted that "indeed, in its formal republicanism and its relative religious
toleration, as well as in its militant commercial imperialism, the Commonwealth was the near-embodiment of their interests and ideals."[891]

The Commonwealth Republic, along with its republican liberties,
would become the aspired goal and national slogan of the 1680s radicals and Whigs, and merchants would be central to that pluralistic
struggle for inclusivism. The merchants, along with the gentry, benefited the most from the English Revolution, as Christopher Hill has
demonstrated.[892] Religion played a decisive role in the English Civil
War and resultant Commonwealth revolution. "While there were a
host of economic, political and social factors contributing to the civil
wars, it was religious issues that primarily drove the conflict."[893] The
Commonwealth revolution was a religious revolution[894] against popery, idolatry and religious persecutions. John Morrill, the renowned
British historian of the English Civil War, suggested that the English
civil war was "the last of Europe's wars of religion."[895] The Revolution
proscribed all the perceived monuments of superstition and idolatry
introduced by the Anglican Church.[896] The merchant groups were all
for liberty of conscience, and leaned towards the republican pluralism
of the Muslim empires. Their independent religious thinking, autono-

mous, voluntary modes of congregations, like the Ottoman mosques, helped in breaking the monopoly of Anglican Church hierarchy and increased their own participation in congregational matters.[897] The early English and Scottish Presbyterianism (from the Presbyterian form of church government, which is governed by the representative assemblies of elders)[898] and its later radicalism and Unitarianism were reflections of Eastern experiences.[899]

The merchants demanded religious tolerance and republicanism like the Ottoman Empire, and pushed towards a freer, less hierarchical society. Cromwell promised religious pluralism, freedom of conscience and republicanism.[900] To some historians such as Samuel Gardiner and Winthrop Jordan, Cromwell was a champion of religious tolerance and the English Revolution was a benchmark on the high road to liberalism and pluralism. His religious settlements were antithesis of the Catholic and Anglican establishments' severe persecutory policies.[901] With the Army victory, religious independence became semi-official state policy.[902] Initially the Church of England was abolished, independent, autonomous congregations were allowed and religious diversity was tolerated to an extent.[903] To the royalists and conservatives this was an Islamic, Ottoman and republican revolution which destroyed the Christian Church and divine right monarchy. Cromwell was behaving like Muhammad[904] and the Puritans and other dissenting sects were infidels bent on their international Ottoman hegemonic conspiracy. To Cromwell tolerant, pluralistic religious outlook was a reflection of "Godly Rule", an achievement of the highest level and Cromwell was Machiavellian Godly Prince, a good constable and a Constantine.[905]

Cromwell was undecided about the manner of government causing constitutional instability and political anxiety.[906] His initial aggressive commercial policies, novel religious outlook and anti-Anglican and monarchic establishment directives turned the old society upside-down. It was not free for all society though. Persecution of religious dissent was still there, but lesser than the previous periods. The imprisonment of open anti-Trinitarian Unitarian John Biddle and later banishment with pension instead of hanging well demonstrates the difference between Cromwell and Charles I. The relative "freedom of those years did allow a wide variety of religious, political and social views to circulate across society [...] while in 1640 just 22 tracts were printed, in 1642 the total was nearly 2,000. And the potential of these to subvert good order was not lost on those concerned to see it upheld, one writer noting in 1641 that the 'ink-squittering treacherous pamphlets' produced by sects operating outside of the established church 'are the main prop and pillar to uphold the sovereign unsavoury power of their factious conventicles.'"[907] William M. Lamont noted that "The Civil War left a vacuum at the centre: one that the Presbyterians had wished to fill with their discipline, and one that their Erastian opponents had wished to fill with Parliamentary action. Now for the first time – under Cromwell- there was a *deliberate* vacuum at the centre. Cromwell did not use this authority to impose doctrine, but he *did* use his authority to prevent others from imposing *their* doctrines. What one writer has described as 'a curious kind of ecclesiastical anarchy' prevailed, in which there was wide variety in the doctrine preached and in the organisation adopted."[908]

Commonwealth Radicalism

The ensuing religious, social, economic and political instability brought an explosion of divergent radical religious groups such as the Quakers, Baptists, Diggers, Ranters, Fifth Monarchists, Muggletonians, Levellers and Seekers raising radical questions about Christianity, Church, state and society.[909] The socio-religious storm was supplemented by the overseas trade establishments and their changed perceptions of role of religion and society. The overseas traders shared their personal experiences of the Muslim world and how religious freedom and pluralism contributed to freedom of conscience, social cohesion, peace, security and prosperity. The radical religious groups popularised freedom of conscience and hatred of imposed religious conformity, clergy and monarchy.[910] To Orthodoxy, the Quakers and Fifth Monarchits were anti Christian radicals like Muhammad.[911] By the 1650s they turned English society upside-down, revolting against almost all established religious values and social norms. Religious tolerance and republicanism were the declared common goals of all radical groups and these egalitarian/republican goals were disdained by the monarchists, High Churchmen and conservative nobility. The Army kept things under control, while radical merchant groups and radical religious sects supported the Army.

The early seventeenth century was also the time of cultural and material revolution. The Levant and East India Company merchants had radically transformed the English culture and society with their

Eastern imports. The "trade in material goods from the Islamic world changed life in early modern Europe [...] Currants and carpets, coffee and tobacco, silk and cotton, horses and weaponry, were all commodities that had wide cross-cultural circulation and influence [...] tobacco, sugar, coffee and tea; currants, raisins, sweet wine and oil; cotton, wool and silk, both raw and finished; carpets and cushions; dyes, spices and drugs; jewels and precious stones; saltpetre for gunpowder [...] members of the landed and leisured classes in England were entertaining themselves by dressing up in 'Turkish habits.'"[912] Islamic, culture, habits and imports were everywhere; countless Indian, Persian and Ottoman words, both good and bad, were incorporated into English language.[913] Richard Eaton noted that "This was the height of the so-called 'calico craze', when India's cotton textiles were in feverish demand in England and across Europe generally. Indeed, England's sustained commercial connection with India is seen in the many textile-related Indian words that entered the English language in this period – for example, dungaree, chintz, seersucker, calico, pyjamas, shawl, khaki, cummerbund, taffeta, jaconet and bandana."[914]

England became obsessed with Oriental stuff. "Imports from the Islamic world were changing the ways that people in England lived. Drinking coffee, imported from the Ottoman Empire, and tea, imported from the Far East, became national habits. Textiles—English wool, Persian silk, Turkey carpets, Indian cottons—were crucial commodities linking people in Britain with residents of the Islamic world that changed the ways people dressed themselves and how they decorated their houses."[915] The profit-driven merchants imported every profitable item and the closed hierarchical English society became intoxicated with Eastern novelties. The material, cultural invasion and "Oriental Obsession" caused anxieties, especially to the conservative royalists. The Indian cotton, designs, patterns, tea, tobacco, Persian carpets and luxury items and Turkish attires, silk and coffee all amplified the English uniformist and moralist anxieties. "The reasons for those anxieties are perhaps not hard to find, for the consumption of these novel and addictive drugs swiftly and irrevocably introduced new patterns of economic, social, and cultural activity that challenged traditional ways of life, redesigned urban spaces, and opened up unprecedented forms of public encounter and sociability."[916] New eating, drinking and dressing habits modified English identity, social positions, ethical values, religious ideas, business principles, aesthetic qualities and socio-religious connotations. The pious moralists railed against this revolution with religious zeal, obsession and weapons.[917] They connected the Eastern importations, imitations and domestications with Islamic religion, imputing centuries of fears, animosities and stereotype to loath the English consumer with Islamic derogatory epithets. The pervasiveness of cheap, colourful Eastern textiles, with huge varieties of patterns, earned their utmost scorn. "The traditional English textile trades of the Tudor period were transformed by contact with the Islamic world. Both an increasing range and quantity of imported raw and finished materials, as well as developments in production and design techniques, brought work and wealth, comfort and colour, to the daily lives of Britons across the social ranks. Between 1590 and 1630, the number of women working in silk production within greater London was estimated to have risen from 300 to 14,000."[918] The gentry were as addicted to these relatively cheap colourful patterns, as were the masses;[919] the textile revolution[920] diminished traditional social classes, status and practices. "What one historian has called a '"feverish" demand for indiennes,' or painted Indian cottons, raged throughout the century and sparked off predictable controversies. Calico threatened domestic industries and was considered morally suspect since Eastern imports were invariably luxuries, and luxuries threatened traditional practices 'and hence [...] virtue itself.'"[921]

The English public and private spaces were inundated with Islamic imports. "We saw our Persons of Quality dress'd in Indian Carpets, which but a few Years before their Chamber-Maids would have thought too ordinary for them; the Chints were advanc'd from lying on their Floors to their Backs, from the Foot-Cloth to the Petticoat [...] Nor was this all, but it crept into our Houses, our Closets, and Bed-Chambers, Curtains, Cushions, Chairs, and at last beds themselves were nothing but Callicoes."[922] Calico and printed cotton fashions became popular all over Europe, including the Queen of England. "Calicoes, printed cottons, became fashionable throughout Europe in the late seventeenth century, so much so that Daniel Defoe exclaimed that even the queen of England was wearing the cotton prints that had ordinarily been reserved for bed covers and for children and maids."[923] Defoe noted that "these people's obsessions with products from India has now reached the painted calicos, which were formerly used for quilted blankets and the clothing of lower class children. Today they are even used by our finer women. The power of fashion is so great that we see persons of rank wearing Indian cloths even though only the maids were allowed to use them before. The queen herself has been seen in Chinese silk and calico."[924] Seventeenth-century England was modernised by Mughal, Persian and Ottoman fashion, knowledge and modernity.[925]

The Levant and East India company businessmen justified the change due to economic benefits and financial gains; their influence and profits continuously soared due to public consumption and support. These controversies initiated discussions about legitimacy of wealth, luxury, profit and commercialism. The merchants justified their worldly material projects by quoting the Islamic religious concepts of lawful earnings, wealth accumulation, expression and circulation, while the English conservatives challenged the so-perceived anti-Christian devilish material impulses of the Levant and East India company merchants with talks and sermons against luxury and for humble living and earnings. The otherworldly Christian teachings and saintly models were implied to stop the immoral Eastern invasion but the consumer culture, inner strife and religio-political past and persecutions of orthodoxy impeded the progress. Gradually the religious dissent, radicalism and plurality gained strength, popularity and resources. The merchant community stood for liberties, liberal socio-economic and political policies while the orthodoxy vouched for uniformity, humility, good moral English past and Christian way of life. Seventeenth-century England was the Saudi Arabia of the twentieth century, and the English orthodoxy was like the council of conservative *ulamas* (Muslim scholars) hell-bent against Western and American cultural invasion. The imported commercial consumerism and aggressive advertisement culture was too threatening to the old cause, the English Christian way of life.

The resourceful and influential London merchant community was divided into two main groups; the upper tier of the Levant and East India establishments were pro-monarchy conservatives who supported stability and peace, while the middle-class lower tier radical group aided anti monarchy revolution. However, both groups agreed on religious pluralism, pro-trade policies, as well as less formal, less ritualistic, less authoritative and low-church ecclesiastic formulations. The Elizabethan strict policies of required Sunday service attendance, religious police and courts flogging of minor infractions, hefty fines and imprisonments were no longer acceptable. Faith was a private matter, left to individual conscience and incentives like the Ottoman world. Business deals were not dependent upon religious affinities or uniformity; offices and public positions were to be given to the most qualified and effective individuals, irrespective of their religion or spiritual levels. Such was the Ottoman, Safvid and Mughal culture where Jews, Christian Arminians and Greek Orthodox all were active partners in the market economy, national and international trade. The English society had very few foreigners and businessmen. Cromwell permitted Jewish resettlement in England (1655-56) after a long absence with the hope of converting them to Christianity. They were still hated and socially cornered. That suffocating, persecutory and monolithic England needed to change. The merchants and radicals insisted on a pluralistic society with freedom of worship, movement and opportunities. They pushed for an egalitarian, republican and freer society like the Ottomans. They got push back from nobility and conservative royalists. The author of "The Famous Tragedie King Charles I" bellowed:

"No marvell they lap bloud as milke and glory
To be recorded, villaines, upon Story.
"For having kill'd their King, where will they stay
"That thorow God, and Majestie, make way,
"Throwing the Nobles, and the Gentry downe
"Levelling, all distinctions, to the Crowne.[926]

Cromwell wanted union of believers and not pluralism or tolerance of differing beliefs.[927]

Horrified by the socio-religious radicalism, instability and internal warfare between Puritans, radical Protestants, Presbyterians, Quakers, Catholics and Anglican conservatives Cromwell shifted towards authoritative impulses. The hierarchical nobility was alarmed by the classless egalitarian, pluralistic designs of merchants and radical secretaries. This radicalism was stifled by the hierarchical nobility with the help of Cromwell Commonwealth oligarchy. "If they had not been impeded in this, England might have passed straight to something like the political settlement of 1688 - Parliamentary sovereignty, limited monarchy, imperialist foreign policy, a world safe for businessmen to make profits in."[928] The history of England from the middle to the end of seventeenth century was a history of nobility's struggles against the Popish, Louis XIV-like divine right monarchy's overarching authoritarianism on the one hand and merchants, middle-class and radical dissenters' zeal for real democratic, republican empowerment of people or popular sovereignty on the other. Both extremes were detrimental to hierarchical nobility's authority and previleges and they confronted them with enthusiastic unison. The so-called Glorious Revolution was not that revolutionary for radicals or popular sovereignty.[929] It was a transition of power from one monarch James II to a joint monarchy of Mary and William III. It was the victory of nobility (parliament) over popish monarchy, but not the triumph of popular sovereignty over parliament and moanrchy. It did not abolish monarchy, but only limited its scope and powers; it just restored old rights and previleges of nobility and did not initiate new ones.[930] It did not grant religious tolerance to dissenters, but persecuted them.

Many overseas traders and radicals were for popular sovereignty and religious tolerance instead. Both groups of overseas traders (elites as well as middle class radicals) frequently quoted the Ottoman pluralistic model, its ensuing socio-political stability and economic prosperity. They were fully supported by the American colony merchants. In fact, the later American merchant confederation took over the radical leadership and pushed for more autonomy and liberty. The so-called pluralistic Islamic republicanism and revolutionary egalitarian agenda of the 1650s continued throughout the latter half of the seventeenth century, but mostly clandestinely. Radicals such as Henry Stubbe, who fought in the Crowell Army and was a protégé of the republican Sir Henry Vane the Younger (1613-1662) (the Massachusetts Bay Colony's governor, the leading republican parliamentarian of the Civil War and a confidant of Cromwell) was a connection between the American and Eastern merchant's republicanism and Turkism. He defended religious tolerance based on economic factors and heterodox, dissenting traders' roles and contributions to English economy. He would keep the egalitarian fire alive till his death in 1676. The radical pluralist republicans such as Shaftesbury, the first Earl, his protégé John Locke; Algernon Sidney, Lord William Russell and other moderate and radical Whigs and dissenters such as the Socinians and Unitarians would lead the movement to the end of the seventeenth century and beyond.[931]

On the other hand, the High Church monarchist party vehemently opposed religious pluralism as leading to anarchy and insisted upon religio-political uniformity of One King, One Church and One Nation. "Religious toleration is the greatest of all evils, thought Thomas Edwards in 1646. It will bring in first scepticism in doctrine and looseness of life, then atheism. If a toleration be granted, all preaching will not keep heresies out. 'No man knows where these sectaries will stop or stay, or to what principles they will keep.' Later he wrote the considered words: 'We are in a far worse condition than when the enemy was in the height of his success and victories at the taking of Bristol, or ever since the Parliament began.'"[932] They blamed Cromwell as the new rabble-rouser "Muhammad,"[933] his tolerant religious policies and permission of publication of English Quran as Turkish conspiracy against the Christian religion and nation.[934]

The Cromwell Commonwealth failed to fulfill its promised religious pluralism and republicanism[935], and Cromwell became the Lord Protector of England[936] dissolving the Rump Parliament by force in 1653 and imposing his strict policies in a military,[937] dictatorial fashion,[938] "leading to a restoration of the rule of the gentry, and then of King and bishops in 1660."[939] The radical theology of religious radicals and radical republicanism of political activists was too threatening to the gentry's desire for status quo. John Milton, the great supporter of pluralism and republic, wrote his *The Readie & Easie Way* [940] but his Paradise was Lost[941], as will be discussed in details in the later part of this book. Cromwell died in 1658, but his son Richard was not cut for leadership[942] and 1659 saw enormous anarchy and persecutions.[943] The Levant-East India trading complex, and even radical Whigs like Shaftesbury, turned their loyalties to monarchical restoration for the sake of stability and balance of power,[944] went to Holland to invite the King and helped in restoring Charles II to the English throne[945] with promises of religious toleration, freedom of conscience and indulgences. De Krey has observed that the "restoration of monarchy in England was as much an effort to re-establish 'parliamentary government' as it was an effort to re-establish the crown […] The royalist settlements in England, Scotland, and Ireland were partial and punitive settlements that failed, almost from the beginning, to resolve the political and religious instability they were intended to overcome."[946]

Restoration of Monarchy and Dialectical Struggles

The Restoration was facilitated by the republicans and radicals to ensure parliamentarian rule and Protestant tradition. It was an extension of the republican agenda of the 1640s. "What was restored in England in 1660 was, in fact, the unsteady partnership between crown and parliament that the Long Parliament had sought to impose on Charles I in 1641, after a decade without sessions. The English Restoration may have been a reaction against sectarianism, republicanism, the Army, and the fiscal excesses and 'arbitrary government' of partial parliaments; but it was not a reaction against much of what the Long Parliament had achieved, in its first session, against Charles I's mode of government."[947] The monarchy returned in 1660 bringing Charles II in power after nine years of exile in France, Netherland and Spain.[948] The King showed an unrelenting hatred for his father's murderers; he had Cromwell's corpse dug up, hung in chains, and beheaded. Cromwell was defeated, but the love for republicanism, rationalism, religious tolerance and freedom were not. The Revolution and Interregnum had intellectually and permanently transformed England, and English society was divided into numerous ideological groups. The religious and political radicals demanded abolition of Anglican Church and divine right monarchy, restoration of religious tolerance and popular sovereignty. The religio-political moderates strove to establish a Venetian-type oligarchy where parliament, gentry and merchants played active roles in limiting the Crown and Church's authority. The center-right conservatives could live with a mildly authoritarian Church and monarchy for the sake of continuity, stability and peace but limiting it by the parliamentarian authority. Both groups advocated religious tolerance, rationalism and low-church natural theology. The extreme right royalists attempted to establish divine right monarchy, High Anglican Church, supernatural dogmatic theology and elaborate ritualism. The far-left radical republicanism and popular sovereignty were defeated due to their destablising effects; stability, security and peace were preffered through restoration of a relatively limited monarchy. The ensuing warfare between the parliament and Crown resulted in the Glorious Revolution of 1688 and later constitutional victory of the parliament that heralded the enlightenment. Science, enlightenment and modernity were all products of English Revolution and Interrgenum. Christopher Hill noted that "the radicals were defeated, but science survived. 'All before 1650 is ancient,' the historian of technology declares, 'all after modern.'"[949]

Charles II promised religious tolerance but could not deliver it; he was an opportunist who rode popular sentiments for his political gains. The monarchy was demystified due to the English Civil War and Charles I's execution. The Crown maintained public support with an image of moderation, respect for constitution, parliament, local governments, civil liberties, urban citizenship and charity. This was just the façade. For Charles II and a number of his powerful courtiers "toleration was a tactic for controlling the population, and it was usually wedded to a long-term conformist policy."[950] He also restored the Anglican Church lock, stock and barrel, again an opportunistic move to galvanise support of Anglicans and preserve his divine right prerogatives. The alliance between the King and Anglican Church proved fatal for the dissenters. Charles II longed for an authoritative Catholic England just like his father Charles', and his 1662 Act of Uniformity and the 1664 Conventicle Act crushed religious dissent.[951] The Anabaptists, Seekers, Quakers, Fifth Monarchists and Socinians were imprisoned, slaughtered and tortured.[952] In 1672 he flexed his muscles against the parliament, but was resisted by Shaftesbury and Anglicans. After realising his army's disloyalty and parliament's pressure, Charles offered tolerance for both Catholics and Protestant dissenters, excluding radical dissenters such as Socinians and Unitarians. He wanted to release pressure from his Catholic co-religionists by his tolerant policies, along with the Protestant nonconformists to increase support among the Catholics and nonconformist Protestants. The move was blocked by the Anglican Church and Parliament. "For eighteen months he fought for this moderate settlement only to be defeated by the determination of the rigorist Anglican majority in the Cavalier Parliament, by the lukewarmness of his advisers, and by the self-destructive behavior of Richard Baxter and the Puritan leaders."[953] The Parliament enacted the Clarendon Code to shore up the position of the re-established Church of England. "The Church of England was effectively restored as well, with trappings such as church courts. Many Presbyterian and Independent clergymen were ejected from their pulpits, and members of all Protestant churches except the Church of England became known as Nonconformists. Efforts by the king to relieve pressure on Catholics were thwarted by Parliament with measures such as the Test Act of 1673, which required Church of England orthodoxy from all office-holders. Panics such as the Popish Plot of 1678 led to the execution of many Catholics. Much of the rest of this reign and that of James II, who came to the throne in 1685, was spent in jockeying for position between Protestants and Catholics."[954] The decades of the 1670s, according to N. H. Keeble "quickly slipped into disappointment, disillusionment and resentment,"[955] and brought England's old troubles back to the forefront. Socio-political and religious instability were the norm inside England,[956] while outside England the traders and colonisers focused on business and expansion. Religious coercion was the norm inside England, while the Levant and East India company merchants were enjoying religious tolerance and freedom of liberty in the Muslim world. Mark Goldie has stated that "Restoration England was a persecuting society."[957] De Krey observed that the "most violent persecution of Protestants since the 1550s, in both England and Scotland, actually occurred in the mid-1680s. The fact that this persecution was carried out by other Protestants made it no easier for dissenters to bear."[958] Debates about religious tolerance and coercion inundated England during the 1680s. The Crown as well as Anglican Church's insecurity led to severe persecutory policies. A large number of nonconformists and dissenters, over a million according to Algernon Sidney, supported the Whig parliamentarians due to Charles's religious persecutions.[959] The Presbyterians, Independents joined the Baptists, Quakers, Unitarians and Socininas to secure a freer denominational future.

The Anglican Church and Protestant politicians were wary about Charles II's secret Catholic leanings. The patriotic MP's and parliamentarians felt that Protestantism was under siege due to Catholic universal monarchical designs of Louis XIV. Charles II's support of Louis XIV's war of 1772-1774 against the Dutch quicly became unpopular. Many Reformed Protestants, within and without the Anglican Church, maintained that the Anglican clergy also preferred coercive Catholicism over Protestantism. They felt that Charles II was repeating the pro-Catholic authoritarian policies of his executed father. Sir Robert Filmer's pro-divine right *Patriarcha* and Tory authors Sir Roger L'Estrange and John Dryden's royalist wrtings were opposed by the works of John Locke, James Tyrrell, William Penn, Henry Neville, Slingsby Bethel and others. A storm of anti-Catholic and anti-monarchy pamphleteering gripped England during the 1680s. Locke's *Two Treatises of Government* and *Letter Concerning Toleration* were the products of

1680s. The Whig opposition of 1679-1681 to Charles's arbitrary government and anti-Protestant agenda were meant to stop French Catholic popery and influences.[960] Jurgen Habermas "located the first fully functioning modern public sphere in the commercial and political world of post-1689 England."[961] The print, publications and coffeehouses facilitated merchandising of politics and engaged the public attention to possible Catholic French interventions. Charles ruled without the parliament after 1681. He purged the government of Whig sympathisers, manipulated London Sheriff's elections, installed loyalists in county governments and severely persecuted Whig republicans such as Algernon Sidney and Lord Russell. The Levant Company merchant Dudley North - who spent over 20 years in Turkey - was installed as London Sheriff, oversaw the trials of Sidney, Russell and other dissenters and later on monitored and developed Charles and James II's fiscal and trade policies. East India Company Governor Josiah Child was another loyalist who played a significant role in securing loans, formulating trade policies and financial instruments for Charles and James II. They supported Charles and James II's tolerationist policies though, and might have been a force behind such pluralistic and relatively republican actions. Their support of the King divided the Company into loyalist Tories and opposing Whigs. The successful trade ventures of Levant, East India and other overseas companies and their custom and tax money enabled the Crown its long-running financial shortfalls. Charles II flexed his muscles to an arbitrary style of government, just like his Catholic French cousin Louis XIV.

Charles II's secret promises of conversion to Catholicism,[962] his being on six million French livras salary of Louis XIV to thawart Dutch policies,[963] his brother and heir James, Duke of York's open Catholicism and Charles's persecutory policies sparked the Exclusion Crises in which the Whigs insisted on excluding James from the throne and the Tories supported his inclusion. England was divided between polar political tendencies of Whigs and Tories. Shaftesbury[964] and other radical Whig's desperate Rye House Plot to murder Charles and James in 1683 resulted in the brutal execution of many Whig leaders such as Sir Thomas Armstrong, Sir William Russel,[965] Algernon Sidney, James Holloway, John Ayloffe and exile of others such as Sir John Cochrane, Robert Ferguson, Earl of Shaftesbury, John Locke and many others.[966] The conservative royalists, Anglican and monarchical establishments blamed Whigs of executing the international conspiracy of Islamic republicanism, overthrowing the monarchy and Anglican Church to replace it with Ottoman Unitarianism and pluralism, as Humberto Garcia has amply demonstrated.[967] Charles dissolved the Parliament in 1681 and ruled with an iron fist till 1685, when he died as a childless Catholic. He was succeeded by his openly Catholic, hardheaded but brave brother James II (1633-1701) who ruled with absolutist mindset in the name of divine right monarchy. "James was in fact a bigot. His government of Scotland in the early 1680s had seen a most severe repression and extensive use of judicial torture against Protestant Dissenters ('conventiclers'). Worse still, James believed himself to be a moderate."[968] He tried to use popular radical pluralistic sentiments to galvanise support for his monarchy; the Catholic King decreed tolerance of Catholics and Protestant nonconformists such as Quakers, Baptists and Congregationalists,[969] a tiny minority in the Protestant majority country seeing "an opportunity to transform the English nation and to liberate his co-religionists by leading a public campaign for liberty of conscience."[970] This was by far the most liberal treatment of dissent. "To win over the Dissenters, a Declaration of Indulgence was issued giving them full religious freedom."[971] He also tried to install Catholics and loyalists to city, town and county offices by hook or by crook. His active military duties in the Catholic French and Spanish armies against the Protestant English armies of Cromwell, his open Catholicism and authoritarianism made him suspect from the outset and his pro Catholic toleration policies added fuel to the fire.

James's toleration policies had profound impacts in the decades to come, but backfired during his time.[972] He required the Anglican bishops to read the decree publicly in the Church services. This was a bad time to impose Catholicism or toleration of dissent on the Protestant majority. His French Catholic cousin Louis XIV revoked the Edict of Nantes in 1685, persecuting and maiming thousands of French Protestant Huguenots and expelling between 200, 000 to 400,000. Around 50,000 of them settled in London as refugees. Considering the move of James II as a Catholic anti-Reformation hegemonic plot, seven Anglican bishops petitioned to be excused. "The great majority of the English clergy followed the lead of the seven bishops in refusing to read the king's *Declaration* during divine service."[973] The historian Mark Goldie has dubbed this earlier phase the "Anglican Revolution."[974] The

Bishops were imprisoned in the Tower of London but soon released as a result of public and Whig pressure. The birth of James' son James Francis, conspiracy theories about the botched birth, and his potential of inheriting the English Crown and continuing the Catholic absolutist monarchy enraged the anti-Catholic rioters and Whig MPs.[975] They demanded his removal and replacement by his Anglican daughter Mary and her Dutch husband William of Orange. Prince William was invited[976] to replace James as the English King. William landed in England on November 5 of 1688 with 35000 men, supported by Protestant army officers and nobility, and was declared a joint monarch with Mary. The Parliament abolished the monarchy by birth, exiled James II to France and established William of Orange and Mary as the sovereigns appointed by the parliament.

The Glorious Revolution, Anglican Monarchy and Church

The bloodless Glorious Revolution[977] ended the long English Catholic dynasty and declared that no Roman Catholic would ever be ascending to the English throne and no English monarch would be allowed to marry a Roman Catholic wife. This way "the substantive acceptance of parliamentary monarchy was achieved."[978] It was not a real republican revolution, with popular sovereignty and religious tolerance for all, but it curtailed monarchical absolutism and gave parliament authority in the scheme of governance. The result was a limited, constitutional monarchy. It took England almost a century and countless human lives to replace Catholic divine right monarchy with a limited parliamentary monarchy, and it would take another century or so before England gave religious tolerance and liberty to non-Protestant dissenters such as Catholics, Unitarians and Socininans. The Penal Law against them was lifted in 1770 and Catholics were allowed to vote for and sit as Members of Parliament in 1829, and (along with other nonconformists) to take up Oxford and Cambridge fellowships in 1871. "In 1974, the law was changed to clarify that Roman Catholics were once again permitted to hold Wolsey and More's office of Lord Chancellor, and in 2013 changed again to allow a (hypothetical) Catholic to marry the heir to the throne."[979] England was not as enlightened until the nineteenth century as Whiggish historians have made it to be.

The monarch was still powerful but not the sole authority. It was a limited monarchy, an extension of the English Civil War and Revolution's Commonwealthism. The parliament, with its upper and lower houses, shared the authority. For the first time in English history the monarch was to be under the legislative powers of the parliament; this was considered revolutionary. "The Glorious Revolution involved three basic issues: who should be king of England? What should be the nature of the kingship or in what ways should the government be reformed? And what should be the relationship between the Anglican Church and other Protestant groups? Also important was the question of the nature of the Convention, that is, the body irregularly elected in January 1689 to settle the nation's affairs. Underlying these issues were theoretical questions concerning succession theory, allegiance, consent, conscience, and the concepts of trust and original contract."[980]

Henry Stubbe in the 1670s and John Locke, Deists, Socinians and Unitarians in the 1680s responded to these fundamental questions in light of the century long English debates about Ottoman Islamic republicanism and religious pluralism, as will be detailed in the coming pages. This way a century-long struggle between the Catholic minority and the Protestant majority, between an absolutist monarchy and republican leaning parliament and between the absolutist *Old Regime* and republican outlook came to an end. It also mitigated the century-long uncertainty, division, mistrust, instability, insecurity and religious polarisation. The Glorious Revolution was a "turning point. It may have achieved little that any of the parties sought after or fought for. It may have done even less to transform political and social institutions. But it deeply affected the intellectual values, at least of the political élite."[981]

The Church of England lost its old triumphalism, self-assurance, pomp and might. "Unable to punish those who were not its members, and unable to compel men and women to be its members, the Church of England was a spent spiritual force."[982] Milton's Lost Paradise was at least partially regained. The republican cause achieved partial triumph over the theocracy. "John Milton heroically confronted a God who appeared to have guided his people in the 1640s and 1650s only to betray them in 1660. *Paradise Lost* looked at the Omnipotent Creator who let man fall, *Paradise Regained* looked at the temptation of Christ in the wilderness, at the false worldly ways in which Man might proclaim the gospel. Perhaps republicans had been tempted into the wrong paths. *Samson Agonistes,* most poignantly of all, studied a man given great gifts by God who failed to use them in His service. Just as Samson dallied with Delilah and was shorn of his strength, so the republicans had been distracted by the things of the flesh in the 1650s and had missed their chance to do God's will."[983] In the 1680s, the republican cause was partially triumphant.

During the long half-century since the Interregnum, Henry Stubbe and John Toland Islamised Christianity. Toland and John Locke demystified Christianity and Locke and Newton rationalised and naturalised Christianity. The processes of Islamisation, demystification and rationalisation of Church Christianity were mutually interconnected, interrelated and intertwined through the persons of Henry Stubbe and Shaftesbury and groups such as Deists, Unitarians and Socinians. They all agreed that the historical Church Christianity was the root cause of all problems; the original Christianity of Jesus was nothing but a moral anthology. Consequently, the Christian faith was uprooted from its supernatural, Trinitarian, Incarnational, Augustinian and medieval foundations, depoliticised, anthropomorphised and moralised. "Christianity was being depoliticised and demystified. The characteristic Anglican tracts of the late seventeenth century had titles like *The Reasonableness of Christianity* and *Christianity not Mysterious.* Where God had been in the very warp and woof of nature and life, he now became the creator who set things going, and the spirit who worked within the individual and kept him obedient to moral rules. Sermons stressed the merits of neighbourliness and charity."[984] Instead of Church doctrinal uniformity the Ottoman pluralism was propagated. Religious tolerance was demanded and defending and religion was privatised and sort of secularised. "From the Dissenting side, John Locke, pleading for religious toleration, defined a church as a voluntary society of men, meeting together to worship God in such fashion as they deemed appropriate. Religion had become an unthreatening matter, almost a hobby. The authorities need not concern themselves with what consenting adults did in private meetings. The Puritans of previous generations could not have conceived anything so anaemic."[985]

An absence of monarchical abuse and Church policing allowed English Protestants to think for themselves, decide for themselves and make use of their will, power and energy. The anthropomorphic revolution brought focus to man and his immediate surroundings, and diminished the power and reach of persecuting Church and monarchy. The focus was transferred from the heavens to the earth, from supernaturalism to naturalism and from unintelligible mysteries to rational moralism. This was an intellectual and theological revolution. "When John Locke wrote in his second *Treatise of Government* (1690) that 'all men are naturally in a state of perfect freedom to order their actions and dispose of their possessions and persons as they think fit without asking the leave or depending upon the will of any man' he was proclaiming a message only made possible by the disillusionment with old ideals, but a message which was to make much possible in the decades to come."[986] The reformation of Reformation was partially complete. It removed the last hurdle by demolishing the theological scaffolding of the supernatural absolutism both secular and spiritual. This theological and intellectual revolution was facilitated by the Islamic anti-Trinitarian, moral and republican belief system espoused by English merchants, traders, *politike*, intellectuals, dissenters and philosophers due to specific English circumstances and conditions.

The seventeenth century, due to its religious and political instability, was ripe for ideas of stability, peace, prosperity and religious accommodations. Religious tolerance and freedom of conscience were the two main themes discussed throughout the long seventeenth century,[987] and were championed by different groups at different times for different goals and agendas.[988] In the early part of the century, it was used by the merchants, Protestant nonconformists and Catholics against the hegemonic and persecutory designs of the Anglican Church of Archbishop Laud[989] and absolute monarchy of Charles I, while in the later part of the century it was employed by Charles II and James II to galvanise support of Protestant nonconformists, some pro-diversity Anglicans and to release pressure from the Catholics. The kings' tolerant policies were now opposed by the Anglican Church establishment and Whig parliament. The debate about religious tolerance and pluralism which was fueled by the Levant and East India merchants' experience in the Muslim world remained an integral part of English social, intellectual, religious and political landscape throughout the century. It was internalised and domesticated to the extent that by the end of the century it became an integral part of English social imagination and religio-political vocabulary. The Levant and East India company merchants' long experience with Ottoman, Mughal and Safvid religious pluralism and republicanism was handy and provided helpful ideas and tools to English politicians, intelligentsia and religious leaders to analyse, dissect, appropriate and reject according to their specific needs and agendas.

Religious tolerance was the bedrock of the early English Enlightenment and its debates, arguments, examples and precedents were reflected through the Muslim world's realities, experiences, religious concepts and moral philosophy.[990] The seventeenth-century early English Enlightenment and its foundational principles were reflection of such a cross-cultural metamorphosis. To understand the nature and extent of this cross-cultural exchange and assimilation process let us look at some of the seventeenth-century English institutions such as Turkish coffeehouses, their Islamic connections, their egalitarian impacts and how they were equally popularised and demonised in the English society.[991]

Turkish Coffeehouses

Coffee came to England along with Eastern silk, spices, cotton, tobacco, sugar, horses and other exports. The Eastern wealth, imports, cultural habits and ideas revolutionised the English culture, society and thought patterns. The popular English culture of seventeenth-century coffeehouses epitomised the "Oriental Obsession" and ensuing social, cultural and political transformations.

Soon after its introduction in the 1650s the Turkish berry and Muhammadan soup became symbols of republican dissent and egalitarianism. "How does one explain the rapid proliferation of coffeehouses in Restoration and Augustan England? The political turbulence of the period was partly responsible. The coffeehouse arrived in England three years after the execution of Charles I, and its growing popularity coincided with the Stuart restoration, the Exclusion Crisis, the Glorious Revolution, the bitter partisan struggles of Anne's reign, and the explosion of political journalism that marked the Augustan era. Born in an age of revolution, restoration, and bitter party rivalries, the coffeehouse provided public space at a time when political action and debate had begun to spill beyond the institutions that had traditionally contained them."[992] By the 1680s, coffeehouses had become the centres of political activism. "During the Exclusion Crisis, as is well known, each political move that was made, and some that were not, was revealed, debated, celebrated, and vilified in the coffeehouses."[993] Cities, universities, towns and villages were engrossed in coffee culture and consumerism; this exclusively Ottoman novelty had stormed English markets and sociability. During the Exclusion Crisis it was estimated that throughout England, 100 tuns of coffee were consumed per year. Coffee had "so generally prevailed" within three decades of its introduction "that bread itself, though commonly with us voted the staff of life, is scarcely of so universal use." One pamphleteer marveled that "the dull planet Saturn has not finished one revolution through the orb since coffee-houses were first known amongst us, yet 'tis worth our wonder to observe how numerous they are already grown, not only here in our metropolis, but in both universities and most cities and eminent towns throughout the nation."[994] Scotland and Ireland were as fascinated with coffeehouses as the mainland England. "Coffeehouses existed not only in the metropolis but also in the universities, county towns, and trading centers throughout the three kingdoms."[995] Coffee represented the extent of cross-cultural exchanges and transformations which resulted from the overseas trade.

Levant Trade and Coffee

The Levant merchants, chaplains, ambassadors and English travellers consumed Turkish coffee while in the Ottoman Empire and brought it to England along with their pluralistic and republican ideas. William Biddulph,[996] Dr. Edward Pococke,[997] Henry Blount and others wrote about it and popularised it among the virtuosi. The first coffeehouse "Angel" was opened in Oxford in 1650, along with the Oriental scholarship and vibrant experimental, alchemical and scientific community.[998] The first London coffeehouse was established in 1652 by Pasqua Rosee, the Greek servant of renowned Levant Company trader Daniel Edward who lived and traded in Izmir, Turkey during the 1640s. Edward was known for his Puritan anti-royalist tendencies and resisted royalist policies and faction in Izmir.[999] On his return home, Edward used to invite his big circle of family and friends to his place, entertain them with Turkish coffee and delights and share with them his Ottoman experiences and stories. He opened the first London coffee shop in his servant's name as the Company rules did not permit his retailing business.[1000] It became a sudden hit, both as a medical cure as well as a facilitator of social interactions. There were over 2000 coffee houses in London by the end of the seventeenth century, in addition to countless others all around the country.[1001] "No wonder John Houghton thought that "there are few trades in London that employ more houses, and pay greater rents," than coffeehouses."[1002]

The coffeehouse was not just another alehouse, tavern or inn but a novel institution in itself.[1003] It was a specifically Turkish place with hanging signs of "the Turk Head", "the Sultan Head,"[1004] "the Sulta-ness-head", Turkish tobacco pipes, sherbet, tea, chocolate and even opi-um.[1005] Francis Bacon, Thomas Herbert, Henry Stubbe, William Petty, Robert Southwell and other virtuosi leaders praised opium, its sooth-ing energy, virtues, potentials, medicinal uses and admired the ways in which "the drug putatively made the Turks 'strong and long in Venus exercises.'"[1006] Stubbe also wrote extensively about the medical benefits of chocolate served at the coffeehouses. "Unlike 'hot' coffee, chocolate was thought to be cold and dry, and prone to provoking the blood flow, all of which were conducive to the stimulation of sexual ardor in Ga-lenic physiology."[1007] Stubbe, in his *The Indian Nectar, Or a Discourse Concerning Chocolata*,[1008] refuted the puritanical critics of chocolate on medical bases.[1009] The medical discussion around coffee, chocolate, tea, sherbet and opium revolved around Turks, Ottoman and Mughal Em-pires. Some of the coffeehouses were named after Ottoman cities such as Smyrna. The seventeenth-century London coffee houses closely re-sembled the coffeehouses of Istanbul with their roasted coffee's special aroma, Turkish Sultan's portrait, Quranic verses and Islamic symbols.

The Englishmen were exposed to Turkish Islamic culture and sym-bolism while in the coffee shop. They represented the Anglo-Ottoman cross-cultural metamorphosis blurring the geographical separation into a virtual cross-cultural experience and interaction. The burgeoning and bustling coffeehouses epitomised the allure of Islam and Ottoman power in an instable, insecure and impotent post revolution England of 1649-50. The egalitarian, non-hierarchical, cross-cultural and diverse atmosphere of the coffeehouses with their entertaining stories and nar-rations of egalitarian pluralistic Ottoman society and religious freedom were threatening to a hierarchical English society inundated with re-ligious, social and political persecutions.[1010] The coffeehouse clientele included people from diverse social backgrounds including virtuosi, scholars, intellectuals, journalists, parliamentarians, lawyers, poets, merchants, city workers, sailors, patrons and gentry without any social distinction or discrimination.[1011] First come first serve policy and causal seating arrangements empowered many lower class individuals and gave them a sense of freedom. Coffeehouses became the Noah's Ark of Lon-don. All sat like their Ottoman counterparts, sipped the Turkish berry and shared their ideas, experiences and concerns.[1012] These "Penny Universities"[1013] transformed the socio-political and intellectual landscape of Restoration England;[1014] England was turbaned. "The 1650s had introduced coffee houses into England, and with coffee came the turban, since coffee house keepers often wore turbans as an advertising ploy."[1015] Gerald MacLean noted that "sometimes proprietors dressed as Turks or Arabs; sometimes these proprietors were Levantines. It was not uncommon to see even English coffee house customers wearing turbans, and indeed, Ottoman headgear became a fashionable alternative to the ubiquitous wigs sported by post-Restoration men of fashion. The portraits of many writers and artists such as Samuel Pepys, Alexander Pope and William Hogarth show these men wearing turbans."[1016] Countless Levant Company traders, workers, officers, travellers and converts put on their Turkish dress with turban and headed every night to their favourite coffeehouses.[1017] In "1663 Edmund Verney was keen to obtain an authentic turban via his brother in Aleppo […] In November 1666, Samuel Pepys was evidently surprised to find Sir Philip Howard 'dressing himself in his night-gown and Turban like a Turke; but one of the finest persons that I ever saw in my life'. Clothing clearly continued to signal national and religious identity, yet John Evelyn was evidently pleased when, in October the next year, King Charles appeared at court in 'the Eastern fashion of Vest [...] after the Persian mode."[1018] The so-called "turned Turk" phenomenon increased already existing English anxieties due to its connection with conversions to Islam.

"When Coffee once was vended here,
The Alcoran shortly did appear:
For our Reformers were such Widgeons,
New Liquors brought in new Religions"[1019]

For the Anglican Church leadership, monarchists and proponents of socio-religious conformity, the coffeehouses, the Mahomettan berry and Turkish symbolism were nothing short of a cultural and intellectual invasion.[1020] "This was the means by which the Great Sultan, still very much a pretender to universal monarchy in high church rhetoric, could undermine the English polity by perverting English religiosity."[1021] Coffee bewitched the English consumer, turning them into Turks.[1022] The Turk Heads represented Islam's dynamism and cultural vitality in the face of a divided, instable and insecure England both politically and religiously. The cheap, causal, inclusive coffeehouses with their Turkish habits, religion and cultural invasion had dramatically transformed the English socio-cultural landscape of the 1650s as the Indian textile, tobacco, spices and Barbary horses and sugar had done in the 1630s. To some, it compromised English national cultural identity,[1023] and the coffee-drinking apes compromised English identity and religion.[1024] "The "hot love" between the brown "Groom [coffee] [...] [a] *Turkish Renegade*" and its "fair [...] *Christian* [...] Bride" bewitched the whole of the nation and turned it into "Whore[s]" in "Bawdy-houses [coffeehouses]."[1025]

The coffeehouses provided a sober alternate and emancipatory environment to the hierarchical and suffocating English society, serving as democratic bodies and pluralistic sociability places. They enhanced English civility, polity, manners, socio-communicative skills, general knowledge and specialised skills. To their opponents the "heathenish liquor", the "smoke hole" had turned the Englishmen into "perfect Turk" denying "Divinity," abandoning their "morality [...] piety and virtue."[1026] The supporters contended that the coffeehouses provided them with an escape mechanism from socio-cultural and religious constraints of their suffocating society. They talked about the cultural, religious and intellectual superiority of the Turks over English, who were marred in supernatural unintelligible dogmas and restrained by their Church and state. This was threatening to both English Church and state especially because the religious dissenters such as the Quakers, Seekers, Socinians and Deists frequented the coffeehouses. They used this public sphere for their clandestine ideas and plans.

The Centers of Dissent

The coffeehouses were also the meeting place of political dissenters and trouble makers. For instance, the republican James Harrington and his Rota Club daily "met at Miles's Coffeehouse in the New Palace Yard. James Harrington, along with his friend and fellow traveller in republican politics, Henry Neville, were both early aficionados of the new coffeehouses and they quickly saw the new institution as a suitable venue for the propagation and discussion of their ideas and their politics."[1027] The coffeehouses were the new public sphere of freedom and dissent. "A prototype of the coffeehouse as public sphere was the Turk's Head in London, where the arch-republican James Harrington founded the Rota Club in 1659. The club, whose other members included John Milton, took its name from Harrington's proposal in his utopian *Commonwealth of Oceana* (1656) to establish term limits for Members of Parliament. The club met around an oval table and debated political issues of the day. Samuel Pepys, a frequent visitor there, described how in the heat of debate the members would decide an issue by casting their votes in a ballot box. The radicalism and proto-democratic sociability of the Rota Club helps explain why Restoration coffeehouses came to be viewed as havens for political and religious dissent. Puritan writers reinforced this reputation by repeatedly praising the sobering virtues of coffee over the intoxicating effects of alcohol. These very qualities led royalist critics to associate coffeehouses with incessant talk, places where irresponsible chatterboxes subjected the affairs of church and king to relentless criticism."[1028] Harrington's republican state ideal was discussed and cooked in the coffeehouse environment and in the company of overseas traders, travellers and officers who had firsthand experience of the Ottoman pluralism and republicanism.

The Anglican Church leadership and royalists encouraged the alehouses "for its mellowing and tranquilizing effects"[1029] while the republicans, anti-clerical and anti-monarchy radicals lauded the coffeehouses for their soothing and sobering qualities. One poet complained that "by this Arabian berry, / Comes the neglect of Malago and Sherry." It was said that "an honest drunken cur" - a common Restoration type - "hates coffee as Mahometism, and thinks it a lesser sin to be drunk, than to drink to make him sober."[1030] The Church and Crown wanted people drunk, easy-going and busy with sports because it enabled them to rule the masses with ease.[1031] The egalitarian, republican, Muhammadan, emancipatory coffee culture was detrimental to the Church and Crown's absolutists policies. The subversive, radical and clandestine coffee culture was totally identified with - and hated like - Muhammadanism. Coffeehouses remained the hotbeds of anti-Anglican Church and anti-monarchy sedition throughout the second half of the seventeenth century. "This discursive ideal provided a model for coffeehouse conversation for the rest of the Stuart era."[1032]

The subtle, subversive, radical culture of the Rota Club was carried to other scholarly bodies such as the Royal Society. Michael Hunter has estimated that "eleven out of twenty seven, or nearly 40 percent, of the identifiable Rota-men went on to become Royal Society Fellows,"[1033] the Society which was established by Charles II in opposition to Rota Club and its republican politics.[1034] Henry Stubbe chastised the Royal Society members due to their perceived royalism and clericalism.[1035] He was too Muhammadan and radical to countenance royal loyalties or clerical establishments as the Royal Society Fellows tolerated. The exclusion from the Royal Society of Thomas Hobbes, Stubbe's model and friend, was another bone of contention. On the other hand, the Royal Society members did not consider themselves as courtiers but independent scholars and scientists. Fellows like Robert Boyle engaged with Stubbe on multiple levels, but did not subscribe to his religio-political radicalism. They intended a gradual, systematic, invisible, epistemological transformation without radically breaking with traditional religio-political structures. They were far more calculated, cautious and scrupulous than Stubbe's firebrand radicalism. They equally populated the coffeehouses, though. For instance, John Locke, Christopher Wren, Peter Staehl of Strasbourg, Dr. John Wallis and some other Royal Society members were all independent coffeehouse habitué from their Oxford days.[1036] "Robert Boyle, Robert Hooke, Henry Oldenburg, and other members of the Royal Society could often be found in coffeehouses, particularly Garraway's, discussing 'philosophy.'"[1037] The Royal Society Fellow's saturation with Eastern manuscripts, languages, alchemical experiments, natural sciences and strong business ties with the East India and Levant companies were further supplemented by Turkish coffeehouses. Coffee houses were like "a kind of Athenian school."[1038] Their intellectual, clandestine reformation efforts were discussed in the coffeehouse environment. They researched about the health impacts of coffee, assembled in coffeehouses and shared the alternative society of the coffee culture.

Their Oxford fellow and later critic Henry Stubbe was also addicted to coffeehouses. "The physician and polemicist Henry Stubbe scoffed at the naivete of the foreign inquiries and armchair speculations made by the incipient Royal Society, calling them "newe speculators" with little experience of foreign lands or cultures."[1039] He ridiculed and criticised both the Royal Society and the Rota Club members for indulging in theoretical speculations without proper knowledge and experience of the foreign lands, unlike the overseas traders.[1040] Henry Stubbe, who fought in the army of Oliver Cromwell, was a coffeehouse habitué who used the coffeehouses as springboards for his subversive anti-Trinitarian, anti-clerical, anti-monarchy, anti-absolutist religious pluralism, political republicanism, Islamism and Turkism. He came across countless turbaned Turks, anti-Trinitarian merchants, Muhammadan Christians and disgruntled English virtuosi in his daily visits to various coffeehouses over a long period of time. His firsthand knowledge of Islam, Prophet Muhammad, Turkish religious pluralism and republicanism through his frequent encounters with turbaned Turks in the coffeehouses was supplemented by his access to Oxford Bodleian Library's Arabic and Islamic manuscripts - where he worked for a while - and his exposure to Dr. Edward Pococke's relatively pro-Islamic objective teachings and works. John Toland, another radical enlightenment leader, was notoriously connected with coffeehouses which he abandoned only very late in his life due to severe chastisement from friends and foes. The subversive activities of the so-called Muhammadan fanatics dressed in Turkish attires, frequenting the coffeehouses decorated with Turkish symbolism and inundated with discussions of religious pluralism, rationalism and republicanism, to the conservatives, was nothing short of Antichristian cultural and religious revolution. Unable to stop the repulsive Ottomania, the Anglican and monarchist opponents regarded the foreign coffee places as dangerous, sheltering vermin like "the mad Fifth-monarchy [...] Harringtons Rota," [and] virtuosi,"[1041] and "antichrist[s]," undermining Christian culture."[1042] To them, these aspiring Turks were anti-Christian and anti-England.[1043]

State officials reacted to this Islamic invasion of the English society by ordering the burning of hundreds of copies of Alexander Ross' English translation of the Quran, Socinian Recovian Catechism, persecution of Unitarians, Quakers and their parliamentarian, academician and knightly sympathisers.[1044] The widespread coffeehouse negative sentiments against the Trinity, Bible, Church and monarchy were worrisome to the religious and political authorities and they suppressed them with strict blasphemy laws.[1045] The coffeehouses became the Internet, Reddit and Google of the seventeenth century. The English inflammatory Islamophobic anxieties, anti-Turkish, anti-Oriental and anti-republican rhetoric culminated in Charles II's 1675 ban on coffeehouses.[1046] But the republican, Whiggish coffee culture was so widespread and powerful that the ban was rescinded just a week later.

Coffeehouses all across Britain were the center of Francophobic, anti-Catholic and anti-popery propaganda. Shaftesbury's fight for constitutional monarchy, Protestant succession, civil liberties and religious toleration were all waged from St. John's coffeehouse. The Whig republicanism of Shaftesbury, Earl of Salisbury, Thomas Papillon, Samuel Barnardiston and their pedigree like Henry Stubbe and John Locke was introduced, organised, disseminated and popularised from their base in St. John's Coffeehouse. Shaftesbury's 1670s neo-Harringtonianism,[1047] Whig politics and toleration philosophy were all cooked in the coffeehouse. It replaced Harrington's balanced republic of the Few (the King) and the Many (House of Lords) with a "three-way balance between the One (the king), the Few (the House of Lords) and the Many (the House of Commons). The Lords would play an especially crucial role, preserving the balance between the king and the Commons by preventing the possible corruption of the Commons by royal patronage. Playing this role, the Lords would be the representatives and purveyors of ancient prudence, preventing the court, the representative of modern prudence, from destroying the constitution and establishing monarchical absolutism."[1048] Neo-Harringtonianism was not geared towards establishment of a democratic republic but towards a reformed, curtailed, limited constitutional monarchy. It was an extension of the mid-century English Revolution, and its political juntas aspired Venetian style oligarchy. Both Henry Stubbe and John Locke sought for limited monarchy, worked for Shaftesbury and compiled letters and pamphlets for him. John Locke's *A Letter from a Person of Quality to his Friend in the Country* (1675) written for Shaftesbury and owned by Shaftesbury was distributed in all coffeehouses.[1049] Stubbe's *Further Justification of the Present War with the Netherlands* (1673), *A Further Justification of the Present War against the United Netherlands, Newberry Case* (1673)[1050] and "*The History of the United Provinces of Achaia,*"[1051] all written on behest of Shaftesbury were discussed, distributed and popularised at London coffeehouses. Shaftesbury, the Founding Father of the Whig opposition party along with his pedigree, such as Locke and Stubbe, were fully engaged in demanding religious tolerance, freedom of conscience and limited monarchy, the fundamental themes of later Enlightenment. The bedrock fundamental ideas of the Enlightenment were probably pushed by overseas traders, owned by their Whig ideologues and cooked and disseminated through the public sphere of the Turkish coffeehouses.

The royalists, High Church leaders and the Crown all joined their efforts to stop the radical agenda. "Convinced that coffeehouses were hotbeds of anti-royal, anti-Anglican sedition, Charles II and his ministers launched a campaign to suppress them. In a letter to parliament (1673) Charles condemned coffeehouses as 'pernicious and destructive,' places where people 'sit half the day, and discourse with all companies that come in of State matters, talking of news and broaching of lies, arraigning the judgments and discretion of their governors, censuring all their actions, and insinuating into the ears of the people a prejudice against them.' In 1675, as the earl of Shaftesbury and his Whig followers plotted opposition strategy from their headquarters at John's Coffeehouse in London, the crown issued a proclamation closing the city's coffeehouses. But the measure provoked such a storm of protest, both inside and outside parliament, that the crown was forced to revoke it ten days later."[1052] Both Charles II and James II[1053] went to great length to suppress the sadistic, seditious, rebellious, antichristian, atheistic and heterodox culture of the coffeehouses.[1054] They were fully supported in this by the High Church leadership and high-flying royalists. To them, it became a national security issue, as they blamed the coffeehouse owners of participating in the international republican conspiracy, and blamed some of leaking national security secrets to Algerian pirates and English renegades.[1055]

Contrary to that, Whig historians, leaders and later on David Hume,[1056] considered the ban as absolutists' efforts to suppress freedom of conscience, liberty, rational discourse and pluralistic world view. The historian James Ralph thought the goal was "to extinguish the light of reason, [and] subdue the power of reflection."[1057] Coffeehouses fostered a culture of sobriety, clarity, alertness and hard work in the drunken English society, and popularised a culture of freedom, liberty, rationality, pluralism and importance of public sphere. The authority of the Church and state was challenged and finally subdued by this culture. It also created a mercantile, business and commercial culture like Istanbul, Cairo and Izmir coffeehouses. "Coffeehouses also belonged to the world of commerce, which is another reason why coffeehouses had become so popular in London by the early eighteenth century."[1058] The Lloyd's coffeehouse transitioned into Lloyd's of London and the Jonathan Coffeehouse supplemented the London Royal Exchange.

They also served as the print media centers of the seventeenth century.[1059] The English frequented the "coffeehouses to find jobs, conduct business, exchange information, or celebrate important events of their lives. These were places where baptisms and marriages were celebrated, newspapers circulated, stock traded, crimes plotted, votes solicited, ministers attacked, labourers employed, wars debated, freemasons initiated [...] principle public space, open to anyone who could pay for their drink."[1060] They were the modern British pubs of the seventeenth century. The coffeehouses became the "bourgeois public sphere"[1061] and the "public sphere of the Enlightenment"[1062] diffusing Enlightenment ideas through the print media and open sociability. They promoted English Enlightenment and its republican values.[1063] It represented a decisive break with the *Old Regime's* religious and political persecutory policies and forged the way for a more inclusive, pluralistic and republican society.[1064] The London coffeehouses were firmly identified with radical pluralism, republicanism and anti-monarchism. The identification was so close that the end of republicanism looked like the end of coffeehouses too. The Muhammadan berry became a republican allegory.

Coffeehouses and Stuart Monarchy

The coffeehouses and their rich merchant owners played an important role in the overthrow of Stuart monarchy.[1065] The new monarch Prince William of Orange was no less concerned with the radical environment and foreign culture of the coffeehouse. "The accession of the Protestant and Stuart Queen Anne in March 1702 did not quell anxieties about the role of public opinion among the kingdom's political elite, but the early eighteenth-century state could afford a greater degree of complacency with regard to its coffeehouses than the more seriously embattled regimes of Charles II, James II, and William and Mary."[1066] The Turkish coffeehouses played a significant part in fomenting the social, political and religious diversity so cherished by the Enlightenment leaders. Dorinda Outram's "Coffee Houses and Consumers: The Social Context of Enlightenment"[1067] highlights the important role played by the overseas trade[1068] and coffee houses in formulating and disseminating the Enlightenment ideas in England and Europe.

Henry Stubbe, who would later champion Islamic republicanism and Muhammadan Christianity, was a product of Levantine heritage, Oriental scholarship, Cromwell Commonwealth's republican pluralism, religious tolerance, anti-Church and anti-monarchical establishments, coffeehouse culture of Islamism, Turkism, Orientalism, Shaftesbury's Whiggism, radical resurgence and resistance. His radical republican journey started with his Puritan family, Westminster Head Master Dr. Busby's fascination with Oriental languages including Arabic, Dr. Pococke's Oxford lectures, Levantine Oriental scholarship and Islamic works, and Sir Henry Vane Junior and later Shaftesbury's patronage. This egalitarian ideal took him to Cromwell's anti- monarchy army, later working for Puritan efforts to de-monopolise worship and knowledge, religious tolerance and pluralism, his defense of republican parliamentarian and Commonwealth leader Sir Henry Vane the Younger,[1069] his pamphleteering for the rights of dissenting traders and sects, his close coordination with radical leaders such as Shaftesbury, his compilation of *An Account of the Rise and Progress of Mahometanism, and a Vindication of him and his Religion from the Calumnies of the Christians,* his defenses of Islamic republicanism and his propagation of Turkish government model as an ideal for English limited monarchy, civil religion and revolution. Stubbe epitomises the long seventeenth century's struggle against the absolutism of Church and monarchy which culminated in the early Enlightenment of the late seventeenth and early eighteenth century. Stubbe is the connection between Dr. Busby's Orientalism, Dr. Pococke's Levantine scholarship, Interregnum, the wealthy merchants and shippers,[1070] Restoration, religious radicalism of Deists, Socinians and Unitarians, relative republicanism of Harrington, radical republicanism of Henry Vane Junior and political radicalism of Whigs like Shaftesbury and Sidney, as James Jacob has very well demonstrated. Stubbe is the epitome of social, cultural, religious and political radicalism which ushered the English Enlightenment. He is also the model of Islamism, Turkism and Orientalism, which shaped and steered the long seventeenth-century socio-religious and political debates. Stubbe, along with Locke, Toland and many other Enlightenment figures, was the product of these debates and controversies and not the founder of them. He worked through the English thought patterns, which were prevalent during the seventeenth century, and strove to realise a pluralistic republic and enlightened monarchy, like that of Muhammad. Eighteenth-century enlightened European monarchs such as Frederick II of Prussia were the outcome of this limited monarchy ideology. The enlightenend monarchies applied the Stubbian and Lockean republican principles in their states, which culminated in the later High Enlightenment. Muhammad, the wise legislator and enlightenment Prophet, was equally popular with the eighteenth-century enlightenment figures as he was with the seventeenth-century intellectuals. The French *philosophes* of the 1750s used the Oriental manuscripts, travelogues, examples and ideas as much as the early enlightenment figures did. Muhammad was as much revered by eighteenth-century Romantists as was he invoked by Stubbe, Toland and early Unitarians. Humberto Garcia's treatment and analysis of Edmund Burke, Samuel Taylor Coleridge, Robert Southey, Mary Shelley and other eighteenth-century intellectual's thoughts and works well substantiate the claim.[1071] The seventeenth-century exposure to Islam and Muhammad was more pronounced due to special geo-political circumstances of the century.

The sixteenth- and seventeenth-century Northern Europe was more intertwined with the Muslim East than the previous two centuries. As discussed above, the Dutch, French and English traders, merchants and workers were all over the Muslim World. Their long interactions with Muslim world furnished them with enough knowledge of Islamic anti-Trinitarianism, anti-Fall, anti-Incarnational man Christology and limited republicanism. Many of these merchants, chaplains and workers acquired influential positions in Dutch, French and English societies. They implicitly and publicly encouraged reformation of persecuting European society based on Islamic tolerant model.[1072] Their overseas interactions with Muslims played a major role in bringing about the reformation of Reformation. Additionally, the migration of Transylvanian Unitarians and Socinians to Amsterdam, London and other European cities supplemented the cross-cultural transmission of ideas. Englishmen such as Paul Best,[1073] who travelled to Transylvania and championed anti-Trinitarianism, religious liberty and freedom of conscience and worship along with English dissenters since the Interregnum, pushed for religious reforms and plurality. The Ottoman Unitarian, pluralistic and republican model was aspired and quoted by all. Europe was able to break away from its intellectual stagnation with the help of external resource portfolios and tributaries; the global Muslim bridge to other civilisations was a key element in this historical breakthrough. Europe's transition from the incarnational, supernatural and abstract transcendental theology to anthropomorphic, universal moralism and prophetic, messianic, moral Christology was fundamental to early and later high Enlightenment. The modernity project was made possible with the resultant human empowerment, participation and initiatives. Islamic theology, philosophy, sciences, political thought and spiritual moralism were helpful tools for the enlightenment leaders and were well absorbed, appropriated and re-oriented by many of them. The Enlightenment, in a sense, was a religious revolution.

Chapter 4

Enlightenment:
A Religious Revolution

Enlightenment scholars have long argued that the eighteenth-century Enlightenment was a complete reformation of the sixteenth-century Reformation. First and foremost, it was a theological revolution as theology was central to early Enlightenment in spite of its outward varieties and expressions. J. G. A. Pocock noted that the "Enlightenment cannot be understood apart from theology."[1074] J. C. D. Clarke, Charles Taylor, Jonathan Israel, D. Van Kley and many other leaders in the field have emphasised the religious nature of the seventeenth- and eighteenth-century debates which led to the Enlightenment. The Enlightenment leaders completely overhauled the Church Christianity by rejecting its central supernatural dogmas and its practical insistence upon the worldly kingdom. The Enlightenment was a series of ideological struggles against the central problem related to the absolute Church and monarchy. "In close but extremely various relations with an indictment of Nicene theology – and ultimately of the central doctrines of the Incarnation, the Atonement and the Trinity – as encouraging the belief that a kingdom not of this world might nevertheless be exercised in it, there went a series of programmes for developing a culture of the mind, founded on method and manners, letters and law, and the critical capacity of reading the texts of European civilisation, which should enable it to function independently of Christian theology and anchor the life of the mind in the life of civil society. This repudiation of theology is, however, intimately related with the theology it repudiates and varies in character as it appears in, and attempts to substitute itself for, cultures enduringly Catholic or Protestant, Anglican, Calvinist or Lutheran."[1075] William Lecky has well summarised this ideological struggle between Christian theology and Enlightenment moral vision.[1076]

The Enlightenment was an action upon - and reaction to - the old Christian system of belief, and in the end served as a rejection of it and advocated for its replacement with a Unitarian, moral, rational, natural and republican theology. "If we examine the Church in the fourth and fifth centuries, we find it almost exclusively occupied with minute questions concerning the manner of the co-existence of the two natures in Christ. If we examine it in the middle ages, we find it absorbed in ritualism and pilgrimages. If we examine it at the Reformation, we find it just emerging beneath the pressure of civilisation from this condition; yet still the main speculative test was the doctrine concerning the Sacrament, which had no relation to morals; and the main practical test on the Continent, at least, was the eating of meat on Fridays. In the present day, with the great body of laymen at least, such matters appear simply puerile, because they have no relation to morals."[1077] It was a total break with old thought patterns and a reformation of Christianity on rational, moral and republican lines. Three distinct classes of change were visible. The first was "the gradual evanessence of doctrines that collide with our moral sense. The second is the decline of the influence of those ceremonies, or purely speculative doctrines, which, without being opposed to conscience, are at least wholly beyond its sphere. The third is the substitution of the sense of right for the fear of punishment as the main motive to virtue."[1078]

Enlightenment and Destruction of Old Regime

The Enlightenment in a sense was the destruction of the *Old Regime* Trinitarian and monarchical Christianity. Margarete Jacob argued that the clandestine writings of radical thinkers "fed the flames of [...] massive conflagration intended to destroy the Christian Churches and their doctrines."[1079] Voltaire's letter to Frederick the Great of Prussia, whose name and nearly half-century reign from 1740 to 1786 were "virtually synonymous with the advent and advance of the Enlightenment in Prussia,"[1080] summarised the sentiments of the Enlightenment leaders. "Your majesty will do the human race an eternal service in extirpating this infamous superstition [Christianity]. I do not say among the rabble, who are not worthy of being enlightened and who are apt for every yoke; I say among the well-bred, among those who wish to think."[1081] Frederick II's "sceptical, antagonistic attitude towards the Church as an institution." [...] "demythologised Christian faith,"[1082] and his rejection of "the chief doctrines of Christianity, such as the Trinity, Christ's divinity and humanity, and redemption,"[1083] was a practical manifestation of the aspired enlightenment. This was the Enlightenment which Kant envisaged. "What is enlightenment?" Immanuel Kant asserted that enlightenment could be partially conceptualised as a temporal epoch, one whose salient characteristics, especially in regards to religion, were manifested in the personal opinions and public policies of his royal Prussian sovereign. "We do not live in an enlightened age, but in an age of enlightenment – the century of Friedrich."[1084]

Therefore, Enlightenment with all its complexity, diversity, multifaceted approach and designs universally focused upon dismantling the Church dogmatic Christianity.[1085] The Enlightenment leaders all across Europe focused upon three central Christian dogmas: original sin, Trinity, divine right king and clerical establishment. These were the pivots around which the Enlightenment reformation of Church Christianity mostly revolved. Matthew Kadane, in his *Original Sin and the Path to Enlightenment*, makes it crystal-clear that the difference between the pre-Enlightenment confessional Europe and Enlightened Europe was "the rejection of the doctrine of original sin [...] antagonism to the doctrine of original sin helped to define the Enlightenment."[1086] Isaiah Berlin noted that "what the entire Enlightenment has in common is denial of the central Christian doctrine of original sin, believing instead that man is born either innocent and good, or morally neutral and malleable by education or environment, or, at worst, deeply defective but capable of radical and indefinite improvement by rational education in favourable circumstances, or by a revolutionary reorganisation of society."[1087] Ernst Cassirer identified "the concept of original sin' as 'the common opponent against which all the different trends of the philosophy of Enlightenment join forces."[1088] There is a scholarly consensus, then, that rejection of original sin was central to eighteenth-century Enlightenment.[1089]

Matthew Kadane, Justin Champion and others have shown that anti-Trinitarian struggle was also central to the Enlightenment.[1090] Champion has noted the centrality of anti-clericalism in the Enlightenment struggle. Champion's book *The Pillars of Priestcraft Shaken* addresses this important aspect of Enlightenment. Therefore, total rejection of the central Christian tenets such as the Trinity, Incarnation, Original Sin, Atoning Death, Grace-based Salvific Scheme, Divine Right Monarch and Church were the main tributaries of the early eighteenth-century Enlightenment. J. Israel stated that "Theological debate, then, lay at the heart of the Early Enlightenment. Theology dominated the correspondence between Newton and Locke, and was the exclusive topic of conversation when they first met; for while they shared what has been called 'a rationalistic approach to religion', vast work, it seemed clear to both, lay ahead defining precisely what this meant for Man, religion, and society in the new context."[1091] He further observed that "It was neither science, then, nor new geographical discoveries, nor even philosophy, as such, but rather the formidable difficulty of reconciling old and new in theological terms, and finally, by the 1740s, the apparent collapse of all efforts to forge a new general synthesis of theology, philosophy, politics, and science, which destabilised religious belief and values, causing the wholly unprecedented crisis of faith driving the secularisation of the modern West."[1092] The anti-Christian religious Enlightenment preceded the republican, democratic, liberal political Enlightenment, and was the main backdrop of it. "The redefinition of human nature; the stress on sociability, rationality, moral conduct and improvement; the deflation of religion's mysteries — these notions add up to a definition of the Enlightenment that twenty-first century historians would easily recognise."[1093]

Continental Socinians,[1094] Unitarians, Deists and other heterodox radical dissenters played a central role, especially from 1670s to 1720s, in realising the early Enlightenment.[1095] The Protestant nonconformist dissenters were included in the toleration acts of William and Mary but the Unitarians, Socinians and Catholics were excluded and mostly suffered the persecutory consequences. They led the debates about heterodoxy, religious liberty and freedom of conscience. All the foundational debates of later Enlightenment were initially launched, discussed, debated and hashed out from the 1650s to the 1720s. The later High Enlightenment of 1750s and onward was an offshoot and consolidation of early Enlightenment revolutionary ideas. Jonathan Israel notes that radical enlightenment figures "represent the extreme, most uncompromising fringe of the general trend in culture and ideas towards rationalisation and secularisation. But their less radical colleagues undoubtedly had a far greater impact on attitudes and popular culture. In fact, neither the Reformation of the sixteenth century nor the so-called 'High Enlightenment' of the post-1750 period - often little more than footnotes to the earlier shift - even begins to compete with the intellectual upheaval of the Early Enlightenment in terms of sheer impact, and the depth and extent of the intellectual and spiritual changes it brought about. It may be that the story of the High Enlightenment after 1750 is more familiar to readers and historians, but that does not alter the reality that the later movement was basically just one of consolidating, popularising, and annotating revolutionary concepts introduced earlier. Consequently, even before Voltaire came to be widely known, in the 1740s, the real business was already over."[1096] This was a period (1650s to 1720s) of break with the past medieval Christian system and ushering of a new era of freedom, liberty and rationalism. During this phase, the absolutist Church lost it monopoly on religion and accommodated dissenting Protestant sects and in the 1770s the non-Protestant dissenters such as Socinians and Unitarians were accommodated. Israel states that "the period 1650-80 is designated the phase of transition or 'crisis of the European mind' preceding the onset of the Enlightenment, and the period 1680-1750 the more dramatic and decisive period of rethinking when the mental world of the west was revolutionised along rationalistic and secular lines. By the 1750s, all major intellectual innovations and accomplishments of the European Enlightenment were well advanced if not largely complete."[1097]

The Enlightenment was a doctrinal reformation of Christianity on monotheistic, rational and moral grounds ushering an era of subjective, individualistic and rational approach to faith and religion. The enlightened rational approach dissolved the supernatural, dogmatic and incarnational Christianity of the medieval times into a Unitarian, rational and moral Christianity of the posterity. Faith and religion were not discarded but transformed.[1098] The process of transformation was long and bloody. The absolute Church did not give in that easily; it kept on resisting the change by multilayered and multi-faceted responses, and tried to re-orient, re-interpret, co-opt, adopt and manipulate enlightenment ideas - such as reason,[1099] rational discourse, liberty, freedom of conscience, morality, virtue, justice, consent, faith and accountability - to maintain its power and allure. The process of Reformation and counter-reformation, enlightenment and counter-enlightenment spanned over centuries and finally resulted in the religious tolerance, acceptance of diversity and difference of opinion, "by putting so much pressure on the category of belief, reformers turned articles of faith into objects of critical reflection and debate, setting into motion a tortuous, bloody, and still unfinished historical process enabling the emergence of a secular sphere of toleration [...] As a consequence of these developments, Western civilisation is now characterised by a degree of ideological diversity and social atomisation that would be considered intolerable by the generations that lived before secularism's triumph."[1100] Many Europeans digested, absorbed and appropriated a great deal of these conflicting ideals, beliefs and practices, and the medieval, totalitarian, supernatural and dogmatic Christianity was reformed in the process.

The Anthropomorphic Shift

Charles Taylor, one of the most influential philosophers and social scientists of our times, noted that "belief in God isn't quite the same thing in 1500 and 2000."[1101] Modern man still believed in God but that God was quite divergent from the medieval Orthodox Christianity. The focus was brought from the supernatural, creedal, incarnational Christianity to more natural, moral, utilitarian and human faith. The pendulum now swung all the way to exclusive humanism where God was looked at from the perspective of human sense of self fulfillment. This anthropomorphic shift[1102] highlighted man, his worldly happiness, good and goals as part of the divine plans. A balance between the hereafter and now and then was realised at times, gravitating more towards happiness in this material life. This transcendental anthropomorphism brought the focus on man as the crown of God's creation, dignity, realities, concerns and happiness; human happiness and felicity were not antithetical to faith and religion, but a fundamental part of God's plan. Success and happiness in this life was as significant of a religious duty as success in the life to come. God's plan and cosmos was rational, natural, purposive, moral and comprehensible. It was not mysterious, supernatural, mutable, dogmatic and unintelligible. Reason was the universal gift of God; its proper use facilitated the true understanding of the book of creation as well as the book of revelation. The irrational, unintelligible, paradoxical, supernatural and incomprehensible was antithetical to God's plan for humanity. Man was the most important part of God's religious plan and in the saga of salvation. His moral participation in the affairs of communal reformation and transformation was necessary for his eternal salvation; this salvation was not solely dependent upon the atoning death of Christ and mediation of Church but more upon human virtue and righteousness.[1103]

This anthropomorphic shift was against the bare transcendentalism of the medieval Christianity where man was totally at the mercy of the transcendental God, predestined, depraved, in desperate need of salvation through God's sacrificial acts. "Orthodox Christianity sees us as needing rescue. In this it can seem to treat us as children. Mercy, as a personal connection conflicts with the supremacy of a high code. Christianity seems not compatible with human dignity."[1104] Both the incarnational scheme, central Church role in the salvific scheme and its alliance with the abusive monarchs were sufficient enough proofs that historical Christianity was subversive to human dignity, morality and freedom. "From here it would be easy to take the step that orthodox, communion-defined Christianity really belongs to an earlier age; that it makes little sense, and is hard to sustain today."[1105]

The break with the Roman Christian past was a sort of transcendental anthropomorphism, where God and faith were employed to increase human freedom, participation and happiness. "If God's purposes for us encompass only our own good, and this can be read from the design of our nature, then no further mystery can hide here. If we set aside one of the central mysteries of traditional Christian faith, that of evil, of our estrangement from God, and inability to return to him unaided, but we see all the motivation we need already there, either in our self-interest well understood, or in our feelings of benevolence, then there is no further mystery in the human heart."[1106] Even the seventeenth-century Anglican Latitudinarian Bishop John Tillotson (1630-1694), a close friend of the Unitarian John Locke and Thomas Firmin, noted that "nothing is more likely to prevail with wise and considerate men to become religious, than to be thoroughly convinced, that religion and happiness, our duty and our interest, are but one and the same thing considered under different notions."[1107]

Man still believed in a transcendental reality but, a different kind of transcendence;[1108] it was a sort of attenuated Deism, a bit degraded or de-intensified form of Providential Deism. "Exclusive humanism in a sense crept up on us through an intermediate form, Providential Deism; and both the Deism and the humanism were made possible by earlier developments within orthodox Christianity."[1109] It also led some to a total disenchantment with God as an idea but the majority made a smooth transition from medieval creedalism to human moralism. This anthropomorphic shift was the foundation of early modernity[1110] and was most pronounced among the Unitarians. "Parallel to and overlapping with Deism was a drift towards Unitarianism. The temper [...] and even a lot of the theological beliefs, were found in other churches as well, but the defining theological beliefs of Unitarianism reflect the shift clearly [...] Unitarianism, like the Arianism which inspired it, can be seen as an attempt to hold on to the central figure of Jesus, while cutting loose from the main soteriological doctrines of historical Christianity."[1111]

This Unitarian shift away from incarnational theology of historical Christianity to human, moral and prophetic Christology was the cornerstone of the later Enlightenment. Their human Jesus was approachable, imitable and moral; he allowed human freedom, initiative, participation and empowerment. "What is important about Jesus is not that he inaugurates a new relation with and among us, restoring or transforming our relation to God. That is not what salvation can mean. What it properly amounts to is our acceding to rational principles of conduct in law and ethics, and our becoming able to act on these. Jesus' role in this is that of a teacher, by precept and example. His importance is as an inspiring trailblazer of what we will later call Enlightenment. For this he doesn't need to be divine; indeed, he had better not be, if we want to maintain the notion of a self-contained impersonal order which God in his wisdom has set up, both in nature and for human society. Incarnation would blur the edges of this."[1112] This anthropomorphic shift did not deny the Crucifixion, but diminished its metaphysical significance. "Of course, the Crucifixion can't be read out of the story [...] but it has to be an *accident de parcours;* not the main point. This fits well with the whole shift within the anthropocentric climate in the significance given to the life of Christ: what is important is not what he *does* (atone, conquer death, take captivity captive), but rather what he *says* or *teaches.* The slide to Unitarianism, and then beyond this to a humanism of which Christ can be one of the 'prophets,' belongs to this massive shift in the centre of gravity of the life of Jesus."[1113] The Islamic, prophetic and messianic Christology was finally appropriated and glorified as a liberal and moral approach to religion.

The later Unitarianism and early Socinianism, in this attenuated sense, was fairly widespread in England especially among the elites since the Interregnum. It influenced the clergy as well as laity. Countless dissenting heterodox as well as non-dissenting orthodox leaders either subscribed to it or tacitly sympathised with this theological shift. "Unitarianism wasn't confined to Unitarians. But it is not surprising to see that the members of this confession were among the social élites of Dissent, both in England and America; and also that they contained a disproportionate number of the élite figures involved in reform of various kinds in nineteenth-century Britain (closely followed by the Quakers)."[1114] Many Presbyterians, Calvinists, early Baptists, Quakers and other confessing Christians subscribed to this human, moral and prophetic Christology.

Paul Hazard had noted that the French religious landscape was equally infected with Unitarian/Socinians. "Nowhere could a single synod succeed in stemming the tide of Socinianism. If there was any truth in what was alleged about the diminution of the sect, *qua* sect; if to the outward view it seemed to have contracted, that was only in its superficial aspect. Inwardly, its influence had greatly increased. Its ideas were seeping insensibly into men's minds, leading them to substitute a rationalistic for a religious view of things."[1115] The French Catholic Biblicist Richard Simon noted that the Socinians believed that "'*Calvin and the other early Reformers left their work but half-done*' [...] Richard Simon saw one thing clearly enough, and that was that the Reformation continued to reform itself."[1116] Likewise, Holland, Germany and many other countries were infatuated with rational discourse of Socinianism/Unitarianism. Great scholars such as Poiret, Pufendorf and Jurieu "saw Socinianism everywhere; and perhaps after all he was not far wrong, so widespread and so unmistakable was the general lapse into rationalism."[1117] The Unitarian impact in regards to rational thinking was tremendous; David Martin observed that "relative to their size, which was never very great, Unitarians have acquired more entries in the *Dictionary of National Biography* than any other body."[1118]

The same anthropomorphic shift continued in the eighteenth century. The Socinian, Unitarian and Arminian rational discourse was "destined to prevail throughout the whole of the first half of the eighteenth century. Past and gone are the days when Descartes, conscious that his views were calculated to bear him away into vague, uncharted regions, voluntarily imposed on himself some prudent restraints [...] The day of heterodoxy has dawned, of every kind of heterodoxy, the day of the malcontents, the rebels who during the reign of Louis

XIV had multiplied out of sight and had been awaiting the hour of their emancipation; of learned men, who declined to accept tradition at its face value, and insisted on enquiring into its credentials; of the Jansenists, who were to kindle new fire from their dim but never wholly extinguished embers; of the Biblical exegetists; of the philosophers; the day of Pierre Bayle!"[1119] Once divorced from the long Church tradition and encouraged to think for themselves, the Protestants diversified tremendously. Consequently, Protestantism went through a "perpetual and progressive disintegration."[1120] Many new and foreign ideas were welcomed, appropriated and absorbed.

Some French *Philosophes* and pantheistic Deists stretched it too hard towards materialism and a sort of atheism, but the majority of radical - as well as moderate - enlighteners kept it within the boundaries of faith, God, salvation and morality. The same struggle continues to this day; currently "the multi-cornered debate is shaped by the two extremes, transcendent religion, on one hand, and its frontal denial, on the other."[1121] The story of this transformation and struggle is too complex and multifaceted; mine is but one account of that complex story.

The resultant anti-Trinitarian ethical monotheism or humanistic moralism with its emphasis upon republican values was so drastically un-Christian that the Orthodoxy called it un-belief, infidelity and atheism, while in reality it was no atheism at all.

Anti-Trinitarianism and Enlightenment

The Unitarian ethico-rational monotheism freed Europe of supernatural Christian mysteries with its absolutist abusive policies and allowed religious pluralism and diversity. This theological revolution was as significant as the scientific revolution in the natural sciences. For instance, Isaac Newton was as revolutionary in his Unitarian theology as in his natural sciences. In reality, his scientific works were reflection of his strict, monotheistic, Unitarian theology. The resultant Enlightenment was a theological rupture with the Trinitarian Christian past. "This was the second revolution in religious knowledge, the birth of modern belief, perhaps no less important a rupture in Western thought than the scientific revolution with which it occasionally intersected."[1122] It ushered in an era of personal, individual, subjective and private belief, based upon rationalistic credibility rather than upon religious or political authority.[1123] This freedom of thought, subjectivity

and individualism constituted the core of later liberalism, modernity and democracy. G.W.F. Hegel observed that "the principle of the
modern world at large is freedom of subjectivity."[1124] The freedom,
subjectivity and rational credibility were greatly hampered by the
pre-modern Catholic and Protestant Churches. The Enlightenment
was a revolution against both Churches and their dogmatic hegemony.
Shagan noted that "while Catholics disciplined populations to believe,
Protestants disciplined populations of unbelievers. Modern belief did
not emerge from either of these models, but rather in reaction against
the stark regime they jointly created."[1125]

The end result was neither disbelief nor atheism but an endless plurality and diversity of belief. It was a sort of relativised, personalized
and privatised belief. "Western modernity is characterised not by a decline of belief but by its boundless proliferation: today belief is everywhere, but in forms that would not have been recognised as belief in
previous eras. This proliferation of belief does not imply that religion
remained the cornerstone of Western civilisation; on the contrary,
modern belief was the sharp edge that perforated Christianity, breach-
ing the wall that had separated religion from profane ways of knowing.
This is [...] a considerable revision of the ordinary view that in modernity religion has been relegated to a separate, private sphere. Secularisation in the West was not about the segregation of belief from the
world, but the promiscuous opening of belief to the world."[1126] The end
product of Enlightenment was the liberal, secular Christianity with its
rational, natural and moral bent far removed from the supernatural,
dogmatic and incarnational Christianity of the medieval Church. The
contemporary anti-liberal doctrinal evangelism and right-wing extremism is detrimental to Enlightenment principles and philosophy;
medieval history is repeating itself. The Enlightenment reformation of
the Church Christianity was more in line with Islamic Unitarian rationalism than the medieval Trinitarian Christianity.

Anti-Trinitarianism and Islam

Islam had already offered reformation of the dogmatic Christianity
in the seventh century, and continuously loathed Christendom for its
supernatural, paradoxical and absolutist fallacies. The long, historical,
well developed and well couched Islamic reformative scheme was a
helpful tool for the Enlightenment leaders and they skillfully used it

for their specific struggles and agendas. Islam, Muhammad and the Islamic world played a vital role in Europe's transition from the Trinitarian Incarnational theological and absolutist political outlook to an anthropomorphic, natural, moral and republican outlook. The Enlightenment leaders acted upon and reacted to many Islamic beliefs, concepts, ideas and intentionally or unintentionally appropriated, absorbed and reoriented some of them as a whip to indict the historical Christianity. The Islamic "Other" was too relevant and overwhelming to be ignored.[1127]

The later part of the seventeenth century was also the period when both radical and moderate enlightenment leaders, consciously or unconsciously, interacted with the Islamic ideas and themes the most due to close trade, economic and political interactions with the Muslim world. They closely interacted with Islamic faith and tradition to create a rational, monotheistic, republican "Unitarian-Islamic syncretism," to use Justin Champion's term, which was absorbed in so many ways by various dissenting parties including the Socinians, Unitarians and Deists and through them by the European elites. Muhammad, the "Unitarian Prophet,"[1128] as John Tolan names him, was owned and appropriated by the Unitarians, Socinians and early Deists and through them by the radical as well as moderate enlightenment figures.

The founders of Socinianism, Unitarianism and Deism all had their Islamic connections. Paul Best, the early English Unitarian's Transylvanian visit and connections are well-documented. The Socinians and Unitarians's close connection with Ottoman Transylvania are well recorded. The English Deist Charles Blount's father Henry Blount travelled through the Ottoman Empire, engrossed himself in Turkish life style, wrote about Islam, Ottoman culture and customs and helped his son in compiling deistic treatises. John Locke's best friend James Tyrrell (1642-1718), a known Whig political philosopher and historian, was Charles Blount's brother-in-law. His sister was married to Blount and Locke frequently lodged at Tyrrell residence.[1129] John Locke, Henry Stubbe and many other known leaders of Enlightenment studied under Dr. Edward Pococke, the Oxford Arabic Chair. Dr. Pococke's long diplomatic stints in Muslim Aleppo and Constantinople, as well as his thorough interests in Islamic history, theology, law, political system and the Arabic language made him the most erudite, authentic and proficient authority of his time on Islam. His multiple books on Islam were probably the main source of Locke, Stubbe and other Oxford graduates' knowledge of and interactions with Islam in addition to a multitude of other books available at that time. Other Levant Company chaplains such as Dr. John Covel and Robert Huntington were John Locke and Isaac Newton's friends, supplied information and manuscripts especially scientific ones to Locke, Robert Boyle and other Royal Society fellows who are known to have used the travelogues and Oriental manuscripts in their writings.[1130] The overseas chaplains' detailed diaries and works were filled with eyewitness accounts of the Ottoman Empire, its people, culture, religion and government. Dr. Covel was Cambridge vice chancellor and Newton worked under him. Newton's Cambridge politics was closely coordinated with Dr. Covel.[1131]

These Islamic interactions and the overall English milieu facilitated the transition of Locke, Newton, Stubbe and many others from Anglican Protestant Christianity to their heterodox Unitarian Islamic outlook. They became thorough Unitarian heretics.[1132] Islam, Socinianism and Unitarianism were so intermeshed during the second half of the seventeenth century and early eighteenth century (in England, France, Germany and Holland) that instead of using the term "Islamic" the writers of that period just used the term "Unitarian" to talk about Islam. For instance, Edward Gibbon used Unitarian instead of Islamic in many places of his history monograph *The History of Decline and Fall of the Roman Empire*.[1133] Eighteenth-century English, French and American Enlightenment leaders were heir to this rational, republican, monotheistic Unitarian Islamic syncretism. The process began with the Protestant Reformation.

The sixteenth-century Reformation's "upshot was rather that Roman Catholicism, even at its best, was a perverted form of Christianity."[1134] The Reformers opened a floodgate of scepticism, rendering centuries of Church traditions, culture and authority suddenly null and void. The theological upheavals caused by the Reformation, and the ensuing doctrinal controversies and religious wars, resulted in a total loss of traditional structures of authority and references of meaning.[1135] The resultant frustration, instability and insecurity created an atmosphere of acceptance of foreign ideas, including Islamic ones, to resolve internal problems. "The Reformation endured and brought endless doctrinal controversies in its wake— about Christ, the sacraments liturgy, sin and grace, salvation, the church, ministry, scripture, and authority. The controversies obliterated the existing, shared framework of beliefs within which new intellectual challenges and influences might be confronted, appropriated, and discriminatingly assimilated, as neo-Platonism had been in early medieval monasteries or Aristotelianism in thirteenth-century universities."[1136] The Islamic anti-Trinitarian republican ideas, starting with Michael Servetus, filled the vacuum in so many ways, especially for the persecuted dissenters. The Islamic model of religious tolerance was extremely attractive to the abused, *sola scriptura* individualistic dissenters. Their century's long struggles for liberty facilitated the separation of Church from state, and the subsequent privatisation of faith and worship was cherished by the later generations.[1137]

Seventeenth- and eighteenth-century Europe was marred by Habsburg/Catholic hegemonic designs and fledgling Protestant Churches and nation state's efforts to assert themselves. Inter-Protestant strife was no less chaotic, destructive and apocalyptic; the Protestant states and Churches were as absolute and persecutory as their Catholic counterparts.[1138] Religious and political dissent was heavily punished as a crime against the society and Crown. Citizenship, property and other basic rights were dependent upon membership of national churches, while non-conformists were severely tortured and persecuted. Margarete Jacob notes that "in the 1680s the promotion of absolutist policies in France and Britain threatened the stability of all of northern and western Europe and the religious independence of Protestants in England, Ireland, the Dutch Republic, and potentially in the German states west of the Rhine."[1139] The persecutions of Protestants in Catholic France resulted in countless human miseries. Louis XIV's policies of forced conversion through financial incentives, socio-economic and finally military pressure filled Protestants with fear and horror. They sent a wave of Protestant refugees all around Western Europe. "After the revocation of the Edict of Nantes in 1685 thousands of exiled French Protestants fled to the Dutch Republic and England—to name only the countries with the highest concentrations—and they carried with them experiences of persecution vivid and shocking to the modern imagination. Children deemed convertible were detained by the French authorities; the laity was actually forbidden to emigrate thus forcing families to separate as escape routes were found for some and not others. Elderly Protestants were thrown in prison; the clergy was expelled sometimes with two days' notice or that was how long it took a leading and endangered Protestant clergyman, Jean Claude, to leave France."[1140] The French authorities "strung up their victims, men and women, by their hair or by their feet, to the rafters in the roof, or the hooks in the chimney, and then set fire to bundles of moldy hay heaped up beneath them [...] They flung them into huge fires which they lit for the purpose, and left them there till they were half-roasted. They fastened ropes underneath their arms and lowered them into wells, pulling them up and down till they promised to change their religion."[1141] Paul Hazard inquired: "Was the King of France then unaware that Faith is a gift that comes from on high, and that nothing that man can do can make or destroy it; that violence and coercion can only create unbelievers, or hypocrites, or else engender in the hearts of the sincere a staunchness, a longanimity that no suffering which man can inflict will ever avail to overcome? Does he not know that by perpetrating such atrocities he has put himself beyond the pale, in the eyes of every European country: and that having scandalously violated both the solemn covenant of his predecessors, and the law of nations, his promises and his treaties will henceforth be credited by none?"[1142]

Such a torturous, inhumane and un-dignifying treatment of Protestants in the Catholic areas and Catholics in the Protestant areas was commonplace. The French brutalisation of Protestants was perhaps the harshest of all. "Well over 200,000 French Protestants made the journey out of France, and those who stayed behind were imprisoned or submitted to conversion. These were the events that form the essential background to understanding the Enlightened critique of Christianity as it emerged with virulence in the period of the 1680s. From that moment onward, the critique only became more pointed, more strident, sometimes less anonymous, but always suspicious of clerical authority and often bitter. It lay at the heart of the crisis provoked by monarchical absolutism."[1143] Persecution of dissenters in England was no less torturous.

Both the Church and state were equally oppressive of dissent.[1144] This constant abuse and torturous persecution produced anger, resentment and radicalism, especially among the dissenters, their families and sympathisers.[1145] The Christian religion and history had provided the foundations for such an oppressive society. As the problem of human rights, empowerment and religious tolerance was directly connected with the Christian religion, and as theology was the cornerstone of power structures, enlightenment efforts had to deal with the Christian religion, its theology and institutions to bring down the scaffolding of that oppressive society and oligarchy. The problem of power was really a problem of religious nature, and that needed a religious solution. Therefore, the political abuse and chaos resulted in a sort of theological radicalism. The radical anger was further fueled by a stifling censorship machine.

The Christian Europe was a suffocating society where religious freedom, public debate and printing were closely monitored and supervised. "From the mid-Sixteenth century onwards, Europe was a civilisation in which formal education, public debate, preaching, printing, book-selling, even tavern disputes about religion and the world, were closely supervised and controlled. Virtually nowhere, not even in England or Holland after1688, was full toleration the rule, and hardly anyone subscribed to the idea that the individual should be free to think and believe as he or she thought fit."[1146] People were spied on, and their private, personal and confidential conversations were used to indict them of blasphemy, to torture and burn them alive on the stake. It was a suffocatingly inhumane society; absolute submission to the Church and state was required of all.

The radical and moderate dissenters demanded a reformation of Protestant Reformation by allowing religious liberty and freedom of publication and conscience. The Ottoman liberties of freedom of worship and religious print were quoted, and the Islamic reformative scheme came in handy to European Enlightenment figures dealing with debilitating supernatural, mysterious, irrational, absolutist and intolerant Church Christianity and aiming to reform it on lines of simplistic, tolerant, minimalistic, republican primitive Christianity of Jesus. That primitive Christianity was the ideal model of the enlightenment figures because the problem of Christian persecutions, heresies and inquisition was heralded by the Church and state alliance of the fourth century when the Roman empirical structures and Christian religious institutions were merged in an unholy alliance. As seen above, the Islamic faith blamed the same on the Roman Christianity and claimed itself to be the reformer of that absolutist, Trinitarian, dogmatic and supernatural Christianity. The Enlightenment figures accepted Islam as the heir to that original, simplistic and republican Christianity. Islam became the enlightened ideal and Muhammad became the enlightened Prophet. "Indeed, the figure of Muhammad and the text of the Qur'ān could inspire interest and esteem, particularly from those who criticised the power of the Church in European society or who deviated from its accepted dogmas. Sixteenth-century Unitarian Michael Servetus mined the Qur'ān for arguments against the doctrine of the Trinity; condemned by the Catholic inquisition, he escaped only to be burned at the stake in Calvin's Geneva. In the midst of bloody confessional wars that were tearing Europe apart, some looked to the introduction toleration of religious diversity grounded in the Qur'ān and practiced by the Ottomans as a model Europeans should follow. Various authors of the seventeenth and eighteenth centuries, in England, France, and elsewhere, portrayed Muhammad as a reformer who abolished the privileges of a corrupt and superstitious clergy, showed tolerance to Jews and Christians, and reestablished the true spirit of monotheism. In the eighteenth and nineteenth centuries, he is increasingly portrayed as a 'great man,' a sort of Arab national hero, bringing law, religion, and glory to his people. Many of these authors are interested less in Islam and its prophet per se than in reading in Muhammad's story lessons that they could apply to their own preoccupations and predicaments."[1147] The Enlightenment reformation of the Reformation went through the Islamic faith and tradition back to the first-century Jewish, Unitarian Christianity, the supposed original Christianity of Jesus.

Additionally, Islamic republicanism was a living reality in the sixteenth, seventeenth and eighteenth centuries. The Ottoman, Safvid and Mughal Muslim empires were minimalistic, tolerant, overpowering and alluring, especially in the seventeenth century. The Mediterranean was an Ottoman lake and the gateway to the Muslim East. The English, Dutch and French Protestants were heavily engaged in the Muslim empires and an eye witness to the tolerance given to interfaith as well as intra-faith dissent. Protestants in Hungary and other East European countries were enjoying religious freedom under the Ottoman Millet system, while Protestants in Catholic areas and Catholic and Protestant dissenters in the Protestant areas were persecuted. That is why the Ottoman Islamic minimalistic and republican model was very attractive to the persecuted European dissenters, such as Socinians and Unitarians, whose historical connections with the Ottoman Empire were well-documented. In fact, the Hungarian and East European Unitarians fought in Ottoman armies against the Habsburg Catholics during the long siege of Vienna. Even the Protestant English ambassador to the Sublime Porte Sir Edward Barton participated in

Ottoman military expeditions (1596) against the Catholic Habsburg Empire in Hungry and Eger.[1148]

Moreover, the French-Ottoman alliance against the Habsburg Empire was a popular topic of discussion throughout Europe. Catholics across Europe blamed the Protestants of allying themselves with Ottoman-Muslim republicanism against the divinely-sanctioned, Bible-preserving Habsburg monarchy and Christian Catholic Church. As the Catholics blamed all Protestants of Turkism, the Protestant Churches and states accused local dissenters of Turkism. They accused republican-leaning dissenters such as the Unitarians, Socinians and Deists of Turkish affiliations against the Christian authoritative Church and monarchies. They blamed the dissenters for Christian disunity, anarchy and chaos. Consequently, both the Catholic and Protestant authorities implied heavy-handed policies against the dissenters in the name of maintaining Christian unity. They depicted the Islamic republicanism as the archenemy of Christian unity, and a leading factor of internal anarchy and disunity. This way, the internal European socio-political power struggle was transformed into warfare between the Christian absolute Church and monarchy and Islamic republicanism, cherished by the free-thinking freedom fighters and secular libertarians. It was a strange alliance, but a reality created by the historical circumstances. The dissenters used Islamic republicanism to analyse, dissect, criticise and reject Christian traditions to make room for themselves in European society on equal footing. The centuries-long debates and controversies provided enough fodder and material for both the dissenters and monarchical vanguards to appropriate and digest Islamic religious and political themes to the extent that by the late seventeenth and early eighteenth century the Islamic ideas and concepts were mostly internalised and Christianised.[1149] Catholics used Islam to substantiate some of their doctrines rejected by the radical Protestants such as the Immaculate Conception. The Protestants used Islam to indict Catholics of idolatry and saint worship. Islam was Europeanised, Christianised, used and abused but not neglected. Muhammad and Turks were the most discussed, used and abused figures from the sixteenth century onward Europe.

Europe appropriated these Antichristian ideas, in accordance with its specific cultural needs and conditions, and was enlightened, partially based upon many ready-made Islamic ideals. Of course, the appropriation process and its intensity varied with different European reformers; eighteenth-century radical reformers such as Henry Stubbe, John Toland, Socinians, Unitarians and early Deists were the closest to the Islamic reformation scheme. They equated the pristine, original Christianity of Jesus with Islam, and reformed the historical, Church Christianity based on that Islamic reformative model. They openly quoted Muslim scriptures, Islamic history, Christology and republicanism to delineate their reformative designs. On the other hand, moderate enlightenment leaders such as John Locke, Newton and others changed the Christian dogmas from within, rarely referring to Islam or its scriptures directly; however, the end result was the same. Their strain of reformed Christianity was freed from the so-called fundamental Christian dogmas such as the original sin, justification through the atoning death of Jesus Christ, Trinity, divinity of Jesus and absolute determinism or salvation through grace and election. These reformers believed that Christ was a role model, a law-giver rather than a grace-giver, a messiah and a prophet, an heir to long universal monotheistic prophetic tradition and nothing but an exalted human being who could be called Lord and Son of God like rabbis and kings of antiquity. They contended that the pristine Christianity of Jesus and early Nazarenes was thoroughly corrupted by the Roman era priestcraft, with the help of various Church Councils and Synods.[1150] The resultant Trinitarian, incarnational and ecclesiastical Christianity became a useful tool in the hands of power-hungry church leaders and their royal allies. The absolute church and monarchs subdued the Christian masses by imposing irrational doctrines such as the Trinity and original sin, and by monopolising both the sacred and profane public spaces. Severe punishments were introduced, such as burning alive on the stake, to curb any possible dissent - whether religious or temporal - while the boundaries between the sacred and profane were effectively blurred. The tyrannical monopolisation of both religious and secular realms led to a concentration of knowledge and its interpretations in the hands of a few elites - mostly the religious pundits. Christianity needed a thorough reformation to allow rationalism, monotheism and republicanism to take their due course. Both the moderate and radical Enlightenment figures shared the same reformative scheme with its broader thematic elements, but differed only in the tactics. They were two sides of the same coin.

Seventeenth-century reformers like John Locke, Isaac Newton, Henry Stubbe, John Toland and many English and French Deists such as Henri Boulainvilliers, d'Argenson, Du Marsais, jean-Baptiste de Mirabaud, Nicolas Boindin, Jean Levesque de Burigny, Louis de Brehant, comte de Plelo (1699-1734), the Chevalier de Ramsay and other known French deists such as Voltaire[1151] contended that the sixteenth-century Reformation needed additional doctrinal reformation. They purged Christianity of the remaining incarnational reservoirs, the remnants of ancient Christian Platonic grafting, and brought it in line with the supposed pristine Christianity of Jesus Christ and his original followers, the *Nasara* or Nazarenes.[1152] This Christianity was nothing but a moral tradition in line with the universal monotheistic prophetic tradition. Their Christianity was a Unitarian, Socinian, Deistic and Islamic syncretism. In other words, it was a Muhammadan Christianity, as Henry Stubbe and John Toland termed it, in direct opposition to the traditional Church Christianity. This hybrid rational monotheism, along with its natural outlook, republican government system, ethical anthropology, moral soteriology and rational teleology was the hallmark of the Continental Enlightenment. The national Enlightenments were quite complex and multifaceted processes with unique characteristics, salient features and specific directions. But the Unitarian religious and republican political transformation was elemental to all these national Enlightenments, and hence Continental in nature. Therefore, the early Enlightenment, secular liberalism, republicanism and modernity project owed more to the Unitarian Islamic syncretism than Spinoza's supposed materialism, as Jonathan Israel insists, or on John Locke's liberal works, as the majority of scholarship in the field of Enlightenment studies contends. Both Spinoza and Locke were the products of the Unitarian Islamic theology, scriptural criticism, anti-clericalism and republicanism. They worked through Islamic republican tropes and cultural enmeshments to support the ongoing struggle of dissenters such as the Unitarians, Socinians and Deists. I agree with Humberto Garcia, Justin Champion and others' wonderful corrective works of such a misplaced, Eurocentric, dominant scholarly narrative and agree with their interpretation of *Historia monotheistica* and Islamic republicanism as the main source of English Enlightenment. These were the two main themes implied - openly or tacitly - by radical and moderate enlightenment figures in England and France. The leading Founding Fathers of the French Republic and American Republic such as Napoleon Bonaparte, Benjamin Franklin, John Adams, Thomas Jefferson and Thomas Paine inherited this Unitarian, Deistic, Islamic strand of the English Enlightenment and its reformed Christianity, and built the French and American republics on the moral and political foundations of this newly reformed Christianity. Let us now turn to this Unitarian Islamic syncretism which was realised in the seventeenth- and eighteenth-century England.

Chapter 5

English Enlightenment and Unitarian Islamic Syncretism

The Unitarian Islamic syncretism was a hybrid of Islamic ethical monotheism, prophetic Christology, biblical criticism, anti-Trinitarianism, anti-clericalism and anti-monarchy couched in a Christian vocabulary, with due respect to and considerations of Christian cultural sensitivities. This hybrid was realised by the collective efforts, struggles and sacrifices of the Socinians, Deists, Unitarians and overseas merchants of the seventeenth- and eighteenth-century Europe. This was a mixture of internal as well as external influences. The Islamic catalyst was pretty visible though. Shaftesbury, Stubbe, Toland, Hobbes, Locke, Newton, Harrington, Middleton, Bolingbroke, Milton, Unitarians, Socinians, Deistics and many other anti-clerical and anti-monarchy individuals and sects in part or in total participated in this long seventeenth-century struggle modeled on Islamic republicanism. Europe's long march against the oppressive Church and monarchy, and its transition from absolutist to liberal, democratic, modern project passed through a long love affair with the Islamic republican model. The powerful Catholic Church, which resisted the anti-Trinitarian and republican influences of the Islamic world throughout medieval times, was initially weakened by the Church and state struggles for authority, failed Crusades and Protestant Reformation, while the Protestant national churches and states were crippled by internal struggles for power, freedom and liberty. The English Civil War, Interregnum, overseas trade, emergent middle class of traders and continuous conflicts between the Crown and parliaments facilitated the transition.

The paradigm shift was made possible by the constant warfare between the Christian sects, the ensuing chaos, deformation, destruction of Christendom and the resultant socio-cultural shock, instability and insecurity. The Church both Catholic and Protestant and multiple Protestant sects were directly blamed for this destructive chaos which touched almost everybody's life in Europe. It forced the Europeans to accept one another and tolerate religious differences. However, this acceptance of religious plurality needed to be intellectualised, and the theorisation and legitimisation process of toleration greatly helped the Enlightenment Project. Moreover, European's encounter with other nations, especially the neighbouring Islamic Orient gave them an access to an alternate religio-historical narrative. Many European travellers were fascinated with the Moghul and Ottoman empires and wrote detailed accounts of Muslim religion, customs, habits, culture and politics; these accounts helped in making the Christian claims to divine authority relative rather than absolute. As the Europeans were exhausted by the religious warfare and Christian scaffolding, the alternate Islamic narrative and arrangements were refreshing and attractive. The external "other" was helpful in mirroring the internal fiasco and was used as a whip to indict the perceived internal enemy and to realise the needed internal changes. On the way, many of its ideas, ideals and outlooks were intentionally or un-intentionally absorbed, appropriated and owned.

Seventeenth-century radical enlightenment figures such as Stubbe, Toland, Deists such as Charles Blount and Unitarians such as Stephen Nye and Arthur Bury did not hesitate to quote the Quran, Prophet Muhammad, Islamic history and teachings during their deconstruction process as well as the reconstruction process. They openly demanded a change based on the Islamic/Muhammaden model. They rejected the suffocating, intolerant and absolutist traditional Church Christianity, and instead desired a pristine, rational, natural, minimalistic and tolerant Muhammadan Christianity, epitomised by the Ottoman Empire's pluralism and republicanism. The radical agenda was furthered by the dissenters such as the Socinians, Unitarians and Deists. Both the moderate and radical enlighteners had close Socinian or Unitarian links, but some hesitated to publicly confess such links to avoid Church persecutions. John Locke and Isaac Newton were too cautious, calculated and prudent to sacrifice their careers and social clout to go through the humiliating persecutions and tortures unleashed upon Unitarians, Socinians and other dissenters. The brutal, tortorous and barbaric hanging, drawing and quatering death of the 20--year-old Edinburgh student Thomas

Aikenhead in 1697 was a constant reminder for them.[1153] This was too much of a punishment for tacit anti-Trinitarianism and Islamism.

The Socinians and Unitarians were openly called "crypto-Muslims", "Turks", "Moors" and "Muhammadens", the terms denoting Muslims in sixteenth- to eighteenth-century Europe.[1154] Many moderate as well as radical enlighteners were named by their opponents as "Turks", "Socinians", "Unitarians", Mahometen" and straightforward Muslims. For instance, Locke, Newton, Blount, Stubbe and Toland were named "Turks," "Socinians," "Unitarians," "Arians" and "Muhammadan Christians" by their opponents. Joseph Priestley and Thomas Jefferson for instance were called straightforward Muslims.[1155]

The mainstream moderate enlightenment figures, such as Locke and Newton, were able to bring about a partial change in England that resulted in a mixed monarchy sharing political powers with the parliament and the gentry through the mechanism of a constitution. This enlightenment trend neither broke with the traditional monarchy nor with the traditional Christianity, but tried to reform it from within while using outside - mostly Islamic - models. The Islamic doctrines and ideas were Christianised and contextualised; this moderate trend was the source and the aspired model of the American Revolution. The moderate enlighteners were less effective in the French arena where the Most Christian King and hegemonic Catholic Church ruled with iron fist, meting out swift and harsh punishments to any and every kind of dissent. The French monarchical and clerical radicalism was met with equal brutality by the French radical revolutionaries. The French de-Christianisation and use of monotheistic, rational, Islamic hybrid was open and violent. Ali Bonaparte epitomised this strand of radicalism.

Radicals like Henry Stubbe, Henri de Boulainvilliers, and later on Napoleon Bonaparte did not hesitate to publicise their sheer appreciation for Islamic monotheism, rationalism, constitutionalism and ethical republicanism. They graciously admired Prophet Muhammad as the enlightenment hero who brought about the perfect reformation of the corrupted traditional Christianity, far ahead of the partial 16th century European Reformation. Jonathan Israel observes that "the Radical Enlightenment [...] entertained a curiously schizoid view of Islam and Mohammed. On the one hand, from the late Seventeenth century and culminating in Boulainvilliers' Vie de Mahomed ('Londres', 1730), a work widely diffused through Europe-and republished in English (London, 1731) and Italian (Venice, 1744)-Islam is viewed positively, even enthusiastically, as a purified form of revealed religion, stripped of the many imperfections of Judaism and Christianity and hence reassuringly akin to deism."[1156] Muhammad was the model of English Whiggism; John V. Tolan noted that "over the course of the seventeenth century [...] various Whig intellectuals came to see the prophet Mahomet as a model reformer, one who smashed 'priestcraft,' the grasping greed of a clerical class that built its power on the ignorance and superstition of the masses. Mahomet, far from establishing a new religion, offered a purified monotheism stripped of abstruse doctrines and idolatrous rites. He abolished the privileges of the clergy and reestablished a direct relationship between God and his believers. In all these things, reason was his supreme guide. This vision, most fully expressed by Stubbe and Toland, met fierce opposition from those who defended the privileges of Anglican Church, who reaffirmed the traditional view of Mahomet as a dangerous impostor and did not hesitate to paint their opponents as new Mahomets. In the eighteenth century, Mahomet plays a similar role in France; opponents of the wealth and power of the Catholic Church present Mahomet's purified, anticlerical monotheism as an antidote to French ills."[1157]

Islam and Muhammad were ideal models, but contemporary Muslims were not, due to their human shortcomings. In reality, the constant seventeenth-century struggle between Whiggish republican and Tory conservative ideologies was in a sense a fight between Turkish Muhammad and the Church hegemonic Christianity. From Shaftesbury to Stubbe, Toland to Locke, all republican-leaning enlightenment figures employed, in one way or the other, Muhammad, Turks and Islam as a whip as well as a model to correct the English problems. Henry Stubbe and Napoleon Bonaparte are reported to have declared their conversion to Islam; Napoleon became "Ali Bonaparte" and declared his conversion in a public statement while in Egypt. Many academicians try to highlight the political motives behind Napoleon's conversion to Islam[1158] but his last words of total appreciation of Islamic ethical monotheism, rationalism and Prophet Muhammad's splendid legal, political and moral legacy refute or at least mitigate such claims of political expediency.[1159] It suffices to quote Juan Cole, a contemporary authority on Bonaparte, who confirms that "Bonaparte's admiration for the Prophet Muhammad, in contrast, was genuine."[1160] Even if his conversion is accepted as a political stunt, it still substantiates the close links maintained and affinities harboured by the radical Deists and Unitarians with the Unitarian faith of Islam. Islam and Muhammad were used as catalysts of sweeping changes during the early and high Enlightenment periods. Muhammad was the Prophet of Enlightenment, as John Tolan has noted.

Muhammad, the Prophet of Enlightenment

Islam, Muhammad, the Quran and Turks were some of the most discussed terms and concepts in Enlightenment-era Europe. The Prophet of Islam, Muhammad, can be described as the most discussed and quoted figure during the Enlightenment centuries. Matthew Dimmock notes that "Mahomet was well known in early modern England. Routinely rejected, reclaimed, defamed, defended and used as a polemical tool, in his various forms Mahomet could be imagined as French, Spanish, German, Arabian or Persian, and he might be Muslim, Protestant or Roman Catholic – but most importantly [...] he was repeatedly imagined as English, and summoned to appear in England. The bewildering variety of guises in which Mahomet appears in English writings presents a distinctively new perspective on this period."[1161] Prophet Muhammad was widely invoked all over Christendom. In the "early modern period between 1450 and 1750, Mahomet becomes a defining and often divisive figure. Aside from those celebrated individuals in the interconnected theological and political worlds of Christendom – Biblical patriarchs, saints, potentates – he is the most well known and frequently invoked in this three-hundred-year span. Almost everyone knew of Mahomet. He is depicted in numerous divergent forms in poetry, drama and prose of different genres; he is invoked from pulpits, related in stories, declaimed by travellers and polemically paralleled with Christ, Luther, various popes and almost every English monarch of the period. His image appears in political and religious tracts and pamphlets, in chronicle histories and in English prayerbooks, and hangs on the wall of at least one noble household. In early modern and enlightenment England he is ubiquitous to the point that his invocation becomes a shorthand for a whole range of associations."[1162] John V. Tolan's recent book *Faces of Muhammad* well demonstrates the point. Dimmock further illustrates that "Mahomet and 'his' religion were not simply something alien or 'other' but might be imagined as mutually reinforcing monotheism or even, in some early enlightenment writing, as an authentic true Christianity. Shared Abrahamic roots connected the two religions, making Mahomet and his doctrine uncannily familiar. What we now call Islam became the 'dark bubble' of Christianity, an encroaching other world, a mirror image enabling a sustained reflection on Christian faults and Christian depravity."[1163] Muhammad's erastian church and state model was highly relevant to Henry VIII's England. In a "post-Reformation English context he [Muhammad] gains an extraordinary vitality because – like Henry VIII and most of his successors – Mahomet was simultaneously a spiritual and secular leader. Writing about Mahomet and Mahometanism in England in these years was never simply about engaging with those beyond Christendom. It offered a means of cementing and projecting, but also critiquing, English political and religious structures."[1164] In addition to Prophet Muhammad, the Muslim scripture Quran was also very popular during this period.[1165]

The same can be said about France and many other continental countries. Ian Coller notes that "From the mid-Sixteenth century onward, France joined a loose alliance with the Ottoman Empire, fostering ongoing contacts in diplomacy, military training, and trade with a Muslim power. Beginning in the 1720s, philosophers began to investigate the life and teachings of the Prophet Muhammad in new ways that undermined older theological understandings. Trade and diplomacy produced travellers' accounts that shaped the ideas of Enlightenment thinkers. Radical philosophical ideas about Islam came together with diplomatic and commercial knowledge of Muslim societies to produce a sea change in conceptions about Muslims and Islam that would become entangled with the revolutionary transformation."[1166] The landscape was the same in Germany, Italy and even Spain, albeit secretly.

Muslim presence was felt all over England and France, and Muslim names, relatives, connections and stories were all across France. "Connections could be more intimate. Places and families across France carried names like Le Turc and Sarrazin, traces of medieval Muslim presence in Languedoc and Provence, or the Ottoman fleet that wintered in Toulon in 1543. Members of many French families—among them the Rousseau, Chénier, and Laclos families—spent extended periods living in Muslim cities for trade or diplomacy. Some—like Louis XVI's foreign minister, the Countde Vergennes, former ambassador to Istanbul, and

Louis de Chénier, father of revolutionaries André and Marie-Joseph Chénier—brought Ottoman Christian wives back to France. Others, like the famous Count de Bonneval, moved to Istanbul and converted to Islam. At the other end of the social ladder, convicts and Protestants sentenced to serve in the galleys of Marseille and Toulon found themselves labouring alongside 'Turks'—Muslims purchased from slave traders in Malta or Italy. Muslims were, in the words of a recent historian, Europe's 'familiar strangers.'"[1167] The Muslim world and society was "the most expansive and influential in the Afro-Eurasian hemisphere."[1168] Marshall Hodgson, the famous historian, noted that a visitor from Mars visiting at that time "might well have supposed that the human world was on the verge of becoming Muslim."[1169]

Overseas Trade, Piracy and Turning Turk

Hundreds of thousands of French, Dutch and Englishmen worked in the Muslim Ottoman, Safvid and Mughal Empires, Africa and the Far East (English, Dutch and French Levant and East India Companies),[1170] dealing with Muslims on land and on sea.[1171] They turned many parts of the Muslim East into "a little England,"[1172] France and Netherlands. "From the Atlantic coast to the Valley of the Nile, and from Istanbul to Salee, Britons lived and worked among the Muslims."[1173] Fernand Braudel noted that there "was suddenly an invasion of the East by the West."[1174] Britain was not yet a big power and early British merchants, workers and travellers were mesmerised by the Muslim world, its society, prosperity and systems.[1175] For the early modern English, the Ottoman Empire was "the fabulously wealthy and magnificent court from which the sultan ruled over three continents with his great and powerful army."[1176] Captivity was another main source of interactions, inter-cultural and inter-faith exchanges.

Many Europeans were captives of the Barbary States. Robert C. Davis has shown that "between 1530 and 1780 there were almost certainly a million and quite possibly as many as a million and a quarter white, European Christians enslaved by the Muslims of the Barbary Coast."[1177] Many accepted Islam to avoid slavery or to benefit from the financial possibilities.[1178] "Britons held in North Africa converted to Islam and lived on, or died in captivity, unless they escaped or were ransomed and returned home."[1179] Many of them rejected offers of safe return to their homelands due to new realities and opportunities, but kept regular contacts with their relatives and friends back home.[1180] "Religiously and culturally changed as they were, their compatriots could not but believe that they had continued to retain something of old England or Spain in their hearts—and if not something of their previous Christianity, then a clear memory of their country's customs."[1181] The European diplomates, merchants and workers kept in touch with the renegades and utilised their experience, clout and networks to enhance their opportunities and successes. M. Pugh notes that during "the Seventeenth and Eighteenth centuries an estimated 20,000 Englishmen were captured by the corsairs, most of them ending up as slaves."[1182]

Maartje van Gelder, in *The Republic's Renegades: Dutch Converts to Islam in Seventeenth-Century Diplomatic Relations with North Africa*, has demonstrated that many Dutch renegades and converts played an important diplomatic role between the Dutch and the Barbary States. "Dutch converts to Islam acted as informants, intermediaries, and at times even informal diplomats, thereby facilitating and shaping cross-confessional diplomatic relations between the North African polities and the Protestant Dutch Republic, a relative newcomer to Mediterranean affairs."[1183] Voluntary conversion to Islam was widespread among the Dutch. "Whereas coerced conversion fitted European narratives of an aggressive Islam, voluntary apostasy did not; yet it was a pervasive phenomenon in the Ottoman Empire and the independent kingdom of Morocco. Conversion by pronouncing the *shahada* (declaration of faith), and usually circumcision if the convert was male, was often followed by taking a new name, gifts of clothing and money, marriage to a Muslim spouse, and integration into local patronage networks. Changing faith was not just a religious but also a social and political practice during which converts constructed ties with their new religious community."[1184] Likewise, Algeria and Tunis attracted many Dutch converts. "A similar pattern is discernible in North Africa: men, often with maritime experience, moved to its ports, converted, and joined the corsairing fleets searching for economic gains, social ascent, and perhaps levels of political power that they could never hope to obtain in their native countries."[1185]

Some of the known corsairs came from England and Dutch Republic. Asan Agha and John Ward[1186] were English converts,[1187] and had a huge contingent of English renegades at their disposal. Dutch converts such as Admiral Joseph Rais, born as Gerrit Jacobsz in the town of Enkhuizen, represented Tunis during negotiations with Dutch authorities. The Dutchmen Danseker,[1188] Claes Compaen, Moerad Rais (Jan Jansz), Vice-Admiral Matthijs van Bootel, Soliman Rais (De Veenboer), Xabano Flamengo, Fendri Shaban, Hendrick Jansen, Murat Picinino Rais and many other Dutch converts reached the height of their power and prestige in the Barbary States.[1189] "In April 1611, the States of Holland discussed the fact that one Simon Maartenszoon Stuijt served as the captain of several corsairing ships in the Bay of Marmora; in 1613, a Dutch captive related that eight of the thirty-five ships of the Algerian corsairing fleet were commanded by Dutch *rais;* in 1625-1626, a Dutch envoy reported that eight of the fifty Algerian *rais* hailed originally from the Low Countries, including Seffer Rais alias Thomas the Pickpocket, from Harlingen, Regeb Rais from The Hague, and Seliman Buffoen alias Jacob the Brothelkeeper, from Rotterdam."[1190] Indeed "several were so successful in their pursuits as North African pirates that they became the objects of keen interest in the popular Dutch press."[1191] Ibn abi Dinar, the famous seventeenth-century Tunisian historian, attributed the success of the Tunisian fleet to Dutch, English and other European converts.[1192]

These "converts maintained business relations or correspondence with Christian family members and friends [...] the liminal position of converts and their ability to cross and recross not just religious but also political and social boundaries. It is this ability that has seen them cast as yet another category of cultural intermediaries or brokers"[1193] They visited their families, closely helped the Dutch ambassadors in North Africa and corresponded with the State General and Prince Maurice of Orange.[1194] "During a career that spanned three decades, the privateer Jan Jansz became Moerad Rais, the North African corsair who evolved from aggressor to protector, adviser, and diplomatic mediator to the Dutch."[1195] The Dutch converts, like their French and British counterparts, aggressively engaged in proselytisation, converting multitudes of their countrymen to Islam.[1196] They married in the Muslim world, lived with their Muslim spouses and children and brought some of their Dutch and British family members to live with them.[1197] At times they spent entire winters in the Dutch Republic, had religious debates with their friends and relatives and refused to change their Islamic religion or to return to Christianity.[1198] Van Gelder after quoting many examples stresses "how common such encounters between the converted and their Christian kin and former compatriots could be. These examples indicate the frequency and apparent ease with which these interactions took place, whether in the Dutch Republic or in North Africa. Renegades continued to engage with Christian Dutchmen and to be identifiable by their Dutch origins."[1199]

Likewise, there were countless Muslims slaves in Europe and America.[1200] "That the Barbary corsairs captured thousands of Europeans is not in question; but then, the Europeans captured and enslaved more. That the actions of the Barbary corsairs were motivated by greed and economic need are not in question; but they were also undertaken in retaliation for the violence committed against them by Europeans— government-sponsored acts of empire as well as disparate attacks of pirates and privateers."[1201] The East and West especially the Mediterranean basin were intersected in so many ways and their cultures, customs and religions were quite familiar.

Nabil Matar[1202] and Gerald MacLean have shown close interactions and intersections between Europeans and Muslims of the seventeenth and eighteenth centuries. Matar noted that "throughout the Elizabethan and Stuart periods Britons had extensive interaction with Turks and Moors."[1203] He further noted that "so extensive was the commercial and diplomatic coordination between the queen and the sultan that Europeans suspected her of planning to offer him 'safe port in England, by means of which to set his foot also into the Western Empire.' In 1590 King James VI of Scotland was 'perswaided that no Christian Prince [except Queen Elizabeth] ever had in the Turk suche great estimation'; and by the end of the century, the Pope viewed Elizabeth as "a confederate with the Turk.'"[1204] Francis Bacon, the father of English empiricism, strongly defended English ties with the Grand Turk and hailed Muslim anti-saint images, and other idolatrous practices of the Catholic Church.[1205]

Nobody can exactly gauge the type of information transmitted back to England, but one thing is certain; that the Englishmen knew a great deal about Islam and the Muslim world. "But there is little doubt that the information about Muslims that was available to Britons in the Age of Discovery provided them with a window on an un-Christian but powerful empire with an unchallenged but challenging religion that was both unthreatened and threatening. It was not an empire England could possess, but one it had to watch and guard against. While Britons traveled and traded between London and Salee, or Plymouth and New

England, or Bristol and Guinea, and as they expanded their 'discovery' of the world, they were constantly aware of the Muslim Other, as buyer and seller, partner and pirate, captive and captor."[1206] The Muslim Barbary States were instrumental and integral to such close and intimate interactions, "until the middle of the seventeenth century, the Barbary States and the rest of the Islamic Mediterranean were instrumental in refashioning the British self-image and determining historical, political and commercial choices."[1207] The influence of the Barbary States on English literature, culture, politics, religion and identity was tremendous.[1208]

Pugh observed that "it is now clear that in 1619, in Algeria alone, there were 200,000 Christian converts – 'Renegados' or 'Levantines' as they were known, with a further 500 joining them each year. Christians who did not believe in the Trinity were often called 'Mahometans', which created the impression of even more Muslims. All this was embarrassing. Contemporaries asked whether it meant that Islam was the superior religion."[1209] The Levant Compnay chaplain - and later vice chancellor of Isaac Newton's Cambridge University - Dr. John Covel's observations about a single day of large Christian conversions to Islam in the Ottoman Empire were telling.[1210] "It is our shame, for I believe all Europe have not gained so many Turkes to us these 200 yeares; for, though the Ch. of Rome boast their Emissaryes here (as, indeed, there are many, many), Jesuits, Dominicans, Franciscans, yet, believe me, they have other designes than converting of Turkes."[1211] Throughout the sixteenth and seventeenth centuries Europeans flocked to the Muslim East and converted in bands; merchants, skilled workers, soldiers, clergy and high officials succumbed to the allure of the Islamic world. The renowned French historian F. Braudel observed that "Men flocked from Christendom to Islam, which tempted them with visions of adventure and profit [...] On coming into contact with Islamic countries, Christians were often seized with the urge to turn Moslem. In the *presidios* on the African coast, Spanish garrisons were decimated by epidemics of desertion. On Djerba in 1560, before the fort surrendered to the Turks, a number of Spaniards had already joined the enemy, 'abandoning their faith and their comrades'. Not long afterwards at La Goletta, a plot to surrender the position to the Infidel was uncovered. Small boats frequently left Sicily with cargoes of candidates for apostasy. At Goa the same phenomenon was observable among the Portuguese. The call was so strong that it even reached the clergy. The 'Turk' who accompanied one of His Christian Majesty's ambassadors back to France, and whom the Spanish authorities were advised to capture en route, was a former Hungarian priest. It cannot have been such a very rare occurrence: in 1630, Pere Joseph was asked to recall the Capuchins living in the Levant, 'lest they turn Turk'. From Corsica, Sardinia, Sicily, Calabria, Genoa, Venice, Spain, from every point in the Mediterranean world, renegades converged on Islam. There was no comparable flow in the other direction."[1212] Pugh asked: "Why were there so many converts from Christianity to Islam and so few from Islam to Christianity? Despite a widespread belief in England that the Turks practised forcible conversion, in fact generally they did not seek converts from vanquished opponents, preferring simply to collect taxes, fines or services from them. The idea was spread by slaves who had been ransomed or escaped, and then claimed to have been the victims of compulsory conversion. In fact, converts were usually willing, especially if they had experienced religious persecution in Europe. Protestants were especially appreciative of Muslim society; it was relatively tolerant, had no idols or monastic orders, and was based on individual study of the religion instead of passive acceptance of it from priests. But the main advantage lay in linking oneself to a more powerful empire and a superior civilisation. Converts found that the relatively egalitarian spirit of Islam allowed employment and advancement for those from modest backgrounds. In Morocco, the royal executioner was one 'Absalom'; as a former butcher from Exeter, he evidently had the right skills!" [1213]

Some converts, like English John Ward, became extremely wealthy and influential.[1214] Many Christian converts reached the pinnacle of their power and influence in the Ottoman Empire, as Tobias P. Graf has amply demonstrated. They kept closely connected with their relatives back in Europe, and many of their friends, relatives and colleagues visited them in Istanbul, Aleppo and Budapest.[1215] Adrian Tinniswood has shown that countless English, Dutch and French Christians had turned Turk[1216] and Matthew Dimmock,[1217] Matthew Birchwood,[1218] Daniel J. Vitkus, Samuel C. Chew[1219] and Nabil Matar in his *Islam and Britain* and many others have demonstrated the height of alarm it caused in London and elsewhere. Jonathan Burton, in *English Anxiety and the Muslim Power of Conversion: Five Perspectives on 'Turning Turk' in Early Modern Texts*,[1220] has amply shown that many of these converts were impressed by the superior, rational and systematic Islamic religion rather than just secular interests. The scholars of this period tend to trivialise these spiritual and religious dimensions. Burton raises the possibility that "Christians could have been moved by theological debate."[1221] Burton demonstrated that the Muslim Christian theological debates occurred both in England and France, and involved the high echelons of society,[1222] and that some of the converts belonged to high noble families and clergy. The Moorish delegate Ahmad Ibn Qasim al-Hajari's 1611 debates all over France[1223] and Moroccan ambassador to Low Countries Ahmad bin Abd Allah's dialogue with Maurice, Prince of Orange and his brother-in-law Immanuel of Portugal, and his subsequent polemic text *Muhamedani Epistola,* are good examples of such high-level discourse.[1224] Nabil Matar noted that religious dialogue between Muslim kings and their Christian counterparts was not uncommon.[1225]

Consequently, there were many Muslim converts in France, Netherland and England. "In 1611, Thomas Coryate wrote about the numerous Muslims in London who could be identified by the 'rowle of fine linen wrapped together upon their heads'—their turbans."[1226] Another English writer in1641 decried these "Divelish and Demnable" London Muslims along with 29 other heretical sects. These Muslims along with their many other anti-Trinitarian "Christian Turks" and "Mahometan Christian" fellows were permanent fixtures in the early seventeenth century London.[1227] Ottoman Turkish and Barbary cultures, customs, clothes and expressions were pretty common in London and Paris.[1228] "Clearly the Moors and Turks were "everywhere,"—not just in the literary imagination of English dramatists and poets, but in the streets, the sea towns, the royal residences, the courts, and the jails of Elizabethan, Jacobean and Caroline England and Wales."[1229] As noted above, the coffeehouses with Turkish turban and "Muhammadan berry" were all around London.[1230] They were the Starbucks of that time and were frequented by many turbaned Englishmen.[1231] Such Ottomania and Orientalism was a long lasting English tradition.

King Henry VIII used Turkish clothes on special occasions. "Turbans were worn at the Tudor court. On Shrove Sunday in 1533, the youthful king Henry VIII, along with the Earl of Essex, hosted a banquet at Westminster 'for all the Ambassadours, whiche then wer here'. Henry and his companion presumably aimed to startle the foreign envoys when they 'came in appareled after Turkey fasshion, in long robes of Bawkin, powedered with gold, hattes on their heddes of Crimsoyn

Velvet.'"[1232] Queen Elizabeth frequently dressed in the special dress sent to her from Istanbul by Roxelana (Hurrum Sultana), Sultan Sulayman the Magnificent's wife, including hijab. "She was so fascinated by things Islamic that she requested from her ambassador in Istanbul some Turkish clothes; like her father, she wanted to dress in the oriental fashion."[1233] The Turkish clothes and Ottomania validated English monarchs' anti-Catholic and anti-Habsburg sentiments and policies. Many English and Scottish travellers ventured into the Islamic world especially for pilgrimage to the Holy Lands and returned with Islamic dresses and habits. "Meanwhile, travelling Englishmen started returning from the Levant fully 'attired in Turkish dress complete with turban': after all, whenever they went into the domains of Islam, they dressed in Muslim attire. The first engraving that survives of a Christian from Britain dressed in Muslim clothes and turban shows the Scottish traveller William Lithgow who visited the Levant in 1612. 'I clad in Turkish manner,' wrote Henry Blount in his 1636 account of his *Voyage into the Levant*."[1234]

Turkish clothes were fashionable among the royals and elites. King Charles II (1630 – 1685) was known for dressing up in Persian and Turkish clothes.[1235] "At the same time, the first coffee shop selling the 'Turkish berry' opened in Oxford; a few years later, King Charles II started wearing clothes designed in the 'Persian' fashion. In 1681–2, the Moroccan ambassador was widely feted and taken to see the Royal Society— where he signed his name on the visitors' chart—and the University of Oxford."[1236] Later on we will see that the Unitarians tried to present to this Ambassador a detailed letter about Islamic Unitarian similarities against the calumnies of Trinitarians. Countless English merchants, consuls and even ambassadors' Eastern fascinations and assimilations have already been discussed above. Islam, Muslims and Muslim culture were a known commodity, as the "leisured classes in England were entertaining themselves by dressing up in 'Turkish habits'[…] Imports from the Islamic world were changing the ways that people in England lived. Drinking coffee, imported from the Ottoman Empire, and tea, imported from the Far East, became national habits. Textiles—English wool, Persian silk, Turkey carpets, Indian cottons— were crucial commodities linking people in Britain with residents of the Islamic world that changed the ways people dressed themselves and how they decorated their houses. The intimate adoption of these commodities, their penetration into everyday lives, represents a largely unacknowledged relationship between Britain and the Muslim world."[1237] Some English ladies were married to Muslim rulers and converts. "In the second half of the Seventeenth century one of the wives of the dey of Algiers was English, and so too was one of the harem of Mulay Ismail, the powerful ruler of Morocco. She bore him two sons. In 1682 a Christian convert to Islam by the name of Hamed Lucas accompanied the Moroccan ambassador Mohammad bin Hadou to London, and during his stay married an English servant girl."[1238] Matar further noted that "in numerous plays there are references to Muslim-Christian and Muslim-English marriages—marriages that could not have taken place or even been dramatised between Britons/Christians and unconverted Jews or American Indians."[1239]

Christian-Muslim marriages were also widespread in the Mughal Empire; many East India Company officials, employees and workers were married to their Indian Muslim wives. The same is reported of some European workers in Levant[1240] and the Barbary States. These officers and workers must have converted to Islam, otherwise marriage with a Muslim woman would have not been permitted. French, Dutch and English merchants and officers dressed in Eastern clothes, adopted Eastern habits, cultural expressions and even wrote poetry in Eastern languages. It is pertinent to note that many merchants who made their fortunes in the Muslim East especially those who broke the monopoly of the early East India Company Royalists since 1648 were anti-Trinitarian, anti-clerical Whig radicals who supported the anti-monarchy revolutions of 1649 and then the Glorious Revolution of 1688-1689.[1241] The English dissenters, radical merchants, Low Churchmen and Whig parliamentarians worked closely against the royalist elite merchants, High Churchmen, nonjurors and Tories.[1242]

Many merchants and officers practiced polygamy and maintained large harems while in the Muslim world.[1243] "When in the Indian capital, Ochterlony liked to be addressed by his full Mughal title, Nasir-ud-Daula (Defender of the State), and to live the life of a Mughal gentleman: every evening all thirteen of his consorts used to process around Delhi behind their husband, each on the back of her own elephant. With his fondness for hookahs and nautch girls and Indian costumes, Ochterlony amazed Bishop Reginald Heber, the Anglican Primate of Calcutta, by receiving him sitting on a divan wearing a '*cho-*

ga and *pagri'* while being fanned by servants holding peacock-feather *punkhas.* To one side of Ochterlony's own tent was the red silk harem tent where his women slept, and on the other side the encampment of his daughters, all, according to the Bishop, 'hung around with red cloth and thus fenced in from the eyes of the profane.'"[1244] General Ochterlony's wife Mubarak Begum went to perform Hajj in Mecca.[1245]

They brought their wives and children back to Europe; this practice continued until very late in the nineteenth century, when after the general mutiny of 1857 the British were prohibited from such practices. The contemporary British historian William Dalrymple's *White Mughals* well substantiates this Muslim Christian hybrid.[1246] He showed that "of the Bengal Wills from 1780 to 1785 preserved in the India Office, one in three contains a bequest to Indian wives or companions or their natural children. It can safely be assumed that many more kept Indian mistresses without wishing to leave a formal legal record of the fact."[1247] He further noted that "for nearly three hundred years Europeans coming out to the subcontinent had been assimilating themselves to India in a kaleidoscope of different ways."[1248] These Christian Muslim families, on their return to England, moved in the high echelons of British society, enjoying high-profile connections and influences. One such family was the Kirkpatrick family; Kitty Kirkpatrick, the daughter of Kirkpatrick and his Muslim wife Khair un Nisas, was born as Muslim. "She had initially been brought up as Sahib Begum, a Muslim noblewoman in Hyderabad, before being shipped off to England at four years old, baptised on her arrival in London and thenceforth completely cut off from her Matarnal relations. Instead she had been absorbed into the upper echelons of Victorian literary society, where she had fascinated her cousins' tutor, the young Thomas Carlyle, and formed the basis for the heroine Blumine, 'a many tinted radiant Aurora [...] the fairest of Oriental light-bringers,' in Carlyle's novel *Sartor Resartus.*"[1249]

The cultural and political influence of the Muslim empires in the seventeenth and eighteenth centuries was immense. "The Turks and Moors belonged to the most powerful of all the non-Christian civilisations with which Britons were engaged. They also belonged to the international community of trade, diplomacy, and military rivalry that marked England's foray into the age of Mediterranean and Atlantic discovery. Although from the Elizabethan period on the English were beginning to develop their anglocentric view of the world, they were deeply aware that they had to contend with a powerful and sometimes confrontational and aggressive islamocentrism—from Salee to London, from Tunis to Istanbul, and from Bristol to New England, Turks and Moors reminded them that the world did not revolve around Albion."[1250]

The situation in France was pretty much the same.[1251] The French leaders were willing to replace obsolete and irrational Christian dogmas and practices with more enlightening and liberating Islamic teachings, but were hesitant to elevate the contemporary Muslims to that level of sophistication and enlightenment. The role of Islam was more symbolic, fluid and multifaceted.[1252] The Muslim enemies were too useful to be discarded. Islam, Muhammad, Islamic Unitarianism, ethical salvation schemes, republicanism and religious tolerance were employed by almost all segments of European religious and political landscape to propagate or defend their ideals or to attack, ridicule or berate their opponents' Islamic republicanism. Indeed, Islam and Ottomans were the obsessions of seventeenth- and eighteenth-century Europe both positively and negatively. They were the "others" against whom Europe mirrored its failures, successes and aspirations.

In the eighteenth century, many Europeans - especially some of the known radical enlighteners - began to see Muhammad as a statesman, a legislator and a true messenger of God and his religion, Islam, as the rational religion of justice, good will and republican values. Their main predicament was organised Christianity and the *Old Regime*, with their mysterious interpretations of man, God, politics and universe. The royals and clergy claimed special knowledge of those mysteries and hence superiority over the masses; those challenging that superiority, whether religious or political, were severely persecuted. The reformers needed an alternate interpretation of man, God and universe to replace the irrational, mysterious Christian interpretations; Islam, Muhammad and Quran were their best bet, due to their relative historical authenticity and relevance. Consequently, the reformers turned to them. Islam was equally an element of subversion, deformation, destruction and at the same time reformation and reconstruction. It was the "other" that defined and mirrored the enlightenment in so many ways and forms.

Chapter 6

Islam and the Early English Enlightenment

Radical and moderate English enlightenment figures alike agreed that Islam was a genuine heir to the universal, monotheistic, prophetic tradition and republicanism. Islam was the antidote to Christian theological and political excesses and cure for the abusive political and religious hierarchy.

Mainstream English enlighteners, such as Locke and Newton, were neither as public as their radical English fellows such as Stubbe or Toland, nor as radical as the French revolutionaries. They were more cautious, subtle, calculated and thoughtful, and did not throw out the baby along with the bathwater. J. Israel states that "among its primary spokesmen were Newton and Locke in England, Thomasius and Wolff in Germany, the 'Newtonians' Nieuwentijt and 's-Gravesande in the Netherlands, and Feijoo and Piquer, in Spain. This was the Enlightenment which aspired to conquer ignorance and superstition, establish toleration, and revolutionise ideas, education, and attitudes by means of philosophy but in such a way as to preserve and safeguard what were judged essential elements of the older structures, effecting a viable synthesis of old and new, and of reason and faith."[1253] Israel noted that Locke and Newton were moderate in their tactics but radical in their theology and philosophy.[1254] Their Christian reformation scheme was no less radical than Stubbe, Toland, Socinians and Unitarians; in reality, they were closet Unitarians.

They felt that the God of the Bible and Church Christianity was inadequate for their rational religious and democratic political needs. That God was intolerant of dissent, religious plurality and freedom, claiming to be the only political sovereign, granting governmental authority at whims without any considerations of qualifications, accountability and mutuality. He did not recognise natural human rights, freedoms and liberties, his commandments, instructions and covenants were tyrannical, autocratic and draconian, and his ways were arbitrary, selective and discriminatory. He preferred certain people over others, and preferred faith, submission and obedience over morality, righteousness and virtue. They wanted instead a God, faith and Bible that allowed diversity, toleration, morality, human rights and equality. They deconstructed and decoded the Christian God, Bible and theology to reconstruct it on relatively liberal, democratic and republican lines. The politics of the seventeenth and eighteenth centuries accelerated the theological transformation. The new Christianity was totally at odd with the old, Church Christianity; it was more rational, less supernatural, authoritarian and persecutory. They built the new Enlightenment culture based on this revised and reformed belief system, purging the traditional Christianity and its systems from supernatural elements, irrational dogmas and persecutory instincts without discarding the outer shell. They accomplished this in the name of a return to the original, pristine and simple Christianity of Jesus and the first-century Church. They did not de-Christianise England like their French counterparts, but re-Christianised it on the original, simple and pure lines. The end product was not the historical, traditional Church Christianity practiced in Europe for centuries, but a totally different animal, far removed from the dogmatic, irrational, intrusive and abusive Church Christianity and closer to the monotheistic, ethical, liberating, universal prophetic tradition. It was rather a simple, minimal, tolerant, egalitarian, rational, Unitarian, Muhammaden Christianity; crafted, couched and suited to English needs, culture and society.

They were neither irreligious nor atheists but infidels who rejected the Christian dogmas, institutional authority and scriptural foundations. It is not appropriate to call them Christian rationalists, Christian Deists or Christian liberals, as they did not subscribe to the fundamentally-central tenets of Christianity; their belief system was not a subset of Church Christianity. They demolished the fundamental roots of the word "Christianity" by rejecting Christ's divinity, atoning death and salvific efficacy. If denying every fundamental belief of Christianity does not make them un-Christian then what does? In the eighteenth century there was no such thing as Christianity by association; adherence to the fundamental dogmas of Christianity in conformity with the Church interpretations was required. They appropriated the word Christianity, Jesus, Scripture and salvation to their peculiar understandings and hybrid belief system, totally divergent from the historical Christianity. They were neither fully Christians nor fully Deists per strict, narrow and official definitions of the categories. Their theological and political views were more akin to Muslim thought patterns. This is how their opponents described them as crypto-Muslims and Turks. The assimilation and appropriation of Islamic ideas was intentional, conscious and calculated.

Islam was a known commodity to the English Protestants; English encounters with Islam and Muslims in the Holy Land during the Crusades were not trivial. Later on, the Ottoman armies were at the doorsteps of Vienna, the gateway to Western Europe by 1529, and continued the push until the 1680s. The Protestant Hungarian rebel Imre Tokoly (1657-1705), the Prince of Transylvania, known as Count Teckely in England, had sought out Ottoman Sultan Mehmed IV's protection and help against the Catholic Hapsburg monarchs. He fought along with the Ottomans against the Catholics until the battle of Zenta in 1697, and lived under the Ottoman auspices until his death in 1705. He, like the Hungarian King John Sigismund Zápolya (1540 -1571), preferred the Unitarian Islamic faith and relatively tolerant Islamic law in opposition to the Trinitarian and intolerant Catholic Austrians.[1255]

The Euro-Ottoman affairs had their resonance all around Europe, including England. The Protestant alliances with Ottoman Muslims were widely discussed in Europe, and the Anglo-Ottoman alliance was widely discussed in English drama. In England the Muslims and their so-called secret hegemonic agendas were connected with the Whig parliamentarians; for instance, Count Teckely was often identified with the English republicans, the Whigs who were dubbed as seditious "Teckelites" or as the Protestant allies of the Turco-Islamic cause. The anonymous writer of *The rebels association in Hungary for reformation of religion and advancement of Empire* (1682), invoked such a close collaboration in the following words: "The Teckelites are in Discipline and Principles much the same with those they call Whigs in *England*, Religion being the ground of their Exorbitances. Under pretence of Religion (which is indeed but Rebellion,) they will Levy Arms against the Emperour, and for Defence of the Gospel, join with the Turk against their Christian Sovereign."[1256] Shaftesbury, Stubbe,

Locke and other dissenting Whigs were all depicted as Turk infidels, bent on overthrowing the Christian Church and monarchy and replacing it with Turkish republican model.

Matthew Birchwood and Nabil Matar have consistently shown that "images of Islam and the dreaded Ottoman Turk have played a crucial role in the formation of national identity and religious difference in Restoration England."[1257] Humberto Garcia has proven beyond doubt that "English radical Protestantism achieved historical, philosophical, and ideological coherence, in part, through its sympathetic identification with what I am calling Islamic republicanism, a flexible and malleable trope that casts Mahomet's revolutionary reestablishment of the Christian prophetic monarchy as the epitome of English constitutional virtue."[1258] He has also noticed that the above mentioned satire *The rebels association* "seeks to expose the defense of a limited Protestant monarchy as a false pretense for concealing an international conspiracy between radical Protestants and Muslims intent on overthrowing Christendom, renewing the English Civil War, and welcoming an Ottoman invasion."[1259] To the Royalists Muhammad was "a rabble-rouser and a revolutionary; he is Cromwell [...] Indeed, Mahomet is Cromwell, or perhaps Cromwell is Mahomet."[1260] Islam, Quran and Muhammad were integral to the intellectual landscape of seventeenth-century England. The Whigs were accused of extending the Ottoman universal monarchy to England.

Garcia further noted that "with the formation of the Hungarian-Ottoman alliance, English representations of Islam became central to ideological debates regarding monarchal and religious authority."[1261] It confirmed "Tory fears about a Muslim-Protestant alliance on the brink of establishing a revolutionary regime in England."[1262] Garcia showed how Islamic republican model anticipated the Glorious Revolution and hence the English Enlightenment. "Tory burlesques offer a crucial site for investigating how the trope of Islamic republicanism lent narrative coherence to a series of national crises that, in historical hindsight, anticipated the Glorious Revolution of 1688. Radical Protestants deployed Islamic republicanism as a way of rewriting Christian prophetic history in tolerationist and constitutionalist terms, providing them with a convenient ideological framework with which to make sense of national crises as they arose. In reducing radical Whiggism to a vulgar obsession with the Mahometan 'good old cause,' Tory burlesques were, in effect, publicising 'secrets' about Islam's ubiquitous impact on England's political unconscious."[1263] Shaftesbury's circle, including Stubbe and Locke, was the representative of this Islamic republican model, Stubbe being the radical stalwart of it. Garcia has demonstrated that the "satirical figuration of English reformers as Teckelite infidels has its political and literary roots in Henry Stubbe's defense of Islam—*The Rise and Progress of Mahometanism* (circa 1671; published in 1911)."[1264] James Jacob has shown the originality of Stubbe's Islamic hybrid.

Henry Stubbe and John Locke: The Pococke and Shaftesbury Pedigrees

John Locke and Henry Stubbe were the exact contemporaries. Both went to Westminster School, Christ Church College, and were Dr. Pococke's students and colleagues at Oxford. The historical Westminster School was the most reputable school of London, where Arabic was part of the curriculum along with Latin and Hebrew. Its headmaster, Richard Busby (1606-1695), was a graduate of Christ Church Oxford where he studied Arabic with Matthias Paser (1598-1658). Paser hailed Arabic as the language of natural sciences and Oriental wisdom, while Busby compiled Arabic and Hebrew grammer and incorporated them into the school curriculum with great enthusiasm. All students of Westminster School were required to take Arabic and all the celebrated alumni - and the list is very long[1265] - who played significant role in English politics, clerical circles and business were exposed to the Arabic program. Both John Locke[1266] and Henry Stubbe learned Arabic as part of school curriculum, even though Stubbe's proficiency was greater than Locke.[1267] Both Arabic and Hebrew were part of selecting King's Scholars for Oxford and Cambridge Universities. G. Russell has shown that Locke was King's Scholar to Oxford and must have had Arabic for his minor and major election competition, though he used Latin and Hebrew more often.[1268] Edward Pococke, the rationalist Arabist and renowned Continental Orientalist, was Locke's ideal of knowledge, scholarship and humility.[1269] Locke had the utmost respect and admiration for Dr. Pococke as his friend and mentor.[1270] Likewise, Henry Stubbe was a product of Pococke and quoted his works on Islamic history, theology and philosophy in his writings. In spite of his royal loyalties, Anglican commitments and pragmatic missionary overtures Pococke was known for his objective treatment of the Muslim history, theology, law and civilization. Locke, Stubbe and other students of Pococke were heirs to this relative objectivity.

Both Locke and Stubbe worked for Shaftesbury, the First Earl; Locke was Shaftesbury's secretary while Stubbe worked as a pamphleteer. Even though Locke's father was a puritan who fought in the English Civil War, Locke mostly remained royalist and against religious tolerance until he met Shaftesbury who advised him to "apply himself to the study of ecclesiastical and political affairs, which might have some relation to the business of a minister of state. And Mr. Locke succeeded so well in these studies, that his Lordship began to consult him on all occasions of that nature. He not only took him into his library and closet, but brought him into the company of the Duke of Buckingham, my Lord Halifax, and other noblemen of the greatest wit and learning, who were pleased as much with his conversation as my Lord Ashley."[1271] Locke's biographer, Maurice Cransto, noted that Locke learned his political liberal views from Shaftesbury. "I have searched in vain for evidence of Locke's holding liberal views before his introduction to Lord Shaftesbury in 1666. There is much to show that Locke held such views soon afterwards; and I cannot help wondering if he learned them from Shaftesbury. For it is certainly not the case... that Shaftesbury learned his liberalism from Locke."[1272] Richard Ashcraft showed the type of profound respect, adulation and unmatched loyalty Locke showed to Shaftesbury for the sixteen years he worked for him.[1273] Ashcraft attributed Locke's radical political and republican views to Shatesbury's companionship and training and Leopold van Ranke observed that "Locke's principles are those of Shaftesbury."[1274]

Shaftesbury was well acquainted with the Continental geopolitics and deeply involved in English political affairs. Shaftesbury was connected with the merchant circle of Levant and East India Company through his stepmother Mary Moryson, one of the daughters of wealthy London textile merchant Baptist Hicks and co-heir of his fortune.[1275] Hick was a friend of Sir Thomas Smythe, the Governor of the Levant and East India Company, a Mercer to Queen Elizabeth and King James I and an active politician in London politics. Both had Chipping Campden connections, the famous wool trading center and market town in Cotswold district of Gloucestershire. Hick's famous mansion of Campden was burned to ashes by the Royalists in the Civil War. Both Smythe and Hicks were buried in Chipping Campden Wool

Church of St. James. Through his stepmother, Cooper (Shaftesbury) gained wealth and an important political connection in the form of her grandson, the future 1st Earl of Essex. Shaftesbury himself was involved in overseas trade and plantation,[1276] and was well connected with London merchants. Sir Thomas Pilkington (died 1691), the London merchant elected as London Sherriff in 1681, showed great partiality in returning the grand jury in Shaftesbury's trial of high treason (24 November 1681) and was reprimanded by the judges and the Court. Shaftesbury was given shelter and a secret hiding place in a London merchant Watson's Wood Street house when the Rye House Plot was exposed, and another Levant Company merchant Sir Dudley North was installed by royalists as London Sherriff to arrest Shaftesbury and other plotters.[1277]

Shaftesbury believed in "'a secret universal Catholic league carried on by the clergy for the utter extirpation of the Protestant religion out of the world.' This design, so far as it pertains to England, it is noted, 'cannot be carried on without the full concurrence of the English Court.' It is Shaftesbury's leadership in organising the opposition to both these forces which establishes the political dimensions for the theoretical arguments contained in the exclusionist pamphlets and tracts of the 1680s."[1278] Alliances with or sympathies for the enemies (Ottomans) of your enemies (Catholic Habsburg) was quite natural in the world of geopolitics, even though we do not have direct evidences of such propensities from Shaftesbury's own writings - which are very rare anyway, as he burned all his papers to avoid persecution during his high treason trial. However, we have substantial circumstantial evidence, especially from the Tory dramatists, that Shaftesbury was the head of seditious English "Teckelites," the masterminds of anti-monarchy Islamic republican consipiracy. His grandson James Harris (1709–80) was a known Turkophile and Arab historian. In his *Posthumous Philological Inquiries* (1781) he dedicated three chapters to Middle Eastern matters, written in a spirit of open-mindedness and generosity.

Chapter 7

Henry Stubbe and Muhammadan Christianity

Both Henry Stubbe and John Locke were the best reflections of Shaftesbury's religious and political ideas. Just like Stubbe and Locke's Unitarianism, Shaftesbury died in exile in Amsterdam as an anti-Trinitarian Arian. Arianism was a generic seventeenth-century category used to represent Unitarians, Socinians and other anti-Trinitarians. We do not have many written works of Shaftesbury, because he burnt all his papers when arrested on the charges of high treason and put in the Tower of London, as well as all proof of his anti-Crown subversive activities, but Stubbe and Locke were a good reflection of his ideas and ideals. Stubbe and Locke also shared Robert Boyle's friendship; Boyle was Stubbe's patron and friend[1279] and Locke's close working relationships with Boyle and Royal Society fellowships are well-recorded. Both Stubbe and Locke also shared Boyle's fascination with alchemy. Stubbe and Locke pretty much shared the common connections and circle of friends since their childhoods, moving in the same socio-political elite circles. Nabil Matar observed that "the two men were exact contemporaries: both were born in 1632, studied at Westminster School, matriculated at Christ Church, Oxford, and were pupils of the orientalist Edward Pococke; indeed, both were at Christ Church between 1656 and 1660, Stubbe as a librarian at the Bodleian, and Locke from 1652 as the beneficiary of a studentship (effectively a life fellowship), taking his BA in 1656 and his MA in 1658."[1280]

Islam and Muslims loomed large on the horizon of Shaftesbury, Henry Stubbe and John Locke's century. The Ottoman-Habsburg rivalry and its impact upon the emergence, continuity and subsequent victory of Protestantism, the so-called Calvino-Turkism,[1281] the flourishing of Protestantism, anti-Trinitarianism and finally radical Unitarianism of Ferenc David in Transylvania under the auspice of Ottomans,[1282] the Franco-Ottoman alliance and joint naval ventures against Charles V, Francis I of France's efforts to convince Henry VIII of England to join that alliance, Queen Elizabeth's correspondence and friendly overtures to Sultan Murad III, Mehmed III and his mother Safiye Sultan, her suggestions of a natural religious affinity between the Ottoman Muslims and English Protestants and an Anglo-Ottoman alliance against the Catholic Spain,[1283] the indirect role that Ottoman fleet played in the English defeat of the Spanish Armada of 1588,[1284] the Levant and East India Companies, their embassies, factors and trade with the Ottomans, Mughals and Persians,[1285] the Ottoman-Dutch contacts in the early phases of Dutch revolt against Philip II of Spain, William of Orange's requests for help and Sultan Suleiman's subsequent expressions of religious affinity and support,[1286] the Dutch slogan "Rather Turkish than Papist"[1287] and use of Turkish flag on their warships, French, English and Dutch capitulations and ensuing multiplications of trade opportunities in the vast Ottoman Empire,[1288] the embassy of Sir Thomas Roe and subsequent East India Company's significant trade with the Mughal Empire,[1289] the English overtures to the Persian Safavid Empire, English struggles against and treaties with the Barbary States,[1290] the problems connected with piracy, slavery, apostasy and conversion, Spanish Inquisition and forced conversion of Muslims and Jews in Spain and, later on their expulsion and the Dutch Inquisition[1291] were all political realities of sixteenth- and seventeenth-century Europe. John Locke and Stubbe lived these realities and could not have escaped their broader implications. The erratic internal English affairs and political upheavals of the seventeenth century must have caused unrelenting sense of instability, insecurity and fear in the British society of Locke's era. Seventeenth-century England was yet to be an empire of international scope, and the terrible Turks were still in a dominant position, knocking at the gates of Vienna. The Protestant alliances with Ottoman Muslims against the Christian Catholics were widely discussed in the European newspapers and theater. In England, the Tories connected Muslims and their so-called secret hegemonic agendas with the Whig parliamentarians. Count Teckely was often identified by the English dramatists with English republicans, the Whigs who were dubbed as seditious "Teckelites" or as the Protestant allies of the Turco-Islamic cause. The English coffeehouses, visible and pervasive

Indian, Persian and Ottoman material culture, constant and continuous invocation of Islam, Muhammad and Turks for or against republican Whigs and in religious debates, captives, converts and merchants were all frequent reminders of things Islamic to seventeenth-century English society. Stubbe and Locke were at the center of these politico-religious storms.

Stubbe, the Father of Muhammadan Christianity

Henry Stubbe was the father of early Whig Islamic republicanism and Muhammadan Christianity. He, unlike the indirect subtle Islamic influence upon Locke, represents the direct Islamic influence. Stubbe (1632–1676), the most radical reformer and influential English thinker, is believed to have converted to Islam.[1292] Stubbe completed in 1674 his famous book *An Account of the Rise and Progress of Mahometanism, and a Vindication of Him and His Religion from the Calumnies of the Christians*. He was closely working with Shaftesbury at that time. Its parts were in circulation among the freethinkers since 1671, and both Justin Champion and J. R. Jacob place this work in the "broad context of the Unitarian-Islamic syncretism."[1293]

Stubbe was a radical reformer who wanted to eradicate the supernatural, absolutist and hierarchical Church Christianity and replace it with Islamic, rational, simple, minimal, ethical monotheism and limited republicanism. He was a sort of wing leader of the so-called international, Protestant and Muslim republican conspirators who supposedly wanted to replace the English monarchy with Ottoman republicanism and Christianity with Turkish faith. Stubbe propagated a return to the primitive Christianity of Jesus via the authentic channels of Islam, advocating for a policy of full toleration for dissenters, as practiced by the Muslim Ottomans and popularised by Anthony Ashley Cooper, the First Earl of Shaftesbury (1621-1683). Shaftesbury, the patron of Stubbe and Locke fought for a limited monarchy, toleration and religious freedom.[1294] He was arrested for a number of times for high treason, escaped to Amsterdam and died there. Locke followed him to Amsterdam. James R. Jacob shows that "Stubbe's career rests on his defense of Mahomet, depicted as a wise legislator who founded a tolerant republican monarchy."[1295] These might very well have been a reflection of Shaftesbury's views, as the founder and father of the opposition Whig party and its main ideologue.

Stubbe was a revolutionary who changed the long anti-Muhammad and anti-Islamic European landscape and introduced Muhammad and Islam with a balanced, nuanced approach. Nabil Matar noted that "This little-known physician [...] undertook a "Copernican Revolution (in Kants use of the phrase) in the study of Islam."[1296] Stubbe introduced Muhammad and Islam as the monotheistic reformers of the Christian excesses and Islamic civilisation as a fresh, independent and glorious civilisation.[1297] Stubbe used Islam as a whip to indict the Christian Church, religion and society and to bring about a radical, natural, rational, monotheistic and republican revolution.[1298] "Far from corrupting or deforming Christianity, 'Mahomet' tried to return to its purest expression."[1299]

Stubbe argued that the Islamic concept of divine unity was the pristine message of salvation preached by all the Prophets starting with Adam and Noah and culminating in Muhammad.[1300] The Unitarian Christianity of Jesus was corrupted by the Roman Church of the fourth century and the ensuing Trinitarian controversies weakened the Christian community. The intolerant Eastern Christian community was chaotically divided on sectarian lines "so Mahomet happily perceived the opportunity in Christian division to re-establish true religion and abolish idolatry. Mahomet, convinced of the unity of God, 'accomplish'd himself in civil and military prudence' through his travels and converse, and erected a 'new religion and empire' amidst the decay and debauchery of Eastern Christianity. Stubbe continued to note that the theology Mahomet established was compatible with original Nazarene and Arian Christianity."[1301] Muhammad transformed the superstitious Arab culture on natural, rational lines and protected them from supernatural mysteries and cumbersome ceremonies. Muhammad "did ingeniously accommodate to his ends those superstitious usages which were imprinted in the breasts of the Ismaelites', towards the worship of one God. The Koran was the embodiment of 'rational belief', and Mahomet commended for 'on the one hand not clogging men's faith with the necessity of believing a number of abstruse notions which they cannot comprehend, and which are often contrary to the dictates of reason and commonsense; nor on the other hand loading them with the performance of many troublesome, expensive and superstitious ceremonies.'"[1302]

Stubbe vehemently attacked the Christian dogma of the Trinity and divinity of Jesus and - just like Michael Servetus - called it tri-theism and paganism. "Christianity was then degenerated into such a kind of paganism as wanted nothing but the ancient sacrifices and professed polytheism, and, even as to the latter, there wanted not some who did make three gods of the Trinity. Others made a goddess of the Virgin Mary. The reverence to the saints differed little from that of the pagans to their heroes and lesser gods, and images were brought into churches then, though not by public authority. And it is no less remarkable that obscure persons had several times been promoted by fraud or indifferent means to the Empire."[1303] He argued "that all the first Christians, and even the apostles themselves, were taught and did teach that Christ was a mere man (which was their tenet) and that the truth of this doctrine was continued in the church until the days of Pope Victor who was the thirteenth bishop of Rome after Peter, and that Zephyrinus his successor did alter and corrupt that truth—if it be true which the Arians said that none but idiots and simple persons believed any such thing, and that till the decision at Nicaea the more knowing Christians did not hold him to be really God."[1304] The Apostles "taught that there was but one God, and that they were too dull to comprehend or invent those subtle distinctions of essence and person, consubstantiation, eternal generation, and if it be certain that the Fathers after the Nicene Council were not agreed concerning the meaning of those uncouth words, and that the world was long after dissatisfied with the use of them, and that such as Gregory Nazianzen and Basil were shy how they taught the deity of the Holy Ghost or of Christ or touched upon the Trinity [...] if we take notice how differently the Fathers explicate themselves upon that point, and how much the other works of Athanasius do differ from the Creed which goes under his name, we may very well doubt concerning their judgment if not conclude the contrary."[1305] The Roman paganistic beliefs, rituals, priests and institutions were Christianised, turning Christianity into a paganistic religion.[1306] He noted that Prophet Mohammad was sent by God to rectify Christian corruptions, and his theology was in line with the original message of Jesus and his original followers, the Nazarene (Quranic *Nasaara*). Prophet Muhammad "told them [...] that [...] the introduction of idols was a novel practice, that the prophets and patriarchs, especially Abraham, Isaac, and their father Ismael, did worship God without associating any with Him; that all associating of others with the great God, either in worship or in essence or both, was idolatry and therefore the Coreischites and other Arabians that did worship these idols were idolaters. So were those Christians who either held a trinity of persons or trinity of gods or did hold the deity of the Virgin Mary. So also were the Jews who did associate Ozair or Ezra to the great God, saying that he was the son of God."[1307] Stubbe's *Originall* was a comparative study of Islam. It was "not just a history of Mahomet but a history of religion culminating in Mahomet, and organised around four 'great revolutions' – the acceptance of Christ by a number of Jews as the messiah; the Jewish rebellion against the Romans in Jerusalem and Alexandria, resulting in a greater divide between Jewish and Christian traditions and practises; Constantine's revolution, reducing Christianity to the Nicene Creed; and Mahomet's revolution, re-establishing an original purity."[1308] The decline of original Christianity, especially the corruptions of Christian scriptures and the introduction of irrational dogmas such as the Trinity and Church abuses, spurred the advance of Islam. While "most of Christianity was sunk in superstition and internecine war, Mohammed accomplished the fourth revolution, the invention, establishment and expansion of Islam."[1309]

The Muhammadan republican revolution served as a reformation of both the Jewish and Christian excesses in the matters of law and doctrines. Mohammed's intelligence and thoughts are "not to be scorned but admired." Jacob sees in Stubbe a synthesis of "Mohammed's simple creed, Hobbes's natural religion and the deistical confessions of Cherbury and Blount."[1310] As noted above, Stubbe was a connection between Islam's Unitarian republicanism detailed in Pococke and John Seldon's works, Hobbes's natural religion and enlightened monarchy, Harrington's republic, Lord Cherbury and Charles Blount's deism and Shaftesbury's anti-Trinitarian Whig republicanism. His subversive republican career stretched from English Civil War to the late 1670s, early Exclusion Crises and later the Rye House plot to assassinate King Charles II and his brother James II. His sudden accidental death deprived him of an active participation in the later upheavals which led to the Glorious Revolution, but he was ideologically and spiritually there. Stubbe was the luminary of early Enlightenment ideas, and his radical manuscript clandestinely moved among Whig as will as Tory freethinkers and reformists.

Stubbe gave a detailed and accurate account of Muslim concept of *al-Tawhid* (Oneness and Unity of God), Islamic acts of devotions,

Shari'ah laws, customs and practices. He defended the Quran's eloquence.[1311] The Quran was the greatest miracle of Muhammad. Stubbe counted and defended some of the miracles of Prophet Muhammad,[1312] and noted the way Muslims interpreted the Christian Bible to substantiate Muhammad's coming.[1313] He concluded his *Account* observing that: "This is the sum of Mahometan religion, on the one hand, not clogging men's faith with the necessity of believing a number of abstruse notions which they cannot comprehend, and which are often contrary to the dictates of reason and common sense: nor on the other hand loading them with performance of many troublesome, expensive, and superstitious ceremonies, yet enjoining a due observance of religion, as the surest method to keep men in the bounds of their duty both to God and man."[1314] Muhammad's religion was a reflection of Jesus' command of loving God and neighbour.

In addition to being a spiritual leader Muhammad was also a wise civic leader. Stubbe argued that Prophet Muhammad was a wise legislature, leader and a spiritual prince who ushered Islamic republicanism. Muhammad was the "wisest legislator that ever was."[1315] Garcia noted that "Islamic republicanism begins with Henry Stubbe's *The Rise and Progress of Mahometanism* (c. 1671), a subversive work that portrays Mahomet as a wise legislator who reinstituted primitive Christianity's republican order. Accordingly, Christianity began as egalitarian Jewish sect with Ebonite and Arian leanings that refused the corrupt doctrine of Trinity as decreed by the Nicene Council in ad 325."[1316] Matthew Dimmock noted that "Stubbe's Mahomet is a pragmatic visionary, a benevolent leader of multiple talents prepared to compromise in order to achieve the greater good – someone whom we might call an 'Enlightenment man.'"[1317]

Muhammad, the Protestant Prophet

Stubbe considered Prophet Muhammad a true reformer of Christianity centuries before Luther's partial reformation. "Mahomet, though he did not force the Christians to his religion, yet he told them that such as believed in Isa ought to live according to his precepts with great humility, piety, and unconcernedness for the pomp and vanities of this world, that they ought neither to seek nor retain honour nor riches or go to war, or intermeddle with state affairs—these things being inconsistent with the doctrine of Isa; such as pursued those courses not being really Christians, since Christianity lies not so much in open profession of reverence and worship as in the practice of a holy life."[1318]

Muhammad, the Protestant Prophet, promulgated religious pluralism, tolerance, acceptance and civil public arena with civilising effects. John Tolan observed that "Stubbe's work is not merely an academic exercise in the history of religion, of course; it is a polemical work aimed at the Anglican Church and the monarchy. Like Mahomet, the king should strip the priests of their power and ban superstitious doctrine, returning to the simple, rational monotheism of the early Christians. He should also allow for the practice of diverse cults, just as the 'Mahometans' do. Charles II should become a new Mahomet."[1319] Stubbe, knowingly or unknowingly, was internally supporting the external Ottoman and Barbary leader's call to Charles and James II to convert to Islam and implement universal, Islamic, tolerant, republican government system in England. The Ottoman and Moroccan leaders' inviting and proselytizing letters to Kings Charles and James II are well documented. Islam was the intended solution for the Anglican restrictive dogmatic and suffocating policies, and Muhammadan civic republicanism was the needed cure for English persecutions. "Mahometanism is modeled after the egalitarian teachings of the 'Judaizing Christians,' the first practitioners of Christ's simple faith. As such, Mahomet granted liberty of religion to Jews and Christians living in his empire after paying a small tribute. He began the Reformation eight hundred years before Luther. Appearing in Coleridge's 'Mahomet' over a century later, Stubbe's Protestant Prophet resurrected civic republicanism. In solving the problem of particularity, Islam offers an attractive counterpoint to the restrictive policy of Anglican toleration."[1320] Islam was the aspired natural and civic religion. "According to Stubbe, Mahometanism is a natural faith worthy of admiration. The Prophet's civic laws have accomplished in less than a century what Trinitarian Christians could not in over a millennium: his laws have anchored a state-sponsored (rather than ecclesiastical) toleration policy for all religious minorities on a solid constitutional foundation that originated with Noah's covenant as prophetically renewed by Abraham, Moses, and Christ. Like Teckely, Stubbe treats Islamic toleration as the antidote to the religious and political contentions that have plagued Europe and England since the Protestant Reformation."[1321]

Stubbe's work was transpired and influenced by the Ottoman Hungarian alliance and he sincerely wanted that experience repeated in England. "Stubbe promoted such an agenda during the same period that Protestant Hungarians were interested in forming an alliance with the Ottomans. *The Rise and Progress of Mahometanism* makes three controversial claims: (i) Islam revived Arian Christianity, an anticlerical version of messianic Judaism that upheld Christ as a human prophet and, as a result, was marginalized by the persecution of corrupt Trinitarian churches; (ii) the decline of Christianity and the rise of Islam are a result of the combined influence of trinitarianism and the clergy, political ideologies that serve to legitimate the rise of despotic monarchies; and (iii) Mahomet, a wise legislator, replaced Christian dogmas with popular myths pertaining to the restoration of constitutional law. For Stubbe, Islam is a natural religion worthy of admiration. The Prophet's civic laws have accomplished in less than a hundred years what Trinitarian Christians have failed to achieve in over a millennium: his laws have anchored a state-sponsored (rather than ecclesiastical) model of toleration for all religious minorities on a solid constitutional foundation that originated with Noah's covenant as prophetically renewed by Abraham, Moses, and Christ."[1322]

Stubbe was less of an Islamic missionary and more of an English reformer who, like countless other concerned leaders, was more interested in religious tolerance and European unity. "Stubbe treats Islamic toleration as the much-needed antidote to the religious and political contentions that have plagued Europe and England since the onset of the Protestant Reformation. Not surprisingly, Anglican polemicists attacked Teckelite politics as an instance of Protestant conversion to Islam under the pretense of promoting toleration. Indeed, Stubbe's manuscript lacks the kind of proselytising rhetoric that typically accompanies Anglican polemics on Islam. Rather than suggesting that Muslims must be converted to the true Protestant faith, he foregrounds the need for Christians to come closer to Islam's pristine tolerationist principles."[1323] Stubbe, employing Islamic terminologies, concepts and history presented a complete model of European reformation based upon the Islamic republican model. "His work suggests that Christians have more to gain from Islam's reformist outlook than Muslims do from the false teachings of Trinitarian Christology. In this case, his heretical views can be interpreted literally as his de facto conversion to

Islam."[1324] This republican model, with all its antecedents, would resonate well with the later moderate and radical enlightenment figures, with certain diverging subtleties.

Stubbe was extremely impressed by the Islamic concept of religious pluralism and toleration for other religious traditions, "it is manifest that the Mahometans did propagate their empire, but not their religion, by force of arms, and, albeit they did not permit others than Musulmen to enjoy any military or civil commands in their territories or entire conquests, yet the Christians and other religions might peaceably subsist under their protection if they paid the tribute demanded. In Spain the Mozarabick Christians always lived quietly and safely under them, and others in their other kingdoms and dominions, an inviolate justice being preserved towards them; and though the rich and potent nobility and rulers were destroyed or reduced to nothing, which was done to prevent future rebellions, yet it is observed by Scaliger—and it is an assured truth—that the vulgar Greeks live in a better condition under the Turk at present than they did under their own emperors when there were perpetual murders practiced on their princes and tyranny on their people. But they are now secure from injury if they pay their taxes, and it is more the interest of the princes and nobles than of the people at present which keeps all Europe from submitting to the Turks."[1325] Stubbe, who was actively involved in the politics of his time and well connected with the English elites, underscored the level of appreciation for Muslim Ottoman Turks and their republican government system in England. He further noted that "Mahomet did give protection and security to the pagans, Magicians, and Jews, and Christians also which swore fealty to him and paid him yearly tribute. Moreover, that he sent Omar to the Christians to assure them that they should live securely under his dominion, and that he would esteem their lives as the lives of his Moslemin and of their goods as the goods of those others: to this purpose, there is extant a compact or league betwixt Mahomet and the Christians, published in France by Gabriel Sionita and reprinted by Johannes Fabricius a Dantzicker, which is by him affirmed to be most authentic, and mentioned by Selden [...] The sum of it is that the Christians submitting to him and paying their tributes duly shall live and enjoy the liberty of their religion without any molestation, and that there shall be a perpetual amity betwixt the Musulmen and them."[1326] Stubbe emphasised that

Mohammad never imposed his religion upon others, as long as they were not idolatrous or paid a moderate tribute (*jizyah*). "The security which he gave to the Jews and Christians that they might live quietly under him without molestation brought a great deal of riches into the publick treasury, and those securities were observed with so inviolate a faith that it was a great invitation to the next neighbours to come under his government."[1327]

Stubbe wanted Europeans to follow the tolerant path of the Muslim Turkish Empire and allow freedom of religious beliefs, expression, worship, and freedom of conscience. "So favourable are the conditions of Muslim rule [...] that Christians in contemporary Europe would prefer, if given the choice, Muslim rule to their own."[1328] Stubbe was close to the dissenting merchant community and wrote pamphlets about religious tolerance, based upon economic reasons and benefits. He was well aware of the English dissenters' desire to implement Turkish Islamic government model in England. The royalists and Tories were also conscious of the Whig allure with Ottoman republicanism and they highlighted, pinpointed and exposed it at every possible opportunity. To Stubbe, the interests of the kings and princes "at present keeps all Europe from submitting to the Turks."[1329] Had it not been to the persecutory policies of the national monarchs and if the choice was given to the masses, they would have chosen the pluralistic, freer, powerful and prosperous Ottoman government over the suffocating English monarchy and Church. Stubbe represented in 1670's the popular English sentiments against their church and state which John Beale expressed in 1650's. Muhammad's government system was the ideal for the waring Europe; the long-lasting sectarian wars, conflicts and destruction could be stopped by the tolerant, republican and democratic policies of Islam. Muhammad did not accomplish the task of diversity and pluralism by dint of force but by means of persuasion. His government was not despotic, tyrannical and autocratic but inspiring and prophetic. "Stubbe also praises the sort of government Mohammed established. It was rule by one man but it was not government by a monarch, an emperor or an army general. Rather it was government by a prophet, an inspired leader. As such his power was absolute but not tyrannical because he ruled by a natural prudence that freed men from superstition, injustice and onerous exactions, and instead nurtured learning, tolerance and prosperity: he is far from depriving any

Ismaelite [Arab] of his liberty, that he would set even a bird free if he saw him encaged, and so remote from ambition and avarice that the greatest pleasure he takes in having anything is that he may give it away to some more indigent Moslemin."[1330] Therefore Muhammad's religion and his government must be a Christian ideal, "a government based upon natural prudence to match 'the religion of Noah' and of nature."[1331] Stubbe saw Islamic egalitarian republicanism as the solution to Restoration England's thorny problems. "Stubbe's republic was to be ruled by the virtuous who were seen to be inspired men in the same sense that Mohammed was – at once dedicated, worthy and shrewd. The new prophetic rule and the old republican and civic ideal were both intended to set up governments in which virtue would rule; power would be harnessed in both to virtue; and the result would be to create not only virtuous rule but also virtuous men and women, public virtue and a virtuous state, if not republican virtue. The emphasis in Stubbe's Account upon almsgiving and the resulting levelling up and down is probably also a holdover from his pre-Restoration attack on tithing and his republican egalitarianism."[1332] Hobbes' enlightend monarch was a reflection of Stubbe's Muhammad.

Stubbe was not alone in his desire to assimilate Islamic religious and political ideals to English society,[1333] and he had many influential partners in this movement. "Nor is Stubbe's manuscript the only example of an attempt to bring Muslim ideas and institutions to bear on English affairs in the 1670s. There was considerable interest at court in the 1670s and 1680s in things Islamic, from coffee to costumes to religious doctrine. Viscount Conway, who was a Privy Councillor for Ireland at the time, commissioned his brother-in-law, Sir John Finch, Ambassador to Constantinople, to write a series of reports concerning Muslim customs and culture with a view to suggesting the ways in which they might be applied in England to the reform of political and religious institutions. In 1675, Sir John complied after some delay, and the letters exist in manuscript in the British Library."[1334] John Finch's philosopher sister Anne Conwey, a student and colleague of Cambridge Platonist and theologian Henry More and a well-connected figure among the Continental intelligentsia, was interested in Islam, Ottoman culture and Kabbala. She converted to Quakerism and died as a Quaker. Sarah Hutton attributed Anne Conway's anti-Trinitarian Islamic sympathies to Henry Stubbe and her brother John Finch.[1335] It is interesting to note that Viscount Conway, Secretary of State for the Northern Department, was the principle patron of Henry Stubbe.[1336] His family connections with Islam, Ottomans and reformation in England on Ottoman lines may very well have shaped Stubbe's Islamism and Ottomanism. Conway tried to purchase Stubbe's library immediately after Stubbe's sudden accidental death.[1337] Stubbe's original patron Sir Henry Vane the Younger - the staunch republican, pluralist governor of the Massachusetts Bay Colony, the friend of Roger William, one of the founders of Harvard College, the confidant of Oliver Cromwell and later critic of Cromwell's authoritarianism - was himself engaged in trade, and was closely connected with English merchants. Vane championed religious tolerance in the American colony, fought against the imposition of the Presbyterian Church as the official Church of England during Cromwell Protectorate and worked towards religious and political reforms. He vouched for universal religious tolerance including Jews, Muslims and all Catholic and Protestant dissenters. In 1659, a Royalist satire against Sir Henry Vane castigated him as 'Alcoran Vane'; in a 1661 satire, Vane was again caricatured as one who had sought to change the laws of Britain into laws of "Mahomet. Stubbe was heavily engaged in Sir Vane's religious and political reforms and pamphleteering campaigns. Mordechai Fiengold noted that "by mid-1659 Stubbe was conscripted by Sir Henry Vane into heavy political and religious pamphleteering."[1338] His other patron Robert Boyle was fascinated with Eastern alchemy, natural sciences and Arabic language. Boyle's natural, anti-dogmatic and moral Christianity might have resembled Stubbe's Muhammadan Christianity. John Finch was a fellow of Royal Society and a fellow alchemy seeker; he, along with Robert Boyle, Henry Stubbe, Henry More, William Harvey and renowned physician, natural philosopher, chymist, Christian kabbalist and court diplomat Francis Mercury Van Helmont, tried to cure Anne Conway.[1339] Stubbe's other patron, the Earl of Shaftesbury, was a republican Whig accused of championing Ottoman Islamic republicanism. It will not be far-fetched to conclude that Stubbe's pro Islamic and pro Ottoman views were a product of these patrons with diverging interests but united in a general religio-political reformative scheme based on Eastern, Islamic knowledge, wisdom and experiences. Muslim ideas were sought after equally by the natural philosophers, intellectuals and policymakers for implementation in Stubbe's England; Stubbe very much embodied and championed that reformative trend. Levant Company ambassadors, merchants and workers were equally interested in the Ottoman government model and pluralistic society. John Finch, the Levant company ambassador in Istanbul, wrote detailed reports about Ottomans and Islam and sent them to his influential sister Ann Convey and his high-ranking cousins and uncles. Finch seemed to be in possession of Stubbe's manuscript, as he quoted portion from it in his reports. Stubbe represented the influential, republican leaning but reserved English intelligentsia in their Islamism, Ottomanism and reformism.

Stubbe's *Account* was a theological and political prescriptive critique of European religion and government. "England would be better off if religious authority were vested in the civil sovereign, as under Islam, just as Mohammed did; moreover, the sovereign should enforce a rational religion, a 'Mahometan Christianity' which would represent a return to the Apostolic church. Again just as Mohammed did, the sovereign should allow for toleration of opinion beyond the enforcement of this doctrinal minimum, this rational religion of nature."[1340] Stubbe was reflecting upon the English challenges from the prism of Islam and suggesting Islamic solutions to England's theological, political and social problems. His Islamic republicanism was particularly attractive to the English dissenters who were discriminated against and persecuted due to their heterodoxy. The dissenters could not own property, hold state offices or benefit from tax laws. Garcia noted that "Stubbe's account offers a reassuring message for English nonconformists: in an age dominated by Trinitarian persecution, only Islam's tolerant principles can guarantee a constitutional republicanism that would allow them to become citizens equally entitled to rights, property, and privilege. These ideas are revolutionary because they implicitly suggest that Islamic law should replace and supplement ineffective Christian regimes."[1341]

Muhammadan Christianity and Natural Law

Thomas Hobbes, John Locke, John Toland and many other Deists, Socinians, Unitarians, Quakers, Presbyterians and other dissenters struggled for the same goals; it is therefore no wonder that their natural law, civic religion and theories of reason were strikingly similar to Henry Stubbe's Muhammadan Christianity. "From Stubbe to Reid, Mahometanism was a useful bricolage medium for a diverse group of writers from various political and religious backgrounds. John Toland, Lady Mary Wortley Montagu, Edmund Burke, Samuel Taylor Coleridge, and

Percy Shelley variously understood Mahometanism to provide both a model and an idiom for the definition of political liberty. In this context, English radicalism is defined not as a linear history of ideas but as a series of subversive practices and eclectic discursive techniques that are culturally situated."[1342] Henry Stubbe set the stage for the later Unitarian, Islamic republicanism, set its agenda and provided it with adequate material and directions; Stubbe was a nation in himself.

Jacob rightly observes that in his *Account*, Stubbe "turns true religion inside out. Trinitarian Christianity is dismissed as hopelessly corrupt and false in favour of Islam, which is represented as the religion of Christ and the Apostles. There are some striking similarities between Stubbe's 'Mahometan Christianity' and Hobbes' natural religion set out in Chapter 31 of *Leviathan*. There Hobbes says that men can reasonably acknowledge God's existence as creator and governor of the universe and that he should be worshipped further through prayer and thanksgiving. Men are not to inquire into the nature of God because finite beings cannot comprehend the infinite. Such efforts in the past have led to 'volumes of disputation' rather than truth - to heat, not light. Hobbes also speaks of God's 'natural punishments.' To wit: 'he that will do anything for his pleasure, must engage himself to suffer all the pains annexed to it.' Hobbes and Stubbe have both produced a pared-down faith."[1343] Hobbes criticised the theologians (Schoolman) for deceiving the common men with absurd terms such as the Trinity, transubstantiation and the nature of Christ, "let him take a Schoolman into his hands and see if he can translate any one chapter concerning any difficult point; as the Trinity, the Deity, the nature of Christ, transubstantiation, free will, etc., into any of the modern tongues, so as to make the same intelligible [...] When men write whole volumes of such stuff, are they not mad, or intend to make others so?"[1344] He doubted the authenticity of the Christian scriptures and called God, Moses and the Apostles the real Trinity. To Hobbes, the greatest worship of God is conformity to His laws and not belief in the Trinity or God's atoning death, "obedience to His laws (that is, in this case to the laws of nature) is the greatest worship of all. For as obedience is more acceptable to God than sacrifice; so also to set light by His commandments is the greatest of all contumelies. And these are the laws of that divine worship which natural reason dictateth to private men."[1345]

It is pertinent to mention that Stubbe and Hobbes were close friends and Stubbe translated chapters of Hobbes Leviathan to Latin.[1346] On "occasions Hobbes even incorporated Stubbe's critique."[1347] John Tolan noted that "Stubbe was a friend and admirer of Thomas Hobbes, with whom he corresponded frequently; in the 1650s, Stubbe was at work on a Latin translation of Hobbes'ss *Leviathan*. His Mahomet fits well the model of the benevolent monarch portrayed in the *Leviathan*, using the precepts of a simple, natural religion to enforce morality and uphold authority, without handing over power to a caste of grasping priests. Hobbes proposed a civic, natural religion devoted to the honour of the one God, in which vain disputations about his nature would be prohibited, since 'volumes of disputation about the nature of God [...] tend not to His honour, but to the honour of our own wits and learning; and are nothing else but inconsiderate and vain abuses of His sacred name.' Stubbe's Mahomet is a Hobbesian monarch who returns to a simple form of natural monotheism in accordance with the religion of the primitive Christians."[1348]

It is therefore no wonder that Hobbes' ideas about natural religion were strikingly close to Stubbe's 'Mahometan Christianity,' which was Stubbe's ideal civil religion. Jacob has shown that Stubbe's central doctrines consisted of "the beliefs of 'the most primitive' Christians, revived by Mohammed."[1349] Stubbe might have influenced Hobbes's ideas of natural religion, law and social contract in light of Stubbe's perceptions of Prophet Muhammad's religion, law and governing principles. Both Hobbes and Stubbe were trying to get rid of the corrupt priests and kings and replace them with a just spiritual prince. Hobbes indebtedness to Stubbe on this point is unquestionable. Stubbe contrasted "the religious policy of Islam with that of the Christianised Roman empire. In the latter for political reasons the emperors from Constantine onwards had allowed the clergy to claim a spiritual authority separate from their own civil authority, and this had led to ignorance, superstition, contention and a weakening of the empire. Mohammed, on the other hand, placed control of religion in the hands of the civil ruler and the result was the opposite [...] 'What a discourse might be made upon his [Mohammed's] uniting the civil and ecclesiastical powers in one sovereign!' This of course is Hobbes's prescription, set out in the last half of *Leviathan,* and the influence of that book on Stubbe is again unmistakable."[1350]

Muhammad, the Machiavellian Prince

To Stubbe, Prophet Muhammad was that Machiavellian prince who had accomplished the task of combining the sacred and civil authority. Muhammad's historical model could save England of its religious and political ills. "For Stubbe, Mahomet's Machiavellian republic can help guide a Country politics determined to protect England's virtuous commonwealth from corrupt ministers, despotic kings, intolerant Anglicans, parasitic aristocrats, monied interest, and standing armies."[1351] Garcia further observed that "Stubbe has no qualms about justifying Islam's rise to geopolitical domination, because the true opponents to the Christian faith are the Trinitarians, the 'enemies to all human Learning': St. Athanasius, for his false teachings about the 'son of God,' and Emperor Constantine, for rigging the Nicene Council elections in favour of the Trinitarian heresy. Stubbe argues that Islam was spread not through the sword but by the word."[1352]

Stubbe and English Deism

Stubbe was also the source of Charles Blount's deism. Blount's father Sir Henry Blount, who according to Charles Gildon was "the *Socrates* of the Age for his aversion to the reigning Sophisms, and Hypocrisies, Eminent in all Capacities, the best Husband, Father, and Master, extreamly ageeable in Conversation, and just in all his dealings,"[1353] had extensively traveled in the Ottoman Empire and stayed long in Muslim Levant. His *A Voyage Into the Levant* was "reprinted seven times before 1671."[1354] Henry Blount was well-versed in Muslim religion, habits and culture. He "became famous for abstaining from any drinks other than water and coffee. 'For the first forty years of his life he was a boon companion,' one biographer reports, 'and much given to railery; but in the other forty, of a serious temper, and a water drinker."[1355] He dressed in Turkish clothes and abstained from alcohol. He helped Charles Blount in compiling his Deistic works. Charles Blount himself intended to compile a biography of Prophet Muhammad, as reported by Pierre Bayle in his *Dictionary*; the father of English Deism was an Islamophile, like his friend Henry Stubbe.

Henry Stubbe read the Voyage and benefitted from it. Stubbe, a friend of Charles Blount, helped in refining Blount's Unitarian deism; This Unitarian Deism would later become the predominant religious ideology of many of the Founding Fathers of French and American republics. Jacob observes: "There are more striking similarities between Stubbe and the early deism of Charles Blount."[1356] Blount's natural religion consisted of the following points. "Natural religion is the belief we have of an eternal intellectual being, & of the duty which we owe to him, manifested to us by our reason, without revelation or positive law: The chief heads whereof seem contained in these few particulars.

1. That there is one infinite eternal God, Creator of all things.
2. That he governs the world by Providence.
3. That 'tis our duty to worship & obey him as Creator and Governor.
4. That our worship consists in prayers to him, & praise of him.
5. That our obedience consists in the rules of right reason, the practice whereof is moral virtue.
6. That we are to expect rewards and punishments hereafter, according to our actions in this life; which includes the soul's immortality, and is proved by our admitting providence.
7. Seventhly, that when we err from the rules of our duty, we ought to repent & trust in God's mercy for pardon."[1357]

This seems to be an exact summary of the Islamic articles of faith. Jacob notes that "Blount's formulation shares with Stubbe's 'Mahometan Christianity' all of the points that Hobbes's natural religion does, and more besides."[1358] Blount's Deism and Hobbes's natural religion were closely identical with Stubbe's "Mahometan Christianity." Therefore, early Deism and the natural, civic religion of Blount, Hobbes, Locke and other Unitarians was closely identified with the Mohammadan Christianity of Stubbe and John Toland. Jacob notes that "These strong similarities between Stubbe's 'Mahometan Christianity' and Blount's natural religion argue, however, for a close connection between the two thinkers, especially as they were contemporaries."[1359] After a detailed discussion of these striking similarities and Blount's friendship with Stubbe, Jacob concludes that "Stubbe must now be reckoned as one of the founders of English deism, though his creed wore the guise of 'Mahometan Christianity."[1360] Therefore, the close affinity of early Deism with Muhammadan Christianity is not an accident.

Jacob also shows that Bristol Quaker leader George Bishop, in his article *A Looking-Glass for the Times* published in 1668, recognised

Stubbe as "the source of many of his own Quaker ideals."[1361] Early Quakers had historical connections with Islam; the Quaker leader George Fox quoted many verses from the Quran, and later on Thomas Paine would combine his Quaker upbringing with his radical deistic ideology because of their similarities. Early "English Deism" was a proto-copy of Stubbe's "Mahometan Christianity." Stubbe's ideal of "Mahometan Christianity" resonated with many other English dissenters in addition to Quakers, Deists, Socinians, and Unitarians. This Deistic, Unitarian, rational "Mahometan Christianity" will become the rallying cry of the Enlightenment period against the abusive Trinitarian Christianity of the Church and monarchy. The comprehensive "Mohamoten Christianity" had all ingredients of the Enlightenment and offered solutions to Christendom's religious as well as political problems such as Trinitarianism, depraved human nature and religious persecutions.

Stubbe and English Civil Religion

Likewise, the English civil religion tradition also started with Stubbe. James A. Jacob has shown that Stubbe, borrowing mostly from John Selden, Thomas Hobbes, and James Harrington "developed and advocated a civil religion which would survive the Restoration, undergoing several mutations in the course of the 1660s and 1670s. Stubbe's civil religion was based upon a "deistical minimum, common to the Jews, the Muslims and the primitive Christian."[1362] Stubbe had argued that Moses and Jesus were civil republican monotheists like Muhammad; the original Jewish, Christian, and Islamic messages were the one and same Unity of a transcendent, just God and equality of his creatures. Stubbe, in *An Account,* argued that Jesus was sent to rectify Jewish excesses and that Prophet Mohammad came to "revive ancient Christianity."[1363] Henry Care (1646/7-1688), the famous anti-Catholic Whig propagandist, English writer and journalist, was also influenced by Stubbe. Care's the Weekly Pacquet of Advice from Rome, the English Liberties (1680) and The Excellent Priviledge of Liberty (1687) reflected Stubbe's Turkophilism and Islamism. Care's praises of Islamic rationalism, minimalism, limited republicanism, toleration, diversity and empire building against the persecuting, irrational, dogmatic, absolutist popery of both the Catholic and Protestant churches echoed Stubbe's Muhammadan Christianity and Turkophilism. Care made the Turks appear the more civil – even more "Christian" – power.[1364]

Stubbe was very influential in many ways. Matar observed that "P. M. Holt saw Stubbe's interest in Islam as a product of the mid-seventeenth-century civil wars, while James R. Jacob argued that *Originall* reflected the change in Restoration England that gave rise to a 'secular conception of history' inspired by Hobbes. Stubbe, added Jacob, wrote his treatise after he began to identify with the radical movement in English religious thought that included figures like John Milton, Andrew Marvell, Algernon Sidney, and Lord Shaftesbury. For Jacob, *Originall* was intended as a message to Charles II about proper governance at the same time that it could be viewed as the link between 'radical Protestantism' and Deism. Citing Jacob, Christopher Hill agreed, as did Justin A. I. Champion: the *Originall* is part of the 'radical' religious developments that led to the early English deists, and belongs in the trajectory that led to the Socinian tracts of the 1690s and to John Toland's *Nazarenus* (1718). Humberto Garcia argued that the beginnings of the Enlightenment in England can be traced, in some measure, to Stubbe and his views on Islam."[1365] Stubbe's reformative scheme included all the ingredients of early Enlightenment; it rejected Church Christianity with all its central dogmas, insisted upon religious tolerance and pluralism and offered a republican model of governance and civic society. His Mohammadan Christianity was the model of early Deism, natural religion and rights and civic religion. John Locke, Isaac Newton and other moderate enlightenment figures tacitly incorporated these themes into their reformation plans, and the resulting Enlightenment was a product of such an appropriation.

It was mainly due to Stubbe that from early on Islam was considered, as H. Garcia argues, "the natural ally of the Radical Enlightenment, an underground international movement that tended to borrow the legends, stories, and motifs associated with various prophetic strains of near-eastern monotheism in order to define its theological and political heterodoxy in republican-constitutionalist terms."[1366] Stubbe heavily influenced later radical dissenters such as Socinians, Deists and Unitarian's views of Islam and Muhammad. "C. E. Bosworth argued that Stubbe's rejection of Trinitarianism stemmed from admiration of the Great Tew Circle, especially Lord Falkland and William Chillingworth, both of whom are mentioned in *Originall*. Although they may not, as H. John McLachlan observed, 'have been antitrinitarian in theology, their Latitudinarianism may be regarded as a step in the direction of Arianism and Socinianism.' Jacob and Champion concurred with Bosworth, confirming Stubbe's place within the rising trends of Socinianism, Deism, and Whiggism in the Restoration period. As Champion noted, Socinian tracts were widely available in the 1660s and 70s, and writers in the 1690s such as Arthur Bury, William Freke, and Stephen Nye identified 'Unitarianism with monotheistic Islam."'[1367] Stubbe was a link between the later radical enlightenment figures and Dr. Edward Pococke and other authors of "Republic of Letters".[1368] Stubbe was the "Father of Unitarian Islamic syncretism"[1369] and Islamic republicanism, the two main themes and ideologies of the early Enlightenment in England which lingered well into the eighteenth century. Stubbe, like John Selden, was influenced by Islamic Unitarian theology,[1370] and- also like John Selden - praised Islamic theology, republican values and religious tolerance.

Stubbe was among the founding propagators of religious tolerance and pluralism in Britain. He supported a full-fledged policy of religious tolerance for all sects just like the Ottoman Empire, at a time when leaders like John Locke considered toleration a taboo leading to social disruption, violence and anarchy.[1371] Stubbe encouraged Locke to accept the religious tolerance as early as 1659, but Locke refused to join the movement. Stubbe's insistence upon the Muslim Ottoman example of total religious freedom, in line with Islamic religion and history, was perhaps an addendum to his previous efforts. Matar observed that "it is tempting to treat Stubbe's *Originall* as a continuation of the letter exchange with John Locke. After reading Stubbe's *Essay in Defence of the Good Old Cause* (1659), Locke wrote Stubbe a letter in which he expressed "admiration" for the "strength and vigour" of the style, but complained about the extent to which Stubbe was willing to go in advocating toleration (in this case for the Quakers). At that point in time, Locke still believed that religious differences in the state would result in anarchy and violence."[1372] It took John Locke almost thirty years to publicly agree and write about a truncated version of Stubbe's religious tolerance, which even then did not extend tolerance to Catholics and atheists.[1373] Stubbe's treatise on Muhammad and Islam's republican, tolerant and rational policies might have been a response to leaders like John Locke, who initially opposed religious tolerance as anarchic.[1374] It is the irony of fate that Stubbe, with his comprehensive appeal for religious tolerance, was mostly ignored by the historians of religious freedom while Locke with his late, attenuated appeal is considered the founding father of religious pluralism, tolerance and Enlightenment. Likewise, the long Islamic history of religious tolerance and pluralism is seldom acknowledged while the late, partial and ambiguous eighteenth-century European policies of religious tolerance are underscored as the foundations of human liberty, republican values and democratic systems.[1375] This is how the Whiggish, linear, arbitrary and biased historical narratives are created to fan specific historical agendas. The Whiggish naratives make the past subservient to the demands of progressive present, as H. Butterfield has well demonstrated.

In their efforts to glorify the present they intentionally or subconsciously mutilate the past, make the crooked straight, the rough places plain, refurbish the lost causes, reinvigorate failed arguments, fabricate noble sacrifices, artificially open unopened doors, untried passages and dark narrow alleys, create fanciful characters, destroy historical characters and facts to replace them with malleable trops and figures. Whiggish modern historians committed theft and played havoc to the real history in their efforts to rewrite history on Eurocentric lines. Real heroes were destroyed, suppressed and ignored to create and highlight characters and mythologies congenial to Eurocentrism. The modern political spinning and intellectual red herring is nothing new; it has precedents in the eighteenth- and nineteenth-century Whiggish British and American historiography of teleological Christian, Protestant, Anglican, constitutional, libertarian, scientific, progressive, modern and miraculous Eurocentric world.[1376]

Additionally, the seventeenth century was the century of Arabic translations to Latin and English. The Arab and Islamic influences were rampant. The modern historians are hesitant to give Islam and Arabs their due place in the history of ideas and want to present England and Europe as the sole proprietors of Enlightenment and modernity projects. They totally ignore the Islamic contributions, burying those who were at the forefront of such a movement.[1377] The contemporary historians of that period are willing to give all credit to ancient Greco-Roman writers such as Aristotle, Plato and Cicero but are at a loss to acknowledge their Muslim interlocutors, commentators and interpreters who transmitted that knowledge with fundamental additions, modifications and assimilations to Christendom. They tend to ignore centuries of Muslim contributions to human civilisation and progress including close encounters and appropriations from the sixteenth century to the eighteenth century. This is nothing short of theft of history, as Jack Goody demonstrates.[1378] Stubbe along with Islamic faith deserves a rightful place in the unfolding of the English Enlightenment.

To Anthony Wood, the earliest biographer of Stubbe, he was "the most noted person of his age that these late times have produced."[1379] Stubbe died in 1676, but his influence continued through the remainder of the Restoration and after the Revolution of 1688–1689, until at least 1720. "Perhaps the influence of the *Account* was more profound than it initially appears."[1380] He was the source of "the early English deism of Charles Blount and the civil religion or 'Mahometan Christianity' of John Toland, and hence charted the intellectual links between the radical Protestantism and subversive naturalism represented by Stubbe and the deism and vitalistic materialism or pantheism (to use Toland's words) of the early Enlightenment. Stubbe is a key connection between the radicalism of the mid-century English revolution with the radicalism of the early eighteenth century. The principal medium of this connection [...] was Stubbe's manuscript 'An Account of the Rise and Progress of Mahometanism,' which circulated underground between the 1670s and 1720."[1381]

Charles Blount copied and transmitted Stubbe's manuscript to other freethinkers and radical Whigs. "Charles Blount, one of the most active of the radicals during the Exclusion, crisis and a prominent member of the Green Ribbon Club, had read and copied at least portions of Stubbe's Account of the Rise and Progress of Mahometanism by 1678. In that year he wrote a letter to Hobbes and another to John Wilmot, Earl of Rochester, himself a notorious libertine and freethinker, which consisted mainly of extracts from Stubbe's manuscript."[1382] Stubbe's manuscript exerted tangible influence upon Blount's "Oracles of Reason" and upon the writings of other members of Shaftesbury's circle, such as Albertus Warren and Clifford. There is a crystal-clear line stretching from Shaftesbury to Stubbe to deistic, radical Whigs. James Jacob noted that "there is then an ideological continuity between Stubbe, the sometime court pen, sometime 'country' spokesman, and the radical Whigs of the Exclusion crisis - so profound in fact that one wishes he had lived to take part in the campaign organised by the Green Ribbon Club, for one knows that he would have been there, alongside Blount and the others, at its active center. Indeed the evidence - Stubbe's all but certain collabouration with Shaftesbury in the autumn of 1673, the publication of *A Caveat for the Protestant Clergy* under his name in 1678, the clandestine circulation of Stubbe's manuscript, and the writings of Blount and Warren - all points to more than an ideological affinity and influence but a continuity of actual political organisation emanating from and revolving around the First Earl himself."[1383] John Locke was an important member of Shaftesbury's circle, and continued Shaftesbury's reformation after his sudden death in Amsterdam.

Chapter 8

John Toland and Mohammadan Christianity

John Toland (1670–1722) furthered Stubbe's historical thesis of Mohammadan Christianity in his famous book *Nazarenus: or Jewish, Gentile and Mahometan Christianity, Containing the History of the Ancient Gospel of Barnabas [...] Also the Original Plan of Christianity Explained in the History of the Nazarens [...] with [...] a Summary of Ancient Irish Christianity*, written in 1718. Toland was a known Deist, Socinian and republican radical reformer; Justin Champion observed that "throughout the 1690s, and the early 1700s, working closely with powerful political figures like the third Earl of Shaftesbury, Robert Harley and Sir Robert Molesworth, Toland became one of the most consistent and vocal publicists for Protestant liberties and the Hanoverian succession. During the 1700s he continued this public role writing (amongst many contributions) detailed defences of [...] the Toleration Act, as well as fierce attacks upon the 'popery' of the High Church party in Convocation and Parliament. Alongside this explicitly political writing, Toland was involved in the production of works of profound erudition and scholarship. Much of this material was circulated in clandestine form amongst a circle of elite figures that included Sophia of Hanover (the successor apparent to the British Crown), Prince Eugene of Savoy (leading military strategist of the Protestant cause), and English gentlemen like Anthony Collins. Ultimately this erudition, which was also published in print form, earned Toland a significant and contentious reputation in the European 'republic of letters.'"[1384]

Toland was an activist of international connections, scholarship and repute,[1385] and his works and thought were important reflections of the eighteenth-century intellectual landscape.[1386] His main focus was to demolish the dominant traditional Christian system of absolute Church and monarch. He made "a mighty shout of defiance"[1387] against traditional Christianity, and broke the nexus between sacred knowledge and Church authority.[1388] The absolute submission to both Church and king was demanded in the name of God, as promulgated by St. Augustine, and continually followed over the centuries by Christendom. Toland aimed at the theological roots of the whole Christian system to replace it with Islamic Unitarian republicanism.[1389] Toland engaged all levels of authority (Biblical, Sacerdotal, political, cultural and social) to shake up the entire Christian system of power and authority: "Rupturing, capturing and transforming the logic of such cultural procedures was a discursive manoeuvre that had profound and explicit social and political consequences…Toland conducted a sustained and public assault upon the clerical cultural system for making authority. By embroiling his priestly opponents in public debate he dislodged the mortar that bound the stones of Christian order."[1390] He accomplished the difficult task with a mixture of scholarship, sincerity and subterfuge, and was more influential than some of his Deistic and Socinian compatriots.[1391] Toland was very influential in a number of important ways; his ideas and thoughts provoked many local controversies and initiated national and international upheavals. He was well read all across Europe as well as in Istanbul.[1392] Toland's "writings had 'alarm'd all sober well-meaning Christians, and set the whole clergy against him.'"[1393] Toland, like Stubbe, realised an anti-Church Christianity revolution.

Huge Trevor-Roper notes that in the 1690s "there began in England a concerted attack both on the central doctrines and on the external proofs of orthodox Christianity. From one quarter, the divine inspiration of the Bible was questioned. Thereby the historic context and cosmological significance of Christ's mission were made to tremble. From another, the doctrine of the Trinity, which had become the badge of orthodoxy in the fourth century, and had been defended by fire and faggot ever since, was openly challenged. With it, not only the authority of the Fathers who had invented and imposed it, but the divinity of Christ himself, was put in doubt. These challenges were not indeed new, but they were now delivered far more forcefully than before, from inside as well as outside the established Church; and they aroused a forceful response. In that last decade of the Seventeenth century, 'Arian' – that is, anti-Trinitarian – works were ritually condemned in both universities; new Blasphemy Acts were passed by Parliament in a vain attempt to stay the infection; and the alarm of the establishment was increased by the appearance of an alternative religion only loosely connected with traditional Christianity and quite incompatible with Trinitarian doctrines: 'the religion of Nature,' or 'deism.'"[1394] Deistic Christianity was identical to Toland's Muhammadan Christianity and infected English society like a bush fire; unfortunately, many historians of the period tend to minimise its reach, influence and implications.[1395] "Anti-Trinitarianism was more pervasive and spread more diversely in Europe and in England than any other single unorthodox view. It was seemingly everywhere and came from every quarter. It was part of the armory of unlearned religious radicals and also educated divines and laymen."[1396] It spread like a storm.

John Toland was the immediate instigator of the above sketched storm. In 1696 he had published *Christianity not Mysterious* to debunk the Christian mysteries, supernatural dogmas and their clerical guardians.

Trevor-Roper credits this book with causing the deistic uproar.[1397] It "shattered the complacent 'reasonableness' of mainstream Anglican theology."[1398] Paul Hazard noted that Tolad was a "queer personage indeed, this John Toland! He had got drunk on 'reason'; it had gone to his head. Christianity not mysterious was his war cry, in the book that made him famous in 1696. 'No mystery about Christianity,' he gave out, and that for the plain and sufficient reason that there are no mysteries, they simply don't exist. Mystery—the very word is pagan, like so many others we have clung to. It either means a superstition of some sort, and should be stamped out, or it denotes some problem by which we are temporarily baffled, but must sooner or later resolve. Either Christianity is reason, and is part and parcel of the universal order, sloughing off all that is extraneous thereto—tradition, dogmas, rites, creed, faith; or else it could not exist, since nothing in the world can be above reason, or contrary to it."[1399] Indeed, this was a huge storm against the historical Christianity, which centered on supernatural mysteries. The Christian Church, its dogmas, monarchy and absolutism were all exposed and targeted.

The work was "published without Toland's name or details of either publisher or bookseller between December 1695 and June 1696. Draft 'papers' had possibly been sent to John Locke in late March 1695, via his friend John Freke. Reports about Toland's work were widespread in Oxford through the year [...] By early June the book was being attacked from London pulpits for its 'most arrogant and impudent treatment of God and the Holy Scriptures' [...] By August the book had been announced on the Continent. To accompany this revelation a 'second edition enlarg'd' was published with Toland's name on the title-page. He revelled in the celebrity."[1400] In mid-May 1697 the Grand Jury of Middlesex condemned *Christianity not mysterious* in the company of two other anonymous works: *The Reasonableness of Christianity* and *A Lady's Religion*. Toland's book especially provoked an angry response from the Church of England, Parliament and both monarchs William and Mary. The swift and harsh response showed how the publication of *Christianity not mysterious* "perturbed the authority of public religion."[1401] Ultimately a Blasphemy Act was officially enacted in 1698.

Both Locke's "*Reasonableness of Christianity*" and Toland's "*Christianity not Mysterious*" were taken as subversive works against the Holy Trinity and other Christian mysteries.[1402] Bishop Stillingfeet "attempted to tar Locke's work with Toland's intellectual consequences [...] Locke merely commented that Toland 'says something which has a conformity with some notions in my book.'"[1403] Locke was an active part of the anti-Trinitarian storm but prudent enough to avoid its persecutory consequences. Toland like Stubbe was an open canon.

Toland had a bigger target in mind other than just rejecting the Trinity; he wanted to shake up the very foundations of the politics of knowledge, and tried to replace all supernatural Christian mysteries with things simple, reasonable and accessible to all men. Toland "had declared that 'religion is a plain & easy thing, & that there is not so much in it, as Priestcraft would persuade: taking it for granted to be part of this Doctrine, that what is to be done in order to Salvation, is as easy, as what is to be known, is plain.'"[1404] The motive was to unpick "deference and tutelage to the clerical 'Doctor.' The combination of epistemological confidence (every man may believe according to his own sense) and political liberty (establishing toleration) would establish a system of intellectual liberty. This was central to Toland's lifetime project. Importantly, for Toland the liberty enshrined in this process of enlightenment was prompted by the act of reading."[1405] He wanted the Christians to think for themselves and to read and understand the Bible by themselves, as their Muslim counterparts did, without the manipulative medium of the clergy.[1406] To accomplish this goal of individual liberty and comprehension, Toland rejected the Christian mysteries and dogmas which inhibited the truth from the second century all the way to the eighteenth century. "Toland established how manipulation of the concepts of mystery had been institutionalised by the Christian clergy after the second century. As he commented 'here's enough to show how Christianity became mysterious, and how so divine an institution did, through the craft and ambition of priests and philosophers, degenerate into mere paganism.' Priestly fraud monopolised 'the sole right of interpreting scripture and with it [a] claim'd infallibility, to their body,' unfortunately, as Toland noted, 'and so it continues, in a great measure, to this day.'"[1407] Toland's book destroyed both biblical as well as clerical authority to liberate Christians of centuries' suffocations. Some called it a Deistic work, while the others dubbed it as Socinian;[1408] both deists and Socinians stood for anti-Trinitarian republicanism.

Toland and New Testament Criticism

In *Amyntor: Or a Defence of Milton's Life* (1699) he went further by clearly denying the authenticity and validity of the New Testament itself. He classified the New Testament material into three categories: orthodox, apocryphal, and fictitious. Jonathan C. Birch noted that Toland, borrowing from the pioneer researches of French Richard Simon and German Johan Albrecht Fabricius, doubted the historicity and authenticity of Bible and anticipated the later German and Continental schools of biblical criticism.[1409] Toland anticipated the Eighteenth century German pietism and related textual, source, form and literary biblical criticisms of Johann Salomo Semler (1725–1791), Johann Gottfried Eichhorn (1752–1827), Johann Philipp Gabler (1753–1826), and Georg Lorenz Bauer (1755–1806) and G. E. Lessing (1729–1781), Ferdinand Christian Baur (1792–1860), Albert Schweitzer (1875–1965) and others' quest for historical Jesus.[1410] Like the Quran and Muslim theologians, Toland accused the Church of corrupting and compromising the Bible. The old Quranic criticisms of the Bible were getting acceptance in Europe, due to Reformation debates about the *sola scriptura,* Catholic efforts to uphold Church tradition and authority by insinuating scriptural insufficiency and literal incompetence in matters of doctrine and faith. Radical reformers like Toland were furthering Catholic arguments to bring down both Church and Bible; to them, both Catholic and Protestant clerical establishments were corrupt, like the corrupted scriptures.

Toland maintained that the present New Testament was canonised centuries after Jesus or his original followers and was not a reliable source for Jesus' life, theology, politics and preaching. He blamed the fourth-century Christian priests for grafting heathenistic supernatural, mysterious dogmas on the simple monotheistic message of Jesus. He also blamed the following clerical generation for maintaining the sacred fraud. "To the priests fell the honour, not of establishing heathenism, but of maintaining it, and of introducing its various rites. The modes of worship of the gods, says Toland, 'were afterwards manag'd by the Priests so as to make their imagin'd Intimacy with Heaven more valu'd, and to get Revenues settled on themselves'. 'Moreover', he adds, after the manner of Blount, 'there was not wanting sometimes a mutual Compact between the Prince and the Priest', which bound the priests to preach the absolute power of the prince and the fear of hell, to contribute to the stability of the state."[1411] Charles Blount's deism and Toland's Muhammadan Christianity were both directed against the Anglican Trinitarian royalist establishment's claims to authentic revelation and authority.

Toland and Primitive Christianity

After demolishing the foundations of Christian system of knowledge, authority and politics, Toland re-established them on the basis of the primitive Christianity of Jesus. Toland contended that the original followers of Jesus were "Nazarenes" who followed the Gospel of Barnabas.[1412] This Gospel "offered proof of this close correspondence between pure primitive Christianity and early Islam."[1413] These primitive Christians followed the Law of Moses in conformity with the universal law of nature propagated by all the prophets since Adam. Radical reformers such as Stubbe, Toland and Deists, as well as moderate reformers such as Locke and Newton, used Primitive Christianity as a model of reforming the historically corrupted Church Christianity. Diego Lucci noted that "in their attempts to revive "true religion," Locke and several English deists, such as Toland, Tindal, Chubb, Morgan, and Annet, focused on the relationship between the Law of Nature, the Law of Moses, and Christ's teaching [...] Locke and the English deists aimed to recover true religion from long-lasting distortions. However, their rethinking of the relationship between the Law of Nature, the Mosaic Law, and Christ's message led to different conceptions, uses, and appropriations of natural religion, Mosaic Judaism, and primitive Christianity in their attempts to restore what they perceived as true religion."[1414] These Deists regarded "the religion of nature as universal, eternal, necessary, and sufficient. Accordingly, they argued that Christ had merely confirmed natural religion. Though, they claimed that the religion of nature had suffered from frequent distortions throughout the centuries, both before and after Christ's reaffirmation of the Law of Nature. Appropriating Christ's message to his own philosophy, each of these deists identified primitive Christianity with his own version of natural religion. In describing Jesus as a moral philosopher who had simply restated the Law of Nature without adding anything to it, these authors aimed to grant historical dignity to their respective versions of deism, which they maintained against the ecclesiastical traditions, priestly frauds, and abstruse doctrines that had perverted what Toland called 'the original plan of Christianity.'"[1415] Toland portrayed Mosaic Judaism "as being on a par with primitive Christianity, given that both the Law of Moses and Christ's precepts were compatible with, and indeed based on, the Law of Nature."[1416] This natural, Mosaic and Christian law was preserved by Muhammad in the Quran. Therefore, the original message of Moses, Jesus and Muhammad was the one and the same ethical monotheism. This line of thought was in opposition to the Pauline, Augustinian and Church insistence upon Christian unique Trinitarian salvific scheme and Church's unique role in the grace-based universal salvation. Ethical laws of Moses and Jesus were complemented by the natural laws understood and comprehended by human reason, and hence in no need of the atoning death of Jesus or the mediatorial offices of Church and clergy. Toland, like the Deists, destroyed all Christian claims of scriptural, ecclesiastical and monarchical authority and connected man directly with God through reason and moral laws.

Toland and Gospel of Barnabas

In 1709 Toland discovered a manuscript of the Gospel of Barnabas in Amsterdam through his acquaintance with Prince Eugene of Vienna who possessed that manuscript. Toland began work on *Nazarenus* in 1710 based upon his study of the Gospel of Barnabas. Justin Champion showed that Toland "readily employed this text as evidence, following Stubbe's argument, of the continuity of Judaic, Christian and Islamic theology."[1417] James Jacob totally agreed.[1418] Toland, like Stubbe, believed that the pristine message of divine unity, charity, and moral responsibility was a common thread between all the Prophets, starting with Adam,[1419] and successive prophets came to rectify periodic human excesses and omissions. Jesus came to correct Jewish excesses, and Mohammad came to rectify Christian corruptions. He insisted that the "fundamental doctrines of Mahometanism to have their rise, not from Sergius the Nestorian monk (a person who has hitherto serv'd for a world of fine purposes) but from the earliest monuments of the Christian religion."[1420] Muhammad rectified St. Paul's supernatural, apostatic grafting upon Christianity. Toland maintained that the original followers of Jesus were Nazarene or Ebionites who were "mortal enemies to Paul [...] whom they stil'd an Apostate [...] and a transgressor of the Law [...] representing him as an intruder on the genuine Christianity...a stranger to the person of Christ, yet substituting his own pretended Revelations to the doctrines of those with whom Christ had convers'd, and to whom he actually communicated his will."[1421] Toland concluded, "Mahometans believe concerning Christ and his doctrine, were neither the inventions of Mahomet, nor yet of those Monks who are said to have assisted him in framing of his Alcoran but that they are as old as the time of the Apostles having been the sentiments of whole sects or Churches."[1422] Muhammad did not borrow the so-called heretical Arian Christology from Syrian monks of his time, but was a proper heir to the universal prophetic tradition of ethical monotheism preached by Jesus and preserved by his immediate disciples. To Toland, Muhammad was a true Christian. "'Mahometans' to be 'a sort of Christians, and not the worst sort neither.'"[1423] Muhammad was a Protestant, Unitarian Prophet, as Stubbe had contended before him.

Harrison summarises Toland's position on Islam and Gospel of Barnabas in the following words: "It was from this document, he believed, that the Mahometans derived their doctrines. Islam was a religion much maligned, said Toland, there being many myths and fables about it 'to which the Musulmans are utter strangers'. The truth was that Islamic doctrines were based not on the heterodox opinions of a Nestorian monk, as Medieval tradition would have it, but on 'the earliest documents of the Christian Religion'. The document in question was, of course, the Gospel of Barnabas, which Toland declared was 'in a very great part the same book' as the 'Gospel of the Mahometans' (presumably the Qu'ran). The Mahometans, moreover, 'openly profess to believe the *Gospel:* tho they charge our copies with so much corruption and alteration'. Toland's reasonings led him to the conclusion that the 'Mahometans', like the Jews, were really 'a sort or sect of Christians', and he even hinted that they were closer to the original plan of Christianity than was historical Christianity itself, the latter having suffered alteration through contact with paganism and being in addition based upon corrupted documents. It is not hard to see how Toland got his reputation for being a 'Mahometan' Christian."[1424]

The title "Mahometan Christians" got popularised in the later part of the seventeenth century to denote those anti-Trinitarians who called for a return to the original Unitarian Christianity of Jesus and his early disciples. The Unitarian phenomenon was quite widespread, as seen above, extending to dissenters as well as non-dissenting conformists and Church leaders. Toland greatly popularised the idea of Muhammadan Christianity due to his scholarship, erudition and sincerity. He sincerely believed that Islam was the true heir to the original Christianity of Jesus. Jacob notes that "like Stubbe, Toland argued that this first Christianity of Jesus and his immediate followers survived in pockets in the late Roman empire and was eventually appropriated by Mohammed to become the basis of Islam."[1425] Toland like Stubbe drew a straight historical line from Jesus to Muhammad, excluding the entire Roman Christian tradition from this legitimate Unitarian Christianity.

Islam was identical with the natural religion which allowed natural human reason to connect with God through divine signs, symbols and manifestations prevalent in the book of creation; Christendom needed to follow suit. "Ideal Christianity, Toland had insisted, did not coincide with the Church of England, or any other form of positive Christianity, but was to be identified with a practice of natural religion which could take place under the guise of any number of religious traditions. This equating of genuine Christianity with natural religion became a platform of later deist thought. The classic statement of this thesis is Matthew Tindal's *Christianity as Old as the Creation: or the Gospel, a Republication of the Religion of Nature* (1730."[1426] Paul Hazard noted that Toland wanted to replace Christianity with a more rational, republican and less supernatural religion; he wanted to be a Muhammad. "His dream was to become the founder of a religion, a sort of Mahomet; but he lacked the power and prestige. Yet what a hater he was, using all the resources of a ready tongue and a nimble wit to envenom his vituperations. And how he loathed priests, every single one of them, from the tribe of Levi onwards; for the Levites, too, were tricksters, nothing more nor less. On the priesthood he poured forth all the vials of his wrath. He denounced them for liars and malefactors; he was anti-clerical to the marrow of his bones."[1427] The Church of England, which considered itself the repository of all truth, could not tolerate Toland's sheer anti-clericalism and total opposition to its' "totalising theological dogma and religious exclusivism."[1428] The Church leaders dubbed him an absolute infidel and a Mahometan. "John Toland, in particular, was singled out as an infidel. One 'Dr South' apparently dubbed him 'a certain *Mahometan Christian*', while John Norris, in his critique of *Christianity not Mysterious,* thought him a Socinian who might as well be a Mahometan. Jean Gailhard, who thought to dismiss both Toland and the Socinians with one protracted stroke of the pen, noted that the Jews were 'enemies to our Lord Jesus', who with Mahometans and Socinians join in blasphemy."[1429]

It is pertinent to note that the Quran relayed a successive prophetic monotheistic history in which prophet after prophet followed each other as rectifiers of immoralities, sins and human transgressions. From Adam to Noah to Abraham, Moses, Jesus and Muhammad they conveyed the same Unitarian message of divine unity, human morality, accountability and final reward and punishment. The Quran also claimed that Jesus had prophesised the coming of Muhammad and his reformation of Christianity; Toland propagated the same Quranic narrative.[1430] Champion observes that "Toland deployed the Islamic notion of the succession of the prophets as the authors of new institutions each increasingly perfect, 'tho' in substance it still be one and the same religion.'" Toland accepted the Islamic charge that Jesus' prophecy of Mahomet, that he would come 'to complete or perfect all things', had been erased from Scripture by the priests."[1431] Here again Toland was following the Stubbean arguments, as discussed above. Toland considered the Muslims as the true followers of pristine Christianity and reformers of corrupted Church Christianity. He was keen to see Muslims tolerated in Europe as Christians and Jews were tolerated throughout the Muslim Empire. Muslims "might with as much reason and safety be tolerated at London and Amsterdam, as the Christians of every kind are so tolerated at London and Amsterdam, as the Christians of every kind are so tolerated at Constantinople and throughout all Turkey."[1432]

Toland, at the time of writing his Nazarene, was a Unitarian who believed in a linear prophetic monotheism, culminating in Prophet Muhammad. Islam was the most refined, reformed and pure form of the original Jewish and Christian ethical monotheism. Champion rightly observes that "Stubbe and Toland can thus be seen to place the historical past of Judaism, Christianity, and Islam into a Polybian framework."[1433] Furthermore, "both works set out to present an unbiased view of Islam, rejecting the slanders of the medieval canon identified in Prideaux's work. It must be remembered that especially when Toland's work was published it was into a public arena which had perceived Islam through the distorting lens of Prideaux's polemic."[1434]

Toland and Mahometan Christianity

Both Stubbe and Toland used Islam or 'Mahometan Christianity' as their ideal for a civil religion that would eliminate the corrupted Trinitarian Christianity, its stifling dogmas and absolutist political theology. "There was a close link between Stubbe's civil religion and Toland's. In both Christianity could and should be divested of its adventitious mysteries - 'unintelligible jargon,' as Toland said - and made to yield a Scriptural minimum in harmony with natural law, which could then serve as the basis of 'a natural religion,' tolerant, reasonable and dedicated to civil ends rather than priestly ones - the advancement of learning, national power and prosperity."[1435] Jacob further notes that "what was prescribed, instead, was a religion enjoining toleration, in which people would be instructed in the wisdom of the ancients for the pursuit of moral and political goals in this life. Much of the inspiration for this was Harringtonian, and Stubbe must be credited with reviving civil religion, couched in Harringtonian language, during the Restoration."[1436] The rector of St. Nicholas Church in Guildford, Thomas Mangey (1688–1755), condemned Toland's work: "His expression of the Mahometan Christianity is the only passage in this book which I do not condemn, provided he would mean by it not the Muselmans on the other side of the water, but the Socinians here. These may truely and properly be termed Mahometan Christians."[1437] To the Church and monarchical establishments, the widespread anti-Trinitarian, rational, natural law, civil religion, tolerant and republican movement of seventeenth-century England, with all its varieties, was an offshoot of the Ottoman conspiracy, directed at promoting anarchy, instability and degradation of state and Church authority to be replaced with Islamic republicanism of the Ottoman Empire. The merchants, nonconformists, Deists, Socinians and Unitarians all were part of the same international conspiracy; their demands of a return to the primitive Christianity were the veneer of a bigger subvervise and heinious plot of the international Islamic caliphate.

The identification of Jesus' primitive Christianity with Islam became a standard after Stubbe and Toland. It was often argued "that Mahomet was a better Christian than most, that he properly understood the relations between state power and clergy, that he had happily stripped power away from a corrupt and grasping clerical elite, and that he put into place a policy of toleration that was still practiced by the Ottomans and that should be imitated by enlightened European monarchs. Stubbe transformed the prophet of Islam into a republican revolutionary, and subsequent writers (Bury, Nye, Toland, and others) would confirm and elaborate upon this transformation. In the eighteenth century, several French intellectuals will use Muhammad in the same way to attack the preeminent place of the Catholic Church in France."[1438] Stubbe and Toland's Mohametan Christianity was embraced by the Socinians, Unitarians and Deists of the Eighteenth century; they were often called Muhammadan Christians.

John Locke, Isaac Newton and Milton's Socinian and Unitarian beliefs were a product of this Unitarian, Socinian, Deist and Islamic syncretism, in which Islamic theology and religious thought patterns were pretty visible. This Unitarian-Islamic hybrid was the rational theism which influenced the later generations of Deists, Unitarians and Socinians in England, France and America. This monotheistic and republican syncretism constituted the foundations of the English, French and American Enlightenments. Both its radical and moderate leaders agreed upon some broader points. They agreed: (1) that the supernatural, Trinitarian and incarnational Christianity was a corrupted version of the original, Unitarian, natural and moral Christianity of Jesus and his disciples. (2) This corruption occurred in the fourth century when the Christian religion was coopted by the Roman Empire. (3) The Bible was compromised in various ways. (4) The Church tradition and Church Fathers' writing were neither a genuine reflection of the original, monotheistic message of Jesus nor of the biblical text. (5) There was a universal, moral, successive prophetic tradition. (6) The Trinitarian

Christian belief system was irrational, paradoxical and absolutist. (7) The vanguards of historical Christianity (both clerical and monarchical establishments) were usurpers of authority and betrayers of the Lord. (8) The Christian divisions into Catholic, Protestant and confessional national churches and the resultant wars were detrimental to the Christian faith and society. (9) Christian religious persecutions were inhumane, irreligious and abusive. (10) The incarnational scheme of original sin and redemptive death of Christ was antithetical to human freedom, dignity and morality. (11) Historical Christianity needed theological as well as political reformation and a total break with the medieval past. (12) Islamic ethical monotheism, nomianism, naturalism, rationalism and republicanism were true heirs to the original Jewish, Christian and prophetic traditions. (13) Islam was the ideal but the contemporary Muslims were not. (14) The Ottoman Empire, in spite of its shortcomings, was a good republican model to be pursued, especially in regards to religious tolerance and pluralism. (15) Christianity must be reformed but not destroyed. (16) Reason was the arbiter to resolve the countless theological confusions and confessional jargons. (17) A stable, natural and rational order was needed in natural sciences and theology to empower the individuals and to avert the manipulation of priests and princes. (18) Church and knowledge must be democratised and anthropomorphised. (19) Clerical mediation between man and God was unnecessary. (20) No absolute monarchy and Church were promulgated by the Scriptures. (21) The human, prophetic and messianic Christology was the alternate. (22) A minimal, civic and all-embracing religion was the way out of religious conflicts, persecutions and debacles. (23) Faith and religion were private entities and could not be imposed from outside. (24) Virtuous sociability and not faith was publicly required. (25) Church and state should focus on social virtues rather than creedal uniformity. Almost all reformers agreed with give and take on the above points. This moral, theological and political consensus would form the basis of later English, French and American Enlightenments and both American and French republics.

Stubbe's ideal of "Mahometan Christianity" and his works were highly influential among the English thinkers of his time. Champion wrote: "We know that Charles Blount plagiarized a section in his *Oracles of Reason* (1693) and also that he sent Rochester extracts of the Account [...] An unnoticed influence can be found in Sir John

Finch's correspondence with Lord Conway between 4 and 14 February 1675. These letters give a 'politic' account of the growth of Islam including a presentation of the Islamic notion of the unipersonality of God [...] Mahomet is referred to as both a wise prince and legislator. There also may be the possibility that William Temple read and adopted Stubbe's work."[1439] Toland's works furthered that influence into multiple directions and popularised it in the public arena and sphere. These public debates coupled with material culture of "Oriental Obsessions" played havoc to the traditional institutions of ecclesiastical and monarchical establishments.

Nabil Matar, in *Islam in Britain*,[1440] and Jacob in *Henry Stubbe* have proven beyond doubt that an interest in Islamic ideas, philosophy, sciences, and institutions was prevalent among the English intelligentsia since the 1660s. G. A. Russell, in her book *The 'Arabick' Interest of the Natural Philosophers in the Seventeenth-Century*, has shown that the sixteenth and seventeenth centuries were the age of Arabic in England, when thousands of Arabic manuscripts were translated into Latin and English for multiple purposes by a variety of scholars and scientists. John Tolan noted that "in England as elsewhere in Europe, the study of Arabic, and the translation of key texts, had taken root over the fifteenth and sixteenth centuries. Guillaume Postel (1510–1581) in Paris, Joseph Scaliger (1540–1609) in Leiden, Pococke (1604–1691) in Oxford, and others had breathed new life into the study of Arabic letters and Muslim history and had translated key texts."[1441] This direct Islamic influence, Socinian missionary zeal, Deists and Unitarian controversies and a culture of "Oriental Obsession" apparently influenced many English thinkers of that era, including John Locke, Isaac Newton and many others. Their reformative scheme was broadly Unitarian in which Stubbean Mohammadan Christianity was quite visible.

Chapter 9

John Locke:
The Unitarian Heretic

John Locke (1632-1704), the Unitarian heretic, was an integral part of Unitarian republican movement. His educational background, intellectual associations, political affiliations and social interactions were closely identical to Stubbe. Locke was introduced to the Arabic language at Westminster, along with Latin and Hebrew; his Oxford exposure to Dr. Edward Pococke[1442] may have strengthened that connection. Pococke's long diplomatic stints in Aleppo and Constantinople, his command of Islamic theology, history, law and his erudition[1443] may well have enhanced Locke's insatiable curiosity for knowledge of other religions and cultures, especially that of Islam. Pococke was Locke's model and mentor, as seen above. Locke was also well connected with a number of other Levant Company chaplains, and commissioned them to collect manuscripts from the Muslim world.[1444] Chaplain Robert Huntington was Locke's fellow in Oxford and collected manuscripts for Locke while in Aleppo and Istanbul. Chaplain John Luke, who later became the chair of Arabic at Cambridge, was also actively involved in securing manuscript for Locke and Robert Boyle.[1445] Locke was acquinted with John Finch and Paul Recaut, the fellow Royal Society members and longterm Levant Company officials to the Ottoman Empire.

Locke's Westminster and Oxford colleague and one-time close friend Henry Stubbe's radical views especially regarding Unitarian primitive Christianity, post-Constantine Nicaean Church's abuses, corruptions and absolutism, subsequent Islamic reformation of Christian dogma and Islamic republicanism could have impacted Locke's outlook. Both were simultaneously at Oxford, moved in the circle of Shaftesbury and worked for him. Stubbe's correspondence with Locke on toleration is well-documented.[1446] His *An Account of the Rise and Progress of Maho-*

metanism, and a Vindication of him and his Religion from the Calumnies of the Christians may well have been read by Locke, though there is no surviving evidence that he possessed a copy or read it; many of Locke's Deist and Unitarian friends had access to it. It might very well have been written on behest of Shaftesbury, who also commissioned Locke to write about government and religious toleration. It supplemented Pococke Junior's English translation of Ibn Tufayl's philosophical novel Hayy bin Yaqzan (1671) which was highlighted by the Royal Society in 1674. Both Locke and Ibn Tufayle insisted upon autodidacticism, self-education, natural state, antidogmatic rational discourse and liberal, tolerant religious approach. Stubbe's antidogmatism, rationalism and tolerationism were quite identical to Locke's overall approach. Stubbe and Locke's 1670s works were two sides of the same coin.

The possibility of Locke glancing over the more radical and synthetic works of John Toland is greater and recorded. Toland visited him at Oates, even though Locke seemed to have aversion to some of his personality traits.[1447] Locke's reading of Deistic corpus, his close friendship with Matthew Tindal and Anthony Collins (he "numbered his days by Collins' friendship."),[1448] his substantive interactions with the Socinian and Unitarian writings and his ensuing partial or total subscription to their theological outlook are historical facts. The bulk of Locke's library consisted of theological works, and the Socinian/Unitarian works constituted perhaps the most important part of this library. In reality Locke's transition from an orthodox Anglican to a Unitarian heretic went through the writings of Deists, Socinians and Unitarians.

John Marshall has documented the proof of Locke's immersion in the Socinian and Unitarian writings of contemporary figures such as Bury, Freke and Nye, who in turn were quite sympathetic to Islamic tradition.[1449] He possessed almost all the works of major Socinian intellectuals of his time. Marshall observed that "Locke possessed works by all of the major Socinian writers, including eight titles by Faustus Socinus himself, nine works by John Crell, perhaps Socinus's most important follower, seven by Jonas Schlichting, five by Valantin Smaltz, joint editor of the *Racovian catechism*—the closest that the Socinians, who explicitly supported varying interpretations of Scripture, came to an official statement of doctrine—and two books by JohnVolkel, including his compendium of Socinian thought, *De vera religione*. He possessed no less than three editions of the *Racovian catechism*. His collection of especially Socinian, but also of occasional Arian works included the Arian ecclesiastical history of Christopher Sand, the Socinian-influenced work of George Enyedi, and various Socinian works by John von Wolzogen, Martin Ruar, Samuel Przypkowski, Samuel Crell, and Andreas Wissowatius the younger, and the *Bibliothe cafratrum Polonorum,* a nine-volume collection of the major writings of Socinus, Crell, Schlichting, and von Wolzogen."[1450]

John Marshall is the renowned authority on Locke's silences, aberrations, deletions and unorthodox interpretations of Trinitarian texts. Like Socinians, Locke's denial of Christ's divinity, plurality of persons in the godhead, co-equality, pre-existence in the orthodox sense, incarnation, and utterly unorthodox interpretations of Christ's messiahship, all led to his clandestine Unitarianism. In these central theological precincts, Locke is evidently closer to the Unitarian Islamic syncretism, to use Justin Champion's phrase,[1451] than to the Trinitarian theology. Locke is as radical in his theology as is he in his political thought, though he is more conscious of the dangers involved and cautious of his position and surroundings than some other radical enlightenment figures. Allison Coudert notes that "John Locke left an unfinished manuscript surveying Islamic doctrine. He realised that since Charles II was expanding trade with Muslim North Africa the prevailing prejudicial view of Islam was neither accurate nor helpful. He asked his friend James Tyrrell for a description of the Moroccan ambassador's visit to England, which had caused a great stir because the ambassador had defied stereotypes and shown himself to be extraordinarily polite, erudite, and, in a word, civil."[1452] Jonathan Edward and Charles Leslie were broadly correct in identifying Locke's Islamic affinities and sources, especially the Quran, which Locke possessed.[1453]

Locke and Travel Literature

In addition to the above sketched sources on the Islamic faith, Locke possessed many contemporary travel writings containing firsthand information about Islamic world, especially the Ottoman and Mughal Empires. Locke was engrossed in travelogues; like Robert Boyle and other Royal Society fellows, Locke had one of the largest collections of travel literature in his library.[1454] Ann Talbot noted that "Locke valued it highly because in a library of 3,641 books he had 275 works that could be classified as travel or geography. Locke's library was mainly theological in character, and only 269 of his books could be classified as what we would regard as philosophy, making the travel books a considerable proportion of the whole, and it is difficult to believe that this does not reflect Locke's intellectual interests. If we want to know the historical Locke then we have to understand what travel literature meant to him. It is clear that it was important to him."[1455] David Paxman described Locke as omnivorous reader of travel books.[1456]

Locke was extremely interested in other nations' cultures, habits, beliefs and morals, and his intense study of travelogues seemed to have helped him transition from a Trinitarian royalist to an anti-absolutist revolutionary advocating for active resistance.[1457] Locke was a product of local, supernatural and absolutist tradition, and through most of his life subscribed to this limited ideology.[1458] His evolution to a universal, natural and republican outlook, well-reflected in his mature writings, was partly facilitated by his exposure to global societies, especially the Orient.[1459] In fact, the Royal Society fellows, the French *Philosophe* and almost all Enlightenment leaders read, analysed and quoted the travel literature, and owed much to it. There was a strong connection between travel literature and the seventeenth- and eighteenth-century European natural philosophy, sociology, anthropology, theology and political thought. The detailed travelogues about the Ottoman, Persian and Mughal Empires constituted the major bulk of this genre. "Travellers to the Ottoman Empire often described a thriving, prosperous state where subjects of different faiths and languages lived in harmony; shouldn't England follow this example?"[1460] As seen above, Englishmen were fascinated with Islamic Orient and obsessed with its material luxury, prosperity, vastness, pluralism and religious tolerance. Albrecht Classen noted that "no European country or culture could truly match up with the Muslim world to the East. In many respects life in the Turkish lands proved to be much more sophisticated, well established, more orderly, better protected, and secured from external problems than in the West [...] even a number of major intellectuals raised trenchant questions as to the alleged superiority of Christianity over Islam, such as Locke and Newton, but they could not afford to speak up more explicitly and had to guard themselves against immediate repercussions from the courts in their own country, especially because the Church closely guarded its absolute supremacy also in legal and political terms."[1461]

Locke had to be especially careful, as he was suspected of religious and political heterodoxy and being spied on.

Travel accounts of Richard Hukluyt (1553–1616),[1462] Samuel Purchas (1577? –1626),[1463] Thévenot, Roe, Terry, Coryat and Pyrard[1464] all contained ample information about Muslim religious, political, social, cultural and economic institutions. Locke owned Paul Rycaut's "The Present State of the Ottoman Empire"[1465] and befriended Rycaut. Both were members of the Royal Society. He also read Terry's detailed accounts of East Indies.[1466] Locke was enthusiastic about these narratives and incorporated some of the information into his writings, as Ann Talbot has shown.[1467] All these sources agreed-upon the universal religious toleration practiced by the Ottomans and Mughals based upon Islamic teachings. Terry and Coryat's early seventeenth-century (1616) *Multan* and *Agra* encounters[1468] and Coryat's aggressive anti-Muhammad outbursts in a local mosque were quite telling of the ease with which they could berate and barrage the Islamic faith with full immunity in the Mughal Empire,[1469] while in 1697 Edinburgh a young Thomas Aikenhead was tortured and hanged for confiding in his friends of possible heterodoxy.[1470] Locke was horrified and shaken by Aikenhead's dismemberment and mutilation. Throughout his mature writings Locke would quote the truboned nations[1471] (Muslims) for their sobriety, sincerity of worship and religious tolerance.[1472]

Since the inception of Oriental trade in the 1580s, travelogues and English writers had used the Muslim Orient as a whip to highlight English religious persecutions, internal strife and absolutism.[1473] For instance, Richard Knolles used Ottoman prosperity, military might and pluralism as a whip to indict Christendom of its internal disunity, religious persecutions and immoralities. In his 1603's *The Generall Historie of the Turkes* Knolles greatly admired the Turks while criticising the Christendom. At the end of the second edition of 1610, "Knolles added a 'Discourse on the greatness of the Ottoman Turkes', summarising the conclusions he drew from his work. Here, as throughout the *Historie,* the mirror of Ottoman organisation and personal humility is held up to reflect the disunity, the incompetence and the general sinfulness of Christian Europe. Knolles' frame of reference is religion. For him, Ottoman superiority is due primarily to 'the Just and Secret Judgement of the Almighty', brought down by 'the small care the Christian Princes [...] have had of the common state of the Christian Commonweal' in continually warring amongst themselves. Only after placing the blame fairly and squarely upon Christian shoulders, does Knolles acknowledge the strengths of the Turks."[1474] Since then, the travellers and writers fascinatingly highlighted the religious tolerance and co-existence prevalent in the Muslim world to indict Europe's religious persecutions in the name of unity and social cohesiveness, "many of these travellers were impressed by the sophistication and wealth they saw and expressed admiration at the tolerance shown to a confusing mix of Jewish, Christian, and Muslim communities speaking a Babel of languages. And travellers noted that some of the English and other Europeans who gained their freedom (or who came voluntarily) were happy to stay on and did quite well in the Ottoman army and administration. Indeed, the Ottomans and their Barbary allies seemed to offer more possibilities for advancement and enrichment than many European societies."[1475] Erasmus, Costello, Servetus, Grotius, Stubbe, Toland, Deists, Socinians, Unitarians and even politicians such as William of Orange and Maurice of Nassau had quoted the tolerant Turkish model and its positive ramifications for societal harmony.[1476] The cautious Locke had no hesitation in repeating the same example in his *Letter Concerning Toleration*.[1477] Tolan noted that "while Locke, unlike Stubbe and other Deists and Unitarians, offers no theological assessment of Islam or Muhammad, he clearly sees Islamic religious tolerance as a positive model for Anglican England."[1478] John Marshall has recognised that Islam became "central to tolerationist debates in England in the late seventeenth century because of the similarities alleged between Islam and anti-Trinitarianism."[1479] Locke was also well aware of the tolerant Torda Edict and the Ottoman role in its facilitation.[1480]

Muslims in Locke's Horizons

Nabil Matar and Gerald MacLean have depicted the cultural milieu of seventeenth-century England, and Muslim presence therein, well.[1481] Matthew Dimmock has shown that Islam and the Turks took a central position in so many aspects of English life in the sixteenth century.[1482] Matthew Birchwood has consistently shown that "images of Islam and the dreaded Ottoman Turk have played a crucial role in the formation of national identity and religious difference in Restoration England."[1483] Humberto Garcia has analysed the sympathetic literary and cultural representations of Islamic republic and its significant contributions to evolving English self-definition. He has skillfully demonstrated how the "Islamic republicanism reinvents English revolutionary history, providing sociopolitical empowerment for marginalized 'mute witnesses': deists, Unitarians, Gnostics, and Arians, among other forgotten heretics, and heterodox women who championed female-friendly versions of the prophetic past. Islamic republicanism's political reinvention—enabled through reprinted republican tracts and recirculated subversive manuscripts—creates a historical continuity among the 1640s, 1688, 1776, and 1789. This imaginative process ties together the various events that took place between the Eighteenth-century revolutions."[1484]

John Tolan shows the role on the central stage which Muhammad took in the English intellectual discussions of the sixteenth and seventeenth centuries.[1485] Tolan noted that "Europeans' views of Islam and of Muhammad tend to reflect their own preoccupations close to home more than any real interest in or engagement with Muslim history. In England in the seventeenth century, we see fierce debates about Muhammad or the Qur'ān, which in fact are coded polemics about the English kings, the civil war, the role of the Anglican Church, and the place of radical Protestants in English society [...] Muhammad and his primitive community of Muslims came to represent for some Englishmen [...] exemplary anticlerical radical republicans, a free society in which the power and privilege of the Church was abolished and religious freedom was granted to members of different faith communities. The fierce reactions of Prideaux and others, who upheld the traditional negative view of Mahomet, have as much or more to do with their abhorrence of republicanism as they do with their defense of Anglicanism (although clearly the two were closely linked for them)."[1486]

Sir John Finch's correspondence with Lord Conway between 4- 14 February 1675 illustrates the situation.[1487] These letters give a "politic" account of the growth of Islam, including a presentation of the Islamic notion of the unipersonality of God, and the description of Muhammad as both a wise prince and legislator.[1488] Jane D. McAuliffe does show the same significance given to Islamic scripture, the Quran.[1489] Long ago Archibald H. Christie and others had highlighted the Turkish influences upon early modern English costumes, textile, fashion and design.[1490] Deborah Howard,[1491] Lisa Jardine,[1492] Rosamond Mack[1493] and Stefano Carboni[1494] have skillfully documented the importance of Islamic luxury items such as carpets, textile and jewelry in early modern British society.

G. A. Russell clearly shows that the seventeenth century was the "Age of Arabik" in England; her demonstrations of possible influences of Hayy b. Yaqzan upon Locke are quite substantial.[1495] The philosophical novel originally written by Muslim philosopher Ibn Tufayl was translated by Edward Pococke and published in the name of his 21-year-old son Edward Pococke Junior. Locke was Pococke Junior's tutor. Robert Boyle, the Cambridge Platonist Henry More, Levant Company Ambassador Sir John Finch, his anti-Trinitarian Quaker sister and philosopher Ann Conway, Samuel and John Worthington all knew about the translation.[1496] Locke used Hayy bin Yaqzan to refute innate ideas and need for organised religion and church. The novel was very well-received by dissenters all over the Continent. Locke was an outcome and a beneficiary of the cross cultural globalization of England.

Jerry Bentley,[1497] Jack Goody,[1498] Janet Abu Lughod,[1499] Samir Amin[1500] and John Hobson's revisionist approach to Eurocentric interpretations of history[1501] have highlighted the globalisation of Europe rather than Europeanisation of the globe. John Sweetman[1502] and Jerry Brotton[1503] show the Islamic influences upon English art, architecture and paintings. John Locke's influential colleague, Royal Society's founder and president, Christopher Wren determined that the Gothic architectural style was not Gothic but purely Saracenic.[1504] He confessedly incorporated Islamic architectural motifs in the design of St. Paul's cathedral and countless other religious buildings.[1505] Locke was surrounded by things Islamic.

In the English political arena, Prophet Muhammad's ideas were used to redefine Whig principles and to challenge Anglican establishment. James R. Jacob, Nabil Matar and Justin Champion, H. Garcia and John Tolan, as discussed above, demonstrate the role played by Henry Stubbe in this respect and the way he impacted the English discourse on Unitarian theology, civil religion and moral theology. The clandestine defenses of Islamic faith were often published during the Trinitarian controversy of the 1690s, Socinian and Unitarian controversies of 1700 and afterwards. "These debates then, must be examined against the backdrop of key events: the civil war, which culminated with the execution of Charles I in 1649 (the same year that saw the publication of the first English translation of the Qur'ān); the Restoration, which brought Charles II to the throne in 1660; the (unsuccessful) Rye House plot to assassinate Charles II and his brother James in 1683 (the same year as the failed

Ottoman siege of Vienna); James II's Declaration of Indulgence in 1687 (granting freedom of worship to Catholics and dissident Protestants), the Glorious Revolution that deposed James the following year." [1506] John Locke was heavily engaged with these politico-religious events and debates; he could not have escaped them at all. Consequently, he could not have escaped the Unitarian responses to these events and controversies. In reality he actively participated in those controversies, albeit secretly siding with the Socinians and Unitarians who were called Muhammadan, Turks and crypto-Muslims by their opponents. Therefore, Locke's engagement with things Islamic was a given fact.

In short, Locke's society and surroundings were almost certainly engaged with the Islamic tradition and many of his acquaintances had acted and reacted to Islam and in the process appropriated many Islamic ideas, themes, motifs and beliefs to their reformative schemes. In a sense, there were numerous theological, philosophical and political elements derived from Islam in Locke's surroundings, both good and bad, and he could not have ignored them altogether. Appropriation of Islamic themes, just like Stubbe, Toland and Unitarians, was also a real possibility for Locke; after all, Locke worked with and around them. Locke's interaction with Islamic history, culture and religion stretches from his early school to his Oxford days under Dr. Pococke to Shaftesbury's circle to his Socinian, Unitarian and Deistic associations. Let us not forget that Anthony Collin, the articulate Deist of his time, was among Locke's closest friends during the last days of Locke. Therefore, it would not be an exaggeration to state that Locke had a lifelong affair with Islam in various capacities both positive and negative.

There is thus a considerable likelihood that Locke's theological outlook, when gleaned through the backdrop of the above sketched milieu, was to some extent 'Turkish,' to use Jonathan Edward's phrase. His relatively radical Unitarian theology may thus in many ways have been far more Islamic than orthodox. His reasonable Christianity was more Mohammaden than the unreasonable Nicaean or Chalcedonian Christianity, which Locke tried to reform. Locke's mature writings purged Christianity of the orthodox incarnational reservoirs, the remnants of ancient Christian Platonic grafting, and brought it in line with the pristine Christianity of Jesus Christ and his original followers, the Quranic *Nasara* or Nazarenes. There was no room in it for the traditional sense of Trinity, original sin, justification through faith at the expense of good works, absolute predestination, ecclesiastical hierarchy and clerical prerogatives. Locke's Christianity was nothing but a moral tradition in line with the universal monotheistic prophetic tradition. In other words, it was a Monotheistic Christianity, like Judaism and Islam, as Henry Stubbe and John Toland envisaged, in direct opposition to the traditional Trinitarian Christianity. He accomplished the task by sticking to the scriptural text, at the expense of later Church traditions and Councils. In this scriptural hermeneutic Locke was preceded by his Muslim counterparts. For instance, Locke's full trust in the scripture, and the role assigned to reason in understanding it had a well-established precedent in Muslim theologian Abu Hamid al-Ghazali[1507] and other Asha'rite theologians.[1508] Stubbe quoted these Muslim theologians in his *Account* and Dr. Pococke analysed them in his works; they were a known commodity to Locke's circle of friends.

Locke and Islamic Minimalism

There was an echo of minimal Islamic credo in Locke's minimal creed for salvation. Locke's Messiah, as a spiritual king, lawgiver and moral teacher, was closer to the Islamic concept of a reformative Messiah (Jesus) than the orthodox Christian Messiah of divine substance and propositions. Tolan and Garcia have amply demonstrated that Prophet Muhammad was idealised by many European thinkers as the spiritual king, lawgiver and moral teacher, the true prince of Machiavelli.[1509] Muhammad was made equal to Moses and a true heir to his religio-political legacy. Locke seemed to be following the suit.

Interestingly, Locke believed that Islam, like Judaism and Christianity, possessed a genuine divine revelation and was an heir to the monotheistic message of Jesus Christ. Locke stated in his *Discourse on Miracles* that "of such who have come in the name of the one only true God, professing to bring a law from him, we have in history a clear account but of three, viz. Moses, Jesus, and Mahomet. For what the Persees say of their Zoroaster, or the Indians of their Brama (not to mention all the wild stories of the religions farther East) is so obscure, or so manifestly fabulous, that no account can be made of it."[1510] Locke's inclusion of Muhammad in the authentic, divine, monotheistic message at par with Moses and Jesus was the single most important point proving Locke's Islamic affinities; this was a thunderous indictment of the historical Christianity and a bold but disguised assessment of Islam's authenticity.

Muhammad, throughout Christian history, was depicted and berated as the archetype, Antichrist perverter who perverted the original Trinitarian message of Jesus into abstract Unitarianism. Contrary to that, Locke placed Muhammad on the pedestal of authentic monotheism, on par with Jesus and Moses, while placing the fourth-century Church Fathers and the subsequent Trinitarian Church tradition (both Catholic and Protestant) as perverters of Jesus' monotheism. They were heretical, and far removed from the original message of Jesus, but not Muhammad. This was a revolution in line with the radical views of eighteenth-century Socinians, Unitarians and Deists such as Henry Stubbe, John Toland, Arthur Bury, Stephan Nye and others. Indeed, Locke was an active member of the radical Unitarian and Socinian Islamic syncretism, albeit clandestinely. He, like the Unitarians, wanted historical Trinitarian Christianity reformed on Islamic monotheistic lines. Locke was a follower of this Muhammadan Christianity, as Stubbe and Toland would call it. He was a Unitarian heretic, as John Marshall noted.

In his *Reasonableness of Christianity* Locke observed that Islamic monotheism was derived from Jesus. He said that "since our Saviour's time, the 'belief of one God' has prevailed and spread itself over the face of the earth. For even to the light that the Messiah brought into the world with him, we must ascribe the owning and profession of one God, which the mahometan religion hath derived and borrowed from it."[1511] The Quran, which Locke owned, clearly stated that Muhammad had not introduced a new religion but had come to revive the pristine message of Jesus and Moses. To Locke, Muhammad was no heretic nor was the Turk heretic.[1512] Islamic borrowing from the pristine monotheistic faith of Jesus and its reformation of Trinitarian Christian faith was in conformity with Locke's reformatory scheme; it was a reflection of Stubbe, Toland and Unitarians' corrective history.

Islam, Locke thought, was defective due to a lack of miracles, not because of its strict monotheistic theology and messianic Christology. "Now of the three before- mentioned, Mahomet having none to produce, pretends to no miracles for the vouching his mission; so that the only revelations that come attested by miracles, being those of Moses and Christ, and they confirming each other; the business of miracles, as it stands really in matter of fact, has no manner of difficulty in it; and I think the most scrupulous or sceptical cannot from miracles raise the least doubt against the divine revelation of the Gospel."[1513]

I am not sure whether Locke, by this miracle argument, was indirectly proving the authenticity of Muhammad's message or really denying it. Locke published his "*Reasonableness of Christianity*" during 1695 when the Trinitarian Controversy of 1690s was at its peak. During this period of hot Deistic, Socinian, Unitarian and Orthodox controversies, the Unitarians and Socinians refuted the Orthodox claims of Christian authenticity based on its miraculous missionary success by quoting the faster, larger, comprehensive and lasting Islamic victories against the Byzantium Christianity continued by the Ottoman Empire all the way to the pre modern times. Locke's friend and student Anthony Collins, a known deist, and many others Deists and Unitarians such as Matthew Tindal, Stephen Nye, Arthur Bury and William Freke had objected to the Christian claims of supernatural miracles and mitigated the power behind this Lockean claim of Christian authenticity by emphasising the miraculous spread of Islam. Locke was known for his natural and rational interpretations of miracles. It is quite conceivable that Locke's argument of miracles was indirectly aimed at rebutting the Orthodox arguments against his Unitarian, Socinian and Deistic friends.

The most outstanding miracle of Christianity, to Locke, was its worldwide spread. "The marks of his over-ruling power accompany it; and therefore to this day we find, that wherever the Gospel comes, it prevails to the beating down the strong holds of Satan, and the dislodging the prince of the power of darkness, driving him away with all his lying wonders; which is a standing miracle, carrying with it the testimony of superiority."[1514] Regarding this argument of a standing miracle, Locke's Unitarian contemporaries such as Bury and Nye argued that the same or even more miraculous evangelising conquests were attributed to Islam. For instance, Bury argued: "So the victories of the Alcoran over the Gospel must be evidence, that as the religion of Moses was better than that of the Canaanites, and the religion of Christ better than that of Moses; so must the religion of Mahomet be better than that of Christ. Thus may a Mahometan either disarm us of St. Augustine's argument, or restore it against us; for either it is of no force at all or of so much more force for Mahomet, by how much more he hath prevailed over the Churches of Christ."[1515] Locke was well aware of this line of argumentation, as the argument was frequently used during the Trinitarian controversy of the 1690s by the Unitarians. With the standing miracle argument, Locke may well have intended to disarm the orthodox establishment, who since the times of St. Augustine had used this approach to prove the providential support for their ecclesiastical institution. This evangelising miracle, providence and resultant superiority applied more to the Islamic than Christian tradition, as Bury contended.[1516]

Locke's argument of the Gospel's superiority based upon evangelisation becomes more intriguing when placed in the proper historical context. Henry Stubbe had used this argument since the 1670s to dislodge Christian claims of superiority based upon worldwide spread, in favour of Islam's superiority over clerical Christianity. Stubbe used this argument to connect Islam with the pristine Christian message, and to connect the post Constantine Church with pagan corruptions. Islam's rapid spread in the Christian lands and Muslims' continuous dominance over the traditional Christians was used to prove the validity of true monotheistic faith over the Trinitarian tradition. The worldwide speedy spread and continuity of Islam, to Stubbe, was a standing miracle of Islam. Stubbe's Westminster and Christ Church colleague, the then Dean of Norwich, Humphrey Prideaux, vehemently opposed Stubbe and other Deists of his time and their defenses of Islamic faith. He declared Muhammad an absolute impostor. His *The True Nature of Imposture fully display'd in the Life of Mahomet* was initially published in 1697.[1517] In this book Prideaux chastised Muhammad and his English Socinian, Unitarian and Deist followers. Locke's *Discourse on Miracles* was written in 1701, four years after Prideaux's publication. Locke possessed a copy of Prideaux's book and was aware of his argument that Muhammad was an imposter, and that his success was not a sign of providence or Islam's superiority over Christianity, but God's scourge against the sins of Eastern Christianity; Muhammad was the devil, used by God to punish Eastern Christianity's heresy, sectarianism and moral decadence. Locke, by declaring Muhammad as a genuine bearer of divine revelation and as an heir to Christ's monotheism, must have refuted Prideaux's claims or at least did not want to share his sentiments. In his earlier book *Reasonableness of Christianity* Locke was a little restrained and allowed that whilst the Muslim religion was true, for it requires 'the Profession of One God', this was something that was "borrowed or derived" from Christianity. In his *Discourse on Miracles* Locke removed that clause and allowed Muhammad an un-restrained, unqualified and independent authenticity of a divine revelation, just like Moses and Jesus.

I am not sure whether Locke was aware of an inherent contradiction in his standing miracle and related superiority argument. That argument, as seen above, had been frequently used by the radicals and Unitarians to vindicate Islam against the calumnies of Christians, to use Stubbe's phrase, and was historically more applicable to Islam than Christianity. Was Locke imperceptibly following the radical/Unitarian trope or unintentionally falling into self-contradiction? The first possibility is greater than the second, given the meticulous nature of Locke's mature writings. Moreover, by accepting Muhammad's authentic revelation, was Locke's refuting the Christian claim of finality of Christ's message or again falling into self-contradiction? I prefer the first possibility over the second, even though any categorical proof for my assumption is not available; there is plenty of likely circumstantial evidence. In any event, it is quite evident that Locke did not share Prideaux's impostor sentiments, and showed reserved respect for the Prophet of Islam, though believing in the superiority of pristine Christianity over Islam based upon miracles. This was a likely middle position between the two extremes of radical enlightenment figures, such as Stubbe, and orthodox Muslim-bashers such as Prideaux, though I prefer the idea that Locke was indirectly aiding his Deist and Unitarian friends by a dialectic subterfuge. In his *Third Letter* Locke himself refuted the same miracle argument by diminishing the role of miracles in the spreading of Christianity. John Marshall noted that "a significant portion of the *Third Letter* was devoted to a diminution of the role of miracles in the early church by arguing that very few early Christians were 'wrought on' by miracles because most had been converted to Christianity by preaching and the report of miracles. Locke therefore constructed an argument in 1693 that the Gospel had prevailed then and prevailed still 'by its own beauty, force [of argument], and reasonableness.'"[1518]

Locke and Christ's Pre-existence: Some Discussions

Some scholars argue against the view that Locke's theological outlook was more Islamic than Chalcedonian, and that his Jesus was a human Messiah and not divine or God; they contend that Locke confessed Christ's pre-existence and a sort of limited divinity. They confuse Locke's mere use of lofty phrases with either Nicaean Trinitarian contents or with Arian semi-divine interpretations, which a detailed study of Locke's interpretations and elaborations totally refute. For instance,

Arthur Wainwright,[1519] Victor Nuovo and others argue that by the end of his life Locke had come to believe that Christ was a pre-existent person to historical Jesus. Nuovo contends that "in the *Paraphrase*, Locke explicitly asserts Christ's pre-existence."[1520] They insinuate that Locke's concept of preexistence was gravitating towards an Arian semi-divine Christ with divine exaltations and glorifications, albeit secondary and derivative. This interpretation of Christ's preexistence is against the man Christology of Islam. A detailed analysis of Locke's understanding of preexistence makes it crystal-clear that he was not an orthodox believer in the soft or hard divinity of Christ. His sense of preexistence was reverential and not metaphysical.

Firstly, Locke was not fond of emphasising Christ's preexistence. *Paraphrase* is perhaps the only place where he applied preexistence to Christ. The main question is what type of preexistence? Whether Athanasian, Arian or Socinian? I argue that it was neither Athanasian nor Arian, but Socinian and Unitarian in line with Stephen Nye and Isaac Newton's sense of preexistence, both being close friends of Locke.

Secondly, such a notion of preexistence would pitch Locke against the Islamic and Socinian point of view if we only accept orthodox interpretations of metaphysical pre-existence (as co-equality and co-eternity with God in substance). Even the Arian semi-reverential, in time, secondary and derivative preexistence may not be totally far from the reverential preexistence of the Socinians.

The Socinians - as well as Newton - maintained that Christ was not pre-existent in this orthodox, eternal, literal sense but in the monarchical and dominion sense. Locke, like the Socinians, had believed that Christ existed in God from eternity as God's Word and not as a distinct person. By shifting the definition of "person" from substance to "person" as word and consciousness, Locke removed any possibility of co-equality or co-eternity between the persons of Christ and the One and Only God. Christ's pre-existence was relative and not absolute as it related to God's plan of salvation, creation and mercy and in no way or form to God Himself. Christ's generation was before the world and not from eternity. He was created and not begotten; he was called the firstborn of everything and not the unbegotten, unborn eternal God. Victor Nuovo observes that "the Messiah is the second Adam, whose spirit exists before his appearance in the flesh and whose coming was foretold by the prophets."[1521] God created Christ's spirit after the original sin was committed by Adam and Eve and after they were pushed out of the heavens. The "Fall" facilitated the creation of Christ's spirit as the second Adam. Christ's spirit remained with God (and not in God ontologically) until his historical birth as Jesus of Nazareth. "Immediately subsequent to the Fall and coincidentally with the first intimation of the gospel to Adam and Eve, God the Father created the intellectual nature or soul of the Messiah."[1522]

God wanted to save mankind with the divine law and not by the crucifixion of his only begotten Son, as Orthodox Christians claim; God's plans of human salvation were totally moral and not incarnational. "In its residence in the divine bosom united with the Word, the Messiah's intellectual soul must have been informed with the divine law, of which the Messiah, once incarnate, became a perfect teacher, and with the plan of God to save mankind, which included the life of the Messiah in the flesh which the prophets foretold."[1523] Christ's pre-existence was before the creation of other creatures and after the creation of Adam and not from eternity. His creation and preexistence were parts of the divine plans for human salvation, *an office and mission*, and not due to his divine essence or substance, co-eternity or co-equality. There was no sense of eternity in created beings, even if they were created before the other creatures; otherwise Adam, who was also called the son of God in the Gospels, would be a bigger God created before the second Adam, Jesus Christ. Jesus was Messiah and son of God in this very sense. "The phrase 'Son of God' was explained as indicating the Messiah, but not as signifying that Christ was God. The union of Jesus and God was described as 'such a union that God operates in him and by him.' Locke declared that Jesus 'being conceived in the Womb of a Virgin (that had not known Man) by the immediate Power of God, was properly the Son of God.' This paralleled the sonship of Jesus with that of Adam, avoiding subscription to an eternal generation."[1524] Therefore, Christ's pre-existence was related to God's plan of human salvation, reconciliation of humanity with God through moral law, Jesus' voluntary crucifixion for God's pleasure, as a sign of total submission to God's plans, for Jesus' own rewards as crucified Messiah and exaltation by God after resurrection, and to lead humanity by his moral model to salvation. There is nothing much in it for the Orthodox Nicaean or Chalcedonian Trinitarian Christology, or much against the Unitarian/Socinian Christology of exaltation after Crucifixion and Resurrection. Locke, like Newton, seemed bent on exalting Jesus as Lord after resurrection. Nuovo noted that Jesus' "unequivocal affirmation of the preexistence of Christ" is "in a reconsideration of the office of Christ as priest"[1525] and not as God or divine. The whole saga of preexistence is situated in the drama of the Fall, Satan's rebellion against God and enmity towards Adam, God's moral plans for human salvation and Jesus being the moral Lamb of God, voluntarily dying as a moral model of total submission. His God-given dominion over creation is neither eternal nor everlasting; it went through various phases and ups and downs, finally being restored after Jesus' resurrection by God and as an act of reward by God Almighty for his sacrifices and obedience. "Locke's paraphrase states: 'Until the Coming of the due time of that dispensation wherein he had predetermined *to reduce all things again,* both in Heaven and Earth under one Head in Christ' [italics mine]. 'To reduce all things again' is Locke's translation of the Greek verb ἀνακε- φαλαιώσασθαι. He spells out his meaning in his notes: "T is plain in Sacred Scripture, that Christ at first had the Rule and Supremacy over all, and was head over all'. This unitary headship of 'all' under Christ was ended by the rebellion of Satan who took with him 'great Numbers of Angels'. They established their own kingdom in opposition to Christ's kingdom, and exercised sway not only over themselves but also over 'all the Heathen World' as their 'Vassals and Subjects'. Christ's ancient kingdom was supposed to have been restored through the death and resurrection of Christ."[1526]

Locke's use of lofty phrases such as preexistence, dominion and Christ creating things in the heavens and earth must not be taken as indications of Jesus' divinity, eternal dominion or co-equality with God in any way or form. Locke has given these lofty terms somewhat attenuated interpretations totally free of incarnational, Trinitarian and metaphysical contents. "Still, Locke's gloss is undeniably scriptural and it is unequivocal in its expression of the Messiah's pre-existence, if not his divinity. However, this clear assertion is muted somewhat when, in the same explanatory note, Locke tentatively suggests that 'things in heaven' and 'things on earth' might signify Jews and Gentiles, which implies that, notwithstanding his title, Christ's kingdom might be a merely terrestrial one."[1527] The main difference between his *Reasonableness of Christianity* and his later *Paraphrase* is that in *Reasonableness,* Locke diminished the significance of Jesus' priestly offices due to his overall anti-clerical, moral tendencies and in the "*Paraphrase*" he restored that significance, most probably due to Newton's influence. Locke's overall Messianic, prophetic Christological scheme remained stable, but his concept of Messiah went through some evolution over time. Jesus the Son of God and Messiah was sometimes connected with his immediacy in creation as the first born of creation, sometimes with his virgin birth[1528] and finally with his immediacy in resurrection after death. "In the final draft of the *Paraphrase*, however, the emphasis is clearly placed on the resurrection as the distinguishing mark of being the son of God. This indicates a subtle but clear theological shift from the *Reasonableness*."[1529] Locke's final settled position was that all the advantage, glorification and exaltation given to Jesus by God was "through the death and resurrection of Christ and, as a consequence of it."[1530] Parker noted that "in Locke's final draft of his *Paraphrase and Notes on Romans*, 'spirit' comes to mean merely a contrast to the flesh (i.e. not an eternal spirit), and 'son' comes to mean that Jesus was the first to be resurrected (i.e. sonship was not to imply that Jesus was not literally the 'son of God' through a miraculous birth). The orthodox trinitarian connection between the Father, Son and Spirit is thus subtly undermined in Locke's rewriting of his manuscript, a rewriting that bears the influence of his Arian friend."[1531] In the last years of his life Locke, under Newton's influence, gravitated more towards the Socinian/Unitarian position of Jesus' exaltation after the resurrection. This God-given post-crucifixion and resurrection glory, dominion and kingdom were rewards totally void of any Trinitarian, incarnational, supernatural and metaphysical pretensions. It was thoroughly moral, spiritual, derivative and secondary exaltation in conformity with the general Socinian, Unitarian and Newtonian position. Nuovo noted that "Locke interpreted the death of Christ in much the same way."[1532] In the words of John Marshall "his religious position in the *Paraphrase* was still predominantly Socinian, or one which was more Socinian than Arian (or, even if this one part of this note is read in a trinitarian sense, one which was more Socinian than trinitarian)."[1533] Marshall further noted that "Locke's view similarly focused on Christ's death and resurrection as leading to him being 'given' all power. Some of the texts mentioned by Locke in this note and tied to the resurrection and the bestowal of 'all power' on Christ were those which Newton elsewhere discussed in emphasising Christ's resurrection and lordship.

Newton's vision of Christ was centrally moral and monarchical, not metaphysical, as was that of Locke in the *Reasonableness* and still in the *Paraphrase*."[1534] Nuovo agreed that Locke's opinion was Socinian, but his agenda was not.[1535] Marshall categorically placed both his opinion and agenda in the Unitarian camp.[1536]

In short, Locke's moralist union and Christ's pre-existence as "Word or Command of God" was very much in line with the Socinian and Quranic model[1537] once the co-equal of the same divine substance and co-eternal clause was removed from the equation. To the Quran, Jesus was the Word of God and a spirit from Him.[1538] The Quran, like Locke, insisted that all souls were pre-existent to their historical manifestations.[1539] They existed in the spiritual realms long before their union with the material, historical bodies,[1540] and came into being with the command of God,[1541] pre-existed the body and continued into eternity[1542] without ceasing to be, as was the case with human body at death. The prophetic souls enjoyed increased preexistence and eternity as they constituted an important part of God's master plan. Prophet Muhammad is considered pre-existent in this sense.[1543] Similarly the Quran, the Word of God like Jesus, is also considered uncreated and pre-existent.[1544] Orthodox Jews maintain the same for the Torah. "To the Rabbis the Torah existed even before the world was created. It is regarded as one of the six or seven things that were created before the creation of anything in the world and it even preceded the throne of God's glory [...] God consulted the Torah in regard to the creation of the world as an architect consults a blue print."[1545] The Rabbis stated that the "Torah which God had kept by him in heaven for nine hundred and seventy-four generations was a hidden treasure."[1546] This notion of pre-existence is reverential and not ontological.

This qualified reverential and metaphorical glory is very different from the Trinitarian notions of Christ as a distinct person, co-equal with God in eternity and essence. Christ's essence is not of the divine substance and his relative eternity, like other souls, is not absolute like the eternity of God. Locke does differentiate between the two substances as well as eternities; this is clear from his interpretation of 1 Cor. 15:28: "When he has done this, then the Son himself will be made subject to him who put everything under him, so that God may be all in all." He absolutely rejects the Trinitarian interpretation that Jesus possessed two natures, and that Christ's human nature will subject to

God and not the divine nature. Locke, like his friend Isaac Newton, does not see such a concept of two natures presented by the scripture; Locke cannot believe that there are two persons (consciousness) in Jesus that one person will submit to the second person. Jesus has only one human nature, which is conscious of its divinely assigned functions; he is called divine as much as he fulfills those divine functions of reconciling humanity to God through his moral example and not through his atoning death. The reverential divine epithets are functional and connected with Christ's office and relative dominion rather than his divine being and ontology. Christ, the subject of these divine appellations, after fulfilling the divinely assigned functions, will ultimately subject himself to God Almighty who bestowed upon him the divine glory. Therefore, Christ's derived, secondary and finite glory and pre-existence is totally different from the absolute, original and infinite glory of God. Locke's pre-existent Christ is quite void of the Trinitarian embellishments. Marshall notes that "It is important to stress […] that it is not necessarily therefore a trinitarian position, because it does not indicate that Christ was pre-existent to the world, let alone eternally God."[1547] We will see in the coming pages that Newton's concepts of Christ's pre-existence were also reverential and not ontological. Both Locke and Newton exhibited identical views on Christ's pre-existence and were identical to the general Unitarian/Socinian framework.

Diego Lucci contended that Locke's position was neither Socinian nor Arian, but a result of his scriptural hermeneutics and epistemology. Locke "expressed, unsystematically and at times ambiguously, his views on Christ's nature and mission in his public writings on religion, including *The Reasonableness of Christianity* and the unfinished *A Paraphrase and Notes on the Epistle of St Paul*, and in various theological manuscripts. Moreover, he focused on Trinitarian issues in 'Adversaria Theologica,' 'Lemmata Ethica,' and several other manuscripts. Like Socinus and his followers, Locke put a strong emphasis on Christ's resurrection and exaltation. Furthermore, his analysis of Ephesians 1:10 in the *Paraphrase* indicates belief in Christ's pre-existence, thus denoting an incipient Arianism. Conversely, Locke's writings on religion indicate no belief in the Trinity. Briefly, Locke's Christological reflections and his consideration of Trinitarian issues denote a Messianic and non-Trinitarian Christology, which, although presenting Socinian and Arian elements, was essentially grounded in his own reading of Scripture."[1548]

Lucci further noted that "this does not mean that he believed in Christ's *eternal* pre-existence and, thus, this does not make him a Trinitarian. Locke's endorsement of the theory of Christ's pre-existence, in the *Paraphrase* and possibly in 'Adversaria,' might actually denote an Arian notion of Christ as *pre-existent but created* – namely, begotten by God the Father *at a point in time* and, hence, not co-eternal with the Father."[1549] After a lengthy discussion of various options and minute Christological intricacies, Lucci concluded that "in the *Paraphrase* it is essentially Christ's resurrection that distinguishes him as the Son of God. Thus, the *Paraphrase* echoes the Socinian emphasis on Christ's resurrection and exaltation, instead of focusing on his virgin birth. However, there is still a significant difference between Socinianism and Locke's Christology, in that the Socinians conceived of Jesus as created mortal and then made immortal by divine miracle upon his death, while Locke, in the *Reasonableness*, affirmed Christ's immortality since birth, and he never recanted this position. At any rate, what really counts, in the Christology of the *Paraphrase*, is Christ's resurrection and exaltation, not his pre-existence or miraculous birth; and this is certainly a Socinian leitmotif."[1550] As seen above, the spiritual preexistence and immortality is not against the Islamic notions of preexistence and immortality of soul. The Socinian insistence upon Christ's feeble humanity was meant to diminish the Orthodox over exaltation of Jesus as divine.

We will conclude this part of discussion with John Marshall, who observed that "the note itself includes emphasis on Christ's death and resurrection as reinstating him in his power, and leading to his position as head of the Church as what was significant for humans to know. Focus on that exaltation and on Christ's lordship following the resurrection – his headship of the Church and position as lord in the kingdom of God – was thus what this note itself made most important, and the issue of his pre-existence only came up in this one note and nowhere else in the text. Such focus was more distinctive of Socinian emphases than of Arian or trinitarian emphases."[1551] In short, Locke's mention of Christ's preexistence was momentary, non-Trinitarian, non-incarnational, non-supernatural and non-metaphysical. It was totally antithetical to the Orthodox Trinitarian scheme, and too close - if not totally identical - with the Socinian/Unitarian Messianic Christology.

Locke's Messianic Christology

Locke argued in his *Reasonableness of Christianity* (1695) that Jesus was neither God nor divine, but just a Messiah. "Whereby it is plain, that the Gospel was writ to induce men into a belief of this Proposition, *that Jesus of Nazareth was the Messiah*; Which if they believed, they should *have life.*"[1552] This was a transition from an Anglican theological position to a Socinian/Unitarian position. It was heretical, as Jonathan Edwards noted that "he makes our *Saviour* a Coward, he turns the *Epistles* of the *Apostles* into wast paper, he perverts the plain words of the *Gospels,* and he misrepresents and doubts of the most *Fundamental Articles* of the Christian Religion. One would wonder that such wild conceptions should possess any thinking head. It is strange that any serious man can believe these things, and frame such thoughts of Christianity. It is true, that Fundamental Articles of our Belief are few; but there is a difference between *a few* and but *one only.*"[1553] Edwards was correct in his argument that Locke's Messianic Christology was antithetical to the Christian faith as elaborated by the Church for centuries; Locke's Christology was totally Socinian, but Locke denied the charges of being Socinian or having read their books. "Locke's refusal to be branded as having taken his positions because of reading Socinian authors was not merely pragmatic, and probably partly sophistical, however."[1554] Locke's response added fuel to the fire. "I satisfied myself against those heats, with this assurance, that, if there was anything in my book against what any one called religion, it was not against the religion contained in the gospel. And for that, I appeal to all mankind."[1555] Locke turned the table on Edwards, insisting that the Trinitarian and incarnation jargon was not found in the Gospel and was fabricated; this fact could be witnessed by mankind through the use of simple reason and common sense. Locke's indictment of Orthodox irrational, un-scriptural prepositions and creeds was more scathing than the original Christological divergence; it indicated a huge gap between Locke and Edwards' understandings of orthodoxy. Locke's orthodoxy had gone through some fundamental changes; it was confined to the scriptural text which did not contain the incarnational, Trinitarian and supernatural jargons, while Edwards' orthodoxy was thoroughly dependent upon the Church interpretations, traditions and Councils - which to Locke were superfluous.

David Wooten noted that "Locke's main critic was John Edwards who argued that The Reasonableness was entirely silent on the doctrine of the Trinity; it attacked original sin and said nothing about the atonement; it reduced (as Socinians did) the Gospel message to a simple, rational creed, and identified it with the single principle - that Jesus is the Christ – that Hobbes had singled out in Leviathan; it emphasised the Gospels alone and paid virtually no attention to the Old Testament and the Epistles. In short, it was Socinian, and a work that was not an antidote, as Locke claimed, against unbelief, but a dangerous ally to Christianity not Mysterious, written by Toland, a former friend of Locke's who claimed to be arguing from Lockean principles, and who employed them to undermine orthodox Christianity."[1556] Locke was clandestinely promoting the Socinian and Unitarian agendas of Stubbe, Toland and Nye. Wootton further observed that Locke's position was simply Socinian: "Locke's *The Reasonableness* does come uncommonly close to Socinianism [...] Locke's defences of *The Reasonableness* were based on a lie: he owned numerous Socinian works, had obviously read them, and had been influenced by them. To claim that they were arguing not as the members of a sect but as honest Christians was a standard ploy (though something more than a ploy, for it reflected a commitment to open debate and honest argument) of Unitarian propagandists, some of whom were amongst Locke's friends and associates. Some have therefore felt it right to conclude that Locke was to all intents and purposes a Socinian."[1557]

Bishop Stillingfleet accused Locke of being a total Unitarian and Socinian, not only because of his *Reasonableness* but also due to his *Essays*. "In a series of works in the 1690s, Bishop Edward Stillingfleet suggested that Locke's epistemology indirectly favoured Unitarianism, focusing not upon the *Reasonableness*, but upon *An essay concerning human understanding*."[1558] Locke's lengthy defenses against Stillingfleets' charges reinforced the anti-Trinitarian arguments. Maurice Wiles noted that "by showing that Stillingfleet had failed in his attempt to offer an intellectually convincing account of the Trinity, Locke strengthened the two main planks of his own defence. His demonstration of the weakness of Stillingfleet's presentation of Trinitarian doctrine enhanced the credibility of his own contention that it was very difficult to know what the received doctrine of the Trinity to which he was supposed to conform really was, and in doing so it served also to reinforce his long-held conviction that faithfulness to Scripture was the only reliable norm. He rested his case on a readiness to make public retractation of anything in his book that he could be shown 'contained or implied any opposition in it to anything revealed in Holy Writ concerning the Trinity'. But the effectiveness of his argument had a longer-term implication too. It also reinforced the more general conviction of antitrintarians that the doctrine of the Trinity that they were opposing was not just false, but meaningless."[1559] Clearly Locke's agenda was Unitarian, but his tactics were subtler than them.

In 1709, Leibniz also accused Locke's *Essays* of Socinianism. Nicholas Jolley noted that it was "not revealed theology but natural theology and metaphysics which Leibniz has in mind when he accuses Locke of inclining to the Socinians."[1560] Leibniz accused Locke of denying the immateriality of the soul, like the Soncinians. "The equation of immateriality with indestructibility is so fundamental to Leibniz's metaphysics that he does not always feel the need to argue for it or even explain it; for this reason he sometimes refers to Locke's doctrine as a denial of the soul's immateriality and sometimes as a denial of its natural immortality. To argue, as Locke and the Socinians do, that the soul is an accident inhering in the body as a subject, is to render it naturally mortal."[1561] This was a serious charge, and Locke dreaded it.[1562] Edwards went further than Leibniz, and accused Locke of being straightforward Muslim and Turk. Justin Champion observed that "the complicity between Locke and Islam according to Edwards was the notion of the nature and divinity of Christ; the Koran treated Christ purely as a prophet, 'as a great man, one commissioned by God, and sent by him into the world. This is of the like import with our good Ottoman writer the Vindicator saith of our saviour, and this he holds is the sum of all that is necessary to be believed concerning him'. Edwards insisted that Locke was 'confounding Turky with Christendom.'"[1563] Edwards was able to identify Locke's Islamic Christological underpinnings which the scrupulous Locke was willing to propagate but not to confess.

During the latter part of the seventeenth century, the Socinians, Unitarians and Muslims were lumped together as one system of metaphysics. Locke had so many Socinian, Unitarian and Islamic affinities that a cursory reader of his mature writings could obviously identify them. "There were many features of Locke's thought which provoked the charge of Socinianism and which have led modern scholars to follow his contemporaries in comparisons between his writings and Socinian or Unitarian thought, including his credal minimalism, his advocacy of religious toleration, and his views on original sin, on innatism, on eternal torments, and on the possible materiality of the soul. Central to the accusation of Socinianism, however, were two theological concerns. Locke's omission from the *Reasonableness* of Christ's satisfaction for sin, when discussing a series of advantages of Christ's coming, provided the basis for much of the vituperation. Edwards declared that Locke 'gave proof of his being Socinianiz'd by his utter silence about Christ's satisfying for us, and purchasing salvation by vertue of his Deafh.' As serious for Locke's accusers was the possibility that he disbelieved in the Trinity. They feared that, for Locke, Christ was not a person of the coequal, coeternal, and consubstantial Godhead, but instead a divinely inspired prophet, who had come to teach morality and to offer greater or clearer incentives for its practice."[1564] Edwards was not totally wrong in calling Locke an outright Muslim and Turk. The Socinian rational discourse and human, moral Christology were in the air. Many Latitudinarian Bishops and high official, such as John Hales, William Chillingworth and John Tillotson were also accused of Socinianism.[1565] Their Christology was also more Islamic than Chalcedonian; the Socinian insistence upon the Unitarian Islamic metaphysics and Christology was widely known and appreciated. By the end of the seventeenth century, the Socinians started calling themselves "Unitarians."[1566] Locke's Unitarian theology evolved and passed through his Socinian readings and affiliations.

From 1661–1662, Locke recorded his belief in the Trinity in his *Essay on Infallibility,* where he also stated he did not comprehend its arguments or how it was true; the truth of Trinity could not be grasped by the mind or expressed in words other than those God had used to express it in His own words - i.e., in revelation.[1567] By 1682 he had become possibly Arian and Socinian. "Twenty-five years after Shaftesbury's death in 1682, it was asserted by Robert Ferguson that on his deathbed Shaftesbury had declared himself an Arian, believing that Jesus Christ was 'the first creature that God made, and that by him He made the world, rejecting the doctrine of the satisfaction by Jesus Christ's death.' It was said, in an account derived from Ferguson, that Shaftesbury had 'talked all over Arianism and Socinianism, which notions he confessed he imbibed from Mr Locke and his tenth chapter of 'Human Understanding.'"[1568] Locke was Shaftesbury's reader of books. Marshall notes that "it is possible that both Locke and Shaftesbury were Arians, or that

Locke had influenced Shaftesbury to positions identified with both Arianism and Socinianism, and that this dated from the 1670s or early 1680s. It should be noted that in his translation of Pierre Nicole's *Essais de morale,* a work whose meaning he felt free to change to its diametric opposite on other topics, Locke maintained in 1676 the description of Christ as 'God himself dying for them' (and to a double eternity of happiness and misery). If Locke became Arian or Socinian before 1682, it would thus be likely to have been after 1676."[1569] By the 1690s, when Locke had revised his published *Essay,* his views of the Trinity had drastically changed as a result of his reading Socinian works. Marshall argues, "indeed, given his apparently contemporaneous Socinian reading and composition of the *Essay* [...] Locke had the Trinity in his mind in composing the *Essay,* a series of linked arguments about the difficulties of assenting to a true faith."[1570] Locke was quite aware of the Socinians' theological and scriptural arguments against the Trinity, as well as their public opposition to the dogma, and most likely had extended his Socinian sympathies to denying the dogma of the Trinity. Locke had followed the Unitarian Controversy since his return to England from Holland in 1689. He extensively read antitrinitarian Socinian and Unitarian books and struck a close friendship with the antitrinitarian Isaac Newton, shortly after his return from Holland.

Newton shared with Locke two lengthy manuscripts criticising biblical texts that were often cited by the clergy to support the Trinity;[1571] Newton declared such texts were fraudulent insertions into the Bible. Maurice Wiles noted that "the first letter included a short treatise entitled 'An Historical Account of Two Notable Corruptions of Scripture.' The two texts in question were 1 John 5:7 and 1 Tim. 3:16, and, although formally a purely textual discussion, it carried clear antitrinitarian implications."[1572] Locke copied these criticisms and forwarded them to friends such as Jean le Clerc. John Marshall observes "it is quite possible that Newton's willingness to send Locke his manuscript criticisms of Trinitarian texts as early as 1690 indicates that Locke had revealed to Newton that he was antitrinitarian by that date."[1573] Marshall also argues that the absence of any discussion of Trinity in Locke's *Reasonableness of Christianity* was "the result of lengthy and detailed consideration of the Trinity, and that in issuing the *Reasonableness* Locke was consciously willing to give succor to the Unitarian side in the Unitarian Controversy, albeit anonymously."[1574] He further notes that "in October 1694, just before commencing composition of the *Reasonableness,* Locke was surely thinking that the Trinity was not expressed in clear and express words and was not part of the simple truth of the Gospel, and that it should not be imposed; and he was thinking this in connection with thinking about the persuasion of non-Christians to Christianity, one of the central purposes—directed at deists—that he later recorded for the *Reasonableness*."[1575] Arthur Wainwright has also concluded that by the end of his life, especially in his *Paraphrase*, Locke was unequivocally antitrinitarian.[1576]

Just like Stubbe, Toland and the Unitarians, Locke believed in a monotheistic prophetic tradition, and insisted that since times gone by, the unity of God was the only crucial foundation of true faith and that the same unity of the One and Only God must be cherished now. "We must, therefore, examine and see what God requires us to believe now, under the revelation of the gospel; for the belief of one invisible, eternal, omnipotent God, maker of heaven and earth, was required before, as well as now."[1577] Locke insisted upon the divine justice and required good deeds for salvation; mere faith was not sufficient for attaining the needed salvation. "Neither, indeed, could it be otherwise; for life, eternal life, being the reward of justice or righteousness only, appointed by the righteous God (who is of purer eyes than to behold iniquity) to those who only had no taint or infection of sin upon them, it is impossible that he should justify those who had no regard to justice at all whatever they believed."[1578] Jesus did not come to die for man's sins but "to reform the corrupt state of degenerate man; and out of those who would mend their lives, and bring forth fruit meet for repentance, erect a new kingdom."[1579] Locke further argued that it was "not enough to believe him to be the Messiah, unless we also obey his laws, and take him to be our king to reign over us."[1580]

Locke strongly bonded the belief in Unity of the One and Only God and Jesus' Messiahship with morality; morality was nothing but following the laws promulgated by the revelation, and these laws were neither abrogated nor suspended by Jesus. Locke totally rejected the Pauline claim that Jesus had abrogated the law, and that salvation was based upon grace and faith in the redemptive sacrifice of Jesus. Locke instead contended that the eternal rewards - and punishments - were dependent upon conformity to these moral laws. "Open their eyes upon the endless, unspeakable joys of another life, and their hearts will find something solid and powerful to move them. The view of heaven and hell will cast a slight upon the short pleasures and pains of this present state, and give attractions and encouragements to virtue which reason and interest, and the care of ourselves, cannot but allow and prefer. Upon this foundation, and upon this only, morality stands firm, and may defy all competition. This makes it more than a name; a substantial good, worth all our aims and endeavours; and thus the gospel of Jesus Christ has delivered it to us."[1581] In short, Locke promoted a moral, working faith deeply oriented towards and anchored in the life hereafter, a faith in total opposition to both the traditional Catholic as well as Protestant churches. It was far closer to the Islamic salvation scheme than the faith based Christian incarnational scheme.

Locke's *Reasonable Christianity* then was fundamentally different from both the Catholic and Protestant versions of the incarnational, Trinitarian and redemptive faith. The traditional Christianity revolved around the central Christian doctrines of Trinity, justification through grace, original sin, crucifixion and atonement. Locke had strong aversion to these central Christian dogmas, and in total opposition to the traditional dogmas held that the original sin did not taint the good nature of humanity. A child was born with a clean slate without any innate ideas, and learned things and constructed ideas through senses and experience; it was the education and not the original sin which contributed the most to human personality. Therefore, neither the concept of God nor divine rights of kings and bishops were innate to human beings. Both political and religious structures were voluntary human organisations in which human free will and consent were instrumental. Unlike Luther and Calvin, Locke believed that man was neither predetermined nor predestined by God but enjoyed free will; salvation was based upon good deeds and moral choices rather than the atoning death of Christ or arbitrary grace of God. Locke's understandings of the human self, essence and person were too individualistic to accommodate any idea of Trinitarian unity of the Godhead with allowance of distinction in persons or consciousness. Locke was a rationalist and had neither room nor tolerance for irrational mysteries such as the Trinity, or the divinity of a feeble historical man, Jesus of Nazareth. He was not an orthodox Christian as he totally rejected the fundamental Christian doctrines; he was a Unitarian heretic.

Marshall observes that "between the early 1660s and the 1690s he changed from being a trinitarian who very probably held a strong view of the Fall and of original sin — in common with almost all of his contemporaries — to becoming at the least heterodox in his expressions about the Trinity and original sin and very probably in private an Unitarian heretic"[1582] Marshall argues that his Unitarianism might have gravitated more towards Arianism with emphasis upon Christ's reverential pre-existence but not co-eternity or co-equality. "The evidence, however, of Locke's reading, friendships, correspondence, failure to proclaim belief in the Trinity, and careful phrasing about the issue, his interpretation of the atonement, his non-trinitarian interpretations of biblical texts [...] still seem sufficient to suggest that Locke was *probably* unitarian personally. His final work suggests that, if he was unitarian, then a Unitarianism divergent from Socinianism in an Arian direction on pre-existence, but similar in other emphases on Christ, was the most probable kind of Unitarianism with which he ended his life, and this may have been true of his earlier beliefs. Ferguson may have been correct in suggesting that Shaftesbury was Arian, but even more revealing in apparently suggesting that Shaftesbury talked all over Arianism and Socinianism under Locke's influence."[1583] As discussed above, Locke's leaning towards Arianism based upon his understanding of Christ's pre-existence shall not be over emphasised, as it was more reverential than ontological. His Christology differed in so many ways from historical Arianism and was so close to Islamic Socinian hybrid that it may well be called Socinian and Islamic with few minor divergences.

Locke's Islamic Christology

Locke's Christology resembled the Islamic Jesus so much that a cursory read of the Quran or Islamic theology would reveal the striking similarity. Almost all Christian sects, including the most heretical such as the Arians and Monophysites, believed that Jesus possessed some sort of divinity or divine nature. Throughout history, the prevalent dispute over the nature of Jesus has occurred mainly between the advocates of hard and soft divinity. Arius, a Christian ascetic presbyter in Alexandria (250 or 256–336 AD), said Jesus the divine Logos was pre-existent and "performed an essential mediatorial role in the relation of God to [the] world."[1584] Arius, observed Hilaire Belloc, "was willing to grant our Lord every kind of honour and majesty short of the full nature of the Godhead [...] He was granted one might say (paradoxically) all the divine attributes – except divinity."[1585] To Arius, Jesus did not have a human soul. "The soul of Christ was the Logos; only his body was human. As a consequence all that he did and suffered was done and suffered by the Logos."[1586] As a result of Jesus' actions during his earthly life and unswerving devotion to divine will, the Son was given glory and lordship, and would even be called "God" and worshipped; yet to identify him with God's essence is to commit blasphemy. We can conclude with historian William Bright's assertion that Arius was then "speaking of Him as, after all, only the eldest and highest of creatures; not denying to him the title of God, but by limitations and glosses abating its real power."[1587] The Council of Nicea opposed Arianism by maintaining that "the Father and the Son are of the same substance" (*homoousios*).[1588] The main difference between Arian and Orthodoxy was that Arian insisted upon identity and unity of nature, while the Orthodox Fathers insisted upon unity of substance. Locke insisted upon separation of both nature and substance, as his Jesus had only one human nature and substance, totally divergent from divine nature and substance. Locke stated that "concerning his Son Jesus Christ our Lord, who according to the flesh, ie as to the body which he took in the womb of the blessed virgin his mother, was of the posterity and linage of David, according to the spirit of holyness ie as to that more pure and spiritual part, which in him over-ruled all, and kept even his frail flesh holy and Spotless from the least taint of sin and was of an other extraction with most mighty power declared to be the son of god by his resurrection."[1589] The divinely gifted spirit of holiness guided and assisted his body to remain righteous and pure without modifying his human essence and resultantly earned the title of son of god through his death after his resurrection. It was the divine guidance, grace (the Spirit of God, the Holy Spirit) rather than divine essence which purified Jesus' human nature from sinful acts.[1590] Maurice Wiles has noted that "it is also noteworthy that the main questions he poses are in the form of a sharp dichotomy between Christ's absolute divinity and straightforward humanity. The midway Arian proposal of a lower order of divinity is not brought into consideration at all."[1591] Locke's human Jesus, with human nature and essence, was different from the Arian Logos, with divine nature and attributes but human essence. Arian's Jesus was taken over by the divine nature and attributes while Locke's Jesus was a purely human person who was exalted due to his moral, human choices. His human nature did not change, but was purified by absolute submission to the moral commandments of God. This position was more Islamic, Socinian, Unitarian than historical Arianism.

Likewise, the Alexandrian Monophysites of the fourth and fifth centuries did not reject Jesus' divinity or the dogma of the Holy Trinity; they only denied that Jesus had two natures. In opposition to the School of Antioch, which emphasised Jesus' human nature, the Alexandrian Monophysites believed in the merger of the divine and human natures in Jesus at incarnation. To both kinds of Monophysitism (Eutychianism as well as Appollinarianism), at incarnation the human nature of Jesus was "dissolved like a drop of honey in the sea."[1592] Therefore, the Lockean Christology of a pure human, prophetic messiah diverted from all known Christian Christologies except the adoptionist Christology of Dynamic Monarchians such as Theodotus (c. 190) Paul of Samosata,[1593] the Bishop of Antioch.[1594] It mostly resembled the Islamic Christology of a man, prophet and Messiah Jesus. There was no room in it to call Jesus as God or divine, as Arius suggested, or to worship him as God. It was also against the Monophysites, who contended that the divine Logos had dominated the human nature and finally dissolved it. Locke's Jesus was fully human, with full human nature, and without any stretch of divinity or divine nature. Jesus was glorified by God due to his absolute moral submission and given dominion as a result of total unison with God's will. This total human, prophetic, Messiah Christology had no exact precedent in the historical Christianity; it was totally in line with the Quranic Christology. Newton will exhibit the same restrictions and situate Christ's pre-existence and glory in the realms of knowledge, submission and dominion. Additionally, Locke's man was not depraved due to the original sin. Therefore, the need for Trinity or divine intervention for human salvation was absolutely un-necessary. To Locke, Jesus reconciled humanity with God through morality and not by divine nature or satisfaction by Crucifixion. By de-emphasising Jesus' divinity and re-emphasising his humanity, Locke brought Jesus to the terrestrial realms and empowered earthly men to the moral heights. Locke's insistence upon human free will, and the necessity of morality for salvation coupled with total rejection of predestination, dispelled the need for Trinity, Incarnation and atoning death. This was a revolution, turning the historical Christianity upside-down in line with Islamic Christology and anthropology. Even though Locke's Christology showed some unique scriptural elements, it was definitely more Socinian and Islamic than Orthodox Christianity. This rational Christology was the foundation of the eighteenth-century early Enlightenment as seen above.

Historians of this period usually credit the Dutch Arminians for their anti-Calvinist free will theology.[1595] Locke was more radical in denying the predestination, selection and grace in matters of faith and salvation than Arminians. Locke's strong emphasis upon free will and human choices, and his insistence upon human efforts rather than the grace of God in attaining salvation, was at odds with the Dutch Arminian theology. The Arminians, including Hugo Grotius (1583-1645), focused more upon the grace of God while giving less prominence to human agency.[1596] Locke was both anti-Calvinist and anti-Arminian; his theology was rather closer to the Polish Socinians than the Dutch Arminians.[1597] The crypto-Muslim Socinians, like Locke, were anti-Trinitarian rationalist who emphasised human free will and moral agency. Like Muslims they denied Jesus' divinity, emphasised salvation through human efforts and declared Jesus to be a model prophet and messiah.

Locke, Hobbes, Newton and Stubbe knew Islam and its theology very well. Their Oxford teacher Dr. Edward Pococke's[1598] *Arabic History of Bar-Hebraeus(Greg. Abulfaragii historia compendiosa dynastiarum)* was well-received in England. Martin Pugh observed that "Pococke shared the fashionable desire to study religion in a rational and informed manner and was sceptical about Christian mysteries, such as the Trinity. In 1650, he published the Specimen Historiae Arabum, which discussed the culture, literature and history of Islam in a sober, scholarly way for the first time. Taken with the 1649 English translation of the Quran, the book enabled people in England to study an objective account of Islamic thought and civilisation, a huge advance over the absurdities of the medieval era."[1599] The Islamic, human, prophet and Messiah Christology was a common denominator in Socinians, Locke, Hobbes, Newton and Stubbe. Locke then was quite aware of Islamic theology and religion; he also owned a copy of the Quran. Justin Champion and others have shown that John Locke's adversaries saw him as a Muslim who interpreted the Christian Gospel in light of the Koran (Quran). Justin Champion stated that "indeed Edwards in his

Socinianism Unmasked (1696) had confronted John Locke, the author of The Reasonableness of Christianity (1695), firstly as a Socinian, and then by implication as a Moslem. He wrote [...] 'It is likely I shall further exasperate this author when I desire the reader to observe that this lank faith of his is in a manner no other than the faith of a Turk.' Edwards objected to Locke's assertion that there was only one necessary defining credal belief in Christianity accessible to all understandings; i.e., that Jesus is the Messiah. Edwards slyly commented that Locke 'seems to have consulted the Mahometan bible.' We know that Locke possessed an edition of the Quran."[1600] Locke's adversaries, while vilifying his anti-Christian beliefs, also identified the sources from where he derived his Christological doctrine. His adversaries genuinely believed that Locke consulted the "Mahometan bible," rather than the Christian Bible, to formulate his Christological scheme.

As mentioned earlier, Locke rejected the fundamental Christian dogma of original sin in the very beginning of his *Reasonableness of Christianity*. In his *An Essay Concerning Human Understanding,* he at once rejected the Cartesian understanding of innate ideas and the Augustinian understanding of original sin. "It is an established opinion amongst some men, that there are in the understanding certain innate principles; some primary notions, koinai ennoiai, characters, as it were stamped upon the mind of man; which the soul receives in its very first being, and brings into the world with it. It would be sufficient to convince unprejudiced readers of the falseness of this supposition, if I should only show [...] how men, barely by the use of their natural faculties, may attain to all the knowledge they have, without the help of any innate impressions; and may arrive at certainty, without any such original notions or principles."[1601] This was at once a rejection of both innatism and tainted fallen nature due to original sin. Innatism was an "anathema to the ethics of rational discipline."[1602]

Locke's rejection of innatism was also a denial of Trinity and atoning death of Jesus. David Wooten noted that even "Locke's friend Molyneux was somewhat surprised at the account of moral responsibility that Locke gave in the first edition of the *Essay,* in discussing liberty and necessity; by making all sins proceed from defects of understanding Locke had seemed to leave no scope for a theory of human depravity, or (one could add) for original sin, atonement, and predestination."[1603] There was no need for Jesus' atoning death if there was nothing to atone for; it was totally in opposition to the fundamental sacrificial role assigned to Jesus by the orthodoxy. Edwards noted that Locke "gave proof of his being *Socinianifd* by his utter silence about *Christ's satisfying for us,* and purchasing Salvation by vertue of his Death, when he designedly undertook to enumerate the *Advantages* and *Benefits* which accrue to mankind by Christ's coming into the World."[1604] Locke's response was infuriating. "There is not any such word in any one of the epistles, or other books of the New Testament, in my bible, as satisfying, or satisfaction made by our Saviour; and so I could not put it into my 'Christianity as delivered in the Scripture.'"[1605] Trinity, Original Sin and Satisfaction by atoning death: none of these central Christian dogmas were original to the scriptures, but later fabrications. This was a huge indictment of the Church Christianity by Locke, just like his friends Stubbe and Toland before him. If the Trinitarian Incarnational theology of atoning death was not intrinsic and innate to human conscience, then the divine rights of kings and bishops which were founded on that supernatural theology were also null and void. Categorical and unqualified submission to monarch and church were not natural but voluntary consensual prepositions. The king and Church's arguments for obedience from morality, unity, order and uniformity were at once rebutted by Locke's rejection of innate ideas and fallen nature.[1606] There was no innate conscience in man;[1607] rather, it was the result of human education and experiences. Locke argued that human beings were born innocent, without the supposed tainted nature due to men's fall in Adam. Even those who never heard of Jesus or believed in him could learn morality and repentance by the help of natural reason, and attain salvation through good works and repentance. "God had, by the Light of Reason, revealed to all Mankind, who would make use of that Light, that he was Good and Merciful."[1608] People were born in the original state of nature.

Locke's idea of the original state of nature had no resemblance to Christian concept of original sin and fallen nature. Man lived in God's world for God's purposes and the governments were constructed to protect and enhance those God-given rights of life, liberty, property and health. Locke's agents were free with some God-given rights restrained only by natural law; these free agents formed human society based on voluntary consent.[1609] Locke's emphasis upon the individual and collective consent was antithetical to divine right monarchy and absolute Church; Locke empowered man at the expense of monarchy and Church. He advocated popular sovereignty and liberal democracy,[1610] and truly empowered mankind on equal bases by legitimising the role of collective consent in establishing boundaries for civil rulers. The ruler's authority stemmed from people and not from God; people were sovereign. Locke's rational theology and natural religion was the foundation of his liberal, republican political theology. This was a debilitating and destabilising blow to both the Church and monarchical hierarchy.

Locke harmonised the scripture with the liberal democratic theory by rationalising the above discussed Pauline texts and epistles such as 1 Peter 2:13-14 and Romans 13:1-1. He made them republican instead of absolutist, contending that Paul did ask for obedience to the genuine authority, but did not define the lawful authority. This was neither Paul nor Jesus' business to define the political authority as political and civil authority was of this world while Jesus' kingdom was other worldly. Therefore, determination of lawful authority was to be done by the people, the subjects of that authority. He further argued that Paul did not promulgate a political commandment in his epistles, but just showed prudence to avoid Roman persecutions. Locke did not refuse a limited monarchy, as long as the monarch followed a law and was responsible to the parliament.[1611] He used scriptural hermeneutics and rationalisation to render Romans 13:1-1 as a republican verse rather than supporting absolute monarchy. He differentiated between the Gospels and Acts of Apostle and St. Paul's epistles, emphasising the significance of Gospels over the epistles in the areas of beliefs and salvation. He tacitly questioned the coherence of various segments of the Bible, morally and semantically critiqued it and diminished the universal, spiritual efficacy of Paulin Epistles. The epistles were historical, addressing many particularities, and must be read in light of St. Paul's overall philosophy and Gospel's overall message. The later theologians and exegetes' overzealous departmentalisation of epistles and fanciful interpretations were too convoluted and torturous to convey the true intent of Paul. Therefore simple, literal and historical meanings of the epistles must be understood in light of the overall message of the scripture.

Locke's Popular Sovereignty

Locke's popular sovereignty led to the right of self-determination in regards to the form of government and delegation of power and authority. So, it was not God who determined the form of civil government, but the people. This interpretation was antithetical to the Augustinian divine right monarchy believed and practiced by Christendom over the centuries. Throughout the seventeenth century, clerics like Sir Robert Filmer and others were insisting upon the divine rights of kings based upon the Book of *Genesis*, English history and logic. Filmer's *Patriarcha,* which was probably compiled in the 1620s, was posthumously published in 1680 to support Charles II's absolutist and arbitrary policies. Locke wrote his *Two Treatises of Government* to debunk Filmer and other's arguments, and to support Shaftesbury's revolutionary plans and exclusionary designs.[1612] Ashcraft observed that Locke was not a mere closet political philosopher, but practically engaged in radical revolt against Charles II; Locke was a link between the Civil War radicalism of the Levellers and the post-Restoration radicalism of Shaftesbury. "Locke's political theory is much more clearly linked with the political ideas of the Civil War radicals than we have been taught to believe. The Two Treatises viewed in its historical context is, in other words, a good deal more Janus-faced than most interpreters of Locke's political thought have recognised. I shall [...] place the emphasis on the more disturbing and hidden face of Locke's radicalism rather than the familiar one that smiles benignly in anticipation of the triumph of the moderate Whiggism of the eighteenth century."[1613]

Locke's popular sovereignty, and the right of resistance, were as radical as his anti-Trinitarian theology; this was as blasphemous as denying the divinity of Jesus. It was alleged to be Turkish rather than English or Christian. Locke, English and Continental Protestants and the Grand Turk were all members of the same dissenter, disobedient and rabble rouser league, as the satirical "Dialogue Between the Pope and a Phanatick Concerning Affairs in England" emphasized." "The Mufti is of the same mind with our Presbytery concerning Princes, 'That whatsoever Prince obey not the Law of God, he is no true Muscelman or Believer, and being become by his filthy Actions an Infidel, he is ipso facto fallen from his Throne, and no farther Capable of Authority and Government,' and with this Divinity our Turkish Brethren strangled Sultan Ibrahim, in the same year Forty Eight, when we by the same Maxim cut off Charles the First."[1614] The royal, Tory propagandist Roger L'Estrange (1616-1704) in his the *Observator* equated the Whig's rebellion against Charles II and his brother James II as Turkish plots and "Pacqueteers Apology for Turcism", while the Whig propagandist Henry Care in his *Weekly Pacquet* hailed the Turco Islamic ideaolgy of resistance as the essence of true Christianity and Muhammad as the better Christian than the Anglican clergy and Tory royalists. The Tories alleged that the Whigs out-Turked the Turks. Locke, the Whig leader, was a rabble rouser in line with his overall Turkism.[1615] Locke's insistence upon the "social contract" and the right to resist the tyrant was a bombshell. Taylor noted that "it is Locke who first uses this theory as a justification of 'revolution,' and as a ground for limited government. Rights can now be seriously pleaded against power. Consent is not just an original agreement to set up government, but a continuing right to agree to taxation."[1616] Many orthodox religious and political authorities resisted it as a sin against God and Christ.[1617] How could rulers be accountable to people while the Bible categorically stated that their authority stemmed from God, and they were accountable only to him?[1618] Locke's theory of popular sovereignty, social contract and natural laws had long-lasting impacts on modern political thought. Charles Taylor noted that "in the next three centuries, from Locke to our day, although the contract language may fall away, and be used only by a minority of theorists, the underlying idea of society as existing for the (mutual) benefit of individuals, and the defense of their rights, takes on more and more importance. That is, it both comes to be the dominant view, pushing older theories of society, or newer rivals, to the margins of political life and discourse; and it also generates more and more far-reaching claims on political life. The requirement of original consent, via the halfway house of Locke's consent to taxation, becomes the full-fledged doctrine of popular sovereignty under which we now live. The theory of natural rights ends up spawning a dense web of limits to legislative and executive action, via the entrenched charters which have become an important feature of contemporary government."[1619]

Locke also proposed that the government was formed mainly for the protection of common good and interest. This was in total opposition to the Augustinian biblical dogma, which stated that the government and civil authorities were divinely established to curb the violent nature and evil acts of the fallen man. Locke blotted out the original sin, depraved and fallen nature, and the concept of innate ideas to establish the fact that by nature, man was not evil but good. Man was born with a clean slate, and his identity and ideas were formed by his experiences.

Locke did not always have the same anti-innate ideas propensity. He evolved into it after reading the Spanish Muslim philosopher Ibn Tufayl's writings, as Russell has demonstrated. Following Ibn Tofayl's novel *Hayy bin Yaqzan*, which was translated to English as *The Self-Taught Philosopher*, Locke argued that a child was born with a clean slate (*Tabula Rasa*) and one's identity, ideas, and beliefs were the result of one's experiences, society, and education, "of all the men we meet with, nine parts of ten, or perhaps ninety-nine of one hundred, are what they are, good or evil, useful or not, by their education. It is that which makes the great difference in mankind."[1620] This perspective contrasted with both the Catholic and Protestant position that original sin had corrupted Adam's posterity, and that all humans were prone to sin and had no natural tendency to goodness and morality.

Locke's views on human nature conformed to Islamic teachings, as Islam propagated original forgiveness rather than original sin. The Quran, the Muslim scripture, clearly stated that Adam and Eve repented to God after their original mistake and God forgave them. "They said: Our Lord! We have wronged ourselves. If thou forgive us not and have not mercy on us, surely we are of the lost!" (7:23) Then Adam received from his Lord words (of revelation), and He relented toward him. Lo! He is the relenting, the Merciful. We said: Go down, all of you, from hence; but verily there cometh unto you from Me a guidance; and whoso followeth My guidance, there shall no fear come upon them neither shall they grieve." (2:37-38) Prophet Muhammad explained that all children were born in a state of nature and goodness; their immediate environment from parents, teachers, and society made them good or bad. Therefore, human beings were capable of realising morality and righteousness.

Locke did not deny that men were sinful; he argued that their sinfulness resulted from their "vices, Passions, and domineering Interest."[1621] These vices did not need a supernatural or divine treatment, such as Christ's crucifixion, but proper contemplation and education. Further, most men followed the standards of their society and ignored contemplation. They were not inherently deficient in their knowledge and understanding of moral values due to their supposed corrupted nature; they just needed adequate education and strong will to discipline their passions, caprices and desires to make the right moral choices. Taylor noted that "As we move from the Cambridge Platonists through Tillotson to Locke and the eighteenth century, apologetics, and indeed, much preaching, is less and less concerned with sin as a condition we need to be rescued from through some transformation of our being, and more and more with sin as wrong behaviour which we can be persuaded, trained or disciplined to turn our backs on. This concern with a morality of correct conduct has been observed by many historians of the period. Religion is narrowed to moralism."[1622] Locke's position on the role of education, and man's capability of individual moral choices without supernatural intervention, opposed central Christian doctrine, and was in line with the Socinian and Islamic positions. No wonder that in the 1690s, Bishop Edward Stillingfleet vehemently attacked the *Essay* as supporting Socinianism.[1623]

Locke and Religious Tolerance

Locke also advocated religious tolerance and a complete separation between the church and state. As noted earlier, John Marshall, in his magisterial work on Locke and toleration, recognised that Islam was "central to tolerationist debates in England in the late seventeenth century," in part because "the practice of Muslim toleration for Christianity was repeatedly rehearsed by many authors."[1624] Religious tolerance was the "principal mark of the true church,"[1625] because "care of souls cannot belong to the civil ruler, because his power consists wholly in compulsion. But true and saving religion consists in an inward conviction of the mind; without it, nothing has value in the eyes of God. Such is the nature of the human understanding that it cannot be compelled by any external force. You may take away people's goods, imprison them, even inflict physical torture on their bodies, but you will not achieve anything if what you are trying to do by this punishment is change the judgement of their minds about things."[1626] The struggle for religious tolerance was the struggle for restoration of pristine, primitive Christianity and an enlightened future void of Church (both Catholic and Protestant in all its varieties including the seventeenth century Erasmian, Arminian and Dutch trends) and monarchy's abusive constraints. Religious toleration was the cornerstone of true reformation of the Protestant Reformation. Faith needed inner light and persuasion and not force and compulsion. "To accept a doctrine or a form of worship for the salvation of one's soul, one must believe sincerely that the doctrine is true, and that the form of worship will be acceptable and pleasing to God, but no penalty has any force to instil this kind of conviction in the mind. It is light that is needed to change a belief in the mind; punishment of the body does not lend light."[1627]

He insisted that men were obliged to think for themselves, and that "the care of each man's salvation belongs only to himself."[1628] Further, the search for truth was a sublime duty and a meritorious act rewarded by God, and the sincerity of efforts and search received more recompense than the objective truth sought. Locke encouraged everyone to seek the truth on their own rather than from society, church, tradition, or customs, because God did not give anyone authority over others to compel them in matters of faith and religion. Jesus convinced people with the Gospel and not with swords or spears. "If they sincerely desired the salvation of souls, as he did who is the Captain of our salvation, they would walk in his footsteps and follow the excellent example of the Prince of Peace. He sent out his troops to subdue the nations and compel them to come into the church not with swords or spears or any other weapon of violence, but with the Gospel, with the message of peace and with the exemplary force of holiness."[1629]

Locke clearly rejected the Roman Church's claims from Matthew 16:18 that the Church had the authority to interpret the scripture, and that people must follow Church interpretations and traditions to avoid heresy and idolatry. He equally denounced claims by the Church of England and Puritans that they were duty-bound to establish the true religion and implement Christian teachings and dogmas with the help of civil authority. He maintained: "It appears not that God has ever given any such authority to one Man over another, as to compel any one to his Religion."[1630] The Gospels never approved of such a policy, "the Gospel everywhere testifies that the true disciples of Christ must expect persecution and bear it, but I do not remember reading anywhere in the New Testament that the true church of Christ should persecute others or harass them, or compel them to adopt their own doctrines with violence, fire, and sword."[1631] Salvation, faith and belief required voluntary will and consent. Even God cannot force people to believe, let alone the Church. "No one can be compelled to be healthy or prosperous against his will. Even God cannot save people against their will."[1632] The Church arrogance was appalling. "I cannot help but wonder at the unholy arrogance of those who think that they can teach what is necessary to salvation more clearly and plainly than the Holy Spirit, who is the infinite and eternal wisdom." [1633]

Locke argued that religious imposition and lack of religious freedom led to communal confrontation and civil unrest. Civil authority or government must not interfere in religious matters, but focus only upon safeguarding and guaranteeing human external interests such as life, liberty, health, property, and general human welfare. The Church must not intrude in man's privacy and general welfare, as its realms were connected with internal interests such as human salvation. Therefore, the Church and the State were two separate entities with two very different functions and roles. "Church itself is a thing absolutely separate and distinct from the commonwealth."[1634] Church use of violence was contrary to its nature and role as it could gain true followers only through "exhortations, admonitions, and advices."[1635] To Locke "churches have neither any jurisdiction in worldly matters, nor are fire and sword any proper instruments wherewith to convince men's minds of error, and inform them of the truth."[1636]

Civil authorities, magistrates, princes, and kings had no business with saving souls or imposing religious dogmas. "This would be the case at Constantinople; and the reason of the thing is the same in any Christian kingdom. The civil power is the same in every place. Nor can that power, in the hands of a Christian prince, confer any greater authority upon the Church than in the hands of a heathen; which is to say, just none at all."[1637] Beliefs and inner thoughts could never be changed by civil authority or coercion. "There is absolutely no such thing, under the Gospel, as a Christian commonwealth."[1638] It is against human nature to change their beliefs or conform their faiths to the dictates of others. "If the magistrate thinks to save men thus, he seems to understand little of the way of salvation. And if he does it not in order to save them, why is he so solicitous about the articles of faith as to enact them by a law?"[1639] Religion had nothing to do with civil liberties: "No private person has any right in any manner to prejudice another person in his civil enjoyments because he is of another church or religion. All the rights and franchises that belong to him as a man, or as a denizen, are inviolably to be preserved to him. These are not the business of religion. No violence nor injury is to be offered him, whether he be Christian or Pagan. Nay, we must not content ourselves with the narrow measures of bare justice; charity, bounty, and liberality must be added to it. This the Gospel enjoins, this reason directs, and this that natural fellowship we are born into requires of us. If any man err from the right way, it is his own misfortune, no injury to thee; nor therefore art thou to punish him in the things of this life because thou supposest he will be miserable in that which is to come."[1640]

There was no coercion in matters of religion and faith. This Lockean principle of toleration[1641] was in line with the Islamic teachings[1642] and antithetical to the Church history, policies, and practices. Locke repeatedly quoted the example of the Ottoman Empire's tolerance towards followers of other faiths, and advocated religious tolerance for Muslims in England.[1643] "Would anyone say that either church has the right to take away the liberty or property of those who disagree with them (as we see happens elsewhere), or to punish them with exile or death because they have different doctrines or rituals? The Turks meanwhile say nothing and laugh up their sleeves at the cruelty of Christians beating and killing each other."[1644] He insisted that Muslims were sincere truth seekers, and must be given religious freedom to worship the way they wanted to. "Do not think all the world, who are not of your church, abandon themselves to an utter carelessness of their future state. You cannot but allow there are many Turks who sincerely seek truth, to whom yet you could never bring evidence sufficient to convince them of the truth of the Christian religion, whilst they looked on it as a principle not to be questioned that the Alcoran was of divine revelation. This possibly you will tell me is a prejudice [...] This though you blame it as an ill way, yet you can allow in one of your own religion, even to that degree that he may be ignorant of the grounds of his religion. And why then may you not allow it to a Turk, not as a good way or as having led him to the truth; but as a way as fit for him, as for one of your church to acquiesce in; and as fit to exempt him from your force as to exempt anyone of your church from it?"[1645]

The Church of England's leading figures, such as Thomas Lang and Jonas Proast, roundly rejected such notions of toleration and separation of Church and State,[1646] and charged Locke with Socinian affiliations and Islamic orientations.[1647]

It becomes evident from the above discussions that Locke's religio political theology evolved overtime. He was engrossed in religious, spiritual and theological purification as John Dunn, Jeremy Waldron, and many others have shown. His religious orientation and peity were genuine and not a mere façade as Leo Strauss, Thomas Pangle, Michael Zuckert, and others contend. His Christian religious loyalty was sincere but his Unitarian Christianity differed from the Orthodox supernatural and dogmatic Christianity. In the later part of his life he did not have orthodox Christian views; he almost entirely rejected the fundamental Christian doctrines and gave them heterodox interpretations. He engaged in biblical criticism, denied original sin, Trinity, incarnation, atoning death, absolute Church, monarchy and many other central Christian supernatural dogmas. His Christology of Jesus as a human, prophetic Messiah was neither Arian, with all its variations, nor Chalcedonian; it was squarely Islamic. Locke had a copy of the Quran, studied under scholar of Islam Dr. Pococke and showed knowledge of Arabic language and Islamic history, law and theology. He befriended Muslim-leaning Deists, Socinians and Unitarians and sided with them during the long anti-Trinitarian controversies of the 1690s. In reality, he did exactly what Stubbe, Socinians and the Unitarians had espoused and propagated. Therefore, this similarity should not be shrugged off as mere coincidence. He was far removed from the official Christianity and very close to Islamic theological and political outlook. His "Turkish" Messiah, as his opponents dubbed it, was the result of his close Socinian and Unitarian associations, who in turn had close historical and theological Islamic affinities. His public rejection of Socinianism and Unitarian Islamic syncretism should not be taken at face value. He hid his associations, affiliations and sympathies to avoid persecutions and un-necessary distractions, and was scrupulously secret, as David Wootton has observed: "Locke had a great capacity for secrecy. He had first sought to conceal his political commitments from his colleagues in Oxford and had then been obliged not only to go into exile, but to go into hiding to avoid being kidnapped or assassinated. He was used to writing letters in cipher and took elaborate precautions to prevent his private papers from falling into the wrong hands. He was also capable of lying. He lied in an effort to hold on to his Oxford position in 1684. He lied when he told Edwards he had read no Socinian books. He was capable of believing that the Church Fathers had practised a systematic economy with the truth in their exposition of Christian doctrine."[1648] Locke's public ambivalence towards things Islamic could very well be part of his overall strategy of dissimulation to avoid persecutions and distractions. Locke's disguised Islamism is as marked as his Socinian inclinations.

Let us now turn to the Socinians and their Islamic connections.

Chapter 10

Socinianism:
The Muslim Bridge

Locke's Islamic connection could possibly be traced back to his Socinian association. H. J. McLachlan and John Marshall have clearly proved that Locke was an outright Socinian.[1649] J. Israel and many others considered them the heralds of early Enlightenment, and the main tributaries of the radical and high enlightenments.[1650] Israel stated: "For the modern historian, all this powerfully poses the question of whether, and especially how, Socinianism may have aided and abetted the rise of philosophical Deism and hence of the Enlightenment both moderate and radical, particularly in its Dutch, Huguenot, German, and Anglo-American contexts. Even if, as seems likely, many contemporaries overstated the links and affinities between Socinianism and the diverse strands of Deism, *prima facie* it would still seem that Socinianism in significant ways lent added impetus and many new recruits to all wings of the Enlightenment. If, moreover, the more extreme variants of Socinianism were only marginally distinguishable from Deistic 'natural religion', consisting mainly, apart from a drastically reduced minimum of core mysteries, of a spiritually intense moral teaching based on Christ's example, and if Socinian Collegiants like Pieter Balling (d. 1669), Jarig Jelles (*c*.1620–83), and the Amsterdam publisher Jan Rieuwertsz (*c*.1616–87) were undoubtedly disciples and allies of Spinoza, is there not a clear case for reckoning Socinianism among the chief factors generating radical no less than the Arminian and Voltairean currents of the Enlightenment?"[1651]

Socinianism was a system of Christian doctrine named for Fausto Sozzini (Latin: Faustus Socinus), which was developed among the Polish Brethren in the Minor Reformed Church of Poland during the fifteenth and sixteenth centuries.[1652] Influenced by the humanist commentaries of Erasmus, radical Unitarian theology of Servetus and Ottomans, they pushed biblical criticism, antitrinitarianism and primitive biblicism to their logical conclusions. The Socinian anti-clericalism, antitrinitarianism, scripturalism, rationalism and moralism was totally identified with Islam. Martin Mulsow observes that "Socinianism [...] or, broader: anti-trinitarianism was often paralleled to Islam: both the Christian heresy and the Muslim religion reject the doctrine of the Trinity and regard Jesus only as a prophet, not as a god. There are indeed numerous historical connections between both currents. From Michael Servetus onward, the Qur'ān and islamic writings had an impact on the emerging Socinian critique. Antitrinitarians tried to establish a historical genealogy from early (Ebionite) Christianity through Islam (which preserved the true monotheistic idea) to the present."[1653]

In Transylvania, theologian Peter Melius had already warned in 1568 that anti-Trinitarians preached a "Turkish Christ." Theologian Johann Heinrich Hottinger of Zurich published his *Historia Orientalis* in 1660. He dedicated a full chapter to demonstrate Socinian affiliations with Islamic teachings. "It dogmatically explicitly spelled out the parallels between Socinianism and Islam, mainly based on authentic Muslim documents. Already before Hottinger, the latter's teacher Jacob Golius, Johannes Hoornbeck, and others had in some passages in their works emphasised this similarity.[1654] J. Israel observed that "since the Reformation, there had indeed been various recorded instances of Italian, Polish, and German Socinians fleeing Christian for Ottoman lands and embracing the, to them, supposedly familiar tenets of Islam."[1655]

The Racovian Alcoran

The Socinian statement of faith, as manifest in the book *Racovian Catechism,* emphasised the significance of human reason and preferred rationality over revelation. It declared the dogma of the Trinity as irrational, and maintained the uni-personality of God. It also denied Jesus' divinity, emphasising his humanity and messianic role. The book, dedicated to King James I of England, was first published there in 1609, and later was publicly burned. In 1640 the *Laudian Canon* was introduced by the King of England to curb *Racovian*'s impact. John Biddle, the founder of English Unitarianism, translated it into English and published it in 1652. The *Racovian* theology was so similar to the Islamic outlook that prominent English Presbyterian Francis Chennell

(1608–1665), President of St. John's College, Oxford, called it a "Raco-vian Alcoran."[1656]

Thomas Calvert observed that when Christians turn to Islam, "they begin with Arianism and Socinianisme, and then Turcism [Islam] is not so strange a thing."[1657] Such a transition was a commonplace in many areas of Europe, including Holland and England. Consequently, Socin-ianism and Unitarianism were so closely associated with Islam that all those "who ventured into anti-Trinitarian theologies were viewed as crypto-Muslims: as a result, orthodox theologians started seeing Mus-lims wherever they saw Unitarians. A high number of Christians and Britons was reported in English writings to have converted to Islam."[1658]

Therefore, this widespread conversion to Islam was perceived as a serious threat to the English and European political and spiritual realms, and as a precursor to Muslim religious and political domi-nance. Ecclesiastical and monarchical authorities took the threat seri-ously and sponsored polemical literature against Islam, Turks, and all those who subscribed to Islamic political outlook or theology, such as Socinians and Unitarians.

The anonymous author of the *Historical and Critical Reflections upon Mahometanism and Socinianism* did a thorough search of the Islamic and Socinian sources to show they were "impossible to dis-tinguish." [1659] After a detailed discussion of the Islamic doctrines, the author concluded that in the Islamic "Confessions of Faith which I have related, the Socinians find anything that, according to their own Principles, they can condemn as erroneous or impious. Nay, I am per-suaded, that if they acted with Sincerity, they would own that Maho-metans are Orthodox: And indeed they must be so by the Principles of all those who have embrac'd the Socinian Religion. The two sects are proud to be call'd Unitarians; a name that signifies the same thing with both Parties […] The chief of the Sect has acted herein with more Sincerity […] he owns, that the Alcoran speaks of the Unity of God in the same sense, that he spoke of it himself, and that his Predecessors in Poland and Transylvania had spoke of it before him."[1660]

The author further showed that the Socinian arguments against the Trinity are the same common Islamic rational arguments. He wrote that Muslims contended no "human Understanding can perceive or comprehend, that the Father, Son, and Holy Ghost are at the same time, and in the same Essence, one and the same God; and the Omnipotent

God never requir'd nor commanded Man to believe what can neither be perceiv'd nor understood. On the contrary, he hath given Man an Understanding apt to conceive whatever was possible and necessary, and to deny and not conceive what is impossible. We shall see presently the Socinians making use of the same Sophism. Indeed 'tis what they insist most upon."[1661] He clearly denounced the Socinians' tendency to elevate human reason and rational arguments over Christian mysteries substantiated by Christian revelation. To him, this was the old Islamic discourse quite known to Christian scholarship.

He further analysed the Socinians' acceptance of Jesus' crucifixion that the Mahometans deny "puts no great difference between them; since the Socinians don't own the Fruits and Necessity of that Death [...] To deny this Satisfaction, and to deny the Death that made it, is the same." He claimed that the Socinians can never deny the Prophetic mission of Mahomet because "an able Mussulman will shew them the necessity of it, by Principles that are common to both Sects."[1662]

He presented a geographical and historical connection between Socinianism and Islam by observing, "Poland and Germany shar'd with the Turks the Ruins of Dispersion of Venice; but the Turks had the greatest Lot; and indeed they seem'd to have the best Right to it. Michael Servetus, who was the first that dogmatiz'd in the Sixteenth Century against the Mystery of the Trinity, had dip'd into the Alcoran, upon the Briars of which (they are words of Lubinietski) like a Bee, he gather'd the Honey of his Doctrine. He had travel'd from Spain to Africa, doubtless with a design to communicate his Sentiments to the Mahometan Doctors, and profit by their Instructions. We ought not therefore to be surpriz'd, if the Unitarians of Transylvania, in the Infancy of their Sect, cited the Alcoran as one of the Classic Books of their Religion."[1663]

The author further observed that other antitrinitarians such as Francis David who otherwise was an anti-Socinian "made no scruple of citing the Alcoran, to support what he advanc'd concerning the Divinity and Adoration of Jesus Christ. Certainly, says he, as 'tis not without reason said in the Alcoran, that Jesus Christ can give no Assistance to those who worship him, because they would have him pass for God, contrary to the Doctrine which he taught."[1664] The Muslims and Hungarian Unitarians were less dangerous than the English Unitarians and Socinians. "Indeed, Socinianism was often described as even worse than Islam from the perspective of orthodox Christians. Although both made use of similar arguments against the trinity theologically, Unitarianism could be judged as even more inadequate in its understanding of such things as Christology or predestination; as Whitaker put it, in his *The Origin of Arianism,* written towards the end of the Eighteenth century, 'The truth is, that even Mahomet himself, weak and wicked as he was, never ventured out into the high blasphemies of Socinianism.' It was also thought worse because it was potentially more dangerous than Islam, causing Christianity to be destroyed from within."[1665]

The original connection between the Quran and Socinian teachings is historically credible. Lelio Francesco Maria Sozzini (1525–1562), the uncle of Faustus Socinus, knew Arabic and Hebrew and gave a copy of the Quran to Theodore Bibliander (1509–1564), the Swiss orientalist who published the first printed Latin edition of the Quran, in Basel in 1543, based on the medieval translation of Robert of Ketton. Miguel Servet, the original thinker of antitrinitarianism, read and quoted Robert Ketton's Quranic translation. Meggitt notes that "indeed, as some of their critics accurately observed, founding figures within Socinianism more generally had been happy to both acknowledge that the Quran contained the same message of the unity of God that they proclaimed, and to make use of the Quran to support their case. Francis David, for example, used it support his non-adorationist understanding of Jesus, and both Servetus and Socinus made some use of it too. As the Unitarian historiographer of the Polish radical reformation, Stanislas Lubieniecki, could say of Servetus, he 'sucked honey even out of the very thistles of the Koran' in arriving at his doctrine, and in his famous trial in Geneva in 1553 he had to defend his use of the Quran to support his theological thought. La Croze, the French critic of Socinianism, could claim, with some justification, that Unitarians, in the infancy of their sect, 'cited the Alcoran as one of the Classick Books of their Religion,' even if later followers were rather more reticent in acknowledging this debt."[1666]

Miguel Servetus: The Martyr of Liberty

Miguel Servet (Serveto, 1511–1553)[1667] was a Spanish theologian, physician, and humanist. He anticipated the eighteenth-century Enlightenment by denying Jesus' divinity, co-equality with God, original sin, redemptive death, satisfaction by grace and predestination. He argued that Jesus was a human prophet and Messiah, to be emulated in morality. According to Michael Allen Gillespie, Servet was the founding father of modern anti-Trinitarianism, ensuing liberalism and liberty, "it was the anti-Trinitarianism that he defended that ultimately provided the answer to the intolerance and fanaticism at the heart of the Reformation conflict. Moreover, it was his thought, transmuted and transmitted by Italian humanists to Transylvania and Poland that came to play a decisive role in the development of a more liberal outlook in Holland, Britain, and America. In short [...] Michael Servetus was an unacknowledged father or at least forefather of liberalism."[1668] Huge Trevar-Roper, like many other scholars, considered Servet the father of later Socinians who played an important role in the eighteenth-century Enlightenment. "Calvin himself might have Servetus, an early Socinian, burnt in Geneva, but Calvin's followers raged in vain against the followers of Servetus in Holland."[1669] Trevor-Roper observed that the anti-Trinitarian movement, originally initiated by Erasmus and fueled by his student Servet, was older than Calvinism and more comprehensive, lasting and relevant than it. "The tables had been turned on history, and the Socinian Servetus had triumphed in the very capital of his grim enemy, Calvin."[1670]

Miguel Servet came from Spain, where Islamic rule prevailed for centuries, and where still hundreds of thousands of Moriscos lived. Marian Hillar,[1671] Peter Hughes[1672] and S. Ritchie[1673] declare Michael Servetus as an authority on the Quran. They have demonstrated Servetus' interest in and dependence upon the Quran to substantiate his anti-trinitarian theology. John Tolan agreed.[1674] We know that he quoted the exact chapters and verses of the Quran in his *Restoration* and other works. Calvin used this charge, among others, against Servetus to burn him at the stake.

Servetus and the Quran

Servet's work *De trinitatis erroribus* (1531) mentions the Quran several times. In 1543 "Servet read Theodor Bibliander's Latin translation of the Quran that was based on the medieval translation of Robert of Ketton (1143), and quoted Surahs 3, 4, and 5 in his main work, *Restitutio Christianismi* (1553)."[1675] According to Peter Hughes Servetus showed surprising familiarity with the contents of the Quran and it affected his analysis of what was wrong with Christianity.[1676] He considered the doctrine of Trinity as polytheism and used the Quran to refute it. He used the Quranic chapters with their original Arabic names.[1677] Servetus quoted the unreserved Quranic condemnation of Trinity in Surahs 11, 12 and 28 to show that the traditional Trinitarian formula was basically polytheism, making partners with God, and that the Trinity was a later invention as it was unfound in the disciples' generation.[1678] He quoted the exact Quranic words, such as *Ruhullah* (Spirit from God), while referring to Christ and noticed that the claims of Christ's divinity were the main reasons that Muhammad denied Christ's sonship.[1679] Hughes declares him as an "interfaith liberal" who was open to "reading wisdom in the Quran."[1680] "The doctrine of the Trinity, he affirmed, was without warrant of Scripture and without support of reason. He ridiculed it as a piece of nonsense and a fable [...] a being who was three Gods in one was an impossible existence, he held."[1681] Servet noted: "How much this tradition of the Trinity has, alas! been a laughing-stock to the Mahometans, only God knows. The Jews also shrink from giving adherence to this fancy of ours, and laugh at our foolishness about the Trinity; and on account of its blasphemies they do not believe that this is the Messiah who was promised in their law. And not only Mahometans and Hebrews, but the very beasts of the field, would make fun of us did they grasp our fantastical notion, for all the works of the Lord bless the one God. Hear also what Mahomet says; for more reliance is to be given to one truth which an enemy confesses than to a hundred lies on our side. For he says in his *Alcoran* that Christ was the greatest of the prophets, the spirit of God, the power of God, the breath of God, the very soul of God, the Word born of a perpetual virgin by God's breathing upon her; and that it is because of the wickedness of the Jews toward him that they are in their present wretchedness and misfortune. He says, moreover, that the Apostles and Evangelists and the first Christians were the best of men, and wrote what is true, and did not hold the Trinity, or three Persons in the Divine Being, but men in later times added this."[1682] Servet, like Locke and Newton after him, was a scripturalist who depended solely on the scriptures for central doctrines of Christianity; the Catholic Church's tradition, like the later reformists, was no authority in the matters of faith and doctrine. "Servetus was the fruit of the freethinking of his time grafted upon the basal principle of Protestantism, namely the supreme and final authority of the Scriptures."[1683] The Quran substantiated the original monotheistic intent of the Christian scriptures. "The Qur'ān [...] offers a more correct assessment of Christ than do the Trinitarian theologians. Servet subsequently came across a copy of Bibliander's Qur'ān and made extensive use of it in his *Christianismi Restitutio*, published in Vienne in 1553 as an expanded broadside against Trinitarian doctrine that was to provoke the ire of Catholic and Protestant authorities and would eventually cost him his life."[1684] Tolan further noted that "the Qur'ān confirms and complements Servet's antitrinitarian arguments, notably showing how the Trinity was a blasphemous innovation of the early Church and quite alien to the teachings of Jesus and his apostles. Moreover, Muhammad's antitrinitarianism prevented him from recognising Jesus as the Son of God: 'Because of the misguided teachings of the Trinitarians, he dissented from Christianity, which was truly an unfortunate tragedy for the world.'"[1685] To Servet, Muhammad was the real reformer of Christianity and its Trinitarian excesses. "For Servet, Mahomet is better than all of them, Catholic or Protestant, because he is closer to the teaching of Christ; he is a reformer who preaches the unity of God. This does not mean that Servet approves of Islam; Mahomet's dissent from Christianity is a 'tragedy,' but a tragedy for which the responsibility lies with those who preached the absurd doctrines of the Trinity. Obviously it comes as no surprise, he says, if the Turks laugh at us more than at asses and mules, since we have been made like the horse and the mule, which have no intellect."[1686] Such an indictment was too much for Calvin.

Under the leadership of John Calvin, the Turk Servetus was burned at the stake as a heretic, in accordance with the sixth-century Justinian code against anti-trinitarianism. Reformists like Calvin, who originally aimed for religious tolerance, quickly became as intolerant as the old Roman church. Both branches of Christianity persecuted hundreds and thousands of so-called heretics who deviated from or questioned accepted dogmas such as the Trinity. Servetus had denied original sin, predestination, and satisfaction through crucifixion. He valued human dignity, good nature, reason, and good works and through them human autonomy in moral decisions. Servetus insisted that all humans have the right to think individually, express their religious views, and follow their consciences.

Servetus further advanced that the Biblical God had wrongly chosen the Jewish people and graced them with his special covenant. This was arbitrary predestination antithetical to the justice of true God. Both Catholics and Protestants, following the biblical notion of the covenant, extended that supposed God-given grace to certain individuals at the time of creation rather than to a nation or a people such as the Jews. For instance, Calvin completely ruled out that a man can attain salvation through good works, and rather insisted that eternity and salvation was completely determined by God. Servetus vehemently opposed the doctrine of arbitrary predestination and grace while emphasising upon salvation based upon good works and morality. Servetus paid with his life for opposing Calvin and traditional Christian dogmas, but left a legacy of anti-trinitarianism, religious freedom, toleration, and salvation through good works. To John Tolan, he was the martyr of Unitarianism.[1687] Unitarians, such as Ferenc David and Giorgio Biandrata, followed Servet's theology. The Socinians followed them in opposing Orthodox dogmas and emphasising human autonomy, religious tolerance, freedom of religious expression, and conscience.

The same Socinian/Unitarian influence is seen in the writings of Locke,[1688] Newton and other Enlightenment thinkers, through Joseph Priestley and others - all the way to the Founding Fathers of America, such as Benjamin Franklin, Thomas Jefferson, John Adams, Thomas Paine, Ethan Ellan and others.[1689] Islamic teachings regarding religious pluralism, original sin, free will, salvation through good deeds, individual moral responsibility, limited monarchy and republicanism were handy instruments for Servetus, Socinians, and Enlightenment thinkers, especially radical reformists such as Henry Stubbe and John Toland.

Martin Mulsow observes: "Throughout the entire Seventeenth century, it (Socinianism) became the specter of all Christian denominations until it slowly transformed into unitarianism and liberal theology during the Eighteenth and nineteenth centuries." Further, "more interestingly, Socinianism was in fact a precursor to the Enlightenment – and to the Radical Enlightenment as well. Its rationalist opposition to everything that seemed illogical in doctrine, its interpretation of the teachings of Jesus – he was simply viewed as a human being – as some kind of moral philosophy, and its arguments for religious tolerance foreshadow the views of the Eighteenth-century Enlightenment. Indeed, especially during the second half of the Eighteenth century it is possible to see a continuity between Socinians such as Andreas Wissowatius, Samuel Przypkowsky, and Samuel Crell on the one hand, and early Enlightenment figures such as John Locke, Jean Le Clerc, Philipp van Limborch – even Isaac Newton and William Whiston – on the other."[1690] In brief, Michael Servetus and Socinians were the precursors of the eighteenth-century Enlightenment. German theologian Klaus Scholder puts the Socinians alongside the Copernican revolution in its influence on modem critical theology.[1691] Even Voltaire exalted Socinian's countless contributions towards enlightening the intellectual landscape of the Continent.[1692] The Socinians' close, historical and intellectual connections with Islam are well-documented. Therefore, the Islamic influences upon the enlightenment figures cannot be shrugged off as mere accidents. Socinians/Unitarians, even to their worst enemies, were the pathway to Islam. "To Protestant and Catholic critics, the fact that Unitarians cited the Qur'ān and flourished in an Ottoman protectorate confirmed their worst fears. A century later, in 1660, Johann Heinrich Hottinger wrote: "those teachings that have been called from the abyss of the old anti-Trinitarians may pave a way for Islam within the boundaries of Europe." The "Socinians [Unitarians]," he says, "are in fact even worse than Islam."[1693] The constant fight of both Catholic and Protestant leadership against the Socinian/Unitarians opened the Pandora's Box of Islamic refutations of Church Christianity, and facilitated the reach of Islamic ideas to European elites and common readership. Islam was equated with Unitarian rationalism, humanism and republicanism. The "turban wearing Socinians"[1694] were quite influential in Europe. "Sixteenth- and seventeenth-century Europeans could not be indifferent to Islam and its prophet. The danger of much of Europe falling under Ottoman dominion was quite real. The possibility that Europeans would be seduced by Ottoman opulence, by the relative peace that reigned among its numerous religious communities, by the simplicity and rationality of its doctrines, was ominous to both Protestants and Catholics. The intellectual tools they forged to fight this menace, such as Bibliander's Qur'ān, were being used against them by dissident Christians and risked weakening and dividing Christian Europe even further, or so it seemed to some."[1695] Many European elites who fought for the rational and republican values - wittingly or unwittingly -absorbed things Islamic. John Milton was one of those adventurist souls.

Chapter 11

John Milton: The Pious Muslim?

John Milton[1696] (1608–1674) was at first an Arminian, a sixteenth-century soteriological sect of Protestant Christianity, but at his death he left a manuscript *On Christian Doctrine*, not discovered and published until 1825, which showed that he had become a Socinian/Unitarian in belief.[1697] In *On Christian Doctrine*, "Milton rejects the Trinity, denies creation *ex nihilo*, and insists on the common materiality and mortality of body and soul (CP VI: 590). It seems absurd that the idiosyncratic Christian revealed by *de doctrina* – who also opposed infant baptism, scorned paid clergy, renounced state interference in religious affairs, defended divorce, and approved of polygamy — could be heard as a voice of orthodoxy."[1698] Milton, like Locke and Newton, tried to avoid clerical and monarchical persecutions by hiding his heterodoxy, anti-clerical and anti-monarchical radical impulses. Paul Best, John Biddle and other anti-Trinitarians were constantly imprisoned, tortured and persecuted during Milton's life. Constant calls were made for execution of Thomas Hobbes. Milton himself was interrogated about licencing of Socinian *Racovian Catechism*. "The outright denial of the Trinity was indeed a far more serious position: from it would follow, in the eyes of the Calvinists, a complete unraveling of Christian society, beginning with an anarchy of doctrine, and ending with a depraved society, via the idolatry of worshiping Jesus as a person, and the lawlessness implicit in a world without original sin, divine punishment, or Christ's atonement."[1699] But his early commentators, like John Toland and Daniel Defoe, were certain that the poet was anti-Trinitarian.[1700]

On the other hand, he supported Socinian heterodoxy wherever he could. Milton was the government licensor during Cromwell's Commonwealth government and licensed publishing of Socinian *Racovian*

Catechism, the central Socinian religious tract sometimes called the Socinian Bible. "Indeed Milton's licensing of the Socinian *Racovian Catechism* helped introduce antitrinitarianism into public discourse."[1701] He popularised the radical (both political and theological) themes of John Selden, Samuel Purchas, Herbert of Cherbury, Henry More, and Socinians. His anti-Trinitarian, republican, historical and rational critique of the Judeo-Christian tradition was well-reflected in his *Paradise Lost, Paradise Regained* and *Samson Agonistes.*[1702] These works were precursors to the Enlightenment's rational critique and re-evaluation of the Christian religion when placed in their historical context of Socinian, Unitarian and Deist debates about Trinity, original sin, predestination, Christian salvific scheme and religious tolerance. They are clearly anti-Trinitarian, anti-Fall with its antecedents, pro free will and religious tolerance.[1703] "*Paradise Lost* is about the angelic rebellion and the fall of man. But both of these, Milton's language implies, can be viewed as parts of a struggle between polytheism and monotheism."[1704] In *Paradise Regained* Milton's questions, answers, vocabulary, ideas and insinuations are all monotheistic and anti-Trinitarian.[1705] "Antitrinitarianism seems indeed to have been early readers' common complaint. Charles Leslie in 1698 condemned Milton for making 'the Angels ignorant of the blessed Trinity.' […] John Dennis, commenting in 1704 on Book 3.383-95, claimed that "Milton was a little tainted with Socinianism, for by the first verse 'tis evident that he looked upon the Son of God as a created Being." When Bishop Charles Sumner published his translation of the treatise, he listed Newton, Trapp, Todd, Symmons, Warton, and Calton as previous readers who, without ever having seen *de doctrina,* regarded Milton's poetry as heretically Arian. Finally, Thomas Macaulay, commenting on Milton's Arianism just after the treatise was published, asserts that "we can scarcely conceive that any person could have read *Paradise Lost* without suspecting him of [it]."[1706]

Milton's Christology

Milton's Jesus is definitely a created being, void of all divine pretentions and absolute attributes. God the Father is eternally One, self-existent and self-sufficient, while the Son is not co-eternal but contingent and existent in time.[1707] The Son is limited, mutable and localised.[1708] Depending upon the Father's will the Son increases in power, dominion, stature, authority and knowledge; this would not be the case had he been eternal, immutable, infinite and unlimited. His powers, creation and dominion are derivative and secondary. Milton concludes that the Son was begotten not from eternity but "within the limits of time."[1709] This was in line with Arianism: "Arians deny the Son the essential divine attribute of unbegottenness - or eternal existence - and also deny him related attributes such as omnipotence, omniscience, and ubiquity. Inferior to the Father, the Son is not 'very' or 'true' God, but instead, per the formulation in *de doctrina*, 'a God who is not self-existent, who did not beget but was begotten, is not a first cause but an effect, and is therefore not a supreme God' (CP VI: 263-64)."[1710] William Empson observed that "the poem makes the Son and the Father about as unidentical as a terrier and a camel."[1711] Michael Bauman makes a strong case for Milton's Arianism and heterodoxy;[1712] how can the created, finite and derivative Son be equal with God, the infinite eternal Creator?[1713] There is crystal-clear disparity of substance, nature, office, agency, subsistence and function. The derivative, secondary, soft dominion and time-bound reverential pre-existence is antithetical to the everlasting eternity and absolute, non-derivative and self-subsistence divinity of God Almighty. Milton, Locke and Newton are all Socinian heretics in their Christology and attribution of preexistence to Jesus in a reverential manner.[1714] Newton's "arguments are close to those presented in *de doctrina*. He is also, like Locke, a prime example of the wave of antitrinitarian heresy that swept over late-seventeenth and early eighteenth-century England. For Newton as for the author of *de doctrina,* trinitarianism confused causes and as a species of polytheism, was an instance of the gravest sin, idolatry. Both insisted on the Arian position primarily because each viewed God as indivisibly one. As the author of *de doctrina* wryly observes, 'it would have been a waste of time for God to thunder forth so repeatedly that first commandment which said that he was the one and only God, if it could nevertheless be maintained that another God existed as well' (CPvi: 212)."[1715] God's eternal and omnipresent absolute essence, casual priority and universal everlasting dominion are in sharp contrast with the Son. Milton makes God say of Himself, "Who am alone/ From all eternity, for none I know/ Second to me or like, equal much less."[1716] God is far superior and the Son is far inferior in nature, substance and powers. Adam's answers indicate that the truth of God's numeric unity, unique substance and infinite nature are essential truths, needing no further substantiation:

"No need that thou shouldst propagate, already infinite;/And through all numbers absolute, though one."[1717] To Maurice Kelley and Michael Bauman this is a clear anti-Trinitarian statement.[1718] Maurice Kelley observes that Milton "holds a consistent, anti-Trinitarian view of God during all the last period of his life. In the *De Doctrina* (1658-1660) he holds that the Son is neither coessential nor coeternal with the Father," and Ruth Kivette shows the persistence of this anti Trinitarianism in Milton's *Artis Logica* (1672) and *Of True Religion* (1673). In this context, *Paradise Lost* (1667) should be assumed as also anti-Trinitarian; and parallels between Milton's systematic theology, his epic, and his textbook on logic affirm this assumption."[1719]

Like Locke and Newton, Milton exalts Jesus as a result of his willing sacrifices, divinely assigned and sanctioned redeeming acts and unfettering obeidence, "in *Paradise Lost,* once the Father has determined to show humanity mercy, the Son volunteers to act as redeemer and rescue humankind from death and the Father enables him to do so: 'all Power / I give thee' (3.317-18; see also 203-302). Similarly, the Father assigns him the task and provides the means of defeating the rebel angels: 'Two days are therefore past, the third is thine; / For thee I have ordain'd it [...] / [...] Into thee such Virtue and Grace / Immense I have transfus'd' (6.699—704). Creation, too, occurs at the Father's pleasure, through the Son: 'thou my Word, begotten Son, by thee / This I perform' (7.163-64)."[1720] This pre-creation and post-resurrection exaltation is neither eternal nor everlasting. The orthodox emphasis on atoning death and crucifixion is diminished. John Rogers noted that "it is Christ's having offered himself, not actually having died, that reconciles man and God."[1721]

The *Paradise Regained's* subtle anti-Trinitariansm is reflective of Paul Best, John Biddle and Socinians' minimalistic monotheism, as well as the controversies surrounding Milton and his society.[1722] The Unitarian Paul Best (1590 - 1657) was imprisoned several times, and finally died in prison, due to his strong anti-Trinitarian writings. Best contended "that of three coequall persons to be but the Chappell of Rome, for the Church of Christ, and that which keepeth the rest of the world in the Pope's Pownd [...] both the Jews that believe the Old Testament, the Turk, and the Great Mogull, etc., according to the dictate of common intelligence, not corrupt in this kind by a contrary habit, who cannot be brought to believe in a Trinity implying Polytheosie, or Apotheosie, i.e., many gods or man-god. So that the denying of a second Deity or Godhead is not destructive of faith, but onely removes it from a false foundation to a true."[1723] Milton's continuous insistence upon monotheism and derivative time bound existence of Jesus was a clear reflection of the Socinian/Unitarian Christology and a clandestine support to Biddle and Best. Modern scholars who try to impose Orthodoxy upon Milton because he used Orthodox scriptural terms are misplaced.[1724] He, like Locke, did not see the Trinity, satisfaction through grace and atoning death, divinity of Jesus and absolute predestination in the scriptures. Kelley states that "Milton disliked the doctrine of the Trinity: he considered it unscriptural (XV, 262), hastily adopted on the authority of almost a single, dubious text (XIV, 402), and supported by strange and absurd hypotheses that have no foundation in holy writ (XIV, 378). Milton would not appreciate the false aura of orthodoxy with which these anti-Arian phrases invest his views, for his views, a comparison with Earl Morse Wilbur's A History of Unitarianism will show, are not Trinitarian at all. Rather, they constitute a classic example of Renaissance anti-Trinitarianism."[1725] Milton's scriptural phrases are totally void of Trinitarian Incarnational content.

In *De Doctrina Christiana,* Milton repeatedly insisted upon the numerical Oneness of God Almighty. His anti-Trinitarian impulses were abundantly clear: "The numerical significance of 'one' and 'two' must be unalterable and the same for God as for man. It would have been a waste of time for God to thunder forth so repeatedly that first commandment which said that he was the one and only God, if it could nevertheless be maintained that another God existed as well, who ought to be thought of as the only God."[1726] Milton extended John Selden's work on polytheism and Lord Bolingbrook's works on monotheism. He like Deists, Socininas, Unitarians and Locke insisted upon rational treatment of monotheism and theology to make Christianity reasonable. Both internal and external worship belonged to One and Only God. He analysed the fact that the worship could be for one God, or no God or multiple gods. He rejected the logical plausibility of the last two prepositions to insist upon the monotheistic worship and love. "Internal worship means, in the first place, acknowledgement of the one true God and devout affection for him [...] Opposed to this is atheism [...] And polytheism, which means acknowledgment of more than one God."[1727]

Milton's Scripturalism

Milton insistently stuck to the scriptures at the expense of Trinitarian tradition of the Church.[1728] "For my own part, I adhere to the Holy Scriptures alone-I follow no other heresy or sect. I had not even read any of the works of heretics, so-called, when the mistakes of those who are reckoned for orthodox, and their incautious handling of Scripture first taught me to agree with their opponents whenever those opponents agreed with Scripture."[1729] His literal and sole dependence upon the scripture was no less emphatic than Michael Servetus or Socinians. Both Servetus and Socinians claimed that the Trinity, selective predestination, religious persecutions and total human wretchedness were not substantiated by the scriptures. Milton agreed with all these prepositions.

Milton was against religious intolerance, persecution and absolutism; he actively preached republican revolt against persecuting power structures.[1730] Both Biddle and Best were persecuted for their anti-Trinitarian views. The sceptical world of *Samson Agomstes* relayed the Deistic/Socinian love for pluralism and toleration, and a critique of the Christian tradition. "In *Samson Agonistes*, Milton experiments with Edward Lord Herbert of Cherbury's radical expression of the discourse of monotheism, which replaces revelation with rational insight – with an epistemology that supports natural religion. This extreme and proto-deist version of monotheism, like Cherbury's abstract God in the geometric godhead [...] resists narration. With the continued absence of revelation in *Samson Agonistes,* as Samson's despairing 'sense of heaven's desertion' [...] goes unremedied, the possibility of theodicy, the poem's ability to claim with the Chorus that 'just are the ways of God/ and Justifiable to men' [...] collapses. And with the fall of theodicy, the poem opens itself, at least momentarily, to the subversion of the Mosaic distinction—to a reevaluation of the Judeo-Christian revelation itself."[1731] His Arianism indicted the Athanasian Nicaean Creed of corruption and fraud against the original Unitarian message of Jesus and his disciples.

J. B. Pittion showed that Milton's views, scriptural methods and derivative schemes were totally Socinian. He used Socinian arguments against Christ's co-eternity and co-equality with God the Father, and blamed Orthodoxy for wrongly attributing scriptural divine attributes to Jesus. "The intellectual evolution which led Milton to hold anti-trinitarian views was of course entirely his own. But his handling of La Place in chapter v shows that when he wrote the chapter, he was committed to Socinian views against the doctrine of the Trinity."[1732] Martin A. Larson contended that Milton's thoughts were Socinian, but his overall system of belief was a copy of Michael Servetus.[1733] After a lengthy analysis and comparison of their writings, Larson concluded that "there is some kind of relation between Milton and Servetus I am unable to doubt [...] the parallels which have been traced in the present paper are of value in enabling us to define more clearly Milton's theological conceptions and to relate them to the history of Christian dogma. They also illustrate the similarity of result produced when humanistic ethics, Renaissance philosophy, and scriptural Christianity unite in sincere, progressive, and profound minds."[1734] Milton was an heir to the enlightened legacy of Servetus, Unitarians and their Islamic hybrid.

Dennis Danielson explained that Milton was totally against the Calvinist dogma of predestination and popularised human free will. "Milton in Christian Doctrine, that 'neither God's decree nor his foreknowledge can shackle free causes with any kind of necessity'. For otherwise, God himself is made 'the cause and author of sin'; and to refute this conclusion 'would be like inventing a long argument to prove that God is not the Devil.'"[1735] God's foreknowledge did not mean predestination and imposition. "We should feel certain that God has not decreed that everything must happen inevitably. Otherwise we should make him responsible for all the sins ever committed, and should make demons and wicked men blameless. But we should feel certain also that God really does foreknow everything that is going to happen."[1736] To Milton, the Fall with all its implications of human depravity and total dependence upon God's grace and Jesus' crucifixion for salvation "was not necessary."[1737]

Abraham Stoll well summarised the scholarly assessment of Milton's theology and outlook. Milton "has been associated with Arianism, with the anti-trinitarian reformers Michael Servetus and Bernardino Ochino, with Unitarianism and Socinianism, with subordinationism, and with orthodoxy [...] Most frequently, Milton has been called an Arian: Kelley calls *Paradise Lost* 'an Arian document' [...] Hunter and Patrides assert orthodoxy by arguing against Arianism. Recently, Michael Bauman has devoted a book full of meticulous detail to defending the Arian label. Ultimately, I agree with Christopher Hill, who shrugs at the 'great pother' made over how to label Milton's theology, arguing that it is too 'eclectic' to fit a single heresy [...] Here, therefore, Milton will simply be called an antitrinitarian. Yet attention to the fine distinction between Arianism and Socinianism will prove crucial to understanding both Milton's anti-trinitarianism and *Paradise Regained*."[1738] To the majority of scholarship, Milton was an anti-Trinitarian heretic. I agree with Herbert McLachlan that Milton, like Locke and Newton, was a Unitarian heretic.[1739]

Milton and Middle Eastern Culture

Milton was profoundly invested in Middle Eastern culture and imagery.[1740] Muhammad Inani, who translated "Paradise Lost" into Arabic in 1928, molded Milton into an Islamic, Middle Eastern, heterodox poet due to Milton's use of words of Arabic and Persian origin, Islamic imagery and Ottoman motifs.[1741] As discussed above, Islam, Muslims, Quran and Ottomans were well known to the English society of Milton and his "mature works show occasional use of Arabic sources, or at least use of sources themselves dependent upon Arabic material."[1742] The Levant Company merchants, chaplains like William Biddulph, Charles Robson, Dr. Edward Pococke, Thomas Pritchett, Bartholomew Chapple,[1743] ambassadors, Barbary captives and renegades transmitted a great deal of knowledge about Ottomans, their religion and culture to England. The seventeenth century was also the century of Arabic, Persian and Turkish manuscript collections and their translations into Latin and English. The rational, anti-Trinitarian, human Christology of the Ottomans was well known and oft debated in England of Milton times. "Milton could have learned a great deal about Islam and the culture of Muslim peoples from reading works such as Richard Knolles's General History of the Turks (1603), George Sandys's Relation of a Journey (1615), and Andrew More's Compendius History of the Turks (1660) as well as Samuel Purchas's Hakluytus Posthumous."[1744] The Islamic critiques of Christian Trinitarian monotheism and alternative Islamic Unitarian monotheism were employed by English dissenters to dislodge Orthodox Anglican establishment of its absolutist claims; Milton was an integral part of that deconstruction. David Currell noted "there were in the seventeenth century two principal discourses bringing a historically and doctrinally grounded engagement with Islam into English theological contexts: the discourse of monotheism and the discourse of anti-Trinitarianism. One discourse is apparently ecumenical and the other apparently sectarian, although the difference may at times be a matter of perspective, as both challenged the orthodox view of Jesus as the coequal and coeternal Son of God whose mediation is essential to human salvation, and were therefore at the centre of a polemical environment in which Milton was an important participant."[1745] The anti-Trinitarian deconstruction was aimed at the Church and King's claims to supernatural connections and authority. The alternative human Christology was geared towards bringing down the Church and monarch to earthly prepositions of limited constitutionalism and democratisation. The mature Milton was a republican heretic with radical theological and political agendas, just like Stubbe, Toland and Locke after him.

Milton's Trinitarian orthodoxy evolved, just like John Locke's, as a result of anti-Trinitarian and anti-clerical controversies in which Islam and Ottomans were employed as a whip and a corrective measure to internal English fiascos.[1746] Milton's *Paradise Regained* can be reflected through the prism of Socinian, Unitarian Islamic monotheistic hybrid. "Monotheistic narrative" is nevertheless a very enabling rubric through which to encounter a text such as Paradise Regained in the light of Islam, which rules Jesus decisively to the far side of the Mosaic distinction. "This is not Milton's object, but the degree to which his Jesus is cut off from both the Son of Paradise Lost and the divine scaffolding of Paradise Regained—the heavenly and diabolic councils, but even the angelic cheerleaders—is thrown thereby into high relief."[1747]

Additionally, Milton's constant efforts to avoid satisfaction through the atoning death of Christ and total censorship of discussion about the Crucifixion has convinced many scholars of Milton's Socinian Islamic Christology. "Many critics have explored the influence of anti-Trinitarianism's 'new theology of the Son of God' and 'consequent denial of an atonement occasioned by his Crucifixion' upon Milton's 'extravagant avoidance of the subject of Crucifixion' as the indispensable satisfaction for sin required by God, with particular reference to Socinianism. Both the challenge to the orthodox theology of Sonship and the de-emphasis upon crucifixion and satisfaction in evaluating Jesus' importance to humanity constitute homologies between Socinianism and Islam, and some scholarship has pressed beyond homology to explore the historical influence between the Qur'ān, Islamic thought and the development of Socinianism."[1748] Milton was an heir to the Islamic anti-Trinitarian Christology, which was quite prevalent and influential in Milton's milieu. "Anti-Trinitarianism, then, was another vector along which Islam entered Protestant discourse, and not always with a negative valence."[1749] Islamic theology was employed for internal apologetic concerns.[1750] Currell notes that "Islamic theology and Milton's poetry can be seen to participate in this movement, their very discordancy suggesting not a potential completeness so much as a method of probing the tension established by the very structure of monotheistic narrative. Productive conjunctions between Milton and the Qur'ān are possible even at a textual level. The episodes of Satan's rebellion and the war in Heaven and their causal association with the begetting of the Son are largely untethered to scriptural authority, and Milton's licence here takes him very close to the motifs, if not the precise narrative, of the fall of Iblis in the Qur'ān,"[1751] *Paradise Lost* (e.g. 1.582–7, 1.763–6, 9.33–38) rejected the old animosity of the Crusades and envisaged an interfaith union and assimilation. "Milton deliberately figures the Parthian empire as proleptically Islamic. The 'half moons' (PR 3.309) of the Parthian muster suggest the 'Turkish crescent' formation in the briefer snapshot of Eastern military prowess in Paradise Lost (10.434). More significantly, the long geographical survey of the ancient Assyrian, Babylonian, Persian, Emathian and Parthian empires, from 'Indus East, Euphrates West [...] to South the Persian Bay' and a host of major cities tracks closely the extent of contemporary Islamic empires, Ottoman, Persian and Mughal (3.269–93)."[1752] Milton's profound interactions with Eastern imagery, vocabulary, history and motifs along with his anti-clerical, anti-Fall, anti-Trinitarian, ethical monotheistic and republican reformation scheme is identical with the reformative schemes of radical and moderate enlightenment figures, in which Islamic Christology and political thought were quite visible. Milton's Jesus was no less an Islamic Jesus than the human Jesus of Stubbe, Toland and Locke. David Currell identifies Milton's Jesus with the Muslim Jesus.[1753] "As David Quint comments: "Milton invites the reader of book 3 to hear a quiet question and appeal lurking beneath the Son's confidence: surely God will not leave him in the loathsome grave, will he? [...] The confident Son shares his faith directly with the Father, but it is still the same act of faith in which every Christian partakes against doubt before the physical fact of death." It is that question, amplified and focused thanks to Jesus' humanity, that lends Paradise Regained its poignancy and drama. For many readers, the narrative frame or a personal or projected orthodoxy militate against these qualities, but reading through Islam it is plausible to hear Milton's Jesus echoing his Muslim counterpart: "I do not know whether he will save me or not."[1754]

Luwis ʿAwad, the distinguished scholar and former professor of English literature at the University of Cairo, in 1967 declared Milton's works to be entirely in accordance with the teachings of Islam. "When we read *Paradise Lost*, we feel that Milton is a devout Muslim. This is reflected in his rejection of Prelates and their mediation between God and His creatures. You also find Milton as a lover of life on earth. He interprets the Bible in practical and personal ways. He advocates divorce and considers man superior to woman. He also hates the rituals of church and the icons. He draws on the Old Testament, not the New Testament. For these reasons, I have already said that Milton was not Christian, but rather a pious Muslim."[1755] Gerald MacLean is not that sure, but is condescending in a way. "In revising the story of the double fall for his own purposes, he seems to have come close to reproducing key elements of the Quranic version of how evil entered into the human world. The question then follows: how can we be sure that Luwis ʿAwad was wrong to claim that Milton was, in many respects, 'a pious Muslim?'"[1756]

Chapter 12

Isaac Newton:
The Enraged Anti-Trinitarian

Isaac Newton (1642-1727), a close friend of John Locke and a "fellow heretic,"[1757] was also a Socinian and a Unitarian, with minor diverging Arian leanings. He was a friend and colleague of Dr. J. Covel (1638-1722) who was Levant Company's chaplain in Constantinople in 1670, travelled extensively in the Ottoman Empire and collected a lot of manuscripts. Covel probably developed his heterodox views while in the Ottoman Empire.[1758] Covel became chaplain to Princess of Orange in Hague on his return from Constantinople, and then vice chancellor of Newton's Cambridge University. Newton's extensive correspondence with Dr. Covel while in Constantinople is well recorded.[1759] His regular discussions with Dr. Covel were helpful sources of Newton's knowledge about Ottomans, their religion and habits. His Cambridge teacher, mentor and friend Dr. Isaac Barrow had also spent years in Istanbul and other parts of the Ottoman Empire, and was well versed with Islamic religion, theology and culture. Newton succeeded him as the Lucasian Professor of Mathematics at Cambridge. Newton's alchemical enthusiasm and dependence upon Achmet's Arabic dream book and metaphorical interpretations in biblical prophecies have been discussed in the previous pages. Newton's searches for *Prisca theologia* and *Prisca sapientia* were two sides of the same coin. His anti-claricalism, anti-ritualism, anti-traditionalism, anti- supernatural dogmatism, Whiggish republicanism and pluralistic tendencies are well-documented.[1760]

Newton's Unitarian monotheism and anti-Trinitarianism[1761] were more emphatic than even Locke and Milton. Like Locke, he rejected innatism, original sin and the Trinity; his reverential pre-existent Jesus was a human prophet, Messiah and the metaphorical Son of God due to his virgin birth and immediate resurrection after death. He was exalted by God in creation and resurrection, but was neither co-equal nor co-eternal with God. There was only One God and Jesus was His prophetic Messiah. "To be a Christian one had to believe only that Christ was the Messiah prophesied in the Hebrew Bible or Old Testament, the Son of God who had died on the Cross and then been resurrected on the third day."[1762] Rob Iliffe noted that Newton "believed that the central Christian doctrine of the Trinity was a diabolical fraud, and that all of modern Christianity was tainted by its presence. Jesus Christ, the Son of God, was not equal in any sense to God the Father, although he was divine, and was worthy of being worshipped in his own right. Newton did not arrive at these beliefs as a result of pursuing some dilettantish hobby; nor were they the result of studies he pursued at the end of his life. Instead, they lay at the heart of a massive research programme on prophecy and church history that he carried out early in his career. This was at least as strenuous, and, in his eyes, at least as "rational" as his work on physics and mathematics."[1763] Newton believed in the genuine primitive Unitarian Christianity which was corrupted by the Church and Fathers in the Fourth century. Newton also believed that Prophet Muhammad was a genuine prophet sent to the Arabs.[1764] He implemented his Unitarian monotheistic theology of the One and Only Supreme God through his natural philosophy and scientific works.[1765] The Orthodoxy very well recognised Newton's subversive anti-Trinitarianism and scolded him for that.

Newton's Biblicism

Newton was an avid reader of the Bible and theological works; John Locke described Newton as "a very valuable man not onely for his wonderful skill in Mathematicks but in divinity too and his great knowledg in the Scriptures where in I know few his equals."[1766] This was a tremendous testimony about Newton's scriptural and theological erudition from a scrupulous scripturalist and philosopher like John Locke. Newton was extremely interested in Christian theology and dogmatic history. Frank Manuel noted that Newton wrote over one million words on theology and scripture and perhaps much more.[1767]

His biographer Richard Westfall observed that "in a notebook he entered a number of headings that summarised Christian theology: 'Attributa Dei,' 'Deus Pater,' 'Deus Fili us,' 'Incarnatio,' 'Christi Satisfactio,

& Redemptio,' 'Spiritus Sanctus Deus,' and the like."[1768] Newton was obsessed with works related to the Trinity and Christ's person. He labouriously studied the Christian Fathers, their arguments about Trinity and other central Christian doctrines, a "period of intensive study was devoted not just to Scripture, but to the writings of the Fathers of the second, third, and fourth centuries. The volume of his reading was prodigious, and he made extensive notes on his findings."[1769] After a detailed analysis of the central Christian doctrines, Newton rejected them all.[1770] Iliffe observed that "Newton's extensive writings on the Trinitarian corruption of Christianity are among the most daring works of any writer in the early modern period, and they would merit careful study even if they had not been composed by the author of the *Principia*."[1771] He was truly a Christian infidel and a Unitarian heretic. His anti-Trinitarianism and Unitarianism was more pronounced than Locke and he was "part of a Radical Reformation or Radical Enlightenment."[1772]

He was especially focused on the Trinitarian controversy of the fourth century when the Trinitarian saga began, and on the figures of St. Athanasius and Arian who fought it. "More than the doctrine interested him. He became fascinated with the man Athanasius and with the history of the church in the fourth century, when a passionate and bloody conflict raged between Athanasius and his followers, the founders of what became Christian orthodoxy, on the one hand, and Arius and his followers, who denied the Trinity and the status of Christ in the Godhead, on the other; and he read extensively about them."[1773] Maurice Wiles observed that Newton was "passionately anti-Athanasian rather than pro-Arian. Arius is a figure of no great interest to him. But Athanasius was the prime cause of that doctrinal corruption of the church, which caused such practical embarrassment to Newton personally as well as frustrating the purposes of God. Positively, Newton saw himself as a faithful follower of primitive Christianity, which was taught by Scripture and to a large degree practised by the church of the second and third centuries. And that primitive Christianity was, as Whiston observed with reference to Newton in a way Newton would have been reluctant to do, not very different from what had for many centuries been designated 'Arianism.'"[1774]

He fully concentrated upon Christ's relationship with the Father;[1775] his thorough research of the Bible and Church Fathers lead him to doubt the authenticity of both Scripture and dogma. "There was no single one of importance whose works he did not devour. And always, his eye was on the allied problems of the nature of Christ and the nature of God. The conviction began to possess him that a massive fraud, which began in the fourth and fifth centuries, had perverted the legacy of the early church. Central to the fraud were the Scriptures, which Newton began to believe had been corrupted to support trinitarianism."[1776] He charged Athanasius with forgery, whose crime "was the corruption of evidence to make it appear that the new doctrine was much older than it really was. The two scriptural texts whose authenticity Newton had discussed with Locke were both key texts used in support of Trinitarian doctrine. In an accompanying letter Newton listed a further twenty-eight texts, almost all of which had, he believed, been changed to give a Trinitarian sense in the fourth century in the course of the Arian controversy [...] Newton frequently charges Athanasius with forgery."[1777] Newton believed that the "corruptions of Scripture came relatively late. The earlier corruption of doctrine, which called for the corruption of Scripture to support it, occurred in the fourth century, when the triumph of Athanasius over Arius imposed the false doctrine of the trinity on Christianity."[1778]

Newton and Primitive Christianity

Newton observed that the original Christianity of Jesus was Nazarene Unitarian, which later got corrupted by the idolatrous Trinitarian Christianity. The Trinity was idolatry, the gravest of all the sins. "In Newton's eyes, worshipping Christ as God was idolatry, to him the fundamental sin. 'Idolatria' had appeared among the original list of headings in his theological notebook. The special horror of the perversion that triumphed in the fourth century was the reversion of Christianity to idolatry after the early church had established proper worship of the one true God. 'If there be no transubstantiation,' he wrote in the early 1670s, 'never was Pagan Idolatry so bad as the Roman, as even Jesuits sometimes confess.' Newton held that the pope in Rome had aided and abetted Athanasius and that the idolatrous Roman church was the direct product of Athanasius' corruption of doctrine."[1779] Trinity was the utmost disgrace to the One and Only God and hence the gravest of all the sins.[1780] "To Newton, idolatry represented the fundamental sin"[1781] and "the most grievous version of idolatry was to turn the Son of God into God himself."[1782]

Newton, after an exhausted study of the so-called Trinitarian verses in the New Testament and their interpretations by the Church Fathers, concluded that the Fathers manipulated the original words and imposed Trinitarian jargon on the verses, which were not supported by the text. This linguistic fraud and textual violence was the source of the Trinitarian grafting on the simple, Unitarian belief of Jesus Christ. The Roman Church, with its clerical establishment, was solely responsible for this enormous corruption. "In the end- and the end did not wait long- Newton convinced himself that a universal corruption of Christianity had followed the central corruption of doctrine. Concentration of ecclesiastical power in the hands of the hierarchy had replaced the polity of the early church. The perverse institution of monasticism sprang from the same source. Athanasius had patronised Anthony, and the 'homousians' had introduced monks into ecclesiastical government. In the fourth century, trinitarianism fouled every element of Christianity. Though he did not say so, he obviously believed that the Protestant Reformation had not touched the seat of infection. In Cambridge of the 1670s this was strong meat indeed. It is not hard to understand why Newton became impatient with interruptions from minor diversions such as optics and mathematics. He had committed himself to a reinterpretation of the tradition central to the whole of European civilisation."[1783] For this reason, for a while Newton diverted his attention away from his natural philosophy and scientific works to concentrate on the Church theology and its corrupted foundations, to help in reforming Christianity on the original, simple and Unitarian foundations. He became an Arian denying Jesus' divinity and exalting his humanity, reverential dominion and moral efficacy; there was no God but the One and Only Father Who created Jesus, glorified him and bestowed upon him the honourific titles. Jesus was honoured by God before the creation and glorified after his death. Newton collected scriptural texts to emphasise God's unity and Jesus' humanity. "On the scriptural side, a small number of texts or short passages stand out as controlling influences on his understanding of the person of Christ. By and large it is the same selection of scriptural evidence that had shaped Arian understanding in the fourth century. Most formative of all is 1 Cor. 8: 5-6, which speaks of 'the one God, the Father, from whom are all things [...] and the one Lord, Jesus Christ, through whom are all things.' This provides Newton with his basic monotheistic premiss: there is one God, the Father. Newton generalizes the point by insisting that 'whenever it is said in the Scriptures that there is one God, it means the Father.'"[1784]

Newton and Early Christian Apologists

Newton, like the second-century Christian Apologists such as Justin Martyr, Theophilus, Tatian, Aristides and Athenagoras,[1785] differentiated between the ineffable, transcendent and eternal God and finite, begotten and subservient Jesus. Justin, the most renowned of them, for instance insisted that "though Jesus had come from God he was not identical with God."[1786] Jesus was Son of God, Logos and Angel of derivative, secondary and subservient nature. "Justin's God was a transcendent being who could have not come into contact with the utilitarian sphere of man and things. To Justin, it seemed altogether absurd that such a transcendent God could be born of a woman, eat, drink and eventually be mercilessly crucified. However, strict belief in God's transcendence did not stop Justin from thinking of Jesus as divine, and to defend Christ's relationship with God he made use of the then current Christian phraseology calling Jesus the Son of God, Logos and also the Angel. Indeed according to him, Christ was worthy of these titles on account of his wisdom, virgin birth and because he was God's first begotten Logos."[1787] Jesus' divinity was "derivative, and for that reason inferior to the one God [...] In Justin's system there truly was, in the last resort, only one ultimate God. The Logos represented a slightly lower level of divinity, something between the pure divinity of God and the nondivinity of creatures. Justin had made sense of the incarnational picture of Jesus by adopting a hierarchical picture of the world-order in which the Logos stands as a kind of bumper state between God and the world, and it is this fact that makes Justin's Christology problematic."[1788]

Jesus was a pre-existent Logos, God's agent in creation, through whom all creatures were created. Therefore, he could be called Lord and worshipped as divine but in terms of being of second rank. In his *Dialogue with the Jewish Trypho*, he argued the matter at length: "I will give you, my friends, another testimony from the Scriptures certain rational power which is called by the Holy Spirit now Glory of the Lord, again Wisdom, again Angel, again God, again Lord, and Logos. Also he called himself Captain of the host when he appeared to Jesus the Son of Nave in the form of a man. For he can be called by all these names since he serves the Father's will and was begotten of the Father by will."[1789] The unity of purpose and will was antithetical to the later claims of unity of essence and substance. Alois Grillmeier observed:

"In calling the Logos the servant, the apostle, the angel of the absolutely transcendent Father, Justin gives him a diminished transcendence, even if he does not make him a creature. He compares the Logos with Herms, the Logos-interpreter of Zeus [...] There is a *deus inferior* subordinate to the *theos hypsistos*."[1790]

Other apologists, such as Tatian and Hippolytus, followed Justin in his ideas of God's transcendence, ineffability, immutability and otherness while maintaining his inferior Logos Christology. J. N. D. Kelly underlined the two most important points that were common among all the Apologists: "(a) that for all of them the description 'God the Father' connoted, not the first Person of the Holy Trinity, but the one Godhead considered as author of whatever exists; and (b) that they all, Athenagoras included, dated the generation of the Logos, and His eligibility for the title 'Son', not from His origination within the being of the Godhead, but from His emission or putting forth for the purposes of creation, revelation and redemption. Unless these points are firmly grasped, and their significance appreciated, a completely distorted view of the Apologists' theology is liable to result."[1791] The Logos had a beginning in time, a specifically assigned mission and reward. He was not God in essence or substance but divine in his moral efficacy, exaltation, glorification and dominion. The credit of his exaltation and dominion went to God Almighty, who bestowed it upon him.

The Apologists clearly portrayed the Logos as required for the work of creation in subordination to God the Father. They also manifestly limited the Logos as compared to God Himself, to safeguard the indispensable idea of monotheism. There were residuals of Middle Platonism in this Logos interpretation of the Apologists. The Logos was understood in relation to the cosmos and the world to stress God's absolute transcendence, invisibility and unknowableness. Almighty God was too transcendent to directly deal with men and the world. The Logos, a product of God's creative will, was a subordinate mediator, a derivative god. The idea of subordination was fortified by the close linking of the creation of the world with the procession of the Logos, and then by the scheme of salvation or man's redemption through his intermediate agency. Therefore, worship of Jesus as Logos was permitted, like the worship of angels, but not like the worship of One and Only God.

Newton followed Justin Martyr in his derivative, secondary and subservient Christology. He believed that Jesus was the Word of God,

the Logos begotten by God in time and used for the purposes of creation and redemption. This created, pre-existent Logos was not co-equal
with God in substance or eternity but in moral will and obedience. "In
any case the stress is always on the distinct, personal, entitative character of the pre-existent Logos, who is the agent of creation."[1792]

Newton laid down fourteen *Argumenta* in Latin to show God the
Father's ineffability, transcendence and eternity against Jesus' begotten,
finite and derivative nature. Louis Trenchard More argued that these
arguments demonstrated that for Newton, the Son was neither coeternal with, nor equal to, the Father. More listed Newton's salient points as
follows: "(2) Because the Son is called the Word: John 1.1.; (4) Because
God begot the Son at some time, he had not existence from eternity.
Prov. viii. 23, 25; (5) Because the Father is greater than the Son. John
XIV, 28; (6). Because the Son did not know his last hour. Mark XIII, 32-
Matt. XXIV, 36- Rev. 1.1 and V.3.; and (7) Because the Son received all
things from the Father; and (9). Because the Son could be incarnated.
In the second manuscript Newton offered seven *Rationes* against the
traditional formulation including: (1) H*omoousian* is unintelligible.
'Twas not understood in the Council of Nice... nor ever since. What
cannot be understood is no object of belief; (6) The Father is God,
creating and a person; the Son is God, created and a person; and the
Holy Ghost is God, proceeding and a person; *et tamen non est nisi unus
Deus*; and (7) The Person is intellectual substance [*substantia intellec-
tualis*], therefore the three Persons are three substances."[1793]

Jesus' unity with God was nothing else but his sanctification and
creation by God. More insisted that Newton was a Unitarian. "His Unitarianism is, I think, even more pronounced in the following: 'Jesus
therefore by calling himself the Son of God and saying I and the Father
are one meant nothing more than that the Father had sanctified him
and sent him into the world.'"[1794] Newton totally denied the Trinity and
the Triune concept of Godhead by rejecting the multiplicity of persons. "Personally, Newton was an Arian since he states definitely that
the Father and the Son are not one substance; that the Son was created
and therefore of a different substance for, if they were of one substance
then, the Father having created the substance of the Son, He must have
created his own substance. Having placed the source of authority in the
Bible and not in the Councils, he shows that the Holy Ghost is not a
person or substance by calling the two passages in the New Testament

spurious which specifically mention the Holy Ghost as a person."[1795] Newton was totally Unitarian in insisting that Jesus was a Prophet and not ontologically God or divine. "But Newton goes much farther than merely to deny the doctrine of consubstantiation. He had rationally adopted the Unitarian position that Jesus was sent by the Father into the world as a Prophet who differed from the other Prophets only in the immediacy of the message delivered to him. Thus he explains the claim that 'I and my Father are one' as a unity of purpose and not one of identity. Like so many other Unitarians of the day, such as Locke, he here makes a break between reason and practice, since he maintained his affiliation with the Church of England. But, as I have remarked before, I find in this the cause of his refusal to take orders; as a private worshipper he felt he was justified in making reservations which his conscience was too tender to permit him to make as a priest."[1796]

Like the Apologists, Newton allowed reverential worship of Jesus based on God-given dominion. "'Tis not consubstantiality but power and dominion which gives a right to be worshipped."[1797] Jesus Lordship was not eternal; it was granted to him by God after his crucifixion and resurrection. God was eternally God, but Jesus was made Lord in time. God was worshipped as eternally God, while Jesus was venerated as Lord in time. "'Equality with God' […] is understood to refer to his 'being worshipped as Lord'; and that was not true of him earlier but something assumed only after the incarnation and crucifixion. So in distinguishing the worship due to the 'one God' and the 'one Lord', Newton regularly distinguishes between the primary grounds for the offering of each of those two forms of worship: that offered to the one God or Father is for his creation of all things, that offered to the one Lord or Son is because he is the Lamb of God who was slain for us."[1798] God's worship was absolute, while Jesus' veneration was relative. Newton painstakingly insisted upon the distinction between God and Lord in many ways. to avert any possibility of consubstantiality. "And therefore as a father and his son cannot be called one King upon account of their being consubstantial but may be called one King by unity of dominion if the Son be Viceroy under the father: so God and his son cannot be called one God upon account of their being consubstantial."[1799] He argued that such exalting titles and reverential worship was permitted by the first commandment. Newton limited the role of Jesus merely to creation and redemption to avoid over-exaltation and other

Orthodox ambiguities related to the Son's role. "Even the traditional understanding of the intermediary role of the Son is somewhat diminished in Newton's scheme [...] There we find that while we may call Jesus 'God' without transgressing the first commandment, he is not to be worshiped as 'God Almighty', but only in relationship to his office as Monarch, as 'Lord, the Messiah, the Great King, and the Lamb of God.' Christ is not worshiped on the basis of his ontology according to Newton's theology but on the basis of his christological office."[1800]

Even this worship, glorification and exaltation in reality belonged to God, who glorified Jesus. Newton left no stone unturned to differentiate between God and Jesus, and to place Jesus lower than God and a bit higher than man due to his immediacy. "The worship wch we are directed in scripture to give to Jesus Christ Respects his death & exaltation to the right hand of God & is given to him as our Lord & King & tends to the glory of God the father. Should we give the Father that worship wch is due to the Son we should be Patripassians & should we give the Son all that worship wch is due to the father we should make two creators and be all guilty of polytheism & in both cases we should practically deny the father & the Son. We may give blessing & honour & glory & power to God & the Lamb together but it must be in different respects, to God as he is God the father Almighty who created the heaven & earth & to the Lamb as he is the Lord who was slain for us & washed away our sins in his own blood & is exalted to the right hand of God the father. In worshipping them we must keep to the characters given them in the primitive creed then we are safe."[1801]

The Father is eternal, self-sufficient and self-sustaining while the Son is finite, dependent upon and derived from God. "The Father is the ancient of days and has life in himself originally essentially and independently from all eternity, and has given the Son to have life in himself [...] Because the Word of God received life from the Father immediately, both before the world began and at his resurrection from the dead, therefore he is the Son of God in a sense peculiar to himself."[1802] Newton's peculiar, detailed insistence upon Jesus' secondary, derivative and finite nature, his exaltation of Jesus as the first born of creation and the first resurrected of the creation and his emphasis upon Jesus' prophetic mission make him more Socinian/Unitarian than Arian. Like Locke, Newton's terminologies are traditional and more Arian-looking, but their explanations and contents are more Socinian/Unitarian, even moreso than Locke's. We are mostly dealing with his private writings where Newton is mostly interacting with his own thoughts rather than explaining himself to others or for the intent of publications. Newton, even in these condensed private notes and writings, is more Unitarian, Socinian and Islamic-leaning than John Locke. His God is Unique, Eternal, Transcendent and Unitary without equals, partners and resemblance, and his Jesus is nothing but an exalted creature by dint of his office, and not substance or divine essence. This is a totally Unitarian position, more emphatic than historical Arianism. Maurice Wiles observes that "reflection on the scriptural teaching about Christ led Newton into much bolder and more detailed affirmations than it did Locke. And those affirmations are predominantly 'Arian' in character, in the sense that they understand the pre-existent Christ as a distinct being of a secondary divine nature. But they also lay great stress on a worship of Christ as Lord, which is focused more on the dignity awarded to him after and on the basis of his redemptive death [...] On occasion it is emphasised to the exclusion of any reference to Christ's pre-existence in a manner that helps to explain why he might sometimes have been regarded as more Socinian than Arian."[1803] Scott Mandelbrote[1804] and Rob Iliffe have shown Newton's relative use of Unitarian authors such as John Biddle,[1805] Stephen Nye[1806] and similarities with Deists authors such as Herbert of Cherbury and Charles Blount.[1807]

Newton's insistence upon Jesus' humanity, in time creation, natural revival after death, prophetic and messianic role and reverential exaltation, all place him squarely in the Unitarian/Socinian and Islamic camp. He is too emphatic of a Unitarian to be confused with Orthodoxy or Trinitarian. "Jesus Christ a true man born of a woman was crucified [...] and by the same power by which God gave life at first to every species of animal being revived, he appeared to his disciples and explained to them Moses and the Prophets concerning himself, as that he was the Sun of righteousness spoken of by Malachi, the son of man and the Messiah spoken of by Daniel, the servant of God and lamb of God and Redeemer spoken of by Isaiah [...] and is gone into the heavens to receive a kingdom and prepare a place for us, and is mystically said to sit at the right hand of God, that is, to be next to him in dignity, and is worshipped and glorified as the Lamb of God." [1808] Wiles especially noted that "here Christ is portrayed not as the Word who spoke through the prophets, but simply as the man about whom the prophets spoke.

As a careful student of Scripture, Newton found the pre-existence of Christ inescapable, but religiously it does not seem to have been of great importance to him. He enunciates the general principle that 'God does nothing by himself which he can do by another.' The Son is his agent for the tasks of creation and judgement. His distinctive title of 'only begotten Son' derives from the fact that he alone has received life directly from the Father. But he is simply the agent of God, and 'all other beings formed by the Son may be considered as the works of God's hand.' It was his redemptive death that was distinctively Christ's work, and the reason for his special worship."[1809] Therefore, it was not the death of God which saved the sinful, but the voluntary death of an exalted man. This was absolutely a Socinian/Unitarian position, totally in opposition to everything the Church Christianity had ever taught. "Newton seems content to see the crucifixion as the death of a man subsequently raised to the dignity of God's right hand, and made by God the legitimate object of our secondary worship. At such times a Socinian Christ seems to be all he feels the need to affirm. That such a measure of prima-facie inconsistency should appear in jottings made over many years and never prepared for publication or integrated into a single coherent treatment of the theme is hardly surprising. But though one might describe his religious position as predominantly Socinian, there is no doubt that his overall theological position is Arian rather than Socinian. Nor indeed is there any logical inconsistency in an 'Arian' belief in the pre-existence of a divine being, the agent of the Father's creative work, which none the less places its main religious stress on that divine being's redemptive self-giving in crucifixion and on the even greater glory given by the Father as the outcome of it."[1810] This sort of in-time, finite glory is at odds with the eternal, co-equal, Trinitarian glory of Jesus rehearsed in the Nicaean and Chalcedonian formulas.[1811]

Newton and Unitarian Theology

To Newton, the Unitarian theology of One and Only God was truly Christian while the Trinitarian, Incarnational theology was heathenistic. "Such opinions did not derive 'from the Apostles by tradition'; they were 'brought into the Church from the theology of the heathens or Cabbalists in which learned men happened to be educated and instructed before they became Christians.'"[1812] The Roman, paganistic and idolatrous engrafting turned the metaphorical, reverential Son of

God into a real ontological Son of God, the reverential titles used for Jesus into a Triune Godhead and a monarchical dominion into a metaphysical dominion.[1813] "If the Father or Son be called God: they [men skilled in the learning of heathens, cabbalists, and schoolmen] take the name in a metaphysical sense, as if it signified God's metaphysical perfections of infinite eternal omniscient omnipotent: whereas it relates only to God's dominion over us to teach us obedience. The word God is relative and signifies the same thing with Lord and King but in a higher degree. As we say my Lord, our Lord, your Lord, the supreme Lord, the Lord of the earth [...] so we say my God, our God, your God, the supreme God, the God of the earth [...] but we do not say my infinite, our infinite, your infinite, the supreme infinite, the infinite of the earth [...] When therefore the Father or Son are called God, we are to understand it not metaphysically but in a moral monarchical sense."[1814] The transfer of the metaphor of incarnation into a metaphysic of incarnation was categorically paganistic and heathenistic; Newton went further than that in differentiating between God and Lord. "The word God usually signifies *Lord;* but every lord is not a God. It is the dominion of a spiritual being which constitutes a God: a true, supreme, or imaginary dominion makes a true, supreme, or imaginary God. And from his dominion it follows that the true God is a living, intelligent, and powerful Being; and, from his other perfections, that he is supreme, or most perfect. He is eternal and infinite, omnipotent and omniscient; that is, his duration reaches from eternity to eternity; his presence from infinity to infinity; he governs all things, and knows all things that are or can be done."[1815] The Son, begotten in time with finite derivative powers and exaltation, can never be equal to God who is absolutely perfect, eternal, everlasting, omnipotent and omniscient.

The Almighty God is neither anthropomorphic nor corporeal; he is self-existing and the necessary being, the First Cause, the uncaused Cause of everything, the Necessary through Himself while Jesus, the contingent being, is necessary through God. God is "not eternity and infinity, but eternal and infinite, he is not duration or space, but he endures and is present. He endures forever, and is everywhere present; and, by existing always and everywhere, he constitutes duration and space [...] It is allowed by all that the Supreme God exists necessarily; and by the same necessity he exists *always* and *everywhere.* Whence also he is similar, all eye, all ear, all brain, all arm, all power to perceive, to understand, and to act; but in a manner not at all human, in a manner not at all corporeal, in a manner utterly unknown to us. As a blind man has no ideas of colours, so we have no idea of the manner by which the all-wise God perceives and understands all things. He is utterly void of all body and bodily figure, and can therefore neither be seen, nor heard, nor touched; nor ought he to be worshipped under the representation of any corporeal thing."[1816]

Newton's above arguments resemble the Islamic transcendental notions of God,[1817] to the extent that it seems as if they were copied from the arguments of Muslim philosophers and theologians such as Ibn Sina, al-Farabi, Ibn Rushd and al-Ghazali.[1818]

Ibn Sina, for instance, states that "every being, if considered from the point of view of its essence and without consideration of other things, is found to be such that either existence necessarily belongs to it in itself or it does not. If existence belongs to it necessarily, then it is the truth in itself and that whose existence is necessary from itself. This is the Independent Reality. If, on the other hand, existence does not belong to it necessarily, it is not permissible to say that it is impossible in itself after it was supposed existing. But if, in relation to its essence, a condition is linked to it, such as the condition of the nonexistence of its cause, it becomes impossible or, such as the condition of the existence of its cause, it becomes necessary. If no condition is linked to its essence, neither existence nor nonexistence of a cause, then there remains for it in itself the third option, that is, possibility. Thus, with respect to its essence, it would be a thing that is neither necessary nor impossible. Therefore every existent either has necessary existence in essence or has possible existence in essence."[1819] Shams Inati explains the concept in a simple fashion: "The existence of a thing is either necessary or possible (contingent). Necessary existence is such that if the thing to which it belongs is assumed to be non-existent, an impossibility arises. Possible existence is such that if the thing to which it belongs is assumed to be non-existent or existent, no impossibility arises. Ibn Sina mentions that in other contexts 'possible existence' could also be used in the sense of 'being in potentiality.' Necessary existence is either that which always belongs to a thing through that thing itself, or that which always belongs to it through another."[1820]

Causality is the main difference between the two categories (necessary and contingent) of being; the necessary being is not caused while the contingent is caused.[1821] God, the First Mover, is the only necessary being hence not caused.[1822] The creation is contingent and caused by God.[1823] Ibn Sina further states that "if this chain includes an uncaused thing, then this thing is an extremity and a limit. Therefore every chain terminates in that whose existence is necessary in itself."[1824] This transcendental, philosophical and Unitarian argument propounded by Ibn Sina and popularized by the later Muslim philosophers and theologian might have reached Newton through the writings of Moses Maimonides or St. Thomas Aquinas. Both employed it in their theologico philosophical writings.

Richard H. Popkin observed that Newton was influenced by Moses Maimonides.[1825] "Another major and serious influence on Newton's theological views was that of the great medieval Jewish theologian, Moses Maimonides."[1826] Popkin extended the thesis of John Maynard Keynes who gave a lecture on the occasion of the three-hundredth anniversary of the birth of Newton, entitled 'Newton the Man,' Keynes ended the lecture by saying that "Newton was not just a closet Unitarian Arian, but 'was rather a Judaic monotheist of the school of Maimonides.'"[1827] To Abraham Shalom Yahuda "Newton was a Maimonidean. Among Yahuda's Newton manuscripts is one entitled *On Maimonides*. This work consists of notes which Newton took when he read portions of the 17th century Latin edition of Maimonides' *Mishneh Torah*. Maimonides also appears as a frequently cited source throughout Newton's religious writings."[1828] This is not surprising, given the close common Semitic monotheistic consciousness shared by Judaism and Islam, and the close historical connections between the works of Maimonides and his Muslim predecessors.[1829]

Both the Jewish Master Moses Maimonides and the medieval Christian stalwart Thomas Aquinas took the Muslim philosopher's arguments of God as the necessary being and incorporated them into their philosophical schemes. One should not overlook the influence Islamic theology and philosophy had upon medieval Jewish thought, especially that of Karaites, Saadia Gaon, Jacob al-Qirqisani, Isaac Israeli, Solomon Ibn Gabirol, Bahya Ibn Paquda, Abraham bar Hiyya, Joseph Ibn Zaddik, Moses Ibn Ezra, Judah Halevi, Abraham Ibn Daud, Moses Maimonides, Samuel Ibn Tibbon, Shem Tov Ibn Falaquera, Levi ben Gershom (Gersonides), Moses Narboni, and Hasdai Crescas. E. Renan noted that the "Arabic philosophy was never really taken seriously except by the Jews [...] whose literary culture in the Middle Ages is merely a reflection of Muslim culture."[1830] To Arthur Hyman, "by and large Jewish philosophy was a continuation of the philosophy which flourished in the Islamic world"[1831] Oliver Leaman notes that "it is difficult to overemphasise significance which Islamic philosophy had for Jewish thinkers who were working at the same time in the Islamic world, or who were influenced by such work. Many Jewish thinkers wrote in Arabic and their main philosophical authorities were Arabic authors, which is hardly surprising given the pervasiveness of Arabic culture within the Islamic Empire."[1832]

Islam, like Judaism, was an ethical monotheistic tradition where law and theology were crowned as highly prized sciences. There was so much common between the two faith traditions that theological insights, inquiries, concerns and even the legal theories and framework were almost identical. Leaman states that "when we look at the works of thinkers such as Saadiah, Halevi, Maimonides and even Gersonides we can observe the curriculum of Islamic philosophy quite fully represented. They did not just take some of the leading ideas and try to see how far they could use them to make sense of their own philosophical concerns, as was very much the case with many of the major Christian philosophers. The Jewish philosophers went much further than this in their work, often working well within the tradition of Islamic philosophy itself, albeit just as often using it to develop points which were of specifically Jewish concern. Perhaps one of the reasons why Jewish philosophy came to rely so much on Islamic philosophy lies in the proximity of the religions."[1833] Steven Wesserstrom agrees that "another reason for common cause on the part of Jewish and Muslim philosophers was their joint monotheistic opposition to a common pagan adversary. The ostensible impetus of this joint counterforce remains a leitmotif of scholarship on Jewish-Muslim symbiosis."[1834] The transcendental monotheistic tradition of Judaism and Islam were pitched against the Trinitarian tradition of Christianity. The Jewish and Islamic philosophical-theological collaborations against Incarnational, corporeal and anthropomorphic Christian theology were the hallmark of medieval Jewish Muslim symbiosis. Newton sided with the Jewish Muslim transcendental monotheism against the Trinitarian Christianity. Newton was a product of Islamico-Hebraic civilisation. The medieval Jewry was a true reflection of the majority Muslim community in so many ways that it would not be wrong to call the resultant civilisation as an Islamico-Hebraic civilisation, as Mauro Zonta states. "We might speak of 'Hebrew-Arabic' philosophy while considering the great influence of Islamic thought on much of the Jewish philosophical legacy written in the Hebrew language during the thirteenth, fourteenth and fifteenth centuries.[1835]

Moses Maimonides (d. 1204), confessed in a letter addressed to his disciple, Joseph Ben Juda, written in Cairo in 1191, that "he had received lately everything Averroes had written on the works of Aristotle and found that he was extremely right."[1836] Majid Fakhry states that "the two Aristotelians had so much in common, especially in their attitude to Ash'arite Kalam, that readers of Maimonides tended to find Averroes particularly intriguing and to look upon the former as the disciple of the latter."[1837] Maimonides was born and raised in the Muslim Cordoba of Ibn Rushd, and died in the Muslim Cairo. He worked for the Muslim rulers and elites, studying and absorbed many Muslim philosophers and theologians along his studies of the Rabbinic corpus. Maimonides, to Alexander Brodie, "was steeped in Islamic philosophy."[1838] L. V. Berman in his *Maimonides, The Disciple of Alfarabi*, argues that Maimonides was an avid disciple of al-Farabi.[1839] A. Eran shows similarities between al-Ghazali and Maimonides' works on spirituality and soteriology.[1840] S. Harvey illustrates the influence of al-Farabi, Ibn Sina and al-Ghazali upon the fourteenth-century Jewish philosophers and theologians.[1841] To Majid Fakhry, Maimonides was a pure disciple of Ibn Rushd.

St. Thomas Aquinas,[1842] the most known medieval philosophical theologian and the stalwart of scholasticism, was also greatly influenced by Muslim synthetic thought. He widely quoted from Ibn Rushd, Ibn Sina, al-Farabi, al-Ghazali in his writings, acting and reacting to them in a number of ways. He read Latin translations of their works and incorporated many of their ideas, thoughts and arguments into his synthetic project. In short, Newton's arguments about God's necessary being, the cosmological arguments from design and overemphasis upon divine transcendence and total rejection of anthropomorphic and corporeal depictions of God were reflections of Muslim philosophers and theologians, whether assimilated directly through Dr. Pococke's works or via Moses Maimonides or St. Thomas Aquinas. Newton's Christology and overall theological systems were too Islamic and Unitarian to be ignored; his verbiage was orthodox Christian, but the detailed contents were more Islamic than mere Arian. Newton gravitated more towards Jesus' humanity, prophetic mission and moral efficacy than Arians and at times even more than ambivalent Socinians. His exalted Jesus was more natural, human, finite and subservient than the semi-divine, relatively supernatural and omnipotent Christ or Logos of early Arians. Newton's insistence upon eternal, transcendental and unique absolute attributes of God and total separation of Jesus from anything ontologically divine and derivative finite nature, mission-based secondary exaltation and many other non-divine attributes were far more marked and pronounced than Arians, and at times even more than Socinians and Deists. His derivative, natural, prophetic and angelic Christology was in line with the radical Unitarians such as Stephen Nye and early Muhammadan Christians such as Henry Stubbe. It was thoroughly transcendental, monotheistic and natural, and in total opposition to the anthropomorphic, corporeal, supernatural and Trinitarian Christology of the historical Christianity.

Newton and Nicaean Christology

Newton's Christology was a total indictment of the Orthodox Christianity. This was a total deviation from the Church Nicaean Christology and a full swing to the Arian, Unitarian and Socinian camp, though he kept his beliefs to himself and to his selected confidants to avoid the social, financial and religious persecutions common during his times. "It is useful to set Newton's behavior in the early 1670s against the background of his Arianism. He identified himself with Arius, both intellectually and emotionally. He relived the terrible struggles of the fourth century, when doctrine counted for more than charity, came to see Athanasius as his personal nemesis, and learned to hate him fiercely. When questions, which look legitimate to us, about his theory of colours seemed to drive him frantic, the pattern that disagreement took in the fourth century may have determined his conduct. He wished to avoid controversy at all costs. On the most important question of all, he had to avoid controversy."[1843] Newton's boss was an enthusiastic and vocal Trinitarian; he was aggressively anti-Arian and anti-Socinian. Newton concealed his beliefs to avert the confrontation. "Since any discussion was fraught with the danger of ruin, Newton chose silence [...] Newton concealed his views so effectively that only in our day has full knowledge of them become available."[1844]

Newton, a zealous student of prophecies - especially in the Books of *Daniel* and *Revelation* - interpreted them as confirming the Trinitarian apostasy and emperor Theodosius' persecutions of original Unitarian Christians. It was Emperor Theodosius who, after the initial peaceful period of coexistence and Arian ascendancy, patronised the idolatrous Trinitarians, unleashing the state and Church persecutions against the anti-Trinitarian Christians. "The seventh seal, within which the seven trumpets (which also represent successive periods of time) are included, began with the year 380 [...] Until then, trinitarian doctrines, though formulated by Athanasius, had been professed only by a few western bishops led by the Pope. At that time, however, Theodosius became its patron and called the Council of Constantinople in 381 to ratify it."[1845] This was the "Beast" which destroyed the pristine Christianity of Jesus and turned it into the Trinitarian idolatry. Newton considered the Trinity as the utmost injustice to God and Jesus. "The mere thought of trinitarianism, the 'false infernal religion,' was enough to fan Newton into a rage. With it had come the return of idolatry in a more degraded form [...] Superstitions of every sort, fanned and spread by monks with feigned stories of false miracles, accompanied the new worship. 'Idolaters,' Newton thundered at them in the isolation of his chamber, 'Blasphemers & spiritual fornicators.' They pretended to be Christians, but the devil knew 'that they were to be above all others ye most wicked wretched sort of people [...] the worst sort of men that ever reigned upon the face of ye earth till that same time.' 'The first six trumpets and the six vials of wrath corresponding to them represent successive invasions of the Empire,' 'like Furies sent in by the wrath of God to scourge ye Romans,' repeated punishments of an apostate people who whored after false gods."[1846]

Newton reserved the utmost hatred and the worst of epithets for the Trinitarians. It was not the worth or strength of the arguments which carried the Trinity so far and wide, but the arm of the state and base human motives which perpetuated this sacred fraud. "As the passion with which Newton expressed himself suggests, his early treatise on the prophecies was a very personal document. In his view, the triumph of trinitarianism had stretched beyond the limits of doctrine. It had won dominance by allying itself with base human motives, such as 'covetousness & ambition.'"[1847] Christianity was deformed by the corrupt priests and kings; only the Second coming of Jesus was to reform it to its pristine nature. "Only with the second coming will there be a final conversion of the kingdoms of this world to the kingdom of Christ forever."[1848]

Newton was a reformer and proselyte of a private sort; he converted his closest friends and colleagues to his anti-Trinitarian Christianity. Stephan Snobelen, in his *Isaac Newton, heretic: the strategies of a Nicodemite,* greatly highlights Newton's reformatory and recruiting strategies. He observed that "Newton was indeed preaching his faith. It was a strategy of proselytisation carried out almost completely in the private sphere and done so [...] not only for legal and social reasons. This reconstruction of Newton's actions tallies well with his belief that the deeper things of theology should only be handled by the experienced and mature members of the remnant and, even then, only in private [...] men like Humphrey Newton, Locke, Gregory, Haynes, Clarke and Whiston were either given access to, or had knowledge of, Newton's theological manuscripts, thus suggesting one of the uses Newton intended for some of his theological writings, and possibly explaining."[1849] Newton's job, position and work environment prohibited him from publicly berating the Trinitarian theology.[1850]

Newton, like Stubbe, Toland and Locke believed in the successive, monotheistic, prophetic tradition. This fundamentally Islamic, universal, historical narrative of original monotheism through the successive prophetic offices of Adam, Noah, Abraham, Moses, Jesus and Muhammad was a common thread between the eighteenth-century Deists, Unitarians and Socinians. Even a careful writer like John Locke insisted that Muhammad borrowed monotheism from Jesus and Islam was heir to the original Unitarian message of Jesus. This was a clear indication of authenticity of Islamic monotheism against the Trinitarian usurpers of Jesus' message. Newton followed the same line of argument and declared Muhammad to be the prophet sent to the Arabs in line with Jesus' monotheistic tradition. Newton brought down Jesus from the high offices of Godhead to the human offices of a moral prophet and situated him right in the successive, monotheistic prophetic history. "More significant was the implicit deemphasis of the role of Christ, a step which came readily enough to an Arian. Instead of the agent of a new dispensation, Christ was a prophet, like Moses before him, sent to recall mankind to the original true worship of God. As he revised the 'Origines,' Newton set down a number of chapter headings, the last of which was for chapter 11. What was the true religion of the sons of Noah before it began to be corrupted by the worship of false Gods. And that the Christian religion was not more true and did not become less corrupt. In this setting, trinitarianism with its encouragement of the worship of saints and martyrs, indeed with its worship of Christ as God, took on a new meaning. What was trinitarianism but the latest manifestation of the universal tendency of mankind to superstition and idolatry? Through Athanasius, Egypt once again played its nefarious role as the corrupter of true religion. By universalising the Christian experience of the first four centuries, Newton denied it any unique role in human history. The Christian religion rightly understood was not more true than the religion of the sons of Noah, which was founded upon the recognition of God in His creation."[1851] *Prisca theologia* and *prisca sapientia* were one and the same since the beginning of humanity. God's book of revelation and book of creation highlighted divine unity, simplicity, uniqueness and transcendence. The same direct divine sovereighnty was preached by all the successive prophets. The ethical monotheism, simple, natural and rational theology was the hallmark of all prophets. The Christian supernatural, Trinitarian and abnormal theology was an aberration and not the norm. Islam was in line with that Unitarian, natural theology. Newton believed in the authenticity of Prophet Muhammad, and the Quranic monotheistic message. Snobelen notes that "a report deriving from Newton's Cambridge period has him believing that God had sent Muhammad to reveal the One God to Arabs, which echoes the Unitarian *historia monotheistica* of the 1670s-1710s."[1852] This report is cited in J. Edleston, *Correspondence of Sir Isaac Newton and Professor Cotes.*[1853]

As noted above, the seventeenth- and eighteenth-century Unitarians, Socinians and Deists believed that Islam was the true heir to the original, primitive, monotheistic Christianity of Jesus, and that the corrupted Orthodox Trinitarian Christianity of the Church must be reformed on the Islamic lines. Muhammad did not bring a new religion, but revived the original, universal, moral, prophetic, monotheistic message preached by Jesus, Moses and all other prophets. Newton subscribed to this line of argument and was a part of the late seventeenth- and early eighteenth-century Unitarian Islamic syncretism "*historia monotheistica*" hailed by Henry Stubbe, John Toland, Arthur Bury, Stephan Nye and other Unitarians, Socinians and Deists. John Locke and Isaac Newton were the silent supporters of this hybrid rational monotheism. Justin Champion's *Pillars of Priestcraft Shaken* has a complete chapter explaining and delineating this Unitarian Islamic syncretism, and we will return to it in the coming pages. Locke's antrinitarian human Christology, biblical criticism and anti-clerical tendencies were identical to those of Newton. They regularly corresponded and met, cementing their friendship based on mutual religious bonds. "Religion provided what was easily the dominant theme of the correspondence and apparently of their conversation when they met. Locke later told his cousin, Peter King, that he knew few who were Newton's equal in knowledge of the Bible."[1854] Newton privately shared with Locke his total rejection of Trinity and corruption of scriptures, beliefs which Locke totally agreed with.[1855] Locke sent Newton's antitrinitarian work *Origins of Gentile Theology* to his Socinain friend Jean Le Clerc in Amsterdam for publication, but later on Newton stopped the publication for fear of persecution.[1856] Locke shared his third *Letter on Toleration* with Newton and Newton commented on it. Both agreed on the dire need for religious tolerance and accommodation, and that the essence of Christianity was not Trinity but the humanity of Jesus. Loving God and loving one's neighbour summarised that essence. "When Jesus was asked what was the great commandment of the law, he answered that it was to love God, and he added that the second commandment was to love your neighbour. This was the religion of the sons of Noah established by Moses & Christ & still in force."[1857]

Newton contended that "Loving God and Loving one's neighbour" was the universal religion revealed to all the prophets from Noah to Jesus. Trinitarianism or incarnation were not part of this pristine universal religion; therefore, persecuting those Christians who denied Trinity was equal to waging war on Christ. "To impose now any article of communion that was not such from the beginning was to preach another gospel. To persecute Christians for not receiving that Gospel was to make war on Christ. The two great commandments, he insisted over and over, 'always have & always will be the duty of all nations & The coming of Jesus Christ has made no alteration in them.' As often as mankind has turned from them, God has made a reformation - through Noah, Abraham, Moses, the Jewish prophets, and Jesus. Now that the gentiles had corrupted themselves, men must expect a new reformation."[1858] Church Christianity, with its centuries-long persecution of anti-Trinitarian Christians, was an open war against Christ and his Unitarianism. That war needed to stop; therefore, Newton asked for reformation of the corrupted Church Christianity in conformity with the original prophetic tradition. Newton said "and in all the reformations of religion hitherto made the religion in respect of God & our neighbour is one & the same religion (barring ceremonies & forms of government which are of a changeable nature) so that this is the oldest religion in the world."[1859] The knowledge of this ethical monotheism was universal; all humans could identify the moral commandments with the help of natural reason. The salvation depended on following the moral commandments of God, and not on Trinitarian or incarnational belief. "Thus you see there is but one law for all nations the law of righteousness & charity dictated to the Christians by Christ to the Jews by Moses & to all mankind by the light of reason & by this law all men are to be judged at the last day."[1860] This is exactly what Stubbe and Locke emphasized upon. The same Islamic insistence upon the moral laws was very much on the mind of Newton.

As discussed above, Newton did address Jesus as "Lord" as a token of respect and glory, without any divine designations. "Newton argued, we are to believe in one God and in one Lord, Jesus Christ, who is next to him in power and glory. All this was taught from the beginning in the primitive church."[1861] He, like Locke, entertained the pre-existence of Christ in a reverential fashion and in no way or form in the ontological sense. His Jesus was a full human, who was dignified and glorified by God Almighty for a dignified ethical mission. This unity was not the unity of essence, substance or Godhead but a unity of purpose, will and dominion. Jesus' Lordship was God-given and not begotten. "The Arian features of Newton's christology continued to be evident. Although we are to worship Christ as Lord, "yet we are to do it without breaking the first commandment." The true manhood of Christ was important to Newton, who believed that trinitarianism effectively denied his manhood, and with it the reality of his suffering on the cross. However, "he was not an ordinary man but incarnate by the almighty power of God & born of a Virgin without any other father then God himself." That is, Newton had reached back to the primitive church to resurrect a concept of Christ as a human body animated by a divine or semidivine spirit. He rejected any notion of a unity of substance between God the Father and Christ the Son, and asserted instead what he called a monarchical unity "a unity of Dominion, the Son receiving all things from the father, being subject to him, executing his will, sitting in his throne & calling him his God, & so is but one God with the Father as a king & his viceroy are but one king. For the word God relates not to the metaphysical nature of God but to his dominion."[1862]

He did not accept Jesus or any other mediator between man and God; only Almighty God deserved the worship. Newton was emphatically elaborate on this point: "We are therefore to acknowledge one God infinite eternal omnipresent, omniscient omnipotent, the creator of all things most wise, most just, most good most holy: & to have no other Gods but him. We must love him feare him honour him trust in him pray to him give him thanks praise him hollow his name obey his commandments & set times apart for his service as we are directed in the third & fourth commandments. For this is the love of God that we keep his commandments & his commandments are not grievous 1 John 5.3. These things we must do not to any mediators between him & us but to him alone, that he may give his Angels charge over us who being our fellow servants are pleased with the worship which we give to their God. And this is the first & principal part of religion. This always was & always will be the religion of all Gods people, from the beginning to the end of the world."[1863]

Newton's Christianity was free of mysteries, paradoxes, superstitions and supernatural jargons. He desired to revive the simple, original, monotheistic Christianity by purging the Church's Christianity and its scriptures of their corruptions and returning to the original purity of the Gospel of Jesus. "Newton set out at an early age to purge Christianity of irrationality, mystery, and superstition, and he never turned from that path. His study of the prophecies, the work most frequently cited in support of a contrary interpretation of his religion, was in fact one of the cornerstones of his program. True, he undertook to purge Christianity in the name of Gospel purity, but in the light of the role that Arianism played in the early church and the role that it and its offspring played in the Eighteenth century, one cannot view Newton's Arianism in isolation from the intellectual currents of his day. Rather we do him more justice and acknowledge anew his manifest genius by allowing that here too he stood in the van, although the very reform of Christianity he sought to foster was already, in his old age, surging far beyond the limits he had envisaged."[1864]

Newton's Bible mostly consisted of two books: *Daniel* and *Revela-*

tion. The rest of the Bible was mixed up with man's words, and was dubious in nature. "He justified himself in terms of the Bible, but the Bible as he understood it was far removed from the Bible of traditional belief. Where that Bible contained truths beyond reason, Newton summed up true religion in terms that effectively dispensed with all of revelation beyond the prophecies. Christians for centuries had understood divine revelation in terms of a new dispensation foretold in the Old Testament and fulfilled in the New; divine revelation as Newton understood it centered on two books, *Daniel* and *Revelation*, which revealed the almighty dominion of God over history as natural philosophy revealed His dominion over nature. Newton questioned the plenary inspiration of the received canon of books and regarded the historical books of the Old Testament as the compilations of men."[1865] His Christology was humanistic, his soteriology moralistic and his monotheism was simplistic. "Though he wrote at some length about Christ, his interest largely exhausted itself in proving that Christ was not God. His soteriology, the focus of traditional Christian concern, was uninspired and jejune, substituting a mere legal pact for the reconciliation of fallen man to the majesty of God which generations of theologians had explored. The two fundamental duties of true religion, to love God and to love one's neighbour, seem to present the opportunity for spiritual insight."[1866]

Newton's Heterodoxy

Newton refused to take sacraments, seldom attended Church services and kept his heterodox theological views to himself or to his close circle of confidants.[1867] Snobelen noted that "Isaac Newton was a heretic. But like Nicodemus, the secret disciple of Jesus, he never made a public declaration of his private faith-which the orthodox would have deemed extremely radical. He hid his faith so well that scholars are still unravelling his personal beliefs."[1868] He camouflaged conformity to the Church of England's articles of faith in public. "Whereas Newton published statements of his belief in God, he not only kept the unorthodox aspects of his religion to himself, but he exercised some care in London to mask his heterodoxy behind a facade of public conformity."[1869] But his infidelity was not that hidden from the Orthodoxy.[1870] Thomas Hearne noted in 1732: "Sir Isaac Newton, tho' a great Mathematician, was a man of very little Religion, in so much that he is ranked with the Heterodox men of the age. Nay they stick not to make him, with respect to belief, of no better principles than Mr. Woolaston [corrected later to Wolston], who hath written so many vile books and made so much noise."[1871]

Stephen David Snobelen, in *Isaac Newton, Socinianism and the One Supreme God*, has proven beyond doubt that Newton was an Arian leaning towards Socinian.[1872] "Newton's Christology was [...] further from orthodoxy than Socinianism."[1873] There are "Socinian parallels in Newton's theology, historiography, textual criticism, biblical hermeneutics and even his natural philosophy."[1874] He further states that "Newton denied the Trinity and the Socinians were the most intellectually sophisticated anti-Trinitarians of his time."[1875] In addition to Locke, Newton associated with Samuel Krell, the grandson of the known Socinian Jonathan Krell, patronised him, possessed eight Socinian books, had access to his friends Samuel Crell, John Locke and Bishop John Moor's huge Socinian collections, like Socininas wanted to reform the Church Christianity in conformity with the primitive, monotheistic Christianity, used Socinian scriptural hermeneutics, reflected their theological influence in his writings such as *General Scholium* and *Optics* and believed in religious tolerance, just like them. Snobelen advises that "scholars of Newton's theology and natural philosophy must take seriously his use of Socinianism — particularly because it helps explain so much of his thought. One suspects that the last word has not been said on Isaac Newton and Socinianism."[1876]

Just like Locke, Newton rejected the doctrines of original sin, satisfaction through crucifixion, and clerical authority. In his church history Newton stated, "the nature of the satisfaction made by Christ" among a list of adiaphora "more difficult to be understood and not so absolutely necessary to salvation."[1877] Newton believed in the alternate monotheistic and republican narrative; he, like the Socinians, wanted reformation of Reformation on primitive Unitarian principles. "Both the Socinians and Newton were keen to restore the original doctrines of Christianity, and both desired a 'second' reformation."[1878] Newton was more radical in his reformatory scheme than even some of his Socinian fellows.[1879] Snobelen noted that "Newton's Nicodemite strategy of outwardly confirming to orthodoxy while secretly harbouring heretical beliefs mirrors that of such crypto-Unitarians as Stephen Nye, who came of age at the same time as Newton. And Newton's Nicodemism was both passive and active, as he was not only a secret heretic, but his 'Two notable corruptions' and General Scholium reveal that he was also actively engaged in an antitrinitarian reformist programme. His actions thus show that he was directly or indirectly a player in the subversive Socinian-Unitarian agenda in both the 1690s and the 1710s."[1880]

Moreover, Newton's beliefs show affinity with radical and dissenting theologies of Stubbe and other dissenters like the continental radical Reformists and British non-conformists, especially the Unitarians. Snobelen notes that "Much of the antitrinitarian argumentation of writers like John Biddle, who is often termed 'the father of Unitarianism,' and Stephen Nye, is isomorphic with that of Newton. Additionally, Newton's near intervention in the Trinitarian controversy of the late 1680s and early 1690s reveals that he shared some common reformist goals with the British Unitarians. Newton's anti-Athanasian *Paradoxical questions* is part of the same genre as the *Unitarian Tracts* of the 1690s. Newton owned at least one collection of the *Unitarian Tracts* and would have been familiar with the teachings of the movement that produced them – a movement that developed its theology contemporaneously with Newton."[1881]

Newton's close friends knew about his Unitarianism. "Richard Baron, an abrasive unitarian who described Haynes years later as 'the most zealous unitarian; he had ever known, reported that Haynes had told him Newton held the same views, and Haynes himself criticised Newton for not leading a new Reformation."[1882] Maurice Wiles noted that "despite his secretiveness about his theological views, the heretical tendency of Newton's beliefs was not unknown to some of his contemporaries. William Whiston, his successor as Lucasian Professor at Cambridge, described him as one whose study led him to recognise that 'what has long been called Arianism is no other than old uncorrupt Christianity'. Hopton Haynes, on the other hand, Newton's close associate over many years at the Mint, is reported to have said of Newton that he did not believe in Christ's pre-existence, being in that respect a Socinian, and that he much 'lamented Mr Clarke's embracing Arianism, which opinion he feared had been, and still was, if maintained by learned men, a great obstruction to the progress of Christianity.'"[1883] This statement substantiates the fact that Newton and William Whiston were more radical in their human Christology and anti-Trinitarianism than many Arians of their time.[1884] Even the slightest postulate of Jesus' semi-divinity in the sense of Godhead was totally preposterous to Newton.

Newton's close friends and students went public with their heretical Unitarians views, and were persecuted by the Church of England.[1885] The Orthodoxy blamed Newton for his students' heresies. "When Joseph Hallet, alarmed by the spread of Arianism, published in 1735 *An Address to Coriform*-to convince them of their hypocrisy and to lead them to repent, he named two men as the source of the infection, William Whiston and Samuel Clarke. Both were Newton's disciples and known as such. Later another disciple, Hopton Haynes, would publish unitarian tracts, and a more aggressive unitarian, Richard Baron, would lament that Samuel Clarke, who had performed good work in purging Christianity of much absurdity and rubbish, had stopped short in Arianism when a fully rational Christianity lay only another step beyond. But Newton's extended quest, barely hinted at in his published works, had to enter the stream of religious controversy through disciples more daring than he."[1886] Just like his friend Locke, Newton was attacked by Jonathan Edwards as a "Turk" and a "Socinian." "Edwards' attack demonstrates, a theologically-astute contemporary observer had no trouble identifying Newton's theology with Socinianism."[1887]

It is astonishing to see some Orthodox leaders and writers ascribing Trinitarian[1888] beliefs to Newton in the face of such an exhaustive number of solid proofs. Wiles noted that "in the years after his death, a host of orthodox Trinitarians, unwilling to admit that so respected a figure could have been tainted with heresy, did their best to deny his antitrinitarianism. In 1831, when he wrote his *Life of Sir Isaac Newton*, David Brewster had, as he was later to admit, 'no hesitation in coming to the conclusion that he was a believer in the Trinity'. He argued that when, in his discussion of the inauthenticity of 1 John 5:7, Newton pointed out that 'for a long time [...] the faith subsisted without this text,' the context required that 'faith' there must mean 'faith in the particular doctrine of the Trinity.' But that conviction was rudely overthrown by Brewster's examination of Newton's unpublished manuscripts in 1836, where he found expressions of opinion adverse to his own, and, as he judged, to those of the great majority of Newton's admirers."[1889]

In spite of such Orthodox subterfuge and violence to Newton's thought and theology, the majority of contemporary scholarship in the field counts him among the Arians, Socinians and Unitarians of his time.[1890] Newton was an integral part and a product of his seventeenth-century milieu in which Socinians, Unitarians, Muhammadan Christians, Deists and anti-Trinitarian Church leaders played havoc to the Church establishment and English monarchy. Newton, like Locke, was an integral part of this theological revolution against the *Old Regime* and its theological foundations. This anti-Trinitarian, anti-Incarnational and anti-absolutism revolution changed the way Englishmen looked at the Christian religion, theology, insitutions and monarchy. They gradually replaced the Trinitarian God of historical Christianity with a totally different God of ethical monotheism. The theological revolution was as significant as the Newtonian revolution in the natural sciences; in fact, the Newtonian scientific revolution was a result of, and an implementation of Newton's theological revolution, as Stephen Snobelen has amply demonstrated.[1891] Newton's scientific discoveries were a reflection and embodiment of his Unitarian, monotheistic revolution against the the Trinitarian, paganistic and tri-theistic Church Christianity. Newton's famous scientific works such as *The General Scholium*, and the *Principia* were as much subversive critique of the Trinity and other Christian corruptions as his theological treatises.[1892] Jonathan Ewards was appalled at Newton's subtle attacks on the Trinity and the Christian religion as a whole.[1893] Newton's Unitarian revolution was too much to be ignored by the Orthodoxy. Both the theological and scientific revolutions changed the intellectual landscape of Europe, ushering in a new era of rationalism, liberty and republicanism. Newton must be credited with the historical anti-Trinitarian theological revolution as is he credited with revolution in natural sciences. Europe's break with the suffocating absolute Church and monarchy of the Middle Ages and its transition to modernity passes through Locke and Newton, and they shall be credited for that. Their Socinian/Unitarian monotheistic and republican ideologies greatly contributed to ensuing religious tolerance, liberty, constitutional monarchy and human rights.

In England during the Restoration period in 1660, as observed by Justin Champion, Clark[1894] and J. G. A. Pocock, Socinianism and Unitarians[1895] appear to have extended its influence to the highest levels due to their financial power.[1896] As Unitarians and Socinians were not allowed the public and state offices, they were forced to join business and trade. They received help from the middle tier of the Levant, East India and Puritan American merchants who supported Puritan republican theology. Many known, resourceful and well-connected merchants of the later seventeenth century subscribed to the Unitarian/Socinian outlook. Pocock noted that "from the days of John Locke and Archbishop Tillotson there existed a Socinian undercurrent within the church itself, and a hierarchy willing to recognise its presence so long as it confined itself to the serious and by no means clandestine sphere of private discussion as distinct from public profession."[1897] The coterie surrounding the philanthropist Thomas Firmin (1632–1697),[1898] an "avowed Socinian and a Unitarian, included Locke, Tillotson (the future Archbishop of Canterbury), and minor members of the Anglican Church, such as Stephen Nye (1648–1719) and Henry Hedworth (1626–1705). Such was the ubiquity of the movement that Andrew Marvell was able to comment in the same year that 'the Socinian books are tolerated and sell as openly as the Bible.'"[1899] Perhaps the most widespread of Socinian influences was reflected in the Anglican Church's direction of broad religious toleration, and in the tendency of some leading Church leaders to reduce the essentials of Christianity to the minimal important elements such as the Messianic role of Christ, the trend usually referred to as Latitudinarianism.[1900] Many members of the clergy publicly recited the Trinitarian Athanasian Creed, as required by the Church in public worship, thirteen times a year but with a twinge of conscience and without much faith in its validity or authenticity. Reflecting the Socinian/Unitarian theological impact, even Archbishop of Canterbury John Tillotson (1630–1694) said "I wish we were well-rid of it."[1901] Pocock observed that this dialectical environment was the foundational source of early Enlightenment. "Tensions within the established church, between establishment and dissent, and within dissent itself, provide the context in which English Enlightenment must be seen."[1902] The Socinians and Unitarians, along with other rational dissenters, were the instigators and facilitators of the early Enlightenment, and hence of later liberty, democracy and modernity, as G. M. Trevelyan, W. E. H. Lecky and many others have noted.[1903] Newton's connections with the overseas trading companies, their military pursuits and with dissenting merchants of London are well-documented by Merton and others, as discussed above. Newton was an integral part of the Unitarian religio-political and scienctific reformative scheme.

Chapter 13

English Unitarians: Pinnacle
of Islamic Hybrid

The Unitarians since the times of Servetus had believed that Prophet Muhammad was a "Unitarian Prophet" and Islam was a Unitarian reformation of the Roman Christianity. This close connection was made public by the eighteenth-century English Unitarians. John Tolan noted "in the wake of the toleration act, English Unitarians wrote pamphlets defending their beliefs as consistent with primitive Christianity; they of course published these pamphlets anonymously. Like earlier Unitarians such as Miguel Servet, they took antitrinitarian arguments from the Qur'ān and saw Muhammad as a Unitarian reformer. *The Naked Gospel* (1691), probably by Arthur Bury, asks rhetorically 'whether Mahomet or the Christian doctors have more corrupted the Gospel?' His charge against Christian Trinitarian theologians makes clear what the answer is for him."[1904] Other Unitarians, such as Stephen Nye, went further than that. "In the same year, *A letter of resolution concerning the doctrines of the Trinity and the Incarnation*, probably by Stephen Nye, presents Mahomet as closer to the truth of the Gospel than Trinitarian Christianity, in a passage that shows familiarity with Stubbe. Mahomet, he affirms, did not try to create a new religion, 'but to restore the Belief of the Unity of God, which at the time was extirpated among the Eastern Christians, by the Doctrines of the Trinity and Incarnation.' Muslims affirm that they are 'the true Disciples of the Messias or Christ,' while 'Christians are Apostates from the most essential Parts of the Doctrine of the Messias; such as the Unity of God.' God is to be worshipped without use of images. Muslims and Jews 'are perpetually and without hope of regaining them, alienated from us, that they suppose the Trinity to be the Doctrine of all Christians; and from thence conclude, that modern Christianity is no better nor other than a sort of

Paganism and Heathenism.""[1905] Nye was a close friend of Locke; Locke's extensive notes taken from the works of Biddle and Nye demonstrate the level of influence the Unitarian writings had upon Locke.

Like his Socinian associations, Locke's Unitarian affinities are also well-attested. He befriended Anglican theologians such as Arthur Bury (1624–1714), Stephen Nye (1648–1719), and William Freke (1662-1744), who willingly acknowledged the prescriptive value of Islamic reformation, wrote about its validity, and never hesitated to share their thoughts and writing with other thinkers, including Locke. These Unitarians were fully engaged in the Unitarian controversy of 1700 and Locke was also absorbed in it, siding with the Unitarians. "By 1700 Locke possessed eight works by Stephen Nye, including the *Brief History of the Unitarians.* He owned a shoal of slim anonymous tracts like the 1690 *Brief Notes Upon the Creed of St Athanasius*, and its re-daction *The Acts of Great Athanasius*, which assaulted Athanasius, the fourth-century credal formulator of co-equal, coeternal and consub-stantial persons in the Godhead. More significantly, Locke owned five works by Arthur Bury, including the *Naked Gospel.* In the 1690s Locke owned John Biddle's *The Apostolical and True Opinion Concerning the Trinity',* perhaps most famous for its assault upon trinitarians' delu-sions of 'personalities, moods, subsistencies, and such-like brain-sick notions' hatched by Platonists to pervert the worship of God.""[1906] Locke especially read Nye with great enthusiasm, and Nye was the most vol-uble about Unitarian Islamic syncretism. These Unitarian Muslim sympathisers insisted upon Christian reformation in conformity with Islamic monotheism and republicanism. Therefore, Locke was an es-sential part of that reformatory scheme.

John Marshall notes that "between 1687 and approximately 1700 there was a major debate over the Trinity in England which became known as the 'Unitarian Controversy'. This controversy began when the Unitarians took advantage of the relaxation of the press under James II to disseminate their views and it burned particularly fiercely in the early 1690s when many Anglicans, including leading Latitudi-narian Anglicans such as Tillotson, Fowler, Burnet and Stillingfleet, wrote lengthy accounts defending the Athanasian Trinity and in turn provoked further Unitarian works. The Unitarian Controversy was sparked by publication of Stephen Nye's (anonymous) *Brief History of the Unitarians,* which first gave the term 'unitarian' prominence in

England to indicate all those who accented the superiority of God the Father to Jesus Christ and the Holy Ghost, and thus joined the Arians who believed after Arius in a pre-existent but not eternal Christ with the Socinians who followed Socinus in believing that Christ was neither pre-existent nor eternal."[1907]

Locke sent Nye's *Brief History of the Unitarians* to Jean le Clerc in Amsterdam, who reviewed it positively in *Bibliotheque Universelle*. Locke collected the Unitarian books for Benjamin Furly, as is clear from his correspondence with Furly. He discussed these works with Isaac Newton, who himself was heavily engaged in the Unitarian controversy. "In 1690 Locke's notes show that he either discussed three Unitarian works with Newton or procured them for him. It is quite possible that Newton's willingness to send Locke his manuscript criticisms of Trinitarian texts as early as 1690 indicates that Locke had revealed to Newton that he was antitrinitarian by that date."[1908] Moreover, Locke was closely affiliated with the Unitarian publisher Thomas Firmin who had commissioned Stephen Nye's book. "Locke had known the Unitarian merchant Thomas Firmin since 1671 at the latest, and was probably a member of the circle of intellectuals that Firmin hosted in the 1670s and 1680s. In the late 1680s and early 1690s Firmin was the 'great promoter of Socinianism' who commissioned Stephen Nye's *Brief History of the Unitarians* and many of his other works, financed several collections of Unitarian tracts, and almost certainly financed their free distribution as well."[1909] Therefore, Locke was well aware of the Unitarian Islamic syncretism, well absorbed in the Unitarian controversy of 1690s to 1700 and well appreciative of their struggles totally siding with them against their orthodox detractors.

Stephen Nye: The Roaring Unitarian

Stephen Nye (1648–1719), an English clergyman and "rector of Little Hormead for a period of forty years,"[1910] perhaps was the most emphatic Unitarian to refute the Church dogmas, mysteries, and abusive authority. In his *Brief History of the Unitarians, called also Socinians*, first published in 1687 and republished in 1691, Nye categorically denied that the Christianity of his time had anything to do with the original message of Jesus Christ; Trinitarian Christianity was a degradation and depravation of the genuine Christian message of One and Only God. "Nye claimed that the Scriptures were clear that God is one person. In the Scriptures God is referred to in the singular: I, thou, me, him. To interpret these pronouns as referring to a Trinity of persons is 'contrary to custom, grammar and sense'. He dismissed the doctrine of the Trinity as 'absurd, and contrary both to Reason and to itself, and therefore not only false, but impossible. To claim that there are three persons and yet one God was simply "an error in counting." The 'Letter' concluded by tracing a pedigree for unitarianism back to the New Testament, and attempted to demonstrate how the original apostolic doctrine had been corrupted!"[1911]

Nye's extensive publications were sponsored by Thomas Firmin, the Socinian/Unitarian philanthropist who also supported Locke and other Latitudinarian Bishops' works. As seen above, Locke was the other milder side of Henry Stubbe in the 1670s while both were working for Shaftesbury. In the 1680s and 1690s he became the milder side of Stephen Nye's radical revolution while in patronage of Thomas Firmin. Locke was the moderate propounder and expositor of the same radical Unitarian revolution.

Nye was more pronounced Unitarian than Locke, Newton, Socinians and other anti-Trinitarians; he called a spade a spade. "Nye was opposed to what he took to be the tritheism of most contemporary orthodox Trinitarianism, to Arianism which he dismisses 'as only a more absurd and less defensible Tritheism' than the orthodox view, and to the teaching of Socinus whom he describes as 'having not the least tincture of academical, much less of theological learning'. Socinianism was a misnomer for the Unitarianism he himself professed. His own position was of a modalist or Sabellian nature; claiming the authority of Augustine's non-personalized understanding of the Trinity, he believed himself justified in presenting his own Unitarian understanding of the person of Christ as true to traditional Christian teaching."[1912] He argued that Christ can be called God as the embodiment of God's will and absolute submission to God's commandments. The Trinitarian language was reverential rather than metaphysical. "Christ is God, and Man [...] God in respect of God in him [...] not only occasionally assisting [...] but [...] always in Christ, illuminating, conducting and actuating him. More than this is the heresy of Eutyches."[1913]

Nye refuted Old Testament texts cited as proof for the doctrine of the Trinity. He denied that any of the Old Testament books ever predicted the coming of a divine Messiah or a Trinitarian incarnational system of belief. "Nye comments slyly that the 'more learned and judicious trinitarians,' such as Jerome and Bellarmine, agreed with him on this. Moreover, it would be inherently odd, argued Nye, that the Jews were not corrected by Christ for believing God to be one person if God were really three."[1914] He also noted that all New Testament texts quoted to prove Trinity did not prove it and carried alternate Unitarian meanings. Like Newton, Nye blamed St. Athanasius and his priestly party of corrupting the pristine message of Jesus.

The original followers of Jesus were Nazarenes who, like the original Apostles, maintained the unipersonality of God. Nye "invoked the pattern of the Nazarenes, an early Judaeo-Christian sect, as the legitimate ancestors of the Unitarian movement."[1915] That pristine message had only survived in the Turkish or Mahomaten tradition. The "historical model of pre-Nicene Unitarianism, and its links with Islam, was reiterated and reinforced by Nye in his *Letter of Resolution Concerning the Doctrines of the Trinity and Incarnation* (1695)."[1916] He strongly criticised Church teachings such as worship of Mary, saints and images, ecclesiastical authority and tradition, papal supremacy, indulgences, the mystery of transubstantiation, original sin, and satisfaction through crucifixion. "The Apostles' Creed and the Nazarene faith were both the most ancient beliefs and 'the very doctrines that are now called Socinian'. The Athanasian Trinity established at Nicea was the historical font of all Christian corruption. The supremacy of the papacy, worship of the Virgin Mary, saints, images, the mystery of transubstantiation, the authority of Church tradition, papal indulgences and the theology of Christ's satisfaction, were all doctrinal accretions grown out of the corrupt Trinitarian Christology."[1917]

To Nye, all these corruptions were post-Nicean extensions of the corrupt Trinitarian theology, the major stumbling block between Judaism, Islam and Christianity. "Nye insisted that Trinitarianism was a corruption of heathen Platonism which confused 'properties of the Divine nature for persons, or willfully and affectedly allegoris'd them into persons'. The doctrines of the Trinity and Incarnation, according to Nye, were the main obstacles between Christianity and Islam and Judaism."[1918]

Nye defended Islam and Mohammad as true reflections of Jesus' message: "Mahomet had 'no other design in pretending himself to be a prophet, but to restore the belief of the Unity of God. Mahomet proclaimed himself disciple of the 'Messias or Christ' aiming to restore the Unitarian 'true intent of the Christian religion'. Mahomet's success in converting Asia, Africa and part of Europe was not to be attributed to the force of arms but to 'that one truth in the Alkoran, the unity of God. '"[1919] Locke's claims of Muhammad borrowing the Unitarian belief system of Jesus, as discussed above, were a moderate form of Nye's radical argument.

Locke used Nye's and other Unitarian works to defend himself against Bishop Stillingfleet's attacks.[1920] Locke was an ardent reader of Nye taking careful notes and well appreciative of his strong Unitarian arguments against Trinity, original sin, satisfaction by atoning death, predestination, Jesus' humanity, human liberty and freedom, content of natural religion known by reason and many other important Unitarian theological views.[1921] Locke commented on Nye's books and views in his correspondence with friends; in brief, Locke was the moderate side of Nye's radical coin

Arthur Bury's Naked Gospel

Locke was also well acquainted with Arthur Bury, read his works and shared them with friends. For instance, he discussed Bury's *Naked Gospel* with James Tyrrell, Locke's best friend and brother-in-law of Deist Charles Blount. Locke frequented Tyrrell's residence, especially before leaving for Amsterdam.

Bury's 1690 anti-trinitarian work, *The Naked Gospel*, first published anonymously, was commanded to burning at Oxford, and in a complex sequence of events involving legal action, Bury lost his position as rector of Exeter College, Oxford after being expelled initially in 1689. He contended that Christianity had changed so much "that were any Apostle to return into the world, he would be so far from Owning, that he would not be able to understand it [...] Whether Mahomet, or Christian Doctors have more corrupted the Gospel, it is not so plain by the light of Scripture, as it is by that of Experience [...] For when by nice and hot disputes (especially concerning the Second and Third Persons of the Trinity) the minds of the whole people had been long confounded, and by the then late stablishment of Image worship, the scandal was encreased; so that the Vulgar Understandings of the Doctrine of the Trinity appeared no less guilty of Polytheism, than that of Image-worship did of Idolatry."[1922]

Bury's *Naked Gospel* indicted the Christian Scriptures, dogmas, mysteries, as Church corruptions.[1923] He demanded purification of Christian Scripture by purging them of human additions and Church manipulations. This action would clear Christianity of irrational mysteries invented by the priestcraft after the Council of Nicea. Dusting off mysteries would let the original message of Jesus and the Gospel shine. To Bury, that essential message was to love your God and love your neighbour or "repent and believe."[1924] "The result of this would be that, rather than the mysteries of faith which he considered the product of the historical rise of priestcraft after the post-Nicene Athanasian Creed, the simple dogma of the Gospel in its largest edition would be 'repent and believe.'"[1925] Morality and charity, rather than the mysterious dogmas, were needed to attain salvation. The Church was neither the mediator nor the dispenser of grace and salvation; everybody had direct access to God and salvation through love, charity and morality. He concluded his book observing that the "end of all is to determine between Faith and Love [...] Give unto Faith the things that are Faith's and the Love that are Love's [...] Do good to all especially to those that are of the household of Faith."[1926]

In the preface of this book, Bury refuted the Church establishment's claims that Mohammad was an imposter and that Islam was spread with the power of sword rather than God's providence. As seen above, it has been argued since St. Augustine's time that due to merit and divine providence, Christ's message prevailed over the old Jewish message; although Jesus came from a meek background and his early followers were illiterate fishermen, his message succeeded against educated philosophers and powerful kings due to divine providence. Bury used the same argument to defend Islam and Mohammad. He argued: "So the victories of the Alcoran over the Gospel must be evidence, that as the religion of Moses was better than that of the Canaanites, and the religion of Christ better than that of Moses; so must the religion of Mahomet be better than that of Christ. Thus may a Mahometan either disarm us of St. Augustine's argument, or restore it against us; for either it is of no force at all or of so much more force for Mahomet, by how much more he hath prevailed over the Churches of Christ."[1927] Muhammad's reformation of Trinitarian Christianity succeeded due to divine providence. He noted "that to suggest the rise of Islam was not the product of divine providence was in effect to deny the existence of a divine guide [...] Mahomet was 'not an apostate, but a reformer': his task was one of purification. The Islamic prophet was cast in the mould of Christian reformer, professing Christian and monotheistic articles of belief."[1928] Bury rejected Alexander Ross and Humphrey Prideaux's contention that Muhammad was a divine scourage, and insisted on the positive reformatory designs of Muhammad's message. "Bury's analysis was a clever piece of insinuation. Christianity in the East had become corrupt through the manipulation of the Gospel; it was Mahomet's good fortune to re-institute the true gospel, which in Bury's view was Unitarian. In opposition to Ross's providential scheme which presented Islam as a scourge and deformed image of pristine Christianity, Bury considered Islam within its own terms. Islam was not a misshapen mirror image of Christianity, but an object of commendation."[1929]

The positive and reformatory approach of Bury was scolded by the Orthodoxy as the most destructive conspiracy against the Christian religion and world, the epitome of Christian destruction. They accused Bury of being a Quranic exegete and a Muslim conspirator. John Meggitt notes that "On the one hand early Unitarians regularly found themselves described as being virtually synonymous with Muslims, as 'more Mahometan than Christian', with the Racovian Catechism dismissed as the 'Racovian Alcoran'. An important antitrinitarian writing, Arthur Bury's Naked Gospel (1690), could be accused of being so like the Quran that it amounted to no more than 'a Commentary on that Text'. There was a clear attempt to associate this form of dissent with a religion that was largely viewed as a work of 'imposture', something dangerously alluring but blasphemous, diabolical, and – given the dominance of the Ottoman empire and anxiety about the depredations of Barbary slavers – physically threatening."[1930] The Orthodoxy and its vanguard played on public fear by using centuries-old stereotypes against Islam and Muslims by highlighting Ottoman hegemonic designs against England. Unitarian Islamic republicanism was a danger to both Christian faith and politics.

William Freke: The Mystic Unitarian

William Freke (1662-1744) was an English mystical writer, of Wadham College, Oxford and a barrister of the Temple. He was also a friend of John Locke. He suffered at the hands of Parliament in 1694 for his anti-Trinitarian beliefs. William Freke sent his *Brief but Clear Confutation of the Doctrine of the Trinity* to both Houses of Parliament, which fined him and burned the book in response. Justin Champion noted that "William Freke [...] who suffered at the hands of Parliament in 1694 for his anti-Trinitarian beliefs, emphasised the connection between the Unitarian insistence on the unity of God and Islamic monotheism."[1931]

In his *Vindication of the Unitarians,* Freke "subtly equates the Unitarian creed with Islamic monotheism and 'the unity in the Alchoran', while maintaining that orthodox Anglicans, in their support of the corrupt pagan doctrine of the Trinity, are actually endorsing an oppressive 'popery'. Because of their belief in God's unity and their toleration of other non- Muslim religions, the Mahometans have experienced more prosperity, politically, economically, and spiritually, than have the adherents of Western Christendom, whether Catholic, Protestant, or Anglican."[1932] Like Stubbe and Toland, Freke connected Ottoman might, prosperity and success with their Unitarian pluralistic republicanism. This insinuation was detrimental to the authority of Anglican Church and state; both came hard on Freke, and persecuted him with passion.

Freke noted that he had "fallen into 'Arianisme' while searching the New Testament for scriptural evidence for the Trinity. Adopting a commonplace Unitarian argument, he insisted that there was as just a case for the truth of the Trinity as there was for the absurd Catholic mystery of transubstantiation. The notion of a triple Godhead offended all 'Jews, Turks, and Pagans': it was the ground on which Mahomet had based his division from Christianity. As Freke noted, the Koran contained 'above a hundred' indictments of the dogma. One of the central historical arguments was that the Trinity had only become part of Christian creed some three hundred years after Christ's death."[1933] The Quranic criticism of the Trinity, and its detailed arguments, had been employed by the Unitarians since the time of Michael Servetus and were internalised by the Socinian/Unitarians and Deists by the middle of the seventeenth century. Freke was referring to this long tradition of Unitarian Islamic hybrid.

The Trinity was nothing but "the Platonick Philosophy made Christian."[1934] The mankind was at a loss to comprehend it, "the World is made too giddy by this Mystery, to bear such, or any other Reasoning."[1935] It was imposed upon Christians by Roman might and manipulations.[1936] They fabricated the supernatural Church tradition against the simple scripture, manipulated the Councils and created the facts which were not part of the divine truth, "You must excuse me therefore, if I think

Tradition to be too much a Nose of "Wax, to be alledg'd against Scripture."[1937] Freke was appalled that the Church of England had de-emphasised the role of good works and re-emphasised repetition of unintelligible creedal formulas: "See how your Mystery has missed you, Sir, that Men should be sav'd, only by parrotting over a few unintelligible words."[1938] Christianity's focus upon original sin and fallen nature at the expense of God's forgiveness and love is "fitter for paganism than Christianity" and can be preached only "by a dead anathematising implicit Faith."[1939] Unlike the Church's riches and resources, the Unitarians had only the truth on their side; they neither showed the arrogance of knowledge nor practiced the politics of knowledge. They had truth as clear as the day light, but the Church was afraid of that truth.[1940] The Church had made a nonsense of the First Commandment and introduced the absurdity of multiple persons in the Godhead. The Protestant scriptural evidences for the Trinity were as feeble as the Catholic evidence for transubstantiation.[1941] Both Churches maintained and preserved the mysteries by persecutions and not by the force of the argument. "Mystery and Persecution are the Devil's Twins, and stand and fall both together; Persecution without Mystery were too cruel, and Mystery without Blood too much Nonsense to be born; 'tis these two are Popery, and the worst of Popery, Transubstantiation without these were an innocent Error."[1942]

Freke criticised the Christian dogma of Christ's two natures and showed the inherent absurdity of making Jesus look like a split personality. "So, what an Answer you have there, that the Son was tempted as to his Manhood, but not as to his Godhead; And pray then where was the Godhead all the while, like Baal's asleep; or was the Man Christ now and then as it were possessed by Fits? Methinks I am assum'd to handle the Absurdities of this Hypothesis, they make me giddy when I consider them."[1943] Consequently he recommended replacing this confusing Trinitarian jargon with the simple Unitarian faith of Islam. Meggitt observes that "it is also important to note that although the claims about the affinities between Unitarianism and Islam were intended to be damning, they were not always understood that way by Unitarians themselves. Although some could be 'enraged' by the association with Islam, William Freke, for example, was happy to praise Muhammad and the Quran for defending the unity of God against the errors of trinitarian Christians, and Stephen Nye could talk favourably about

Muhammad as someone who set out 'to restore the Belief of the Unity of GOD, which at that time was extirpated among the Eastern Christians, by the Doctrines of the Trinity and Incarnation [...] Mahomet meant not his Religion should be esteemed a new Religion, but only the Restitution of the true Intent of the Christian Religion'. Bury could say that 'Mahomet professed all the articles of the Christian faith.'"[1944]

Anti-Trinitarianism was closely connected with Islam since Michael Servetus's time. This close identification became a norm by the eighteenth century to the extent that they were used interchangeably by the Orthodoxy, as well as by the leading writers of that time. "Such language reflected the common assumption, found even on occasions where they were not targets of polemic, that antitrinitarian Christianity had a strong affinity with Islam. Indeed, somewhat later, we can find Gibbon using the term 'Unitarian', in his famous *The History of the Decline and Fall of the Roman Empire*, to refer to Muhammad, picking up on language that can be found at the beginning of Eighteenth century, if not before."[1945] There was a direct and continuous line of Muhammadan Christians from Henry Stubbe, John Toland to Stephen Nye, Arthur Bury, William Freke and many other Unitarians and Socinians. These Christian infidels were highly involved in the religious controversies of the late seventeenth and early eighteenth century. These were well supported by the moderate enlighteners such as Locke, Newton and Milton. The master plan of Church Christianity's reformation was a shared concern of both the radicals and moderates, and the end result of their struggles against the Orthodoxy was also identical; the only difference was tactics.

The moderates maintained an outward façade of Orthodoxy and an artificial social distance from the radicals, to avoid controversies and to preserve their time and energies for the bigger reformatory project. They were genuinely afraid of instability, chaos and anarchy caused by radicals during the English Civil War, Revolution and even during the Interregnum. The moderate reformers were further divided into three main groups. The far-right Latitudinarians employed dogmatic terminologies such as the Trinity, incarnation, grace, crucifixion, redemption, episcopacy, salvation through the Church, divine right monarchy etc., but rationalising, relativising, diluting and broadening their meanings, conceptual parameters and implications. The center-left reformers, such as Locke and Newton, minimised use of dogmatic theology and phrases, shunned the Trinity, rejected original sin and incorporated heterodox interpretations of orthodox dogmas. Both groups avoided any link or connection with Islamic religious or political theology or open confrontation with Anglican Church. The far-left Unitarians and Latitudinarians, such as Nye, Arbury and Freke, did exactly what Locke and Newton did in secret and with an abundance of caution. They did it publicly and in a confrontational manner. They also identified their Islamic affiliations, sympathies and sources. "Divided among themselves into three main separate factions contending for the middle ground, they were at the same time engaged in fending off traditionalists on one flank and radicals on the other. Hence it became a typical feature of intellectual conflict that moderates endeavoured to shield themselves against conservatives by stressing, even exaggerating, the gulf dividing them from the universally reviled and abhorred radicals while, simultaneously, traditionalists sought a tactical advantage, in their public discourse, by minimising the gap separating the latter from the moderates as much as possible."[1946] The English Enlightenment was the result of this tripartite struggle. The Unitarian Islamic hybrid of the radical and moderate enlightenment figures gradually succeeded and won over the hearts and minds of some enlightened monarchs, intellectuals and traders finally oozing into the greater European community.

Epistle Dedicatory: The Culmination of Unitarian Islamic Imagination

The *Epistle* (1682), which was presented to the Moroccan ambassador was a culmination of this Unitarian Islamic syncretism, which in turn was central to the reformatory movement of this period. Justin Champion observed that "the historical connection between the Nazarenes and Islam was to form the central theme in the work of both Henry Stubbe and John Toland. While the work of Arthur Bury, William Freke and Stephen Nye displays no reluctance to identify Unitarianism with monotheistic Islam, the most radical case of Unitarian-Islam syncretism is to be found in the enigmatic Epistle Dedicatory to his Illustrious Excellency Ameth Ben Ameth (1682)."[1947] The Muslim ambassadors and emissaries were a commonplace in London since the early seventeenth century. Their visits were well publicised, sermonised and ceremonised. "The visits of Muslim ambassadors and emissaries to London, along with Jewish and Christian subjects sent by Muslim potentates, produced magnificent processions and exhibits of horses, slaves, turbans, scimitars, priests, jurists, and cuisines. The majority of visitors came from North Africa, with Ottoman, Safavid, and Indian emissaries trailing behind. The most elaborate procession was described in The Arrivall and Intertainements of the Embassador, (1637) Alkaid Jaurar Ben Abdella (an emissary from Morocco, whom king Charles preferred to meet rather than the Polish ambassador whom he kept languishing for months."[1948]

The 1681 visit of Moroccan ambassador Muhammad bin Haddu to London was lengthy and significant.[1949] The ambassador was accompanied by English Muslim converts such as Lucas and James, stayed in England for six months, intermingled with English leaders, merchants and commoners, visited chapels and cathedrals and received exceptional welcomes from top officials as well as common people. His secretary was awarded an honourary degree from Cambridge University as a token of respect.[1950] Matar observes that "he had learned enough to change his views about the Protestant religion and to take those changes back with him to Morocco. As much as Londoners were learning about Islam from him, so was he learning about Christianity from them."[1951] He further notes that "the visit of the Moroccan ambassador to London on 29 December 1681, Muhammad bin Haddu, raised expectations of improved relations between Mulay Ismail and King Charles II. Indeed, such were the hopes that a group of Unitarians approached the ambassador with an indictment of Trinitarian Christianity and praise for Islam. They believed that if the Moroccans would see eye to eye with them over matters of religion, there would ensue fruitful cooperation between the two countries. Religion, for the Unitarians, did not have to be a separator, for they and the Moors were not too dissimilar given their rejection of the doctrine of the Trinity and the godhood of Jesus."[1952] The *Epistle* was the preface to a bundle of three papers delivered to the Ambassador by Nöel Aubert de Versé. John Meggitt states that "Sometime in the summer of 1682, just as a Moroccan ambassador was about to leave for home after a lengthy and successful visit to England, some Unitarians in London attempted to deliver a bundle of papers to him. On hearing that they were concerned with religious matters, he declined to accept them, and so, unread, they passed into the hands of the Master of the Ceremonies, Sir Charles Cotterell, and from him to a Church of England priest, Thomas Tenison. When, over a decade later, Tenison became Archbishop of Canterbury, they found their way into the holdings of the library of Lambeth Palace, where they can still be consulted today."[1953]

Nöel Aubert de Versé was an intriguing figure with Unitarian/Socinian affiliations. He "was born in Le Mans, France, sometime between 1642 and 1645, to a moderately wealthy Catholic family. Initially educated at an Oratory college in Le Mans, he went to Paris to pursue medical studies. Whilst there, he encountered Protestantism, and in 1662 he converted to the Reformed faith. He subsequently abandoned his medical training to enrol in the Protestant Academy of Sedan, where he encountered anti-Trinitarian and Socinian works. He was to be associated with these ideas for the rest of his life."[1954] De Verse was active in Amsterdam, Paris and London. He was well acquainted with both moderate and radical enlightenment figures such as Pierre Bayle, Jean le Clerc, John Locke and actively participated in the ongoing intellectual debates of his time. "Settling in Amsterdam, he worked for the Elzevier press and produced a Latin translation of Richard Simon's *Histoire critique du Vieux Testament* (1678). During this period he also wrote of number of works, including *Le protestant pacifique* (1684), an argument for religious toleration; *L'impie convaincu* (1685), a critique of Spinoza; and *Traité de la liberté de la conscience* (1687), a defence of liberty of individual conscience."[1955] He authored the Dedicatory Epistle and came to London to deliver it to the Ambassador. "He also made a number of trips, including one to England in 1682 in order to present the Moroccan ambassador with Unitarian papers, among them the so-called Epistle dedicatory, a text of which he was the sole or chief author."[1956] The Epistle, written on behalf of the Unitarians, was "concerned with the relationship of Unitarian Christianity to Islam. In addition to explaining why the three accompanying treatises are being presented to the ambassador, it describes the state and nature of Unitarian Christianity, emphasises the commonalities between Islam and Unitarian Christianity over and against Trinitarian Christianity, both Catholic and Protestant, and ultimately claims that Unitarian Christianity is superior to Islam which, in the letter's view, contains a number of defects that the writers offer to correct."[1957]

The Unitarian authors wrote: "Be pleased to observe that all ye Christians throughout Persia, Armenia, Mesopotamia, those called of S. Thomas, & some Hollanders & Portugases in Asia, these yt lieu among ye Greecks in Europe, even your neighbouring Christians in Nubia, all those together, wch farr exceed ye Trinity- Asserting Christians, doe maintaine with us that Faith of one Soverain God, one onely in Person & Essence. And why should I forget to add you Mahumetans who also consent with us in ye Belief & worship of an one onely Supreme Deity, to whome be glory forever, Amen."[1958] Justin Meggitt observed that "the authors then identify themselves as belonging to 'the Sect of Christians called Unitarians' (p. v) and congratulate the ambassador and his retinue for being 'fellow Worshippers of that sole Supreme Deity of the Almighty Father and Creator,' and for preserving, unlike Christians in the 'Western part of the world,' 'the excellent Knowledge of that Truth touching a belief on an only Sovereign God (who hath no distinction or Plurality in Persons)' (p. v). The ambassador is informed of a letter written some years earlier by another Moroccan ambassador in answer to some queries about his religion from two Christian princes, one Protestant and one Catholic, the Latin text of which they have included as the second document in their collection (the *Epistola Ameth Benandala Mahumetani*). This letter both expounds Islamic beliefs and criticises the failings of the faith of Catholics and Protestants. However, the authors complain that 'such errors, we Unitarians do abhor as well as the Mahumetans, in which we must agree in such even against our fellow Christians.'"[1959]

The Epistle underscored the historical, theological and intellectual affinities between Islam, Unitarians and general anti-Trinitarian Christians. Justin Champion noted that letter was "a succinct account of the perceived links between the theologies of Islam and the Unitarians [...] they shared the necessary common truth in accepting 'the religion of an only one Godhead' which brought them to a closer fraternity with each other than with Trinitarian Christianity. The defence of one God 'without personalities or pluralities' was a pristine and original tradition that included, 'not only all the patriarchs down from Adam until Moses, not only all the Jews under the written law and the Old Testament to this very day, were still worshippers of an only one God (without a Trinity of persons), but that also all the Primitive Christians, in and after Christ and his Apostles' time'. In distinction from the post-Constantinian 'backsliding Christians' who believed in 'three co-equal and self-subsisting persons, whereof everyone is an absolute and infinite God', original Unitarians like Paul of Samosatus and Marcellus

Bishop of Ancyra upheld a monotheism that was maintained by Mahomet."[1960] Further, the authors explained, "'in the West and North we are not so numerous, by reason of the inhumanity of the clergy' (p.xi); there are many in Poland, Hungary, Holland and England, but the threat of persecution means that they cannot be open (p. xii)."[1961] The Unitarians were willing to be the ambassadors of Islam in the West, and worked to extend the political power of the Ottoman Sultan in Northern Europe. "The writers plead with the ambassador to make the documents known to 'the fittest Persons of your Countrymen' (p. xiii) – even though they contain only 'a Scantling of what the more learn'd of our Unitarian Brethren cou'd say' (p. xiii), and to become an ambassador 'in the Cause and the Religion of the Supreme Monarch of the World' (p. xiii)."[1962] The author of the Epistle clearly subscribed to the so-called Stubbian international conspiracy of Islamic republicanism, which wanted to replace the English and European monarchies with Ottoman republicanism and Christianity with Islamic Unitarianism. Shaftesbury, Locke, Unitarians, Socinians and radical Whiggs were all suspected of that international republican conspiracy.

The letter was a reflection of perceived affinity between the Unitarians and Muslims and their disdain of Trinitarianism. "The *Epistle Dedicatory* clearly reflects the major tropes that characterised the relationship between Unitarianism and Islam as understood by early Unitarians. It is, in most respects, not innovative but rather representative of early Unitarian views, notably in the way it identifies fundamental commonalities between the two religions, embracing rather than rejecting something central to anti-Unitarian polemic."[1963] The perceived notions of similarity, and their active use by the early Unitarians, were significant indications of Islam's centrality in the Unitarian/Socinian's reformatory scheme. This enlightend reformation of Christianity was founded on Islamic lines. Meggitt noted that "the Epistle is significant because it is the first time that we see Islam as foundational in the genesis of a major Christian denomination and the formation of its emergent identity. The Epistle has been called the 'Primary document of English Unitarianism' by the influential Unitarian historiographer Alexander Gordon ('Primary document', p. 464) and, although it is not the case that it is the first time the word 'Unitarian' was used in English (it appeared almost a decade earlier in H. Hedworth, Controversy ended, London, 1673, p. 53), it represents a significant moment in the development of Unitarian self-consciousness, a key point in the movement's transition from the 'sporadic Antrinitarianism' of preceding years to becoming a 'comprehensive school of thought' (Gordon, Heads of English Unitarian history, p. 13). Clearly Islam was in some sense central to this transformation."[1964]

The centrality of Islam in the Unitarian/Socinian anti-Trinitarian theological scheme was unparalleled in Christian history. "There is no other example of the genesis of a major Christian movement in which Islam, or indeed any other non-Christian religion, was a central, defining interlocutor, other than the birth of the early Christian church itself – although even there the parallel breaks down, as Christianity was initially a messianic sect *within* Judaism. At the very least the story of the origins of early English Unitarianism is not solely one of intra-Christian struggles, of arguments about reason and the scripture – or rather not solely *Christian* scripture."[1965] It was a total break with the supernatural Christianity's dogmatic past. Islam was as central to Unitarianism as Unitarianism was central to the early Enlightenment. The Epistle provides "evidence of the rhetorical weight of Islam in intra-Christian polemics."[1966] The same applies to the Socinians, early Deists and other anti-Trinitarians. They used, abused, acted upon and reacted to Islam and Muslims in so many ways that on the way many Islamic concepts, ideas and ideals were appropriated and internalised by them. Islam became their obsessive "other."

Like Stubbe, Toland, early Deists and Unitarians, the Epistle was full of praises for Prophet Muhammad and his preservation of the original Gospel of Jesus, "the text indicates a high estimation of Muḥammad, even if it is one that would not find favour with Muslims. He is not only someone raised up by God as a 'Scourge of those idolising Christians' (p. vii) – a common trope in Christian interpretations of Muḥammad since the emergence of Islam – but is also recognised as a 'Preacher' of the 'Gospel of Christ' (pp. vii-viii). Indeed, the authors' high estimation of Muḥammad provides grounds for their unusual theory of interpolation: as a man of 'judgement that had proved itself in other things so conspicuously,' Muḥammad could not be responsible for the 'many and frequent repugnancies, as are to be seen in those Writings and Laws that are nowadays giv'n out under his name' (p. viii)."[1967] The *Epistle* chided the later Muslim cultural engraftings upon the pristine, simple, rational and compassionate teachings of Muhammad represented in some books of Muhammad's biographies. Muhammad was too pure and lofty to have preached such mythological precincts.

Islam was truly an aspirational model for both the Socinians and Unitarians, due to its simple monotheism, republican values such as religious tolerance and moral salvific scheme and Prophet Muhammad was the model lawgiver. The early Unitarians looked at this closeness in a total positive way. Meggitt states that "indeed, as the authors of the *Epistle Dedicatory* had noted, Socinianism had thrived under Islamic rule, and rather than this being evidence of the intolerance of trinitarians, as the letter and other Unitarian literature claimed, their critics saw this as conclusive proof that the Unitarians were Muslims in all but name. For its opponents, Socinianism was virtually indistinguishable from Islam, the differences largely 'imperceptible.'"[1968] This historic fact was well recognised by their Orthodox opponents. The Trinitarians considered the Socinians and Unitarians as the bridge and gateway to Islam, "it was claimed that Unitarianism 'makes way for Mahometanism' that Unitarianism inevitably led from Christianity to Islam. As Thomas Calvert remarked, 'If any Christians turne Mahometans they begin with Arianisme, and Socinianisme, and then Turcisme is not so strange a thing'. And, as conclusive proof of this, famous converts from antitrinitarianism to Islam were paraded as proof, notably Adam Neuser and Paul Alciat – although actually it was only true of the former, a prominent Reformed Protestant theologian from Heidelberg. Such a perception does not seem to have been one held solely by trinitarian Christians, as Ottoman Muslims expressed much the same view. Leibniz, for example, recounted reading about how a Turk, on hearing a Polish Socinian talk about his faith, wondered why he did not get circumcised and become a Muslim."[1969]

The undelivered letter was printed in newspapers and books to cause an alarm against the Unitarian, Socinian, Whiggish, Republican and Islamic conspiracy against Christianity, Anglican Church and British monarchy. The Socinians and Unitarians were allying themselves with the "Mahometans magnifying the Koran in considering it reconcilable with the Gospel if the doctrine of the Trinity was laid aside. The Socinians were in 'mere complacency with those infidels.'"[1970] Jonathan Edwards championed the orthodoxy's cause, blaming John Locke and his Socinian, Unitarians accomplices of preaching and promoting the

"Turkish" faith at the expense of Christian faith. Bishop Stillingfeet's attacks on Locke's Socinian motives were no less piercing.

Unitarian's Turkish Faith

Francis Fullwood blamed the Unitarians of exhibiting more enthusiasm for Turkish faith than the faith of Christians. They were fanatics and enthusiasts like Mahometans.[1971] Charles Leslie was aghast by this unholy alliance between the Unitarians and Muslims. He "treated the Unitarians 'as scouts amongst us for Mahomet'. The Unitarians could 'in no propriety be called Christians; that they are more Mahometans than Christians and far greater enemies to Christianity than the Mahometans.'"[1972] The Unitarians were more dangerous than Muslims as they were integral to the Christian society. "Leslie insisted that Islam was less corrosive of Trinitarian Christianity than the English challenge. The Unitarians were reviled for representing the 'Mahometans as the true Christians, and our Christianity as mere paganism and Heathenism'. Contrary to the Unitarian interpretation, where Mahomet was applauded for re-establishing a primitive and pure Christianity, Leslie suggested that the 'Alkoran is a system of Arianism' and therefore 'vile heresy.'"[1973] Socinians went further than even the Muslims, recalled Leslie, in uprooting the Christian faith by degrading Christ's redemptive role and by humanising Jesus to mere moral model of no divine pretensions. "Leslie's ironic argument that Mahomet was a more orthodox ancestor than the Nazarenes or Ebionites. The Alkoran certainly applauded Christ as Messiah, but the Socinians overstated this applause, 'as Mahomet improved Arianism, so the Socinians have exceeded even the Alkoran in their contempt of Christ.'"[1974] The Socinians' human, moral Christology naturalised the role of Christ's to the extent that he was no different than Muhammad. Leslie "pointed out the dangers of the Unitarian elision of Mahomet and Christ: many 'say that there is no greater ground to believe in Christ than Mahomet.'"[1975]

Anglican Orthodoxy's fight against the Unitarians and Socinains was a fight for survival of Trinitarian Christian faith, orthodoxy and episcopacy. It was "incumbent upon Anglican controversialists to neutralize the moral value of such pasts."[1976] The Anglican Church hierarchy, with all its might and resources, were pitched against the Unitarian, Socinian and Deists anti-Trinitarian, anti-clerical and anti-monarchy republican alliance. Archbishop Tenison, Bishop Edward Stillingfeet, Bishop Wettenhall, Bishop Trelawny, William Sherlock, John Williams, John Tillotson, John Willis, William Jane, Henry Aldrich, Gilbert Burnet, Daniel Whitby, Edward Fowler, Francis Fullwood, Robert South, Jonathan Edwards, Charles Leslie and many other high ranking jurors and non-jurors were fully engaged in refuting the anti-Trinitarians.[1977] They were supported in various capacities by the Royalty, Parliament, educational establishment and lay mobsters. The continuous, long lasting controversy called "Anti-Trinitarian Controversy," or "Socinian Controversy or "Unitarian Controversy," was a multifaceted, comprehensive and exhaustive movement.[1978] It threatened the core of Christianity, Anglican Church, British political institutions and society. Brent S. Sirota notes that "the trinitarian controversy of the 1690s was never simply a contest over the doctrine of the Church of England. The theological imperative to vindicate Trinitarian orthodoxy was from the beginning embedded in what might be thought of as a disciplinary crisis, a series of constitutional and ecclesiological controversies over precisely which civil and religious institutions bore responsibility for undertaking such vindications. The trinitarian controversy was distinctive for the sheer variety of public authorities involved. No less than five sitting bishops participated in the controversy alongside a host of lay and clerical writers. The matter was taken up by the convocation of the province of Canterbury and elicited two separate condemnations from Oxford University convocations, a royal directive to the episcopate, and a parliamentary statute within the space of a decade. For all the attention paid to the controversy as a crisis in English theology and epistemology, this institutional dimension has largely gone unstudied."[1979]

The controversy, and its far-reaching arms, underscored the depth of crises prevalent in the Protestant Church in general, and the Anglican Church in particular. The Reformation severed the Protestants from centuries-old Church traditional authority, and the *sola scriptura* encouraged individualism and autonomy, shattering the monopoly of Church and state in the matters of faith and worship. The political upheavals of the 1640s to the 1690s turned everything upside-down, to use Christopher Hill's phrase.[1980] The multiple anti-Trinitarian controversies shook the very foundations of the Anglican Church demanding a concerted effort from the Church authorities. "The trinitarian controversy must be understood not simply as a doctrinal dispute but as a disciplinary crisis: a far-reaching debate over not only the content of orthodoxy but also the constitutional apportionment of responsibilities for its enforcement."[1981] The blame of "turning Turk" was tossed between the Orthodoxy and dissenters of all kinds. To defend Trinitarian absolutism was in fact a defense of Anglican Church and State. Anti-Trinitarian controversies of the late seventeenth and early eighteenth century were directed at Church and state authority and subsequent persecutions. They were an extension of the early seventeenth-century English Civil War and Commonwealth revolution. From the early seventeenth-century merchants to Paul Best, John Biddle, Henry Stubbe, John Toland, Shaftesbury, John Locke, Isaac Newton, Socinians, Unitarians and Deists all participated in this republican struggle in various capacities and forms. The goal was same, but the means and methods were different. The Enlightenment was a product of such a long and bloody dialectical struggle. It was not the love of Islam or Ottomans but the longing for an inclusive, tolerant and republican England which steered the century long struggles.

Catholic writers blamed the entire Protestant faith, especially the Anglican Church, of turning Turk and Socinian.[1982] This was a time of crises for both the Church and state. Many Anglican leaders believed that Unitarians like Nye, Locke, Firmin and Socinians were part of an international Islamic conspiracy, bent on destroying the entire Christian faith. "Henry Maurice, Archbishop William Sancroft's domestic chaplain, predicted that Firmin and his ilk would not be satisfied until the Nicene Creed, 'the spring of all the doctrines, which makes up your mystery and their abomination,' was similarly struck out."[1983] Humphrey Prideaux's famous anti-Muhammad diatribe was meant to halt this local, English, Deistic, Unitarian and Socianian conspiracy against the Christian faith. "The historical interpretation of Islam as a triumph of empire was given extended treatment in Humphrey Prideaux's The True Nature of Imposture Fully Displayed in the Life of Mahomet (1697) which addressed the Unitarian assaults upon Trinitarianism of the 1690s. The work sold two editions in the first year of publication, and a tenth edition was on sale by 1722 indicating its popularity as the staple and ubiquitous Anglican defence against the infidels."[1984] Prideaux, an Oxford fellow of Henry Stube and John Locke, was trying to highlight Anglican and Protestant sectarianism and Unitarian onslaught as an extension of the early seventeenth-century English Civil War and the resultant Cromwell republic, which was tolerant and anti-Church like Muhammad. Cromwell abolished the Anglican Church, excuted Charles I and destroyed monarchy; the Unitarian onslaught of 1690s was an extension of that Islamic republican conspiracy against the Church and monarchy. "Prideaux drew an easy parallel between the sectarianism of the 1650s and 1690s, which in turn mirrored the confusion and disunity evident in the Eastern Church at the time of Mahomet. The warning was to beware that God might 'raise up some Mahomet against us for our utter confusion.'"[1985] Tolan also noted that "although Prideaux does not say so, he is responding to the claims of Henry Stubbe, who had presented the Muslim prophet as a reformer and visionary who proposed a renewed monotheistic revelation in a time when Jews and Christians, victims of bickering clerical elites, had strayed from their pristine monotheism."[1986] The Orthodox anti-Muslim rhetoric lumped together the English Socinians, Unitariansans and Deists with the supposed Ottoman conspiracy to destroy Christiandom from within. This was a common trope of the late seventeenth- and early eighteenth-century Anglican establishment.

Adriaan Reelant's *Four Treatises concerning the Doctrine, Discipline, and Worship of the Mahometans* was published in 1712. Reelant totally lumped together the Socinians, Unitarians and Muslims as one body and faith. "Mahomet's central doctrinal position was the 'unity of God' which was merely a revival of the ancient anti-Trinitarian heresy of Paul of Samosatus, Theodotian and Photinus. The Mahometans insisted upon calling themselves 'Unitarians' in opposition to orthodox Christians whom they termed 'Associants'. The Socinians and Mahometans collaborated in insisting upon the corruptions and forgeries in Scripture upon which the Trinity was erected. The radical Unitarian Francis David in his polemics of the 1590s had repeatedly cited the Alkoran against the Trinity. The Racovian Catechism used identical definitions of the unity of God to the Koran. The early heretic Ebionites had fled into Syria to become the first Mahometan converts. The crucial charge against both Unitarian and Mahometan, echoing Prideaux's condemnation, was that they were Pelagian heresies or human theologies, 'more like the moral philosophy of the Pagans, than the doctrine of our Lord and Saviour Jesus Christ.'"[1987] Bishop Edward Stillingfleet was no less emphatic. "We must examine the political implications of these rival theologies. What were the challenges and issues that the Islamic rhetoric masked? Socinian argument rejected the Christian status of the Anglican establishment, considering it a corruption from the veridical model of pre-Nicene Christianity. Contemporary Christianity in the Unitarians' view conflated the ritual and worship of the person of Christ with the practice of religion. The Unitarians demanded a reform of the ecclesiastical establishment to the pattern of primitive morality."[1988] They demanded nothing short of a complete overhaul of the Christian faith. "What they demanded was an alteration in faith to satisfy divine prescriptions."[1989] The Socinians and Unitarian were bent on reforming the dogmatic, Church Christianity on simple, moral and Unitarian Islamic model.

The Anglican leaders were especially threatened by the Socinain, Unitarian human Christology. This trend brought to the earth both Jesus and the Church, and both theology and ecclesiology. "This Christology required that sacerdos was to be present in the temporal Church, identified in the priesthood. Elevating the competence of human reason to perceive the example of Christ and follow its precepts undermined the Trinitarian distinction between sacerdos and laity. The conception of Christ's sacrifice as a total propitiation of sins elevated the Church on earth to ministrators of this divinity: to undermine the sacrifice of Christ was to undercut the authority of the human priesthood."[1990] The Unitarians were literally there to "'subvert Christianity."'[1991] They subverted hierarchy in Church, monarchy and social order; the hierarchical ideology was a matter of faith and disbelief. Charles Leslie in the voluminous *Socinian Dialogues*, "stated, with uncharacteristic succinctness, that the crux of the debate was 'no less whether what we worship is God or a creature, whether we adore the true or false God, and are the grossest Idolaters in the world.'"[1992] Newton, Toland, Stubbe and Nye's indictment that the Trinity was gross idolatry was now ratcheting and resonating in Leslie's defenses. To him, Socinian's humanistic moralism was atheistic. "His complaint was that this reduced all to morality: if Christian behaviour was given such a wide circumference then it could include anyone who acted in a virtuous manner. Leslie pointed out, 'so that if a Mahometan, Jew or Pagan, leads a good moral life, he has the very essence of a Christian, and then no doubt is a Christian, let his system of faith be what it will.' This was the high road to subversion and atheism."[1993]

Leslie was correct in identifying a growing radical trend in England which, unlike Locke, Nye and Bury, was propagating a total break with Christian faith, institutions and culture. This trend was following the radical ideas of Henry Stubbe, John Toland and some other Deists. "Stephen Nye and Arthur Bury was not to overthrow Christianity but to reform its deviant Trinitarianism. There was a more radical enterprise which, in appealing to the history of Mahomet, suggested not just an end to Trinitarian theology but also to the very idea of a 'Christian' society. In Mahomet No Impostor (1720), written under the assumed Arabic name of Abdulla Mahumed Omar, the Anglican denigration of Mahomet epitomised in Prideaux's True Nature of Imposture (1697) was subject to radical analysis."[1994]

The *Epistle Dedicatory*, together with Stubbe's *Originall & Progress of Mahometanism*, were clandestinely distributed in England by 1701 and, by 1784, "the Epistle was employed to demonstrate that Unitarians were a fifth column that would soon recognise Muhammad's prophethood (Horsley, Letters, p. 151), repeating Leslie's claim at the begining of the century that Unitarians were 'Scouts amongst us of Mahomet' (Socinian controversy discuss'd, p. xxx), and drawing upon the common trope that Islam was a political, as much as a religious, threat."[1995] In short, Socinians, Deists, Unitarians and anti-Trinitarians were closely identified with Islam and Muslims, called Muhammadan Christians, Turks, Moors and straightforward Muslims throughout the seventeenth and eighteenth centuries. They were considered integral to an international Islamic monotheistic and republican conspiracy against Christendom, its religious and political institutions.

The English Abdulla Mahumed Omar and "Mahomet No Imposter"

Some scholars have connected *Mahomet No Imposter* to George Sale, who later translated the Quran to English.[1996] The author of *Mahomet No Imposter* seemed well-equipped with Islamic religion, history and customs. He demolished the imposter artifice built by Prideaux, and constructed an alternate positive portrait of Muhammad and his religion. It was Christian faith which was paganistic, tri-theistic, ceremonial and idolatrous; contrary to that, Islam was monotheistic, moralistic, simplistic and minimalistic. "As Abdalla Mahumed Omar wrote to his fictional Moslem correspondent in Mecca commenting on Prideaux's work, 'it is no new matter to find a Christian author railing at the Great Prophet, and heaping together a company of false and scandalous reflections, to render him and his religion odious to their own people.' According to Omar, Mahomet had re-established an economy based upon faith in 'one eternal God, the Creator of all things.' Opposed to this the Christians were more intent upon upholding heathenish dogmatism, and promoting idolatry rather than establishing 'moral institutions.' The Islamic faith could be reduced to two central doctrines, the unity of God and 'the moral duties that are to regulate our actions towards one another.' The binary choice presented by Omar was between a conception of religion which was primarily ceremonial, or one which established a system of social duties and harmony."[1997] Islam was a reflection of Newton, Locke and Nye's minimal Christianity of loving God and loving one's neighbour.

As seen above, these Unitarian thinkers appreciated and were interested in simple, minimalistic, rational and natural Islamic monotheism, morality, religious toleration, rational and ethical scheme of salvation, republican interpretations of man, state and society, and limited government and monarchy. Orthodox Christianity not only excluded them from faith and salvation, as well as from society and government, but also persecuted them for their love of freedom, liberty, pluralism, republicanism and natural theology. These persecuted dissenters looked outside the Christendom for analysis, comparison and solutions and found a ready-made complete system of theology, cosmology and politics in Islam; they wanted that model implemented in England and Europe.

The Muslim world of the seventeenth and eighteenth centuries was not weak like the modern-day Muslim world; it was powerful and threatening. Many British citizens had the firsthand knowledge of the Muslim world and its religious and political allures. Therefore, they struggled to reform Trinitarian Christianity on Unitarian Republican Islamic foundations. The dissenters, whether Deists, Socinians, Unitarians or others, owned Islam as their own to bring about the revolution called the Enlightenment. The early Enlightenment was really a religious and theological revolution, which shattered the old Christian system of belief and politics and built it upon natural, rational, Islamic republican lines. Islam was a constant, continuous trope and theme in these long decades of struggle between the authoritarian, persecutory and absolutist Church and monarchical institutions and the English heterodox dissenters. The so-called secularisation project went through this Unitarian Islamic republicanism and through the model of Prophet Muhammad, as Garcia noted that "our secular predecessors often hailed the Prophet an Enlightened Promethean hero."[1998] Garcia, in opposition to the oft repeated, dominant, Eurocentric narrative, offers "an alternative story about the emergence of Islamic-inspired secularisation in Eighteenth-century Britain. This story should not be read as a subaltern approach to "histories from below" or as a victimisation narrative about an overpowering West and a correspondingly subjugated East. Rather, I foreground Islam's contribution to the English Enlightenment [...] I challenge an exclusionist Judeo-Christian Enlightenment by engaging with precolonial perceptions of Islam."[1999] Garcia defines Islamic republicanism as "a term that describes how radical Protestants in Eighteenth-century England self-consciously recast Islam in constitutional-nationalist terms."[2000]

The expression Islamic republic "evokes the political disillusionment that originally characterised the negative freethinking response to Latinate-Roman Christianity."[2001] The Islamic republicanism was not an imaginary construct but a real, firsthand experience. The "positive (and negative) perceptions of Islam were conditioned by Anglo-Islamic encounters in India, Ottoman Europe, and elsewhere in the Muslim world. As a result, the radical Enlightenment was in constant dialectical engagement with Islam."[2002] Garcia argued that "mid Seventeenth-century radical Protestant dissent—plebeian and sectarian movements that spurned the Church of England's authority—informed country and commonwealthean opposition to Britain's Whig-Walpolean oligarchy in the 1730s and '40s, the American democratic upheavals, and French Jacobin politics despite its defeat in 1660. If 1789 or 1688 repeats history, then how does one account for the transmission of radical ideas in this period? This [...] argues that Islamic republicanism is enabled by a heterodox biblical hermeneutics associated with (but not confined to) the English deist movement. To think about what lies between the revolutions involves long and complicated national debates about Mahometanism, a supplementary prophetic faith that helped transmit and renew radical ideas in England."[2003]

The early Deists, like their Socinian and Unitarian compatriots, were equally religious, pious and concerned Christians. They were neither matarialists nor atheist, as is usually stated. The early Deists, such as Charles Blount and others, agreed with Stubbe and Toland about the possibility of reforming Church Christianity in conformity with Islamic ethical monotheism and republican values. "By the Eighteenth century, many deists preferred Mahometanism over the dogmatic Christianity codified in the Anglican church and state. Thomas Morgan, Matthew Tindal, and Peter Annet variously employed Islamic *tawhid*, or unity of God, to discredit the scriptural basis of revelation, liturgical practices, apostolic succession, the Trinity, the incarnation, miracles, and original sin. In particular, they used Islamic toleration as a beating stick against English toleration—the entitlement to freedom of conscience that, in practice, excluded many nonconformists from citizenship. Because of the Corporation (1662) and Test (1673) Acts—which remained in effect after the 1689 Toleration Act—the Anglican state barred Unitarians, Quakers, Catholics, and antitrinitarians from holding public office, obtaining legal preferment, and earning degrees from Oxford and Cambridge."[2004] These persecuted anti-Trinitarians formed a common cause with Islamic republicanism to realise their liberty, freedom and rights. Their struggle for human rights and religious freedom thrusted them close to Islamic world, ideas and institution. For this reason, "deism not only implies a preference for natural religion over scriptural authority and revealed truth but also an open-ended investigation in which various primitive monotheisms—Arian, Ebonite, Jewish, or Islamic—can be used to explore republican-democratic models that promote civic equality despite confessional affiliation and socioeconomic differences. By reading the scriptures beside profane histories, deists helped shape the *Historica monotheistica*, a comparativist study that challenges Christocentric history and politics. Radical dissenters used this study to question the theological authority of an exclusionist Anglican establishment. From Stubbe onward, deism implied a temper or attitude toward England's toleration policy and religious plurality rather than a systematic creed."[2005]

The simple, rational, minimalistic and universal Islamic monotheism solved the problem of particularities and localism for the Deists. "The deists solved this problem by insisting that a universal and reasonable religion, in its 'natural' and simple form, would avoid ascribing a partial will to an arbitrary God. This tidy solution would require not only an unbiased comparative investigation of Judaism, paganism, and Islam, but also the categorical denial of the belief that Jesus was the Son of God. Deists could not accept that this divine mediator determined human history, and that his sacrifice has atoned for humanity's original sin through God's forgiveness. The deist solution to the problem of particularity requires the wholesale rejection of original sin, the Trinity, the incarnation, divine revelation, and the atonement. In their imagination, these erroneous 'pagan' doctrines were concocted by priests, popes, and kings to dupe their subjects into voluntary submission."[2006] Once free of the localised, specified and brutalised Trinitarian faith system, the reformers were able to connect with the universal monotheistic history epitomised by Muhammad. "For deists [...] Christendom's fragmentation from within and without its porous borders is not a problem, because Mahometanism and the Protestant Reformation symbolise the providential unfolding of the *Historica monotheistica*. Mahomet, as well as Christ, is one among many prophets belonging to Abraham's natural religion. In other words, if Christian Europe is to overcome religious pluralism as the subject of political and theological contention, it must abandon its obsession with a particular time and event: a diachronic history that is grounded on Christ's incarnation in first-century Jerusalem. Instead, deists concluded that, ideally, religious plurality is the universal essence of history: a synchronic monotheism that interprets Islam's worldwide triumph as anticipating the Protestant Reformation. In their imagination, Muhammad is an earlier and more radical reformer than Luther."[2007]

Muhammad's reformation was in conformity with the moral schemes of Moses and Jesus; therefore, pristine Judaism, Christianity and Islam stood for the same ethical monotheism and democratic value system. Islam was a bridge between true Judaism and Christianity, and the true voice of the voiceless dissenters. "In English political life, Islam is one of the principal mediums for imagining cultural transmission and transformation. Converting to a Mahometan is therefore a process of radical self-fashioning for those who believe that England's constitutional model has excluded them from participating in the symbolic rites of Anglican citizenship. For many English nonconformists, Islam offers a renovated constitutional idiom for reclaiming political subjectivity and national identity, reworking the universal ideals of liberty, equality, and fraternity into a new vocabulary for redefining the power struggle among state sovereignty, church authority, and the people. Employed in this manner, Islamic republicanism augments English nonauthoritarian liberty while dispensing with exclusionist and oppressive Christian policies."[2008]

Islamic natural, earthly and ethico-moral, egalitarian ideals were the aspired goals of the downtrodden, pressurised, demonised, deprived and persecuted by the oppressive Church and state alliance. "Islamic republicanism reinvents English revolutionary history, providing sociopolitical empowerment for marginalized 'mute witnesses': deists, Unitarians, Gnostics, and Arians, among other forgotten heretics, and heterodox women who championed female-friendly versions of the prophetic past. Islamic republicanism's political reinvention—enabled through reprinted republican tracts and recirculated subversive manuscripts—creates a historical continuity among the 1640s, 1688, 1776, and 1789. This imaginative process ties together the various events that took place between the Eighteenth-century revolutions. Mythical accounts about Mahometanism's worldwide triumph constitute a lived cultural heritage that underwrites the English social imaginary."[2009]

Historica Monotheistica and Islamic Republicanism

Islamic republicanism and *Historica monotheistica* were the two major themes greatly discussed during Europe's early Enlightenment. Islamic republicanism, as discussed above, greatly contributed to English, French and American Enlightenments, and hence to the French and American Revolutions. The *Historica monotheistica* represented a universal Unitarian prophetic tradition, and Islamic republicanism stood for its historical preservation in the Islamic faith. The pluralistic Ottoman Empire stood as its historical model; such a Unitarian Islamic republicanism was the general conceptual framework of the early and high Enlightenment. "From the late Seventeenth to the mid-nineteenth century, Islamic republicanism captivated the radical Anglo-Protestant imagination and redefined reformed orthodoxy in England, North America, and the transatlantic world, only to be silenced by the anti- Islamic sentiments that gripped Victorian culture after the 1857 Indian Mutiny."[2010]

It is commonly argued that Enlightenment thinkers such as Locke, Newton, Stubbe, Toland and others were neither theologians nor religiously-oriented, that they were secular political thinkers who wanted to replace religion with reason. This Whiggish, modern secularistic interpretation of early Enlightenment is misplaced. A detailed analysis of writings of Locke, Newton, and other English thinkers of the sixteenth and seventeenth centuries shows that they were in fact religiously-oriented pious theologians, who wanted to reform Christianity for religious reasons rather than banish it altogether. The alliance between the Church and state and the redefinition of this bondage were central to their desires for viable political changes. Monarchical sovereignty and Church authority were mutually interconnected; the idea of dismantling the theological foundations of Church doctrines concurrently eroded the foundations of ecclesiastical authority and monarchical sovereignty. In this viewpoint, a correct conception of God, man, and human nature was a fundamental premise for morality and good character, and a deviant conception of God, man, and human nature was the source of immoral, capricious human behavior. The reformers understanding of God and religion was based on the central characteristic belief in the necessity of inducing a virtuous and moral social, political, and economic life. Moral reformation of the individual and society was elemental in their scheme of transformation. Cumbersome rituals, irrational mysteries, and corrupt dogmas were antithetical to morality and good character. They were not against Christianity as such but against the supernatural, dogmatic and ceremonial Roman Christianity. Therefore, these thinkers tried to reform Christianity rather than throwing it out of the window. They tried to do so by importing heterodox theological perspectives from outside. The Islamic model and sources were helpful tools and they used them well for their reformation agendas.

In short, Locke, Newton, Stubbe, Toland, Deists, Socinians and Unitarians were anti-clerical, anti-dogmatic and anti-monarchy Christians. They denounced fundamental Church dogmas such as the Trinity, Jesus' divinity, original sin, ecclesiastical authority, biblical inerrancy, and salvation through the redemptive death and crucifixion of Christ. Their Christianity was far removed from the official Church Christianity; in reality it was no Christianity per orthodox definitions. It was also no Deism, as espoused by some later radical deists, who rejected divine providence, revelation in all forms, miracles, prayers, rewards and punishments in the afterlife and spiritualism. Contrary to that, Locke, Newton and many other enlightenment ideologues and early Deists believed in divine providence, authentic rational revelation, partial scriptures, miracles, prayers, personal relationship with God, spirituality, reward and punishment in the afterlife.[2011] They did not fit in the strict categories of Christians or materialist Deists. They were rational Unitarian theistic in line with ethical, rational, minimal and Unitarian monotheism of Islam. They were Muhammaden Christians and so were they called by their opponents. This conscious or unconscious Islamic subscription needs to be recognised and appreciated.

In addition to rejecting the central religious tenants of Church Christianity, they also scorned its socio-political framework. They hated its clerical as well as monarchical hierarchy, its religious and political persecutions, its interpretations of authority, man and government, its top-down government system and its cumbersome ceremonies and practices. In short, they demolished the entire Christian system from within to replace it with rational, Unitarian monotheism; religious tolerance and pluralism; limited republicanism and liberal, democratic and bottom-up government system; confidence in man, his liberty, freedoms, human rights, equality, justice; simple and straightforward morality, virtues and worship. This was their understanding of the natural religion in opposition to the super natural Christian system of God, man and society. They kept the outer skeleton of the Christian system but replaced almost all the inner elements with appropriated, modified and Christianised Islamic ideas and concepts. The end result was the "Muhammaden Christianity" espoused equally by the radical as well as moderate enlightenment figures.

This Unitarian Muslim hybrid continued throughout the long eighteenth century, culminating in Joseph Priestley, Richard Price[2012] and many other Unitarians. The English Unitarians were closely identified with Muslims and excluded from citizenship. "With the gradual formation of an Anglican nationalism in Eighteenth-century England, orthodox polemicists used the image of Unitarians as 'Mahometans' as a prime justification for their exclusion from citizenship. Once again orthodox polemicists panicked about a possible Muslim-Unitarian plot to thwart the state, especially after the French Revolution. The Epistle to the Moroccan ambassador and *A Letter of Resolution* continued to haunt the Unitarian psyche."[2013] Samuel Horsley openly criticised Joseph Priestley as the epitome of Muslim theology and an enemy of Christ. Joseph Priestley's house, library, laboratory and chapel were torched to ashes during the Birmingham riots. "The most acute manifestation of this resurgence can be found in the polemical exchanges between Joseph Priestley, who converted to Socinianism during his ministry at Leeds and wrote prolifically in favour of Unitarian theology, and Samuel Horsley, the archdeacon of St. Albans who was elevated to Bishop of Rochester in 1793 for his defense of Anglican dogmas. In this eight-year controversy (1783–91), Horsley launched a smear campaign against the English Unitarian movement by maintaining that Priestley, a prominent philosopher and scientist of the age, was secretly preaching the Mahometan faith. To elucidate the subtle connections among antinationalist sentiments, dissenting politics, and Islamic republicanism, this renewed Mahometan-Unitarian conspiracy can be traced in the theological writings of Priestley, whose mind, as one late-Victorian historian puts it, charts 'the mental pilgrimage' of late-Eighteenth-century Unitarianism."[2014] Horsley stigmatized Priestley "as a disguised Mahometan who seeks to overthrow church and state [...] In the Unitarian writings of the last century, it is allowed of Mahomet, that he had no other design than to restore the belief of the unity of God.—Of his religion, that it was not meant for a new religion, but for a restitution of the true intent of the Christian.—Of the great prevalence of the Mahometan religion, that it has been owing not to force and the sword, but to that one truth contained in the Alcoran, the unity of God."[2015] Horsley continued that "like their late-Seventeenth-century predecessors, Priestley and his Socinian cohort are involved in a new conspiracy with Mahometan enemies intent on overthrowing England's Christian rule. To support this latest conspiracy theory, Horsley refers to the Unitarian Epistle printed in Leslie's earlier tract as indisputable proof, deploying an earlier polemical strategy bent on discrediting dissenting claims to Anglican citizenship and property rights."[2016] Priestley's *An history of the corruptions of Christianity* (1782) was dubbed a Muslim treatise against Christianity, because like Nye before him, Priestley identified the fourth century's clerical establishment as the main culprits of the Christian fraud. They deviated from the original message of Jesus by inserting Trinitarian jargon into the simple Unitarian message of the original Nazerene. Reverend James Barnard "satirically states that Priestley should acknowledge the Muslims as his 'brethren' and include them in his next edition of *An History of the Early Opinions concerning Jesus Christ* (1786). Some orthodox polemicists pointed out that Priestley's defense of Chris's prophetic status must be proof that he accepts the revealed truth of the Quran and that Islam is preferable to Christianity. As one writer sarcastically puts it, "the real creed of the Unitarian [...] is—There is one God, and Priestley is his prophet; and it is a matter of moonshine to a Christian, whether Priestley or Mahomet be exalted in that honour."[2017]

Justin Meggitt well summarises the impact of the *Epistle Dedicatory* to Unitarian Christian relationships throughout the Eighteenth century both in England and America. "The contents of the *Epistle* continued to be used by opponents of Unitarianism in both England and the United States to argue that Unitarians were indistinguishable from Muslims, or indeed, worse than Muslims (Whitaker, *Origin of Arianism disclosed*, pp. 399-400; Wilkins, *The trial of the Unitarians*, p. 4), that they could not be judged Christians (T.C.S., 'Letter to a Mahometan ambassador'; Feltus, *Historical documents*). The *Epistle* and its association of Unitarianism with Islam was sometimes used to the material disadvantage of the former. For example, it was quoted in evidence in the House of Lords to demonstrate that Unitarians should be debarred from being either the trustees or beneficiaries of Lady Hewley's charities, a significant source of assistance to dissenters (Gurney and Gurney, *Lady Hewley's charities*, pp. 171–3). The text dogged a number of Unitarian initiatives: a Unitarian version of the New Testament published by Thomas Belsham in 1808 was referred to as the 'gospel of Mohammed' and likened to the Quran, and the address to the Moroccan ambassador was used to justify speaking about it in such a manner (Anon., 'Article XV', p. 72; Norris, *A practical exposition*, p. 232)."[2018] He also demonstrates that the Unitarian Islamic identification and syncretism was at times denied by some Unitarian leaders, but mostly acknowledged and appreciated by the majority. "However, from the outset some Unitarians acknowledged that the *Epistle* was genuine and that there was nothing in it of which to be ashamed (Emlyn, *An examination of Mr. Leslie's last dialogue*, p. 21) and this was continued throughout the 18th century (Rutt, *Theological and miscellaneous works of Joseph Priestley*, vol. 18, p. 248). This more positive interpretation of the *Epistle* was clearly shared by Gordon when, towards the end of the 19th century, he brought attention to it once again after some decades of neglect by both Unitarians and their critics, and identified it as the 'primary document' of Unitarianism."[2019]

Joseph Priestley was an heir to this long tradition of Unitarian Islamic syncretism. By 1790, he self-consciously knew that his detractors considered him "half a Mahometan."[2020] Priestley had to escape to America due to his support for French and American revolutions and for being a Mahometan. In spite of his constant and continuous efforts to distance himself from Islam, the charge of being an Islamophile remained stuck to Joseph Priestley; he transmitted the same to the Founding Fathers of America. This was the Christianity with its Socinian/Unitarian/Deistic bent, theology and political outlook, which was transmitted to some of the most influential Founding Fathers of America through Locke's writings, Deistic, Unitarian and Muslim associations but more importantly via Joseph Priestley's preaching. These Founding Fathers suffered the same fate and were vilified as crypto-Muslims, Turks, atheists and infidels.

In conclusion, we can state that the Unitarian Islamic republican syncretism was the fundamental source of English and the ensuing French and American Enlightenments.

Endnotes

1   Eric R. Wolf, *Europe And The People Without History*, Berkeley, University of California Press, 2010, p. 5

2   Anthony Pagden, *Lords of All the World: Ideologies of Empire in Spain, Britian, and France, C. 1500-1800*, New Haven, Yale University Press, 1995, 11; and *passim*, ch. 1, 'The Legacy of Rome,' 11-28; also David Armitage, *The Ideological Origins of the British Empire*, Cambridge, Cambridge University Press, 2009, 195ff ; Thomas James Dandelet, *The Renaissance of Empire in Early Modern Europe*, Cambridge, Cambridge University Press, 2014, p. 276

3   See Max Weber, *The Protestant Ethics and the Spirit of Capitalism*, trans. By Talcott Parsons, London and New York, Routledge, 2005, p. xlii (certain types of rationalisation have developed in the Occident). See Joseph M. Bryant, "The West and the rest revisited: Debating capitalist origins, European colonialism and the advent of modernity", *Canadian Journal of Sociology* 31(4), 2006, pp.403–444.

4   See Weber, *The Protestant Ethics* for details.

5   Weber, *Ibid*, p. xvi

6   M. H. Mackinnon, "*The Longevity of the Thesis*: A Critique of the Critics" in H. Lehmann & G. Roth (eds,), *Weber's Protestant Ethic: Origins, Evidence, Contexts*, Cambridge, Cambridge University Press, 1993, p. 212

7   M. Weber, "Anticritical Last Word on the Spirit of Capitalism," *American Journal of Sociology*, 83, v.5, (1978), p. 1124

8   Weber, *The Protestant Ethics*, p. xvi

9   Weber, *The Protestant Ethics*, p. xvii

10   Weber, *Ibid*, p. xvii

11   Weber, *Ibid*, p. xvii

12   Weber, *Ibid*, p. xvii

13   Weber, *Ibid*, xvii

14   Weber, *Ibid*, xxxix

15   Weber, *Ibid*, xxxix

16   Weber, *Ibid*, xxxix

17   Weber, *Ibid*, xvii

18   Mackinnon, "*The Longevity of the Thesis*: A Critique of the Critics" in H. Lehmann & G. Roth (eds,), *Weber's Protestant Ethic*, p. 215

19   JRD Coffey, 'Religious Thought', 'in *The Oxford Handbook of the English Revolution*' ed. by M. J. Braddick, Oxford, Oxford University Press, 2015, pp. 447-465, p. 453

20   See details in Mackinnon, "*The Longevity of the Thesis*, p. 216

21   Mackinnon, "*The Longevity of the Thesis*, p. 223

22   See F. Rachfahl, "Kalvinismus und Kapitalismus," inj. Winckelmann, ed., *Die Protestant Ethik II* (Hamburg, 1972), 57-148; and, F. Rachfahl, "Nochmals Kalvinismus und Kapitalismus," in Winckelmann, *Protestant Ethik,* 216-282

23   L. Brentano, *Die Anjange des modemen Kapitalismus* (Leipzig, 1916), 134, 136.

24   W. Sombart, The Quintessence of Capitalism: A Study of the History and Psychology of the Modern Business Man, New York,The Classics,1967, 105ff; W. Sombart, *The Jews and Modern Capitalism,* New York, Martino Fine Books, 2015

25   G. Simmel, *The Philosophy of Money,* New York, Routledge, 2011

26   H. M. Robertson, *Aspects of the Rise of Economic Individualism:* A Criticism of Max Weber and his School, New York, Kelley and Millman, 1959, 10ff

27   K. Samuelson, *Religion and Economic Action:* The Protestant Ethic, the Rise of Capitalism and the Abuses of Scholarship, Toronto, University of Tornoto Press, 1993

28   A. Hyma, *Christianity, Capitalism and Communism,* Ann Arbor, Mich., University of Michigan,1937; A. Hyma, *Renaissance to Reformation,* Grand Rapids, Mich., Wm. B. Eerdmans Publishing, 1951

29   R. H. Tawney, *Religion and the Rise of Capitalism*, New York, Routledge, 1998

30   H. R. Trevor-Roper, *Religion, Reformation and Social Change*, London, Macmillan, 1972, p. 21ff

31   H. Luthy, "Once Again: Calvinism and Capitalism," in R. W. Green, ed., *The Weber Thesis Controversy*, Toronto, University of Toronto Press, 1973, p. 98-99

32   See details in Mackinnon, "*The Longevity of the Thesis*: A Critique of the Critics" in H. Lehmann & G. Roth (eds,), *Weber's Protestant Ethic*

33   Mackinnon, "*The Longevity of the Thesis*: A Critique of the Critics" in H. Lehmann & G. Roth (eds,), *Weber's Protestant Ethic*, p. 243

34   Samir Amin, *Eurocentrism: Modernity, Religion and Democracy, A Critique of Eurocentrism and Culturalism*, translated by Russell Moore and James Membrez, New York, Monthly Review Press, 2009, p. 27

35   Samir Amin, *Eurocentrism*, P. 27. "The arguments Weber advances, in this respect, are confused, despite their apparent precision. They are, moreover, perfectly reversible, analogous to those previously advanced to explain the backwardness of China in terms of Confucianism, then fifty years later to explain the take-off of that country in terms of the same Confucianism! Superficial historians have explained the success of the Arab civilisation of the Middle Ages by way of Islam, while contemporary journalists, even more superficially, explain the stagnation of the Arab world by the same Islam. Culturalism has no possible univocal response to any of these great historical challenges. In fact, it has too many, because it can prove any formulation and its opposite." Amin, *Ibid*, p. 27

36   See John A. Hall, *Powers and Liberties: The Causes and Consequences of the Rise of the West*, London, Blackwell, 1985; M. Mann, "European Development: Approaching a Historical Explanation." in Jean Baechler, Michael Mann, and John Hall, *Europe and the Rise of Capitalism*, London, Blackwell, 1988; M. Mann, The Sources of Social Power: A History of Power from the Beginning to A.D. 1760 , Cambridge, Cambridge University Press, 2012, v. 1; Eric Jones, The European Miracle: Environments, Economics, and Geopolitics in the History of Europe and Asia, Cambridge University Press, 2003

37   David S. Landes, *The Wealth and Poverty of Nations*, New York, W. W. Norton and Company1998, p. xxi

38   H. R. Trevor-Roper, *The rise of Christian Europe*. London, Thames and Hudson, 1965, p. 21

39   See Joseph Needham, *Science and civilisation in China*, Pt 2, vol VII, Cambridge, Cambridge University Press, 2004

40   M. Elvin, *The pattern of the Chinese past*, London, Eyre Methuen, 1973

41   F. Braudel, *Civilisation and capitalism*, 15th–18th century, London, Phoenix Press, 1979

42   Wolf, *Europe And The People Without History*, p. 5

43   Wolf, *Ibid*, p. 1

44   See Saumitra Jha, *Financial Asset Holdings and Political Attitudes: Evidence from Revolutionary England, The Quarterly Journal of Economics* (2015), 1485–1545. doi:10.1093/qje/qjv019

45   Daron Acemoglu, Simon Johnson and James Robinson, *The Rise of Europe: Atlantic Trade, Institutional Change, and Economic Growth*, The American Economic Review, Vol. 95, No. 3 (Jun., 2005), pp. 546-579, P. 561

46   See John M. Hobson, *The Eastern Origins of Western Civilisation*, Cambridge, Cambridge University Press, 2004

47   Jack Goody, *The Theft of History*, Cambridge, Cambridge University Press, 2006, p. 61

48   See H. Butterfield, *The whig interpretation of history*, London, G. Bell and Sons, 1931; his *The Englishman and his history*, Cambridge, Cambridge University Press, 1944 and *George III and the historians*, London: Collins, 1957

49   See Butterfield, *The whig interpretation of history*, p. 5

50   See J. W. Burrow, A liberal descent. *Victorian historians and the English past*, Cambridge: Cambridge University Press, 1981; H. T. Colbourn, *The lamp of experience. Whig history and the intellectual origins of the American revolution*, Chapel Hill: North Carolina Press, 1965

51   Goody, *The Theft of History*, p. 1; ; J. M. Blaut, *The Coloniser's Model of the World: Geographical Diffusionism and Eurocentric History*, New York, Guilford Press, 1993 and *Eight Eurocentric Historians*, New York, Guilford Press, 2000

52   See Samir Amin, *Eurocentrism*; J. M. Blaut, *The Coloniser's Model of the World*

53   Goody, *The Theft of History*, p. 8

54   See Avihu Zakai. *The Rise of Modern Science and the Decline of Theol-*

ogy as the 'Queen of Sciences' in the Early Modern Era, Reformation &
Renaissance Review 9.2 (2007) 125–151, doi:10.1558/rrr.v9i2.125

55   See details in A. O. Lovejoy, *The Great Chain of Being : A Study of the
      History of an Idea*, Cambridge, Mass., Harvard University Press, 1936;
      E. M. W. Tillyard, *The Elizabethan World Picture*, New York, Rout-
      ledge, 2017

56   S. F. Mason, "Science and Religion in Seventeenth Century England"
      in *The Intellectual Revolution of the Seventeenth Century* edited by
      Charles Webster, New York, Routledge, 1974, p. 200

57   St Thomas Aquinas, *Summa contra gentiles,* trans. by members of the
      Dominican Order, 4 vols (London, 1923-9), iii, pt I, chaps 78-82, pp.
      195-207-

58   Depending upon diverging Catholic or Proetstant or Greek Ortho-
      dox views.

59   David C. Lingberg and Ronald L. Numbers eds., *God and Nature:
      Historical Essays on the Encounter between Christianity and Science*,
      Berkeley, University of Califorinia Press, 1986, p. 169

60   See William Edward Hartpole Lecky, *History of the Rise and Influence
      of the Spirit of Rationalism in Europe,* London, D. Appleton and Com-
      pany, 1919, v. 1, p. 119

61   See details in Terence L. Nichols, *The Sacred Cosmos: Christian Faith
      and the Challenge of Naturalism*, Eugene, WIPF & STOCK, 2003, p. 43

62   Mason, "Science and Religion in Seventeenth Century England", p. 207

63   See details in Mason, "Science and Religion in Seventeenth Century
      England", p. 206ff

64   See details in P. N. R. Zutschi, "The Avignon Papacy" in M. Jones
      (ed.), *The New Cambridge Medieval History. Volume VI c.1300–c.1415*,
      Cambridge: Cambridge University Press, 2000, pp. 653–673

65   See Norman P. Zacour and Harry W. Hazard eds., *A History of the Cru-
      sades*, Vol. V: The Impact of the Crusades on the Near East, Madison,
      WI and London: University of Wisconsin Press, 1985

66   See Maria Rosa Menocal, *The Ornament of the World, How Muslims,
      Jews, and Christians Created a Culture of Tolerance in Medieval Spain*,
      New York, Back Bay Books, Little Brown and Company, 2002

67   See William Manchester, *A World Lit Only by Fire: The Medieval Mind*

and the Renaissance: Portrait of an Age, Boston, Little, Brown and Company, 1993

68   See Hobson, *The Eastern Origins of Western Civilisation,* P. 115ff

69   Ronald Findlay and Kevin H. O'Rourke eds., *Power and Plenty: Trade, War and the World Economy in the Second Millennium,* Princeton, Princeton University Press, 2007, p. xxii

70   C. H. Haskins, *The Renaissance of the Twelfth Century,* London, Harvard University Press, 1955, p. 7

71   Haskins, *The Renaissance of the Twelfth Century,* p. 7; Charles Burnett, "Arabic into Latin: the Reception of Arabic Philosophy into Western Europe" in Peter Adamson and Richard C. Taylor (eds.), *The Cambridge Companion to Arabic Philosophy,* Cambridge, Cambridge University Press, 2006, p. 370ff

72   Haskins, *The Renaissance of the Twelfth Century,* p. 278

73   A. S. McGrade (ed.), *The Cambridge Companion to Medieval Philosophy,* Cambridge, Cambridge University Press, 2006, p. 21

74   Eric John Holmyard (ed.), *The Works of Geber,* translated by Richard Russel, London, Dent, 1928, digitalized by the University of Michigan on July 13, 2007, p. xv

75   Dorothee Metlitzki, *The Matter of Araby in Medieval England,* New Haven, Yale University Press, 1977, p.54

76   Haskins, *The Renaissance of the Twelfth Century,* p. 281

77   See Simon Barton and Peter Linehan (eds.), *Cross, Crescent and Conversion: Studies on Medieval Spain and Christendom in Memory of Richard Fletcher,* Leiden, Brill, 2008, p. 53ff;

78   Haskins, *The Renaissance of the Twelfth Century,* p. 11

79   Haskins, *The Renaissance of the Twelfth Century,* p. 285; also see Eva R. Hoffman, *Pathways of Portability: Islamic and Christian interchange from the tenth to the twelfth century,* Oxford, Blackwell Publishers, Art History ISSN 0141-6790 Vol. 24 No. 1 February 2001 pp. 17-50

80   See Charles Burnett, "Arabic into Latin: the Reception of Arabic Philosophy into Western Europe" in Peter Adamson and Richard C. Taylor (eds.), *The Cambridge Companion to Arabic Philosophy,* Cambridge, Cambridge University Press, 2006, p. 370ff

81   Haskins, *The Renaissance of the Twelfth Century,* p. 290

82   See Jeremy Johns, *Arabic Administration in Norman Sicily*, Cambridge, Cambridge University Press, 2002

83   Haskins, *The Renaissance of the Twelfth Century*, p. 283

84   Haskins, *The Renaissance of the Twelfth Century*, p. 284

85   See George Saliba, *Islamic Science and the Making of European Renaissance*, London, MIT Press, 2007, p. viiiff especially chapter 6 "Islamic Science and the Renaissance Europe: The Copernican Connection".

86   Haskins, *The Renaissance of the Twelfth Century*, p. 290-291

87   See details in Rena D. Dossett, *The Historical Influence of Classical Islam on Western Humanistic Education, International Journal of Social Science and Humanity*, Vol. 4, No. 2, March 2014

88   See details in Erika Rummel (Ed.), *Biblical Humanism and Scholasticism in the Age of Erasmus*, Brills, Leiden, 2008, p. 1

89   G. H. R. Parkinson (Ed.), *The Renaissance and the Seventeenth-century Rationalism*, London, Routledge, 1993, p. 1

90   George Makdisi, *The Scholastic Method in Medieval Education: An Inquiry into its Origins in Law and Theology*, Speculum, v. 49, No.4, October, 1974, p. 648

91   See Zulfiqar Ali Shah, *St. Thomas Aquinas and Muslim Thought*, Swansea, Claritis Books, 2021

92   See David B. Burrell, *Thomas Aquinas and Islam, Modern Theology*, 20:1, Oxford, Blackwell, January 2004; Jon McGinnis, Avicenna, Oxford, Oxford University Press, 2010; Jean-Pierre Torrell, *Aquinas's Summa, Background, Structure and Reception*, translated by Benedict M.Guevin, Washington D. C., The Catholic University of America Press, 2005, p. 82; Robert Hammond, *The Philosophy of al-Farabi and Its Influence on Medieval Thought*, New York, Hobson Book Press, 1947

93   Quoted in Hamid Naseem Rafiabadai and Aadil Amin Kak, *The Attitude of Islam Towards Science and Philosophy*, New Delhi, Sarup and Sons, 2003, P. 43

94   Quoted by Haider Bammate, *Muslim contribution to Civilisation*, Indiana: American Trust Publications, 1976, p. 23

95   See Muammer Eskenderoglu, *Fakhr al-Din al-Razi and Thomas Aquinas on the Question of the Eternity of the World*, Leiden, Brills, 2002; Majid Fakhry, *al-Farabi: Founder of Islamic Neoplatonism, His Life,*

Works and Influence, Oxford, Oneworld, 2002; Hamid Naseem Rafi-abadi, *Emerging From Darkness: Ghazzali's Impact on the Western Philosophers,* New Delhi, Sarup & Sons, 2002; Joseph Owens: "Aquinas as Aristotelian Commentator," in *St. Thomas Aquinas. 1274-1974. Commemorative Studies* (Toronto: Pont. Ins!. Med. Stud., 1974) V. 1; Richard C. Taylor, *Arabic / Islamic Philosophy In Thomas Aquinas's Conception Of The Beatific Vision* In Iv SenT., D. 49, Q. 2, A. 11, *The Thomist* 76 (2012): 509-50, p. 540-541

96   See Nakosteen, *History of Islamic Origins of Western Education,* A.D. 800-1350, Boulder, University of Colorado Press, 1978

97   Goody, *The Theft of History,* p. 236

98   Quoted in Asma Afsaruddin and A. H. Mathias Zahniser (eds.), *Humanism Culture and Language in the Near East,* Winona Lake, Indiana, Eisenbrauns, 1997, p. 21

99   Goody, *The Theft of History,* p. 234

100   Michael G. Carter, "Humanism and the Language Sciences in Medieval Islam" in Asma Afsaruddin and A. H. Mathias Zahniser (Eds), *Humanism Culture and Language in the Near East,* p. 27

101   Carter, *Humanism,* p. 28-38

102   George Makdisi, *The Rise of Colleges,* Institutions of Higher Learning in Islam and the West, Edinburgh, Edinburgh University Press, 1981

103   Goody, *The Theft of History,* p. 228

104   Goody, *The Theft of History,* p. 228

105   Goody, *The Theft of History,* p. 231

106   Goody, *The Theft of History,* p. 232

107   Quoted in Goody, *The Theft of History,* p. 228

108   See George Saliba, *Islamic Science and the Making of European Renaissance*

109   Jerry Brotton, *Renaissance: A Very Short Introduction,* Oxford, Oxford University Press, 2006, p. 13

110   Brotton, *Renaissance,* p. 19

111   Jacob Burckhardt, *The Civilisation of the Renaissance in Italy,* tr. S. G. C. Middlemore, revised and edited by Irene Gordon, London, Macmillan, 1904, Part II, p. 122

112   Burckhardt, *Civilisation, Part II, The Development of the Individual,* p. 122

113   Burckhardt, *Civilisation, Part II, The Development of the Individual*, p. 122

114   Brotton, *Renaissance*, p. 8

115   Hobson, *The Eastern Origins of Western Civilisation*, P. 115

116   Brotton, *Renaissance*, p. 19

117   Hobosn, *Eastern Origins*, p. 116

118   Hobosn, *Eastern Origins*, p. 116-117

119   Janet L. Abu-Lughod, *Before European Hegemony*, Oxford, Oxford University Press, 1989, p. 108

120   Abu-Lughod, *Before European Hegemony*, p. 67

121   Abu-Lughod, *Before European Hegemony*, p. 67

122   See Abu-Lughod, *Before European Hegemony*, p. 67

123   Gerald MaLean (Ed.), *Re-Orienting the Renaissance: Cultural Exchanges with the East*, New York, Palgrave Macmillan, 2005 p. 6

124   See John North, *The Ambassadors' Secret: Holbein and the World of the Renaissance*, London, Phoenix, 2004

125   See details in Geraldine A. Johnson, *Renaissance Art, A Very Short Introduction*, Oxford, Oxford University Press, 2005, p. 70-74

126   R. J. Knecht , *Francis I*, Cambridge, Cambridge University Press, 1982, p. 187-190

127   See Roger Bigelow Merriman, *Suleiman the Magnificent 1520-1566*, Worcestershire, Read Books, 2007

128   See Knecht, *Francis I*, p. 187

129   See Knecht, *Francis I*, p. 187; Frangipani returned with the following answer from Suleiman, on 6 February 1526: "I, the khan and sultan of Mediterranean, Black Sea, Anatolia, Karaman, Kurdistan, land of persian, Damascus, Aleppo, Egypt, Mecca and Medina, Jerusalem and all of the lands of arabian, yemen and all of many other countries; Son of the Bayezıd, Son of the Sultan Selim, Shadow of the God, Sultan Suleiman Khan and you, governor of the France, Francis...You have sent to my Porte, refuge of sovereigns, a letter by your faithful agent Frangipani, and you have furthermore entrusted to him sundry verbal communications; you have informed me that the enemy has overrun your country and that you are at present in prison and a captive, and you have here asked aid and succors for your deliverance. (...) Take courage

then, and be not dismayed. Our glorious predecessors and our illustrious ancestors (may God light up their tombs!) have never ceased to
make war to repel the foe and conquer his lands. We ourselves have
followed in their footsteps, and have at all times conquered provinces
and citadels of great strength and difficult of approach. Night and day
our horse is saddled and our saber is girt. May God on High promote
righteousness! May whatsoever He will be accomplished! For the rest,
question your ambassador and be informed..."

130   Gabor Agoston and Bruce Master (eds.), *Encyclopedia of Ottoman Em-
       pire,* New York, Facts On File, 2009, p. 542

131   *Encyclopedia of Ottoman Empire,* p. 542

132   A. Nuri Yurdusev et al., *Ottoman Diplomacy: Conventional or Uncon-
       ventional?,* New York, Palgrave Macmillan, 2004, p. 23

133   See Knecht, *Francis I,* p. 214

134   See Robert A. Kann, *A History of the Hapsburg Empire,* 1526-1918,
       Berkeley, University of California Press, 1980, p. 62

135   Brotton, *Renaissance,* p. 6-7

136   See Rosamond E. Mack, *Bazaar to Piazza: Islamic Trade and Italian
       Art, 1300-1600,* Berkeley, University of California Press, 2001

137   See Mack, *Bazaar,* p. 84

138   Brotton, *Renaissance,* p. 7

139   Brotton, *Renaissance,* p. 7

140   Brotton, *Renaissance,* p. 21

141   Brotton, *Renaissance,* p. 22

142   Brotton, *Renaissance,* p. 22

143   Brotton, *Renaissance,* p. 22-23

144   W. M. Watt, *Islamic Surveys: The Influence of Islam on Medieval Europe,*
       Edinburgh, Edinburgh University Press, 1972, p. 2; See also G. MacLean,
       Re-Orienting the Renaissance: Cultural Exchanges with the East, p. 6

145   Watt, *The Influence of Islam on Medieval Europe,* p. 84; See also S. M.
       Ghazanfar, *Medieval Islamic Thought,* New York, Routledge Curzon,
       2003, p. 182

146   Adam S. Francisco, *Martin Luther and Islam: A Study in Sixteenth-Cen-
       tury Polemics and Apologetics,* Brill, Leiden, 2007, p. 40

147 See Mark Greengrass, *Christendom Destroyed. Europe 1517-1648.* London, Penguin Books, 2014, p. 45, 340, 540ff

148 See Adam S. Francisco, *Martin Luther and Islam: A Study in Sixteenth-Century Polemics and Apologetics*; D. D. Grafton, (2017), *Martin Luther's sources on the Turk and Islam in the midst of the fear of Ottoman imperialism.* Muslim World, 107: 665-683. doi:10.1111/muwo.12215; see F. Guerin "Re-orienting the Reformation? Prolegomena to a History of the Reformation's Connection with the Islamic World" in N. R. F. Al-Rodhan (ed.), *The Role of the Arab-Islamic World in the Rise of the West,* London, Palgrave Macmillan, 2012, p.38-60

149 Tijana Krstic, *Contested Conversions to Islam: Narratives of Religious Change in the Early Modern Ottoman Empire,* Stanford, Stanford University Press, 2011, p. 77

150 See Nabil Matar, *Renaissance English Soldiers in the Armies of Islam.* Explorations in Renaissance Culture, (1995), 21, 81-95.

151 See Kaspars Klavins, The importance of Islamic civilization at the crossroads of European thinkers: 16th and 17th centuries, "Scholarly Papers"/ University of Latvia // Oriental Studies, Vol. 803. Riga, 2015, p. 8

152 See D. D. Grafton, (2017), *Martin Luther's sources on the Turk and Islam in the midst of the fear of Ottoman imperialism.* Muslim World, 107: 665-683. doi:10.1111/muwo.12215

153 See Ivan Kalmar, *Early Orientalism: Imagined Islam and the Notion of Sublime Power,* New York, Routledge, 2011, p. 54

154 D Niţulescu, *The Influence of the Ottoman Threat on the Protestant Reformation...*, https://digitalcommons.andrews.edu/cgi/viewcontent. cgi?article=1098&context=arc

155 Stephen A. Fischer-Galati, *Ottoman Imperialism and German Protestantism*, 1521-1555, Cambridge, Massachusetts, Harvard University Press, 1959, p. 112

156 See Steven Ozment, *The Age of Reform 1250-1550: An Intellectual And Religious History Of Late Medieval And Reformation Europe,* London, Yale University Press, 1980, chapter 8

157 Kenneth Setton, *Lutheranism and The Turkish Peril, in Europe and the Levant in the Middle Age and the Renaissance*, London, Variorum Reprints, 1976, 3.

158 Quoted in *The Armenian Review,* Volume 42, Hairenik Association,

1990 - Armenia, digitalized by the University of Virginia on June 26, 2007, p. 77

159   Abraham Ascher, Tibor Halasi-Kun, Béla K. Király, *The mutual effects of the Islamic and Judeo-Christian worlds: the East European pattern,* New York, Brooklyn College Press, 1979, p. 58

160   Jae Jerkins, *Islam in the Early Modern Protestant Imagination,* Eras, Edn 13, Issue 2, June 2012, p. 13

161   See Jerry Brotton, *The Sultan and the Queen: The Untold Story of Elizabeth and Islam,* New York, Penguin Books, 2016, p. 103ff

162   Jack Goody, *Islam in Europe,* Malden: Polity Press, 2004, p.162.

163   Jonathan Burton, *Traffic and Turning: Islam and English Drama, 1579-1624.* Delaware, University of Delaware Press, 2005. p. 64; Brotton, *The Sultan and the Queen,* p. 2

164   Jerkins, *Islam in the Early Modern Protestant Imagination,* p. 16

165   Brotton, *The Sultan and the Queen,* p. 2

166   Karen Ordahl Kupperman, *The Jamestown Project,* New Haven: Cambridge: University Press, 2007, p. 40

167   See Virginia Mason Vaughan *Performing Blackness on English Stages,* 1500–1800, Cambridge, Cambridge University Press, (2005)

168   Martin Luther, "War Against the Turk." *Works of Martin Luther,* Volume V. Trans. C. M. Jacobs. Cologne, Germany, Lindemann Press, 2007

169   Tijana Krstic, *Contested Conversions to Islam,* p. 87

170   Kaspars Klavins, *The importance of Islamic civilization at the crossroads of European thinkers: 16th and 17th centuries,* p. 9

171   Bela K. Kiraly (ed.), *Tolerance and Movements of Religious Dissent in Eastern Europe,* East European Monographs, New York, Columbia University Press, 1976

172   Kiraly, *Tolerance and Movements of Religious Dissent in Eastern Europe,* p. 199

173   Kiraly, *Tolerance and Movements of Religious Dissent in Eastern Europe,* p. 200

174   See D Nițulescu, *The Influence of the Ottoman Threat on the Protestant Reformation* ..., https://digitalcommons.andrews.edu/cgi/viewcontent. cgi?article=1098&context=arc; Stephen A. Fischer-Galati, *Ottoman Im-*

perialism and German Protestantism, 1521-1555, p. 112; Kenneth Setton, *Lutheranism and The Turkish Peril, in Europe and the Levant in the Middle Age and the Renaissance,* p. 3.

175   See F. Guerin "Re-orienting the Reformation? Prolegomena to a History of the Reformation's Connection with the Islamic World" in N. R. F. Al-Rodhan (ed.), *The Role of the Arab-Islamic World in the Rise of the West,* 2012, p.38-60

176   See George Huntson Williams, *The Radical Reformation,* London, Weidenfeld & Nicolson, 1962, p. xxxi.

177   See details in Sarah Mortimer and John Robertson eds., *The Intellectual Consequences of Religious Heterodoxy 1600–1750,* Leiden, Brills, 2012; Sarah Mortimer, *Reason and Religion in the English Revolution: The Challenge of Socinianism,* Cambridge, Cambridge University Press, 2010, p. 2ff

178   Mortimer, *Reason and Religion in the English Revolution,* p. 2

179   See details in Earl Morse Wilbur, *Our Unitarian heritage: An introduction to the history of the Unitarian movement,* Boston, Beacon Press, 1963, p. 55ff; Bibliotheca dissidentium: The Heidelberg antitrinitarians : Johann Sylvan, Adam Neuser, Matthias Vehe, Jacob Suter, Johann Hasler edited by André Séguenny, Jean Rott, Irena Backus, V. Koerner, 1980 ; http://pacificuu.org/wilbur/ahu/book1/index.html

180   See Susan J. Ritchie, *Children of the Same God: The Historical Relationship Between Unitarianism, Judaism, and Islam,* Boston, Skinner House Books, 2014

181   See Michael White, *The Pope & the Heretic: The True Story of Giordano Bruno, the Man Who Dared to Defy the Roman Inquisition,* New York, William Morrow, 2002, p. 7ff

182   See White, *The Pope & the Heretic,* p. 27ff

183   Frances Yates, *Giordano Bruno and the Hermetic Tradition,* Chicago, University of Chicago Press, 1964

184   Yates, *Giordano Bruno and the Hermetic Tradition,* p. 49ff, 450ff

185   *Cause, Principle and Unity,* by Giordano Bruno edited by R.J. Blackwell and Robert de Lucca, with an Introduction by Alfonso Ingegno. p.x. Cambridge University Press, 1998, p. x

186   *Cause, Principle and Unity,* by Giordano Bruno edited by R.J. Blackwell and Robert de Lucca, p. x

187   See Lecky, *History of the Rise and Influence of the Spirit of Rationalism in Europe*, v.1, p. 164ff

188   Samir Amin, *Eurocentrism*, p. 27

189   See details in John Coffey ed., *The Oxford History of Protestant Dissenting Traditions: The Post Reformation Era 1559-1689*, Oxford, Oxford University Press, 2020, vol. 1, p. 357ff

190   See details in Sarah Mortimer and John Robertson eds., *The Intellectual Consequences of Religious Heterodoxy 1600–1750*, p. 9ff

191   Lecky, *History of the Rise and Influence of the Spirit of Rationalism in Europe*, v.1, p. 80

192   S. F. Mason, "Science and Religion in Seventeenth Century England", p. 206-207

193   See details in John Coffey ed., *Oxford History of Protestant Dissenting Traditions*, p. 392ff

194   John Coffey ed., *Oxford History of Protestant Dissenting Traditions*, p. 392

195   See Matthew Birchwood, Staging Islam in England: Drama and Culture, 1640-1685, Cambridge, D. S. Brewer, 2007, p. 182; See James Mather, Pashas: Traders and Travellers in the Islamic World, New Haven, Yale University Press, 2009, p. 175ff; Noel Malcolm, Useful Enemies: Islam and the Ottoman Empire in Western Political Thought, 1450-1750, Oxford, Oxford University Press, 2019; Nabil Matar, Islam in Britain, 1558–1685, Cambridge, Cambridge University Press, 1998, p. 14-15; Matthew Dimmock, New Turkes: Dramatizing Islam and the Ottomans in Early Modern England, New York, Routledge, 2005, p. 207ff; Christopher J. Walker, Reason and Religion in Late Seventeenth-Century England: The Politics and Theology of Radical Dissent, London, I.B. Tauris, 2013

196   Jonathan Scott, *England's Troubles: Seventeenth Century English Political Instability in European Context*, Cambridge, Cambridge University Press, 2004, p. 253

197   In Bridget Heal and Anorthe Kremers eds., *Radicalism and Dissent in the World of Protestant Reform*, Göttingen, Vandenhoeck & Ruprecht, 2017, p. 201ff

198   See Lecky, *History of the Rise and Influence of the Spirit of Rationalism in Europe*, v.1, p. 149ff

199   See Barbara J. Shapiro, *A Culture of Fact: England,* 1550-1720, London, Cornell University Press, 2000

200   Mark Greengrass, *Christendom Destroyed.* Europe 1517-1648, p. 46

201   Robert J. Topinka, *Islam, England, and Identity in the Early Modern Period: A Review of Recent Scholarship,* Mediterranean Studies, "https://www.jstor.org/stable/i40051739" Vol. 18 (2009). p. 114; see Samuel C. Chew, *The Crescent and the Rose: Islam and England During the Renaissance,* New York, Octagon Press, 1937, vii; Emily C. Bartels, *Speaking of the Moor: from Alcazar to Othello,* Philadelphia, University of Pennsylvania Press, 2009; Nabil I. Matar, *Britain and Barbary, 1589-1689,* Gainesville, University of Florida Press, 2005; and Barbara Fuchs, *Exotic Nation: Maurophilia and the Construction of Early Modern Spain,* Philadelphia, University of Pennsylvania Press, 2008

202   Coffey ed., *Oxford History of Protestant Dissenting Traditions,* p. 391

203   In Bridget Heal and Anorthe Kremers eds., *Radicalism and Dissent in the World of Protestant Reform,* p. 223

204   See Jonathan I. Israel, *Radical Enlightenment: Philosophy and the Making of Modernity 1650-1750,* Oxford, Oxford University Press, 2001, p. 573

205   See Justin A. I. Champion, *The Pillars of Priestcraft Shaken: The Church of England and its Enemies, 1660-1730* (Cambridge Studies in Early Modern British History) 1st Edition, Cambridge, Cambridge University Press, 2014

206   See Lecky, *History of the Rise and Influence of the Spirit of Rationalism in Europe,* v.1, p. 121ff

207   See details in Margaret C. Jacob, *Newtonians and the English Revolution 1689-1720,* New York, Cornell University Press, 1976, p. 22ff

208   See Jacob, *Newtonians and the English Revolution 1689-1720,* p. 271ff

209   Noel Malcolm, *Useful Enemies,* p. 417

210   See John Coffey ed., *Oxford History of Protestant Dissenting Traditions,* p. 377ff

211   See Joachim Jeremias, *New Testament Theology,* John Bowden, trans. (New York: Charles Scribner's Sons, 1971; John N. D. Kelly, *Early Christian Doctrines,* New York, Harper and Brothers, 1958; Charles F. D. Moule, *The Origin of Christology,* Cambridge: Cambridge University Press, 1977

212   See John Hick, "A Remonstrance in Concluding," *Jesus in History and Myth*, R. J. Hoffmann, G. A. Larue, eds., Buffalo, Prometheus Books, 1986; John Hick, ed., *The Myth of God Incarnate,* Philadelphia, The Westminster Press, 1977

213   See details in Zulfiqar Ali Shah, *Islam's Reformation of Christianity,* Swansea, Claritis Books, 2021, chapter 1 & 2.

214   See Geza Vermes, *Jesus the Jew: A Historian's Reading of the Gospels,* Minneapolis, Fortress Press, 1981

215   See S. Angus, *The Mystery Religions: A Study in the Religious Backgrounds of Early Christianity,* New York, Dover Publications, 1975; W. H. C. Frend, *The Rise of Christianity,* Fortress Press, Philadelphia, 1984; Arthur Darby Nock, *Early Gentile Christianity and its Hellenistic Background,* New York, Harper Torchbooks, 1964

216   See details in Zulfiqar Ali Shah, *A Study of Anthropomorphism and Transcendence in the Bible and Quran: The Concept of God in Judaic, Christian and Islamic Traditions,* London, International Institute of Islamic Thought, 2012, p. 189 ff

217   See Shah, *A Study of Anthropomorphism and Transcendence in the Bible and Quran,* p. 232 ff

218   See Shah, *A Study of Anthropomorphism and Transcendence in the Bible and Quran,* p. 265

219   See *Augustine,* 'Unfinished Work in Answer to Julian', in *Answer to the Pelagians III* (*The Works of St. Augustine: A Translation for the 21ˢᵗ Century,* volume I/25), introduced, translated and with notes by Roland J. Teske, New City Press, New York, 1999; *Augustine, On Christian Teaching,* translated, introduced and with notes by R. P. H. Green, Oxford University Press, Oxford, 2008; R. A. Markus, *Sacred and Secular: Studies on Augustine and Latin Christianity,* Ashgate Variorum, Farnham, 1994

220   See James Boyce, *Born Bad: Original Sin and the Making of the Western World,* Black Inc., Collingwood, Australia, 2014

221   Diarmaid MacCulloch, *Reformation: Europe's House Divided 1490–1700,* Penguin, London, 2003; Euan Cameron, *The European Reformation* (second edition), Oxford University Press, Oxford, 2012, p. 15; Tatha Wiley, *Original Sin: Origins, Developments, Contemporary Meanings,* Paulist Press, New York & Mahwah, 2002; Hieko A. Oberman, *Luther: Man between God and the Devil,* translated by Eileen Walliser-Schwarzbart, New Haven, Yale University Press, 1989

222   See John Calvin, *Institutes of the Christian Religion,* translated by John Allen, First American Edition, London, 1813

223   See Jean Delumeau, *Sin and Fear: The Emergence of a Western Guilt Culture 13th to 18th Centuries* translated by Eric Nicholson, New York, St. Martin's Press, 1990

224   See R.I. Moore, *The Formation of a Persecuting Society: Power and Deviance in Western Europe AD 950–1250,* Oxford, 1986, Wiley-Blackwell, p. 6; see also Edward Peters, *Heresy and Authority in the Middle Ages,* London, University of Pennsylvania Press, 1980; Edward Peters, *Torture,* New York: Basil Blackwell, 1985

225   William Edward Hartpole Lecky, *History of the Rise and Influence of the Spirit of Rationalism in Europe,* v. 1, p. 156

226   See John Howard Yoder, *The Politics of Jesus,* Cambridge, William B. Eerdmans, 1994, p. 142

227   See Ernst Bammel and C. F. D. Moule eds., *Jesus and the Politics of His Day,* Cambridge, Cambridge University Press, 1984, p. 374

228   See Cornelius M. Stam, *Commentary on the Epistle of Roman,* Steven Point, WI, Berean Literature Foundation, 1984, p. 267-268

229   See Bammel and C. F. D. Moule eds., *Jesus and the Politics of His Day,* p. 374

230   See Cornelius M. Stam, *Commentary on the Epistle of Roman,* p. 268

231   See Charles Hodge, *Commentary on the Epistle to the Romans,* Albany, Books For The Ages, 1997, p. 631-632

232   See Douglas J. Moo, *The Epistle to the Romans,* Grand Rapids, MI, William B. Eerdmans, 1996, p. 790

233   Moo, *The Epistle to Romans,* p. 791

234   See Bammel and C. F. D. Moule eds., *Jesus and the Politics of His Day,* p. 263

235   See details in Lecky, *History of the Rise and Influence of the Spirit of Rationalism in Europe,* v. 1, p. 146ff

236   Ian Hunter, John Christian Laursen, and Cary J. Nederman eds., *Heresy in Transition,* Burlington, VT, Ashgate Publishing Company, 2005, p. 1; for a useful overview, see John B. Henderson, *The Construction of Orthodoxy and Heresy: Neo-Confucian, Islamic, Jewish, and Early Christian Patterns,* Albany, SUNY Press, 1998

237   See David M. Gwynn, *Christianity in the Later Roman Empire: A Source Book,* London, Bloomsbury, 2015, p. 50

238   Stephen Williams and Gerard Friell, *Theodosius, The Empire at Bay,* London, Routledge, 1994, p. 31

239   Clyde Pharr trans., *The Theodosian Code,* London, Oxford University Press, 1952, p. 440

240   Clyde Pharr trans., *The Theodosian Code,* P. 77

241   Ian Hunter, *Heresy in Transition,* p.1

242   Williams and Gerard Friell, *Theodosius,* 38

243   See Richard Lim, "Christian Triumph and Controversy" in G. W. Bowersock, Peter Brown and Oleg Grabar eds., *Interpreting Late Antiquity: Essays on the Postclassical World,* London, Balkan Press of Harvard University Press, 2001, p. 208

244   See Perez Zagorin, *How the Idea of Religious Toleration Came to the West,* New Jersey, Princeton University, 2003, P. 23

245   Richard Lim, "Christian Triumph and Controversy" in G. W. Bowersock, Peter Brown and Oleg Grabar, *Interpreting Late Antiquity: Essays on the Postclassical World,* p. 208

246   Michael Gaddis, *There Is No Crime for Those Who Have Christ,* Berkeley, University of California Press, 2005, p. 133

247   Zagorin, *How the Idea of Religious Toleration,* p. 29

248   Philip Schaff, *Augustin: The Writings Against the Manichaeans and Against the Donatists,* New York: The Christian Literature Publishing Co., 1890, p. 817

249   See Alexandra Walsham, *Charitable Hatred: Tolerance and Intolerance in England 1500-1700,* Manchester, Manchester University Press, 2006, p. 2 ff

250   Schaff, *Augustine,* p. 817

251   Schaff, *Augustine,* p. 817

252   Gaddis, *There Is No Crime,* p. 134

253   Schaff, *Augustine,* p. 817-818

254   See Zagorin, *How the Idea of Toleration,* p. 30

255   See Edward Peters, *Inquisition,* New York, Free Press, 1988

256   Zagorin, *How the Idea of Toleration,* p. 32; W. J. Sheils, ed., *Persecution*

and Toleration. Studies in Church History, 21, Oxford, Blackwell, 1984.

257   See Peter Brown, "St. Augustine's Attitude to Religious Coercion." *The Journal of Roman Studies*, vol. 54, 1964, pp. 107–116., www.jstor.org/stable/298656, p. 107

258   Brown, *Augustine's Attitude*, p. 110

259   See Karen Sullivan, *Truth and the Heretic. Crises of Knowledge in Medieval French Literature*, Chicago, University of Chicago Press, 2005; W. L. Wakefield, *Heresy, Crusade and Inquisition in Southern France, 1100–1250*, London, Allen & Unwin, 1974, http://hdl.handle.net/2027/heb.01080.0001.001

260   See William Tabbernee, *Fake Prophecy and Polluted Sacraments*, Boston, Brill, 2007, p. 335

261   See J. A. S. Evans, *The Age of Justinian*, London, Routledge, 1996, p. 246

262   See Evans, *The Age of Justinian*, p. 240

263   Evans, *Age of Justinian*, p. 249

264   See Christine Caldwell Ames, *Righteous Persecution: Inquisition, Dominicans and Christianity in the Middle Ages*, Philadelphia, University of Pennsylvania Press, 2009

265   See John Coffey, *Persecution and Toleration in Protestant England 1558-1689*, New York, Routledge, 2000; Alexandra Walsham, *Charitable Hatred: Tolerance and Intolerance in England 1500-1700*

266   Jonathan Israel, *Radical Enlightenment: Philosophy and the Making of Modernity 1650-1750*, Oxford, Oxford University Press, 2001, p. 4

267   Jonathan I. Israel, *Enlightenment Contested: Philosophy, Modernity and the Emancipation of Man 1670-1752*, Oxford, Oxford University Press, 2006, p. 69

268   See William J. Bulman, *Anglican Enlightenment: Orientalism, Religion and Politics in England and its Empire*, 1648-1715, Cambridge, Cambridge University Press, 2015, p. 4

269   John Robertson, *The Case for the Enlightenment: Scotland and Naples 1680-1760*, Cambridge, Cambridge University Press, 2005, p. 28

270   See Bulman, *Anglican Enlightenment*, p. 4

271   See Robertson, *The Case for the Enlightenment*, p. 31; see Ole Peter Grell and Roy Potter eds., *Toleration in Enlightenment England*, Cambridge, Cambridge University Press, 2000, p. 1ff

272   Huge Trevor-Roper, *History and the Enlightenment,* London, Yale University Press, 2010, p. 71

273   See Bulman, *Anglican Enlightenment,* p. xii-xiii

274   See Gertrude Himmelfarb, *The Roads to Modernity: The British, French and American Enlightenments,* New York, Vintage Books, 2005, Preface

275   John William Draper, *History of the Conflict Between Religion and Science,* p. xiii; also see Alfred G. McKinney, Mohammed, *The Myths,* New York, i Universe Inc, 2007, p. 28

276   See Thomas Dixon, Geoffrey Canter, and Stephen Pumfrey (eds.), *Science and Religion: New Historical Perspectives,* Cambridge, Cambridge University Press, 2010, p. 113

277   Lecky, *History of the Rise and Influence of the Spirit of Rationalism in Europe,* v. 1, p. 98

278   See Draper, *History of the Conflict,* chapter III, p. 68-101

279   Martin Pugh, *Britain and Islam: New Haven,* Yale University Press, 2019, p. 4

280   See details in Lecky, *History of the Rise and Influence of the Spirit of Rationalism in Europe,* v. 1, p. 92ff

281   See Lecky, *History of the Rise and Influence of the Spirit of Rationalism in Europe,* v. 1, p. 150ff

282   Lecky, *History of the Rise and Influence of the Spirit of Rationalism in Europe,* v. 1, p. 148ff

283   Pugh, *Britain and Islam,* p. 7

284   Draper, *History of the Conflict,* p. 84

285   See John V. Tolan, Faces of Muhammad: *Western Perception of the Prophet of Islam from Middle Ages to Today,* Princeton, Princeton University Press, 2019

286   See Surah al-Kahf, verse 4 "And to warn those who say, "God has begotten a son." (18:4)

287   Draper, *History of the Conflict,* xiii

288   Draper, *History of the Conflict,* xiv

289   Toshihiko Izutsu, *God and Man in the Quran: Semantics of the Quranic Weltanschauung,* Tokyo, Keio University, 1964, p. 136

290   Franz Rosenthal, *Man Versus Society in Early Islam,* edited by Dimitri Gutas, Leiden, Brill, 2015, p. 565

291   See L. Rosen, *Justice of Islam: Comparative Perspectives on Islamic Law and Society,* Oxford, Oxford University Press, 2000 p. 70

292   See details in Rosenthal, *Man Versus Society in Early Islam,* chapter II, "The Muslim Concept of Freedom Prior to the Nineteenth Century", p. 21ff

293   Patricia Crone, *God's Rule, Government and Islam,* New York, Columbia University Press, 2004, p. 6

294   Crone, *God's Rule,* p. 14

295   See Imam Feisal Abdul Rauf, *What is Right With Islam,* New York, HarperCollins, 2004, p. 45ff

296   See Toshihiko Izutsu, *Ethico-Religious Concepts in the Qur'ān,* McGill-Queen's University Press, 2002; Fazlur Rahman, *Major Theme of the Quran,* Minneapolis, Bibliotheca Islamica, 1994

297   See Mohammad Omar Farooq, *Towards Our Reformation: From Legalism to Value-Oriented Islamic Law and Jurisprudence,* London, International Institute of Islamic Thought, 2011, p. 36ff; for a different perspective see Jacques Ellul, *Islam and Judeo-Christianity: A Critique of Their Commonality,* Translated by D. Bruce MacKay, Eugene, OR, Cascade Books, 2015, p. 69ff

298   Pugh, *Britain and Islam,* p. 10

299   Imam Feisal Abdul Rauf, *Defining Islamic Statehood, Measuring and Indexing Contemporary Muslim States,* London, Palgrave Macmillan, 2015, p. 67ff

300   Amina Wadud, "Freedom and Responsibility: An Islamic Perspective" in *Freedom and Responsibility, Christian and Muslim Explorations* edited by Simone Sinn and Martin L. Sinaga, Minneapolis, Luther University Press, 2010, p. 27

301   See C. G. Weeramantry, Islamic Jurisprudence, An International Perspective, London, Macmillan Press, 1988, p. 113-125; David Pearl, *A Textbook on Muslim Personal Law,* London: Croom Helm,1979, pp. 41–57, 77–84, 100–120; Sayed Khatab and Gary D. Bouma, *Democracy in Islam,* New York, Routledge, 2007, p. 24-25

302   See Muhammad Shafiq, *The Role And Place of Shura In The Islamic Polity,* Islamabad, Islamic Studies, Vol. 23, No. 4 (Winter 1984), pp. 419-441

303   Ilyas Ahmad, The Social Contract and the Foundations of the Islamic State, *The Indian Journal of Political Science*, Vol. 4, No. 2 (October—December, 1942), pp. 132-169

304   Feisal Abdul Rauf, *Defining Islamic Statehood*, p. 63ff

305   See details in Azizah Y. al-Hibri, *Islam and American Constitutional Law: Borrowing Possibilities or a History of Borrowing*, University of Pennsylvania *Journal of Constitutional Law* 1.3 (1999): 492-527.

306   Sayed Khatab and Gary D. Bouma, *Democracy in Islam*, p. 18-19

307   Sayed Khatab and Gary D. Bouma, *Democracy in Islam*, p. 19

308   Sayed Khatab and Gary D. Bouma, *Democracy in Islam*, p. 19-20

309   Sayed Khatab and Gary D. Bouma, *Democracy in Islam*, p. 20

310   Sayed Khatab and Gary D. Bouma, *Democracy in Islam*, p. 20

311   J. Wellhausen, *The Arab Kingdom and Its Fall*, translated by Margaret Graham Wier, Calcutta, Calcutta University Press, 1927, p. 8-9

312   See M. H. Kamali, *Caliphate and Political Jurisprudence in Islam: Historical and Contemporary Perspectives*. Muslim World, 106, 2016, p. 384–403. doi:10.1111/muwo.12145; For Shi'ite concept of "Deputyship of Imam" see Abdulaziz A. Sachedina, *The Just Ruler (al-Sultan al-'Adil) in Shi'ite Islam*, Oxford, Oxford University Press, 1998, p. 29ff

313   See Hugh Kennedy, Caliphate, *The History of an Idea*, New York, Basic Books, 2016, p. chapter 1

314   See details in Sayed Khatab and Gary D. Bouma, *Democracy in Islam*, p. 7-23

315   See details in Anis Ahmad, *Islam's political order: the model, deviations and Muslim response : al-Khilāfah wa al-mulākīyah*, Islamabad, Institute of Policy Studies, Islamabad, 2018

316   See Imam Feisal Abdul Rauf, *Defining Islamic Statehood, Measuring and Indexing Contemporary Muslim States*, p. 30ff

317   John L. Esposito, *What Everyone Needs to Know About Islam*, Oxford, Oxford University Press, 2002, p. 70; Juan Cole, Muhammad: Prophet of Peace Amid the Clash of Empires, New York, Nation Books, 2018. p. 172, 181; Karen Barkey, Empire of Difference: The Ottomans in Comparative Perspective, Cambridge, Cambridge University Press, 2008, p. 153; Karen Barkey, Islam and Toleration: Studying the Ottoman Imperial Model, International Journal of Politics, Culture, and Society, (2005), 19:5-19

318   Esposito, *What Everyone Needs to Know About Islam*, p. 70-71

319   See details in Karen Armstrong, *Muhammad: A Biography of the Prophet*, San Francisco, Harper Collins, 1992, p.11; Norman Daniel, *Islam and the West: The Making of an Image*, Edinburgh, Edinburgh University Press, 1989, p.297 ff

320   See Charles D. Gunnoe Jr., *Thomas Erastus and the Palatinate: A Renaissance Physician in the Second Reformation*, Leiden, Brills, 2011; Christopher J. Burchill, *The Heidelberg Antitrinitarians*. Bibliotheca Dissidentium, vol, XI, ed., Andre Seguenny. Baden-Baden: Editions Valentin Koemer, 1989

321   See Zachary W. Schulz, *The English In The Levant: Commerce, Diplomacy, And The English Nation In The Ottoman Empire, 1672-1691*, A Ph.D. Dissertation Submitted to the Faculty of Purdue University, West Lafayette, Indiana, 2018, p. 130

322   See details in Saumitra Jha, *Financial Asset Holdings and Political Attitudes: Evidence from Revolutionary England, The Quarterly Journal of Economics* (2015), 1485–1545. doi:10.1093/qje/qjv019; Daron Acemoglu, Simon Johnson, and James Robinson, "The Rise of Europe: Atlantic Trade, Institutional Change and Economic Growth," American Economic Review, 95 (2005), 546–579.

323   See William Dalrymple, *The Anarchy: The Relentless Rise of the East India Company*, New York. Bloombury, 2019, p. 3ff

324   F. P. Wilson, *The Plague in Shakespeare's London*, new edn, Oxford, Oxford University Press, 1963

325   See J. F. D. Shrewsbury, *A History of Bubonic Plague in the British Isles*, Cambridge, Cambridge University Press, 1970

326   See C. Bridenbaugh, *Vexed and Troubled Englishmen*, Oxford, Oxford University Press,1968

327   See details in Keith Thomas, *Religion and the Decline of Magic: Studies in Popular Beliefs in Sixteenth and Seventeenth Century England*, London, Penguin Books, 1991, p. 21ff

328   See William Manchester, *A World Lit only by Fire*

329   See Christopher Hill, *The World Turned Upside-down: Radical Ideas During the English Revolution*, London, Penguin Books, 1972

330   See details in Keith Thomas, *Religion and the Decline of Magic: Studies in Popular Beliefs in Sixteenth and Seventeenth Century England*, p. 3

331   Nabil Matar, "England and Religious Plurality: Henry Stubbe, John Locke and Islam", https://www.cambridge.org/core. https://doi.org/10.1017/S042420840005018X, p. 181

332   See Keith Thomas, *Religion and the Decline of Magic Studies in Popular Beliefs in Sixteenth and Seventeenth Century England,* p. 3. Even the more prosperous and progressive Dutch were considered so. See Claudia Schnurmann, "Wherever profit leads us. To every sea and shore. . .': The VOC, the WIC, and Dutch Methods of Globalisation in the Seventeenth Century," *Renaissance Studies* 17 (2003): 474–93; here 483. Cf. Andre Gunder Frank, *ReOrient: Global Economy in the Asian Age,* Berkeley, University of California Press, 1997.

333   William Dalrymple, *The Anarchy: The Relentless Rise of the East India Company,* 3

334   Paul Hazard, *The Crisis of the European Mind: 168-1715* translated by J. Lewis May, New York, New York Review Books, 2013, p. 5

335   See John Morrill, *The Nature of the English Revolution,* New York, Routledge, 2013, p. 2-3

336   See Richard L. Greaves, *Society and Religion in Elizabethan England,* Minneapolis, University of Minnesota Press, 1981, p. 332

337   See Greaves, *Society and Religion in Elizabethan England*

338   See B. Coward, *The Stuart Age – England, 1603–1714* 5th edition ch.4. New York, Routledge, 2017

339   Hill, *The World Turned Upside-down,* p. 13

340   J. H. Plumb, *The Growth of Political Stability in England 1675–1725,* London, Macmillan,1967, p. 13

341   Jonathan Scott, *England's Troubles: Seventeenth Century English Political Instability in European Context,* p. 47

342   See Scott, *England's Troubles,* p. 90. "For the fact that in crucial respects, moreover, it was religious passions that drove political ones there were several reasons. One was that, weak though the monarchy may have been, the English protestant church was more recent. It was a product of the still unfolding and embattled reformation. If the national boundaries of politics were therefore permeable and half-formed, those of religion were frailer still. Not all members of the Church of England agreed with one another. All agreed, however, that they were protestants: participants in a European reformation process and identity."

343 John Locke, *Two Tracts*, ed. Philip Abrams, Cambridge, Cambridge University Press, 1967, p.160–1.

344 See *The Correspondence of John Locke*, ed. E. S. de Beer (8 vols., Oxford 1976–89), vol. I, p. 82; W. Spellman, *John Locke*, London, Springer, 1997.

345 William J. Bulman, *Enlightenment and Religious Politics in Restoration England*, History Compass 10/10 (2012): 752–764, 10.1111/j.1478-0542.2012.00873.x, p. 755

346 See Bulman, *Enlightenment and Religious Politics in Restoration England*, p. 755

347 Hill, *The World Turned Upside-down*, p. 98

348 Geoffrey Parker, *The Military Revolution*, Cambridge, Cambridge University Press,1988, p. 135, Dalrymple, *Anarchy*, p. 15

349 See details in Rhoads Murphey, *Ottoman Warfare*, 1500-1700, New Jersey, Rutgers University Press, 1999; Gábor Ágoston, *Guns for the Sultan: Military Power and the Weapons Industry in the Ottoman Empire*, Cambridge, Cambridge University Press, 2005; Mesut Uyar, and Edward J. Erickson. *A Military History of the Ottomans: From Osman to Atatürk*, Wisconsin, Pleager Security International, 2009.

350 Conrad Russell, *Unrevolutionary England*, 1603-1642, London, Hambledon Press, 1990, p. 183

351 Conrad Russell, *Unrevolutionary England*, 1603-1642, p. 184

352 "Under Charles I and Archbishop Laud, however, there was a concerted campaign to remodel the British churches. In matters of doctrine, the Laudians rejected the predestinarianism of Zwingli and Calvin, preferring the teaching of the Greek Fathers and the Dutch Arminians who had emphasised the synergy of divine grace and human freewill in salvation. In matters of worship, Laudians sought to infuse 'the beauty of holiness' into Protestantism through choral music, elaborate vestments, liturgical rites and restoration of altars. Communicants were to kneel at the altar rails, and receive the elements from the priest, thus imbibing a high view of both the eucharist and the priestly office. In matters of discipline and government, the Laudians asserted the authority of the higher clergy over parish pastors, often justifying this by a divine right (*jure divino*) theory of episcopacy that cast doubt on the legitimacy of the ministry in Europe's non-episcopal Reformed churches. These policies involved a fundamental realignment of the *Ecclesia Anglicana*." JRD Coffey, , 'Religious Thought', 'in The Oxford

Handbook of the English Revolution' ed. by M. J. Braddick, p. 447

353   See JRD Coffey, 'Religious Thought',

354   See Charles W. A. Prior and Glenn Burgess eds, *England's Wars of Religions*, Revisited, Burlington, Ashgate, p. 47; Anthony Milton, *Laudian and Royalist Polemic in Seventeenth-Century England: The Career and Writings of Peter Heylyn*, Manchester, Manchester University Press, 2007; Johann P. Sommerville, 'The Royal Supremacy and Episcopacy "iure divino", 1603–1640', *Journal of Ecclesiastical History*, 34 (1984): pp. 548–58.

355   See Charles W. A. Prior and Glenn Burgess eds, *England's Wars of Religions*, Revisited, p. 100; also see Theodore D. Bozeman, *To Live Ancient Lives*, Chapel Hill, University of North Carolina Press, 1988, p. 26

356   See John Morril, *The Nature of English Revolution*, New York, Routledge, 2013, p. 9

357   Scott, *England's Troubles*, p. 52

358   John Morril, *The Nature of English Revolution*, p. 2. "After chronic instability and civil war for much o f the fifteenth century (the consequence o f the complicated marital affairs of Edward III and John of Gaunt and the consequence of the Lancastrian *coup d'etat* o f 1399), the country teetered on the brink of civil war for much o f the sixteenth century as the doubtful legitimacy o f H enry VIII's daughters and the childlessness of all three of his children made a War of the English Succession an ever-present threat. In 1559 a heretic bastard Queen (three damning qualities) was trying to secure the throne and was faced by a formidable rival in Mary o f Scotland, married to King Francis II o f France. If Francis had fathered a child by Mary before he died unexpectedly of an ear infection at the age o f nineteen, there would have been a single heir to the thrones of France, Scotland and England, a circumstance that would have ensured that the great Habsburg/Valois struggle would have been fought out on British soil." P. 2

359   "The period from 1569 to 1642 was the longest period ever without a major rebellion; the period 1605 to 1641 the longest without the conviction of a peer of the realm for treason; the number of trials for treasons declined decade by decade from the late sixteenth century through to the 1630s. Where else in the early seventeenth century were few or no royal officials killed in discharging their duties? Was not England alone in not having no-go areas for unaccompanied tax-collectors? Were there not more dead bodies on stage at the end of a production of *Hamlet* than following any collective act of violence in the

period up to 1642? Where else was the arbitration o f the royal courts so completely accepted? Riots declined in number, in the num ber of those involved and in intensity after the turn o f the sixteenth century. Englishmen were notorious throughout Europe for being litigious. They were litigious because they were law-abiding." Morrill, *Nature of English Revolution,* p. 5

360   "By the 1620s, the centre o f gravity o f European power politics had moved eastward again, to the Rhineland and to Bohemia: invasions o f the British Isles, even assistance to rebels, were not on the agenda o f over-com m itted continental m onarchs." Morrill, *Nature of English Revolution,* p. 3

361   See Nicholas Tyacke, *Anti-Calvinists: The Rise of English Arminianism, c.1590-1640,* Oxford, Clarendon Press, 1987; Kenneth Fincham and Nicholas Tyacke, *Altars Restored: The Changing Face of English Religious Worship,* 1547-c.1700, Oxford, Oxford University Press, 2007; Anthony Milton, *Catholic and Reformed: The Roman and Protestant Churches in English Protestant Thought,* 1600-1640, Cambridge, Cambridge University Press, 1995; Jean-Louis Quantin, *The Church of England and Christian Antiquity: The Construction of a Confessional Identity in the 17th Century,* Oxford, Oxford University Press, 2009.

362   See John Morril, *The Nature of English Revolution,* p. 10

363   See details in JOHN ADAMSON: *The Noble Revolt: The Overthrow of Charles I.* London: Weidenfeld & Nicolson, 2007

364   See Mark Häberlein, *A 16th-Century German Traveller's Perspective on Discrimination and Tolerance in the Ottoman Empire,* 2008, https://www.researchgate.net/publication/237274589_A_Sixteenth-Century_German_Traveller's_Perspective_on_Discrimination_and_Tolerance_in_the_Ottoman_Empire and his K.H. Dannenfeldt, *Leonhard Rauwolf: Sixteenth-Century Physician,* Botanist, and Traveller, Cambridge, Mass. Harvard University Press,1968. "During his stay in the Syrian city of Aleppo in the mid-1570s, the German traveller Leonhard Rauwolf, a physician from the imperial city of Augsburg, heard a remarkable story about the Ottoman sultan Suleyman. According to Rauwolf, Suleyman once discussed with his advisers whether the Jews in his territories should be tolerated or exterminated. Most members of his council expressed the opinion that the Jews did not merit toleration since they burdened the people with their abominable usurious practices. The sultan then asked his councillors to regard the forms and colours of the flowers that were arranged in a bouquet in their

midst. Did they share his opinion that each flower in its particular shape and colour added to the beauty of the others? When the councillors agreed, the sultan pointed out to them that he ruled over many different nations – Turks, Moors, Greeks and others. Each of these nations contributed to the wealth and reputation of his kingdom, and in order to continue this happy situation, he deemed it wise to continue to tolerate those who were already living together under his rule. His advisers liked this proposition so well that they unanimously accepted it." *Leonhard Rauwolf: Sixteenth-Century Physician*, p. 202-203

365   Häberlein, *A 16ᵗʰ-Century German Traveller's Perspective on Discrimination and Tolerance in the Ottoman Empire*, p. 120; G. Adams, *The Huguenots and French Opinion, 1685-1787. The Enlightenment Debate on Toleration*, Waterloo, Ontario 1991, pp. 63-64; O.P. Grell, B. Scribner (eds.), *Tolerance and Intolerance in the European Reformation*. On the situation of Jews, see J.I. Israel, *European Jewry in the Age of Mercantilism, 1550-1750*, Oxford, Oxford University Press,1985.

366   Andrew Lake, *The First Protestants in the Arab World: The Contribution to Christian Mission of the English Aleppo Chaplians 1597-1782*, Melbourn School of Theology, 2015, P. 32; William Biddulph, *The Travels of Certaine Englishmen into Africa, Asia and to the Blacke Sea* London: Aspley, 1609; Theophilus Lavender, "The Travels of Four Englishmen and a Preacher ". Chap. 12 In *A Collection of Voyages and Travels*, edited by Anon. Voyages and Travels Published from the Earl of Oxford's Library. London: Thomas Osborne, 1745, p. 794-95

367   See Simon Mills (2011) *The English Chaplains at Aleppo: Exploration and Scholarship between England and the Ottoman Empire*, 1620–1760, Bulletin for the Council for British Research in the Levant, 6:1, 13-20, p. 13; Charles Robson, Nevves from Aleppo: A letter written to T. V. B. of D. Vicar of Cockfi eld in Southsex· By Charles Robson Master of Artes, fellow of Qu: Col: in Oxford, and preacher to the Company of our English Merchants at Aleppo. Containing many remarkeable occurrences obserued by him in his iourney, thither (London, 1628), 14–15

368   See details in John Coffey, *Puritanism And Liberty Revisited* : The Case For Toleration In The English Revolution, *The Historical Journal*, 41, 4 (1998), pp. 961-985, p. 973ff

369   Extortion was common, "there is evidence that some monarchs extorted money by demanding loans or presents in return for renewing or extending the EIC's trading monopoly during the period of royal control in the 1600s. Also some monarchs encouraged 'interlopers' to enter the

EIC's market undermining its profits. Moreover, the narrative history suggests that renegotiation of the charter, bribes, and the like often occurred in the wake of a monarch change, implying such events raised the risk of extraction." Dan Bogart and Marco Del Angel, *Monarchs, institutional change, and the trade of the English East India Company,* http://www.socsci.uci.edu/~dbogart/eic_shipping_oct212019.pdf, P. 2

370   Saumitra Jha, *Financial Asset Holdings and Political Attitudes: Evidence from Revolutionary England,* p. 1494; Glenn Burgess, *The Politics of the Ancient Constitution: An Introduction to English Political Thought, 1603–1642,* University Park: Pennsylvania State University Press, 1992; Samuel Rawson Gardiner ed., *Parliamentary Debates in 1610,* Edited, from the *Notes of a Member of the House of Commons,* vol. 81, London: Camden Society, 1862.

371   "The loan in 1641 to Charles I came just before the Civil War between the monarchy and parliament. The loan in 1643 to the Long Parliament happened just after the start of the Civil War. The loan in 1659 to the Council of State was made shortly after the death of Oliver Cromwell, England's leader during its brief Republic. Finally, the loan in 1662 to Charles II came two years after the Restoration of the Monarchy in 1660." Dan Bogart and Marco Del Angel, *Monarchs, institutional change, and the trade of the English East India Company,* p. 7

372   See Dan Bogart and Marco Del Angel, *Monarchs, institutional change, and the trade of the English East India Company,* p. 7-8

373   Saumitra Jha, *Financial Asset Holdings and Political Attitudes: Evidence from Revolutionary England,* p. 1494; Theodore K. Rabb, *Enterprise and Empire: Merchant and Gentry Investment in the Expansion of England, 1575–1630,* Cambridge, MA, Harvard University Press, 1967, p. 71-75

374   See Saumitra Jha, *Financial Asset Holdings and Political Attitudes: Evidence from Revolutionary England,* p. 1502ff

375   Philip Lawson, *The East India Company: A History,* New York, Routledge, 1994, p. 74

376   Saumitra Jha, *Financial Asset Holdings and Political Attitudes: Evidence from Revolutionary England,* p. 1494; Christopher Hill, *The Century of Revolution: 1603–1714,* New York: Routledge, 1961, p. 48-50; T. K. Rabb, *Jacobean Gentleman: Sir Edwin Sandys, 1561-1629,* Princeton, NJ: Princeton University Press, 1998.

377   Saumitra Jha, *Financial Asset Holdings and Political Attitudes: Evidence from Revolutionary England,* p. 1495; David L. Smith, *The Stuart Par-*

liaments, 1603–1689, London: Arnold, 1999, p. 53-55

378   Saumitra Jha, *Financial Asset Holdings and Political Attitudes: Evidence from Revolutionary England,* p. 1496; James D. Fearon, "Bargaining over Objects that Influence Future Bargaining Power," Mimeo, APSA general meetings, 1996, p. 48-49

379   John Morril, *The Nature of English Revolution,* p. 14

380   See John Coffey, "The Toleration Controversy during the English Revolution" in C. Durston and J. Maltby, eds, *Religion in Revolutionary England,* Manchester University Press, 2006. P. 42-68.

381   See details in John Coffey ed., *Oxford History of Protestant Dissenting Traditions,* Part 1, p. 41-73

382   See John Coffey, *Puritanism And Liberty Revisited,* p. 978ff

383   See J. C. Davis, Religion and the Struggle for Freedom in the English Revolution, *The Historical Journal* 35,3 (1992), p. 507-530

384   John Coffey, *Puritanism And Liberty Revisited,* p. 973; Franklin Hamlin Little, Anabaptist View: A Study in the Origins of Sectarian Protestantism, p. 47, 54; Bard Thompson and George H. Bricker, eds. Lancaster Series on the Mercersburg Theology, vol. 1, The Principle of Protestantism, by Philip Schaff, United Church Press, 1845.

385   John Coffey, *Puritanism And Liberty Revisited,* p. 973

386   Quoted In John Coffey, *Puritanism And Liberty Revisited,* p. 964

387   Quoted in John Coffey, *Puritanism And Liberty Revisited,* p. 965

388   Roger Williams, *The bloudy tenent of persecution* [1644], ed. E. B. Underhill, London, 1848, p. 2.

389   Roger Williams, *The bloudy tenent of persecution,* p. 2; also Oscar S. Straus, *Roger Williams: The Pioneer of Religious Liberty,* New York, Century Co, 1894

390   Quoted in Don M. Wolfe, *Milton in the Puritan Revolution,* New York, Humanities Press, 1963, p. 87

391   Quoted in Don M. Wolfe, *Milton in the Puritan Revolution,* p. 87

392   S. Fisher, *Christianismus redivivus, Christendom both unchrist'ned and new christ'ned* (1655), pp. 533-51, quotations at pp. 534, 537

393   Richard Ashcraft, *Revolutionary Politics and John Locke's Two Treatises of Governemnt,* New Jersey, Princeton University Press, 1986,

chapter 4, p. 143ff

394   Richard Ashcraft, *Revolutionary Politics and Locke's Two Treatises of Government: Radicalism and Lockean Political Theory,* Political Theory , Nov., 1980, Vol. 8, No. 4 (Nov., 1980), pp. 429-486 p. 458

395   Quoted in John Coffey, *Puritanism And Liberty Revisited,* p. 969

396   https://quod.lib.umich.edu/e/eebo2/A67478.0001.001/1:2?rgn=-div1;view=fulltext, p. 11; also *The Writings of William Walwyn,* (eds) Jack R. McMichael & Barbara Taft, University of Georgia Press, Athens, Georgia, 1989, p. 26; Peter Richard Pick, *Interjections Of Silence: The Poetics And Politics Of Radical Protestant Writing,* 1642-1660, Ph.D. dissertation submitted to The University of Birmingham, School of English, 2000, p. 52

397   *The writings of William Walwyn,* ed. J. R. McMichael and B. Taft, Athens, GA, 1989, pp. 57-9, 164.

398   Don M. Wolfe, *Milton in the Puritan Revolution,* p. 76

399   Quoted in John Coffey, *Puritanism And Liberty Revisited,* p. 969

400   John Coffey, *Puritanism And Liberty Revisited,* p. 970

401   See details in Blair Warden, *God's Instruments: Political Conduct in the England of Oliver Cromwell,* Oxford, Oxford University Press, 2012, p. 73ff

402   See details in Blair Worden, *God's Instruments: Political Conduct in the England of Oliver Cromwell,* Oxford, Oxford University Press, 2012, p. 64ff

403   John Coffey, *Puritanism And Liberty Revisited,* p. 964

404   Williams, *Bloudy tenent,* p. 46.

405   For Congregationalism see Zakai, Religious Toleration and Its Enemies: The Independent Divines and the Issue of Toleration during the English Civil War, *Albion:* A Quarterly Journal Concerned with British Studies, Vol. 21, No. 1 (Spring, 1989), pp. 1-33, p. 31

406   John Coffey, *Puritanism And Liberty Revisited,* p. 976

407   John Morril, *The Nature of English Revolution,* p. 16

408   See H. Garcia, *Islam and English Enlightenment,* Baltimore: John Hopkins University Press, 2012, p. 133ff; On the Quaker fascination with Ibn Tufayl's book, see Nawal Muhammad Hassan, *Hayy Bin Yaqzan and Robinson Crusoe: A Study of an Early Arabic Impact on English Literature,* Baghdad: Al-Rashid House, 1980, 5–6. In *The True Christian Divinity* (1678), the Quaker apologist Robert Barclay identifies the views

expressed in *Hayy ibn Yaqzan* with the Quaker teachings of the "inner light." On the connection between Quakerism and Mahometanism, seen as two heresies that share the same republican spirit, see Francis Bugg, *Hidden things brought to light, whereby the Fox is unkennell'd: and the bowells of Quakerism ript up, laid open, and expos'd to publick view* (London, 1707), 175, 202, and *Life and Actions of Mahomet in Four Treatises concerning Mahometanism* (London, 1712), 29. A discussion on Islam and Quakerism in seventeenth-century England is provided in Nabil Matar, "Some Notes on George Fox and Islam," *The Journal of the Friends' Historical Society* 55 (1989): 271–76.

409   "Campaigns (mainly peaceful and impractical) were launched for the abolition of the rights of primogeniture, for granting security of tenure to tenant farmers, for the return to common use of the ancient common lands which had been enclosed over the previous century by landlords and larger farmers, and for strengthening the position of independent small producers and craftsmen at the expense of entrepreneurs and pro-to-capitalist merchants. Underpinning such demands for social reform was a radical extension of notions of social contract. The leaders of the Levellers argued that rulers were not appointed by God (as Charles I had argued) nor in agreement between king and people (as many Parliamentarians had argued) but in an agreement among the people themselves. The Levellers asserted that abuses of power by all existing institutions (the standing Parliament as well as the king) invalidated their right to govern. What was needed was a new social contract - what they called (in a very literal sense) the Agreement of the People - by which all who wished to enjoy political rights opted into an agreement by which limited powers to maintain order would be accorded to *elected* governors. The mechanism of selection (the extent of democracy) was less important than the end - the accountability of all who exercised authority, the rigidly fixed and non-renewable terms of office which would prevent the concentration of power in particular hands, a hatred of 'professionals' in government (e.g. lawyers and judges who claimed to be able to mediate justice through their mastery of arcane legal language and procedures)." John Morril, *The Nature of English Revolution*, p. 19

410   See Blair Worden, "Oliver Cromwell and the Cause of Civil and Religious Liberty" in Charles W. A. Prior and Glenn Burgess eds., *England's Wars of Religions, Revisited*, p. 231 ff

411   See J. C. Davis, *Religion and the Struggle for Freedom in the English Revolution;* also Zakai, *Religious Toleration and Its Enemies: The Independent Divines and the Issue of Tolerationduring the English Civil War*

412   See Philip Baker and Elliot Vernon eds, *The Agreements of the People, the Levellers and the Constitionl Crises of the English Revolution,* London, Palgrave Macmillan, 2012, p. 51

413   See Rachel Foxley, John Lilburne and the Citizenship of 'Free-Born Englishmen, *The Historical Journal,* Vol. 47, No. 4 (Dec., 2004), pp. 849-874

414   See Philip Baker and Elliot Vernon eds, *The Agreements of the People, the Levellers and the Constitionl Crises of the English Revolution,* chapter 2 & 3

415   See details in *Huge Trevor-Roper, Archbishop Laud 1573-1645,* London, Macmillan Press, 1988

416   See details in Scott Sowerby, *Making Toleration: The Repealers and the Glorious Revolution,* Cambridge, Mass., Harvard University Press, 2013, p. 18ff

417   JRD Coffey, , 'Religious Thought', p. 452

418   Qouted in Coffey, 'Religious Thought', p. 447

419   Coffey, 'Religious Thought', p. 447

420   Coffey, 'Religious Thought', p. 452

421   George Yerby, *The Economic Causes of the English Civil War: Freedom of Trade and the English Revolution,* New York, Routledge, 2020, p. 1

422   Quoted in Noel Malcolm, *Useful Enemies,* p. 301

423   Noel Malcolm, *Useful Enemies,* p. 302

424   See Yerby, *The Economic Causes of the English Civil War,* p. 2-3

425   Saumitra Jha, *Financial Asset Holdings and Political Attitudes: Evidence from Revolutionary England,* p. 1486; Douglass C. North, and Barry R. Weingast, "Constitutions and Commitment: Evolution of Institutions Governing Public Choice," *Journal of Economic History,* 49 (1989), 803–832.

426   Stone, Lawrence, "The Bourgeois Revolution of Seventeenth Century England Revisited," *Past and Present,* 109 (1985), 44–54, p. 44

427   Raghuram G. Rajan, and Luigi Zingales, *Saving Capitalism from the Capitalists: Unleashing the Power of Financial Markets to Create Wealth and Spread Opportunity,* New York, Crown Business, 2003

428   Daron Acemoglu, Simon Johnson and James Robinson, *The Rise of Europe: Atlantic Trade, Institutional Change, and Economic Growth, The*

American Economic Review, Vol. 95, No. 3 (Jun., 2005), pp. 546-579; Robert Brenner, *The Civil War Politics of London's Merchant Community, Past & Present,* No. 58 (Feb., 1973), pp. 53-107 and his *Merchants and Revolution: Commercial Change, Political Conflict, and London's Overseas Traders 1550-1653,* London, Verso, 2003

429   Barrington Moore, *Social Origins of Dictatorship and Democracy: Lord and Peasant in the Making of the Modern World,* Boston: Beacon, 1966

430   R. H. Tawney, 'The Rise of the Gentry, 1558–1640," *Economic History Review,* 11 (1941), 1–38.

431   See Martin Finch, *Animadversions* upon Sir Henry Vanes Book, entituled The Retired Mans Meditations: Examining his Doctrine concerning Adam's Fall, Christs Person, and Sufferings, Justification, Common and Special Grace; and Many Other Things in his Book (1656).

432   See Margaret A Judson, *The Political Thought of Sir Henry Vane the Younger.* Philadelphia: University of Pennsylvania Press, 1969; George Sikes, *The Life and Death of Sir Henry Vane, Kt.* London, 1662

433   Yerby, *The Economic Causes of the English Civil War,* p. 12

434   John Morril, *The Nature of English Revolution,* p. 22-23

435   See John Tolan, https://www.historytoday.com/miscellanies/muhammad-republican-revolutionary

436   Daron Acemoglu, Simon Johnson and James Robinson, *The Rise of Europe: Atlantic Trade, Institutional Change, and Economic Growth,* p. 550

437   Stephen Alford, "A Politics of Emergency in the Reign of Elizabeth I" in Glen Burgess and Matthew Festenstein eds., *English Radicalism 1550-1850,* Cambridge, Cambridge University Press, 2007, p. 19

438   See Cesare Cuttica and Glenn Burgess eds., *Monarchism and Absolutism in Early Modern Europe,* New York, Routledge, 2012, p. 8ff

439   See Morril, *Nature of English Revolution,* p. 2ff

440   Christopher Hill, *Intellectual Origins,* p. 7

441   Christopher Hill, *Intellectual Origins,* p. 7

442   Saumitra Jha, *Financial Asset Holdings and Political Attitudes: Evidence from Revolutionary England,* p. 1493

443   See John Sweetman, *The Oriental Obsession: Islamic Inspiration in British and American Art and Architecture 1500-1920,* Cambridge, Cambridge University Press, 1991; Mark Hutchings, *Turks, Repertories, and the Early*

Modern English Stage, London, Palgrave Macmillan, 2017; Maxine Berg, 'New Commodities, Luxuries and their Consumers in Eighteenth-Century England', in Maxine Berg and Helen Clifford, eds., *Consumers and Luxury: Consumer Culture in Europe, 1650-1850* (Manchester, 1999), pp. 63-85; Beverly Lemire, *Fashion's Favourite: The Cotton Trade and the Consumer in Britain,* 1660-1800, Oxford, Oxford University Press, 1991

444   Saumitra Jha, *Financial Asset Holdings and Political Attitudes: Evidence from Revolutionary England,* p. 1493; Rabb, *Enterprise and Empire: Merchant and Gentry Investment in the Expansion of England,* 1575–1630

445   Saumitra Jha, *Financial Asset Holdings and Political Attitudes: Evidence from Revolutionary England,* p. 1505ff

446   See Daron Acemoglu, Simon Johnson and James Robinson, *The Rise of Europe: Atlantic Trade, Institutional Change, and Economic Growth,* p. 564ff

447   See Saumitra Jha, *Financial Asset Holdings and Political Attitudes: Evidence from Revolutionary England,* p. 1539-40

448   See Hill, *Intellectual Origins,* p. 7ff

449   R. Baxter, *Reliquiae Baxterianae* (ed. M. Sylvester, 1696), i. p. 89.

450   M. H. Carré, *Phases of Thought in England,* Oxford, Clarendon Press, 1949, p. 224

451   Hill, *Intellectual Origins,* p. 12

452   See Wesley Frank Craven, *Dissolution of the Virginia Company: The Failure of a Colonial Experiment.* Gloucester, Massachusetts: Peter Smith, 1964; *The Virginia Company of London, 1606–1624.* Williamsburg: *Virginia 350th Anniversary Celebration Corporation,* 1957; Karen Ordahl Kupperman, *The Jamestown Project.* Cambridge, Massachusetts: The Belknap Press of Harvard University Press, 2007

453   See Samuel M. Bemis, *The Three Charters of the Virginia Company of London,* Baton Rouge, Louisiana State University Press, 2009

454   See Dalrymple, *Anarchy,* p. 15ff

455   Alison Games, *The Web of Empire: English Cosmopolitans in an Age of Expansion 1560-1660,* Cambridge, Cambridge University Press, 2008, p. 49; See Daniel Goffman, *The Ottoman Empire and Early Modern Europe,* Cambridge, Cambridge University Press, 2004, p. 194 ff

456   Matthew Dimmock, *Mythologies of the Prophet Muhammad in Early Modern English Culture,* Cambridge: Cambridge University Press,

2013, p. 9-10; Birchwood, Staging Islam in England: Drama and Culture, 1640-1685, p. 96

457 Allison P. Coudert, "Orientalism in Early Modern Europe", in Albrecht Classen ed., *East Meets West in the Middle Ages and Early Modern Times: Transcultural Experiences in the Premodern World*, Boston, De Gruyter, 2013, p. 718

458 See Maxine Rodinson, *Europe and the Mystique of Islam*, London, I. B. Tauris, 2002

459 Allison P. Coudert, "Orientalism in Early Modern Europe", p. 718

460 Robert C. Davis, *Christian Slaves, Muslim Masters: White Slavery in the Mediterranean, The Barbary Coast, and Italy, 1500–1800. Early Modern History: Society and Culture*, London, Macmillan Palgrave, 2004, p. 28

461 Allison P. Coudert, "Orientalism in Early Modern Europe", p. 719

462 See Francis Knight, *Relation of Seaven Years Slaverie Under the Turks of Argeire suffered by an English captive merchant* (London: printed by T. Cotes, for M[ichael]. S[parke]. Iunior, 1640), 19.\; Francis Knight, *Relation of Seaven Years Slaverie Under the Turks of Argeire suffered by an English captive merchant* (London: printed by T. Cotes, for M[ichael]. S[parke]. Iunior, 1640), p. 19; Joseph Morgan, *A Complete History of Algiers* (1728–1729; New York: Negro University Press,1970), p. 617ff; Allison P. Coudert, "Orientalism in Early Modern Europe", p. 720ff

463 See F. Ahmad, "Ottoman perceptions of the capitulations 1800-1914," *Journal of Islamic Studies*, 11,1 (2000), 1-20; Maurits H. van den Boogert, The Capitulations and the Ottoman Legal System: Qadis, Consuls, and Beraths in the 18th century. Leiden: Brill, 2005; Despina Vlami, *Trading with the Ottomans: The Levant Company in the Middle East*, Bloomsbury, 2014

464 See Michael Talbot, *British Ottoman Relations, 1661-1807: Commerce and Diplomatic Practice in Eighteenth Century Istanbul*, Woodbridge, Boydell Press, 2017, p. 25ff, "In the past, the chief of the nobles of the queen of the said province [vil.yet] [of England] came to and arrived at our threshold of the workings of felicity – which is the refuge of asylum of the sultans of the world and the place of retreat of the sovereigns of the globe – with her gentlemen and her ships with her tribute, and the gifts that she had sent were gladly accepted. In the time of my ancestor who dwells in heaven in the paradise of the mercy of the merciful protector of all things, Sultan Murad Khan (may his tomb be pleasant to him), a man was sent to our Threshold of Felicity manifesting friend-

ly, sincere, and agreeable affection, asking that their gentlemen might come and go at the Porte, [and] a positive response was given. In the time of the same aforementioned [sultan], noble commands were given, saying that 'at the stopping places and stations, at the crossings and at the gateways, at sea and on land, no one should trouble them'. P. 25

465   See Samuel Chew, *The Crescent and the Rose, p. 155ff*

466   See Beni Prasad, *History of Jahangir*, Allahabad, 1962, Dalrymple, *Anarchy*, p. 15ff

467   Andrew Lake, *The First Protestants in the Arab World: The Contribution to Christian Mission of the English Aleppo Chaplians 1597-1782*, p. 17

468   See Maartje van Gelder, The Republic's Renegades: Dutch Converts to Islam in Seventeenth-Century Diplomatic Relations with North Africa, *Journal of Early Modern History* 19 (2015) 175-198, p. 190-91

469   See Thomas Malloch, *Finch and Baines: A Seventeenth Century Friendship*. Cambridge: Cambridge University Press, 1917, p. 62-63; Marjorie Hope Nicholson, ed. *Conway Letters: The Correspondence of Anne, Viscountess Conway, Henry More, and Their Friends, 1642-1684,* New Haven: Yale University Press, 1930, 458-59; Alfred C. Wood, *A History of the Levant Company,* New York, Barnes and Noble, Inc, 1964, 98

470   Allison P. Coudert, "Orientalism in Early Modern Europe", p. 724

471   Nabil Matar, *Islam in Britain, 1558–1685*, p. 4

472   George F. Abbott, *Under the Turk at Constantinople: A Record of Sir John Finch's Embassy, 1674–1681*, London, Macmillan, 1920, p. 303.

473   See Dalrymple, *Anarchy*, p. 18

474   See Geoffrey Parker, *The Military Revolution, p. 108*

475   "The Grand Signior possesses such vast territories… It being a great mistake to say that his territories lie waste, and are not populous. Asia Minor… that is now entirely in his possession, is as full of people, as ever it was. Smyrna is very populous; and Aleppo counts within its walls thirty thousand fighting men. Constantinople, its advantageous situation being more convenient and suitable for so great a monarchy, then any other city of the known world, has its number of inhabitants answerable to its vast extent… As for his treasures, they are very considerable, for he is the most absolute monarch in the world, and disposes sovereignly of whatever his subjects, or rather his slaves, are possessed of. The trade of Constantinople brings him in vast sums of

money... The Christians, to get favour with the Grand Signior in order to promote their trade with the infidels, are often at exceeding great, and sometimes unwilling, expenses. For nothing is done at Constantinople, but by money. And money, which is powerful everywhere, is their Almighty." David Abercromby, *The Present State of the German and Turkish Empires* (London, 1684), 51-53

476   Allison P. Coudert, "Orientalism in Early Modern Europe", p. 729-30

477   Sir Thomas Roe and Dr John Fryer, *Travels in India in the 17ᵗʰ Century*, London, 1873, p. 103-104; also Sir William Foster, *The Embassy of Sir Thomas Roe to India 1615–9, as Narrated in his Journal and correspondence*, New Delhi, 1990, Dalrymple, *Anarchy*, p. 17

478   Quoted in Dalrymple, *Anarchy*, p. 17

479   Samuel Purchas, *Hakluytus Posthumus or Purchas His Pilgrimes, Contayning a History of the World*, 20 vols, Glasgow, 1905, part 1, IV, pp. 334–9, Dalrymple, *Anarchy*, p. 18

480   Dalrymple, *Anarchy*, p. 22-23

481   See Dalrymple, *Anarchy*, p. 15ff

482   See Dalrymple, *Anarchy*, p. 23

483   Dalrymple, *Anarchy*, p. 23

484   See William Letwin, *The Origin of Scientific Economics*, London, Economics, 1963, p. 37.

485   Dalrymple, *Anarchy*, p. 24

486   Dalrymple, *Anarchy*, p. 24

487   Dalrymple, *Anarchy*, p. 24; also see *Narrative of the Capture of Calcutta from April 10 1756 to November 10 1756*, William Tooke, BL, OIOC, O.V. 19, Bengal 1756, pp. 5–46; Rajat Kanta Ray, *The Felt Community: Commonality and Mentality before the Emergence of Indian Nationalism*, New Delhi, 2003, p.233.

488   Dalrymple, *Anarchy*, p. 24; *Narrative of the Capture of Calcutta from April 10 1756 to November 10 1756*, pp. 5–46

489   See Dalrymple, *Anarchy*, p. 106

490   Dalrymple, *Anarchy*, p. 106; *Concerning the Loss of Calcutta*, BL, OIOC, HM vol. 66, pp. 821–4; G. J. Bryant, *Emergence of British Power in India 1600–1784: A Grand Strategic Interpretation*, Woodbridge, BOYE6, 2013, pp. 118–21

491   Colin Newbury, *Patrons, Clients and Empire: Chieftaincy and Over-Rule in Asia, Africa, and the Pacific,* Oxford, Oxford University Press, 2003, p. 12.

492   See details in Anna Winterbottom, *Hybrid Knowledge in the Early East India Company World,* London, Palgrave Macmillan, 2016, p. 13. "Thus, the history of the Company at the beginning of this period was directed more by the local political realities in which each settlement was embedded than by commands from and events in distant London."

493   See Parker, *Military Revolution,* p. 135ff

494   See Parker, *Military Revolution,* p. 117ff

495   See Michael Harrigan, *Veiled Encounters: Representing the Orient in 17ᵗʰ Century French Travel Literature,* Amsterdam, Rodopi, 2008; See "The Voyages and Travels of the Ambassadors", Adam Olearius, translated by John Davies (1662)

496   See Gerald MacLean and Nabil Matar, *Britain and the Islamic World 1558-1713,* Oxford, Oxford University Press, 2011, p. 91 ff

497   See Alistair Maeer, "Instruments of Acquisition and Reflections of Desire: English Nautical Charts and Islamic Shores, 1650-1700" In Justin Quinn Olmstead ed., *Britain in the Islamic World: Imperial and Post-Imperial Connections,* London, Palgrave Macmillan, 2019, p. 27ff

498   See Goffman, *The Ottoman Empire and Early Modern Europe, p. 195 ff*

499   James D. Tracy, *The Rise of Merchant Empires: Long Distance Trade in the Early Modern World 1350-1750,* Cambridge, Cambridge University Press, 1993, p. 103

500   See Nicolas Canny, *The Origins of Empire: British Overseas Enterprise to the Close of the Seventeenth Century,* Oxford, Oxford University Press, 2001, p. 1

501   See Alison Games, *The Web of Empire,* p. 47

502   See Lisa Jardine and Jerry Brotton, *Global Interests: Renaissance Art Between East and West,* London, Reaktion Books, 2000, p. 60ff

503   See Canny, *The Origins of Empire,* p. 60 ff

504   See Ralph Davis, *Aleppo and Devonshire Square: English Traders in the Levant in the Eighteenth Century,* London: Macmillan, 1967; Geoffrey Berridge, *British Diplomacy in Turkey, 1583 to the Present, Leiden, Brill, 2009;* Alfred C. Wood, *A History of the Levant Company,* New

York: Barnes and Noble, Inc, 1964; Christine Laidlaw, *The British in the Levant, Trade and Perceptions of the Ottoman Empire in the Eighteenth Century,* New York, Tauris Academic Studies, 2010; Roger North, *The Lives of the Norths*, Vol. II, ed. Augustus Jessopp, London, Gregg International Publishers Limited, 1969; Alexander Russell, *The Natural History of Aleppo and Parts Adjacent*, Vol II, London, Gregg Publishing, 1969; A.C. Wood, *A History of the Levant Company*, Oxford, Oxford University Press, 1935

505   Mortimer Epstein, *The English Levant Company: Its Foundation and its History to 1640,* New York: Burt Franklin, 1968; James Mather, *Pashas: Traders and Travellers in the Islamic World,* New Haven, Yale University Press, 2009

506   See Alison Games, *The Web of Empire*, p. 51 ("The first important pragmatic advantage that the English gained from their earliest trade forays in the Mediterranean came from the experience merchants acquired through their work in the Levant Company. Merchants learned in the Mediterranean how to secure trade privileges from a powerful empire, and they mastered the challenges of organising a complex and multifaceted trade over long distances. Th e East India Company subsequently acquired its leadership and much of its capital from the Levant Company and experienced Levant traders applied their knowledge to later trade eff orts in the Indian Ocean." Games, *The Web of Empire,* p. 51-52

507   Wesley Frank Craven,. *The Virginia Company of London*, 1606–1624. Williamsburg: *Virginia 350th Anniversary Celebration Corporation*, 1957; Wesley Frank Craven, *Dissolution of the Virginia Company: The Failure of a Colonial Experiment*. Gloucester, Massachusetts: Peter Smith, 1964

508   Douglass C. North and Robert Paul Thomas. *The Rise of the Western World: A New Economic History*. Cambridge, England: Cambridge University Press, 1973; Morgan, Edmund S. American Slavery, *American Freedom: The Ordeal of Colonial Virginia*. New York: W. W. Norton and Company, 1975; Alison Games, *The Web of Empire*, p. 53 ("In India, in Japan, and elsewhere we find the English adhering to this Mediterranean model. And, indeed, we find it in America, where the English first ventured for purposes of trade, and where many of the first colonial leaders came with experience in the Levant. This Mediterranean model endured for generations in places where the English were a minority and where trade depended on local alliances, from the cold waters of Hudson Bay to West African trading ports." Games, p. 53

509   Alison Games, *The Web of Empire*, p. 47

510   See Zachary W. Schulz, *The English In The Levant: Commerce, Diplomacy, And The English Nation In The Ottoman Empire, 1672-1691,* A Ph.D. Dissertation Submitted to the Faculty of Purdue University, West Lafayette, Indiana, 2018

511   See Daniel Goffman, *Izmir and the Levantine world, 1550–1650,* Seattle, WA, University of Washington Press, 1990)

512   See Edhem Eldem, Daniel Goffman and Bruce Masters eds., *The Ottoman City Between East and West: Aleppo, Izmir, and Istanbul,* Cambridge, Cambridge University Press, 1999

513   Richard Grassby, *The Business Community of Seventeenth-Century England.* Cambridge: Cambridge University Press, 1995, p. 271

514   See Andrew Thompson, The *Oxford History of Protestant Dissenting Traditions,* Volume II: The Long Eighteenth Century c. 1689-c. 1828, Oxford, Oxford University Press, 2018, p. 11-12; Grassby, *Business Community,* p. 271-273

515   "Dissent was disproportionately represented in London. They constituted 15-20 per cent of the electorate, 35 per cent of Company directors, 32 per cent of importers, three-eighths of the aldermen, 27 per 20 cent of holders of short-term debt and 25 per cent of bank subscribers.20 It also proved hard for the Established Church to compete in the provincial 21 towns with Dissenters In addition there was a substantial community of alien Protestant immigrants and refugees." Grassby, *Business Community,* p. 273

516   See Grassby *Business Community,* p. 273-74; Michael R. Watts, *The Dissenters,* vol. 2, *The Expansion of Evangelical Nonconformity,* Oxford, Oxford University Press, 1995, p. 271

517   Grassby *Business Community,* p. 276

518   Andrew Lake, *First Protestants,* p. 1

519   See Wood, *A History of the Levant Company,* p. 222-3

520   See P.M. Holt, 'The Study of Arabic Historians in Seventeenth Century England: The Background and Work of Edward Pococke', *Bulletin of the School of Oriental and African Studies,* 19.3, 1957, pp. 444–55

521   See details in Colin Wakefield, "Arabic Manuscripts in the Bodlian Library: The Seventeenth Century Collections" in G. A. Russell (ed.), *The 'Arabick' Interest of the Natural Philosophers in Seventeenth-Century England,* Leiden, Brill, 1994, p. 134ff

522   At the Bodleian Library of Oxford University, there were hundreds of Arabic manuscripts, as well as dozens of Persian and Turkish ones, available during the 17th century. These included works on Islamic law and Arabic grammar; the lexicography of Al-Firuzabadi and Al-Jawhari; works on Arabic poetry; the Indian literary work Kalila and Dimna; the proverbs of Al-Maydani and Maqama of Al-Hariri of Basra; the medical works of Al-Razi, Avicenna, Ibn al-Baitar, Hunayn ibn Ishaq, Al-Majusi, Ibn al-Jazzar, Abu al-Qasim al-Zahrawi, Ibn Zuhr, Maimonides and Ibn al-Nafis; the astronomical works of Ibn al-Banna, Ibn al-Shatir, Al-Farghani and Alhazen; the Masudic Canon by Abu Rayhan Biruni and the Book of Fixed Stars by Al-Sufi; several Ottoman scientific works by Taqi al-Din Muhammad ibn Ma'ruf; occult and alchemical works; the Secretum Secretorum; Al-Safadi's biographical dictionary Al-Sihah; the historical works of Al-Tabari, Al-Isfahani, Al-Makin, Ibn Khallikan, Al-Dhahabi, Al-Waqidi, Ibn al-Shina, Al-Utbi, Ibn al-Jawzi, Ibn al-Athir, Sibt ibn al-Jawzi, Ibn Abi Usaibia, Bar-Hebraeus, Al-Tunaynai, Ibn Duqmaq, Ibn Taghribirdi, Al-Suyuti, Al-Jannabi, Ibn Hayyan, Ibn Miskawayh, Ibn Hajar al-Asqalani and Al-Maqrizi; the History of Time by Al-Masudi and volume five of Ibn Khaldun's historiographical work Kitab al-Ibar; the historical and geographical works of Abu al-Fida; the Sahih al-Bukhari and Quranic commentaries; the Algebra by Al-Khwarizmi and the mathematical works of Nasir al-Din al-Tusi; the Encyclopedia of the Brethren of Purity and Avienna's The Book of Healing; the works of Ibn Bajjah and Ibn Tufail; geographical works of Ibn Khordadbeh and Ibn Hawqal; .[37] A Latin translation of two of Ali Qushji's works, the Tract on Arithmetic and Tract on Astronomy, was published by John Greaves in 1650. https://www.wikiwand.com/en/Reception_of_Islam_ in_Early_Modern_Europe; G. A. Russell, *The 'Arabick' Interest of the Natural Philosophers in Seventeenth-century England*, p. 162

523   See Wakefield, "Arabic Manuscripts in the Bodlian Library: The Seventeenth Century Collections", p. 134

524   See Wakefield, "Arabic Manuscripts in the Bodlian Library: The Seventeenth Century Collections", p. 130

525   See Wakefield, "Arabic Manuscripts in the Bodlian Library: The Seventeenth Century Collections", p. 130-31

526   See Toomer, *Eastern Wisdom and Learning*, p. 281ff

527   See Wakefield, "Arabic Manuscripts in the Bodlian Library: The Seventeenth Century Collections", p. 135

528   Simon Mills, "Learning Arabic in the Overseas Factories: The Case of the English" in Jan Loop, Alastair Hamilton and Charles Burnett eds., *The Teaching and Learning of Arabic in Early Modern Europe,* Leiden, Brills, 2017, p. 280; see also D. Goffman, *Britons in the Ottoman Empire 1642–1660,* Seattle, 1998, p. 216.

529   Andrew Lake, *First Protestants,* p. 56

530   John Covel, "Dr. Covel's Diary (1670-1679)," in *Early Voyages and Travels in the Levant,* ed. Theodore Bent, New York, The Hakluyt Society, 1964

531   See Alie, Remi, "'Empire without end': John Finch, *Orientalism,* and Early Modern Empire, 1674-1681" (2017). *Electronic Thesis and Dissertation Repository,* p. 121; Jonathan Israel, *Radical Enlightenment: Philosophy and the Making of Modernity 1650-1750,* Oxford, Oxford University Press, 2001, 8

532   See Zachary W. Schulz, *The English In The Levant: Commerce, Diplomacy, And The English Nation In The Ottoman Empire, 1672-1691,* P. 90ff

533   Simon Mills, "Learning Arabic in the Overseas Factories: The Case of the English", p. 277

534   Simon Mills, "Learning Arabic in the Overseas Factories: The Case of the English", p. 283

535   William Dalrymple, *The Anarchy: The Relentless Rise of the East India Company,* New York. Bloombury, 2019; Alfred Mervyn Davies, *Strange destiny: a biography of Warren Hastings* (1935)

536   See Keith Feiling, *Warren Hastings,* London, Macmillan, 1954, pp. 1–11; Jeremy Bernstein, *Dawning of the Raj: The Life & Trials of Warren Hastings,* Chicago, I. R. Dee, 2000, pp. 32–5.

537   See P.J. Marshall, 'Warren Hastings as Scholar and Patron', *Statesmen, Scholars and Merchants: Essays in Eighteenth-Century History presented to Dame Lucy Sutherland,* eds A. Whiteman, J.S. Bromley, and P.G.M. Dickson, Oxford, 1973, pp. 242–62

538   See Simon Mills, "Learning Arabic in the Overseas Factories: The Case of the English", p. 236ff; C. Ravis, *A Discourse of the Orientall Tongues,* London, 1648, p. 30.

539   See Simon Mills, "Learning Arabic in the Overseas Factories: The Case of the English", p. 278

540   Anonymous, *A True Account of the Irregular Proceedings at Guild-Hall,*

About the Swearing the Two Pretended Sheriffs Mr. North and Mr. Rich, London, 1682

541   See Richard Grassby, *The English Gentleman in Trade: The Life and Works of Sir Dudley North, 1641-1691,* Oxfor, Clarendon Press, 1994; Linda T. Darling, "Ottoman Politics through British Eyes: Paul Rycaut's 'the Present State of the Ottoman Empire,'" *Journal of World History* 5, no. 1 (1994): 71-97; Ben Coates, *The Impact of the English Civil War on the Economy of London, 1642-50,* Burlington, Ashgate Publishing Company, 2004

542   See Suzanne J. Farmer, "Sir Dudley North in Loyal Principle Exceeding: A Political Merchant in the First Age of Party, *International Social Science Review:* vol. 92, Issue 2, article 1 and her Ph. D. dissertation "Sir Dudley North: Merchant Politics In The First Age Of Party" submitted to The University of Mississippi, department of History, 2011

543   See Roger North, *The Life of the Honourable Sir Dudley North* (London, 1744)

544   "Finch was part of an extensive, politically influential clan. His older brother was Heneage Finch, first Earl of Nottingham and Lord Chancellor from 1675-1682 under Charles II. Heneage's son, Sir Daniel Finch, was a frequent correspondent with his uncle John, and later became Lord President of the Council under George I. John's first cousin, Heneage Finch, third Earl of Winchelsea, and his other first cousin, Sir Daniel Harvey, both served as previous ambassadors to the Levant. Indeed, Finch was replacing Daniel Harvey as ambassador. Rounding out his familial circle of notables was *Anne Conway,* his sister and famed Cambridge Platonist philosopher, who had married Sir Edward Conway, first Earl of Conway and eventual Secretary of State for the Northern Department." ; Zachary W. Schulz, *The English In The Levant: Commerce, Diplomacy, And The English Nation In The Ottoman Empire, 1672-1691,* A Ph.D. Dissertation Submitted to the Faculty of Purdue University, West Lafayette, Indiana, 2018, p. 130

545   See Sarah Hutton, *Anne Conway: A Women Philosopher,* Cambridge, Cambridge University Press, 2004, p. 107

546   See Daniel O'Connor, *The Chaplains of the East India Company, 1601-1858,* London, Continuum, 2012; Penelope Carson,*The East India Company and Religion,* 1698–1858, Woodbridge, Boydell Press, 2012

547   https://en.wikisource.org/wiki/Dictionary_of_National_Biography,_1885-1900/Addison,_Lancelot

548   See John Julian: *Dictionary of Hymnology*, 2nd edition, London: John Murray, 1907, p. 19

549   See Simon Mills, "Learning Arabic in the Overseas Factories: The Case of the English", p. 279

550   See Richard Grassby, *The Business Community of Seventeenth-Century England*, p. 219ff

551   Robert Brenner, *The Civil War Politics of London's Merchant Community, Past & Present*, No. 58 (Feb., 1973), pp. 53-107, p. 54ff; Perry Gauci, *The Politics of Trade: The Overseas Merchant in State and Society, 1660-1720*. Oxford: Oxford University Press, 2001

552   See Richard Grassby, *English Merchant Capitalism in the Late Seventeenth Century. The Composition of Business Fortunes, Past & Present*, No. 46 (Feb., 1970), pp. 87-107, p. 101

553   See Robert Brenner, *The Civil War Politics of London's Merchant Community*, 77ff

554   Dalrymple, *Anarchy*, p. 23

555   See Robert Brenner, *The Civil War Politics of London's Merchant Community*, 72ff

556   See Gary S. De Krey, *Restoration and Revolution in Britain: A Political History of the Era of Charles Ii and the Glorious Revolution*, New York, Palgrave Macmillan, 2007, 101, 12-16

557   Gauci, *The Politics of Trade: The Overseas Merchant in State and Society, 1660-1720*, p. 9

558   See Gary S. De. Krey, *A Fractured Society: The Politics of London in the First Age of Party 1688-1715*. Oxford: Clarendon Press, 1985, p. 76-81, 101, 116; Zachary W. Schulz, *The English In The Levant*, p. 71ff

559   Schulz, *The English In The Levant*, p. 68

560   See Gauci, *The Politics of Trade: The Overseas Merchant in State and Society, 1660-1720*; Robert Brenner, *The Civil War Politics of London's Merchant Community*

561   Ralph Davis, *Aleppo and Devonshire Square*, p. 222

562   Paul Hazard noted: "It was an East gravely distorted by the European view of it; nevertheless, it retained enough of its original impressiveness to loom forth as a vast agglomeration of non-Christian values, a huge block of humanity which had constructed its moral system,

its concept of truth, on lines peculiarly its own. This was one of the reasons why the conscience of the old Europe was stirred and perplexed, and why, seeking to be thrown into confusion, it obtained what it sought." *Crisis of Eropean Mind,* p. 28

563   See Ivo Kamps and Jyotsana G. Singh eds., *Travel Knowledge: European "Discoveries" in the Early Modern Peried,* New York, Palgrave, 2001; Gerald MacLean, *The Rise of Oriental Travel: English Visitors to the Ottoman Empire 1580-1720,* New York, Palgrave Macmillian, 2004; Samuel Chew, *The Crescent and the Rose: Islam and England during the Renaissance,* Oxford, Oxford University Press, 1937; Brandon H. Beck, *From the Rising of the Sun: English Images of the Ottoman Empire to 1715,* New York, P. Lang, 1987; Orhan Burian, "Interest of the English in Turkey as Reflected in English Literature of the *Renaissance,*" Oriens 5 (1952): 208-29.

564   Daniel J. Vitkus, "Trafficking With The Turk: English Travellers In The Ottoman Empire During The Early Seventeenth Century" in Ivo Kamps and Jyotsana G. Singh eds., *Travel Knowledge: European "Discoveries" in the Early Modern Peried,* p. 35

565   Quoted in Daniel J. Vitkus, "Trafficking With The Turk: English Travellers In The Ottoman Empire During The Early Seventeenth Century", p. 37

566   See Daniel J. Vitkus, "Trafficking With The Turk: English Travellers In The Ottoman Empire During The Early Seventeenth Century", p. 48ff

567   See Daniel Carey, *Compiling nature's history: Travellers and travel narratives in the early royal society, Annals of Science,* 1997, 54:3, 269-292, DOI: 10.1080/00033799700200211

568   Michael Hunter. *The Royal Society and its Fellows, 1660–1700: The Morphology of an Early Scientific Institution.* (British Society for the History of Science Monographs, Volume 4.) Oxford: The Alden Press. 1994, p. 118-121Michael Hunter, *The Royal SocieO' and Its Fellows 16601700,* 2nd edn (London, 1994)

569   Daniel Carey, *Compiling nature's history: Travellers and travel narratives in the early royal society,* p. 282

570   See Daniel Carey, *Compiling nature's history: Travellers and travel narratives in the early royal society,* p. 273ff; Winterbottom, Hybrid Knowledge, p. 141ff

571   See Gerald MacLean, *The Rise of Oriental Travel: English Visitors to the Ottoman Empire, 1580–1720*; Jas Elsner, and Joan-Pau Rubiés, *Voyages and Visions: Towards a Cultural History of Travel,* London: Reaktion

Books, 1999; Muzaffar Alam, and Sanjay Subrahmanyam, *Indo-Persian Travels in the Age of Discoveries*, 1400–1800, Cambridge and New York, Cambridge University Press, 2007; K. Raj, *Relocating Modern Science: Circulation and the Construction of Knowledge in South Asia and Europe, 1650–1900*, Basingstoke, Palgrave Macmillan, 2007; Harold J. Cook, *Matters of Exchange: Commerce, Medicine, and Science in the Dutch Golden Age, New Haven*, CT, Yale University Press, 2007.

572   Daniel J. Vitkus, "Trafficking With The Turk: English Travellers In The Ottoman Empire During The Early Seventeenth Century", p. 38

573   Daniel J. Vitkus, "Trafficking With The Turk: English Travellers In The Ottoman Empire During The Early Seventeenth Century", p. 35

574   Sir Henry Blount, *A Voyage into the Levant:A Breife Relation of a journey, Lately Peiformed by Master H[enry] B[lount], Gentleman,Jrom England by the way of Venice, into Dalmatia, Sclavonia, Bosnia, Hungary, Macedonia, Thessaly, Thrace, Rhodes and Egypt unto Gran Cairo: With Particular Observations Concerning the moderne condition of the Turkes and other people under that Empire* (London, 1636), p. 2

575   Henry Blount, *A Voyage into the Levant, p. 3*

576   Henry Blount, *A Voyage into the Levant, p. 15*

577   Henry Blount, *A Voyage into the Levant, p. 15*

578   C. F. Beckingham, "The Near East: North and Northeast Africa," ch. 14 in vol. 1 of David B. Quinn, ed., *The Hakluyt Handbook,* London, Hakluyt Society, 1974, p.*184.*

579   See Samuel Chew,*The Crescent and the Rose, chapter 3&4*

580   Daniel J. Vitkus, "Trafficking With The Turk: English Travellers In The Ottoman Empire During The Early Seventeenth Century", p. 39

581   See James J. Porter, ed. By Sir George-Larpent Bart, *Turkey: Its History and Progress: From The Journals and Correspondence of Sir James Porter, Fifteen Years Ambassador at Constantinople; continued to the Present Time, with A memoir of Sir James Porter,* London, Hurst and Blackett Publishers, 1854, v. II, p. 27-33

582   See Frederick G. Whelan, *Enlightenment Political Thought and Non-Western Societies: Sultan and Savages,* New York, Routledge, 2009, p. 82ff; James J. Porter, *Turkey: Its History and Progress, v. II, pp. 27ff, 65ff, 71ff*

583   *Gerald MacLean,* "Ottomanism before Orientalism? Bishop King

Praises Henry Blount, Passenger in the Levant"in Ivo Kamps and Jyot-sana G. Singh eds., *Travel Knowledge: European "Discoveries" in the Early Modern Peried,* p. 85ff

584   *MacLean,* "Ottomanism before Orientalism", p. 86

585   Goffman, *Ottoman Empire and Early Modern Europe,* p. 224

586   Goffman, *Ottoman Empire and Early Modern Europe,* p. 225

587   See Goffman, *Ottoman Empire and Early Modern Europe,* p. 228 ff

588   See Pamela H. Smith and Paula Findlen, eds., *Merchants and Marvels: Commerce, Science and Art in Early Modern Europe,* New York, Rou-tledge, 2002; Pamela H. Smith, "Science on the Move: Recent Trends in the History of Early Modern Science." *Renaissance Quarterly,* vol. 62, no. 2, 2009, pp. 345–375; Kapil Raj, "Colonial Encounters and the Forging of New Knowledge and National Identities: Great Britain and India, 1760–1850," in *Nature and Empire: Science and the Colo-nial Enterprise,* ed. R. M. MacLeod, Chicago, University of Chicago Press, 2001; and Raj, *Relocating Modern Science: Circulation and the Construction of Knowledge in South Asia and Europe, 1650–1900,* New York, Palgrave, 2007; Joseph Needham, 'The Roles of Europe and China in the Evolution of "Ecumenical Science"', in idem, *Clerks and Craftsmen in China and the West,* Cambridge: Cambridge University Press, 1970, p. 397; George Basalla, 'The Spread of Western Science', *Science,* no. 156 (5 May 1967), pp. 611–22; and idem, 'The Spread of Western Science Revisited', in Antonio Lafuente, Alberto Elena, and María Luisa Ortega, eds, *Mundialización de la ciencia y cultura nacion-al* (Aranjuez, Madrid: Doce Calles, 1993), pp. 599–603.

589   See R. Hooykaas (1987). *The Rise of Modern Science: When and Why?, The British Journal for the History of Science,* 20, pp 453-473, doi:10.1017/S0007087400024225, p. 453-454

590   See David Washbrook, "From Comparative Sociology to Global History: Britain and India in the Pre-History of Modernity." *Journal of the Econom-ic and Social History of the Orient,* vol. 40, no. 4, 1997, pp. 410–443

591   See details in R. Hooykaas, *Religion and the Rise of Modern Science,* Edinburgh, Scottish Academic Press, 1972; R. Hooykaas, *Selected Studies in History of Science,* Coimbra, Coimbra University Press, 1983

592   See R. Hooykaas, 'Pitfalls in the historiography of geological science', *Nature et Histoire,* (1982), 19-20, pp. 21-33;

593   See Richard Foster Jones, *Ancients and Moderns: A Study of the Rise of*

Modern Science in the Seventeenth Century, New York, Dover Publications, 1982

594 See Herbert Butterfield, *The Origins of Modern Science, 1300–1800,* New York, Free Press, 1957; Alexandre Koyré, *From the Closed World to the Infinite Universe,* New York, Harper, 1958; idem, *Metaphysics and Measurement: Essays in Scientific Revolution,* Cambridge, MA, Harvard University Press, 1968; A. Rupert Hall, *The Scientific Revolution 1500–1800: The Formation of the Modern Scientific Attitude,* London, Longmans, Green & Co., 1954, published in its second edition as *The Revolution in Science,* Harlow: Longman, 1983; Robert S. Westfall, *The Scientific Revolution in the 17th Century: The Construction of a New World View,* Oxford, Clarendon Press, 1992; and Marcus Hellyer, ed., *The Scientific Revolution: The Essential Readings,* Oxford, Blackwell, 2003. For a critical appraisal of this quest for origins, see Andrew Cunningham and Perry Williams, 'De-centring the "Big Picture": The Origins of Modern Science and the Modern Origins of Science', *British Journal for the History of Science,* vol. 26, no. 4 (1993), pp. 407–32; and Steven Shapin, *The Scientific Revolution,* Chicago & London, University of Chicago Press, 1996.

595 Butterfield, *The Origins of Modern Science,* p. 7

596 See John William Draper, *History of the Conflict Between Religion and Science,* New York, D. Appleton and Company, (1875); Andrew Dickson White, *A History of the Warfare of Science with Theology in Christendom,* 2 volumes, Cambridge, Cambridge University Press, 2009; William Edward Hartpole Lecky, *History of the Rise and Influence of the Spirit of Rationalism in Europe,* London, D. Appleton and Company, 1919

597 Ian G. Barbour, *When Science Meets Religion,* San Francisco, HarperSanFrancisco, 2000; Gary Ferngren, (editor). *Science & Religion: A Historical Introduction.* Baltimore: Johns Hopkins University Press, 2002; Richard H. Jones, *For the Glory of God: The Role of Christianity in the Rise and Development of Modern Science.* Lanham, Maryland: University Press of America, 2011; David C. Lindberg, and Ronald L. Numbers, eds., *God & Nature: Historical Essays on the Encounter Between Christianity and Science,* Berkeley, University of California Press, 1986; Lindberg and Numbers, "Beyond War and Peace: A Reappraisal of the Encounter between Christianity and Science," *Church History* 55 (1986): 338–354; Richard S. Westfall, *Science and Religion in Seventeenth-Century England.* New Haven: Yale University Press, 1958;

598 S.F. Mason, (1953) The scientific revolution and the protestant reforma-

tion.—I, *Annals of Science*, 9:1, 64-87, DOI: 10.1080/00033795300200033

599   Don O'Leary, *Roman Catholicism and Modern Science: A History*, New York, Continuum, 2006; Benjamin Wiker, The Catholic Church & Science: Answering the Questions, Exposing the Myths, Charlotte, Tan Books, 2011

600   See details in Blair, Ann. 2004. "Science and Religion." In *Cambridge History of Christianity, Vol. 6: Reform and Expansion, 1500-1660*, edited by Ronnie Po-Chia Hsia, Cambridge: Cambridge University Press, 2004.

601   See Robert K. Merton, *Science, Technology and Society in Seventeenth Century England*, Bruges, St. Catherine Press, 1938; *The Intellectual Revolution of the Seventeenth Century* edited by Charles Webster, New York, Routledge, 1974; Christopher Hill, *Intellectual Origins of the English Revolution Revisited*, Oxford, Oxford University Press, 1997

602   See James R. Jacob and Margaret C. Jacob, *The Anglican Origins of Modern Science: The Metaphysical Foundations of the Whig Constitution: Isis*, Vol. 71, No. 2 (Jun., 1980), pp. 251-267

603   See Charles Webster, *The Great Instauration, Science, Medicine and Reform, 1626-1660*, London: Duckworth, 1975; Lotte Mulligan, *Puritans and English Science: A Critique of Webster,*: Isis, Vol. 71, No. 3 (Sep., 1980), pp. 456-469; Perceptive criticisms of the analyses have been made by M. M. Knappen, Tudor Puritanism, Chicago, University of Chicago Press, 1939, 478; James Conant, "The Advancement of Learning during the Puritan Commonwealth," Proceedings of the Massachusetts Historical Society, LXVI (1936- 41), 29-30; and Theodore K. Rabb, "Puritanism and the Rise of Experimental Science in England," Cahiers d'Histoire Mondiale, VII (1962), 50ff.

604   B. J. Shapiro, 'Latitudinarianism and science in seventeenth-century England', *Past and Present*, (1986) 40, 16-41;

605   See William Lamont, *Godly Rule: Politics and Religion, 1603–1660*, New York, Macmillan, 1969; Charles Webster, The Great Instauration

606   See "Introduction" of *The Intellectual Revolution of the Seventeenth Century* edited by Chales Webster

607   See Pamela H. Smith and Paula Findlen, eds., *Merchants and Marvels: Commerce, Science and Art in Early Modern Europe*, New York, Routledge, 2002; Kapil Raj, "Colonial Encounters and the Forging of New Knowledge and National Identities: Great Britain and India, 1760–1850,"

in *Nature and Empire: Science and the Colonial Enterprise,* ed. R. M. MacLeod, Chicago, University of Chicago Press, 2001; and Raj, *Relocating Modern Science: Circulation and the Construction of Knowledge in South Asia and Europe, 1650–1900,* New York, Palgrave, 2007; Joseph Needham, 'The Roles of Europe and China in the Evolution of "Ecumenical Science"', in idem, *Clerks and Craftsmen in China and the West,* Cambridge: Cambridge University Press, 1970, p. 397; George Basalla, 'The Spread of Western Science', *Science,* no. 156 (5 May 1967), pp. 611–22; and idem, 'The Spread of Western Science Revisited', in Antonio Lafuente, Alberto Elena, and María Luisa Ortega, eds, *Mundialización de la ciencia y cultura nacional,* Aranjuez, Madrid, Doce Calles, 1993, pp. 599–603.

608   Raj, *Relocating Modern Science,* p. 6-7; see also Roy Porter and Mikuláš Teich, eds, *The Scientific Revolution in National Context,* Cambridge, Cambridge University Press, 1992; and idem, eds, *The Enlightenment in National Context,* Cambridge, Cambridge University Press, 1981.

609   Raj, *Relocating Modern Science,* p. 7; see also David Washbrook, 'From Comparative Sociology to Global History: Britain and India in the Pre-History of Modernity', *Journal of the Economic and Social History of the Orient,* vol. 40, no. 4 (1997), pp. 410–43; Christopher Alan Bayly, *Imperial Meridian: The British Empire and the World, 1780–1830* (London: Longman, 1989)

610   See Robert K. Merton, *Science, Technology and Society in Seventeenth Century England,* chapter IX, p. 543ff . "This insistent reiteration of the economic significance as well as the practical applications of scientific and mathematical theory is a noteworthy reflection of that spirit of economic rationalism which has become increasingly apparent since at least the seventeenth century. Scientists seek not only technical efficiency, but consider as well the economic advantages of a strictly rational adaptation of means to ends. It is an expression of the attitude justly ascribed to Newtonians of instituting an " active and practical science having for its end the assurance, by the knowledge of natural laws, of our domination over nature," plus the conception of a rationalised economy (as found in the discussions of HOBBES and LOCKE)." Merton, p. 553

611   See Raj, *Relocating Modern Science,* p. 28ff; see also Jan Golinski, *Making Natural Knowledge: Constructivism and the History of Science,* Cambridge, Cambridge University Press, 1998. Steven Shapin and Simon Schaffer, *Leviathan and the Air-Pump: Hobbes, Boyle and the Experimental Life,* Princeton, Princeton University Press, 1985; Adir Ophir and Steven Shapin, 'The Place of Knowledge. A Methodological Survey', *Sci-*

ence in Context, vol. 4, no. 1 (1991), pp. 3–21; and Steven Shapin, 'Placing the View from Nowhere: Historical and Sociological Problems in the Location of Science', *Transactions of the Institute of British Geographers,* vol. 23 (1998), pp. 5–12. Harry M. Collins, *Changing Order: Replication and Induction in Scientific Practice,* London, Sage, 1985, p. 143.

612   Robert K. Merton, *Science, Technology and Society in Seventeenth Century England,* p. 556

613   See Merton, *Science, Technology and Society in Seventeenth Century England,* p. 557ff

614   See Merton, *Science, Technology and Society in Seventeenth Century England,* p. 589ff

615   See See Merton, *Science, Technology and Society in Seventeenth Century England,* p. 596ff

616   Raj, *Relocating Modern Science,* p. 8

617   See Steven Shapin, *The Scientific Revolution,* Chicago, University of Chicago Press, 1998, p. 123-124

618   Shapin, *The Scientific Revolution,* p. 123-124

619   Shapin, *The Scientific Revolution,* p. 124

620   Shapin, *The Scientific Revolution,* p. 125

621   See Ann Blair, "Science and Religion." In *Cambridge History of Christianity;* Draper, *History of the Conflict Between Religion and Science*

622   Merton, *Science, Technology and Society in Seventeenth Century England,* p. 461

623   See details in Merton, *Science, Technology and Society in Seventeenth Century England,* p. 416ff

624   See B. J. Shapiro, 'Latitudinarianism and science in seventeenth-century England'

625   See M. C. Jacob, *Newtonians and the English Revolution 1689-1720,* p. 22ff

626   Thomas Sprat, *The History of the Royal Society of London,* 2nd ed, London, 1702, p. 371

627   Kearney, "Puritanism, Capitalism and Scientific Revolution" in *Intellectual Revolution of the Seventeenth Century* edited by Webster, p. 240

628   Raj, *Relocating Modern Science,* p. 16

629   Raj, *Relocating Modern Science,* p. 16

630   "Because of their commercial activity, European trading companies
       were obliged to develop intimate connections with traders and trading
       groups in other parts of the world, particularly in the Indian Ocean
       world, where Europeans were one of many players in the thriving re-
       gional commercial networks which pre-existed their appearance in
       the region. This gave rise to new groups of specialised intermediar-
       ies only through whom did European trading houses have access not
       only to local commodities, but also to specialised knowledges crucial
       to their survival and to sustained trade.36 These knowledges included
       the identification and value of potentially lucrative products, ranging
       from plants, herbs, and animals, to manufactured commodities, their
       geographical distribution, accounting and trading conventions, the
       maintenance and repair of ships and navigation, to name but a few.
       It is important to notice that the geographies of trade and knowledge
       networks thus largely overlapped not only in Europe but also in the
       Asian and Indian Ocean worlds, and it is this crucial shared connec-
       tion which underwrote the intercultural knowledge encounter in the
       region." Raj, *Relocating Modern Science,* p. 18-19

631   Raj, *Relocating Modern Science,* p. 18

632   "Attracted to the East initially by the lucrative spice and luxury-com-
       modity trade, Europeans discovered a world that was, all said and
       done, familiar to them, one already dominated by trade and the pres-
       ence of Muslims, their perennial, yet well-known, rivals. However, it
       was also a world in which they formed but one very small commercial
       group among many long-established trading communities of differ-
       ent racial, religious, and regional origins, who constituted an intricate
       and dynamic world of commerce—based largely on botanical prod-
       ucts—extending across the Indian Ocean.6 European survival in the
       region thus depended on the development of an ongoing and durable
       relationship between their merchants, missionaries, and travellers, and
       various regional agents—rulers, merchants, bankers and interpreters,
       but also skilled workmen and savants. For in the Indian Ocean world,
       specialised knowledge, particularly relating to botany, medicine, and
       alchemy, was already formalized and circulated from the Arabian pen-
       insula to China within constituted specialised communities, each with
       its own civility. And early-modern European physicians, surgeons,
       and, later, naturalists in the region readily acknowledged this fact." Raj,
       Relocating Modern Science, p. 30-31

633   Raj, *Relocating Modern Science,* p. 57

634   Pamela H. Smith, "Science on the Move: Recent Trends in the History of Early Modern Science." *Renaissance Quarterly,* vol. 62, no. 2, 2009, pp. 345–375, p. 368. The Israeli Historian of early modern era and Science Avner Ben-Zaken has also emphasized the "cross- cultural account of early modern science. "With the expansion of empires, establishment of trading companies in the East, and extension of print culture, early modern intellectual practices went beyond monastic contemplation in a closed room. Scholars extensively exchanged books, manuscripts, letters, and instruments, and traveled to other intellectual centers to study and to historical sites and exceptional geographic locations to do further research. Merely an exchange of material objects could set off unintended and uncontrolled processes of circulation, such that scientific ideas and practices traversed cultural boundaries." Avner Ben-Zaken, Cross-Cultural Scientific Exchanges in the Eastern Mediterranean 1560-1660, Baltimore, John Hopkins University Press, 2010, p. 3

635   Smith, "Science on the Move: Recent Trends in the History of Early Modern Science, p. 368

636   Smith, "Science on the Move: Recent Trends in the History of Early Modern Science, p. 369

637   Smith, "Science on the Move: Recent Trends in the History of Early Modern Science, p. 371

638   Smith, "Science on the Move: Recent Trends in the History of Early Modern Science, p. 375

639   Smith, "Science on the Move: Recent Trends in the History of Early Modern Science, p. 375

640   See T. K. Rabb, "Religion and the Rise of Modern Science" in Webster, *The Intellectual Revolution of the Seventeenth Century,* p. 262-279

641   Richard L. Greaves, Puritanism and Science: The Anatomy of a Controversy, *Journal of the History of Ideas,* Vol. 30, No. 3 (Jul. - Sep., 1969), pp. 345-368, p. 368

642   Quoted in Greaves, Puritanism and Science: The Anatomy of a Controversy, p. 368, also in Jones, *Ancients and Moderns,* p. 228-29. For a stimulating discussion of the parallel between political and scientific revolutions, see Thomas S. Kuhn, *The Structure of Scientific Revolutions,* Chicago, University of Chicago Press, 1996, p. 91-109. Kuhn observed that "One aspect of the parallelism must already be apparent.

Political revolutions are inaugurated by a growing sense, often restricted to a segment of the political community, that existing institutions have ceased adequately to meet the problems posed by an environment that they have in part created. In much the same way, scientific revolutions are inaugurated by a growing sense, again often restricted to a narrow subdivision of the scientific community, that an existing paradigm has ceased to function adequately in the exploration of an aspect of nature to which that paradigm itself had previously led the way. In both political and scientific development the sense of malfunction that can lead to crisis is prerequisite to revolution." Kuhn, *The Structure of Scientific Revolutions,* p. 92

643 See Kuhn, *The Structure of Scientific Revolutions,* p. 92ff

644 "True knowledge was all in some sense a knowledge of God; Truth was one, its unity guaranteed by the unity of God. Reason and revelation were not in conflict but were supplementary. God's attributes were recorded in the written Word but were also directly reflected in the nature of nature.Natural philosophy thus had immediate theological meaning for Newton and he deemed it capable of revealing to him those aspects of the divine never recorded in the Bible or the record of which had been corrupted by time and human error. By whatever route one approached Truth, the goal was the same. Experimental discovery and revelation; the productions of reason, speculation, or mathematics; the cryptic, coded messages of the ancients in myth, prophecy, or alchemical tract - all, if correctly interpreted, found their reconciliation in the infinite unity and majesty of the Deity. In Newton's conviction of the unity of Truth and its ultimate source in the divine one may find the fountainhead of all his diverse studies." (B. J. T. Dobbs, *The Janus Faces of Genius: The Role of Alchemy in Newton's Thought,* Cambridge, Cambridge University Press, 1991, p. 6

645 See details in Dobbs, *The Janus Faces of Genius*

646 S. Gaukroger, *The Emergence of a Scientific Culture,* Oxford: Oxford University Press, 2005, P. 23

647 See Peter Harrison (2008) *Religion, the Royal Society, and the Rise of Science, Theology and Science,* 6:3, 255-271, DOI:10.1080/14746700802206925, p. 5ff; Peter Harrison, 'Physico-theology and the Mixed Sciences: The Role of Theology in Early Modern Natural Philosophy', in Peter Anstey and John Schuster (eds.), *The Science of Nature in the Seventeenth Century,* Dordrecht, Springer, 2005, pp. 165-183; Ann Blair, 'Mosaic Physics and the Search for a Pious Natural Philosophy in the Late Re-

naissance', *Isis* 91 (2000), 32-58.

648   Harrison, *Religion, the Royal Society, and the Rise of Science,* p. 5

649   Harrison, *Religion, the Royal Society, and the Rise of Science,* p. 6

650   See Nicolas Copernicus, *On the Revolutions.* Trans. Edward Rosen. Baltimore, MD: Johns Hopkins University Press, 1978; *God & Nature: Historical Essays on the Encounter between Christianity and Science,* edited by David C. Lindberg and Ronald L. Numbers; Peter Dear, *Revolutionising the Sciences: European Knowledge and Its Ambitions,1500–1700.* Princeton, NJ: Princeton University Press, 2001

651   Stephen F. Mason, *Some Historical Roots of the Scientific Revolution, Science & Society,* Vol. 14, No. 3 (Summer, 1950), pp. 237-264, P. 255; Robert K. Merton, *Science, Technology and Society in Seventeenth Century England,* Bruges, St. Catherine Press, 1938, p. 433 and 459.

652   See John Calvin as cited in John H. Brooke, *Science and Religion: Some Historical Perspectives,* Oxford: Oxford University Press, 1991, p. 96

653   Immanuel Kant, *Critique of Pure Reason,* trans. P. Guyer and A.W. Wood, Cambridge, Cambridge University Press, 1998, p. 99

654   See Gary B. Deason, 'Reformation theology and the Mechanistic Conception of Nature,'in *God & Nature: Historical Essays on the Encounter between Christianity and Science,* eds. David C. Lindberg and Ronald L. Numbers, p.169–170; Harold P. Nebelsick, *The Renaissance, The Reformation and the Rise of Science,* Edinburgh:T & T Clark, 1992

655   See Ernan McMullin, 'Galileo on Science and Scripture,' in *The Cambridge Companion to Galileo,* ed. Peter Machamer, Cambridge, Cambridge University Press, 1998, p. 300ff

656   J. Kepler, *New Astronomy,* 1609. Trans. by William H. Donahue, Cambridge, Cambridge University Press, 1992,p. 66

657   See Copernicus, *On the Revolutions,* p. 4–5

658   Galileo Galilei, *Letter to the Grand Duchess Christina ... Concerning the Use of Biblical Quotations in Matters of Science,* 1615. In *Discoveries and Opinions of Galileo* trans. Stillman Drake. New York: Anchor Books, 1957, p. 192–193

659   E. McMullin,"Galileo on Science and Scripture," p. 300

660   See Kenneth J. Howell, *God's Two Books: Copernican Cosmology and Biblical Interpretation in Early Modern Science,* Notre Dame: Universi-

ty of Notre Dame Press, 2002

661   Yahuda MS. 41, f. <7r>, Jewish National and University Library, Jerusalem. The manuscript, written mainly in English with some Latin parts and Greek quotations, is dated back to the early 1690s and consists of *c.* 28,550 words, 47 pp. on 29 ff. A complete transcription of the manuscript is available online at: http://www.newtonproject.sussex.ac.uk/view/texts/normalized/THEM00077.

662   Richard H. Popkin, "Newton's Biblical Theology and His Theological Physics," in Scheurer and Debrock (eds.), *Newton's Legacy,* pp. 81-97, p. 87.

663   See Dobbs, *The Janus Faces of Genius,* p. 74, 76, 202, 237

664   "Primitive Christianity is a simplistic and natural religion intent upon establishing morality rather than worldly advancement. Christ's yoke was easy and innocent of persecution. From this pristine original the priesthood with the corrupt apparatus of pagan philosophy and scholastic 'jargon' turned religion into a trade. False miracles, idolatry, ghosts and goblins created a priestly empire over the minds of the laity. The clergy 'deified their dreams'. In this manner the sacerdotal order set up an independent interest, creating a double kingdom upon which they forged a tyranny that extended to civil affairs. It was this triple analysis (of an original primitive natural religion, of priestly corruption and priestly tyranny) that was to form the backbone of the Freethinking impeachment of the Church." (Justin Champion, *Pillars of Priestcraft Shaken,* p. 136)

665   James E. Force noted that, "Newton's theology, not just his religion, influences his science every bit as much as his science influences the rigorous textual scholarship of his theology." (James E. Force, "Newton's God of Dominion: The Unity of Newton's Theological, Scientific, and Political Thought," in James E. Force and Richard H. Popkin (eds.), *Essays on the Context, Nature, and Influence of Isaac Newton's Theology,* Dordrecht, Kluwer Academic Publishers, 1990, pp. 75-102 , p. 78

666   Betty Jo Teeter Dobbs, "Newton's Alchemy and His 'Active Principle' of Gravitation," in Scheurer and Debrock (eds.), *Newton's Scientific and Philosophical Legacy,* Dordrecht, Kluwer Academic Publishers, 1988, p. 56; Betty Jo Teeter Dobbs and Margaret C. Jacob (eds.), *Newton and the Culture of Newtonianism,* Atlantic Highlands, New Jersey, Humanities Press International, 1995

667   See details in Lawrence M. Principe, "Reflections on Newton's Alchemy in Light of the New Historiography of Alchemy." In J. E. Force and S. Hut-

ton, eds. *Newton and Newtonianism*. Dordrecht: Kluwer Academic Publishers, 2004, p. 214; his *The Aspiring Adept: Robert Boyle and his Alchemical Quest*. Princeton: Princeton University Press, 1998 and *Chymists and Chymistry: Studies in the History of Alchemy and Early Modern Chemistry*. Sagamore Beach, MA: Science History Publications, 2007

668   Kristine Louise Haugen, Apocalypse (A User's Manual): Joseph Mede, *the Interpretation of Prophecy, and the Dream Book of Achmet,* September 2010, The Seventeenth century 25(2):215-39, p. 231

669   See details Principe, *Aspiring Adept*, 159-61; Paul Timothy Greenham, *A Concord of Alchemy with Theology: Isaac Newton's Hermeneutics of the Symbolic Texts of Chymistry and Biblical Prophecy,* Ph. D. dissertation submitted to Institute for the History and Philosophy of Science and Technology (IHPST) University of Toronto, 2015, p. 37ff; Irene Zanon, *The Alchemical Apocalypse of Isaac Newton,* Ph. D. dissertation submitted to Università Ca' Foscari Venezia, 2013, p. 143ff

670   See Mark Greengrass, Michael Leslie, and Timothy Raylor, eds., *Samuel Hartlib and Universal Reformation: Studies in Intellectual Communication,* Cambridge, Cambridge University Press,1994; Charles Webster, Great Instauration, p. 501ff

671   See G.H. Turnbull, *Samuel Hartlib: A Sketch of his Life and his Relations to J.A. Comenius,* Oxford, Oxford University Press, 1920; his Hartlib, *Dury and Comenius: Gleanings from Hartlib's Papers,* Liverpool, University Press, 1947; his "Samuel Hartlib's Influence on the Early History of the Royal Society," *Notes and Records of the Royal Society,* 10 (1952-3), 101-30; R.H. Syfret, "The Origins of the Royal Society," *Notes and Records of the Royal Society,* 5 (1947-8), 75-137; Charles Webster, *The Great Instauration: Science, Medicine and Reform,* 1626-1660, London, Peter Lang Publishing,1974 and his"Introduction," in Webster, ed., *Samuel Hartlib and the Advancement of Learning,* London, Cambridge University Press, 1970; *Dictionary of National Biography* (repr., London: Oxford University Press, 1949-50), 9, 72-3. Dorothy Stimson, "Hartlib, Haak, and Oldenburg: Intelligencers," Isis, 31 (1940), 309-26; and http://galileo.rice.edu/Catalog/NewFiles/hartlib.html

672   See details in Mark Greengrass, Michael Leslie, and Timothy Raylor, eds., *Samuel Hartlib and Universal Reformation, p. 95ff*

673   See Mark Greengrass, Michael Leslie, and Timothy Raylor, eds., *Samuel Hartlib and Universal Reformation, p. 213ff*

674   See Mark Greengrass, Michael Leslie, and Timothy Raylor, eds., *Sam-*

uel Hartlib and Universal Reformation, p. 151ff

675   See Daniel Andersson, *Learning Arabic and Learned Bilingualism in Early Modern England: The Case of John Pell* in Jens Braarvig and Markham J. Geller eds., *Studies in Multilingualism*, Lingua Franca and Lingua Sacra, Max Planck Research Library for the History and Development of Knowledge - Studies 10, Open Access, January 1, 2018, p. 214-15

676   See R.H. Syfret, "The Origins of the Royal Society," *Notes and Records of the Royal Society*, 5 (1947-8), 75-137; John J. O'Brien, Samuel Hartlib's influence on Robert Boyle's scientific development, *Annals of Science*, 1965, 21:1, 1-14;

677   See Andrew J. Mendelsohn, "Alchemy and Politics in England 1649—1665." *Past & Present*, no. 135 (May 1992): 30–78, p. 51

678   See details in Sylvia Brown ed., *Women, Gender and Radical Religion in Early Modern Europe*, Leiden, Brill, 2007, p. 285ff

679   See Hill, *Intellectual Origins*, p. 16

680   Robert K. Merton, *Science, Technology and Society in Seventeenth Century England*, p. 498

681   Merton, *Science, Technology and Society in Seventeenth Century England*, p. 503

682   See detailed analysis in Gidion Preudenthal and Peter Mclaughlin eds., *The Social and Economic Roots of the Scientific Revolution: Texts by Borris Hessen and Henryk Grossmann*, New York, Springer, 2009, p. 4ff

683   Hill, *Intellectual Origins*, p. 16

684   Hill, *Intellectual Origins*, p. 33

685   See details in Francis R. Johnson, Gresham College: Precursor of the Royal Society, *Journal of the History of Ideas*, Vol. 1, No. 4 (Oct., 1940), pp. 413-438

686   Hill, *Intellectual Origins*, p. 39

687   See Daniel Andersson, *Learning Arabic and Learned Bilingualism in Early Modern England: The Case of John Pell*, p. 214ff

688   See details in David Thomas and John Chesworth eds, *Christian Muslim Relations, A Biographical History*, Leiden, Brill, 2016, vol. 8, p. 52ff

689   See David Thomas and John Chesworth eds, *Christian Muslim Relations, A Biographical History*, vol. 8, p. 445

690   See details in David Thomas and John Chesworth eds, *Christian Muslim Relations, A Biographical History,* vol. 8, p. 445ff

691   See David Thomas and John Chesworth eds, *Christian Muslim Relations, A Biographical History,* vol. 8, p. 54 and 302

692   Hill, *Intellectual Origins,* p. 41; Bedwell recommended the study of Arabic, among other reasons, because of the importance of Arabic science (J. B. Mullinger, *The University of Cambridge from…1626 to the decline of the Platonist Movement,* 1911, pp. 93–94)

693   See Hill, *Intellectual Origins,* p. 42

694   Hill, *Intellectual Origins,* p. 44

695   See Hill, *Intellectual Origins,* p. 49ff

696   Qouted in Hill, *Intellectual Origins,* p. 56

697   See Richard P. Ross, *The Social and Economic Causes of the Revolution in the Mathematical Sciences in Mid-Seventeenth-Century England,* p. 56ff

698   See Merton, Science, *Technology and Society in Seventeenth Century England;* Eva G. R. Taylor, Tudor Geography, 1485-1583 (1930; reprint, New York, Octagon Books, 1968); A. R. Hall, *Ballistics in the Seventeenth Century,* Cambridge, Cambridge University Press, 1952), pp. 1-58; Eva G. R. Taylor, *Mathematical Practitioners of Tudor and Stuart England,* Cambridge, Cambridge University Press 1954, pp. 7-25, 165-92, 311-51; David W. Waters, *The Art of Navigation in England in Elizabethan and Early Stuart Times,* London, Hollis & Carter, 1958, pp. 78-250; Henry J. Webb, *Elizabethan Military Science: The Books and the Practice,* Madison, University of Wisconsin Press, 1965. p. 9

699   Ross, *The Social and Economic Causes of the Revolution,* p. 60-61

700   See Ross, *The Social and Economic Causes of the Revolution,* p. 65

701   Ross, *The Social and Economic Causes of the Revolution,* p. 65

702   Stephen F. Mason, Some Historical Roots of the Scientific Revolution, *Science & Society,* Vol. 14, No. 3 (Summer, 1950), pp. 237-264, p. 237

703   Mason, Some Historical Roots of the Scientific Revolution, p. 253-254

704   Mason, Some Historical Roots of the Scientific Revolution, p. 256

705   Anna Winterbottom, *Hybrid Knowledge in the Early East India Company World,* p. 15-16

706   "The Royal Society shared many other features with the EIC, including

its Baconian commitment to keeping detailed vernacular records of all meetings and correspondence. Both institutions kept libraries including numerous works of travel in other European languages and collections of material objects sent from abroad. In London, the EIC had a storehouse or museum of specimens sent to them in this period by their servants abroad. Though references to it are rare, it seems to have been a considerable collection according to a contemporary account of the visit of an Italian duke.83 The Royal Society also had a 'repository' of curiosities, animal, vegetable, and mineral, sent to them from around the world, a collection that was eventually transferred to the British Museum.84 It is clear that objects flowed freely between the collections of the two organisations, which in some cases overlapped. Between 1672 and 1675, the Royal Society shared Gresham College with some of the EIC's collections.85 On occasion, the Royal Society was consulted by agents of the EIC to interpret some of these objects. This was the case in 1680, when the fellows were asked to determine the 'virtues', or useful properties, of a bezoar stone that had been presented to the EIC by the Sultan of Bantam, Abdulfatah Ageng." Anna Winterbottom, *Hybrid Knowledge in the Early East India Company World,* p.16

707   See Jan Golinski, *Making Natural Knowledge: Constructivism and the History of Science,* 2nd edn., Chicago, The University of Chicago Press, 2005; Anna Winterbottom, *Hybrid Knowledge in the Early East India Company World,* p.16

708   See Stevin Shapin, *The Scientific Revolution,* Chicago, University of Chicago Press, 1998, p. 4

709   Richard P. Ross, *The Social and Economic Causes of the Revolution in the Mathematical Sciences in Mid-Seventeenth-Century England, Journal of British Studies,* Vol. 15, No. 1 (Autumn, 1975), pp. 46-66,, p. 66

710   Ross, *The Social and Economic Causes of the Revolution,* p. 66

711   Ina Baghdiantz MaCabe, *Orientalism in Early Modern France: Euraasain Trade, Exoticism and the Ancient Regime,* Oxfordf, BERG, 2008, p. 115; also see Nicolas Dew, Orientalism in Louis XIV's France, Oxford, Oxford University Press, 2009, p. 168ff

712   See M. B. Hall, *Arabick Learning in the Correspondance of the Royal Society, 1660-1676"* in G. A. Russell (ed.), *The 'Arabick' Interest of the Natural Philosophers in Seventeenth-Century England,* p. 147

713   See Anna Winterbottom, *Producing and Using the "Historical Relation of Ceylon": Robert Knox, the East India Company and the Royal Soci-*

ety, The British Journal for the History of Science, Vol. 42, No. 4 (Dec., 2009), pp. 515-538

714   See Royal Society. *Philosophical transactions: giving some accompt of the present undertakings, studies and labours of the ingenious in many considerable parts of the world.* London: Printed by T.N., begun in 1665; Peck, Linda Levy. *Consuming splendor: society and culture in seventeenth-century England.* Cambridge, UK; New York, Cambridge University Press, 2005.

715   See Toomer, *Eastern Wisdom and Learning,* p. 248ff

716   See Miles Ogborn, *Indian Ink: Script and Print in the Making of English East India Company,* Chicago, University of Chicago Press, 2007, p. xvii ff

717   See details Royal Society, *Arabic Roots,* Curator Rim Turkmani, June 2011, https://royalsociety.org/-/media/exhibitions/arabick-roots/2011-06-08-ar-abick-roots.pdf; Rim Turkmani, Arabic Roots of *the Scientific Revolution,* https://muslimheritage.com/arabic-root-sci-revolution/; Miles Ogborn, *Indian Ink: Script and Print in the Making of English East India Company,* p. xviii ff

718   Miles Ogborn, *Indian Ink: Script and Print in the Making of English East India Company,* p. 4

719   See details in Miles Ogborn, *Indian Ink: Script and Print in the Making of English East India Company,* p. xv ff "Within his extensive corre-spondence we do indeed find that Boyle's world was also the world of the English East India Company." Also see Michael Hunter (ed.) *Robert Boyle by Himself and His Friends with a Fragment of William Wotton's Lost Life of Boyle,* London, William Pickering, 1994

720   See Michael Hunter, *Boyle Studies: Aspects of the Life and Thought of Robert Boyle (1627-1691),* Burlington, Ashgate, 2015, p. 84

721   See details in M. B. Hall, *Arabick Learning in the Correspondance of the Royal Society, 1660-1676"* in G. A. Russell (ed.), *The 'Arabick' Interest of the Natural Philosophers in Seventeenth-Century England,* p. 147ff ; Michael Hunter, See Michael Hunter, *Boyle Studies: Aspects of the Life and Thought of Robert Boyle (1627-1691),* p. 92

722   See Russell (ed.), *The 'Arabick' Interest of the Natural Philosophers in Seventeenth-Century England,* p. 234

723   Royal Society, *Arabic Roots,* Curator Rim Turkmani, June 2011, https://royalsociety.org/-/media/exhibitions/arabick-roots/2011-06-08-ara-bick-roots.pdf; Toomer, *Eastern Wisdom and Learning,* p. 247

724   Victor J. Katz ed., *The Mathematics of Egypt,* Mesopotamie, China, India and Islam: A Source Book, Princeton, Princeton University Press, 2007, p. 4

725   See Toomer, *Eastern Wisdom and Learning,* p. 255ff

726   See details Royal Society, *Arabic Roots,* Curator Rim Turkmani, June 2011, https://royalsociety.org/-/media/exhibitions/arabick-roots/2011-06-08-arabick-roots.pdf; Rim Turkmani, Arabic Roots of *the Scientific Revolution,* https://muslimheritage.com/arabic-root-sci-revolution/

727   See M.B. Hall, 'Arabick Learning in the Correspondence of the Royal Society, 1660–1677', in Russell, *The 'Arabick' Interest of the Natural Philosophers in 17ᵗʰ-Century England,* p.154

728   See Angus Armitage, Edmond Halley, London, Thomas Nelson, 1966; Noel Coley, "Halley and Post-Restoration Science". *History Today.* 1986, 36 (September): 10–16; Alan H. Cook, Edmond Halley: *Charting the Heavens and the Seas.* Oxford: Clarendon Press, 1998; Michael N. Fried, Edmond Halley's *Reconstruction of the Lost Book of Apollonius's Conics: Translation and Commentary,* New York, Springer-Verlag, 2012

729   Royal Society, *Phil. Trans.* 1695 19:160-175; doi:10.1098/rstl.1695.0023; see details in Raymond Mercier, "English Orientalists and Mathmatical Astronomy", in G. Russell (edit.), *The 'Arabick' Interest of the Natural Philosophers in Seventeenth-Century England,* pp. 158-214.

730   Michael Hunter and Michael Cooper eds., *Robert Hooke: Tercentennial Studies,* New York, Routledge, 2006, p. 219

731   William Bray (Ed.), *Diaries of John Evelyn.* London, 1852, Vol I, p352: *11 May 1661*

732   See details in Michael Hunter and Michael Cooper eds., *Robert Hooke,* p. 227ff

733   Michael Hunter and Michael Cooper eds., *Robert Hooke,* p. 221

734   Richard Steele, *The Lover.* London, 1714, 27ᵗʰ April 1714, No 27

735   See Nabil Matar, *Islam in Britain,* p. 38

736   M. B. Hall, *Arabick Learning in the Correspondance of the Royal Society, 1660-1676"* in G. A. Russell (ed.), *The 'Arabick' Interest of the Natural Philosophers in Seventeenth-Century England,* p. 147

737   See Mayling Stubbs, John Beale, Philosophical Gardener of Hereford-

shire: part I, Prelude to the Royal Society (1608-1663), in: *Annals of Science* 39 (1982), pp. 463-89; id., John Beale, Philosophical Gardener of Herefordshire: part II, The improvement of agriculture and trade in the Royal Society (1663-1683), in: *Annals of Science* 46 (1989), pp. 323-63; Michael Leslie, *The Spiritual Husbandry of John Beale, in: Culture and Cultivation in Early Modern England,* eds, Michael Leslie and Timothy Raylor (Leicester, Leicester University Press, 1992), pp. 151-72; Rhodri Lewis, 'The Best Mnemonicall Expedient'. John Beale's art of memory and its uses, in: *The Seventeenth Century* 20 (2005), pp. 113-44; and William Poole, Two Early Readers of Milton: John Beale and Abraham Hill, in: *Milton Quarterly,* 38 (2004), pp. 76-99, at pp. 77-88

738   See Dmitri Levitin, *Ancient Wisdom in the Age of New Science: Histories of Philosophy in England,* c. 1640-1700, Cambridge, Cambridge University Press, 2015, p. 476ff

739   Mayling Stubbs (1982) John Beale, philosophical gardener of Herefordshire, *Annals of Science,* 39:5, 463-489, p. 468

740   See David Thomas and John Chesworth eds., *Christian-Muslim Relations: A Biographical History,* vol. 8, p. 302

741   See details in *Mayling Stubbs,* John Beale, p. 473 ff

742   Dmitri Levitin, 'Radical' History Writing in 1650s England: The Case of John Beale" in *Radicalism and Dissent in the World of Protestant Reform,* p. 190

743   For recent work on Lady Ranelagh's religious attitudes, see Ruth Connelly, A Proselytising Protestant Commonwealth: The Religious and Political Ideals of Katherine Jones, Viscountess Ranelagh, in: *The Seventeenth Century,* 23 (2008), pp. 244-264; id., 'A Wise and Godly Sybilla': Viscountess Ranelagh and the Politics of International Protestantism, in: *Women, Gender and Radical Religion,* ed. Sylvia Brown (Leiden, 2007), pp. 285-306. For Evelyn, see John Spurr, 'A sublime and noble service': John Evelyn and the Church of England, in: *John Evelyn and his Milieu,* eds, Frances Harris and Michael Hunter (London, British Library, 2003), pp. 145-163.

744   Dmitri Levitin, 'Radical' History Writing in 1650s England: The Case of John Beale", p. 177

745   Beale to Hartlib, 26 March 1659, Hartlib Papers 51/102; Dmitri Levitin, 'Radical' History Writing in 1650s England: The Case of John Beale" in *Radicalism and Dissent in the World of Protestant Reform,* p. 177

746   Quoted in Dmitri Levitin, 'Radical' History Writing in 1650s England: The Case of John Beale", p. 177;

747   *Beale to Lady Ranelagh*, undated [1659?], Hartlib Papers 27/16/12 https://www.dhi.ac.uk/hartlib/view?docset=main&docname=27A_16&term0=transtext_plantacion#highlight

748   *Ibid.*, HP27/16/ir-12

749   See Dmitri Levitin, 'Radical' History Writing in 1650s England: The Case of John Beale", p. 179

750   See *Ibid.*, HP 27/16/9"-10; Dmitri Levitin, 'Radical' History Writing in 1650s England: The Case of John Beale", p. 179-80

751   *Beale to Lady Ranelagh,* undated *[c.* 1659], HP 27/17

752   Dmitri Levitin, 'Radical' History Writing in 1650s England: The Case of John Beale", p. 181

753   See Dmitri Levitin, 'Radical' History Writing in 1650s England: The Case of John Beale", p. 178 and for Socinian influence on Beale Sarah Mortimer, *Reason and Religion in the English Revolution,* p. 59ff

754   Sarah Mortimer, *Reason and Religion in the English Revolution,* p. 60

755   Sarah Mortimer, *Reason and Religion in the English Revolution,* p. 62

756   *Beale to Lady Ranelagh,* undated (c. 1659), HP 27/16/3^ See also Beale to Hartlib, undated, HP 62/7/r

757   Quoted in Dmitri Levitin, 'Radical' History Writing in 1650s England: The Case of John Beale", p. 185

758   See details Dmitri Levitin, 'Radical' History Writing in 1650s England: The Case of John Beale", p. 185-186

759   Dmitri Levitin, 'Radical' History Writing in 1650s England: The Case of John Beale", p. 188

760   Quoted in Dmitri Levitin, 'Radical' History Writing in 1650s England: The Case of John Beale", p. 188

761   Beale to [Evelyn?], 18 November 1658, HP 39/2/68"-69 https://www.dhi.ac.uk/hartlib/view?docset=main&docname=39B_02_068&term0=transtext_rationable#highlight

762   Dmitri Levitin, 'Radical' History Writing in 1650s England: The Case of John Beale", p. 188

763   Beale to [Evelyn?], 18 November 1658, HP 39/2/68"-69 https://www.

dhi.ac.uk/hartlib/view?docset=main&docname=39B_02_068&ter-
m0=transtext_rationable#highlight

764   Dmitri Levitin, 'Radical' History Writing in 1650s England: The Case
      of John Beale", p. 189; see Henry Oldenburg, The Correspondence of
      Henry Oldenburg, 13 vols., ed. and trans. A. Rubert Hall and Marie
      Boas Hall (Madison, WI: University of Wisconsin Press, 1965), vol.
      1, p. 410; Nabil Matar, Islam in Britain, p. 106; The Letters of Daniel
      Defoe, ed. George Harris Healey (Oxford: Clarendon Press, 1955), p.
      46; Matar, Islam in Britain, p. 107

765   Dmitri Levitin, 'Radical' History Writing in 1650s England: The Case
      of John Beale", p. 190

766   Dmitri Levitin, 'Radical' History Writing in 1650s England: The Case
      of John Beale", p. 190

767   Dmitri Levitin, 'Radical' History Writing in 1650s England: The Case
      of John Beale", p. 190-91

768   Beale to Evelyn, undated [1664], BL MS Add. 78312, fol. 20

769   See John Coffey ed., Oxford History of Protestant Dissenting Traditions,
      p. 391

770   Paul Hazard, Crisis of European Mind, p. 16-17

771   Paul Hazard, Crisis of European Mind, p. 17

772   See details in G. J. Toomer, Eastern Wisdom and Learning: The Study
      of Arabic in Seventeenth-Century England, Oxford, Clarendon Press,
      1996, p. 108ff

773   Toomer, Eastern Wisdom and Learning, p. 114

774   See Toomer, Eastern Wisdom and Learning, p. 191ff

775   Allison P. Coudert, "Orientalism in Early Modern Europe", p. 749; On the
      role of alchemy in fostering the scientific revolution, see Betty Jo T. Dobbs,
      The Foundations of Newton's Alchemy: or, "The Hunting of the Green Lyon",
      Cambridge, Cambridge University Press, 1975; eadem, The Janus Faces
      of Genius: The Role of Alchemy in Newton's Thought, Cambridge, Cam-
      bridge University Press, 1991; Richard S. Westfall, "Newton and Alche-
      my, Occult and Scientific Mentalities in the Renaissance, ed. Brian Vickers
      (Cambridge: Cambridge University Press, 1984); Lawrence M. Principle,
      The Aspiring Adept: Robert Boyle and his Alchemical Quest (Princeton,
      NJ: Princeton University Press, 1998); Bruce T. Moran, Distilling Knowl-
      edge: Alchemy, Chemistry, and the Scientific Revolution (Cambridge, MA:

Harvard University Press, 2006); William R. Newman, *Promethean Am-bitions: Alchemy and the Quest to Perfect Nature* (Chicago and London: The University of Chicago Press, 2004).

776   See Michael Hunter ed., *Archives of the Scientific Revolution: The For-mation and Exchange of Ideas in the Seventeenth-Century Europe,* Woodbridge, Boydell Press, 1998, p. 43

777   Michael Hunter ed., *Archives of the Scientific Revolution: The Forma-tion and Exchange of Ideas in the Seveneteenth-Century Europe,* p. 35

778   See Hill, *Intellectual Origins,* p. 90ff

779   Garcia, *Islam and English Enlightenment,* p. 132

780   See William R. Newman, and Lawrence M. Principe, *Alchemy Tried in the Fire: Starkey, Boyle, and the Fate of Helmontian Chymistry.* Chica-go: The University of Chicago Press, 2002.

781   See Stanton Marlan, *The Philosophers' Stone: Alchemical Imagina-tion and the Soul's Logical Life.* Doctoral dissertation. Pittsburgh, Penn.: Duquesne University, 2014

782   See Dobbs, *The Janus Faces of Genius,* p. 5

783   "Great efforts went into dissolving gold for transmutation, and Robert Boyle would quote the alchemical saying:

       "It is harder to destroy gold than make it". The possibility of trans-mutation of the noble metal was accepted by such distinguished sev-enteenth century scientists as Johannes Kepler (1571-1630), Robert Boyle (1627-1691), G W [Gottfried Wilhelm] Leibniz (1646 -1716), and, for at least thirty years of his life, Sir Isaac Newton (1642 -1727)." *Good as gold: Sir Isaac Newton's alchemy, Perception,* 1989, volume 18, pages 697-702

784   See Eric John Holmyard, *Makers of Chemistry. Oxford: Clarendon Press, 1931.*See Matar, Islam in Britain, p. 93; also see Kavin van Bladel, The Arabic Hermes: From Pagan Sage to Prophet of Science, Oxford, Oxford University Press, 2009

785   See Hill, *Intellectual Origins,* p. 95; Louis Trenchard More, Boyle as Alchemist, *Journal of the History of Ideas,* Vol. 2, No. 1 (Jan., 1941), pp. 61-76, p. 63ff

786   See Stephen Gaukroger, *The Emergence of a Scientific Culture: Science and the Shaping of Modernity 1210-1685,* Oxford, Oxford University Press, 2006, p. 360ff

787   See William R. Newman, 'The Alchemical Sources of Robert Boyle's Corpuscular Philosophy', *Annals of Science* 53 (1996), 567–85; Louis Trenchard More, Boyle as Alchemist, p. 62ff

788   Locke's corresspondance with Robert Boyle and Isaac Newton about alchemical recipes, plants collections and experimentations for gold are well-documented in his letters to them. See E. S. De Beer, *The Correspondence of John Locke*, (Oxford: Oxford University Press, 1979),vol.1, p. 230; Louis Trenchard More, Boyle as Alchemist, *Journal of the History of Ideas*, Vol. 2, No. 1 (Jan., 1941), pp. 61-76, p. 73

789   F. Sherwood Taylor, "An Alchemical Work of Sir Isaac Newton," in *Ambix*, Vol. 5, (1956), pp. 61-64, p. 62.

790   Both quotations here are from William R. Shea, "Introduction: Trends in the Interpretation of Seventeenth Century Science," in M. L. Righini Bonelli and William R. Shea (eds.), *Reason, Experiment, and Mysticism*, New York, Science History Publications, 1975, p. 6

791   William Eamon, *Books of Secrets in Medieval and Early Modern Science*, Sudhoffs Archiv, Bd. 69, H. 1 (1985), pp. 26-49, p. 27

792   See William Eamon, *Science And The Secrets Of Nature: Books Of Secrets In Medieval And Early Modern Culture*, Princeton, Princeton University Press, 1994, p. 18ff

793   "Secretum secretroum extolled the practical benefits of knowledge of nature, and it implied that knowledge of human invention and of nature was an essential part of understanding God. It also advanced the idea of an ancient knowledge that had come down to the sons of Seth (Adam's son), which was subsequently lost and only partly recovered by the Greeks, the Arabs, and now the Christian academics. The book persuaded Bacon the greatest attainment of any truth-seeker was to regain that pristine understanding, or prisca sapientia [...]." (Philip Ashley Fanning, *Isaac Newton and the Transmutation of Alchemy: An Alternate View of the Scientific Revolution*, Berkeley, California, North Atlantic Books, 2009, p. 7.) Actually, this last sentence could be also applied to best describe the ultimate aim of Newton and other natural philosopher's research into alchemy and human knowledge.

794   Eamon, *Books of Secrets in Medieval and Early Modern Science*, p. 27

795   See E. J. Holmyard, *Alchemy*, Toronto, Penguin Books, 1957, p. 58ff; Kaspars Klavins, The importance of Islamic civilization at the crossroads of European thinkers: 16th and 17th centuries, p. 12

796   Eamon, *Science And The Secrets Of Nature*, p. 38

797   See Dobbs, *The Janus Faces of Genius*, p. 253-255. "That religious rationale for the study of nature may in turn have sustained and validated the nascent scientific enterprise in a still Christian Europe until the time arrived when science no longer had need of such support." (Dobbs, *The Janus Faces of Genius*, p. 255)

798   Dobbs, "Newton's Alchemy and His 'Active Principle' of Gravitation," in Scheurer and Debrock (eds.), *Newton's Legacy*, p. 73; see also Dobbs, *The Foundations of Newton's Alchemy*, pp. 210-213. Richard Westfall's reference books, also quoted by Dobbs in "Newton's Alchemy and His 'Active Principle' of Gravitation" (note 63, p. 80), are: Richard S. Westfall, *Force in Newton's Physics. The Science of Dynamics in the Seventeenth Century*, London: Macdonald; New York: American Elsevier, 1971; pp. 323-423; *Idem*, "Newton and the Hermetic Tradition," in *Science, Medicine and Society in the Renaissance. Essays to honour Walter Pagel*, ed. By Allen G. Debus (2 vols.; New York: Science History Publications, 1972), II, pp. 183-198.

799   Eamon, *Books of Secrets in Medieval and Early Modern Science*, p. 47-48

800   See Stephen Gaukroger, *The Emergence of a Scientific Culture*, p. 255ff; See Keith Hutchison, 'What Happened to Occult Qualities in the Scientific Revolution?', *Isis* 73 (1982), 233–53; Ron Millen, 'The Manifestation of Occult Qualities in the Scientific Revolution', in M. J. Osler and P. J. Farber, eds, *Religion, Science, and Worldview* (Cambridge, 1985), 185–216; John Henry, 'Occult Qualities and the Experimental Philosophy: Active Principles in Pre-Newtonian Matter Theory', *History of Science* 24 (1986), 335–81; idem, 'Robert Hooke, The Incongruous Mechanist', in Michael Hunter and Simon Schaffer, eds, *Robert Hooke: New Studies* (Woodbridge, 1989), 149–80; and J. E. McGuire, 'Force, Active Principles and Newton's Invisible Realm', *Ambix* 15 (1968), 154–208.

801   Keith Thomas, *Religion and the Decline of Magic*, p. 241ff

802   Ann Talbot, *Great Ocean of Knowledge*, p. 45

803   "Isaac Newton studied alchemy from about 1668 until the second or third decade of the eighteenth century. He combed the literature of alchemy, compiling voluminous notes and even transcribing entire treatises in his own hand. Eventually he drafted treatises of his own, filled with references to the older literature. The manuscript legacy of his scholarly endeavour is very large and represents a huge commitment

of his time, but to it one must add the record of experimentation. Each brief and often abruptly cryptic labouratory report hides behind itself untold hours with hand-built furnaces of brick, with crucible, with mortar and pestle, with the apparatus of distillation, and with charcoal fires: experimental sequences sometimes ran for weeks, months, or even years. As the seventeenth- century epithet "philosopher by fire" distinguished the serious, philosophical alchemist from the empiric "puffer" or the devious charlatan or the amateur "chymist," so may one use the term to characterise Isaac Newton. Surely this man earned that title if ever any did." (Dobbs, *The Janus Face of Genius,* p. 1

804   See Daren Oldridge, *The Supernatural in Tudor and Stuart England,* New York, Routledge, 2016

805   See details in Keith Thomas, *Religion and the Decline of Magic*

806   See William Eamon, *Science And The Secrets Of Nature,* Introduction, p. 1-12

807   "I very much like the science of alchemy which is, indeed, the philosophy of the ancients. I like it not only because, by melting metals, and decocting, preparing, extracting, and distilling herb and roots, it produces profits; but also because of its allegorical and secret meaning. This is quite excellent and touches upon the resurrection of the dead at the Last Day. For, just as in a furnace the fire extracts and separates the various parts of a substance, and carries upwards its spirit, life, sap and strength, leaving behind at the bottom the unclean matter, the dregs, like a dead, worthless corpse; so God, at the day of Judgment, will separate everything with fire, the righteous from the unrighteous. The Christians, the righteous, will ascend to Heaven, where they will enjoy everlasting life; but the wicked and the unrighteous, like dross and dirt, will remain in Hell, and there they will be damned." (Martin Luther, *Tischreden oder Colloquia,* (published 1556), quoted in P. G. Maxwell-Stuart (ed.), *The Occult in Early Modern Europe. A Documentary History,* Basingstoke, Macmillan, 1999, p. 202)

808   Dobbs, *The Janus Faces of Genius,* p. 7

809   "During the sixteenth century alchemy underwent an important change. Dee and others still tried to make gold; but the alchemical terms were increasingly used to express a mystical rather than a practical experience – they were considered hieroglyphics for the soul's search and for ultimate union with God. The philosopher's stone *is* Christ, the union of the male and female principles *is* the union of the soul with God, and so on for all alchemical terms and symbols."

(Liselotte Dieckmann, "Renaissance Hieroglyphics," in *Comparative Literature*, Vol. 9, No. 4 (Autumn, 1957), pp. 308-321, p. 316.)

810 E. J. Holmyard, *Alchemy*, p. 14 ; also see Arthur E. Waite, *The Secret Tradition in Alchemy: its Development and Records*, London, Kegan Paul, Trench, Trubner & co., ltd.; New York, A. A. Knopf, 1926, p. 405. Waite stated: "[…] it should be remembered that the work of metallic transmutation has been compared by alchemists themselves to that of God in the cosmos and that the staged of the one are affirmed to be an exact reproduction or counterpart of the other. We should remember also that Alchemy in all its departments is dealing with subjects – whether spiritual or material – which are *ex hypothesi* fallen, and that this is true indifferently of so-called base metals and of humanity in the base life. The thesis is that regeneration is an analogous process in every kingdom – that metals are reborn, transmuted or redeemed, and that what happens in their case is in correspondence – *mutatis mutandis* – with the higher work of God in the soul."

811 See Sam Kean, Newton, The Last Magician: The great man of science had more than a passing interest in alchemy, *Humanities*, January/February 2011, Volume 32, Number 1

812 See V. Schettino (2017) Isaac Newton and Alchemy. *Substantia* 1(1): 69-76. doi: 10.13128/Substantia-12

813 See Andrew J. Mendelsohn, "Alchemy and Politics in England 1649—1665." *Past & Present*, no. 135 (May 1992): 30–78.

814 Richard Popkin, Introduction, I.E. Force and R.H. Popkin (eds), *Newton and Religion: Context, Nature, and Influence*, Amsterdam, Kluwer Scientific Publ;ishers, 1999, p. xi-xii

815 See Avner Ben-Zaken, "Intellectual, Scientific and Technological Relations between Christian and Muslim Civilizations 1580-1822" in David Thomas, & John Chesworth, *Christian-Muslim Relations. a Bibliographical History.* Volume 13 Western Europe (1700-1800), Boston: Brill, 2019, p. 38

816 Popkin, Introduction, I.E. Force and R.H. Popkin (eds), *Newton and Religion: Context, Nature, and Influence,* p. xiii

817 Popkin, Introduction, I.E. Force and R.H. Popkin (eds), *Newton and Religion: Context, Nature, and Influence,* p. xiii

818 See J. A. I. Champion, "Acceptable to inquisitive men": Some Simonian Contexts for Newton's Biblical Criticism, 1680-1692, I.E. Force and

R.H. Popkin (eds), *Newton and Religion: Context, Nature, and Influence*, p. 77-96

819   See Schettino, *Isaac Newton and Alchemy*, p. 74: "The underlying idea in Newton's understanding was that of a *prisca sapientia*. Newton believed that in the earliest times the truth about the natural world was revealed and was in the possession of mankind and that, dissipated in the arcane philosophy, was to be sought in the wisdom of the ancients by a correct interpretation of the occult language of alchemy andthe accurate interpretation of the sacred scriptures."

820   See Paul Timothy Greenham, *A Concord of Alchemy with Theology: Isaac Newton's Hermeneutics of the Symbolic Texts of Chymistry and Biblical Prophecy*, doctoral thesis submitted to Institute for the History and Philosophy of Science and Technology (IHPST), University of Toronto, 2015

821   See R. Markley, "Newton, Corruption, and the Tradition of Universal History"in I.E. Force and R.H. Popkin (eds), *Newton and Religion: Context, Nature, and Influence*, p. 121-144

822   Garcia, *Islam and English Enlightenment*, p. 133

823   Garcia, *Islam and English Enlightenment*, p. 133

824   See Justin Champion, *Republican Learning: John Toland and the crisis of Christian culture*, 1696-1722, Manchester University Press 2003, p. 165-235

825   See Dobbs, *The Foundations of Newton's Alchemy*, p.48

826   Harrison, *Religion, the Royal Society, and the Rise of Science*, p. 5

827   See Dobbs, *The Foundations of Newton's Alchemy*, p.48-60

828   Schettino, *Isaac Newton and Alchemy*, p. 69; see also Gaukroger, *The Emergence of a Scientific Culture*, p. 468ff

829   Quoted in Schettino, *Isaac Newton and Alchemy*, p. 70-71

830   See J. Andrew Mendelsohn, *Alchemy and Politics in England 1649-1665*, p. 32ff

831   See Brian Vickers, "Analogy versus Identity: The Rejection of Occult Symbolism, 1580-1680", in Vickers (ed.), Brian Vickers (ed.), *Occult and Scientific Mentalities in the Renaissance*, Cambridge, Cambridge University Press, 1984, p. 108; Lyndy Abraham, *Marvell and Alchemy Brookfield*, VT, Aldershot, 1990; Hill, *Intellectual Origins of the English Revolution*, esp. pp. 122-3, 148-9; P. M. Rattansi, "Paracelsus and the

Puritan Revolution", *Ambix,* xi (1963), pp. 24-32; Keith Thomas, *Religion and the Decline of Magic,* London, Penguin, 1971, pp. 227, 270-1; Charles Webster, "English Medical Reformers of the Puritan Revolution: A Background to the 'Society of Chymical Physitians' ", *Ambix,* xiv (1967), pp. 16-41.

832   See details in J. Andrew Mendelsohn, *Alchemy and Politics in England 1649-1665,* p. 30ff and 62ff

833   See Dobbs, *The Foundations of Newton's Alchemy, p.78* and Mendelsohn, *Alchemy and Politics in England,* p. 73

834   See Dobbs, *The Foundations of Newton's Alchemy, p.91*

835   Christopher Hill, *Intellectual Origins of the English Revolution Revisited,* Oxford, Oxford University Press, 1997, p. 3

836   See Heterdoxy in *Early Modern Science and Religion*

837   See Dobbs, *The Foundations of Newton's Alchemy, p.91-92*

838   F. A. Yates, *The Rosicrucian Enlightenment,* London, Routledge,1972, p. 257

839   See Rob Iliffe, *Priest of Nature: The Religious Worlds of Isaac Newton,* Oxford, Oxford University Press, 2017, p. 121ff

840   S. Snobelen, "The True Frame of Nature," in John Brooke, and Ian MacLean eds., *Heterodoxy in Early Modern Science and Religion,* Oxford, Oxford University Press, 2005 p. 257

841   See Dobbs, *The Foundations of Newton's Alchemy, p.108ff*

842   See Eamon, *Science And The Secrets Of Nature,* p. 42ff

843   Deborah E. Harkness, "Alchemy and Eschatology: Exploring the Connections between John Dee and Isaac Newton" in I.E. Force and R.H. Popkin (eds), *Newton and Religion:Context, Nature, and Influence,* p. 1

844   Kristine Louise Haugen, *Apocalypse* (A User's Manual): Joseph Mede, *the Interpretation of Prophecy, and the Dream Book of Achmet,* p. 215

845   See details in Iliffe, *Priest of Nature,* p. 228ff

846   Haugen, *Apocalypse (A User's Manual),* p. 223

847   Haugen, *Apocalypse (A User's Manual),* p. 225

848   Haugen, *Apocalypse (A User's Manual),* p. 232

849   See Haugen, *Apocalypse (A User's Manual),* p. 232-233

850   Richard H. Popkin, *The Third Force in Seventeenth-century Thought,*

Leiden, E. J. Brill, 1992, pp. 181-182

851   Newton stated: "It was the judiciously learned & conscientious Mr Mede who first made way into these interpretations, & him I have for the most part followed. ffor what I found true in him it was not lawful for me to recede from, & I rather wonder that he erred so little then that he erred in some things. His mistakes were chiefly in his Clavis, & had that been perfect, the rest would have fallen in naturally." Yahuda MS. 1.1, f. <8r>

852   Yahuda MS. 1.1, f. <1r>, http://www.newtonproject.ox.ac.uk/view/texts/diplomatic/THEM00136

853   See Steven M. Oberhelman, ed., *The Oneirocriticon of Achmet: A Medieval Greek and Arabic Treatise on the Interpretation of Dreams,* Lubbock, TX: Texas Tech University Press, 1991

854   Maria V. Mavroudi, *The So-Called Oneirocriticon Of A C H M E T: A Byzantine Book On Dream Interpretation And Its Arabic Source,* doctoral thesis presented to Harvard University, 1998; Maria Mavroudi, A Byzantine Book on Dream Interpretation: The Oneirocriticon of Achmet and Its Arabic Sources, *The Medieval Mediterranean: Peoples, Economies and Cultures,* 4001453, vol. 36, Leiden: E. J. Brill, 2002

855   "I call it established, ffor such the exact consent of the afforesaid three Nations in these records argue it to be, since there uses not to happen any such consent in doctrines which severall nations or severall men in the same nation frame according to their privat imaginations. To which consideration may their consent with such interpretations as are to be collected out of Scripture may be added as a pledge of their certainty|legitimatenes in the rest." Yahuda Ms. 1.1a, fols. 1r-2r. See details in Paul Timothy Greenham, *A Concord of Alchemy with Theology: Isaac Newton's Hermeneutics of the Symbolic Texts of Chymistry and Biblical Prophecy,* p. 129ff

856   Greenham, *A Concord of Alchemy with Theology,* p. 141

857   "I received also much light in this search by the analogy between the world natural & the wor[l]d politique. ffor the mystical language was founded on this analogy & will be best understood by considering its original." Newton, Keynes Ms. 5, fols. Ir-IIr; also see J. Andrew Mendelsohn, Alchemy and Politics in England 1649-1665, *Past & Present,* No. 135 (May, 1992), pp. 30-78

858   See details in Dobbs, *The Foundations of Newton's Alchemy, p. 48ff*

859   See details Garcia , *Islam and English Enlightenment,* p. 134ff

860 See details in Anna Winterbottom, *Producing and Using the "Historical Relation of Ceylon": Robert Knox, the East India Company and the Royal Society,* p. 523-24 and 538

861 Anna Winterbottom, *Hybrid Knowledge in the Early East India Company World,* p. 6; John Richards, 'Early Modern India and World History', *Journal of World History,* 8 (1997), 197–209; Lynn A. Struve (ed.) *The Qing Formation in World-Historical Time* (Cambridge, MA: Harvard University Asia Center, 2004); Sanjay Subrahmanyam, *From the Tagus to the Ganges* (New Delhi: Oxford University Press, 2005

862 See Sanjay Subrahmanyam, *From the Tagus to the Ganges*

863 See Jack Goody, *Renaissances: The One or the Many?,* Cambridge, Cambridge University Press, 2010

864 David Armitage and Michael J. Braddick, 'Introduction', in Armitage and Braddick (eds.) *The British Atlantic World: 1500–1800,* Hampshire, Palgrave Macmillan, 2002, 1.

865 Paul Hazard stated: "…nowhere are there to be found records of travel more engrossing, despite their leisurely style, than the narratives of Chardin. This man, a jeweller and the son of a jeweller, who went to Persia to look for a market for his watches, his bracelets, his necklaces and his rings, this Protestant who found himself an exile from France as a consequence of the Revocation of the Edict of Nantes, was by Nature of a roving disposition. He knew Ispahan better than he knew Paris, and, what was more, he liked it better. The upshot of it all was that any man, however narrow and unimaginative, must have had it borne in upon him from his narrative that far away in distant Asia there were human beings in no way inferior to himself, however widely their mode of life might differ from his own. The notion of "superiority" on which he had hitherto been brought up, as it were, was now no longer valid. Henceforth he must think in other terms. "Difference" not "superiority" was now the appropriate word; a striking psychological readjustment. Yes, in Persia everything is different; those meals you take by the roadside, the strange remedies prescribed by the native physician, the caravansary where you put up for the night, everything is different—clothes, festivals, funerals, religion, justice, laws, all different! Now, these Persians are not barbarians. On the contrary, they are people of extreme refinement, civilised, perhaps almost over-civilised, and, maybe, a little weary of having been so for so long. Chardin underlines the reality, the genuine character of this "other world". He acquaints his reader "with everything that merits the attention of this Europe of ours concerning a country

which we might well call another world, not only because it is so far away, but also because its customs, its standards of life, are so different from our own." *Crisis of European Mind,* p. 18

866   MaCabe, *Orientalism in Early Modern France: Euraasain Trade, Exoticism and the Ancient Regime,* p. 113

867   MaCabe, *Orientalism in Early Modern France: Euraasain Trade, Exoticism and the Ancient Regime,* p. 113

868   MaCabe, *Orientalism in Early Modern France: Euraasain Trade, Exoticism and the Ancient Regime,* p. 113

869   See Sanjay Subrahmanyam, *Europe's India: Words, People, Empires 1500-1800,* London, Harvard University Press, 2017, especially "Introduction: Before and Beyond "Orientalism"; Richmond Barbour, *Before Orientalism: London's Theater of the East,* 1576-1626, Cambridge, Cambridge University Press, 2003

870   See Edward Said, *Orientalism,* New York, Vintage, 1979

871   See Richard Grassby, The *Business Community,* p. 91ff

872   Richard Grassby, The *Business Community,* p. 93

873   Richard Grassby, The *Business Community,* p. 92

874   Richard Grassby, The *Business Community,* p. 92

875   Andrew Lake, *First Protestants,* p. 8-9

876   Andrew Lake, *First Protestants,* p. 9

877   See Wallace, Dewey D. "Socinianism, Justification by Faith, and The Sources of John Locke's The Reasonableness of Christianity." *Journal of the History of Ideas*, vol. 45, no. 1, 1984, pp. 49–66.

878   See https://quod.lib.umich.edu/e/eebo2/A47737.0001.001?view=toc

879   See Andrew Lake, *First Protestants,* p. 32

880   See details in Humberto Garcia, *Islam in the English Radical Protestant Imagination 1660-1830,* Ph. D. dissertation submitted to University of Illinois, Urbana-Champaign, 2007, p. 8. ""Islamic Republic" functions as a metaphorical substitute for frustrated political desires from within England's metropolitan culture: the failure of Cromwell's Interregnum government followed by the restoration of the Stuart monarchy and the high Anglican Church; the loss of civil liberties for many nonconformists barred from holding public office, property rights, and legal preferments due to the enforcement of the Test and Corporation Acts;

and, later on, the growing disillusionment with the setbacks of the French Revolution in conjunction with the mounting of a reactionary conservatism in England during the 1790s and the Napoleonic Wars. During these moments of political anguish, radical dissenters who wish to replace the *ancien regime* with the "good old days" of revolution look toward Islam as an alternative repository of secular values. As such, Islam embodies a "rational" theo-political ideal that, in their imagination, is not only more historically accurate than the dubious teachings of the Church and the Bible, but more durable, dependable, and equitable than the "universal" doctrines of "human rights," Lockean individualism, and liberal-Anglican toleration. For many Englishmen and (especially) Englishwomen, disappointed with the "false universals" of liberty, equality, and fraternity, the Islamic East— rather than Europe, England, or America— marks the symbolic site of a secular, progressive modernity."

881   Dalrymple, *Anarchy,* p. 14

882   Dalrymple, *Anarchy,* p. 14

883   Alison Games, *The Web of Empire,* p. 54-55

884   Alison Games, *The Web of Empire,* p. 64

885   See Goody, *Theft of History,* chapter 7, p. 180ff

886   See Robert Brenner, *The Civil War Politics of London's Merchant Community,* p. 63ff

887   John J. Schroeder, War Finance in London, 1642-1646, *Historian,* 1959 Vol. 21; *Iss.* 4, p. 371; see also his "London and the New Model Army, 1647,", *The Historian,* Vol. 19, No. 3 (May, 1957), pp. 245-261

888   Schroeder, War Finance in London, p. 361

889   Schroeder, War Finance in London, p. 370

890   https://en.wikisource.org/wiki/Dictionary_of_National_Biography,_1885-1900/Chambers,_Richard

891   Robert Brenner, *The Civil War Politics of London's Merchant Community,* p. 97

892   Hill, *The World Turned Upside-down,* p. 13 "Although there was considerable popular support for Parliament in the 1640s, the long-term consequences of the Revolution were all to the advantage of the gentry and merchants, not of the lower fifty per cent of the population…"

893   Andrew Bradstock, *Radical Religions in Cromwell's England: A Concise History from the English Civil War to the End of Commonwealth,* New York, I. B. Tauris, 2011, p. xiv

894   See Glen Burgess and Matthew Festenstein eds., *English Radicalism 1550-1850,* p. 12 "It is arguable that all significant political conflict in the early modern period occurred between groups whose difference was primarily confessional. In this world, what we take to be radicalism was most often the dramatic political impact of extreme religious beliefs, beliefs that were followed sometimes without regard for political and social order. What distances this from modern radicalism is the fact that it was often unpolitical or even antipolitical, relying not on human agency but on God to transform the world. It was animated not by a vision of human freedom and equality, but by a vision of community with God."

895   John Morrill, *The Nature of the English Revolution,* New York, Routledge, 1993, p. 68.

896   See details in Bradstock, *Radical Religions in Cromwell's England,* p. xiv

897   See Brenner, *The Civil War Politics of London's Merchant Community,* p. 100

898   See Walter L. Lingle, and John W. Kuykendall, *Presbyterians: Their History and Beliefs,* Atlanta: Westminster John Knox Press, 1978; James H. Smylie, *A Brief History of the Presbyterians.* Louisville, KY: Geneva Press, 1996

899   "In theological terms, the Calvinist 'orthodoxy' that generally prevailed in 1689 was abandoned.

       In its place, ministers developed Arminian understandings of salvation, in which human free will had a central role, and Arian definitions of God, according to which Christ was subordinate to God the Father. As the century advanced, '[s]tep by step the descent was made from the highest Arianism to the lowest Socinianism', entailing a more complete denial of the Trinity. Without adequate church courts, Presbyterians were unable rigorously to scrutinise candidates for ordination, and the ministry was filled with men of increasingly heterodox opinions." Andrew Thompson, The *Oxford History of Protestant Dissenting Traditions,* Volume II, p. 11

900   See Bradstock, *Radical Religions in Cromwell's England: A Concise History from the English Civil War to the End of Commonwealth."*

901   See Jeffrey R. Collins, The Church Settlement of Oliver Cromwell, *His-*

tory, Vol. 87, No. 285 (January 2002), pp. 18-40, p. 19; S. R. Gardiner, *History of the Commonwealth and Protectorate, 1649–1656* (4 vols., 1903 reprinted by Witney, Windrush Press, 1988), v. iii, p. 24; W. A. Jordan, *The Development of Religious Toleration in England* (4 vols., Cambridge MA, 1932–40), v. iii. P. 144-7; William Lamont, *Godly Rule: Politics and Religion, 1603–1660,* New York, Macmillan, 1969, p. 143.

902   See Andrew Bradstock, *Radical Religions in Cromwell's England,* p. xiii

903   See details in Collins, The Church Settlement of Oliver Cromwell, *History,* p. 20ff

904   See John Tolan, https://www.historytoday.com/miscellanies/muhammad-republican-revolutionary

905   See William Lamont, *Godly Rule,* p. 141ff

906   See Scott, *England's Troubles,* p. 158

907   Bradstock, *Radical Religions in Cromwell's England,* p. xiii

908   William Lamont, *Godly Rule,* p. 143

909   See Hill, *The World Turned Upside-down,* p. 14; Bradstock, *Radical Religions in Cromwell's England,* p. 1ff

910   See Hill, *The World Turned Upside-down,* p. 18ff; Joyce Lee Malcolm ed., *Struggle for Sovereignty: Seventeenth Century English Political Tracts,* (2 volumes) Indianapolis, Liberty Fund, 1992

911   See Dimmock, *Mythologies of the Prophet Muhammad in Early Modern English Culture,* p. 176ff; Andrea Bernadette, *Women and Islam in Early Modern English Literature.* Cambridge: Cambridge University Press, 2008. p. 58

912   MacLean and Matar, *Britain and Islamic World,* p. 199

913   See Dalrymple, *Anarchy,* p. 14; https://en.wikipedia.org/wiki/List_of_English_words_of_Hindi_or_Urdu_origin

914   Richard M. Eaton, *India in the Persianate Age, 1000–1765,* London,- Penguin Random House, 2019, p. 373

915   MacLean and Matar, *Britain and Islamic World,* p. 199

916   MacLean and Matar, *Britain and Islamic World,* p. 200

917   See details in MacLean and Matar, *Britain and Islamic World,* p. 200ff

918   MacLean and Matar, *Britain and Islamic World,* p. 209

919   See P.C. Floud, 'The origins of English calico printing', *Journal of the So-ciety of Dyers and Colourists*, 76 (1960); A.I. Tchitcherov, *India: Chang-ing Economic Structure in the Sixteenth to Eighteenth Centuries: Outline History of Crafts and Trade* (New Delhi, Manohar Publishers, 1998); S. Robinson, *A History of Dyed Textiles*, London, Studio Vista, 1969

920   R. Chenciner, *Madder Red: A History of Luxury and Trade. Plant Dyes and Pigments in World Commerce and Art,* Richmond, Curzon, 2000; N. B. Harte and K. G. Ponting, (eds.), *Textile History and Economic his-tory: Essays in Honour of Miss Julia de Lacy Mann,* Manchester, Man-chester University Press, 1973; S.D. Chapman, (ed.), *The Textile In-dustries. II. Cotton, Linen, Wool and Worsted,* London and New York, 1997; D.A. Farnie and D.J. Jeremy, (eds.), *The Fibre that Changed the World: The Cotton Industry in International Perspective, 1600-1990s,* Oxford, Oxford University Press, 2004; T. Osumi, *Printed Cottons of Asia: the Romance of Trade Textiles,* Tokyo, Charles E. Tuttle Compa-ny, 1963; J. Irwin and P.R. Schwartz, *Studies in Indo-European Textile History,* Ahmedabad, Calico Museum of Textiles, 1966; Giorgio Riello and Tirthankar Roy, *How India Clothed the World: The World of South Asian Textiles, 1500–1850,* Leiden, Brills, 2009; Jennifer Harris ed., *A Companion to Textile Culture,* New Jersey, Wiley Blackwell, 2020

921   MacLean and Matar, *Britain and Islamic World,* p. 210

922   MacLean and Matar, *Britain and Islamic World,* p. 213

923   Ina Baghdiantz MaCabe, *Orientalism in Early Modern France: Euraas-ain Trade, Exoticism and the Ancient Regime,* p. 223

924   Quoted in Robert Chenciner, *Madder Red: A History of Luxury and Trade,* London, Curzon, Caucasus World, 2000, 186

925   See Eaton, "Conclusion and Epilogue" in *India in the Persianate Age, 1000–1765*

926   Quoted in Birchwood, Staging Islam in England: Drama and Culture, 1640-1685, p. 56; The Famous Tragedie of King Charles I (London, 1649), A4r

927   See Blair Worden, *God's Instruments: Political Conduct in the England of Oliver Cromwell.* Oxford, Oxford University Press, 2012, p.69-70

928   Hill, *The World Turned Upside-down,* p. 14

929   See details in Gary S. De Krey, Political Radicalism in London after the Glorious Revolution, *The Journal of Modern History,* Vol. 55, No. 4 (Dec., 1983), pp. 585-617, p. 585ff; Thomas B. Macaulay, *The History of England*

from the Accession of James the Second, 5 vols. (London, 1849-61); George M. Trevelyan, *The English Revolution, 1688-89* (London, 1938); and David Ogg, *England in the Reigns of James II and William III,* Oxford, Clarendon Press, 1955; Lucile Pinkham,*William III and the Respectable Revolution: The Part Played by William of Orange in the Revolution of 1688,* Cambridge, Mass., Harvard University Press, 1954; Maurice Ashley, *The Glorious Revolution of 1688,* London, Scribners, 1966; and John Carswell, *The Descent on England: A Study of the English Revolution of 1688 and Its European Background,* London, John Day, 1969; J. R. Jones, *The Revolution of 1688 in England,* London, Weidenfeld and Nicolson, 1972; and J. P. Kenyon, *Revolution Principles, The Politics of Party 1689-1720,* Cambridge, Cambridge University press, 2009

930   See details in J. R. Jones, *The Revolution of 1688 in England,* p. 7ff

931   See Humberto Garcia, *Islam in the English Radical Protestant Imagination;* also Gary S. De Krey, Between Revolutions: Re-appraising the Restoration in Britain, *History Compass* 6/3 (2008): 738–773, 10.1111/j.1478-0542.2008.00520.x

932   Hill, *The World Turned Upside-down,* p. 98

933   https://www.historytoday.com/miscellanies/muhammad-republican-revolutionary

934   "(Christian Reader) though some, conscious of their own instability in Religion, and of theirs (too like Turks in this) whose prosperity and opinions they follow, were unwilling this should see the Press, yet am I confident, if thou hast been so true a votary to orthodox Religion, as to keep thy self untainted of their follies, this shall not hurt thee: And as for those of that Batch, having once abandoned the Sun of the Gospel, I believe they will wander as far into utter darkness, by following strange lights, as by this Ignis Fatuus of the Alcoran. Such as it is, I present to thee, having taken the pains only to translate it out of French, not doubting, though it hath been a poyson, that hath infected a very great, but most unsound part of the Universe, it may prove an Antidote, to confirm in thee the health of Christianity." https://www.historytoday.com/miscellanies/muhammad-republican-revolutionary

935   See C. Hill, *Century of Revolution: 1603-1714,* London, T. Nelson, 1961, pp. 154-5.

936   See details K. O. Morgan ed., *Oxford History of Britain,* p. 276ff. ""By executing Charles, Cromwell cut himself off from justifications of political authority rooted in the past; by acknowledging that a free vote of those

who held the franchise would restore the king, that is by refusing to base his authority on consent, Cromwell cut himself off from arguments of the present. His self-justification lay in the future, in the belief that he was fulfilling God's will. But because he believed that he had such a task to perform, he had a fatal disregard for civil and legal liberties. To achieve the future promised by God, Cromwell governed arbitrarily. He imprisoned men without trial. When George Cony, a merchant, refused to pay unconstitutional customs duties, Cromwell imprisoned him and his lawyer to prevent him taking his case to court. When Parliament failed to make him an adequate financial provision, he taxed by decree. When the people would not respond voluntarily to the call to moral regeneration, he created Major-Generals and set them to work. Hence the supreme paradox. Cromwell the king-killer, the reluctant head of state, the visionary, was begged by his second Parliament to become King Oliver." P. 276

937   Winston Churchill, *A History of English Speaking Peoples*, London, Dodd, Mead & Company, (1956), p. 314

938   David Sharp, *Oliver Cromwell*, Portsmouth, Heinemann, 2003, p. 60

939   Hill, *The World Turned Upside-down*, p. 15

940   See Joyce Malcolm, *Struggle for Sovereignty*, v. 1, p. 506ff

941   See John Broadbent, *Paradise Lost: Introduction*, Cambridge, Cambridge University Press, 1972; C. A. Patrides, *Approaches to Paradise Lost: The York Tercentenary Lectures*, University of Toronto, 1968

942   See Gary De Krey, *London and the Restoration: 1659-1683*, Cambridge, Cambridge University Press, 2005, p. 4

943   See John Christian Laursen and Cary J. Nederman eds., *Beyond the Persecuting Society*, p. 264ff

944   See Tim Harris. "Cooper, Anthony Ashley," in the *Oxford Dictionary of National Biography* edited by H. C. J. Matthew and Brian Harrison, Oxford University Press, 2004, p. 202-203

945   See Brenner, *The Civil War Politics of London's Merchant Community*, p. 107

946   De Krey, *Between Revolutions*, p. 744

947   De Krey, *Between Revolutions*, p. 744

948   See Gary De Krey, *London and the Restoration: 1659-1683*, p. 3ff

949   Hill, *Intellectual Origins*, p. 112

950   Bulman, *Enlightenment and Religious Politics in Restoration England*, p. 754

951   See Kenneth O. Morgan ed., *The Oxford History of Britain*, Oxford, Oxford University Press, 2010, p. 379ff

952   See Albert Cassell Dudley, "Nonconformity Under the 'Clarendon Code'," *The American Historical Review* 18, no. 1 (Oct., 1912): 65-70.

953   Morgan ed., *Oxford History of Britain*, p. 379

954   John Christian Laursen and Cary J. Nederman eds., *Beyond the Persecuting Society*, p. 173; see also J. P. Kenyon, *The Popish Plot*, London, St. Martin's Press,1972 and *The Stuarts*, London, B. T. Batsford, 1958

955   N. H. Keeble, *The Restoration: England in the 1660s*, Oxford, Blackwell, 2002, p. 5

956   See Morgan ed., *Oxford History of Britain*, p. 380ff

957   M. Goldie, 'The Theory of Religious Intolerance in Restoration England' in Grell et al. (eds.), *From Persecution to Toleration*, p. 331

958   De Krey, *Between Revolutions*, p. 748

959   See De Krey, *Between Revolutions*, p. 749-50; *Letters of the Honourable Algernon Sydney, to the Honourable Henry Savile* (1742), 165; [William Popple], *Some Free Reflections upon Occasion of the Public Discourse about Liberty of Conscience* (1687), 7 [my attribution]; J. Locke, 'An Essay on Toleration' (1667) in [J.] Locke, *Political Essays*, ed. M. Goldie, Cambridge Texts in the History of Political Thought, Cambridge, Cambridge University Press, 1997, 156; *Some Necessary Disquisitions and close Expostulations* (1688), 8.

960   See De Krey, *Between Revolutions*, p. 755

961   De Krey, *Between Revolutions*, p. 757; see J. Habermas, *The Structural Transformation of the Public Sphere: An Inquiry into a Category of Bourgeois Society*, trans. T. Burger with the assistance of F. Lawrence, Cambridge, MA: MIT Press, 1989

962   See Morgan ed., *Oxford History of Britain*, p. 380ff

963   See J. Scott, *Algernon Sidney and the Restoration Crises, 1677-1683*, Cambridge, Cambridge University Press, 2002, p. 35ff

964   See Morgan ed., *Oxford History of Britain*, p. 383ff

965   See Lois G. Schwoerer, "William, Lord Russell: The Making of a Martyr, 1683–1983." *Journal of British Studies* 24.1 (1985): 41-71.

966   See Doreen J. Milne, (1951). "The Results of the Rye House Plot and Their Influence upon the Revolution of 1688: The Alexander Prize Es-

say", *Transactions of the Royal Historical Society*. 5. 1: 91–108; Richard Ashcraft, *Revolutionary Politics and Locke's Two Treatises of Government*, Princeton, Princeton University Press,1986, pp. 376

967   See Garcia, A Hungarian Revolution in Restoration England: Henry Stubbe, Radical Islam, and the Rye House Plot, The Eighteenth Century, Volume 51, Numbers 1-2, Spring/Summer, 2010, pp. 1-25

968   Morgan ed., *Oxford History of Britain,* p. 384

969   See Scott Sowerby, *Making Toleration: The Repealers and the Glorious Revolution,* p. 3ff

970   Sowerby, *Making Toleration,* p. 3; Morgan ed., *Oxford History of Britain,* p. 385

971   Morgan ed., *Oxford History of Britain,* p. 386

972   "The long-term effects of James's policies were profound. Among the most significant was the legislative enactment of religious toleration for Protestant nonconformists in England in May 1689, six months after James's departure from England and three months after the enthronement of William and Mary. This shift should not be attributed to John Locke's writings on toleration, which first appeared in print that same year. Although Locke's *Epistola de Tolerantia* was published at Gouda a few weeks before the passing of the Toleration Act, it was not translated into English until several months afterward and had no demonstrable effect on the parliamentary debate. Rather, it was James II 's toleration campaign that forced the hand of the almost entirely Anglican parliament and led it to grant a set of concessions to nonconformists." Sowerby, *Making Toleration,* p. 10

973   Sowerby, *Making Toleration,* p. 7

974   Mark Goldie, "The Political Thought of the Anglican Revolution," in Robert Beddard, ed., *The Revolutions of 1688,* Oxford, Clarendon Press, 1991, 107–108.

975   See Morgan ed., *Oxford History of Britain,* p. 386ff

976   See details Sowerby, *Making Toleration,* p. 6ff

977   See Geoffrey Holmes ed., *Britain after the Glorious Revolution: 1689-1714,* London, Macmillan, 1969; David Hempton, *Religion and Political Culture in Britain and Ireland: From the Glorious Revolution to the Decline of Empire,* Cambridge, Cambridge University Press, 1996; Lois G. Schwoerer, Locke, *Lockean Ideas, and the Glorious Revolution, Journal of*

the History of Ideas, Vol. 51, No. 4 (Oct. - Dec., 1990), 531-548.

978   Morgan ed., *Oxford History of Britain,* p. 401

979   Peter Marshall, *Heretics and Believers: A History of the English Refor-mation,* London, Yale University Press, 2017, p. 577

980   Schwoerer, Locke, *Lockean Ideas, and the Glorious Revolution,* p. 532

981   Morgan ed., *Oxford History of Britain,* p. 398

982   Morgan ed., *Oxford History of Britain,* p. 393

983   Morgan ed., *Oxford History of Britain,* p. 394

984   Morgan ed., *Oxford History of Britain,* p. 395

985   Morgan ed., *Oxford History of Britain,* p. 395

986   Morgan ed., *Oxford History of Britain,* p. 398

987   See Ole Peter Grell and Roy Porter, *Toleration in Enlightenment Eu-rope,* p. 1 ff

988   See For introduction to the sixteenth- and seventeenth-century de-bates, see O.P. Grell and B. Scribner (eds), *Tolerance and Intolerance in the European Reformation,* Cambridge, Cambridge University Press, 1996; O.P. Grell, J.I. Israel and N. Tyacke (eds), *From Persecution to Toleration: The Glorious Revolution and Religion in England,* Oxford, Clarendon Press, 1991; W.K. Jordan, *The Development of religious Toleration in England,* 4 vols., Cambridge, Mass., Harvard University Press, 1932–40; reprint Gloucester, Mass., 1965; E. Labrousse, 'Reli-gious Toleration', in P.P. Wiener (ed.), *Dictionary of the History of Ideas,* 5 vols., New York, Macmillan, 1974: IV, 112–21; H. Kamen, *The Rise of Toleration,* London, McGraw-Hill, 1967; J.C. Laursen and C.J. Neder-man (eds), *Beyond the Persecuting Society,* Philadelphia, University of Pennsylvania Press, 1998. See also R.I. Moore, *The Formation of a Per-secuting Society: Power and Deviance in Western Europe AD 950–1250,* Oxford, Wiley-Blackwell, 1986.

989   See Noel D. Johnson and Mark Koyama eds., *Persecution and Toleration: The Long Road to Religious Freedom,* Cambridge, Cambridge University Press, 2019, 9.3 "The Emergence of a Modern State in England"

990   See Karen Bird, The Concession of Toleration, Muslims and the Brit-ish Enlightenment, *Limina,* volume 22.2, 2017, p. 15ff ; Karen Barkey, Islam and Toleration: Studying the Ottoman Imperial Model, *Inter-national Journal of Politics, Culture, and Society,* Vol. 19, No. 1/2, The

New Sociological Imagination II (Dec., 2005), pp. 5-19: DOI 10.1007/ s10767-007-9013-5; K. Abou el Fadl, *The place of tolerance in Islam*. In J. Cohen & I. Lague (Eds.), *The place of tolerance in Islam* (pp. 3–23). Boston, MA: Beacon, 2002; T. Ali, *Theological distractions*. In J. Cohen & I. Lague (Eds.), *The place of tolerance in Islam* (pp. 37–41); Juan Pablo Domínguez, *Introduction: Religious toleration in the Age of Enlightenment*, History of European Ideas, 2017, 43:4, 273-287, DOI: 10.1080/01916599.2016.1203590

991   See Mary Lynn Pierce, *Controversy In Seventeenth-Century English Coffeehouses: Transcultural Interactions With An Oriental Import*, Dissertation Submitted to the Faculty of the Department of History, the University of Arizona, 2015; Alexander Mirkovic, *From Courtly Curiosity to Revolutionary Refreshment: Turkish Coffee and English Politics in the Seventeenth century*, A thesis submitted in partial fulfillment of the requirements for the degree of Masters of Arts, Department of History, University of South Florida, 2005

992   James Von Hon Melton, *The Rise of the Public in Enlightenment Europe*, Cambridge, Cambridge University Press, 2001, p. 241

993   Steve Pincus, "Coffee Politicians Does Create": Coffeehouses and Restoration Political Culture, *The Journal of Modern History*, Vol. 67, No. 4 (Dec., 1995), pp. 807-834, p. 821

994   Steve Pincus, "Coffee Politicians Does Create": Coffeehouses and Restoration Political Culture, *The Journal of Modern History*, Vol. 67, No. 4 (Dec., 1995), pp. 807-834, p. 812

995   Steve Pincus, "Coffee Politicians Does Create": Coffeehouses and Restoration Political Culture, *The Journal of Modern History*, Vol. 67, No. 4 (Dec., 1995), pp. 807-834, p. 833

996   See Brian Cowan, *The Social Life of Coffee: The Emergence of British Coffeehouses*, London, Yale University Press, 2005, p. 5ff

997   See Cowan, *The Social Life of Coffee*, p. 23

998   See Cowan, *The Social Life of Coffee*, p. 25

999   See Paul Rycaut, *The History of the Turkish Empire, from the Year 1623, to the Year 1677* (London: J. D., 1687), pp. 67–74. See also Alfred C. Wood, *A History of the Levant Company* (Oxford: Oxford University Press 1935), pp. 90–2; and Gwilym Prichard Ambrose, *The Levant Company mainly from 1640–1753* (B. Litt dissertation, University of Oxford, 1932), pp. 241–57

1000 See S. D. Smith, "The Early Diffusion of Coffee Drinking in England," in *Le commerce du café avant l'ère des plantations coloniales*, ed. Michel Tuchscherer (Le Caire: Institut Français D'archéologie Orientale, 2001), 245-68; Cowan, *The Social Life of Coffee*, p. 49

1001 See Steve Pincus, "Coffee Politicians Does Create": Coffeehouses and Restoration Political Culture, *The Journal of Modern History*, Vol. 67, No. 4 (Dec., 1995), pp. 807-834, p. 813ff

1002 Steve Pincus, "Coffee Politicians Does Create": Coffeehouses and Restoration Political Culture, *The Journal of Modern History*, Vol. 67, No. 4 (Dec., 1995), pp. 807-834, p. 813

1003 See Brian Cowan, The Rise of the Coffeehouse Reconsidered, *The Historical Journal*, Vol. 47, No. 1 (Mar., 2004), pp. 21-46, p. 21

1004 See Cowan, *The Social Life of Coffee*, p. 115ff

1005 See *Endless Queries: or, An End to Queries* (London: n.p. 1659), pp. 3–4.

1006 Cowan, *The Social Life of Coffee*, p. 39

1007 Cowan, *The Social Life of Coffee*, p. 43

1008 https://www.google.com/books/edition/The_Indian_Nectar_Or_a_Discourse_Concern/QyhVAAAAcAAJ?hl=en

1009 See Cowan, *The Social Life of Coffee*, p. 43

1010 See Cowan, *The Social Life of Coffee*, p. 102. "Unlike the formal social interactions prescribed by a visit to the great house, coffeehouse visits were more spontaneous and less rigidly ritualized. The protocols of recognising rank and precedence were abandoned within the coffeehouse, a convenient social fiction which was celebrated in a broadside which proclaimed the "Rules and Orders of the Coffee-House": "First Gentry, tradesmen, all are welcome hither, / And may without affront sit down together: / Preeminence of place, none here should mind, / But take the next fit seat that he can find: / Nor need any, if finer persons come, rise up to assigne to them his room" (Figure 15). This convention was not meant to promote social "leveling," as many of the early detractors and modern historians of the coffeehouses have assumed, but it was rather a means by which the genteel manners of the new metropolitan "Town" were to be distinguished from what were perceived to be the excessive and stifling formalities of the past."

1011 "These secular establishments were places where the authority of the church did not reach, and yet they were places to which people were inevitably drawn - to eat and drink, to play and revel, to talk, argue, exchange views.49 Worse still, they attracted men of every status, even the poor, whom the alehouses especially catered for.50 The fear then was that such places were indeed lay conventicles, levelling in tendency, where all men were priests and one man's opinion was as good as another's. In such an environment heresy, irreligion and sedition, Glanvill and others maintained, might and would flourish." Jacob, Henry Stubbe, p. 84

1012   See Anon., *News From the Coffee- House; In which is shown their several sorts of Passions, Containing News from all our Neighbour Nations, A Poem* (London: E. Crowch, 1667), The British Library, London, and EEBO; Anon., *The Coffee-House of News-Mongers Hall* (London: 1672). English coffeehouses, also known as penny universities, were cheap. Customers could afford to frequent them daily and sometimes several times a day.

1013   John Houghton of the Royal Society confided that "a worthy friend of mine (now departed) who was of good learning" was convinced that the "coffee houses had improved useful knowledge as much as" both universities." Pincus, "Coffee Politicians Does Create, p. 833

1014   See Aytoun Ellis, *The Penny Universities; A History of the Coffee-houses*. London: Decker & War-burg, 1956.

1015   MacLean and Matar, *Britain and the Islamic World*, p. 221

1016   Gerald MacLean, *Looking East: English Writing and the Ottoman Empire before 1800* (New York: Palgrave Macmillian, 2007), p. 59

1017   See Gerald MacLean, *Looking East*, 59ff. Several illustrations, as in *The Coffee House* by Markman Ellis, show some of the men wearing a turban. Samuel Pepys, one of the regular patrons of London coffeehouses, and some of the Turkey merchants, based on some illustrations, are believed to have worn turbans on occasions when attending the coffeehouses. Even in France, upon the introduction of coffee during the reign of Louis XIV, imitating Turkish robes and turbans had gained enthusiasm among the upper classes. See Bennet and Bealer, *The World of Caffeine*, 71.

1018   MacLean and Matar, *Britain and the Islamic World*, p. 221

1019   Anon., *The Character of a Coffee-house wherein is contained a description the persons usually frequenting it, with their discourse and humors, as also the admirable vertues of coffee, By an Eye and Ear Witness* (London: 1665), 2. Available in the British Library and in Early English Books Online (EEBO).

1020   See venom against heretics in Ralph Josselin, *The Diary of Ralph Josselin, 1616-1683*, ed. Alan Macfarlane, New York, Oxford University Press, 1976, 366ff; John Spurr, *The Restoration Church of England, 1646-1689*, New Haven & London: Yale University Press, 1991, 26ff

1021   Steve Pincus, "Coffee Politicians Does Create": Coffeehouses and Restoration Political Culture, *The Journal of Modern History*, Vol. 67, No. 4 (Dec., 1995), pp. 807-834, p. 826

1022   See Jonathan Burton, *Traffic and Turning: Islam and English Drama, 1579-1624*, Newark, University of Delaware Press, 2005

1023   See Anon., *A Cup of Coffee*, London, 1662. In *Envisioning Power: Ideologies of Dominance and Crisis*, Berkeley, University of California Press, 1999, 65-67

1024   See M.P. John Starkey, *A Character of Coffee and Coffee-Houses* (London, 1661), 1; Anon., *The Coffee Scuffle, Occasioned by a Contest Between a Learned Knight, and a Pitiful Pedgogue* (London, not dated), 6, 8, 12; M.P., *A Character of a Coffee and Coffee-Houses*, 8-9.

1025   Anon., *A Broad-side against COFFEE; Or, the Marriage of the Turk* (London: 1667), 1. Bowdy house was a slang for brothels.

1026   *The Character of a Coffee-House*, 4-5. Similar to coffeehouses in the Ottoman cities, smoking tobacco was commonplace in English coffee establishments.

1027   Cowan, *Social Life of Coffee*, p. 96

1028   James Melton, *Rise of Public in Enlightenment Europe*, p. 241-42

1029   James Melton, *Rise of Public in Enlightenment Europe*, p. 242

1030   Poor Robins Character of an Honest Drunken Curr (London, 1675), p. 7.

1031   See Steve Pincus, "Coffee Politicians Does Create": Coffeehouses and Restoration Political Culture, *The Journal of Modern History*, Vol. 67, No. 4 (Dec., 1995), pp. 807-834, p. 825ff

1032   Cowan, *Social Life of Coffee*, p. 97

1033   Michael Hunter, *Science and Society in Restoration England* (Cambridge: Cambridge University Press, 1981, 77.

1034   See details in Cowan, *Social Life of Coffee*, p. 98ff

1035   See Cook, H. (1989). *Physicians and the new philosophy: Henry Stubbe and the virtuosi-physicians.* In R. French & A. Wear (Eds.), *The Medical Revolution of the Seventeenth Century* (pp. 246-271). Cambridge:

Cambridge University Press. doi:10.1017/CBO9780511897078.010

1036   See Cowan, *Social Life of Coffee,* p. 91

1037   Steve Pincus, "Coffee Politicians Does Create": Coffeehouses and Res-
       toration Political Culture, *The Journal of Modern History,* Vol. 67, No.
       4 (Dec., 1995), pp. 807-834, p. 820; Henry Oldenburg to Robert Boyle,
       October 6, 1664, Oldenburg Correspondence (n. 34 above), 2:249;

1038   Samuel Butler: *Characters,* ed. Charles W. Davis, Cleveland, Case
       Western Reserve University Press, 1970, p. 257

1039   Cowan, *Social Life of Coffee,* p. 12

1040   See Cowan, *Social Life of Coffee,* p. 98

1041   Anon., *The Coffee Scuffle, Occasioned by a Contest Between a Learned
       Knight, and a Pitiful Pedgogue* (London, not dated), p. 6, 8, 12.

1042   Anon, *The Coffee Scuffle, p. 5,* 8-10.

1043   Anon.,*The Character of A Coffee-House. With the Symptoms of a Town-
       Wit* (London, 1663), 2. The source also refers to such proprietors as
       apes imitating the Turks

1044   See Bernard Capp, *England's Culture Wars,* Oxford, Oxford University
       Press, 2012, 88.

1045   See Capp, *England's Culture Wars, p. 99ff*

1046   "Whereas it is most apparent, that the Multitude of Coffee-Houses of late
       years set up and kept within the Kingdom, the Dominion of Wales, and
       the Town of Berwick on Tweed, and the great resort of Idle and disaffected
       persons to them, have produced very evil and dangerous effects; as well
       for that many Tradesmen and others, do therein mis-spend much of their
       time, which might and probably would otherwise by imployed in and
       about their Lawful Callings and Affairs; but also, for that in such houses,
       and by occasion of the meetings of such persons therein, diverse False,
       Malitious and Scandalous Reports are devised and spread abroad, to the
       Defamation of His Majesties Government, and to the Disturbance of the
       Peace and Quiet of the Realm; his Majesty hath thought it fit and necessary,
       That the said Coffee-houses be (for the future) put down and suppressed."
       See http://www.theoldfoodie.com/2006/12/king-bans-coffee.html

1047   See J. G. A. Pocock, 'Contexts for the Study of James Harrington/ *II
       Pensiero Politico, 2* (1978), pp. 20-35; *The Machiavellian Moment: Flor-
       entine Political Thought and the Atlantic Republican Tradition,* Princeton,
       Princeton University Press, 2017, Introduction and chapters 12-14

1048 Jacob, Henry Stubbe, *Radical Protestantism and the Early Enlightenment,* p. 117

1049 See Pincus, "Coffee Politicians Does Create, p. 828; Steve Pincus, *A Letter from a Person of Quality in "The English Debate over Universal Monarchy,"* in *A Union for Empire,* ed. John Robertson, Cambridge, Cambridge University Press, 1995, pp. 48-50.

1050 https://www.google.com/books/edition/A_Justification_of_the_Present_War_Again/--dCAQAAMAAJ?hl=en

1051 https://www.google.com/books/edition/The_History_of_the_United_Provinces_of_A/p8FCAAAAcAAJ?hl=en

1052 James Von Hon Melton, The *Rise of Public in Enlightenment Europe,* p. 242, see also Aytoun Ellis, *The Penny Universities: A History of the Coffee-House,* London, Martin Secker & Warburg Ltd, 1956, p. 91.

1053 See Cowan, *Social Life of Coffee,* chapter 7, p. 209ff

1054 See Cowan, *Social Life of Coffee,* chapter 7, p. 193ff

1055 See Cowan. *Rise of Coffeehouses Reconsidered,* p. 199

1056 "The King observing the people to be much dissatisfied yielded to a petition of the coffee-men. .. and the proclamation was recalled." David Hume, *The History of England* (Indianapolis, 1983) 6:296

1057 James Ralph, *The History of England,* 2 vols. (London, 1744), v.1, p. 297.

1058 James Von Hon Melton, The *Rise of Public in Enlightenment Europe,* p. 244

1059 See James Von Hon Melton, The *Rise of Public in Enlightenment Europe,* p. 245

1060 James Von Hon Melton, The *Rise of Public in Enlightenment Europe,* p. 226

1061 Dorinda Outram, *The Enlightenment.* Cambridge, Cambridge University Press, 1995, p. 11

1062 Outram, *The Enlightenment, p. 20*

1063 See Cowan. *Rise of Coffeehouses Reconsidered,* p. 22ff

1064 See Cowan. *Rise of Coffeehouses Reconsidered,* p. 23ff

1065 See Markman Ellis, *The Coffee-House: A Cultural History,* Ashland, OH, Poenix, 2005 and his *Eighteenth Century Coffee-House Culture: Restoration Satire,* New York, Routledge, 2006

1066 Cowan, *Social Life of Coffee,* p. 216

1067   Outram, *The Enlightenment, p. 10ff*

1068   See Outram, *The Enlightenment, p. 62ff*

1069   See details in Jason Peacey, *Politicians and Pamphleteers: Propaganda During the English Civil Wars and Interregnum.* Burlington, VT: Ashgate Publishing, 2004, p. 82

1070   See Jacob, Henry Stubbe, *Radical Protestantism and the Early Enlightenment,* p. 114

1071   See Garcia, *Islam and the English Enlightenment 1670-1840*

1072   See Karen M. Bird, *The Concession of Toleration, Muslims and the British Enlightenment, Limina,* Volume 22.2, 2017

1073   See Nigel Smith, "And if God was one of us": Paul Best, John Biddle, and anti-Trinitarian heresy in seventeenth-century England" in David Loewenstein and John Marshall eds., Heresy, *Literature and Politics in Early Modern English Culture,* Cambridge, Cambridge University Press, 2006, p. 160ff

1074   Pocock, *Barbarism and Religion,* v.1, p.8; See Roy Porter, 'The Enlightenment in England' in Porter and M. Teich (eds.), The Enlightenment in National Context, Cambridge, Cambridge University Press, 1981, p. 1–18; also David Spadafora, The Idea of Progress in Eighteenth-Century Britain, New Haven, Yale University Press, 1990; B. W. Young, Religion and Enlightenment in Eighteenth-Century England: Theological Debates from Locke to Burke, Oxford, Oxford University Press, 1998; David Sorkin, The Religious Enlightenment: Protestants, Jews, and Catholics from London to Vienna, Princeton, Princeton University Press, 2008, p. 3ff

1075   Pocock, *Barbarism and Religion,* v.1, p.7-8

1076   "Generation after generation the power of the moral faculty becomes more absolute, the doctrines that oppose it wane and vanish, and the various elements of theology are absorbed and recast by its influence. The indifference of most men to dogmatic theology is now so marked, and the fear of tampering with formularies that are no longer based on general conviction is with some men so intense, that general revisions of creeds have become extremely rare; but the change of belief is not the less profound. The old words are indeed retained, but they no longer present the old images to the mind, or exercise the old influence upon the life. The modes of thought, and the types of character which those modes produce, are essentially and universally transformed. The whole intellectual atmosphere, the whole tenor of life, the prevailing enthusiasms, the conceptions of the imagination, are all changed." Lecky, *History of the Rise and Influence of the Spirit of Rationalism in Europe,* v. 1, p. 145

1077 Lecky, *History of the Rise and Influence of the Spirit of Rationalism in Europe,* v. 1, p. 130

1078 Lecky, *History of the Rise and Influence of the Spirit of Rationalism in Europe,* v. 1, p. 130

1079 M. Jacob, *The Radical Enlightenment. Pantheists, Freemasons and Republicans,* London, George Allen and Unwin, 1981, p. 27.

1080 Andrew Kloes, *Dissembling Orthodoxy in the Age of the Enlightenment: Frederick the Great and his Confession of Faith,* https://www.cambridge.org/core/terms. https://doi.org/10.1017/S0017816015000504

1081 Quoted in D. Daily, *Enlightenment Deism. The Foremost Threat to Christianity*, Pennsylvania, Dorrance, 1999 p. 44.

1082 Andrew Kloes, *Dissembling Orthodoxy in the Age of the Enlightenment: Frederick the Great and his Confession of Faith,* p. 116

1083 Andrew Kloes, *Dissembling Orthodoxy in the Age of the Enlightenment: Frederick the Great and his Confession of Faith,* p. 116

1084 Andrew Kloes, *Dissembling Orthodoxy in the Age of the Enlightenment: Frederick the Great and his Confession of Faith,* p. 102

1085 See D. Van Kley, *The Religious Origins of the French Revolution. From Calvin to the Civil Constitution, 1560–1791,* New Haven and London, Yale University Press, 1996; D. Outram, *The Enlightenment,* Cambridge, Cambridge University Press, 1995; B. Young, *Religion and Enlightenment in Eighteenth-Century England. Theological Debate from Locke to Burke,* Oxford, Clarendon Press, 1998; J. A. Herrick, *The Radical Rhetoric of the English Deists. The Discourse of Scepticism, 1680–1750,* Columbia, University of South Carolina Press, 1997; J. Walsh and S. Taylor: 'The Church and Anglicanism in the "Long" Eighteenth Century', in C. Haydon, J. Walsh and S. Taylor (eds), *The Church of England c.1689–c.1833,* Cambridge, Cambridge University Press, 1993; M. Jacob, *The Enlightenment. A Brief History with Documents,* Boston, Mass., St Martin's/Bedford, 2001, p. 12; D. Berman, in his *A History of Atheism in Britain,* New York, Croom Helm, 1988; J. Champion, *The Pillars of Priestcraft Shaken*; G. R. Cragg, *The Church and the Age of Reason 1648–1789,* Harmondsworth, Penguin, 1970

1086   Matthew Kadane, *Original Sin and the Path to the Enlightenment, Past & Present,* Volume 235, Issue 1, May 2017, Pages 105–140, p. 108

1087   Quoted in Matthew Kadane, *Original Sin and the Path to the Enlightenment,* p. 110

1088   Ernst Cassirer, *The Philosophy of the Enlightenment,* trans. Fritz C. A. Koelln and J. P. Pettegrove, Princeton, Princeton University Press, 1951, p. 141

1089   See John Robertston, 'Hugh Trevor-Roper, Intellectual History and "The Religious Origins of the Enlightenment", *English Historical Review,* cxxiv, 511 (2009), 1389–1421. Cf. the chapter 'Sin and Hell' in Christopher Hill, *The World Turned Upside-down: Radical Ideas During the English Revolution* (London, 1972). J. G. A. Pocock elaborated on Trevor-Roper's point in the case of Eighteenth century Arminianism: J. G. A. Pocock, *Barbarism and Religion,* 6 vols. (Cambridge 1999–2015), i, *The Enlightenments of Edward Gibbon, 1737–1764,* 8–9, 50–71. Also see Michael Heyd, 'Original Sin, the Struggle for Stability, and the Rise of Moral Individualism in Late Seventeenth-Century England', in Philip Benedict and Myron P. Gutmann (eds.) *Early Modern Europe: From Crisis to Stability* (Newark, 2005); and Michael Heyd, 'Changing Emotions? The Decline of Original Sin on the Eve of the Enlightenment', in Penelope Gouk and Helen Hills (eds.), *Representing Emotions: New Connections in the Histories of Art, Music and Medicine* (Burlington, 2005), 123–38. Original sin is just as central to the Enlightenment in twentieth-century anti-Enlightenment thought. See Carl Schmitt, *Political Theology: Four Chapters on the Concept of Sovereignty,* trans. George Schwab (Chicago, 2005) and Carl Schmitt, *The Concept of the Political,* trans. George Schwab (Chicago, 2007).

1090   Kadane, Matthew, "Anti-Trinitarianism and the Republican Tradition in Enlightenment Britain." *Republics of Letters: A Journal for the Study of Knowledge, Politics, and the Arts* 2, no. 1 (December 15, 2010): http://rofl.stanford.edu/node/68; Justin Champion, *The Pillars of Priestcraft Shaken*; Stuart Andrews, *Unitarian Radicalism: Political Rhetoric, 1770–1814,* New York, Palgrave Macmillan, 2003; Michael R. Watts, *The Dissenters,* vol. 2, *The Expansion of Evangelical Nonconformity,* Oxford, Oxford University Press, 1995

1091   J. Israel, *Enlightenment Contested,* p. 65

1092   Israel, *Enlightenment Contested,* p. 65

1093   Matthew Kadane, *Original Sin and the Path to the Enlightenment,* p. 110

1094   See Israel, *Radical Enlightenment,* p. 7 ff

1095   See J. C. D. Clark, *English Society 1660-1832: Religion, Ideology and Politics during the Ancient Regime,* Cambridge, Cambridge University Press, 2000, p. 319 ff

1096   Israel, *Radical Enlightenment,* p. 7

1097   Israel, *Radical Enlightenment,* p. 20

1098   See Ethan H. Shagan, *The Birth of Modern Belief: Faith and Judgment from the Middle Ages to the Enlightenment,* Princeton, Princeton University Press, 2018, p. 1

1099   See John Spurr, "Rational Religion" in Restoration England, *Journal of the History of Ideas,* Vol. 49, No. 4 (Oct. - Dec., 1988), pp. 563-585

1100   Joanna Picciotto, "Implicit Faith and Reformations of Habit." *JMEMS* 46, no. 3 (2016): 513–43." p. 513

1101   Charles Taylor, *A Secular Age,* London, Belknap Press of Harvard University Press, 2007, p. 13

1102   See Taylor, *A Secular Age,* p. 222

1103   For Islamic take on the subject see Ismail R. al-Faruqi, *Al-Tawhid: Its Implications for Thought and Life,* 2nd edn. (Virginia: International Institute of Islamic Thought, 1992)

1104   Taylor, *A Secular Age,* p. 283

1105   Taylor, *A Secular Age,* p. 289

1106   Taylor, *A Secular Age,* p. 223

1107   Quoted in Taylor, *A Secular Age,* p. 226

1108   See Taylor, *A Secular Age,* p. 20

1109   Taylor, *A Secular Age,* p. 19

1110   Taylor, *A Secular Age,* p. 290

1111   Taylor, *A Secular Age,* p. 291

1112   Taylor, *A Secular Age,* p. 291

1113   Taylor, *A Secular Age,* p. 650

1114   Taylor, *A Secular Age,* p. 291

1115   Paul Hazard, *The Crisis of the European Mind: 168-1715* translated by J. Lewis May, New York, New York Review Books, 2013, p. 95

1116   Hazard, *The Crisis of the European Mind*, p. 96

1117   Hazard, *The Crisis of the European Mind*, p. 95

1118   David Martin, *Christian Language and Its Mutations*, Aldershot, Ashgate, 2002, p. 173.

1119   Hazard, *The Crisis of the European Mind*, p. 97-98

1120   Hazard, *The Crisis of the European Mind*, p. 96

1121   Taylor, *A Secular Age*, p. 20; see also Talal Asad, *Formations of the Secular: Christianity, Islam and Modernity*, Stanford, Stanford University Press, 2003; Asad, *Geneologies of Religion: Discipline and Reasons of Power in Christianity and Islam*, Baltimore, John Hopkins University Press, 1993

1122   Shagan, *The Birth of Modern Belief*, p. 4

1123   See Shagan, *The Birth of Modern Belief*, p. 5; See also George Lindbeck, *The Nature of Doctrine: Religion and Theology in a Postliberal Age*, Louisville, Westminister John Knox Press, 1984; Asad, Talal. *Genealogies of Religion: Discipline and Reasons of Power in Christianity and Islam*. Baltimore, John Hopkin University Press, 1993

1124   G.W.F. Hegel, *Elements of the Philosophy of Right*, Editcd by Allen Wood, Translated by H. B. Nisbet. Cambridge, Cambridge University Press, 1991.

1125   Shagan, *The Birth of Modern Belief*, p. 10

1126   Shagan, *The Birth of Modern Belief*, p. 29

1127   See Tolan, *Faces of Muhammad*, p. 2

1128   Tolan, *Faces of Muhammd*, p. 113

1129   See Philip Milton, John Locke and the Rye House Plot, *The Historical Journal*, Vol. 43, No. 3 (Sep., 2000), pp. 647-668, p. 650ff

1130   See T. Birch, *History of the Royal Society of London* (London, 1756-7); Robert D. Purrington, *The First Professional Scientist: Robert Hooke and the Royal Society of London*, Boston, Birkhauser, 2009

1131   See "Newton: The Making of a Politician", http://www.newtonproject.ox.ac.uk/view/contexts/CNTX00002

1132   See John Marshall, *John Locke: Resistance, Religion and Responsibility*, Cambridge, Cambridge University Press, 1994, p. 414

1133   See Edward Gibbon, *The History of the Decline and Fall of the Roman*

Empire, 6 vols, London, William Hallhead, 1788, v., pp. 204, 221, 679.

1134 Gregory, *The Unintended Reformation: How a Religious Revolution Secularized Society*, London, Belknap Press, 2015, p. 86

1135 See Benjamin J. Kaplan, *Divided by Faith: Religious Conflict and the Practice of Toleration in Early Modern Europe*, London, Belknap Press of Harvard University, 2007, p. 15-47

1136 Gregory, *The Unintended Reformation*, p. 43-44

1137 See Gregory, *The Unintended Reformation*, p. 129

1138 See Kaplan, *Divided by Faith*, p. 28ff

1139 Margarete C. Jacob, "The Enlightenment Critique of Christianity: The crisis provoked by monarchical absolutism and established churches" in Stewart J. Brown and Timothy Tackett eds., *The Cambridge History of Christianity: Enlightenment, Reawakening and Revolution 1660-1815*, Cambridge, Cambridge University Press, 2006, v. VII, p. 265

1140 Margaret. Jacob, "The Nature of Early-Eighteenth-Century Religious Radicalism." *Republics of Letters: A Journal for the Study of Knowledge, Politics, and the Arts 1*, no. 1 (May 1, 2009), p. 1: http://rofl.stanford.edu/node/42.

1141 Jean Claude, *An Account of the Persecutions and Oppressions of the Protestants in France*, London, J. Norris, 1686, 19–21, quoted in John Marshall, *John Locke, Toleration and Early Enlightenment Culture*, Cambridge, Cambridge University Press, 2006, 63–64. See also M. C. Jacob, *The Radical Enlightenment: Pantheists, Freemasons, and Republicans*, London, Allen and Unwin, 1981; see also Hazard, *Crisis of European Mind*, p. 84

1142 Hazard, *Crisis of European Mind*, p. 84

1143 Margarete C. Jacob, "The Enlightenment Critique of Christianity: The crisis provoked by monarchical absolutism and established churches", p. 266

1144 See Kaplan, *Divided by Faith*, p. 1ff

1145 See Ryan K. Frace, *The Foundations Of Enlightenment: Transformations In Religious Toleration, Orthodoxy, And Pluralism In Early Modern Scotland, 1660-1752*, Ph.D. dissertation, University of Chicago, Chicago, 2005

1146 Israel, *Radical Enlightenment*, p. 17

1147 Tolan, *Faces of Muhammad*, p. 2-3

1148   See Samuel Chew, *The Crescent and the Rose*, p. 159

1149   See Al-Rodhan (eds), *The Role of the Arab-Islamic World in the Rise of the West*, London, Palgrave Macmillan, 2012 and also Gene W. Heck, Charlemagne, *Muhammad, and the Arab Roots of Capitalism*, New York, Walter de Gruyter, 2006 C. H. Haskins, *The Renaissance of the Twelfth Century*, London, Harvard University Press, 1955, p. 7

1150   See *Henry Stubbe and the Beginnings of Islam, The Originall & Progress of Mahometanism*, edited and introduced by Nabil Matar, New York, Columbia University Press, 2014, p.102ff

1151   See Jonathan I. Israel, *Radical Enlightenment*, p. 573

1152   See Justin A. I. Champion, *The Pillars of Priestcraft Shaken: The Church of England and its Enemies, 1660-1730*

1153   See Michael Graham, *The Blasphemies of Thomas Aikenhead: Boundaries of Belief on the Eve of the Enlightenment.* Edinburgh, 2013

1154   See J. Meggittt, Early Unitarians and Islam: revisiting a 'primary document', *Unitarian Theology II.* 2018, https://doi.org/10.17863/CAM.21403

1155   See Denise A. Spellberg, *Thomas Jefferson's Quran: Islam and the Founders*, New York: Knopf, 2013, p. 200ff

1156   Israel, *Radical Enlightenment*, p. 702. The word "Deism" will be used a lot during this book. So I will mostly use the generic definition given to the term by Pierre Viret (1511-1571), the author of "*Christian Teaching on the Doctrine of Faith and the Gospel*". As a reformed preacher and close friend of John Calvin, Viret separated deism from theism and defined deists as persons who ". . . profess belief in God as the creator of heaven and earth, but reject Jesus Christ and his doctrines." Viret identified "Deism" with Turkish faith. A century later, Viret's definition was republished in Pierre Bayle's (1647- 1706) 1697 *Historical and Critical Dictionary*, which became widely popular in Europe. Deists accepted Jesus as a human, moral and prophetic model but denied his divinity, pre-existence and redemptive death along with almost all supernatural, incarnational dogmas of Christianity. Islam will absolutely fit under this definition of Deism. It will not be far-fetched to claim that the European Deism which played a major role during the Enlightenment centuries was a reflection and a proto-copy of the simple Unitarian creed of Islam.

1157   Tolan, *Faces of Muhammad*, p. 155

1158   "I confess that Bonaparte frequently conversed with the chiefs of the Mussulman religion on the subject of his conversion; but only for the sake of amusement. The priests of the Koran, who would probably have been delighted to convert us, offered us the most ample concessions. But these conversations were merely started by way of entertainment, and never could have warranted a supposition of their leading to any serious result. If Bonaparte spoke as a Mussulman, it was merely in his character of a military and political chief in a Mussulman country. To do so was essential to his success, to the safety of his army, and, consequently, to his glory. In every country he would have drawn up proclamations and delivered addresses on the same principle. In India he would have been for Ali, at Thibet for the Dalai-lama, and in China for Confucius." *Memoirs of Napoleon Bonaparte* by Louis Antoine Fauvelet de Bourrienne edited by R.W. Phipps. Vol. 1, New York, Charles Scribner's Sons, 1889 p. 168-169 Top of Form Bottom of Form

1159 See Juan Cole, *Napoleon's Egypt: Invading the Middle East*, New York, Palgrave Macmillan, 2007, p. 294

1160 Juan Cole, *Napoleon's Egypt, p. 294*

1161 Matthew Dimmock, *Mythologies of the Prophet Muhammad in Early Modern English Culture*, p.1

1162 Dimmock, *Mythologies of the Prophet Muhammad in Early Modern English Culture,* p. 7

1163 Dimmock, *Mythologies of the Prophet Muhammad,* p. 1

1164 Dimmock, *Mythologies of the Prophet Muhammad,* p.1-2

1165 See Noel Malcolm, The 1649 English Translation of the Koran: Its Origin and Significance, *Journal of the Warburg and Courtauld Institutes,* 2012, Vol. 75 (2012), p. 288; Nabil Matar, *Islam in Britain,* p. 83; Nabil Matar noted that from "sectary to antiquarian to Lord Protector, the Quran was a text widely consulted and quoted: it had legitimacy for addressing not only Muslims overseas but Christians in England and the rest of the British Isles. The Quran had become a text on a Briton's reading list... Associated with 'Alcoran" was the Arabic civilization in which Islam had first developed. This civilization had interacted with Christendom throughout the medieval period and the Renaissance: Arabic translations and interpretations of Aristode and Arabic developments in mathematics, astronomy and medicine -the three areas in which the Arabs had excelled - had left their mark on the evolution of European thought... In the seventeenth century, English and Scottish writers frequently praised the usefulness of Arabic to statesman and trader, traveler and scholar alike." (Matar, Islam in Britain, p. 83) Matar further noted that "From the late Elizabethan until the Restoration periods, Islam was invoked and engaged at various intellectual and social levels. Numerous English and Scottish writers translated and prepared texts about Islam, while the reading public turned to "Alcoran" and learned about Muslim political and religious institutions. Islam entered the English discourse in a manner that superseded every other non-Christian civilization which Britons encountered from the Elizabethan until the Restoration periods." (Matar, Islam in Britain, p. 118)

1166   Ian Coller, *Citizens and Muslims: Islam, Politics and the French Revolution,* London, Yale University Press, 2020, p. 15

1167   Ian Coller, *Citizens and Muslims,* p. 16

1168   Ian Coller, *Citizens and Muslims,* p. 16

1169   Marshall G. S. Hodgson, "The Role of Islam in World History," *International Journal of Middle East Studies* 1.2 (1970): 99

1170   See Robert Brenner, *Merchants and Revolution: Commercial Change, Political Conflict, and London's Overseas Traders 1550-1653,* London, Verso, 2003

1171   See James D. Tracy, *The Rise of Merchant Empires: Long Distance Trade in the Early Modern World 1350-1750,* Cambridge, Cambridge University Press, 1990; Sanjay Subrahmanyam ed., *Merchants Network in the Early Modern World,* New York, Routledge, 2016

1172   Matar, *Britain and Barbary,* p. 146-47

1173   Matar, *Turks, Moors and Englishmen,* p. 66

1174   Fernand Braudel, *The Mediterranean and the Mediterranean World in the Age of Philip II,* translated by Sian Reynold, New York, Collins, 1972 p. 799

1175   See Noel Malcolm, "Positive Views of Islam and of Ottoman Rule in the Sixteenth Century: The Case of Jean Bodin," in *The Renaissance and the Ottoman World,* ed. Anna Contadini and Claire Norton, Farnham, Ashgate, 2013, 197; Anders Ingram, *Writing the Ottomans: Turkish History in Early Modern England,* New York, Palgrave Macmillan, 2015, 7–9;

1176   MacLean, *Looking East,* P. 21.

1177   Robert C. Davis, *Christian Slaves, Muslim Masters: White Slavery in the Mediterranean, the Barbary Coast and Italy, 1500-1800,* New York, Palgrave Macmillan, 2004, p. 23; David, *Holy War and Human Bondage: Tales of Muslim Christian Slavery in the Early Modern Mediterranean,*

Oxford, Praeger ABC-Clio, 2009 also see Kaplan, *Divided by Faith*, p. 301 ff; Charles Sumner, *White Slavery in the Barbary States, Enhanced Media*, Reseda, CA, 2017

1178   See Nabil Matar, *Britain and Barbary,* 1589-1689, Gainesville, University Press of Florida, 2005, p. 101 ff; Davis, Christian Slaves, p. 22

1179   MacLean and Matar, *Britain and Islamic World*, p. 126

1180   See Matar, *Britain and Barbary*, p. 102

1181   Matar, *Britain and Barbary*, p. 103

1182   Pugh, *Britain and Islam*, p. 56; see Matar, *Turks, Moors and Englishmen*, p. 42

1183   Maartje van Gelder, The Republic's Renegades: Dutch Converts to Islam in Seventeenth-Century Diplomatic Relations with North Africa, *Journal of Early Modern History* 19 (2015) 175-198, p. 179

1184   van Gelder, *The Republic's Renegades*, p. 181

1185   van Gelder, *The Republic's Renegades*, p. 181

1186   See Adrian Tinniswood, *Pirates of Barbary: Corsairs, Conquests and Captivity in the 17th Century Mediterranean*, New York, Riverhead Books, 2010, chapter 2 and 3

1187   See Stephen Clissold, 1976. "Christian Renegades and Barbary Corsairs." *History Today* 26, no. 8: 508–515. *Historical Abstracts;* C. S. Forester, *The Barbary Pirates*. New York, Random House. 1953

1188   See Adrian Tinniswood, *Pirates of Barbary,* chapter 4

1189   See Virginia W. Lunsford, *Piracy and Privateering in the Golden Age Netherland,* New York, Palgrave Macmillan, 2005, p. 56

1190   van Gelder, *The Republic's Renegades,* p. 186

1191   Lunsford, *Piracy and Privateering in the Golden Age Netherland,* p. 56

1192   van Gelder, *The Republic's Renegades,* p. 182

1193   van Gelder, *The Republic's Renegades,* p. 182-183

1194   See van Gelder, *The Republic's Renegades,* p. 184

1195   van Gelder, *The Republic's Renegades,* p. 194

1196   See Lunsford, *Piracy and Privateering in the Golden Age Netherland,* p. 57

1197   See van Gelder, *The Republic's Renegades,* p. 187

1198   See van Gelder, *The Republic's Renegades*, p. 189ff

1199   van Gelder, *The Republic's Renegades*, p. 189-90

1200   See Matar, *Britain and Barbary*, p. 113 ff

1201   Matar, *Britain and Barbary*, p. 113

1202   See Matar, *Islam in Britain*, p. 16-17, 22

1203   Nabil Matar, *Turks, Moors and Englishmen in the Age of Discovery*, New York, Columbia University Press, 1999, p. 19

1204   Matar, *Turks, Moors and Englishmen in the Age of Discovery*, p. 20

1205   See Samuel Chew, *The Crescent and the Rose*, p. 158

1206   Matar, *Turks, Moors and Englishmen*, p. 81-82

1207   Matar, *Britain and Barbary*, p. 167

1208   See Matar, *Britain and Barbary*, p. 167

1209   Pugh, *Britain and Islam*, p. 59; also see *Adventures of Baron Wenceslas Wratislaw of Mitrowitz*, ed. A. H. Wratislaw (London: Bell and Daldy, 1862), p. 53; Nabil Matar, Islam in Britain, p. 16-17

1210   See John Covel, "Dr. Covel's Diary (1670-1679)," in *Early Voyages and Travels in the Levant*, ed. James Theodore Bent, Burlington, Ashgate, 2010, p. 210

1211   John Covel, "Dr. Covel's Diary (1670-1679)," in *Early Voyages and Travels in the Levant*, p. 210

1212   Braudel, *The Mediterranean and the Mediterranean World*, p. 799-800. Nabil Matar observed that "Converts to Islam both embarrassed and provoked some of the most important writers and theologians of the European Renaissance. While the "direct encounter" with Islam affected the "small men" of Christendom -sailors, fishermen, merchants and soldiers-the intellectual and religious impact of that encounter challenged men whose writings and influence have been instrumental in defining early modern European culture: from Pope Pius II to Martin Luther and John Locke, from John Calvin to Christopher Marlowe, from John Foxe to George Fox, from Cervantes to Shakespeare, Massinger and Dryden - all reflected, to varying degrees in their writings, on the interaction between Christendom and Islam. Furthermore, all recognized that Christians were converting to Islam more often than Muslims were to Christianity and that the "infidels" challenged Europe not only by their sword but by their religious allure." Matar, Islam in Britain, p. 19

1213   Pugh, *Britain and Islam,* p. 59

1214   Matar, *Turks, Moors and Englishmen,* p. 77; Adrian Tinniswood, *Pirates of Barbary: Corsairs, Conquests and Captivity in the 17ᵗʰ Century Mediterranean,* chapter 2 & 3

1215   See Tobias P. Graf, *The Sultan's Renegades: Christian-European Converts to Islam and the Making of the Ottoman Elite, 1575-1610,* Oxford, Oxford University Press, 2017

1216   See Adrian Tinniswood, *Pirates of Barbary: Corsairs, Conquests and Captivity in the 17ᵗʰ Century Mediterranean,* New York, Riverhead Books, 2010, chapter 3 and 4; The Austrian Baron Wenceslas Wratislaw (1576—1635), "who had been imprisoned by the Turks, noted in 1599 that converts to Islam were so numerous that they "regulate the whole dominions of the Turkish emperor." (Adventures of Baron Wenceslas Wratislaw of Mitrowitz, ed. A. H. Wratislaw (London: Bell and Daldy, 1862), p. 53) There were more renegades "in Turkie and Barbary," confirmed in 1614 the barber-surgeon William Davies who had also been imprisoned by the Turks, than "naturall Turkes." (Matar, Islam in Britain, p. 16-17)

1217   Matthew Dimmock, *New Turkes: Dramatising Islam and the Ottomans in Early Modern England,* New York, Routledge, 2005

1218   See Matthew Birchwood, *Staging Islam in England: Drama and Culture, 1640-1685,* Cambridge, D. S. Brewer, 2007

1219   See Daniel J. Vitkus, ed. *Three Turk Plays from Early Modern England.* Cambridge: Columbia University Press, 2000; Vitkus ed. *Piracy, Slavery, and Redemption: Barbary Captivity Narratives from Early Modern England.* New York: Columbia UP, 2001; *Turning Turk: English Theater and the Multicultural Mediterranean, 1570-1630* (New York: Paigrave, 2003); Samuel C. Chew, *The Crescent and the Rose: Islam and England During the Renaissance* (New York: Octagon Press, 1937; Filiz Barin, "Othello: Turks as "the Other" in the Early Modern Period," *The Journal of the Midwest Modern Language Association* 43 No. 2 (Fall, 2010): 37-58; Matthew Dimmock, "The Tudor Experience of Islam." In *A Companion to Tudor Literature* ed. Kent Cartwright. (Malden: Wiley-Blackwell 2010): 49-62; Matthew Dimmock, "Converting and Not Converting "Strangers" in Early Modern London," *Journal of Early Modern History* 17 (2013): 457-78; Jonathan Burton, *Traffic and Turning: Islam and English Drama, 1579-1624,* Newark, University of Delaware Press, 2005; Matthew Dimmock, "materializing Islam on the Early Modern Stage," In *Early Modern Encounters with the Islamic East: Performing Cultures* ed. Sabine Schülting, Sabine Lucia Müller, and Ralf Hertel, Burlington, Ashgate, 2012: 115-132; Jerry Brotton, "Shakespeare's Turks and the Spectre of Ambivalence in the History Plays," *Textual Practice* 28 No. 3. (2014) 531-4; Jerry Brotton, *This Orient Isle: Elizabethan England and the Islamic World.* (St. Ives: Penguin Random House, 2016); Masood, Hafiz Abid. "Islam in Early Modern English Literature: A Select Bibliography." *Islamic Studies* 44 (2005): 553- 629;

1220   Jonathan Burton, "English Anxiety and the Muslim Power of Conversion: Five Perspectives on 'Turning Turk' in Early Modern Texts", *Journal for Early Modern Cultural Studies*, Spring/Summer 2002, Vol. 2, No. 1, A Special Issue on Representations of Islam and the East (Spring/Summer 2002), pp. 35- 67; See Matar, Islam in Britain, p. 40ff

1221   Burton, "English Anxiety and the Muslim Power of Conversion, p. 61

1222   Burton, "English Anxiety and the Muslim Power of Conversion, p. 62 onward

1223   See Burton, "English Anxiety and the Muslim Power of Conversion, p. 62 onward; Nabil Matar, *In the Lands of the Christians: Arabic Travel Writing in the Seventeenth Century,* New York, Routledge, 2003, p. 5 onward

1224   See details in Gerard Wiegers, "The Andalusi Heritage in the Maghrib" in *Poetry, Politics and Polemics: Cultural Transfer Between the Iberian Peninsula and North Africa* edited by Otto Zwartjes, Atlanta, Rodopi, 1996, p. 121

1225   Nabil Matar, *Europe Through Arab Eyes, 1578-1727,* New York, Columbia University Press, 2009, p. 9

1226   Gerald Maclean and Nabil Matar, *Britain and the Islamic World,* 1558-1713, p. 20

1227   See Discovery of 29 Sects, here in London all of which, except the first are most Divelish and Damnable, being these which follow (1641), p. 4; Matar, *Islam in Britain,* p. 46

1228   See Elisabeth A. Fraser, "Dressing Turks in the French Manner", *Mouradgea d Ohssons* Panorama of the Ottoman Empire, in *ARS Orientalis* volume 39 "Globalising Cultures: Art and Mobility in the Eighteenth Century, edited by Nebahat Avcıoğlu and Finbarr Barry Flood, Washington, D.C, Smithsonian Institution, 2010

1229   Matar, *Turks, Moors and Englishmen,* p. 39

1230   See Brian Cowan, *The Social Life of Coffee: The Emergence of British*

Coffee Houses, New Haven & London, Yale University Press, 2005

1231   See Ralph Hattox, *Coffee and Coffeehouses: The Origins of a Social Beverage in the Medieval Near East* (Seattle, WA, 1985); [Charles II], By the King. *A Proclamation for the Suppression of Coffee-Houses* (1675); Gerald MacLean and Nabil Matar, *Britain and the Islamic World 1558-1713,* p. 221ff

1232   Gerald MacLean and Nabil Matar, *Britain and the Islamic World 1558-1713,* p. 216; Mirkovic, Alexander, "From Courtly Curiosity to Revolutionary Refreshment: Turkish Coffee and English Politics in the Seventeenth century" (2005). Graduate Theses and Dissertations.

   https://scholarcommons.usf.edu/etd/774; Lillywhite, Bryant, *London Coffee Houses: A Reference Book of Coffee Houses of the Seventeenth, Eighteenth, and Nineteenth Centuries.* London: George Allen, 1963; Pincus, Steve, "Coffee Politicians Does Create: Coffeehouses and Restoration Political Culture" in *Journal of Modern History,* 6:4 (1995), 807-834; Robinson, Edward Forbes, *The Early History of Coffee Houses in England.* London, 1893; Dana Sajdi, *Ottoman Tulips, Ottoman Coffee: Leisure And Lifestyle In The Eighteenth Century,* London, New York, Tauris Academic Studies, 2007

1233   Matar, *Turk, Moor and Englishmen,* p. 34; see more details in Jerry Brotton, *The Sultan and the Queen: The Untold Story of Elizabeth and Islam*

1234   MacLean and Matar, *Britain and the Islamic World,* p. 216; Brotton, *The Sultan and the Queen,* p. 2ff

1235   See Esmond S. de Beer, King Charles II's Own Fashion: An Episode in Anglo-French Relations 1666-1670, *Journal of the Warburg Institute,* Vol. 2, No. 2 (Oct., 1938), pp. 105-115

1236   MacLean and Nabil Matar, *Britain and the Islamic World,* p. 20

1237   MacLean and Nabil Matar, *Britain and the Islamic World,* p. 199-200

1238   Matar, *Turks, Moors and Englishmen,* p. 41; Matar, *Britain and Barbary,* p. 103

1239   Matar, *Turks, Moors and Englishmen,* p. 42

1240   See for Levant Company Despina Vlami, *Trading with the Ottomans: The Levant Company in the Middle East,* New York, I. B. Tauris, 2015; Christine Laidlaw, *The British in the Levant: Trade and Perceptions of the Ottoman Empire in the Eighteenth Century,* New York, I. B. Tauris, 2010, p. 169 ff

1241   Robert Brenner, "The Social Basis of English Commercial Expansion, 1550-1650" in *Merchant Networks in Early Modern World*, p. 361 ff especially p. 384 onward; Robert Brenner, *Merchants and Revolution: Commercial Change, Political Conflict and London's Overseas Traders, 1550-1653*, part III

1242   See Kaplan, *Divided by Faith*, p. 91, 120

1243   G.V. Scammell, 'European Exiles, Renegades and Outlaws and the Maritime Economy of Asia c.1500-1750', in *Modern Asian Studies*, Vol. 26, No. 4 (1992), pp.641-61; Edward Thompson's *The Life of Charles Lord Metcalfe* (London, 1937), p.101

1244   William Dalrymple, *White Mughals: Love and Betrayal in Eighteenth Century India*, New York, Penguin Books, 2002, p. 30

1245   Dalrymple, *White Mughals*, p. 183

1246   See Dalrymple, *White Mughals: Love and Betrayal in Eighteenth Century India*; William Dalrymple ed., Begums, *Thugs and White Mughals: The Journals of Fanny Parkes*, London, Eland, 2012

1247   Dalrymple, *White Mughals*, p. 34

1248   Dalrymple, *White Mughals*, p. 54

1249   Dalrymple, *White Mughals*, p. xxxix

1250   Matar, *Turks, Moors and Englishmen*, p. 42

1251   Ian Coller, *Citizens and Muslims*, p. 17

1252   Ian Coller, *Citizens and Muslims*, p. 14

1253   Israel, *Radical Enlightenment*, 11

1254   See Israel, *Enlightenment Contested*, p. 43

1255   See details in Gabor Karman and Lovro Kuncevic eds., *The European Tributary States of the Ottoman Empire in the Sixteenth and Seventeenth Centuries*, Leiden, Brills, 2013, p. 375 ff

1256   Humberto Garcia, *Islam and the English Enlightenment*, p. 41

1257   Humberto Garcia, *A Hungarian Revolution in Restoration England: Henry Stubbe, Radical Islam, and the Rye House Plot*, p. 1

1258   *Humberto* Garcia, *Islam and the English Enlightenment*, p. 30

1259   *Garcia, A Hungarian Revolution in Restoration England*, p. 2

1260   Tolan, *Faces of Muhammad*, 139

1261   *Garcia, A Hungarian Revolution in Restoration England,* p. 11

1262   *Garcia, A Hungarian Revolution in Restoration England,* p. 11

1263   *Garcia, A Hungarian Revolution in Restoration England,* p. 20

1264   Garcia, *A Hungarian Revolution,* p. 2

1265   See John Sargeaunt, *Annals of Westminster School,* London, 1898; G F Russell Barker, *Memoir of Richard Busby,* London, 1895; A. Bolton, and H. D. Henry, eds., The Wren Society Vol XI. Oxford, 1934; William Bray ed., *Diaries of John Evelyn,* London, 1852; Edward Smith, Hooke and Westminster, https://www.westminster.org.uk/wp-content/uploads/2018/08/Robert-Hooke-and-Westminster.pdf

1266   See Maurice Cranston, *John Locke, A Biography,* London, 1957

1267   See Gerald James Toomer, *Easterne Wisedome and Learning,* Oxford, 1996

1268   See details in G. A. Russell (ed.), *The 'Arabick' Interest of the Natural Philosophers in Seventeenth-Century England,* p. 237ff

1269   See Russell (ed.), *The 'Arabick' Interest of the Natural Philosophers in Seventeenth-Century England,* p. 239ff

1270   See Russell (ed.), *The 'Arabick' Interest of the Natural Philosophers in Seventeenth-Century England,* p. 240ff

1271   Quoted in Ashcraft, *Revolutionary Politics and Locke's Two Treatises of Government,* p. 433

1272   Maurice Cranston, "The Politics of John Locke," *History Today* (September 1952): p. 620

1273   See Ashcraft, *Revolutionary Politics and Locke's Two Treatises of Government,* p. 432ff

1274   Leopold von Ranke, *The History of England.* 6 vols. (Oxford), 1875, v. 4, p. 166

1275   See Tim Harris. "Cooper, Anthony Ashley," in the *Oxford Dictionary of National Biography,* p. 199-200

1276   See Tim Harris. "Cooper, Anthony Ashley," in the *Oxford Dictionary of National Biography,* p. 202

1277   See Tim Harris. "Cooper, Anthony Ashley," in the *Oxford Dictionary of National Biography,* p. 202ff

1278   Ashcraft, *Revolutionary Politics and Locke's Two Treatises of Government,* p. 434

1279   See Martin Mulsow, "Henry Stubbe, Robert Boyle and the Idolatry of Nature" in Sarah Mortimer and John Robertson eds., *The Intellectual Consequences of Religious Heterodoxy 1600-1750*, p. 121ff

1280   Matar, *England and Religious Plurality*, p. 183

1281   See D. Goffman, *The Ottoman Empire and Early Modern Europe*, p.111; Aziz al Azmeh, *Islam and Modernities*, New York, Verso, 1993, p. 127

1282   See Istvan Gyorgy Toth, "Old and New Faith in Hungary, Turkish Hungary, and Transylvania" in R. Po-chia Hsia (ed.), *A Companion To The Reformation World*, Oxford, Blackwell, 2004, p. 205-222

1283   See Jerry Brotton, *The Sultan and the Queen: The Untold Story of Elizabeth and Islam*

1284   Neil Hanson, *The Confident Hope of a Miracle. The True History of the Spanish Armada*, New York, Knopf, (2003)

1285   See Christine Laidlaw, *The British in the Levant, Trade and Perceptions of the Ottoman Empire in the Eighteenth Century*, London, I. B. Tauris, 2010

1286   See Yosef Kaplan, *The Dutch Intersection: The Jews and Netherlands in Modern History*, Leiden, Brill, 2008, p. 7ff; Benjamin J. Kaplan, *Muslims in the Dutch Golden Age: Representations and Realities of Religious Toleration*, Amsterdam, Amsterdam University, 2006

1287   Benjamin Schmidt, *Innocence abroad: the Dutch imagination and the New World, 1570-1670*, Cambridge, Cambridge University Press, 2001; Charles Ralph Boxer, *The Dutch seaborne empire, 1600-1800*, Abingdon, Taylor & Francis, 1977; U. Ryad, (2017), "Rather Turkish than Papist": Islam as a political force in the Dutch Low Countries in the Early Modern Period. *Muslim World*, 107: 714-736. doi:10.1111/muwo.12218

1288   Goffman *The Ottoman Empire and early modern Europe, p. 196ff*

1289   https://archive.org/details/embassysirthoma00fostgoog

1290   See Nabil Matar, *Britain and Barbary 1589-1689*, Gainesville, University Press of Florida, 2005; Gerald McLean and Nabil Matar, *Britain and the Islamic World 1558-1713*, Oxford, Oxford University Press, 2011, p. 79ff;

1291   Jonathan I. Israel, *The Dutch Republic. Its Rise, Greatness, and Fall 1477–1806*, Oxford, Clarendon Press, (1998)

1292   See Garcia, *Islam and English Enlightenment*, p. 38

1293   Champion, *The Pillars of Priestcraft Shaken*, p.121.

1294 Charles K. Rowley, Bin Wu, *Britannia 1066-1884: From Medieval Abso-lutism to the Birth of Freedom under Constitutional Monarchy, Limited Suffrage, and the Rule of Law,* New York, Springer, 2014; John Spurr (ed.), Anthony Ashley Cooper, *First Earl of Shaftesbury 1621–1683,* Surrey, Ashgate, 2011

1295 Garcia, *A Hungarian Revolution,* p. 2

1296 Nabil Matar, *Henry Stubbe and the Beginnings of Islam: The Origi-nall and Progress of Mahometenism,* New York, Columbia University Press, 2014, p. 1

1297 See Matar, *Henry Stubbe and the Beginnings of Islam,* p. 3; aslo see Tolan, *Faces of Muhammad,* p. 142 ff

1298 See Tolan, *Faces of Muhammad,* p. 133 ff

1299 Tolan, *Faces of Muhammad,* p. 142

1300 Champion, *The Pillars of Priestcraft Shaken,* p.121-22

1301 Champion, *The Pillars of Priestcraft Shaken,* p.122

1302 Champion, *The Pillars of Priestcraft Shaken,* p.122

1303 Matar, *Henry Stubbe and the Beginnings of Islam,* p. 102

1304 Matar, *Henry Stubbe and the Beginnings of Islam,* p. 89

1305 Matar, *Henry Stubbe and the Beginnings of Islam,* p. 89-90

1306 See Matar, *Henry Stubbe and the Beginnings of Islam,* p. 89-90

1307 Matar, *Henry Stubbe and the Beginnings of Islam,* p. 128

1308 Dimmock, *Mythologies of the Prophet Muhammad,* p. 195

1309 Jacob, *Henry Stubbe,* p.69.

1310 Jacob, *Henry Stubbe,* p.70.

1311 Matar, *Henry Stubbe and the Beginnings of Islam,* p. 57

1312 Matar, *Henry Stubbe and the Beginnings of Islam,* p. 211

1313 Matar, *Henry Stubbe and the Beginnings of Islam,* p. 211

1314 Jacob, *Henry Stubbe,* p.71.

1315 Quoted In *Christian-Muslim Relations. A Bibliographical History. Vol-ume 13. Western Europe (1700-1800),* edited by David Thomas and John A. Chesworth, 75–76. Leiden: Brill, 2019, p. 28

1316 Garcia, *Islam and English Enlightenment,* p. 5

1317   Dimmock, *Mythologies of the Prophet Muhammad*, p. 193

1318   Matar, *Henry Stubbe and the Beginnings of Islam*, p. 186

1319   Tolan, *Faces of Muhammad*, p. 146

1320   Garcia, *Islam and English Enlightenment*, p. 9

1321   Garcia, *Islam and English Enlightenment*, p. 37

1322   Garcia, *A Hungarian Revolution*, p. 8

1323   Garcia, *A Hungarian Revolution*, p. 8

1324   Garcia, *A Hungarian Revolution*, p. 9

1325   Matar, *Henry Stubbe and the Beginnings of Islam*, p. 179

1326   Matar, *Henry Stubbe and the Beginnings of Islam*, p. 180; see also Tolan, *Faces of Muhammad*, 146 ff

1327   Jacob, *Henry Stubbe*, p.74.

1328   Jacob, *Henry Stubbe*, p. 74

1329   Jacob, *Henry Stubbe*, p. 74

1330   Jacob, *Henry Stubbe*, p.75.

1331   Jacob, *Henry Stubbe*, p. 75

1332   Jacob, *Henry Stubbe*, p. 76

1333   See Tolan, *Faces of Muhammad*, p. 146

1334   Jacob, *Henry Stubbe*, p.76-77

1335   "One area where Finch's Turkish sojourn may have been decisively influential on Anne Conway was in her awareness of Islam and in her developing an open mind towards Islamic culture. One of the striking features of Anne Conway's religious eirenicism is that it extended not just to Judaism, but also to Islam. She no doubt shared the tolerant view of Henry More who condemns the 'false Zeal' of those who attack non-Christians 'by vilifying and reproaching all other Religions, in damning the very best and most conscientious *Turks, Jews and Pagans* to the Pit of Hell'. But Anne Conway goes beyond More in her concern to emphasise the common ground between faiths, and to remove Christian doctrines that non-Christians found offensive. In her *Principles* she singles out the doctrine of the Trinity as 'a stumbling block and offense to Jews, Turks, and other people." Sarah Hutton, *Anne Conway: A Women Philosopher*, p. 107

1336   See Jacob, *Henry Stubbe*, p. 77

1337   See Hutton, *Anne Conway,* p. 22

1338   Mordechai Fiengold, "Henry Stubbe" in *Oxford Dictionary of National Biography*, v. 53, p. 200

1339   See *Anne Conway, The Principles of the Most Ancient and Modern Philosophy,* translated by A. P. Coudert and Taylor Corse, Cambridge, Cambridge University Press, 1999, p. xff

1340   Jacob, *Henry Stubbe, p.* 75

1341   Garcia, *Islam and English Enlightenment,* p. 40

1342   Garcia, *Islam and English Enlightenment,* p. 10

1343   Jacob, *Henry Stubbe*, p.71.

1344   Thomas Hobbes, *Leviathan: The Matter, Form and Power of a Commonwealth Ecclesiastical and Civill,* London, Andrew Crooke, 1651, p. 50-51

1345   Hobbes, *Leviathan,* p. 225

1346   Jacob, *Henry Stubbe*, p. 18ff

1347   Jacob, *Henry Stubbe*, p.11.

1348   Tolan, *Faces of Muhammad,* 144-145

1349   Jacob, *Henry Stubbe*, p.71.

1350   Jacob, *Henry Stubbe*, p.72-73

1351   Garcia, *Islam and English Enlightenment,* p. 49

1352   Garcia, *Islam and English Enlightenment,* p. 7

1353   Quoted in Gerald MacLean, *The Rise of Oriental Travel: English Visitors to the Ottoman Empire 1580-1720,* p. 122

1354   MacLean, *The Rise of Oriental Travel,* p. 122

1355   MacLean, *The Rise of Oriental Travel,* p. 118

1356   Jacob, *Henry Stubbe*, p.72.

1357   Jacob, *Henry Stubbe*, p.72

1358   Jacob, *Henry Stubbe*, p.72

1359   Jacob, *Henry Stubbe*, p.72

1360   Jacob, *Henry Stubbe, p. 72*

1361   Jacob, *Henry Stubbe*, p.105.

1362   James R. Jacob, *Henry Stubbe, Radical Protestantism and the Early Enlightenment*, Cambridge, Cambridge University Press, 1983, p.2.

1363   Jacob, *Henry Stubbe*, p.65.

1364   See Lois G. Schwoerer, *The Ingenious Mr. Henry Care, Restoration Publicist*, Baltimore & London, The Johns Hopkins University Press, 2001; Laura Perille, *A Mirror to Turke: "Turks" and the Making of Early Modern England"*, Ph. D. thesis submitted to the Department of History at Brown University Providence, Rhode Island, May 2015, p. 269

1365   Matar, *Henry Stubbe and the Beginnings of Islam*, p. 12

1366   Garcia, *A Hungarian Revolution*, p. 2

1367   Matar, *Henry Stubbe and the Beginnings of Islam*, p. 13

1368   Matar, *Henry Stubbe and the Beginnings of Islam*, p. 14

1369   See Matar, *Henry Stubbe and the Beginnings of Islam*, p. 13

1370   See Matar, *Henry Stubbe and the Beginnings of Islam*, p. 31

1371   See details in Ole Peter Grell and Roy Potter eds., *Toleration in Enlightenment England*, Cambridge, Cambridge University Press, 2000, p. 102 ff; John Marshall, *John Locke, Toleration, and Early Enlightenment Culture: Religious Intolerance and Arguments for Religious Toleration in Early Modern and 'Early Enlightenment' Europe*, Cambridge, Cambridge University Press, 2006

1372   Matar, *Henry Stubbe and the Beginnings of Islam*, p. 46

1373   See Marlies Galenkamp, Locke And Bayle On Religious Toleration, www.erasmuslawreview.nl *Erasmus Law Review*, Volume 5, Issue 1 (2012); Perez Zagorin, *How the Idea of Religious Toleration Came to the West*, p. 240 ff

1374   See Matar, *Henry Stubbe and the Beginnings of Islam*, p. 46

1375   See for instance Perez Zagorin, *How the Idea of Religious Toleration Came to the West*, p. 289 ff

1376   See Ernst Mayr, (1990). "When Is Historiography Whiggish?".*Journal of the History of Ideas.* 51 (2): 301–309; J. W. Burrow, A Liberal Descent: *Victorian historians and the English past.* Cambridge: Cambridge University Press, 1981 and his "The Crisis of Reason: European Thought, 1848–1914", New Haven, Yale University Press, 2000

1377   See Matar, *Henry Stubbe and the Beginnings of Islam*, p. 47

1378   See Jack Goody, *The Theft of History*

1379   Jacob, *Henry Stubbe*, p.9.

1380   Dimmock, *Mythologies of the Prophet Muhammad*, p. 198

1381   Jacob, *Henry Stubbe*, p.139.

1382   Jacob, *Henry Stubbe*, p.140

1383   Jacob, *Henry Stubbe*, p.143

1384   Justin Champion, *Republican Learning: John Toland and the Crisi of Christian Culture 1696-1722*, Manchester, Manchester University Press, 2003, p. 3

1385   See Hazarad, *The Crisis of the European Mind*, p. 148 ff

1386   Champion, *Republican Learning*, p. 4

1387   Hazarad, *The Crisis of the European Mind*, p. 149

1388   Champion, *Republican Learning*, p. 13

1389   Champion, *Republican Learning*, p. 13

1390   Champion, *Republican Learning*, p. 14

1391   Champion, *Republican Learning*, p. 14

1392   Champion, *Republican Learning*, p. 17-18

1393   Champion, *Republican Learning*, p. 69

1394   Huge Trevar-Roper, *History and the Enlightenment*, New Haven, Yale University Press, 2010, p. 71

1395   See Nigel Smith, Best, *Biddle and Anti-Trinitarian Controversy*, p. 161

1396   Nigel Smith, Best, *Biddle and Anti-Trinitarian Controversy*, p. 160

1397   Trevar-Roper, *History and the Enlightenment*, p. 71

1398   Champion, *Republican Learning*, p. 69

1399   Paul Hazard, *The Crisis of the European Mind*, p. 148

1400   Champion, *Republican Learning*, p. 70

1401   Champion, *Republican Learning*, p. 71

1402   See Randy Robertson, *Censorship and Conflict in Seventeenth Century England: A Subtle Art of Division*, University Park, Pennsylvania State

University Press, 2009, p. 178 ff

1403   Champion, *Republican Learning*, p. 79

1404   Champion, *Republican Learning*, p. 69

1405   Champion, *Republican Learning*, p. 83

1406   Champion, *Republican Learning*, p. 84

1407   Champion, *Republican Learning*, p. 85

1408   See Robert Rees Evans, *Pantheisticon: The Career of John Toland*, New York, Peter Lang, 1991; Stephen H. Daniel, *John Toland, his methods, manners and mind*, McGill-Queen's University Press 1984; Justin Champion, *Republican Learning: John Toland and the crisis of Christian culture, 1696-1722*; Margaret C. Jacob, review of R.E. Sullivan's John Toland and the Deist Controversy, in: *American Historical Review*, Vol. 88, no.2, Apr. 1983.

1409   See Jonathan C. Birch, *Cracking the Canon: John Toland's 'Lost' Gospels and the Challenge to Religious Hegemony*, in A.K.M. Adam and Samuel Tongue eds. *Looking Through a Class Bible, Postdisciplinary Biblical Interpretations from the Glasgow School*, Leiden, Brill, 2014, p. 99 ff

1410   See William Baird, *History of New Testament Research, Volume One: From Deism to Tübingen.* Fortress Press. 1992; Peter Hanns Reill, *The German Enlightenment and the Rise of Historicism.* Berkeley: University of California Press, 1975; David R. Law, *The Historical-Critical Method: A Guide for the Perplexed.* New York: T&T Clark, 2012; James A Herrick,."Characteristics of British Deism". *The Radical Rhetoric of the English Deists: The Discourse of Scepticism, 1680–1750, Studies in rhetoric/communication. Columbia, South Carolina: University of South Carolina Press, 1997*; Robert B. Stewart, "Introduction". In Stewart, Robert B. (ed.). *The Reliability of the New Testament: Bart D. Ehrman and Daniel B. Wallace in Dialogue.* Minneapolis, Minnesota: Fortress Press, 2011; Mark Allan Powell, *Jesus as a Figure in History: How Modern Historians View the Man from Galilee.* Westminster John Knox Press, 1998; Gerd Theissen, Annette Merz, *The Historical Jesus: A Comprehensive Guide.* Minneapolis, Minnesota: Fortress Press, , 1996

1411   Peter Harrison, *'Religion' and the Religions in the English Enlightenment*, Cambridge, Cambridge University Press, 2002, p. 75

1412   See Diego Lucci, *The Law of Nature,* Mosaic Judaism, and Primitive Christianity in *John Locke and the English Deists, Entangled Religions 8* (2019), er.ceres.rub.de, DOI: 10.13154/er.8.2019.8354

1413   Tolan, *Faces of Muhammad,* p. 150

1414   Diego Lucci, *The Law of Nature,* p. 1

1415   Diego Lucci, *The Law of Nature,* p. 3

1416   Diego Lucci, *The Law of Nature,* p. 3

1417   Champion, *The Pillars of Priestcraft Shaken,* p.126.

1418   Jacob, *Henry Stubbe,* p.154

1419   Toland, *Nazarenus,* p.139.

1420   Toland, *Nazarenus,* p.135.

1421   Toland, *Nazarenus,* p.153.

1422   Toland, *Nazarenus,* p.192.

1423   Harrison, *Religion and Religions,* p. 166; Noel Malcolm stated that for "centuries, Western writers had portrayed Islam as a religion to be explained in terms of human motivation, and their own faith and Church as divine. Toland's radical historicizing of both religions reversed that pattern in a truly shocking way." Noel Malcolm, *Useful Enemies,* p. 326

1424   Harrison, *Religion and Religions,* p. 166

1425   Jacob, *Henry Stubbe,* p.158

1426   Harrison, *Religion and Religions,* p. 167

1427   Hazard, *The Crises of the European Mind,* p. 150

1428   J. C. Birch, *Cracking the Canon,* p. 85-86

1429   Harrison, *Religion and Religions,* p. 144

1430   See Tolan, *Faces of Muhammd,* p. 153

1431   Champion, *The Pillars of Priestcraft Shaken,* p.126.

1432   Toland, *Nazarenus,* p.135.

1433   Champion, *The Pillars of Priestcraft Shaken,* p.122.

1434   Champion, *The Pillars of Priestcraft Shaken,* p.121.

1435   Jacob, *Henry Stubbe,* p.160

1436   Jacob, *Henry Stubbe,* p.160

1437   Champion, *The Pillars of Priestcraft Shaken,* p.127.

1438   Tolan, *Faces of Muhammad,* p. 154

1439   Champion, *The Pillars of Priestcraft Shaken*, p.106; see more details in Alie, Remi, "'Empire without end': John Finch, *Orientalism, and Early Modern Empire*

1440   Matar, *Islam in Britain*, pp.21.

1441   Tolan, *Faces of Muhammad*, p. 142

1442   Leonard Twells, Zachary Pearce, Thomas Newton, Samuel Burdy, (1816). *The Lives of Dr. Edward Pocock: the celebrated orientalist*, Volume 1. London: Printed for F.C. and J. Rivington, by R. and R. Gilbert. Retrieved on August 30, 2018

1443   P. M. Holt, Edward Pocoke (1604-91), the First Laudian Professor of Arabic at Oxford http://oxoniensia.org/volumes/1991/holt.pdf

1444   See E.S. de Beer, ed. *The Correspondence of John Locke*, 8 vols., vol. 1 (Oxford: Oxford University Press, 2010), 352-54; Simon Mills, "The English Chaplains at Aleppo: Exploration and Scholarship between England and the Ottoman Empire, 1620–1760," *Bulletin of the Council for British Research in the Levant* 6, no. 1 (2011), p. 246.

1445   See details in Zachary W. Schulz, *The English In The Levant: Commerce, Diplomacy, And The English Nation In The Ottoman Empire, 1672-1691*, a dissertation Submitted to the Faculty of Purdue University, 2018, p. 119. He stated: "Working in the 1670s, Chaplains Robert Huntington and John Luke acted on orders from John Locke and Robert Boyle to collect further manuscripts, artifacts, and assorted data to expand the sciences and humanities, both at the universities and for these individual men's libraries. For example, in 1670, Huntington sailed to Aleppo to take over Pococke's appointment. Before departing, Huntington received correspondence from both Robert Boyle and John Locke encouraging him to continue Pococke's practice of collecting manuscripts. In his reply to Locke, he asserted that he was eager to fulfill the "commands" and "instructions" both luminaries made of him to obtain various eastern tracts. Moreover, Pococke, Luke, Huntington, and other chaplains went as far as to learn Arabic while in Aleppo. With these language skills, these men sought to better understand the confessional differences that existed between Eastern Christians, Muslims, and Protestants in England. Moreover, they provided them with the ability to further comprehend the society they had immersed themselves in. All the while, these chaplains continually reported their findings to John Locke and others."

1446   Frederick C. Giffin, John Locke and Religious Toleration, *Journal of Church and State*, Vol. 9, No. 3 (Autumn 1967), pp. 378-390, https://

www.jstor.org/stable/23913736; John William Tate, *Liberty, Toleration and Equality: John Locke, Jonas Proast and the Letters Concerning Toleration,* New York, Routledge, 2016, p. 66

1447   John Marshall, *John Locke: Resistance, Religion and Responsibility*, p. 409; Hazard, *The Crises of the European Mind,* p. 149

1448   Marshall, *John Locke, p.454*

1449   Marshall, *John Locke, p. 409*

1450   John Marshall, "Locke, Socinianism, "Socinianism" and Unitarianism" in M. A. Steward (ed.), *English Philosophy in the Age of Locke,* Oxford, Oxford University Press, 2000, p. 118

1451   Champion, *Pillars of Priestcraft,* p. 121

1452   Allison P. Coudert, "Orientalism in Early Modern Europe", p. 726

1453   See Marshall, *John Locke,* p. 415 onward

1454   See John Harrison and Peter Laslett, *The Library of John Locke* (Oxford: Clarendon Press, 1971)

1455   Ann Talbot, "The Great Ocean of Knowledge", *The Influence of Travel Literature on the Work of John Locke,* Leiden, Brill, 2010, p. 3-4

1456   See David B. Paxman, " 'Adam in a Strange Country': Locke Language Theory and Travel Literature," *Modern Philology*, vol. 92, No. 4 (May, 1995): 460–481

1457   See Talbot, "The Great Ocean of Knowledge", p. 10

1458   See Talbot, "The Great Ocean of Knowledge", p. 19

1459   See Ivo Kamps and Jyotsana G. Singh eds., *Travel Knowledge: European "Discoveries" in the Early Modern Peried,* p. 1ff

1460   Tolan, *Faces of Muhammad,* p. 133

1461   Albrechet Classen, "Encounters Between East and West", in Albrecht Classen ed., *East Meets West in the Middle Ages and Early Modern Times:Transcultural Experiences in the Premodern World,* p. 207

1462   https://archive.org/search.php?query=%28Hakluyt+OR+Hackluyt%29

1463   https://archive.org/search.php?query=%28%28subject%3A%22Purchas%2C%20Samuel%22%20OR%20subject%3A%22Samuel%20Purchas%22%20OR%20creator%3A%22Purchas%2C%20Samuel%22%20OR%20creator%3A%22Samuel%20Purchas%22%20

OR%20creator%3A%22Purchas%2C%20S%2E%22%20OR%20ti-
tle%3A%22Samuel%20Purchas%22%20OR%20description%3A%-
22Purchas%2C%20Samuel%22%20OR%20description%3A%22Sam-
uel%20Purchas%22%29%20OR%20%28%221577-1626%22%20
AND%20Purchas%29%29%20AND%20%28-mediatype:software%29

1464   See Ann Talbot, "Locke's Travel Books," *Locke Studies*, vol. 7 (2007): 113–136.

1465   See The history of the Turkish empire from the year 1623 to the year 1677 containing the reigns of the three last emperours, viz., Sultan Morat or Amurat IV, Sultan Ibrahim, and Sultan Mahomet IV, his son, the XIII emperour now reigning / by Paul Rycaut, Esq. ...Rycaut, Paul, Sir, 1628-1700. London: Printed by J.M. for John Starkey ..., 1680.

1466   See Talbot, "The Great Ocean of Knowledge", p. 119ff

1467   See Talbot, "The Great Ocean of Knowledge", p. 108-109

1468   See Edward Terry, *A voyage to East-India*. Wherein some things are taken notice of in our passage thither, but many more in our abode there, within that rich and most spacious empire of the Great Mogol (London: T. W. for J. Martin and J. Allestrye, 1655)

1469   Talbot, "The Great Ocean of Knowledge", p. 119ff; Jerry Bentley, "Euro-peanisation of the World or Globalisation of Europe?" *Religions* 2012, 3, 441–454; doi:10.3390/rel3020441, p. 449ff; "But to returne againe to those Mahometan Priests, who out of zeale doe so often proclaim their Mahomet. Tom Coryat upon a time having heard their Moolaas often (as before) so to cry got him upon an high place directly op-posite to one of those Priests, and contradicted him thus. La alla illa alla, Hasaret Eesa Ben alla, that is, no God, but one God, and the Lord Christ the Son of God, and further added that Mahomet was an Im-postor: and all this he spake in their owne language as loud as possibly he could, in the eares of many Mahometans that heard." (Thomas Co-ryat, *Mr Thomas Coriat to his friends in England sendeth greeting from Agra the capitall city of the dominion of the great Mogoll in the Easterne India, the last of October, 1616* (London: I. Beale, 1618), p. 271-72

1470   "That ... the prisoner had repeatedly maintained, in conversation, that theology was a rhapsody of ill-invented nonsense, patched up partly of the moral doctrines of philosophers, and partly of poetical fictions and extravagant chimeras: That he ridiculed the holy scriptures, calling the Old Testament Ezra's fables, in profane allusion to Esop's Fables; That he railed on Christ, saying, he had learned magick in Egypt, which enabled him to perform those pranks which were called miracles: That he called the New Testament the history of the imposter Christ; That he said Moses was the better artist and the better politician; and he preferred Muhammad to Christ: That the Holy Scriptures were stuffed with such madness, nonsense, and contradictions, that he admired the stupidity of the world in being so long deluded by them: That he rejected the mystery of the Trinity as unworthy of refutation; and scoffed at the incarnation of Christ." Howell, T. B., ed. (1816). "Proceedings against Thomas Aikenhead for Blasphemy". A Complete Collection of State Trials and Proceedings for High Treason and Other Crimes and Misdemeanors from the Earliest Period to 1783, with Notes and Other Illustrations. Vol. 13. Longman, Hurst, Rees, Orme and Brown – via Google Books

1471 See Nabil Matar, John Locke and the Turbaned Nations, *Journal of Islamic Studio* 2:1 (1991) pp. 67-77

1472 See Talbot, "The Great Ocean of Knowledge", p. 108-109

1473 See Samuel Chew, *The Crescent and the Rose, p. 119ff*

1474 Christine Woodhead, 'The Present Terrour of the World'? Contemporary Views of the Ottoman Empire c1600, *History,* vol. 72, issue 234, 1987, p. 20-37, p. 23

1475 Tolan, *Faces of Muhammad,* p. 134

1476 See B. J. Kaplan, *Divided By Faith: Religious Conflict and the Practice of Toleration in Early Modern Europe,* p. 240 ff; Perez Zagorin, *How the Idea of Religious Toleration Came to the West,* Princeton, p. 93ff

1477 See Mark Goldie (ed.), *John Locke: A Letter Concerning Toleration and Other Writings,* Indiana, Liberty Fund, 2010, p. 21ff

1478 Tolan, *Faces of Muhammad,* p. 147

1479 John Marshall, *John Locke, Toleration and Early Enlightenment Culture: Religious Intolerance and Arguments for Religious Toleration in Early Modern and 'Early Enlightenment' Europe,* Cambridge, Cambridge University Press, 2006 p. 393

1480 See Susan J. Ritchie, *Children of the Same God: The Historical Relationship Between Unitarianism, Judaism, and Islam,* Boston, Skinner House Books, 2014; http://www.minnslectures.org/archive/Ritchie/RitchieLecture1.pdf

1481 See Nabil Matar, *Islam in Britain 1558-1685,* p. 1ff

1482   Matthew Dimmock, *Mythologies of the Prophet Muhammad in Early Modern English Culture,* Cambridge, Cambridge University Press, 2013

1483   Garcia, *A Hungarian Revolution,* p. 1; See Matthew Birchwood, Staging Islam in England Drama and Culture 1640-1685, Cambridge, D. S. Brewer, 2007; Daniel Vitkus, *Turning Turk: English Theater and the Multicultural Mediterranean, 1570-1630.* New York: Palgrave Macmillan, 2003

1484   Garcia, *Islam and the English Enlightenment,* p. 11-12

1485   J. V. Tolan, "European Accounts of Muhammad's Life", in Jonathon E. Brockopp (ed.), *The Cambridge Companion to Muhammad,* p. 226-250

1486   Tolan, *Faces of Muhammad,* p. 135

1487   See Matar, *Islam in Britain,* p. 18ff; 82ff; 112ff

1488   See Alie, Remi, "'Empire without end': John Finch, *Orientalism, and Early Modern Empire, 1674-1681*" (2017). Electronic Thesis and Dissertation Repository. 4932. https://ir.lib.uwo.ca/etd/4932

1489   Jane D. McAuliffe (ed.), *The Cambridge Companion to the Quran,* Cambridge, Cambridge University Press, 2006

1490   See Archibald H. Christie, *The Development of Ornament from Arabic Script,* London, 1922; *Traditional Methods of Pattern Designing; An Introduction to the Study of the Decorative Art,* Amazon, CHIZINE PUBN, 2018; *Pattern Design,* New York, Dover Publications, 2011

1491   See Deborah Howard, *Scottish Architecture: From the Reformation to the Restoration, 1560-1660* (Architectural History of Scotland), Edinburgh, Edinburgh University Press, 1995; *Venice & the East: The Impact of the Islamic World on Venetian Architecture 1100-1500,* New Haven, Yale University Press, 2000

1492   Jerry Brotton and Lisa Jardine, *Global Interests: Renaissance Art between East and West,* London, Reaktion Books, 2012

1493   Rosamond E. Mack, *Bazaar to Piazza: Islamic Trade and Italian Art, 1300-1600,* Berkeley, University of California Press, 2001

1494   Stefano Carboni and David Whitehouse, *Glass of the Sultans,* New Haven, Yale University Press, 2001; *Venice and the Islamic World,* 828-1797, New York, *The Metropolitan Museum of Art,* 2007

1495   G. A. Russell (ed.), *The 'Arabick' Interest of the Natural Philosophers in Seventeenth-Century England,* p. 224ff; "Hayy Ibn- Yaqzān raised the possibility of learning without any guidance and teachers, and then

Locke came along and propagated it more widely... The autodidact became a role model for new educational programs with universal claims... a process of exchange and borrowing from sources both near and far combined to construct the edifices of experimentalism and empiricism. The economic network of the Levant Company ... allowed for the circulation of cultural and scientific works that, as oracles of the past, played roles in reinforcing the experimentalist argument still being negotiated, before the canon of empiricism solidified in the form of Locke's Essay Concerning Human Understanding ... This particular medieval work appealed to English experimentalists because it carried within it traces of earlier intellectual and cultural ideas about empiricism, which ranged from the question of self- reliance and self- directed learning to spontaneous generation. The affair of the publication of Philosophus autodidactus also tapped into an already extant history of a utopian literary genre with sources in medieval times" Ben-Zaken, Reading Hayy Ibn Yaqzan, p. 124

1496   See Michael Nahas, A Translation of Hayy B. Yaqzān by the Elder Edward Pococke (1604-1691), *Journal of Arabic Literature*, Vol. 16 (1985), pp. 88-90, p. 88

1497   Jerry H. Bentley, *The Oxford Handbook of World History,* Oxford, Oxford University Press, 2012; "Europeanisation of the World or Globalisation of Europe?"; Kenneth R. Curtis and Jerry H. Bentley (eds.), *Architects of World History: Researching the Global Past,* Oxford, Willy Blackwell, 2014

1498   See Jack Goody, *The Theft of History*

1499   Janet Abu Lughod, *Before European Hegemony: The World System A. D. 1250-1350*

1500   Samir Amin, *Global History: A View from the South,* Oxford, Pambazuka Press, 2011; *Eurocentrism: Modernity, Religion, and Democracy, A Critique of Eurocentrism and Culturalism,* New York, MONTHLY REVIEW PRESS, 2009

1501   See Hobson, *The Eastern Origins of Western Civilisation*

1502   John Sweetman, *The Oriental Obsession: Islamic Inspiration in British and American Art and Architecture 1500-1920,* Cambridge, Cambridge University Press, 1991

1503   Jerry Brotton, *The Renaissance Bazaar: from the Silk Road to Michelangelo,* Oxford, Oxford University Press, 2003

1504   Christopher Wren, *the Junior, 'Parentalia: or, Memoirs of the family of the Wrens'*, viz. of Mathew Bishop, printed for T. Osborn; and R. Dodsley, London, 1750; Miles Danby, 'Moorish style', London. Phaidon, (1995), James Elmes,`Christopher Wren', London, Chapman & Hall.1st edition, 1852; F. Grose, (ed.) `Essays on Gothic architecture by the Rev. T. Warton et al., 3rd ed., London, J. Taylor, at the Architectural Library, 1808

1505   "Christopher Wren and the Muslim Origin of Gothic Architecture"

       http://www.muslimheritage.com/article/christopher-wren-and-muslim-origin-gothic-architecture; Tonia Raquejo, The 'Arab Cathedrals': Moorish Architecture as Seen by British Travellers, *The Burlington Magazine*, Vol. 128, No. 1001 (Aug., 1986), pp. 555-563

1506   Tolan, *Faces of Muhammad*, p. 135

1507   See Michael E. Marmura, "Al-Ghazali" in *the Cambridge Companion to Arabic Philosophy* edited by Peter Adamson and Richard Taylor, Cambridge, Cambridge University Press, 2005; Hamid Naseem Rafiabadi, *Emerging From Darkness: Ghazzali's Impact on the Western Philosophers*, New Delhi, Sarup & Sons, 2002; Thomas Arnold and Alfred Guillaume eds., *The Legacy of Islam*, Oxford, Clarendon Press, 1931; John Renard, *Islam and Christianity: Theological Themes in Comparative Perspective*, Berkeley, University of California Press, 2011

1508   See H. A. Wolfson, *The Philosophy of the Kalam*, Cambridge, Mass., Harvard University Press, 1976; Ismail R. al-Faruqi, Lois L. al-Faruqi, *The Cultural Atlas of Islam*, New York, MacMillan Publishing Company, 1986; Al-Ghazali, *The Incoherence of the Philosophers*, translated by Michael E. Marmura, Provo, Utah, Brigham Young University Press, 2002; Frank Griffel, *Al-Ghazali's Philosophical Theology*, Oxford, Oxford University Press, 2009; Andrew Rippin, *Muslims: Their Religious Beliefs & Practices* (New York: Routledge, 1990

1509   See Tolan, "European Accounts of Muhammad's Life"; Garcia, *Islam and English Enlightenment*, p. 48ff

1510   John Locke, *The Works of John Locke*, London, William Taylor, MDCCXXII, v. III, p. 452

1511   Locke, *The Reasonableness of Christianity: With A Discourse of Miracles and part of A Third Letter Concerning Toleration*, edited by I. T. Ramsey, Stanford, Stanford University Press, 1958, p. 59; Walker further observed that "Locke's positive attitude to Islam raises an interesting idea. Since the philosopher's ideas played a large part in the formulation of the American Constitution, could it be argued that there is an Islamic dimension to that significant document? Perhaps a case can be made for the notion that the United States of America is, at heart, if not an Islamic state, a state with an Islamic dimension to it." Christopher Walker, *Islam and the West: The Dissonant Harmony of Civilizations,* Stroud, Gloucestershire, History Press, 2013, chapter 7, p. 199

1512　See *John Locke, A letter concerning toleration humbly submitted* (London: for Awnsham Churchill, 1689, p. 57; Christopher Walker explained that to Locke, the "Islamic monotheism grew from the Christian gospel; the teaching of both is of the　one and the same God. Locke, who never referred to the Trinity in any of his writings, was saying here that Islam is in effect a cousin to our own belief system and culture, and its view of the divine is similar to that of Christianity. There need be no opposition. We all believe approximately the same thing. We are all on the same side." Christipher Walker, *Islam and the West: The Dissonant Harmony of Civilizations,* Stroud, Gloucestershire, History Press, 2013, chapter 7, p. 199

1513　Locke, *The Reasonableness of Christianity,* p. 81

1514　Locke, *The Works of John Locke,* p. 261

1515　Arthur Bury, *Naked Gospel, 1690,* part 1, preface reprinted by Book on Demand, 2015

1516　See Champion, The *Pillars of Priestcraft Shaken,* p. 108

1517　See Garcia, *Islam and English Enlightenment,* p. 51ff

1518　Marshall, *John Locke,* p. 406

1519　See Marshall, *John Locke,* p.425ff

1520　Victor Nuovo, *Christianity, Antiquity, and Enlightenment: Interpretations of Locke,* New York, Springer, 2011, P. 25

1521　Victor Nuovo, "Locke's Theology 1694-1704" in Stewart ed., *English Philosophy,* p. 199

1522　Victor Nuovo, "Locke's Theology 1694-1704" in Stewart ed., *English Philosophy,* p. 200

1523　Victor Nuovo, "Locke's Theology 1694-1704" in Stewart ed., *English Philosophy,* p. 200

1524　Marshall, Socinianism and Unitarianism in Stewart ed., *English Philosophy,* p. 165

1525 Victor Nuovo, "Locke's Theology 1694-1704" in Stewart ed., *English Philosophy*, p. 210

1526 Victor Nuovo, "Locke's Theology 1694-1704" in Stewart ed., *English Philosophy*, p. 205

1527 Victor Nuovo, "Locke's Theology 1694-1704" in Stewart ed., *English Philosophy*, p. 205

1528 See details in Kim Ian Parker, Newton, *Locke and the Trinity: Sir Isaac's comments on Locke's: A Paraphrase and Notes on the Epistle of St Paul to the Romans*, Scottish *Journal of Theology* / Volume 62 / Issue 01 / February 2009, pp 40 – 52, p. 49

1529 Parker, Newton, *Locke and the Trinity*, p. 49

1530 Victor Nuovo, "Locke's Theology 1694-1704" in Stewart ed., *English Philosophy*, p. 207

1531 Parker,Newton, *Locke and the Trinity*, p. 50

1532 Victor Nuovo, "Locke's Theology 1694-1704" in Stewart ed., *English Philosophy*, p. 194

1533 Marshall, Socinianism and Unitarianism in in Stewart ed., *English Philosophy*, p. 176

1534 Marshall, Socinianism and Unitarianism in in Stewart ed., *English Philosophy*, p. 176

1535 Victor Nuovo, "Locke's Theology 1694-1704" in Stewart ed., *English Philosophy*, p. 211

1536 Marshall, Socinianism and Unitarianism in in Stewart ed., *English Philosophy*, p. 178

1537 Quran, 7:172; 4:171

1538 "O People of the Scripture! Do not exaggerate in your religion, and do not say about God except the truth. The Messiah, Jesus, the son of Mary, is the Messenger of God, and His Word that He conveyed to Mary, and a Spirit from Him. So believe in God and His messengers, and do not say, "Three." Refrain—it is better for you. God is only one God. Glory be to Him—that He should have a son. To Him belongs everything in the heavens and the earth, and God is a sufficient Protector." (Quran 4:171)

1539 See Victor Nuovo, "Locke's Theology 1694-1704" in Stewart ed., *English Philosophy*, p. 188

1540   Quran 7: 172-173

1541   Quran 17: 85

1542   Quran 83:7-18

1543   See Abu Abdullah al Hakim, *al Mustadrak a'la al Sahihayn,* Beirut, al-Kutub al-'Ilmiyyah, 1990, Hadith number 4175

1544   See Shah, *A Study of Anthropomorphism and Transcendence in the Bible and Quran,* p. 551 ff

1545   Shah, *A Study of Anthropomorphism and Transcendence in the Bible and Quran,* p. 62

1546   George Moore, *Judaism* (Cambridge: Harvard University Press, 1970), vol.1, p.247.

1547   Marshall, *John Locke,* p. 426

1548   Diego Lucci, "Locke and the Trinity," *Studi Lockiani. Ricerche sull'età moderna,* 1 (2020), pp. 9-36, p. 11

1549   Lucci, "Locke and the Trinity," p. 16-17

1550   Lucci, "Locke and the Trinity," p. 31

1551   Marshall, Socinianism and Unitarianism in Stewart ed., *English Philosophy,* p. 175

1552   Locke, *Reasonableness,* chap., 4, 24.

1553   Edwards, *The Socinian Creed: or, A Brief Account Of the Professed Tenents and Doctrines of the Foreign and English Socinians.* London, 1697, p. 127

1554   Marshall, "Locke, Socinianism, "Socinianism" and Unitarianism", p. 170

1555   Locke, *Vindication of The Reasonableness of Christianity, &c. from Mr. Edwards's Reflections,* 1695. In *The Reasonableness of Christianity as Delivered in the Scriptures* edited by Victor Nuovo. Bristol, England: Thoemmes Press, 1997, p. 166

1556   David Wooten, "*John Locke: Socinian or natural law theorist?*" in *Religion, Secularisation and Political Thought,* Thomas Hobbes to J. S. Mill, edited by James E. Crimmins, New York, Routledge, 2013, p. 44

1557   Wootton, *John Locke: Socinian of natural law theorist?,* p. 48

1558   Marshall, "Locke, Socinianism, "Socinianism" and Unitarianism", p. 111

1559   Maurice Wiles, *Archetypal Heresy: Arianism through the Centuries,*

Oxford, Clarendon Press, 1996, p. 73

1560 Nicholas Jolley, Leibniz on Locke and Socinianism, *Journal of the History of Ideas*, Vol. 39, No. 2 (Apr. - Jun., 1978), pp. 233-250, Published by: University of Pennsylvania Press, URL: http://www.jstor.org/stable/2708777, p. 234

1561 Jolley, *Leibniz on Locke and Socinianism,* p. 240

1562 Jolley, *Leibniz on Locke and Socinianism,* 233

1563 Champion, *The Pillars of Priestcraft Shaken,* p.112

1564 Marshall, "Locke, Socinianism, "Socinianism" and Unitarianism", p. 111-112

1565 See Marshall, "Locke, Socinianism, "Socinianism" and Unitarianism", p. 112

1566 See Marshall, "Locke, Socinianism, "Socinianism" and Unitarianism", p. 113

1567 See Marshall, "Locke, Socinianism, "Socinianism" and Unitarianism", p. 141 ff

1568 Marshall, "Locke, Socinianism, "Socinianism" and Unitarianism", p. 143

1569 Marshall, "Locke, Socinianism, "Socinianism" and Unitarianism", p. 143

1570 Marshall, *John Locke,* p.350.

1571 See Marshall, "Locke, Socinianism, "Socinianism" and Unitarianism", p. 111

1572 Wiles, *Archetypal Heresy,* p. 76

1573 Marshall, *John Locke,* p. 390.

1574 Marshall, *John Locke,* p. 413.

1575 Marshall, "Locke, Socinianism, "Socinianism" and Unitarianism", p. 139

1576 Arthur Wainwright, *A Paraphrase and Notes on the Epistles of St. Paul to the Galatians, 1 and 2 Corinthians, Romans, Ephesians,* Oxford, Clarendon Press, 1987, Introduction, pp.37–39.

1577 Locke, *The Works of John Locke,* v. II, p. 517

1578 Locke, *The Works of John Locke,* v. II, p. 563

1579 Locke, *The Works of John Locke,* v. II, p. 563

1580 Locke, *The Works of John Locke,* v. II, p. 563

1581 Locke, *The Works of John Locke*, v. II, p. 582

1582 Marshall, *John Locke*, p. xv

1583 Marshall, "Locke, Socinianism, "Socinianism" and Unitarianism", p. 178

1584 Richard A. Norris, Jr., ed. and trans., *The Christological Controversy* (Philadelphia: Fortress Press, 1980), pp.17–18.

1585 Hilaire Belloc, *The Great Heresies*, New York, Sheed & Ward, n.d., p.33.

1586 Arthur C. McGiffert, *A History of Christian Thought*, New York, Scribner's Sons, 1949, vol.1, p.248.

1587 William Bright, *The Age of Fathers,* New York, AMS Press, 1970, vol.1, p.57.

1588 See details in Shah, *Anthropomorphic Depictions,* p. 327 ff

1589 Quoted in Marshall, *John Locke,* p. 424

1590 Diego Lucci stated that "The anti-Trinitarian arguments in "Adversaria Theologica" endorse the theory that Jesus had only a human nature – a theory consistent with Socinian Christology." Lucci, "Locke and the Trinity," p. 16

1591 Wiles, *Archetypal Heresy,* p. 75; John Marshall noted that Locke paraphrased the famous Trinitarian Pauline text "without avowing a divine nature in Christ… One of Locke's notes expanded that the spirit of holiness meant "that more spiritual part he was in him, which by divine extraction he had immediately from God"." This was "unequivocally an antitrinitarian view." Diego Lucci stated that "The anti-Trinitarian arguments in "Adversaria Theologica" endorse the theory that Jesus had only a human nature – a theory consistent with Socinian Christology." See Marshall, *John Locke,* p. 427 and Lucci, "Locke and the Trinity," p. 16

1592 Linda Edwards, *A Brief Guide to Beliefs: Ideas, Theologies, Mysteries, and Movements,* Louisville, Westminster John Knox Press, 2001, p.327.

1593 "Redeemer and Saviour of the human race, and at the same time entered into an eternally indissoluble union with God, because his love can never cease. Now he has obtained from God, as the reward of his love, the name which is above every name; God has committed to him the Judgment, and invested him with divine dignity, so that now we can call him "God" [born] of the virgin." See Shah, *Anthropomorphic Depictions of God,* p. 322

1594 See Shah, *Anthropomorphic Depictions of God,* p. 320 ff

1595   See J.G.A Pocock, *Barbarism and Religion*, v.1, p.8; John Marshall, *John Locke, Toleration and Early Enlightenment Culture: Religious Intolerance and Arguments for Religious Toleration in Early Modern and "Early Enlightenment" Europe*, Cambridge, Cambridge University Press, 2006, p. 234–35.

1596   See F. Leroy Forlines, *Classical Arminianism: A Theology of Salvation*, Nashville, Randall House, 2011; Robert Picirilli, *Grace, Faith, Free Will: Contrasting Views of Salvation*, Nashville, Randall House, 2002

1597   See Marshall, *John Locke*, p. 333 onward

1598   See Edward Pococke and P. M. Holt, The Study of Arabic Historians in Seventeenth Century England: The Background and the Work of Edward Pococke, *Bulletin of the School of Oriental and African Studies*, University of London, Vol. 19,No. 3 (1957), pp. 444-455

1599   Pugh, *Britain and Islam*, p. 55

1600   Champion, *The Pillars of Priestcraft Shaken*, p.112.

1601   John Locke, *An Essay Concerning Human Understanding*, University Park, Pennsylvania State University Press, 1999, p. 27

1602   Taylor, *A Secular Age*, p. 257

1603   Wootton, *John Locke: Socinian or natural law theorist?*, p. 44

1604   *Socinianism Unmask'd*. A Discourse shewing the Unreasonableness of a Tate Writer's Opinion Concerning the Necessity of only One Article of Christian Faith; A n d of his other Assertions in his late book, Entitled, The Reasonableness of Christianity as delivered in the Scriptures, and in his Vindication of it. London, 1696. P. 4

1605   Locke, *Second Vindication of The Reasonableness of Christianity*, 1697. In *The Reasonableness of Christianity as Delivered in the Scriptures* edited by Victor Nuovo, p. 267.

1606   See Conrad Russell, *Unrevolutionary England*, p. 191ff

1607   "Laud, compressing much of the religious unity case, maintained: 'it is impossible in any Christian commonwealth that the church should melt, and the State stand firm. For there can be no firmness without law; and no laws can be binding, if there be no conscience to obey them: penalty alone could never, never, do it. And no school can teach conscience, but the church of Christ'. Hooker regarded the desire to achieve unity in one true religion as an innate idea: 'the generality of which persuasion argueth that God hath implanted it by nature, to the end it might be a spur to our industry in searching and maintaining that religion, from which as to swerve in the least points is error, so the capital enemies thereof God hateth as his deadly foes, and without repentance, children of endless perdition." Conrad Russell, Unrevolutionar England, p. 191-192

1608   Locke, *Reasonableness,* chap. 14, p. 139

1609   See John Dunn, "Consent in the Political Theory of John Locke", *The Historical Journal,* 1967, 10(2): 153–182. Reprinted in his *Political Obligation in its Historical Context: Essays in Political Theory,* Cambridge: Cambridge University Press, 1980, 29–52; Richard Ashcraft, Richard, *Revolutionary Politics and Locke's Two Treatises of Government,* Princeton, NJ: Princeton University Press, 1986

1610   See *John Locke, Two Treatises of Government,* ed. Peter Laslett, Cambridge, Cambridge University Press, 1988

1611   See Mark Goldie, "John Locke and Anglican Royalism", *Political Studies,* 1983, 31(1): 61–85. doi:10.1111/j.1467-9248.1983.tb01335.x

1612   See Ashcraft, *Revolutionary Politics and Locke's Two Treatises of Government,* p. 436ff

1613   Ashcraft, *Revolutionary Politics and Locke's Two Treatises of Government,* p. 431

1614   Qouted in Laura Perille "A Mirror to Turke": "Turks" and the Making of Early Modern England", Ph. D. thesis submitted to the Department of History at Brown University Providence, Rhode Island, May 2015, p. 292

1615   See *A Dialogue Between the Pope and a Phanatick Concerning Affairs in England,* London, Printed for H. Jones, 1681, 10ff; See Laura Perille *A Mirror to Turke,* p. 292-299

1616   Taylor, *A Secular Age,* p. 160

1617   See Hoff Shannon, "Locke and the Nature of Political Authority", *The Review of Politics,* 2015, 77(1): 1–22. doi:10.1017/S0034670514000813

1618   See Charles Taylor, *A Secular Age,* p. 160 ff

1619   Charles Taylor, *A Secular Age,* p. 160

1620   Henry Hallam, *Introduction to the Literature of Europe: In the Fifteenth, Sixteenth, and Seventeenth Centuries, Oxford,* Oxford University Press, 2007, v.2, p.183.

1621   John Locke, *An Essay Concerning Human Understanding,* p. 540

1622   Taylor, *A Secular Age,* p. 225

1623   See Marshall, *John Locke,* p. xviii

1624   John Marshall, *John Locke, Toleration and Early Enlightenment Culture: Religious Intolerance and Arguments for Religious Toleration in Early Modern and "Early Enlightenment" Europe,* Cambridge, Cambridge University Press, 2006, 393.

1625   Richard Vernon (ed.), *Locke on Toleration* translated by Michael Silverthorne, Cambridge, Cambridge University Press, 2010, p. 3

1626   Richard Vernon (ed.), *Locke on Toleration,* p. 8

1627   Richard Vernon (ed.), *Locke on Toleration,* p. 8

1628   John Locke, *The Works of John Locke,* London, (C. and J. Rivington, 1824), v.5, p.41.Top of Form Bottom of Form

1629   Richard Vernon (ed.), *Locke on Toleration,* p. 5

1630   Locke, *Works,* p.123.

1631   Richard Vernon (ed.), *Locke on Toleration,* p. 11

1632   Richard Vernon (ed.), *Locke on Toleration,* p. 18

1633   Richard Vernon (ed.), *Locke on Toleration,* p. 45

1634   Philip Hamburger, *Separation of Church and State,* Cambridge, Mass., Harvard University Press, 2004, p.54.

1635   John Locke, *Two Treatises of Government and a Letter Concerning Toleration* (Digireads.com Publishing, 2005), p.155.

1636   Locke, *Two Treatises,* p.157

1637   Locke, *Two Treatises, Ibid.*

1638   *Locke on Toleration,* p. xv

1639   Locke, *Two Treatises,* p.168.

1640   Locke, *Two Treatises,* p.156.

1641   See details https://oll.libertyfund.org/titles/locke-a-letter-concerning-toleration-and-other-writings

1642   "There is no compulsion in religion" (2:256).

1643   See Karen M. Bird, The Concession of Toleration, Muslims and the British Enlightenment, *Limina,* Volume 22.2, 2017

1644   Richard Vernon (ed.), *Locke on Toleration* translated by Michael Silverthorne, Cambridge, Cambridge University Press, 2010, p. 14

1645   Vernon (ed.), .), *Locke on Toleration,* p. 154-155

1646   See Marshall, *John Locke,* p. 361 ff; Mark Goldie, "John Locke, Jonas Proast and Religious Toleration 1688-1692" in *The Church of England c. 1688-c, 1833,* p. 143ff

1647   See details in *Discourse In Vindication of the Doctrine of the Trinity: With An Answer to the Date Socinian Objections Against it from Scripture, Antiquity and Reason.* And A Preface concerning the different Explications of the Trinity, and the Tendency of the present Socinian Controversie. London,1697.

1648   Wotton, *John Locke: Socinian or natural law theorist?,* p. 58. Perez Zagorin also observed that Locke had "an obsessive concern with secrecy. Till the end of his life he took extreme pains to conceal his authorship of his Two Treatises of Government and certain other writings. As a rationalist and independent thinker in religion he rejected trinitarianism like his friend Newton, and was sympathetic to Socinian arguments against the divine sonship of Christ. To escape accusations of Socinianism, however, which its opponents identified with infidelity and unbelief, he denied any knowledge of Socinian books, a claim that was certainly untrue. In politics too he was sometimes less than honest. As a supporter of the Whig cause in the reigns of Charles II and James II, an intimate of the proscribed Whig leader Lord Shaftesbury, and a political exile and conspirator before the revolution of 1688, he prevaricated on various occasions concerning his opinions and conduct. Nothing but a keen and justifiable fear of persecution could have induced Locke, who held strong moral principles, to dissemble any of his convictions." Zagorin, *Ways of Lying,* p. 328

1649   See Marshall, *John Locke,* p. 342ff; also see Marshall, "Locke, Socinianism, "Socinianism", and Unitarianism" in *English Philosophy in the Age of Locke* edited by Michael Alexander Stewart, Oxford, Clarendon, 2000, p. 111ff. To Noel Malcolm, Socinianism, Deism, or Quakerism are "the modern equivalent of Islam." The famous German polymath and philosopher G. W. Leibniz and the famous French Orientalist M. V. de La Croze maintained in the seventeenth century that Socinians and Deists were Muslims. See Noel Malcolm, *Useful Enemies,* p. 330 and see Maria Rosa Antognazza, *Leibniz on the Trinity and the Incarnation: Reason and Revelation in the Seventeenth Century,* translated by Gerald Parks, London, Yale University Press, 2007, p. 139; Daniel J. Cook, Leibniz and "Orientalism", Studia Leibnitiana, Bd. 40, H. 2 (2008), pp. 168-190, p.

185; Daniel J. Cook: "Leibniz's Use and Abuse of Judaism and Islam", in: Leibniz and Adam. International Colloquium [...] held in Tel Aviv and Jerusalem, from December 29, 1991 to January 2, 1992, ed. by Marcelo Dascal and Elhanan Yakira, Tel Aviv 1993, pp. 283-297.

1650 See Israel, *Enlightenment Contested,* p. 121ff

1651 Israel, *Enlightenment Contested,* p. 121

1652 See Norman Davies, *God's Playground: A History of Poland,* New York, Columbia University Press, 2005, v. 1, p. 144 ff

1653 Martin Mulsow, *Socinianism, Islam and the Radical Uses of Arabic Scholarship,* Al-Qantara, 31(2), July-December 2010, p.549.

1654 Mulsow, *Socinianism,* pp.559–560.

1655 Israel, *Enlightenment Contested,* p. 131

1656 Champion, *The Pillars of Priestcraft Shaken,* p.106.

1657 Nabil Matar, *Islam in Britain 1558-1685,* p.48. Socinianism and Unitarianism were so closely associated with Islam that all those "who ventured into anti-Trinitarian theologies were viewed as crypto-Muslims: as a result, orthodox theologians started seeing Muslims wherever they saw Unitarians. A high number of Christians and Britons was reported in English writings to have converted to Islam." Matar, *Islam in Britain,* p. 48

1658 Matar, *Islam in Britain,* p. 48

1659 David A. Pailin, *Attitudes to Other Religions: Comparative Religion in Seventeenth and Eighteenth Century Britain,* Manchester, Manchester University Press, 1984, p.270.

1660 Pailin, *Attitudes to Other Religions,* p.270–271.

1661 J. Darby, *Four Treatises concerning the doctrine, discipline and worship of the Mahometans: An Abridgment of the Mahometan Religion: A Defence of the Mahometans, A Treatise of Bobovious, Reflections on Mahometansm and Socinianism* (London: B. Lintott, and E. Sanger, 1712), p.188.

1662 Pailin, *Attitudes,* p.271.

1663 Darby, *Four Treatises concerning the doctrine, p. 188*

1664 Darby, *Four Treatises,* pp.189–190.

1665 Meggittt, *Early Unitarians and Islam,* p. 4

1666 Meggittt, *Early Unitarians and Islam,* p. 5

1667   See Lawrence and Nancy Goldstone, *Out of the Flames*, New York, Broadway Books, 2002.

1668   Michael Allen Gillespie, *The Anti-Trinitarian Origins Of Liberalism*, p. 2 https://www.academia.edu/4175803/The_Anti_Trinitarian_Origins_of_Lliberalism?auto=download

1669   Hugh Trevar-Roper, *The Crisis of the Seventeenth Century: Religion, the Reformation and Social Change*, Indianapolis, Liberty Fund, 2001, p. 190

1670   Trevar-Roper, *The Crisis of the Seventeenth Century*, p. 191

1671   Marian Hillar, *The Case of Michael Servetus (1511-1553) - The Turning Point in the Struggle for Freedom of Conscience*, Lewiston, N.Y; Lampeter, U.K.: Edwin Mellen Press, 1997; Hillar, "From the Polish Socinians to the American Constitution," *A Journal from the Radical Reformation. A Testimony to Biblical Unitarianism*, 1994, no. 3, pp. 44-51. Marian Hillar, "The legacy of Servetus: Humanism and the beginning of change in the social paradigm: From Servetus to Thomas Jefferson," in *Miguel Servet. Luz entre tinieblas*, ed. Sergio Baches Opi, Huesca, Instituto de Estudios Sijenenses, 2006, pp. 109-124. Matteo Gribaldi, *Declaratio. Michael Servetus's Revelation of Jesus Christ the Son of God*, translated by Peter Zerner, edited by Peter Hughes and Peter Zerner, Providence, RI: Blackstone Editions and Michael Servetus Institute, 2010. Marian Hillar, "Laelius and Faustus Socinus Founders of Socinianism: Their Lives and Theology." Part 1. *Journal from the Radical Reformation. Testimony to Biblical Unitarianism*, Vol. 10, No. 2. Winter 2002. pp. 18-38. Marian Hillar, "Laelius and Faustus Socinus Founders of Socinianism: Their Lives and Theology." Part 2. *Journal from the Radical Reformation. Testimony to Biblical Unitarianism*, Vol. 10, No. 3. Spring 2002. pp. 11-24

1672   Peter Hughes, "In the Footsteps of Servetus: Biandrata, David, and the Quran", ' *Journal of Unitarian Universalist History*, Cambridge (Mass.), 31 (2006-2007), p. 57-63

1673   Ritchie, *Children of the Same God*, p. 27ff

1674   Tolan, *Faces of Muhammad*, 113

1675   P. Hughes, 'Servetus and the Quran,' *Journal of Unitarian Universalist History*, Cambridge (Mass.), 30 (2005), pp.55–70.

1676   Hughes, 'Servetus and the Quran', p. 55

1677   Hughes, 'Servetus and the Quran', p. 58

1678   Hughes, 'Servetus and the Quran', p. 61; see also Michael Servetus, The

Two Treatises of Servetus on the Trinity: On the Errors of the Trinity, 7 books, A.D. 1531; Dialogues on the Trinity, 2 books; On the Righteousness of Christ's Kingdom, 4 chapters, A.D. 1532, trans. Earl Morse Wilbur, Cambridge, MA: Harvard University Press, 1932; Michael Servetus, Christianismi restitutio, Vienne en Dauphine, Balthazar Arnollett, 1553

1679   Hughes, 'Servetus and the Quran', p. 66

1680   Hughes, 'Servetus and the Quran', p. 67

1681   Martin A. Larson, *Milton and Servetus: A Study in the Sources of Milton's Theology,* PMLA, Vol. 41, No. 4 (Dec., 1926), pp. 891-934 Published by: Modern Language Association Stable URL: http://www.jstor.org/stable/457453,

1682   Quoted in Tolan, *Faces of Muhammad,* p. 114

1683   Quoted in Martin A. Larson, *Milton and Servetus: A Study in the Sources of Milton's Theology,* PMLA, Vol. 41, No. 4 (Dec., 1926), pp. 891-934 Published by: Modern Language Association Stable URL: http://www.jstor.org/stable/457453,

1684   Tolan, *Faces of Muhammad,* 114

1685   Tolan, *Faces of Muhammad,* p. 115

1686   Tolan, *Faces of Muhammad,* p. 115

1687   See Tolan, *Faces of Muhammad,* p. 115

1688   See Marshall, *John Locke,* pp. 344–346.

1689   See Allen Jayne, *Jefferson's Declaration of Independence: Origins, Philosophy and Theology*, Louisville, Kentucky University Press, 1998, pp.10–18.

1690   Mulsow, *Socinianism,* p.553.

1691   See Klaus Scholder, *The Birth of Modem Critical Theology: Origins and Problems of Biblical Criticism at the Seventeenth Century.* John Bowden, tr. Philadelphia, Trinity Press, 1985, p. 26-46.

1692   Jonathan Israel, *Enlightenment Contested,* p.121.

1693   Tolan, *Faces of Muhammad,* 116

1694   See Tolan, *Faces of Muhammad,* 117

1695   Tolan, *Faces of Muhammad,* 119

1696   Herbert McLachlan, *The Religious Views of Milton, Locke and Newton* Manchester, University of Manchester Press, 1941; David Masson, *The*

Life of John Milton. Gloucester, Mass: Peter Smith, 1965

1697   See details in Abraham Dylan Stoll, *Milton and Monotheism,* Doctoral dissertation submitted to Princeton University department of English, 2000, chapter 4, p. 153 ff; Michael Bauman, *Milton's Arianism.* Frankfurt am Main: Verlag Peter Lang, 1986; John Toland, *The Life of John Milton,* London, 1698. Reprinted in Early Lives of Milton, Helen Darbishire, ed., London, Constable, 1932

1698   Stephen B. Dobronski and John P. Rumrich, "Heretical Milton" in Stephen B. Dobranski and John P. Rumrich eds., *Milton and Heresy,* Cambridge, Cambridge University Press, 1998, p. 1

1699   Nigel, Best, *Biddle and Anti-Trinitarian Controversy,* p. 163

1700   Denis Saurat, *Milton, Man and Thinker* (1925; repr., New York: AMS Press, 1975), p. 117–8, 176–7, 257–8, 274; see also George N. Conklin, *Biblical Criticism and Heresy in Milton,* New York: King's Crown Press, 1949

1701   Stephen B. Dobronski and John P. Rumrich, "Heretical Milton", p. 5

1702   See Stanley Fish, *Surprised By Sin: The Reader in Paradise Lost,* 2nd edition. Cambridge, Mass.: Harvard UP, 1997

1703   See details in David Armitage, Armand Himy and Quentin Skinner Eds., *Milton and Republicanism,* Cambridge, Cambridge University Press, 1998; Sharon Achinstein and Elizabeth Sauer, *Milton and Toleration,* Oxford, Oxford University Press, 2007; also Stephen B. Dobranski and John P. Rumrich eds., *Milton and Heresy*

1704   Stoll, *Milton and Monotheism,* p. 1; for monotheism and it implications see E.g. James Henry Breasted, *The Dawn of Conscience,* NY: Scribner, 1933; Richard Niebhur, *Radical Monotheism and Western Culture,* New York, Harper and Row, 1960

1705   See Michael E. Bauman, *Milton's Arianism: "Following The Way Which Is Called Heresy",* Doctoral Dissertation Submitted To The Department Of Theology At Fordham University New York, 1983 especially p. 48 onward

1706   John P. Rumrich, "Milton's Arianism: why it matters" in Stephen B. Dobranski and John P. Rumrich eds., *Milton and Heresy,* p. 76

1707   See John Rogers, "Milton and the Heretical Priesthood of Christ" in Loewenstein and Marshall eds., *Heresy, Literature and Politics,* p. 203 ff

1708   See Rumrich, "Milton's Arianism: why it matters", p. 81; Russell Hillier, M. *Milton's Messiah: The Son of God in the Works of John Milton,* Oxford, Oxford University Press, 2011

1709   See Maurice Kelley, *Milton and the Trinity,* Huntington Library Quarterly , Aug., 1970, Vol. 33, No. 4, pp. 315- 320, p. 318

1710   Rumrich, "Milton's Arianism: why it matters", p. 80

1711   Quoted in Rumrich, "Milton's Arianism: why it matters", p. 82

1712   Michael Bauman, *Miltons Ariansm.* Frankfurt am Main: Verlag Peter Lang, 1986

1713   See details in Rumrich, "Milton's Arianism: why it matters", p. 82ff

1714   See Rumrich, "Milton's Arianism: why it matters", p. 83ff

1715   Rumrich, "Milton's Arianism: why it matters", p. 84

1716   Quoted in Stoll, *Milton and Monotheism,* p. 154

1717   Quoted in Stoll, *Milton and Monotheism,* p. 154

1718   Maurice Kelley, *This Great Argument.* Princeton: Princeton UP, 1941, p. 86; Michael Bauman, *Milton's Arianism,* p. 262-67

1719   Kelley, *Milton and the Trinity,* p. 319-20

1720   Rumrich, "Milton's Arianism: why it matters", p. 85

1721   John Rogers, *Milton and the Heretical Priesthood of Christ,* p. 213

1722   See Nigel Smith, Best, *Biddle and Anti-Trinitarian Controversy,* p. 176ff

1723   Paul Best, *Mysteries Discovered,* 4th ed. London: 1647,5; see Stoll, *Milton and Monotheism,* p. 35

1724   See James H. Sims, "paradise Lost: Arian Document or Christian Poem?" Etudes Anglaises 20 (1967):337-349; Sister / Miriam Joseph, C.S.C., "Orthodoxy in Paradise Lost," Laval Theologique et Philosophique 8 (1952):243-284; and Joseph W. Morris, *John Milton: a Vindication Specially From the Charge of Arianism* (London: Hamilton, Adams & Co., 1862; reprint ed., Folcroft, Pennsylvania, Folcroft Library Editions, 1970

1725   Kelley, *Milton and the Trinity,* p. 318

1726   Quoted in Stoll, *Milton and Monotheism,* p. 6

1727   Stoll, *Milton and Monotheism,* p. 7; also Abraham Stoll, *Milton and Monotheism.* Pittsburgh: Duquesne University Press, 2009.

1728   See *Milton and the Scriptural Tradition,* ed. James H . Sims and Leland

Ryken, Columbia, University of Missouri Press, 1984

1729 Quoted in Martin A. Larson, *Milton and Servetus: A Study in the Sources of Milton's Theology,* PMLA, Vol. 41, No. 4 (Dec., 1926), pp. 891-934 Published by: Modern Language Association Stable URL: http://www.jstor.org/stable/457453,

1730 See *David Loewenstein Representing Revolution in Milton and His Contemporaries: Religion, Politics and Polemics in Radical Puritanism,* Cambridge, Cambridge University Press, 2004

1731 Stoll, *Milton and Monotheism,* p. 211

1732 J. B. Pittion, *Milton, La Place and Socinianism,* p. 145 Downloaded from http://res.oxfordjournals.org/ at University of Iowa Libraries/Serials Acquisitions on July 19, 2015

1733 Martin A. Larson, *Milton and Servetus: A Study in the Sources of Milton's Theology,* PMLA, Vol. 41, No. 4 (Dec., 1926), pp. 891-934 Published by: Modern Language Association Stable URL: http://www.jstor.org/stable/457453,

1734 Martin A. Larson, *Milton and Servetus: A Study in the Sources of Milton's Theology,* PMLA, Vol. 41, No. 4 (Dec., 1926), pp. 891-934 Published by: Modern Language Association Stable URL: http://www.jstor.org/stable/457453,

1735 Dennis Danielson, "The Fall and Milton's Theodicy" in *The Cambridge Companion to Milton* edited by Dennis Danielson, Cambridge, Cambridge University Press, 2004, P. 150

1736 Danielson, *Companion to Milton,* p. 150

1737 Danielson, *Companion to Milton,* p. 152; see details in William Poole, *Milton and the Idea of Fall,* Cambridge, Cambridge University Press, 2005

1738 Stoll, *Milton and Monotheism,* p.157

1739 See McLachlan, *The Religious Views of Milton, Locke and Newton*

1740 See Jeffrey Einboden, A Qur'aˉnic Milton: From Paradise to al-Firdaws, *Milton Quarterly,* Vol. 43, No. 3, 2009, p. 183; Benedict S. Robinson, *Islam and Early Modern English Literature: The Politics of Romance from Spenser to Milton,* New York, Palgrave Macmillan, 2007.

1741 See Einboden, A Qur'aˉnic Milton, p. 184; [Paradise Lost: *The Epic of the English Poet John Milton*]. Trans. Muhammad 'Inaˉnıˉ. Cairo: Al-Hay'eh al-Masriyyeh al'ammeh lil-Kitaˉb, 1982; Awn, Peter J. *Sa-*

tan's Tragedy and Redemption: Iblis in Sufi Psychology, Leiden, Brill, 1983; Dahiyat, Eid Abdallah. "Aspects of John Milton in Arabic." *Milton Quarterly* 18 (1984): 5-13 also *John Milton and the Arab-Islamic Culture*, Amman, Shukayr and Akasheh, 1987

1742　David Currell, *Meditations on Mediation: John Milton and the Muslim Jesus*, English Studies, 2015, 96:1, 44-64, DOI: 10.1080/0013838X.2014.964563, p. 52

1743　See Andrew Lake, *The First Protestants in the Arab World: The contribution to Christian Mission of the English Aleppo Chaplains 1597-1782*

1744　Gerald MacLean, *Milton, Islam and the Ottomans" in Milton and Toleration*, p. 291

1745　David Currell, *Meditations on Mediation*, p. 52-53

1746　See David Currell, *Meditations on Mediation*, p. 53

1747　David Currell, *Meditations on Mediation*, p. 54-55

1748　David Currell, *Meditations on Mediation*, p. 55

1749　David Currell, *Meditations on Mediation*, p. 55

1750　See Michael Lieb, *Theological Milton: Deity, Discourse and Heresy in the Miltonic Canon*, Pittsburgh, Duquesne University Press, 2006., p. 104

1751　David Currell, *Meditations on Mediation*, p. 57

1752　David Currell, *Meditations on Mediation*, p. 59-60

1753　See Tarif Khalidi, ed. and trans., *The Muslim Jesus: Sayings and Stories in Islamic Literature,* Cambridge, MA: Harvard University Press, 2001; Neal Robinson, "Jesus in the Quran, the Historical Jesus, and the Myth of God Incarnate." In *Wilderness: Essays in Honour of Frances Young,* edited by R. S. Sugirtharajah, London, Continuum, 2005

1754　David Currell, *Meditations on Mediation*, p. 62

1755　Quoted in Eid Abdallah Dahiyat, *John Milton and the Arab-Islamic Culture*, p. 68

1756　Gerald MacLean, *Milton, Islam and the Ottomans" in Milton and Toleration*, p. 298

1757　Stephen D. Snobelen, Isaac Newton, heretic: the strategies of a Nicodemite, *British journal for the history of science (BJHS)*, 1999, 32, 381±419, p. 402; Rob Iliffe, *Priest of Nature*, p. 4

1758　See *Early Voyages and Travels in Levant*, p. 271

1759   See *Sir Isaac Newton, Thirteen Letters from Sir Isaac Newton to J. Covel*, D.D. [With a facsimile. Edited by D. Turner.] https://books.google.com/books/about/Thirteen_Letters_from_Sir_Isaac_Newton_t.html?id=Y5lcAAAAcAAJ

1760   See "Newton: The Making of a Politician"

1761   See Rob Iliffe, "The Religion of Isaac Newton" in *Cambridge Companion to Newton* edited by Rob Iliffe and George E. Smith, Cambridge, Cambridge University Press, 2016, p. 485ff

1762   Rob Iliffe, *Priest of Nature,* p. 6

1763   Rob Iliffe, *Priest of Nature,* p. 4

1764   See Snobelen, *Isaac Newton; heretic,* p. 388

1765   See Rob Iliffe, "Newton, God, and the Mathematics of the Two Books." In *Mathematicians and Their Gods.* Edited by S. Lawrence and M. McCartney, 121–55. Oxford, Oxford University Press, 2015

1766   Snobelen, *Isaac Newton: Heretic,* p. 409

1767   See Frank Manuel, *The Religion of Isaac Newton,* Oxford, Oxford University Press, 1974, p. 8-10

1768   S. Richard Westfall, *Never at Rest: The Life of Isaac Newton.* Cambridge, Cambridge University Press, 1994, p. 310

1769   Wiles, *Archetypal Heresy,* p. 79

1770   See Westfall, *Never at Rest, p. 311 onward*

1771   Iliffe, *Priest of Nature,* p. 11

1772   Iliffe, *Priest of Nature,* p. 11

1773   Westfall, *Never at Rest, p. 312*

1774   Wiles, *Archetypal Heresy,* p. 92

1775   See details about Newton's heretical views in James Gleick, *Isaac Newton,* New York, Pantheon Books, 2003, chapter 10

1776   Westfall, *Never at Rest, p. 31*

1777   Wiles, *Archetypal Heresy,* p. 92

1778   Westfall, *Never at Rest, p. 314*

1779   Westfall, *Never at Rest, p. 315*

1780   See details in Iliffe, *Priest of Nature,* p. 138ff

1781   Westfall, *Never at Rest, p. 354*

1782   Iliffe, *Priest of Nature,* p. 141

1783   Westfall, *Never at Rest, p. 315*

1784   Wiles, *Archetypal Heresy,* p. 79

1785   See Shah, *Anthropomorphic Depictions of God,* p. 309 ff

1786   Shah, *Anthropomorphic Depictions of God,* p. 309

1787   Shah, *Anthropomorphic Depictions of God,* p. 309

1788   Richard A. Norris, Jr., ed. and trans., *The Christological Controversy,* Philadelphia, Fortress Press, 1980, p.7.

1789   Quoted from Arthur C. McGiffert, *A History of Christian Thought,* New York, Charles Scribner's Sons, 1960, vol.1, p.113.

1790   Alois Grillmeier, *Christ in Christian Tradition,* John Bowden, trans., Atlanta, John Knox Press, 1975, vol.1, p.110.

1791   John N. D. Kelly, *Early Christian Doctrines,* New York, Harper and Brothers, 1958, pp.100–01.

1792   Wiles, *Archetypal Heresy,* p. 80

1793   Louis Trenchard More, *Isaac Newton: A Biography 1642-1727,* New York, Charles Scribner's Sons, 1934, p. 642-43

1794   More, *Newton,* p. 643

1795   More, *Newton,* p. 644

1796   More, *Newton,* p. 644

1797   Quoted from Wiles, *Archetypal Heresy,* p. 88

1798   Wiles, *Archetypal Heresy,* p. 81

1799   Quoted from Thomas C. Pfizenmaier, *Was Isaac Newton an Arian?,* *Journal of the History of Ideas,* Vol. 58, No. 1 (Jan., 1997), pp. 57-80, University of Pennsylvania Press, URL: http://www.jstor.org/stable/3653988; p. 71; Newton, Yahuda MS 15.7, fol. 154r;

1800   Pfizenmaier, *Was Isaac Newton an Arian?,* p. 72

1801   Pfizenmaier, *Was Isaac Newton an Arian?,* p. 72; Yahuda MS. 15, fol. 46, cf., fol. 68

1802   Wiles, *Archetypal Heresy,* p. 82

1803   Wiles, *Archetypal Heresy,* p. 83

1804 See Scott Mandelbrote, "Eighteenth-Century Reactions to Newton's Anti-Trinitarianism." In *Newton and Newtonianism: New Studies,* edited by J. Force and S. Hutton, 93–111, London, Springer, 2004

1805 See Iliffe, *Priest of Nature,* p. 142

1806 See Iliffe, *Priest of Nature,* p. 367

1807 See Iliffe, *Priest of Nature,* p. 217

1808 Quoted in Wiles, *Archetypal Heresy,* p. 83

1809 Wiles, *Archetypal Heresy,* p. 83

1810 Wiles, *Archetypal Heresy,* p. 84

1811 See Iliffe, *Priest of Nature,* p. 218

1812 Wiles, *Archetypal Heresy,* p. 87

1813 See John Hick, *The Metaphor of God Incarnate,* London, S.C.M. Press, 1993; John Hick, *God and the Universe of Faiths,* London, Macmillan, 1973; John Hick, "A Remonstrance in Concluding," *Jesus in History and Myth,* R. J. Hoffmann, G. A. Larue, eds., Buffalo, Prometheus Books, 1986; John Hick, ed., *The Myth of God Incarnate,* Philadelphia, The Westminster Press, 1977

1814 Wiles, *Archetypal Heresy,* p. 89

1815 *Sir Isaac Newton's Mathematical Principles of Natural Philosophy and his System of the World,* Translated into English by Andrew Motte in 1729, the translations revised by Aorian Cajori, 2 vols., Berkeley and Los Angeles, University of California Press, 1934, v.2, p. 544

1816 *Sir Isaac Newton's Mathematical Principles of Natural Philosophy,* p. 545

1817 See details in Shah, *Anthropomorphic Depictions of God,* chapter 4, p. 399 ff

1818 See Ian Richard Netton, *Allah Transcendent: Studies in the Structure and Semiotics of Islamic Philosophy, Theology and Cosmology,* New York, Routledge, 1995; Duncan B. Macdonald, *Development of Muslim Theology, Jurisprudence and Constitutional Theory,* Beirut, Khayats, 1965; A. K. Kazi, J. G. Flynn, trans., *Muslim Sects and Divisions: The Section on Muslim Sects in Kitab al-Milal wa al-Nihal by Shahrastani,* London, Kegan Paul International, 1984; H. A. Wolfson, *The Philosophy of the Kalam,* Cambridge, Mass., Harvard University Press, 1976; William M. Watt, *Early Islam: Collected Articles,* Edinburgh, Edinburgh University Press, 1990; Majid Fakhry, *Averroes: His Life, Works and Influence,* Oxford, Oneworld, 2001;

1819   Shams Inati, *Ibn Sina's Remarks and Admonitions, Physics and Metaphysics, An Analysis and Annotated Translation,* New York, Columbia University Press, 2014, p. 122

1820   Shams Inati, "Ibn Sina" in S. H. Nasr and Oliver Leaman, eds., *History of Islamic Philosophy,* New York, Routledge, 1996, P. 446

1821   See Shams Inati, *Ibn Sina's Remarks and Admonitions, Physics and Metaphysics, An Analysis and Annotated Translation,* New York, Columbia University Press, 2014, p. 123

1822   See details in Nasr and Leaman, eds., *History of Islamic Philosophy,* p. 446 onward

1823   Inati, *Ibn Sina's Remarks,* p. 124

1824   Inati, *Ibn Sina's Remarks,* p. 124

1825   See details in Matt Goldish, *Judaism in the Theology of Sir Isaac Newton,* Dordrecht, Springer Science+Business Media, 1998, p. 4ff

1826   James E. Force and Richard H. Popkin eds., *Essays on the Context, Nature, and Influence of Isaac Newton's Theology,* London, Kluwer Academic Publishers, 1990, p. 1

1827   James E. Force and Richard H. Popkin eds., *Essays on the Context, Nature, and Influence of Isaac Newton's Theology,* p. 1

1828   James E. Force and Richard H. Popkin eds., Essays on the Context, Nature, and Influence of Isaac Newton's Theology, p. 1-2

1829   Matt Goldish notes that Newton was neither interested in living Jews nor in Jewish theology. "Newton, for example, appealed to *Maimonides'Mishneh Torah* for historical information on the Temple, but he did not show interest in Maimonides' *Guide of the Perplexed* for theological ideas. He used the ancient Jewish Christians as a central example for ecclesiastical serenity and strife, but he made no effort to meet and understand contemporary Jewish Jews, so lately arrived in England. Newton's behavior was typical for his time, then-using Jews and their literature in pragmatic and expedient ways. He was not so much a student of Jewish history and ideas as a consumer of them, picking what fit his needs and ignoring the rest." *Judaism in the Theology of Sir Isaac Newton,* p. 163

1830   Majid Fakhry, *Averroes: His Life, Works and Influence,* Oxford, Oneworld, 2001, p. 132

1831   Arthur Hyman, "Jewish Philosophy in the Islamic World," in Nasr and Leaman eds., *History of Islamic Philosophy,* p. 1200

1832   Nasr and Leaman eds., *History of Islamic Philosophy,* p. 1191

1833   Nasr and Leaman eds., *History of Islamic Philosophy,* P. 1193

1834   Steven M. Wesserstrom, "The Islamic Social and Cultural Context" in *History of Jewish Philosophy,* edited by Daniel H. Frank and O. Leaman, New York, Routledge, 2004, p. 73

1835   See Mauro Zonta, The Relationship of European Jewish Philosophy to Islamic and Christian Philosophies in the Late Middle Ages, *Jewish Studies Quarterly,* Vol. 7, No. 2 (2000), pp. 127-140

1836   Fakhry, *Averroes,* p. 132

1837   Fakhry, *Averroes,* p. 132

1838   Nasr and Leaman eds., *History of Islamic Philosophy,* p. 1298

1839   Zonta, Mauro, "Influence of Arabic and Islamic Philosophy on Judaic Thought", *The Stanford Encyclopedia of Philosophy* (Spring 2011 Edition), Edward N. Zalta (ed.), URL = <http://plato.stanford.edu/archives/spr2011/entries/arabic-islamic-judaic/>.

1840   Zonta, Mauro, "Influence of Arabic and Islamic Philosophy on Judaic Thought", *The Stanford Encyclopedia of Philosophy* (Spring 2011 Edition), Edward N. Zalta (ed.), URL = <http://plato.stanford.edu/archives/spr2011/entries/arabic-islamic-judaic/>.

1841   Zonta, Mauro, "Influence of Arabic and Islamic Philosophy on Judaic Thought", *The Stanford Encyclopedia of Philosophy* (Spring 2011 Edition), Edward N. Zalta (ed.), URL = <http://plato.stanford.edu/archives/spr2011/entries/arabic-islamic-judaic/>.

1842   Fergus Kerr, *Thomas Aquinas: A Very Short Introduction,* Oxford, Oxford University Press, 2009

1843   Westfall, *Never at Rest, p. 318*

1844   Westfall, *Never at Rest, p. 318-19*

1845   Westfall, *Never at Rest, p. 318?*

1846   Westfall, *Never at Rest, p. 323-24*

1847   Westfall, *Never at Rest, p. 324*

1848   Westfall, *Never at Rest, p. 330*

1849   Snobelen, *Isaac Newton: Heretic*, p. 407.. "The assumption that he was restoring some lost and corrupted tradition lay at the heart of Newton's aim to recover a pristine non- Trinitarian Christianity… Newton implicitly placed himself in a line of restorers of the true Noachid religion that included Moses and Christ himself." Rob Iliffe and George E. Smith eds., *Cambridge Companion to Newton,* Cambridge, Cambridge University Press, 2016, p. 501

1850   See Westfall, *Never at Rest, p. 332*

1851   Westfall, *Never at Rest, p. 355-56*

1852   Snobelen, *Isaac Newton; heretic,* p. 388

1853   This report is cited in German in J. Edleston, *Correspondence of Sir Isaac Newton and Professor Cotes*, London, 1850, p. lxxx., https://archive.org/details/correspondenceof00newtrich

1854   Westfall, *Never at Rest, p. 489*

1855   See Westfall, *Never at Rest, p. 491 onward*

1856   See Westfall, *Never at Rest, p. 491 onward*

1857   Westfall, *Never at Rest, p. 821*

1858   Westfall, *Never at Rest, p. 821*

1859   Westfall, *Never at Rest, p. 821*

1860   Westfall, *Never at Rest, p. 822*

1861   Westfall, *Never at Rest, p. 821*

1862   Westfall, *Never at Rest, p. 824*

1863   Westfall, *Never at Rest, p. 825*

1864   Westfall, *Never at Rest, p. 826*

1865   Westfall, *Never at Rest, p. 826-27*

1866   Westfall, *Never at Rest, p. 827*

1867   See Gale E. Christianson, *Isaac Newton,* Oxford, Oxford University Press, 2005, p. 83

1868   Sobelen, *Isaac Newton: heretic,* p. 381

1869   Westfall, *Never at Rest, p. 828*

1870   See Snobele, *Isaac Newton,* p. 412-14

1871   Westfall, *Never at Rest, p. 829*

1872 See this chapter in Martin Mulsow and John Rohls eds., *Socinianism and Arminianism: Antitrinitarians, Calvinists and Cultural Exchange in Seventeenth-Century Europe,* Amsterdam, Brills, 2005

1873 Stephen David Snobelen, *Isaac Newton and Socinianism: Associations with a Greater Heresy* (2003), www.isaac-newton.org.

1874 Snobelen, *Isaac Newton and Socinianism, p. 1*

1875 Snobelen, *Isaac Newton and Socinianism, p. 4*

1876 Snobelen, *Isaac Newton and Socinianism, p. 15*

1877 Quoted from Martin Mulsow and John Rohls eds., *Socinianism and Arminianism,* p. 263

1878 Snobelen, *Isaac Newton, Socinianism, and the One Supreme Giod,* in Martin Mulsow and Jan Rohls ed. *Socinianism and Arminianism: Antitrinitarians, Calvinists and Cultural Exchange in Seventeenth-Century Europe,* Leiden, Brills, 2005, *p.266*

1879 See Snobelen, *Isaac Newton in Mulsow and Rohls ed. Socinianism and Arminianism, p.269*

1880 Snobelen, *Isaac Newton in Mulsow and Rohls ed. Socinianism and Arminianism, p.286*

1881 Snobelen, *Isaac Newton in Mulsow and Rohls ed. Socinianism and Arminianism, p. 284*

1882 Westfall, *Never at Rest, p. 593*

1883 Wiles, *Archetypal Heresy,* p. 77

1884 See details in Robert D. Cornwall and William Gobson eds., *Religion, Politics and Dissent 1660-1832: Essay in Honour of James E. Bradley,* Burlington, Ashgate, 2010, Chapter 1, p. 17 ff

1885 See Cornwall and William Gobson eds., *Relgion, Politics and Dissent 1660-1832,* p. 17 ff

1886 Westfall, *Never at Rest, p. 929-30*

1887 Snobelen, *Isaac Newton in Mulsow and Rohls ed. Socinianism and Arminianism, p.287*

1888 See details in Wiles, *Archetypal Heresy,* p. 78 ff and Thomas C. Pfizenmaier, *Was Isaac Newton an Arian?,* p. 57 onward; See Sir David Brewster, *Memoirs of the Life, Writings and Discoveries of Sir Isaac Newton* (Edinburgh, 1855), ii. 340.

1889   Wiles, *Archetypal Heresy,* p. 77

1890   See D. O. Thomas, *Enlightenment and Dissent,* Aberystwyth, Cambrian Printers, 2000, p. 154 ff; Richard Popkin's Introduction in James Force, *William Whiston, Honest Newtonian* (Cambridge: 1985), p. xiv, and Force likewise in ch. 4; Stephen Snobelen, 'Isaac Newton, Heretic: The Strategies of a Nicodemite' in *The British Journal for the History of Science,* 32/4 (December, 1999), p. 395

1891   See various articles on https://isaac-newton.org/articles/

1892   See https://isaacnewton.ca/newtons-general-scholium/

1893   See "John Edwards' comments on and translation from *Newton's General Scholium in Some remarks on Clarke's last papers* (1714)": https://isaacnewton.ca/newtons-general-scholium/

1894   Clark, *English Society,* p. 319-320

1895   See Andrea Greenwood and Mark W. Harris, *An Introduction to the Unitarian and Universalists Traditions,* Cambridge, Cambridge University Press, 2011, chapter 3, p. 32 ff

1896   See John Seed, "'A Set of Men Powerful Enough in Many Things': Rational Dissent and Political Opposition, 1770–1790," in *Enlightenment and Religion: Rational Dissent in Eighteenth-Century Britain,* ed. Knud Haakonssen (Cambridge: Cambridge University Press, 1996), and "Gentlemen Dissenters: The Social and Political Meanings of Rational Dissent in the 1770s and 1780s," *Historical Journal* 28, no. 2 (1985): 299–325.

1897   Pocock, *Barbarism and Religion,* v.1, p. 297

1898   See *Life of Mr. Thomas Firmin, late Citizen of London* (London, 1698), including *Sermon on his death,* and *An Account of Mr. Firmin's Religion;* Alexander Gordon, 'Thomas Firmin, Unitarian Philanthropist,' in his *Addresses Biographical and Historical* (London, 1922); Harold W. Stephenson, 'A Seventeenth Century Philanthropist,' *U. H. S.* (London), vol. vi; Wallace, *Antitrin.,* iii, 272–389.

1899   Champion, *The Pillars of Priestcraft Shaken,* p.107.

1900   See *The Church of England, c. 1689 – c. 1833,* ed. John Walsh, Colin Haydon, and Stephen Taylor (Cambridge: Cambridge University Press, 1993), chapter 9, p. 209 ff

1901   Robert Wallace, *Antitrinitarian Biography: or Sketches of the Lives and Writings of Distinguished Antitrinitarians, London, E. T. Whitefield, 1850,* p.275.

1902   Pocock, *Barbarism and Religion,* v.1, p. 297

1903   See G. M. Trevelyan, *History of England,* London, Longmans, Green and Co., 1926, 474, 615; W. E. H. Lecky, *A History of England in the 18th Century* 2nd ed., 8 vols., London, Longmans, Green and Co., 1879-1890, 1:177-81; 187-93; W. E. H. Lecky, *Democracy and Liberty* 2nd ed. 2 vols., London, Longmans, Green, and Co., 1896, 1: 434-46, 438, 442.

1904   Tolan, *Faces of Muhammd,* p. 147-148

1905   Tolan, *Faces of Muhammd,* p. 148

1906   Marshall, *John Locke,* p. 391-92

1907   Marshall, *Locke,* p. 389

1908   Marshall, *Locke,* 390

1909   Marshall, *Locke,* p. 391

1910   Wiles, *Archetypal Heresy,* p. 67

1911   Philip Dixon, *Nice and Hot,* p. 106

1912   Wiles, *Archetypal Heresy,* p. 67

1913   S. Nye, *Considerations on the Explication of the Doctrine of the Trinity by Dr Wallis, Dr Sherlock, Dr S—th, Dr Cudworth and Dr Hooker* (London, 1693), p. 7

1914   Philip Dixon, *Nice and Hot Disputes: The Doctrine of the Trinity in the Seventeenth Century,* London, T & T Clark, 2003, p. 106

1915   Champion, *The Pillars of Priestcraft Shaken,*p. 109

1916   Champion, *The Pillars of Priestcraft Shaken,* p.109.

1917   Champion, *The Pillars of Priestcraft Shaken,* p.109-110

1918   Champion, *The Pillars of Priestcraft Shaken,* p.110.

1919   Champion, *The Pillars of Priestcraft Shaken,* p.110.

1920   See Marshall, *Locke,* p. 394ff

1921   See Marshall, *Locke,* p. p. 407ff

1922   Dixon, *Nice and Hot,* p. 108

1923   See Earl Morse Wilbur, *A History of Unitarianism: In Transylvania, England and America Volume II,* Boston, Beacon Press, 1945, chapter 12

1924   Arthur Bury, *The Naked Gospel,* Internet archive, from Princeton Theological Seminary, http://ia700306.us.archive.org/30/items/nakedgospeldisco11bury/nakedgospeldisco11bury.pdf

1925   Champion, *The Pillars of Priestcraft Shaken*, p.8

1926   Bury, *The Naked Gospel*, p.64.

1927   Bury, *The Naked Gospel*, Preface.

1928   Champion, *Pillars*, p. 108

1929   Champion, *Pillars*, p. 108

1930   Justin J. Meggittt, *Early Unitarians and Islam*, Cambridge repository
       https://www.repository.cam.ac.uk/bitstream/handle/1810/275523/
       Meggittt%20%20Early%20Unitarians%20and%20Islam.pdf?se-
       quence=1%26isAllowed=y, p. 3

1931   Champion, *Pillars*, p. 109

1932   Garcia, *Islam and English Enlightenment*, p. 162

1933   Champion, *Pillars*, p. 109

1934   William Freke, *Vindication of the Unitarians, against the late reverend
       author on the Trinity in a letter* (London, 1690, p. 11; also see Wiles,
       Archetypal Heresy, p. 68

1935   Freke, *Vindication*, p. 23

1936   Freke, *Vindication*, p. 23

1937   Freke, *Vindication*, p. 24

1938   Freke, *Vindication*, p. 25

1939   Freke, *Vindication*, p. 25

1940   Freke, *Vindication*, p. 26

1941   Freke, *Vindication*, p. 26

1942   Freke, *Vindication*, p. 27

1943   Freke, *Vindication*, p. 8

1944   Meggittt, *Early Unitarians and Islam*, p. 5

1945   Meggittt, *Early Unitarians and Islam*, p. 4

1946   Israel, *Radical Enlightenment*, p. 12

1947   Champion, *The Pillars of Priestcraft Shaken*, p.110

1948   MacLean and Matar, *Britain and Islamic World*, p. 19

1949   MacLean and Matar, *Britain and Islamic World,* p. 222

1950   See details in Matar, *Britain and Barbary,* p. 160

1951   Matar, *Britain and Barbary,* p. 160

1952   Nabil Matar, *Britain and Barbary,* p. 158-59

1953   Meggitt, *Early Unitarians and Islam,* p. 1

1954   Justin J. Meggittt, 'Nöel Aubert de Versé'. In *Christian-Muslim Relations. A Bibliographical History. Volume 13. Western Europe (1700-1800)*, edited by David Thomas and John A. Chesworth, 75–76. Leiden: Brill, 2019, p. 75

1955   Meggittt, *'Nöel Aubert de Versé'*, p. 75

1956   Meggittt, *'Nöel Aubert de Versé'*, p. 75

1957   Meggittt, 'Epistle Dedicatory'. In *Christian-Muslim Relations. A Bibliographical History. Volume 13. Western Europe (1700-1800)*, edited by David Thomas and John A. Chesworth, 77–85. Leiden: Brill, 2019, p. 79

1958   Lambeth Palace Library, MSS 673, fol. 4, quoted in Matar, *Britain and Barbary,* p. 159

1959   Meggittt, *'Epistle Dedicatory'*, p. 79-80

1960   Champion, *The Pillars of Priestcraft Shaken,* p.111; see more details in Meggittt, 'Epistle Dedicatory', p. 80-81

1961   Meggittt, *'Epistle Dedicatory'*, p. 81

1962   Meggittt, *'Epistle Dedicatory'*, p. 81

1963   Meggittt, *Early Unitarians and Islam,* p. 5

1964   Meggittt, *'Epistle Dedicatory'*, p. 83

1965   Meggittt, *Early Unitarians and Islam,* p. 6

1966   Meggittt, *'Epistle Dedicatory'*, p. 82

1967   Meggittt, *'Epistle Dedicatory'*, p. 82

1968   Meggittt, *Early Unitarians and Islam,* p. 4

1969   Meggittt, *Early Unitarians and Islam,* p. 4

1970   Champion, *The Pillars of Priestcraft Shaken,* p.111

1971   Champion, *The Pillars of Priestcraft Shaken,* p.112.

1972   Champion, *The Pillars of Priestcraft Shaken,* p.113

1973 Champion, *The Pillars of Priestcraft Shaken,* p.113

1974 Champion, *The Pillars of Priestcraft Shaken,* p.113

1975 Champion, *The Pillars of Priestcraft Shaken,* p.114

1976 Champion, *The Pillars of Priestcraft Shaken,* p.114

1977 See Brent S. Sirota. The Trinitarian Crisis in Church and State: Religious Controversy and the Making of the Postrevolutionary Church of England, 1687–1702. *Journal of British Studies,* 2013, 52, pp 26-54 doi:10.1017/ jbr.2012.7; Philip Dixon, *Nice and Hot Disputes: The Doctrine of the Trinity in the Seventeenth Century* especially chapter 3, p. 66 ff

1978 The bibliography of the controversy in John Hunt, *Religious Thought in England from the Reformation to the End of Last Century: A Contribution to the History of Theology,* 3 vols. (London, 1870–71), 2:273–78, lists nearly seventy different pamphlets published between 1689 and 1699.

1979 Sirota. *The Trinitarian Crisis in Church and State,* p. 27

1980 See Christopher Hill, *The World Turned Upside-down,* p. 15 ff

1981 Sirota. *The Trinitarian Crisis in Church and State,* p. 26

1982 See H. J. Maclachlan, *Socinianism in Seventeenth-Century England,* Oxford, 1951; Gerard Reedy, *The Bible and Reason: Anglicans and Scripture in Late Seventeenth-Century England,* Philadelphia, University of Pennsylvania Press 1985, 119–20; on the use of the term by Catholics, see Martin Greig, "Heresy Hunt: Gilbert Burnet and the Convocation Controversy of 1701," *Historical Journal* 37, no. 3 (1994): 569–92.

1983 Sirota. *The Trinitarian Crisis in Church and State,* p. 40

1984 Champion, *The Pillars of Priestcraft Shaken,* p.114

1985 Champion, *The Pillars of Priestcraft Shaken,* p.115; see also Kecia Ali, The Lives of Muhammad, p. 36

1986 Tolan, *Faces of Muhammad,* p. 133

1987 Champion, *The Pillars of Priestcraft Shaken,* p.116

1988 Champion, *The Pillars of Priestcraft Shaken,* p.117

1989 Champion, *The Pillars of Priestcraft Shaken,* p.117

1990 Champion, *The Pillars of Priestcraft Shaken,* p.118

1991 Champion, *The Pillars of Priestcraft Shaken,* p.118

1992 Champion, *The Pillars of Priestcraft Shaken,* p.119

1993   Champion, *The Pillars of Priestcraft Shaken,* p.119

1994   Champion, *The Pillars of Priestcraft Shaken,* p.120

1995   Meggittt, *'Epistle Dedicatory',* p. 83

1996   See David Thomas and John Chesworth eds., *Muslim Christian Relations: A Biographical History,* v. 13, Western Europe, 1700-1800, Leiden, Brills, 2019, p. 326-26

1997   Champion, *The Pillars of Priestcraft Shaken,* p.120

1998   Garcia, *Islam and English Enlightenment,* p. xi

1999   Garcia, *Islam and English Enlightenment,* p. xi

2000   Garcia, *Islam and English Enlightenment,* p. 1

2001   Garcia, *Islam and English Enlightenment,* p. 3

2002   Garcia, *Islam and English Enlightenment,* p. 3

2003   Garcia, *Islam and English Enlightenment,* p. 4-5

2004   Garcia, *Islam and English Enlightenment,* p. 5

2005   Garcia, *Islam and English Enlightenment,* p. 5-6

2006   Garcia, *Islam and English Enlightenment,* p. 6

2007   Garcia, *Islam and English Enlightenment,* p. 7

2008   Garcia, *Islam and English Enlightenment,* p. 11

2009   Garcia, *Islam and English Enlightenment,* p. 11-12

2010   Garcia, *Islam and English Enlightenment,* p. 12

2011   See Hazard, *The Crises of the Europen Mind,* p. 253 ff

2012   See W. Bernard Peach & D. O. Thomas ed., *The correspondence of Richard Price,* 3 vols., Durham, NC & Cardiff, 1983-1994; D O Thomas ed., *Price: political writings,* Cambridge, Cambridge University Press, 1991

2013   Garcia, *Islam and English Enlightenment,* p. 165

2014   Garcia, *Islam and English Enlightenment,* p. 165

2015   Garcia, *Islam and English Enlightenment,* p. 165-66

2016   Garcia, *Islam and English Enlightenment,* p. 166

2017   Garcia, *Islam and English Enlightenment,* p. 168

2018   Meggitt, *Epistle Dedicatory',* p. 84

2019   Meggitt, *Epistle Dedicatory'*, p. 84-85

2020   Garcia, *Islam and English Enlightenment*, p. 168

Bibliography

Abbott, George F. *Under the Turk at Constantinople: A Record of Sir John Finch's Embassy*, 1674–1681, (London, MacMillan, 1920)

Abdul Rauf, *Defining Islamic Statehood, Measuring and Indexing Contemporary Muslim States* (London, Palgrave Macmillan, 2015).

Abdul Rauf, Feisal, *What is Right With Islam* (New York, HarperCollins, 2004).

Abraham, Lyndy, *Marvell and Alchemy Brookfield* (VT, Aldershot, 1990).

Abu Lughod, Janet, *Before European Hegemony: The World System A. D. 1250-1350* (Oxford, Oxford University Press, 1989).

Abu-Lughod, Janet L., *Before European Hegemony* (Oxford, Oxford University Press, 1989).

Acemoglu, Daron, Johnson, Simon and Robinson, James, *The Rise of Europe: Atlantic Trade, Institutional Change, and Economic Growth*, The American Economic Review, Vol. 95, No. 3 (Jun., 2005).

Achinstein, Sharon and Sauer, Elizabeth, *Milton and Toleration*, (Oxford, Oxford University Press, 2007).

Adams, G., *The Huguenots and French Opinion*, 1685-1787. The Enlightenment Debate on Toleration, (Waterloo, Ontario 1991).

ADAMSON, JOHN: *The Noble Revolt: The Overthrow of Charles I.* (London: Weidenfeld & Nicolson, 2007).

Adamson, Peter and Taylor, Richard C. (eds.)., *The Cambridge Companion to Arabic Philosophy*, (Cambridge, Cambridge University Press, 2006).

Adamson, Peter and Taylor, Richard eds., *Cambridge Companion to Arabic Philosophy* (Cambridge, Cambridge University Press, 2005).

Afsaruddin, Asma, and Zahniser, A. H. Mathias (eds.)., *Humanism Culture and Language in the Near East, Winona Lake* (Indiana, Eisenbrauns, 1997).

Agoston, Gabor and Master, Bruce, (eds.)., *Encyclopedia of Ottoman Empire* (New York, Facts On File, 2009).

Ágoston, Gábor, *Guns for the Sultan: Military Power and the Weapons Industry in the*

Ottoman Empire (Cambridge, Cambridge University Press, 2005).

Ahmad, Anis, *Islam's political order: the model, deviations and Muslim response: al-Khilāfah wa al-mulūkīyah* (Islamabad, Institute of Policy Studies, 2018).

Al Hakim, Abu Abdullah, *al Mustadrak a'la al Sahihayn* (Beirut, al-Kutub al-'Ilmiyyah, 1990).

Alam, Muzaffar and Subrahmanyam, Sanjay, *Indo-Persian Travels in the Age of Discoveries, 1400–1800* (Cambridge, Cambridge University Press, 2007).

Al-Faruqi, Ismail R., al-Faruqi, Lois L., *The Cultural Atlas of Islam* (New York: Macmillan Publishing Company, 1986).

Al-Faruqi, Ismail R., *Al-Tawhid: Its Implications for Thought and Life*, 2nd edn, (Virginia: International Institute of Islamic Thought, 1992).

Al-Ghazali, *The Incoherence of the Philosophers*, translated by Michael E. Marmura (Provo, Utah, Brigham Young University Press, 2002).

Al-Hibri, Azizah Y., *Islam and American Constitutional Law: Borrowing Possibilities or a History of Borrowing*, University of Pennsylvania Journal of Constitutional Law 1.3 (1999).

Al-Rodhan, N. R. F. (ed.)., *The Role of the Arab-Islamic World in the Rise of the West* (London, Palgrave Macmillan, 2012).

Ambrose, Gwilym Prichard, *The Levant Company mainly from 1640–1753* (B. Litt dissertation, University of Oxford, 1932).

Ames, Christine Caldwell, *Righteous Persecution: Inquisition, Dominicans and Christianity in the Middle Ages* (Philadelphia, University of Pennsylvania Press, 2009).

Amin, Samir, *Eurocentrism: Modernity, Religion and Democracy*, A Critique of Eurocentrism and *Culturalism*, translated by Russell Moore and James Membrez, (New York, Monthly Review Press, 2009).

Amin, Samir, *Global History: A View from the South* (Oxford, Pambazuka Press, 2011).

Andrews, Stuart, *Unitarian Radicalism: Political Rhetoric, 1770–1814* (New York: Palgrave Macmillan, 2003).

Angus, S., *The Mystery Religions: A Study in the Religious Backgrounds of Early Christianity* (New York, Dover Publications, 1975).

Anstey, Peter and Schuster, John (eds.), *The Science of Nature in the Seventeenth Century* (Dordrecht, Springer, 2005).

Aquinas, St Thomas, *Summa contra gentiles*, trans. by members of the Dominican Order, 4 vols (London, 1923-9).

Armitage, Angus, *Edmond Halley* (London, Thomas Nelson, 1966).

Armitage, David and Braddick, Michael J. (eds.) *The British Atlantic World: 1500–1800* (Hampshire, Palgrave Macmillan, 2002).

Armitage, David, *Armand Himy and Quentin Skinner* Eds., Milton and Republicanism,

(Cambridge, Cambridge University Press, 1998).

Armitage, David, *The Ideological Origins of the British Empire*, (Cambridge: Cambridge University Press, 2009).

Armstrong, Karen, *Muhammad: A Biography of the* Prophet (San Francisco: Harper Collins, 1992).

Arnold, Thomas and Guillaume, Alfred eds., *The Legacy of Islam* (Oxford, Clarendon Press, 1931).

Asad, Talal, *Formations of the Secular: Christianity, Islam and Modernity* (Stanford, Stanford University Press, 2003).

Asad, Talal, *Geneologies Genealogies of Religion: Discipline and Reasons of Power in Christianity and Islam* (Baltimore, John Hopkins University Press, 1993).

Ascher, Abraham, Halasi-Kun, Tibor, Király, Béla K., *The Mutual Effects of the Islamic and Judeo-Christian Worlds: the East European Pattern* (New York, Brooklyn College Press, 1979).

Ashcraft, Richard, *Revolutionary Politics and John Locke's Two Treatises of Government* (New Jersey, Princeton University Press, 1986).

Ashcraft, Richard, *Revolutionary Politics and Locke's Two Treatises of Government: Radicalism and Lockean Political Theory*, Political Theory , Nov., 1980, Vol. 8, No. 4 (Nov., 1980).

Ashcraft, Richard, *Revolutionary Politics and Locke's Two Treatises of Government* (Princeton, Princeton University Press, 1986).

Ashcraft, Richard, *Richard, Revolutionary Politics and Locke's Two Treatises of Government, Princeton* (NJ: Princeton University Press, 1986).

Ashley, Maurice, *The Glorious Revolution of 1688* (London, Scribners Scribner's, 1966).

Augustine, St., '*Unfinished Work in Answer to Julian*', in Answer to the Pelagians III (The Works of St. Augustine: A Translation for the 21st Century, volume I/25)., introduced, translated and with notes by Roland J. Teske, (New City Press, New York, 1999).

Augustine, St., *On Christian Teaching*, translated, introduced and with notes by R. P. H. Green, (Oxford University Press, Oxford, 2008).

Avcıoğlu, Nebahat and Flood, Finbarr Barry eds., *Globalising Cultures: Art and Mobility in the Eighteenth Century* (Washington, D.C, Smithsonian Institution, 2010).

Awn, Peter J., *Satan's Tragedy and Redemption: Iblis in Sufi Psychology* (Leiden: Brill, 1983).

Baechler, Jean, Mann, Michael and Hall, John, *Europe and the Rise of Capitalism* (London, Blackwell, 1988).

Baker, Philip and Vernon, Elliot eds, *The Agreements of the People, the Levellers and the Constitutional Crises of the English Revolution* (London, Palgrave Macmillan, 2012).

Bammate, Haider, *Muslim Contribution to Civilisation*, Indiana: American Trust Publications, 1976

Bammel, Ernst and Moule, C. F. D. eds., *Jesus and the Politics of His Day* (Cambridge, Cambridge University Press, 1984).

Barbour, Ian G., *When Science Meets Religion*, (San Francisco, HarperSanFrancisco, 2000).

Barbour, Richmond, *Before Orientalism, London's Theater of the East, 1576-1626* (Cambridge, Cambridge University Press, 2003).

Barin, Filiz, *"Othello: Turks as "the Other" in the Early Modern Period,"* The Journal of the Midwest Modern Language Association 43 No. 2 (Fall, 2010).

Barkey, Karen, *Islam and Toleration: Studying the Ottoman Imperial Model*, International Journal of Politics, Culture, and Society, Vol. 19, No. 1/2, The New Sociological Imagination II (Dec., 2005).

Bartels, Emily C., *Speaking of the Moor: from Alcazar to Othello,* (Philadelphia, University of Pennsylvania Press, 2009).

Barton, Simon and Linehan, Peter (eds.), *Cross, Crescent and Conversion: Studies on Medieval Spain and Christendom in Memory of Richard Fletcher* (Leiden, Brill, 2008).

Basalla, George, 'The Spread of Western Science', Science, no. 156 (5 May 1967).

Bauman, Michael, *Milton's Arianism*. Frankfurt am Main: (Verlag Peter Lang, 1986).

Beck, Brandon H., *From the Rising of the Sun: English Images of the Ottoman Empire to 1715* (New York, P. Lang, 1987).

Beddard, Robert ed., *The Revolutions of 1688* (Oxford, Clarendon Press, 1991).

Belloc, Hilaire, *The Great Heresies* (New York: Sheed & Ward, n.d.).

Bemis, Samuel M., *The Three Charters of the Virginia Company of London* (Baton Rouge, Louisiana State University Press, 2009).

Ben-Zaken, Avner, *Cross-Cultural Scientific Exchanges in the Eastern Mediterranean 1560-1660,* Baltimore, John Hopkin University Press, (2010).

Ben-Zaken, Avner, *Readin Hayy Ibn-Yaqzan: A Cross-Cultural History of Autodidacticism,* Baltimore, Johns Hopkins University, (2011).

Benedict, Philip and Gutmann, Myron P. (eds.) *Early Modern Europe: From Crisis to Stability* (Newark, University of Delaware Press, 2005).

Bent, James Theodore, *Early Voyages and Travels in the Levant* (Burlington, Ashgate, 2010).

Bentley, Jerry H., *The Oxford Handbook of World History* (Oxford, Oxford University Press, 2012).

Berg, Maxine and Clifford, Helen eds., *Consumers and Luxury: Consumer Culture in Europe,* 1650-1850, (Manchester, University of Manchester Press, 1999).

Berman, David, in his *A History of Atheism in Britain* (New York: Croom Helm, 1988).

Bernstein, Jeremy, *Dawning of the Raj: The Life & Trials of Warren Hastings* (Chicago, I. R. Dee, 2000).

Berridge, Geoffrey, *British Diplomacy in Turkey*, 1583 to the Present, (Leiden, Brill, 2009).

Biddulph, William, *The Travels of Certaine Englishmen into Africa, Asia and to the Blacke Sea London: Aspley* (1609).

Birchwood, Matthew, *Staging Islam in England: Drama and Culture, 1640-1685* (Cambridge, D. S. Brewer, 2007).

Bird, Karen M., *The Concession of Toleration, Muslims and the British Enlightenment*, Limina, Volume 22.2, (2017).

Blair, Ann 'Mosaic Physics and the Search for a Pious Natural Philosophy in the Late Renaissance', Isis 91 (2000).

Blaut, J. M., *Eight Eurocentric Historians* (New York, Guilford Press, 2000).

Blaut, J. M., *The Coloniser's Model of the World: Geographical Diffusionism and Eurocentric History*, (New York, Guilford Press, 1993).

Bonelli, M. L. Righini and Shea, William R. (eds.), *Reason, Experiment, and Mysticism* (New York, Science History Publications, 1975).

Boogert, Maurits H. van den, *The Capitulations and the Ottoman Legal System: Qadis, Consuls, and Berath in the 18th century* (Leiden, Brill, 2005).

Bowersock, G. W., Brown, Peter and Grabar, Oleg, eds., *Interpreting Late Antiquity: Essays on the Postclassical World* (London, Balkan Press of Harvard University Press, 2001).

Boyce, James, *Born Bad: Original Sin and the Making of the Western World*, Black Inc., (Collingwood, Australia, 2014).

Braarvig, Jens and Geller, Markham J. eds., *Studies in Multilingualism, Lingua Franca and Lingua Sacra*, Max Planck Research *Library for the History and Development of Knowledge* – (Studies 10, Open Access, January 1, 2018).

Braddick, M. ed., *The Oxford Handbook of the English Revolution* (Oxford, Oxford University Press, 2015).

Braudel, F., *Civilisation and Capitalism*, 15th–18th century, (London, Phoenix Press, 1979).

Braudel, Fernand, *The Mediterranean and the Mediterranean World in the Age of Philip II*, translated by Sian Reynold, (New York, Collins, 1972).

Breasted, James Henry, *The Dawn of Conscience*, (New York, Scribner, 1933).

Brenner, Robert, *Merchants and Revolution: Commercial Change, Political Conflict, and London's Overseas Traders 1550-1653*, (London, Verso, 2003).

Brenner, Robert, *The Civil War Politics of London's Merchant Community*, Past & Present, No. 58 (Feb., 1973).

Brentano, L., *Die Anjange des modemen Kapitalismus* (Leipzig, 1916).

Bridenbaugh, C., *Vexed and Troubled Englishmen*, (Oxford, Oxford University Press, 1968).

Bright, William, *The Age of Fathers* (New York: AMS Press, 1970).

Broadbent, John, *Paradise Lost: Introduction* (Cambridge, Cambridge University Press, 1972).

Brooke, John H., *Science and Religion: Some Historical Perspectives* (Oxford, Oxford University Press, 1991).

Brooke, John, and Maclean, Ian eds., *Heterodoxy in Early Modern Science and Religion* (Oxford, Oxford University Press, 2005).

Brotton, Jerry, "*Shakespeare's Turks and the Spectre of Ambivalence in the History Plays*," Textual Practice 28 No. 3. (2014).

Brotton, Jerry, *Renaissance: A Very Short Introduction* (Oxford, Oxford University Press, 2006).

Brotton, Jerry, *The Renaissance Bazaar: from the Silk Road to Michelangelo* (Oxford, Oxford University Press, 2003).

Brotton, Jerry, *The Sultan and the Queen: The Untold Story of Elizabeth and Islam* (New York, Viking, 2016).

Brotton, Jerry, *This Orient Isle: Elizabethan England and the Islamic World.* (St. Ives: Penguin Random House, 2016).

Brown, Peter "*St. Augustine's Attitude to Religious Coercion.*" The Journal of Roman Studies, vol. 54, (1964).

Brown, Stewart J. and Tackett, Timothy eds., *The Cambridge History of Christianity: Enlightenment, Reawakening and Revolution 1660-1815* (Cambridge, Cambridge University Press, 2006).

Bryant, J., *Emergence of British Power in India 1600–1784: A Grand Strategic Interpretation,* (Woodbridge, BOYE6, 2013).

Bulman, William J., *Anglican Enlightenment: Orientalism, Religion and Politics in England and its Empire, 1648-1715* (Cambridge, Cambridge University Press, 2015).

Burchill, Christopher J., *The Heidelberg Antitrinitarians.* Bibliotheca Dissidentium, vol, XI, ed., Andre Seguenny. (Baden-Baden: Editions Valentin Koemer, 1989).

Burckhardt, Jacob, *The Civilisation of the Renaissance in Italy*, tr. S. G. C. Middlemore, revised and edited by Irene Gordon, (London, Macmillan, 1904).

Burgess, Glen and Festenstein, Matthew eds., *English Radicalism* 1550-1850, (Cambridge, Cambridge University Press, 2007).

Burgess, Glenn, *The Politics of the Ancient Constitution: An Introduction to English Political Thought,* 1603–1642, (University Park: Pennsylvania State University Press, 1992).

Burian, Orhan, "*Interest of the English in Turkey as Reflected in English Literature of the Renaissance*," Oriens 5 (1952).

Burrell, David B., *Thomas Aquinas and Islam, Modern Theology,* 20:1, (Oxford, Blackwell, January 2004).

Burrow, J. W., *A Liberal Descent. Victorian Historians and the English Past* (Cambridge: Cambridge University Press, 1981).

Burton, Jonathan, "*English Anxiety and the Muslim Power of Conversion: Five Perspec-*

tives on 'Turning Turk' in Early Modern Texts", Journal for Early Modern Cultural Studies, (Spring/Summer 2002), Vol. 2, No. 1

Burton, Jonathan, *Traffic and Turning: Islam and English Drama, 1579-1624* (Delaware, University of Delaware Press, 2005).

Butler, Samuel: *Characters, ed. Charles W. Davis, Cleveland* (Case Western Reserve University Press, 1970).

Butterfield, H., *George III and the Historians* (London: Collins, 1957).

Butterfield, H., *The Englishman and his history* (Cambridge, Cambridge University Press, 1944).

Butterfield, H., *The Whig Interpretation of History* (London, G. Bell and Sons, 1931).

Butterfield, Herbert, *The Origins of Modern Science*, 1300–1800 (New York, Free Press, 1957).

Calvin, John, *Institutes of the Christian Religion*, translated by John Allen, First American Edition, (London, 1813).

Cameron, Euan, *The European Reformation* (second edition), (Oxford University Press, Oxford, 2012).

Canny, Nicolas, *The Origins of Empire: British Overseas Enterprise to the Close of the Seventeenth Century* (Oxford, Oxford University Press, 2001).

Capp, Bernard, *England's Culture Wars* (Oxford: Oxford University Press, 2012).

Carboni, Stefano and Whitehouse, David, *Glass of the Sultans* (New Haven, Yale University Press, 2001).

Carboni, Stefano, *Venice and the Islamic World, 828-1797* (New York, The Metropolitan Museum of Art, 2007).

Carey, Daniel, *Compiling nature's history: Travellers and travel narratives in the early royal society*, (Annals of Science, 1997).

Carré, M. H., *Phases of Thought in England*, (Oxford, Clarendon Press, 1949).

Carson, Penelope, *The East India Company and Religion*, 1698–1858 (Woodbridge, Boydell Press, 2012).

Carswell, John, *The Descent on England: A Study of the English Revolution of 1688 and Its European Background* (London, John Day, 1969).

Cartwright, Kent ed., *A Companion to Tudor Literature* (Malden: Wiley-Blackwell 2010).

Cassirer, Ernst, *The Philosophy of the Enlightenment*, trans. Fritz C. A. Koelln and J. P. Pettegrove, (Princeton, Princeton University Press, 1951).

Champion, Justin A. I., *The Pillars of Priestcraft Shaken: The Church of England and its Enemies, 1660-1730* (Cambridge Studies in Early Modern British History) 1st Edition, (Cambridge, Cambridge University Press, 2014).

Champion, Justin, *Republican Learning: John Toland and the Crisi of Christian Culture 1696-1722*, (Manchester, Manchester University Press, 2003).

Chapman, S.D., (ed.), *The Textile Industries. II. Cotton, Linen, Wool and Worsted* (London and New York, 1997).

Chenciner, R., *Madder Red: A History of Luxury and Trade*. Plant Dyes and Pigments in World Commerce and Art (Richmond, Curzon, 2000).

Chew, Samuel C., *The Crescent and the Rose: Islam and England During the Renaissance* (New York: Octagon Press, 1937).

Christianson, Gale E., *Isaac Newton* (Oxford, Oxford University Press, 2005).

Churchill, Winston, *A History of English Speaking Peoples* (London, Dodd, Mead & Company, 1956).

Clark, J. C. D., *English Society 1660-1832: Religion, Ideology and Politics during the Ancient Regime*, (Cambridge, Cambridge University Press, 2000).

Classen, Albrecht ed., *East Meets West in the Middle Ages and Early Modern Times: Transcultural Experiences in the Premodern World* (Boston, De Gruyter, 2013).

Claude, Jean, *An Account of the Persecutions and Oppressions of the Protestants in France, (London,* J. Norris, 1686).

Clissold, Stephen, 1976. *"Christian Renegades and Barbary Corsairs."* History Today 26, no. 8

Coates, Ben, *The Impact of the English Civil War on the Economy of London, 1642-50,* (Burlington: Ashgate Publishing Company, 2004).

Coffey, John ed., *The Oxford History of Protestant Dissenting Traditions: The Post Reformation Era 1559-1689* (Oxford, Oxford University Press, 2020).

Coffey, John, *Persecution and Toleration in Protestant England 1558-1689* (New York, Routledge, 2000).

Cohen, J. & Lague, I. eds., *The Place of Tolerance in Islam* (Boston, MA: Beacon, 2002).

Colbourn, H. T., *The Lamp of Experience. Whig History and the Intellectual Origins of the American Revolution* (Chapel Hill: University of North Carolina Press, 1965).

Coley, Noel, *"Halley and Post-Restoration Science"*. History Today. 1986, 36 (September).

Coller, Ian, *Citizens and Muslims: Islam, Politics and the French Revolution* (London, Yale University Press, 2020).

Collins, Harry M. *Changing Order: Replication and Induction in Scientific Practice* (London: Sage, 1985).

Collins, Jeffrey R., *The Church Settlement of Oliver Cromwell*, History, Vol. 87, No. 285 (January 2002).

Conant, James *"The Advancement of Learning during the Puritan Commonwealth,"* Proceedings of the Massachusetts Historical Society, LXVI (1936- 41).

Conklin, George N., *Biblical Criticism and Heresy in Milton* (New York, King's Crown Press, 1949).

Contadini, Anna and Norton, Claire eds., *The Renaissance and the Ottoman World*

(Farnham, Ashgate, 2013).

Conway, Anne, *The Principles of the Most Ancient and Modern Philosophy*, translated by A. P. Coudert and Taylor Corse, (Cambridge, Cambridge University Press, 1999).

Cook, Alan H., *Edmond Halley: Charting the Heavens and the Seas.* (Oxford, Clarendon Press, 1998).

Cook, Harold J., *Matters of Exchange: Commerce, Medicine, and Science in the Dutch Golden Age* (New Haven, CT: Yale University Press, 2007).

Copernicus, Nicolas, *On the Revolutions.* Trans. Edward Rosen (Baltimore, MD: Johns Hopkins University Press, 1978).

Cornwall, Robert D. and Gobson, William eds., *Religion, Politics and Dissent 1660-1832: Essay in Honour of James E. Bradley* (Burlington, Ashgate, 2010).

Cowan, Brian, *The Rise of the Coffeehouse Reconsidered*, The Historical Journal, Vol. 47, No. 1 (Mar., 2004).

Cowan, Brian, *The Social Life of Coffee: The Emergence of British Coffeehouses* (London, Yale University Press, 2005).

Coward, B., *The Stuart Age – England*, 1603–1714 (New York, Routledge, 2017).

Cragg, G. R., *The Church and the Age of Reason 1648–1789* (Harmondsworth, Penguin, 1970).

Cranston, Maurice, *John Locke, A Biography* (London, Longmans, Green, 1957).

Craven, Wesley Frank, *Dissolution of the Virginia Company: The Failure of a Colonial Experiment* (Gloucester, Massachusetts, Peter Smith, 1964).

Crimmins, James E., *Religion, Secularisation and Political Thought, Thomas Hobbes to J. S. Mill* (New York, Routledge, 2013).

Crone, Patricia, *God's Rule, Government and Islam* (New York, Columbia University Press, 2004).

Cunningham, Andrew and Williams, Perry, 'De-centring the "Big Picture": The Origins of Modern Science and the Modern Origins of Science', British Journal for the History of Science, vol. 26, no. 4 (1993).

Currell, David, *Meditations on Mediation: John Milton and the Muslim Jesus*, English Studies, 2015, 96:1

Curtis, Kenneth R. and Bentley, Jerry H. (eds.), *Architects of World History: Researching the Global Past* (Oxford, Willy Blackwell, 2014).

Cuttica, Cesare and Burgess, Glenn eds., *Monarchism and Absolutism in Early Modern Europe* (New York, Routledge, 2012).

Dahiyat, Eid Abdallah, *John Milton and the Arab-Islamic Culture.* (Amman, Shukayr and Akasheh, 1987).

Dahiyat, Eid Abdallah. *"Aspects of John Milton in Arabic."* Milton Quarterly 18 (1984).

Daily, D., *Enlightenment Deism.* The Foremost Threat to Christianity, (Pennsylvania,

Dorrance, 1999).

Dalrymple, William ed., *Begums, Thugs and White Mughals: The Journals of Fanny Parkes*, (London, Eland, 2012).

Dalrymple, William, *The Anarchy: The Relentless Rise of the East India Company* (New York, Bloombury, 2019).

Dalrymple, William, *White Mughals: Love and Betrayal in Eighteenth Century India*, (New York, Penguin Books, 2002).

Danby, Miles, *'Moorish style'*, (London, Phaidon, 1995).

Dandelet, Thomas, *The Renaissance of Empire in Early Modern Europe* (Cambridge, Cambridge University Press, 2014).

Daniel Goffman, *The Ottoman Empire and Early Modern Europe,* (Cambridge, Cambridge University Press, 2004).

Daniel, Norman, *Islam and the West: The Making of an Image* (Edinburgh, Edinburgh University Press, 1989).

Daniel, Stephen H., *John Toland, his methods, manners and mind*, (McGill-Queen's University Press, 1984).

Danielson, Dennis, *The Cambridge Companion to Milton*, (Cambridge, Cambridge University Press, 2004).

Dannenfeldt, K.H., *Leonhard Rauwolf: Sixteenth-Century Physician, Botanist, and Traveller* (Cambridge, Mass. Harvard University Press, 1968).

Darby, J., *Four Treatises concerning the doctrine, discipline and worship of the Mahometans: An Abridgment of the Mahometan Religion: A Defence of the Mahometans, A Treatise of Bobovious, Reflections on Mahometansm Mahometanism and Socinianism* (London: B. Lintott, and E. Sanger, 1712).

Davies, Norman, *God's Playground: A History of Poland* (New York, Columbia University Press, 2005).

Davis, Ralph, *Aleppo and Devonshire Square: English Traders in the Levant in the Eighteenth Century* (London: Macmillan, 1967).

Davis, Robert C., *Christian Slaves, Muslim Masters: White Slavery in the Mediterranean, the Barbary Coast and Italy, 1500-1800* (New York, Macmillan Palgrave, 2004).

Davis Robert, *Holy War and Human Bondage: Tales of Muslim Christian Slavery in the Early Modern Mediterranean,* Oxford, Praeger ABC-Clio, 2009

De Beer, E. S., *The Correspondence of John Locke*, Oxford, Oxford University Press, (1976)–89

De Beer, Esmond S., *King Charles II's Own Fashion: An Episode in Anglo-French Relations 1666-1670,* Journal of the Warburg Institute, Vol. 2, No. 2 (Oct., 1938).

De Krey, Gary S., *Between Revolutions: Re-appraising the Restoration in Britain,* History Compass 6/3 (2008).

De Krey, Gary S., *Political Radicalism in London after the Glorious Revolution*, The Journal of Modern History, Vol. 55, No. 4 (Dec., 1983).

De Krey, Gary S., *Restoration and Revolution in Britain*: A Political History of the Era of Charles II and the Glorious Revolution (New York, Palgrave Macmillan, 2007).

De Krey, Gary, *London and the Restoration: 1659-1683*, (Cambridge, Cambridge University Press, 2005).

De. Krey, Gary S., *A Fractured Society: The Politics of London in the First Age of Party* 1688-1715. (Oxford, Clarendon Press, 1985).

Dear, Peter, *Revolutionising the Sciences: European Knowledge and Its Ambitions*, 1500–1700. (Princeton, NJ, Princeton University Press, 2001).

Debus, Allen G. ed., *Science, Medicine and Society in the Renaissance*. Essays to honour Walter Pagel, (New York, Science History Publications, 1972).

Delumeau, Jean, *Sin and Fear: The Emergence of a Western Guilt Culture 13th to 18th Centuries* translated by Eric Nicholson, (New York, St. Martin's Press, 1990).

Dew, Nicolas Nicholas, *Orientalism in Louis XIV's France*, (Oxford, Oxford University Press, 2009).

Dieckmann, Liselotte, *"Renaissance Hieroglyphics,"* in Comparative Literature, Vol. 9, No. 4 (Autumn, 1957).

Dimmock, Matthew, *"Converting and Not Converting "Strangers" in Early Modern London,"* Journal of Early Modern History 17 (2013).

Dimmock, Matthew, *Mythologies of the Prophet Muhammad in Early Modern English Culture*, (Cambridge, Cambridge University Press, 2013).

Dimmock, M., *New Turkes: Dramatizing Islam and the Ottomans in Early Modern England,* (New York, Routledge, 2005).

Dixon, Philip, *Nice and Hot Disputes: The Doctrine of the Trinity in the Seventeenth Century* (London, T & T Clark, 2003)

Dixon, Thomas, Canter, Geoffrey and Pumfrey, Stephen (eds.), *Science and Religion: New Historical Perspectives* (Cambridge, Cambridge University Press, 2010).

Dobbs, Betty Jo T., *The Foundations of Newton's Alchemy: or, "The Hunting of the Green Lyon"*, (Cambridge, Cambridge University Press, 1975).

Dobbs, Betty Jo T., *The Janus Faces of Genius: The Role of Alchemy in Newton's Thought* (Cambridge, Cambridge University Press, 1991).

Dobbs, Betty Jo Teeter and Jacob, Margaret C. (eds.), *Newton and the Culture of Newtonianism* (Atlantic Highlands, New Jersey, Humanities Press International, 1995).

Dobranski, Stephen B. and Rumrich, John P. eds., *Milton and Heresy* (Cambridge, Cambridge University Press, 1998).

Dossett, Rena D., *The Historical Influence of Classical Islam on Western Humanistic Education*, International Journal of Social Science and Humanity, Vol. 4, No. 2,

(March 2014).

Draper, John William, *History of the Conflict Between Religion and Science* (New York, D. Appleton and Company, 1875).

Dudley, Albert Cassell, *"Nonconformity Under the 'Clarendon Code'"* , The American Historical Review 18, no. 1 (Oct., 1912).

Dunn, John, *"Consent in the Political Theory of John Locke"*, The Historical Journal, (1967), 10(2).: 153–182. Reprinted in his Political Obligation in its Historical Context: Essays in Political Theory, Cambridge: Cambridge University Press, (1980)

Durston, C. and Maltby, J. eds, *Religion in Revolutionary England*, (Manchester, Manchester University Press, 2006).

Eamon, William, *Books of Secrets in Medieval and Early Modern Science*, Sudhoffs Archiv, Bd. 69, H. 1 (1985).

Eamon, William, *Science and the Secrets of Nature: Books of Secrets in Medieval and Early Modern Culture* (Princeton, Princeton University Press, 1994).

Eaton, Richard M., *India in the Persianate Age, 1000–1765*, (London, Penguin Random House, 2019).

Edleston, J., *Correspondence of Sir Isaac Newton and Professor Cotes* (London, 1850).

Edwards, J., *The Socinian Creed: or, A Brief Account Of the Professed Tenents and Doctrines of the Foreign and English Socinians*. (London, 1697).

Edwards, Linda, *A Brief Guide to Beliefs: Ideas, Theologies, Mysteries, and Movements*, (Louisville, Westminster John Knox Press, 2001).

Einboden, Jeffrey, *A Qur'a¯nic Milton: From Paradise to al-Firdaws*, Milton Quarterly, Vol. 43, No. 3, (2009).

Eldem, Edhem, Goffman, Daniel and Masters, Bruce eds., *The Ottoman City Between East and West: Aleppo, Izmir, and Istanbul,* (Cambridge, Cambridge University Press, 1999).

Ellis, Aytoun, *The Penny Universities: A History of the Coffee-House* (London, Martin Secker & Warburg Ltd; 1956).

Ellis, Markman, *The Coffee-House: A Cultural History* (Ashland, OH, Phoenix, 2005).

Ellul, Jacques, *Islam and Judeo-Christianity: A Critique of Their Commonality*, Translated by D. Bruce MacKay, (Eugene, OR, Cascade Books, 2015).

Elmes, James, *'Christopher Wren'*, (London, Chapman & Hall.1st edition, 1852).

Elsner, Jas and Rubiés, Joan-Pau, *Voyages and Visions: Towards a Cultural History of Travel* (London, Reaktion Books, 1999).

Elvin, M., *The Pattern of the Chinese Past* (London, Eyre Methuen, 1973).

Epstein, Mortimer, *The English Levant Company: Its Foundation and its History to 1640*, (New York, Burt Franklin, 1968).

Eskenderoglu, Muammer, *Fakhr al-Din al-Razi and Thomas Aquinas on the Question of the Eternity of the World* (Leiden, Brills, 2002).

Esposito, John L., *What Everyone Needs to Know About Islam*, (Oxford, Oxford University Press, 2002).

Evans, J. A. S., *The Age of Justinian* (London, Routledge, 1996).

Fakhry, Majid, *al-Farabi: Founder of Islamic Neoplatonism, His Life, Works and Influence* (Oxford, Oneworld, 2002).

Fakhry, Majid, *Averroes: His Life, Works and Influence* (Oxford, Oneworld, 2001).

Fanning, Philip Ashley, *Isaac Newton and the Transmutation of Alchemy: An Alternate View of the Scientific Revolution* (Berkeley, California, North Atlantic Books, 2009).

Farmer, Suzanne J., *"Sir Dudley North in Loyal Principle Exceeding: A Political Merchant in the First Age of Party, International Social Science Review*: vol. 92, Issue 2, article 1 and her Ph. D. dissertation " *"SIR DUDLEY NORTH: MERCHANT POLITICS IN THE FIRST AGE OF PARTY"* submitted to The University of Mississippi, department of History, (2011).

Farnie, D.A. and Jeremy, D.J., (eds.)., *The Fibre that Changed the World: The Cotton Industry in International Perspective, 1600-1990s*, (Oxford, Oxford University Press, 2004).

Farooq, Mohammad Omar, *Towards Our Reformation: From Legalism to Value-Oriented Islamic Law and Jurisprudence* (London, International Institute of Islamic Thought, 2011).

Feiling, Keith, *Warren Hastings* (London, Macmillan, 1954).

Ferngren, Gary ed., *Science & Religion: A Historical Introduction.* (Baltimore, Johns Hopkins University Press, 2002).

Figgis, J. N., *The Divine Right of Kings* (Cambridge, Cambridge University Press, 1921).

Fincham, Kenneth and Tyacke, Nicholas, *Altars Restored: The Changing Face of English Religious Worship*, 1547-c.1700 (Oxford, Oxford University Press, 2007).

Findlay, Ronald and O'Rourke, Kevin H. eds., *Power and Plenty: Trade, War and the World Economy in the Second Millennium* (Princeton, Princeton University Press, 2007).

Fischer-Galati, Stephen A., *Ottoman Imperialism and German Protestantism, 1521-1555* (Cambridge, Massachusetts, Harvard University Press, 1959).

Fish, Stanley, *Surprised By Sin: The Reader in Paradise Lost, 2ⁿᵈ edition.* (Cambridge, Mass., Harvard University Press, 1997).

Force, J. E. and Hutton, S. eds. *Newton and Newtonianism.* (Dordrecht, Kluwer Academic Publishers, 2004).

Force, James E. and Popkin, Richard H. (eds.), *Essays on the Context, Nature, and Influence of Isaac Newton's Theology*, (Dordrecht, Kluwer Academic Publishers, 1990).

Force, James, *William Whiston: Honest Newtonian* (Cambridge, Cambridge University Press, 1985).

Forester, C. S. , *The Barbary Pirates*. (New York, Random House, 1953).

Forlines, F. Leroy, *Classical Arminianism: A Theology of Salvation*. (Nashville, Randall House, 2011).

Foxley, Rachel, *John Lilburne and the Citizenship of 'Free-Born Englishmen*, The Historical Journal, Vol. 47, No. 4 (Dec., 2004).

Frace Face, Ryan K., *The Foundations of Enlightenment: Transformations in Religious Toleration, Orthodoxy, and Pluralism in Early Modern Scotland, 1660-1752*, Ph.D. dissertation, (University of Chicago, Chicago, 2005).

Francisco, Adam S., *Martin Luther and Islam: A Study in Sixteenth-Century Polemics and Apologetics* (Brill, Leiden, 2007).

Frank, Andre Gunder, *ReOrient: Global Economy in the Asian Age, (Berkeley, University of California Press*, 1997).

Frank, Daniel H. and Leaman, O. eds., *History of Jewish Philosophy* (New York, Routledge, 2004).

Frend, W. H. C., *The Rise of Christianity*, (Philadelphia, Fortress Press, 1984).

Fried, Michael N., *Edmond Halley's Reconstruction of the Lost Book of Apollonius's Conics*: Translation and Commentary, (New York, Springer-Verlag, 2012).

Fuchs, Barbara, Exotic Nation: Maurophilia and the Construction of Early Modern Spain, (Philadelphia, University of Pennsylvania Press, 2008).

Gaddis, Michael, *There Is No Crime for Those Who Have Christ, (Berkeley*, University of California Press, 2005).

Galilei, Galileo, *Discoveries and Opinions of Galileo* trans. Stillman Drake. (New York:, Anchor Books, 1957).

Games, Alison, *The Web of Empire: English Cosmopolitans in an Age of Expansion 1560-1660* (Cambridge, Cambridge University Press, 2008).

Garcia, H., *A Hungarian Revolution in Restoration England: Henry Stubbe, Radical Islam, and the Rye House Plot, The Eighteenth Century*, Volume 51, Numbers 1-2, Spring/Summer, (2010).

Garcia, Humberto, *Islam and the English Enlightenment*, (Baltimore, John Hopkins University Press, 2012).

Garcia, Humberto, *Islam in the English Radical Protestant Imagination 1660-1830*, Ph. D. dissertation submitted to University of Illinois, Urbana-Champaign, (2007).

Gardiner, S. R., *History of the Commonwealth and Protectorate, 1649–1656* (4 vols., 1903 reprinted by Witney, Windrush Press, 1988).

Gardiner, Samuel Rawson ed., *Parliamentary Debates in 1610*, Edited, from the Notes of a Member of the House of Commons, vol. 81, (London: Camden Society, 1862).

Gauci, Perry, *The Politics of Trade: The Overseas Merchant in State and Society*, 1660-1720. (Oxford, Oxford University Press, 2001).

Gaukroger, S. *The Emergence of a Scientific Culture*, (Oxford, Oxford University Press, 2005).

Gaukroger, Stephen, *The Emergence of a Scientific Culture: Science and the Shaping of Modernity* 1210-1685, (Oxford, Oxford University Press, 2006).

Gelder, Maartje van, *The Republic's Renegades: Dutch Converts to Islam in Seventeenth-Century Diplomatic Relations with North Africa*, JOURNAL OF EARLY MODERN HISTORY 19 (2015).

Ghazanfar, S. M., *Medieval Islamic Thought*, (New York, Routledge Curzon, 2003).

Gibbon, Edward, *The History of the Decline and Fall of the Roman Empire*, 6 vols, (London: William Hallhead, 1788).

Giffin, Frederick C., *John Locke and Religious Toleration*, Journal of Church and State, Vol. 9, No. 3 (Autumn 1967).

Gleick, James, *Isaac Newton*, (New York, Pantheon Books, 2003).

Goffman, Daniel, *Izmir and the Levantine world, 1550–1650*, (Seattle, WA, University of Washington Press, 1990).

Goldie, Mark (ed.), *John Locke: A Letter Concerning Toleration and Other Writings*, (Indiana, Liberty Fund, 2010).

Goldie, Mark, *"John Locke and Anglican Royalism"*, Political Studies, (1983).

Goldish, Matt, *Judaism in the Theology of Sir Isaac Newton* (Dordrecht, Springer Science+Business Media, 1998)

Goldstone, Lawrence and Nancy, *Out of the Flames*, (New York, Broadway Books, 2002).

Golinski, Jan, *Making Natural Knowledge: Constructivism and the History of Science* (Cambridge, Cambridge University Press, 1998).

Golinski, Jan, *Making Natural Knowledge: Constructivism and the History of Science* (Chicago, The University of Chicago Press, 2005).

Goody, Jack, *Islam in Europe, (Malden, Polity Press* 2004).

Goody, Jack, *Renaissances: The One or the Many?*, (Cambridge, Cambridge University Press, 2010).

Goody, Jack, *The Theft of History* (Cambridge, Cambridge University Press, 2006).

Gouk, Penelope and Hills, Helen (eds.), *Representing Emotions: New Connections in the Histories of Art, Music and Medicine* (New York, Routledge, 2005).

Graf, Tobias P., *The Sultan's Renegades: Christian-European Converts to Islam and the Making of the Ottoman Elite*, 1575-1610, (Oxford, Oxford University Press, 2017).

Gregory, Brad S., *The Unintended Reformation: How a Religious Revolution Secularized Society,* (London, Belknap Press, 2015).

Graham, Michael, *The Blasphemies of Thomas Aikenhead: Boundaries of Belief on the Eve of the Enlightenment*. (Edinburgh, Edinburgh University Press, 2013).

Grassby, Richard, *The Business Community of Seventeenth-Century England*. (Cambridge, Cambridge University Press, 1995).

Grassby, Richard, *The English Gentleman in Trade: The Life and Works of Sir Dudley North*, 1641-1691, (Oxford, Clarendon Press, 1994).

Greaves, Richard L. *Puritanism and Science: The Anatomy of a Controversy*, Journal of the History of Ideas, Vol. 30, No. 3 (Jul. - Sep., 1969).

Green, R., ed., *The Weber Thesis Controversy* (Toronto, University of Toronto Press, 1973).

Greengrass, Mark, Christendom Destroyed. Europe 1517-1648, (London, Penguin Books, 2014).

Greenham, Paul Timothy, *A Concord of Alchemy with Theology: Isaac Newton's Hermeneutics of the Symbolic Texts of Chymistry and Biblical Prophecy*, Ph. D. dissertation submitted to Institute for the History and Philosophy of Science and Technology (IHPST). University of Toronto, (2015).

Greenwood, Andrea and Harris, Mark W., *An Introduction to the Unitarian and Universalists Traditions*, (Cambridge, Cambridge University Press, 2011).

Greig, Martin, *"Heresy Hunt: Gilbert Burnet and the Convocation Controversy of 1701,"* Historical Journal 37, no. 3 (1994).

Grell, O.P. and Scribner, B. (eds), *Tolerance and Intolerance in the European Reformation* (Cambridge, Cambridge University Press, 1996).

Grell, O.P., Israel, J.I. and Tyacke, N. (eds), *From Persecution to Toleration: The Glorious Revolution and Religion in England* (Oxford, Clarendon Press, 1991).

Grell, Ole Peter and Potter, Roy eds., *Toleration in Enlightenment England* (Cambridge, Cambridge University Press, 2000).

Gribaldi, Matteo, *Declaratio. Michael Servetus's Revelation of Jesus Christ the Son of God*, translated by Peter Zerner, edited by Peter Hughes and Peter Zerner (Providence, RI: Blackstone Editions and Michael Servetus Institute, 2010).

Griffel, Frank, *Al-Ghazali's Philosophical Theology* (Oxford, Oxford University Press, 2009).

Grillmeier, Alois, *Christ in Christian Tradition*, John Bowden, trans., (Atlanta, John Knox Press, 1975).

Grose, F., (ed.). *'Essays on Gothic architecture* by the Rev. T. Warton et al., 3rd ed., (London, J. Taylor, at the Architectural Library, 1808).

Gunnoe Jr., Charles D., *Thomas Erastus and the Palatinate: A Renaissance Physician in the Second Reformation*, (Leiden, Brills, 2011).

Gwynn, David M., *Christianity in the Later Roman Empire: A Source Book,* (London, Bloomsbury, 2015).

Haakonssen, Knud ed., *Enlightenment and Religion: Rational Dissent in Eighteenth-Century Britain*, (Cambridge, Cambridge University Press, 1996).

Habermas, J., *The Structural Transformation of the Public Sphere: An Inquiry into a Category of Bourgeois Society*, trans. T. Burger with the assistance of F. Lawrence,

(Cambridge, MA, MIT Press, 1989).

Hall, A. R., *Ballistics in the Seventeenth Century* (Cambridge, Cambridge University Press, 1952).

Hall, A. Rupert, *The Scientific Revolution* 1500–1800: *The Formation of the Modern Scientific Attitude*, (London, Longmans, Green & Co., 1954) published in its second edition as The Revolution in Science, (Harlow, Longman, 1983).

Hall, John, *Powers and Liberties: The Causes and Consequences of the Rise of the West*, (London, Blackwell, 1985).

Hallam, Henry, *Introduction to the Literature of Europe: In the Fifteenth, Sixteenth, and Seventeenth Centuries* (Oxford, Oxford University Press, 2007).

Hamburger, Philip, *Separation of Church and State*, (Cambridge, Mass., Harvard University Press, 2004).

Hammond, Robert, *The Philosophy of al-Farabi and Its Influence on Medieval Thought* (New York, Hobson Book Press, 1947).

Harrigan, Michael, *Veiled Encounters: Representing the Orient in 17th Century French Travel Literature* (Amsterdam, Rodopi, 2008).

Harris, Jennifer ed., *A Companion to Textile Culture* (New Jersey, Wiley Blackwell, 2020).

Harrison, John and Laslett, Peter, *The Library of John Locke*, (Oxford, Clarendon Press, 1971).

Harrison, Peter, *'Religion' and the Religions in the English Enlightenment* (Cambridge, Cambridge University Press, 2002).

Harte, N. B. and Ponting, K. G., (eds.)., *Textile History and Economic history: Essays in Honour of Miss Julia de Lacy Mann* (Manchester, Manchester University Press, 1973).

Haskins, C. H., *The Renaissance of the Twelfth Century* (London, Harvard University Press, 1955).

Hassan, Nawal Muhammad, *Hayy Bin Yaqzan and Robinson Crusoe: A Study of an Early Arabic Impact on English Literature* (Baghdad, Al-Rashid House, 1980).

Hattox, Ralph, Coffee and Coffeehouses: The Origins of a Social Beverage in the Medieval Near East, Seattle, (WA, University of Washington Press, 1985).

Haydon, C., Walsh, J. and Taylor, S. (eds), *The Church of England c.1689–c.1833*, (Cambridge, Cambridge University Press, 1993).

Hazard, Paul, *The Crisis of the European Mind: 168-1715* translated by J. Lewis May, (New York, New York Review Books, 2013).

Heal, Bridget and Anorthe Kremers eds., *Radicalism and Dissent in the World of Protestant Reform* (Göttingen, Vandenhoeck & Ruprecht, 2017).

Heck, Gene W., *Charlemagne, Muhammad, and the Arab Roots of Capitalism* (New York, Walter de Gruyter, 2006).

Hegel, G.W.F., *Elements of the Philosophy of Right*, Edited by Allen Wood, Translated by

H. B. Nisbet. (Cambridge, Cambridge University Press, 1991).

Hellyer, Marcus ed., *The Scientific Revolution: The Essential Readings* (Oxford, Blackwell, 2003).

Hempton, David, *Religion and Political Culture in Britain and Ireland: From the Glorious Revolution to the Decline of Empire* (Cambridge, Cambridge University Press, 1996).

Henderson, John B., *The Construction of Orthodoxy and Heresy: Neo-Confucian, Islamic, Jewish, and Early Christian Patterns,* (Albany, SUNY, 1998).

Henry, John, 'Occult Qualities and the Experimental Philosophy: Active Principles in Pre-Newtonian Matter Theory', History of Science 24 (1986).

Herrick, J. A., *The Radical Rhetoric of the English Deists. The Discourse of Scepticism Skepticism, 1680–1750* (Columbia, University of South Carolina Press, 1997).

Hick, John ed., *The Myth of God Incarnate* (Philadelphia, The Westminster Press, 1977).

Hick, John, *"A Remonstrance in Concluding,"* Jesus in History and Myth, R. J. Hoffmann, G. A. Larue, eds. (Buffalo, Prometheus Books, 1986).

Hick, John, *God and the Universe of Faiths* (London, Macmillan, 1973).

Hick, John, *The Metaphor of God Incarnate* (London, S.C.M. Press, 1993).

Hill, Christopher, *Intellectual Origins of the English Revolution Revisited* (Oxford, Oxford University Press, 1997).

Hill, Christopher, *The Century of Revolution: 1603–1714* (New York, Routledge, 1961).

Hill, Christopher, *The World Turned Upside-down: Radical Ideas During the English Revolution* (London, Penguin Books, 1972).

Hillar, Marian, *"From the Polish Socinians to the American Constitution,"* A Journal from the Radical Reformation. A Testimony to Biblical Unitarianism, (1994).

Hillar, Marian, *"Laelius and Faustus Socinus Founders of Socinianism: Their Lives and Theology."* Part 1. Journal from the Radical Reformation. Testimony to Biblical Unitarianism, Vol. 10, No. 2. (Winter 2002).

Hillar, Marian, *"Laelius and Faustus Socinus Founders of Socinianism: Their Lives and Theology."* Part 2. Journal from the Radical Reformation. Testimony to Biblical Unitarianism, Vol. 10, No. 3. (Spring 2002).

Hillar, Marian, *"The legacy of Servetus: Humanism and the beginning of change in the social paradigm: From Servetus to Thomas Jefferson,"* in Miguel Servet. Luz entre tinieblas, ed. Sergio Baches Opi, Huesca: Instituto de Estudios Sijenenses, (2006).

Hillar, Marian, *The Case of Michael Servetus (1511-1553). - The Turning Point in the Struggle for Freedom of Conscience,* (Lewiston, N.Y; Lampeter, U.K., Edwin Mellen Press, 1997).

Himmelfarb, Gertrude, *The Roads to Modernity: The British, French and American Enlightenments,* (New York, Vintage Books, 2005).

Hobson, John M., *The Eastern Origins of Western Civilisation* (Cambridge, Cambridge

University Press, 2004).

Hodge, Charles, *Commentary on the Epistle to the Romans*, (Albany, Books For The Ages, 1997).

Hodgson, Marshall G. S., *"The Role of Islam in World History,"* International Journal of Middle East Studies 1.2 (1970).

Hoffman, Eva R., *Pathways of Portability: Islamic and Christian Interchange from the Tenth to the Twelfth Century* (Oxford, Blackwell Publishers, 2001).

Hoffmann, R. J., Larue, G. A., eds., *Jesus in History and Myth*, (Buffalo, Prometheus Books, 1986).

Holmes, Geoffrey ed., *Britain after the Glorious Revolution: 1689-1714* (London, Macmillan, 1969).

Holmyard, E. J., *Alchemy* (Toronto, Penguin Books, 1957).

Holmyard, Eric John (ed.)., *The Works of Geber*, translated by Richard Russel, London, Dent, 1928, digitalized by the University of Michigan on (July 13, 2007).

Holmyard, Eric John, *Makers of Chemistry*. (Oxford, Clarendon Press, 1931).

Holt, P.M., '*The Study of Arabic Historians in Seventeenth Century England: The Background and Work of Edward Pococke*', Bulletin of the School of Oriental and African Studies, 19.3, (1957).

Hooykaas, R., '*Pitfalls in the historiography of geological science*', Nature et Histoire, (1982).

Hooykaas, R., *Religion and the Rise of Modern Science*, (Edinburgh, Scottish Academic Press, 1972).

Hooykaas, R., *Selected Studies in History of Science*, (Coimbra, Coimbra University Press, 1983).

Howell, Kenneth J, *God's Two Books: Copernican Cosmology and Biblical Interpretation in Early Modern Science,* (Notre Dame, University of Notre Dame Press, 2002).

Hsia, Ronnie Po-Chia, *Cambridge History of Christianity*, Vol. 6: Reform and Expansion, 1500-1660, (Cambridge, Cambridge University Press, 2004).

Hughes, P., '*Servetus and the Quran,*' Journal of Unitarian Universalist History, Cambridge (Mass.), 30 (2005).

Hughes, Peter, *"In the Footsteps of Servetus: Biandrata, David, and the Quran"*, Journal of Unitarian Universalist History, Cambridge (Mass.), 31 (2006-2007).

Hunt, John, *Religious Thought in England from the Reformation to the End of Last Century: A Contribution to the History of Theology, 3 vols.* (London, 1870–71).

Hunter, Ian, Laursen, John Christian and Nederman, Cary J. eds., *Heresy in Transition*, (Burlington, VT, Ashgate Publishing Company, 2005).

Hunter, Michael and Cooper, Michael eds., *Robert Hooke: Tercentennial Studies*, (New York, Routledge, 2006).

Hunter, Michael, *Boyle Studies: Aspects of the Life and Thought of Robert Boyle (1627-*

1691), (Burlington, Ashgate, 2015).

Hunter, Michael, ed., *Archives of the Scientific Revolution: The Formation and Exchange of Ideas in the Seventeenth-Century Europe*, (Woodbridge, Boydell Press, 1998).

Hutchings, Mark, *Turks, Repertories, and the Early Modern English Stage* (London, Palgrave Macmillan, 2017).

Hutton, Sarah, *Anne Conway: A Women Philosopher*, (Cambridge, Cambridge University Press, 2004).

Hyma, A., *Christianity, Capitalism and Communism*, (Ann Arbor, Mich., University of Michigan, 1937).

Hyma, A., *Renaissance to Reformation*, (Grand Rapids, Mich., Wm. B. Eerdmans Publishing, 1951).

Iliffe, Rob and George E. Smith, *Cambridge Companion to Newton* (Cambridge, Cambridge University Press, 2016).

Iliffe, Rob, *Priest of Nature: The Religious Worlds of Isaac Newton* (Oxford, Oxford University Press, 2017).

Inati, Shams, *Ibn Sina's Remarks and Admonitions, Physics and Metaphysics, An Analysis and Annotated Translation* (New York, Columbia University Press, 2014).

Ingram, Anders, *Writing the Ottomans: Turkish History in Early Modern England* (New York, Palgrave Macmillan, 2015).

Irwin J. and Schwartz, P.R., *Studies in Indo-European Textile History*, (Ahmedabad, Calico Museum of Textiles, 1966).

Israel, J.I., *European Jewry in the Age of Mercantilism*, 1550-1750, (Oxford, Oxford University Press, 1985).

Israel, Jonathan I., *Enlightenment Contested: Philosophy, Modernity and the Emancipation of Man 1670-1752*, (Oxford, Oxford University Press, 2006).

Israel, Jonathan I., *Radical Enlightenment: Philosophy and the Making of Modernity 1650-1750* (Oxford, Oxford University Press, 2001).

Izutsu, Toshihiko, *Ethico-Religious Concepts in the Qur'an*, (Montreal, McGill-Queen's University Press, 2002).

Izutsu, Toshihiko, *God and Man in the Quran: Semantics of the Quranic Weltanschauung*, (Tokyo, Keio University, 1964).

Jacob, James R. and Jacob, Margaret C. *The Anglican Origins of Modern Science: The Metaphysical Foundations of the Whig Constitution*: Isis, Vol. 71, No. 2 (Jun., 1980).

Jacob, James R. Jacob, *Henry Stubbe, Radical Protestantism and the Early Enlightenment* (Cambridge, Cambridge University Press, 1983).

Jacob, M. C., *The Radical Enlightenment: Pantheists, Freemasons, and Republicans* (London, Allen and Unwin, 1981).

Jacob, M., *The Enlightenment. A Brief History with Documents*, (Boston, Mass., St Martin's/Bedford, 2001).

Jacob, Margaret C., *Newtonians and the English Revolution 1689-1720* (New York, Cornell University Press, 1976).

Jacob, Margaret., *"The Nature of Early-Eighteenth-Century Religious Radicalism."* Republics of Letters: A Journal for the Study of Knowledge, Politics, and the Arts 1, no. 1 (May 1, 2009).

Jardine, Lisa and Brotton, Jerry, *Global Interests: Renaissance Art Between East and West,* (London, Reaktion Books, 2000).

Jayne, Allen, *Jefferson's Declaration of Independence: Origins, Philosophy and Theology*, (Louisville, Kentucky University Press, 1998).

Jeremias, Joachim, *New Testament Theology*, John Bowden, trans., (New York, Charles Scribner's Sons, 1971).

Jha, Saumitra, *Financial Asset Holdings and Political Attitudes: Evidence from Revolutionary England*, The Quarterly Journal of Economics (2015).

John Spurr, *"Rational Religion" in Restoration England, Journal of the History of Ideas*, Vol. 49, No. 4 (Oct. - Dec., 1988).

John, M. Hobson, *The Eastern Origins of Western Civilisation*, (Cambridge, Cambridge University Press, 2004).

Johns, Jeremy, *Arabic Administration in Norman Sicily*, (Cambridge, Cambridge University Press, 2002).

Johnson, Francis R., *Gresham College: Precursor of the Royal Society, Journal of the History of Ideas*, Vol. 1, No. 4 (Oct., 1940).

Johnson, Geraldine A., *Renaissance Art, A Very Short Introduction*, (Oxford, Oxford University Press, 2005).

Johnson, Noel D. and Koyama, Mark eds., *Persecution and Toleration: The Long Road to Religious Freedom*, (Cambridge, Cambridge University Press, 2019).

Jolley, Nicholas, *Leibniz on Locke and Socinianism, Journal of the History of Ideas*, Vol. 39, No. 2 (Apr. - Jun., 1978).

Jones, Eric, *The European Miracle: Environments, Economics, and Geopolitics in the History of Europe and Asia,* (Cambridge, Cambridge University Press, 2003).

Jones, J. R., *The Revolution of 1688 in England*, (London, Weidenfeld and Nicolson, 1972).

Jones, M. (ed.)., *The New Cambridge Medieval History*. Volume VI c.1300–c.1415, (Cambridge, Cambridge University Press, 2000).

Jones, Richard Foster, *Ancients and Moderns: A Study of the Rise of Modern Science in the Seventeenth Century*, (New York, Dover Publications, 1982).

Jones, Richard H., *For the Glory of God: The Role of Christianity in the Rise and Development of Modern Science*, (Lanham, Maryland, University Press of America, 2011).

Jordan, W. A., *The Development of Religious Toleration in England* (4 vols., Cambridge

MA, Harvard University Press 1932–40).

Judson, Margaret A, *The Political Thought of Sir Henry Vane the Younger*, (Philadelphia, University of Pennsylvania Press, 1969).

Julian, John, *A Dictionary of Hymnology*, 2nd edition, (London, John Murray, 1907).

Kadane, Matthew , *Original Sin and the Path to the Enlightenment, Past & Present*, Volume 235, Issue 1, (May 2017).

Kadane, Matthew, "*Anti-Trinitarianism and the Republican Tradition in Enlightenment Britain*." Republics of Letters: A Journal for the Study of Knowledge, Politics, and the Arts 2, no. 1 (December 15, 2010).

Kalmar, Ivan, *Early Orientalism: Imagined Islam and the Notion of Sublime Power*, (New York, Routledge, 2011).

Kamen, H., *The Rise of Toleration*, (London, McGraw-Hill, 1967).

Kamps and Singh, Jyotsana G. eds., *Travel Knowledge:* European "Discoveries" in the Early Modern Period, (New York, Palgrave, 2001).

Kann, Robert A., *A History of the Hapsburg Empire*, 1526-1918, (Berkeley, University of California Press, 1980).

Kant, Immanuel, *Critique of Pure Reason*, trans. P. Guyer and A.W. Wood, (Cambridge, Cambridge University Press, 1998).

Kaplan, B. J., *Divided By Faith: Religious Conflict and the Practice of Toleration in Early Modern Europe* (London, Harvard University Press, 2007).

Kaplan, Benjamin J., *Muslims in the Dutch Golden Age: Representations and Realities of Religious Toleration* (Amsterdam, Amsterdam University, 2006).

Kaplan, Yosef, *The Dutch Intersection: The Jews and Netherlands in Modern History*, (Leiden, Brill, 2008).

Karman, Gabor and Kuncevic, Lovro eds., *The European Tributary States of the Ottoman Empire in the Sixteenth and Seventeenth Centuries*, (Leiden, Brills, 2013).

Katz, Victor J., ed., *The Mathematics of Egypt, Mesopotamie Mesopotamia, China, India and Islam: A Source Book* (Princeton, Princeton University Press, 2007).

Kazi, A. K., Flynn, J. G., trans., *Muslim Sects and Divisions: The Section on Muslim Sects in Kitab al-Milal wa al-Nihal* by Shahrastani (London, Kegan Paul International, 1984).

Kean, Sam, *Newton, The Last Magician: The great man of science had more than a passing interest in alchemy*, HUMANITIES, (January/February 2011), Volume 32, Number 1

Keeble, N. H., *The Restoration: England in the 1660s*, (Oxford, Blackwell, 2002).

Kelley, Maurice, *Milton and the Trinity*, Huntington Library Quarterly, (Aug., 1970) Vol. 33, No. 4

Kelley, Maurice, *This Great Argument*, (Princeton, Princeton University Press, 1941).

Kelly, John N. D., *Early Christian Doctrines*, (New York Harper and Brothers, 1958).

Kennedy, Hugh, *Caliphate, The History of an Idea*, (New York, Basic Books, 2016).

Kenyon, J. P., *Revolution Principles, The Politics of Party 1689-1720* (Cambridge, Cambridge University Press, 2009).

Kenyon, J. P., *The Popish Plot*, (London, St. Martin's Press, 1972).

Kepler, J., *New Astronomy*, 1609. Trans. by William H. Donahue, (Cambridge, Cambridge University Press, 1992).

Kerr, Fergus, *Thomas Aquinas: A Very Short Introduction* (Oxford, Oxford University Press, 2009).

Khalidi, Tarif, ed. and trans., *The Muslim Jesus: Sayings and Stories in Islamic Literature*, (Cambridge, MA, Harvard University Press, 2001).

Khatab, Sayed and Bouma, Gary D., *Democracy in Islam* (New York, Routledge, 2007).

Kiraly, Bela K. (ed.), *Tolerance and Movements of Religious Dissent in Eastern Europe*, East European Monographs, (New York, Columbia University Press, 1976).

Kley, D. Van, *The Religious Origins of the French Revolution. From Calvin to the Civil Constitution, 1560–1791*, (New Haven and London, Yale University Press, 1996).

Knappen, M. M., *Tudor Puritanism*, (Chicago, University of Chicago Press, 1939).

Knecht, R. J., *Francis I*, (Cambridge, Cambridge University Press, 1982).

Koyré, Alexandre, *From the Closed World to the Infinite Universe*, New York: Harper, (1958); idem, *Metaphysics and Measurement*: Essays in Scientific Revolution, (Cambridge, MA, Harvard University Press, 1968).

Krstic, Tijana, Contested Conversions to Islam: Narratives of Religious Change in the Early Modern Ottoman Empire, (Stanford, Stanford University Press, 2011).

Kupperman, Karen Ordahl, *The Jamestown Project*. (Cambridge, Massachusetts, The Belknap Press of Harvard University Press, 2007).

L. Greaves, Richard, *Society and Religion in Elizabethan England*, (Minneapolis, University of Minnesota Press, 1981).

Labrousse, E., 'Religious Toleration', in Wiener, P.P. (ed.), *Dictionary of the History of Ideas*, 5 vols., (New York, Macmillan, 1974).

Lafuente, Antonio, Elena, Alberto and Ortega, María Luisa eds, *Mundialización de la ciencia y cultura nacional*, Aranjuez, (Madrid, Doce Calles, 1993).

Laidlaw, Christine, *The British in the Levant, Trade and Perceptions of the Ottoman Empire in the Eighteenth Century*, (London, I. B. Tauris, 2010).

Lake, Andrew, *The First Protestants in the Arab World: The Contribution to Christian Mission of the English Aleppo Chaplians* 1597-1782, (Melbourn School of Theology, 2015).

Lamont, William, *Godly Rule: Politics and Religion*, 1603–1660, (New York, Macmillan, 1969).

Landes, David, *The Wealth and Poverty of Nations*, (New York, W. W. Norton and Company, 1998).

Larson, Martin A., *Milton and Servetus: A Study in the Sources of Milton's Theology*, PMLA, Vol. 41, No. 4 (Dec., 1926).

Laursen, J.C. and Nederman, C.J. (eds), *Beyond the Persecuting Society*, (Philadelphia, University of Pennsylvania Press, 1998).

Lawson, Philip, *The East India Company: A History,* (New York, Routledge, 1994).

Lecky, William Edward Hartpole, *History of the Rise and Influence of the Spirit of Rationalism in Europe,* (London, D. Appleton and Company, 1919).

Lehmann, H. & Roth, G. (eds,), *Weber's Protestant Ethic: Origins, Evidence, Contexts,* (Cambridge, Cambridge University Press, 1993).

Lemire, Beverly, *Fashion's Favourite: The Cotton Trade and the Consumer in Britain,* 1660-1800, (Oxford, Oxford University Press, 1991).

Leslie, Michael and Timothy Raylor eds., *Culture and Cultivation in Early Modern England* (Leicester, Leicester University Press, 1992).

Letwin, William, *The Origin of Scientific Economics*, (London, Economics, 1963).

Levitin, Dmitri, *Ancient Wisdom in the Age of New Science: Histories of Philosophy in England*, c. 1640-1700 (Cambridge, Cambridge University Press, 2015).

Lieb, Michael, *Theological Milton: Deity, Discourse and Heresy in the Miltonic Canon,* (Pittsburgh, Duquesne University Press, 2006).

Lillywhite, Bryant, *London Coffee Houses: A Reference Book of Coffee Houses of the Seventeenth, Eighteenth, and Nineteenth Centuries*, (London, George Allen, 1963).

Linda T. Darling, "Ottoman Politics through British Eyes: Paul Rycaut's 'the Present State of the Ottoman Empire,'" Journal of World History 5, no. 1 (1994).

Lindbeck, George, *The Nature of Doctrine: Religion and Theology in a Postliberal Age,* (Louisville, Westminster John Knox Press, 1984).

Lindberg, David C. and Numbers, Ronald L. eds., *God & Nature: Historical Essays on the Encounter between Christianity and Science,* (Berkeley, University of California Press, 1986); Lindberg and Numbers, "Beyond War and Peace: A Reappraisal of the Encounter between Christianity and Science," Church History 55 (1986).

Lingle, Walter L. and Kuykendall, John W., *Presbyterians: Their History and Beliefs,* (Atlanta, Westminster John Knox Press, 1978).

Locke, John, *A letter concerning toleration* humbly submitted (London: for Awnsham Churchill, 1689).

Locke, John, *An Essay Concerning Human Understanding*, (University Park, Pennsylvania State University Press, 1999).

Locke, John, *The Reasonableness of Christianity as Delivered in the Scriptures*. Edited by Victor Nuovo. (Bristol, Thoemmes Press, 1997).

Locke, John, *Two Tracts*, ed. Philip Abrams, (Cambridge, Cambridge University Press, 1967).

Locke, John, *Two Treatises of Government, ed. Peter Laslett*, (Cambridge: Cambridge University Press, 1988).

Locke, *Political Essays, ed. M. Goldie, Cambridge Texts in the History of Political Thought* (Cambridge: Cambridge University Press, 1997).

Locke, *The Reasonableness of Christianity: With A Discourse of Miracles and part of A Third Letter Concerning Toleration*, edited by I. T. Ramsey, (Stanford, Stanford University Press, 1958).

Loewenstein, David and Marshall, John eds., *Heresy, Literature and Politics in Early Modern English Culture* (Cambridge, Cambridge University Press, 2006).

Loewenstein, David. *Representing Revolution in Milton and His Contemporaries: Religion, Politics and Polemics in Radical Puritanism* (Cambridge, Cambridge University Press, 2004).

Loop, Jan, Hamilton, Alastair and Burnett, Charles eds., *The Teaching and Learning of Arabic in Early Modern Europe*, (Leiden, Brills, 2017).

Lovejoy, A. O., *The Great Chain of Being: A Study of the History of an Idea*, (Cambridge, Mass., Harvard University Press, 1936).

Lucci, Diego, *"Locke and the Trinity,"* Studi Lockiani. Ricerche sull'età moderna, 1 (2020).

Lucci, Diego, *The Law of Nature, Mosaic Judaism, and Primitive Christianity in John Locke and the English Deists*, Entangled Religions 8 (2019).

Lucci, D., *John Locke's Christianity,* Cambridge, Cambridge University Press, (2020).

Lunsford, Virginia W., *Piracy and Privateering in the Golden Age Netherland* (New York, Palgrave Macmillan, 2005).

Luther, Martin, *"War Against the Turk."* Works of Martin Luther, Volume V. Trans. C. M. Jacobs. (Cologne, Germany, Lindemann Press, 2007).

M. Bryant, Joseph , *"The West and the rest revisited: Debating capitalist origins, European colonialism and the advent of modernity"*, Canadian Journal of Sociology 31(4), (2006).

MaCabe, Ina Baghdiantz, *Orientalism in Early Modern France: Euraasain Eurasian Trade, Exoticism and the Ancient Regime*, (Oxford, BERG, 2008).

Macaulay, Thomas B., *The History of England from the Accession of James the Second, 5 vols.*, (London, 1849-61).

MacCulloch, Diarmaid, *Reformation: Europe's House Divided 1490–1700*, (London, Penguin, 2003).

Macdonald, Duncan B., *Development of Muslim Theology, Jurisprudence and Constitutional Theory* (Beirut: Khayats, 1965).

Machamer, Peter ed., *The Cambridge Companion to Galileo* (Cambridge: Cambridge University Press, 1998).

Mack, Rosamond E., *Bazaar to Piazza: Islamic Trade and Italian Art, 1300-1600*

(Berkeley, University of California Press, 2001).

Maclachlan, H. J., *Socinianism in Seventeenth-Century England* (Oxford, Oxford University Press, 1951).

MacLean, Gerald and Matar, Nabil, *Britain and the Islamic World 1558-1713* (Oxford, Oxford University Press, 2011).

MacLean, Gerald, ed., *Re-Orienting the Renaissance: Cultural Exchanges with the East* (New York, Palgrave Macmillan, 2005).

MacLean, Gerald, *Looking East: English Writing and the Ottoman Empire before 1800* (New York, Palgrave Macmillan, 2007).

MacLean, Gerald, *The Rise of Oriental Travel: English Visitors to the Ottoman Empire*, 1580–1720, Basingstoke, Palgrave, (2004).

MacLean, Gerald, *The Rise of Oriental Travel: English Visitors to the Ottoman Empire 1580-1720*, (New York, Palgrave Macmillian, 2004).

MacLeod, R. M. ed., *Nature and Empire: Science and the Colonial Enterprise*, (Chicago, University of Chicago Press, 2001).

Makdisi, George, *The Rise of Colleges, Institutions of Higher Learning in Islam and the West*, Edinburgh, (Edinburgh University Press, 1981).

Makdisi, George, *The Scholastic Method in Medieval Education: An Inquiry into its Origins in Law and Theology*, Speculum, v. 49, No.4, (October, 1974).

Malcolm, Noel, *Enemies: Islam and the Ottoman Empire in Western Political Thought, 1450-1750*, (Oxford, Oxford University Press, 2019).

Malloch, Thomas, *Finch and Baines: A Seventeenth Century Friendship*. (Cambridge, Cambridge University Press, 1917).

Manchester, William, *A World Lit Only by Fire: The Medieval Mind and the Renaissance: Portrait of an Age*, (Boston, Little, Brown and Company, 1993).

Mann, M., *The Sources of Social Power: A History of Power from the Beginning to A.D. 1760* (Cambridge, Cambridge University Press, 2012).

Manuel, Frank, *The Religion of Isaac Newton* (Oxford, Oxford University Press, 1974).

Markus, R. A., *Sacred and Secular: Studies on Augustine and Latin Christianity*, (Ashgate Variorum, Farnham, 1994).

Marlan, Stanton, *The Philosophers' Stone: Alchemical Imagination and the Soul's Logical Life*, Doctoral dissertation. (Pittsburgh, Penn., Duquesne University, 2014).

Marshall, John, *John Locke, Toleration, and Early Enlightenment Culture: Religious Intolerance and Arguments for Religious Toleration in Early Modern and 'Early Enlightenment' Europe*, (Cambridge, Cambridge University Press, 2006).

Marshall, John, *John Locke: Resistance, Religion and Responsibility*, (Cambridge, Cambridge University Press, 1994).

Marshall, P.J., '*Warren Hastings as Scholar and Patron*', Statesmen, Scholars and Merchants: Essays in Eighteenth-Century History presented to Dame Lucy Sutherland, eds A. Whiteman, J.S. Bromley, and P.G.M. Dickson, (Oxford, Clarendon Press, 1973).

Marshall, Peter, *Heretics and Believers: A History of the English Reformation*, (London, Yale University Press, 2017).

Martin, David, *Christian Language and Its Mutations*, (Aldershot, Ashgate, 2002).

Mason, Stephen F., *Some Historical Roots of the Scientific Revolution*, Science & Society, Vol. 14, No. 3 (Summer, 1950).

Masood, Hafiz Abid, *"Islam in Early Modern English Literature: A Select Bibliography."* Islamic Studies 44 (2005).

Masson, David, *The Life of John Milton*, (Gloucester, Mass, Peter Smith, 1965).

Matar, Nabil (ed.)., *Henry Stubbe and the Beginnings of Islam, The Original & Progress of Mahometanism*, New York, Columbia University Press, (2014).

Matar, Nabil, *"Some Notes on George Fox and Islam,"* The Journal of the Friends' Historical Society 55 (1989).

Matar, Nabil, *Britain and Barbary, 1589-1689*, (Gainesville, University Press of Florida, 2005).

Matar, Nabil, *Europe Through Arab Eyes, 1578-1727*, (New York, Columbia University Press, 2009).

Matar, Nabil, *In the Lands of the Christians: Arabic Travel Writing in the Seventeenth Century*, (New York, Routledge, 2003).

Matar, Nabil, *Islam in Britain*, 1558–1685, (Cambridge, Cambridge University Press, 1998).

Matar, Nabil, *John Locke and the Turbaned Nations*, Journal of Islamic Studio 2:1 (1991).

Matar, Nabil, *Turks, Moors and Englishmen in the Age of Discovery*, (New York, Columbia University Press, 1999).

Mather, James, *Pashas: Traders and Travellers in the Islamic World*, (New Haven, Yale University Press, 2009).

Matthew, H. C. J. and Harrison, Brian, *Oxford Dictionary of National Biography*, (Oxford, Oxford University Press, 2004).

Mavroudi, Maria, *A Byzantine Book on Dream Interpretation: The Oneirocriticon of Achmet and Its Arabic Sources, The Medieval Mediterranean*, (Leiden, Brill, 2002).

Maxwell-Stuart, P. G. (ed.)., *The Occult in Early Modern Europe. A Documentary History*, (Basingstoke, Macmillan, 1999).

McAuliffe, Jane D. (ed.)., *The Cambridge Companion to the Quran*, (Cambridge, Cambridge University Press, 2006).

McGiffert, Arthur C., *A History of Christian Thought*, (New York, Charles Scribner's Sons, 1960).

McGinnis, Jon, *Avicenna*, (Oxford, Oxford University Press, 2010).

McGrade, A. S. (ed.)., *The Cambridge Companion to Medieval Philosophy*, (Cambridge, Cambridge University Press, 2006).

McGuire, J. E., 'Force, Active Principles and Newton's Invisible Realm', Ambix 15 (1968).

McKinney, Alfred G., *Mohammed, The Myths*, (New York, i Universe Inc, 2007).

McLachlan, Herbert, *The Religious Views of Milton, Locke and Newton*, (Manchester, University of Manchester Press, 1941).

McMichael, Jack R. & Taft, Barbara eds., *The Writings of William Walwyn*, (Athens, GA, University of Georgia Press, 1989).

Meggitt, Justin J., 'Nöel Aubert de Versé'. In Christian-Muslim Relations. A Bibliographical History. Volume 13. Western Europe (1700-1800), edited by David Thomas and John A. Chesworth, 75–76. Leiden: Brill, (2019).

Melton, James Von Hon, *The Rise of the Public in Enlightenment Europe*, (Cambridge, Cambridge University Press, 2001).

Mendelsohn, Andrew J., "Alchemy and Politics in England 1649—1665." Past & Present, no. 135 (May 1992).

Menocal, Maria Rosa, *The Ornament of the World, How Muslims, Jews, and Christians Created a Culture of Tolerance in Medieval Spain*, (New York, Back Bay Books, Little Brown and Company, 2002).

Merriman, Roger Bigelow, *Suleiman the Magnificent 1520-1566*, (Worcestershire, Read Books, 2007).

Merton, Robert K., *Science, Technology and Society in Seventeenth Century England*, (Bruges, St. Catherine Press, 1938).

Metlitzki, Dorothee, *The Matter of Araby in Medieval England*, (New Haven, Yale University Press, 1977).

Mills, Simon, "The English Chaplains at Aleppo: Exploration and Scholarship between England and the Ottoman Empire, 1620–1760," Bulletin of the Council for British Research in the Levant 6, no. 1 (2011).

Milne, Doreen J., (1951).. "The Results of the Rye House Plot and Their Influence upon the Revolution of 1688: The Alexander Prize Essay", Transactions of the Royal Historical Society (1951). 5. 1

Milton, Anthony, *Catholic and Reformed: The Roman and Protestant Churches in English Protestant Thought, 1600-1640* (Cambridge, Cambridge University Press, 1995).

Milton, Anthony, *Laudian and Royalist Polemic in Seventeenth-Century England: The Career and Writings of Peter Heylyn*, (Manchester, Manchester University Press, 2007).

Milton, Anthony, *Laudian and Royalist Polemic in Seventeenth-Century England: The Career and Writings of Peter Heylyn* (Manchester, Manchester University Press, 2007).

Milton, Philip, *John Locke and the Rye House Plot, The Historical Journal*, Vol. 43, No. 3 (Sep., 2000).

Mirkovic, Alexander, *From Courtly Curiosity to Revolutionary Refreshment: Turkish Coffee and English Politics in the Seventeenth century* (A thesis submitted in partial fulfillment of the requirements for the degree of Masters of Arts, Department of History, University of South Florida, 2005).

Moo, Douglas J., *The Epistle to the Romans*, Grand Rapids, MI, William B. Eerdmans, 1996

Moore, Barrington, *Social Origins of Dictatorship and Democracy: Lord and Peasant in the Making of the Modern World* (Boston: Beacon, 1966).

Moore, George, *Judaism* (Cambridge: Harvard University Press, 1970).

Moore, R.I., *The Formation of a Persecuting Society: Power and Deviance in Western Europe AD 950–1250* (Oxford, Wiley-Blackwell, 1986).

Moran, Bruce T., *Distilling Knowledge: Alchemy, Chemistry, and the Scientific Revolution* (Cambridge, MA: Harvard University Press, 2006).

More, Louis Trenchard, *Boyle as Alchemist, Journal of the History of Ideas*, Vol. 2, No. 1 (Jan., 1941).

More, Louis Trenchard, *Isaac Newton: A Biography 1642-1727* (New York, Charles Scribner's Sons, 1934).

Morgan, Edmund S., *American Slavery, American Freedom: The Ordeal of Colonial Virginia* (New York: W. W. Norton and Company, 1975).

Morgan, Joseph, *A Complete History of Algiers* (1728–1729, (New York: Negro University Press, 1970).

Morgan, Kenneth O. ed., *The Oxford History of Britain* (Oxford, Oxford University Press, 2010).

Morrill, John, *The Nature of the English Revolution* (New York, Routledge, 2013).

Mortimer, Sarah and Robertson, John eds., *The Intellectual Consequences of Religious Heterodoxy 1600–1750* (Leiden, Brills, 2012).

Mortimer, Sarah, *Reason and Religion in the English Revolution: The Challenge of Socinianism* (Cambridge, Cambridge University Press, 2010)

Moule, Charles F. D., *The Origin of Christology* (Cambridge: Cambridge University Press, 1977).

Mulligan, Lotte, *Puritans and English Science: A Critique of Webster,*: Isis, Vol. 71, No. 3 (Sep., 1980)

Mulsow, Martin and Rohls, John eds., *Socinianism and Arminianism: Antitrinitarians, Calvinists and Cultural Exchange in Seventeenth-Century Europe* (Amsterdam, Brills, 2005).

Mulsow, Martin, *Socinianism, Islam and the Radical Uses of Arabic Scholarship* (Al-Qantara, 31(2), July-December 2010).

Murphey, Rhoads, *Ottoman Warfare, 1500-1700* (New Jersey, Rutgers University

Press, 1999).

Nahas, Michael, *A Translation of Hayy B. Yaqẓān by the Elder Edward Pococke 1604-1691*, Journal of Arabic Literature, Vol. 16 (1985).

Nakosteen, Mehdi, *History of Islamic Origins of Western Education* , A.D. 800-1350 (Boulder, University of Colorado Press, 1978).

Nasr, S. H. and Leaman, Oliver, eds., *History of Islamic Philosophy* (New York, Routledge, 1996).

Nebelsick, Harold P., *The Renaissance,* The Reformation and the Rise of Science (Edinburgh, T & T Clark, 1992).

Needham, Joseph, *Clerks and Craftsmen in China and the West* (Cambridge: Cambridge University Press, 1970).

Needham, Joseph, *Science and Civilisation in China*, Pt 2, vol VII, (Cambridge, Cambridge University Press, 2004).

Netton, Ian Richard , *Allah Transcendent: Studies in the Structure and Semiotics of Islamic Philosophy, Theology and Cosmology* (New York, Routledge, 1995).

Newbury, Colin, *Patrons, Clients and Empire: Chieftaincy and Over-Rule in Asia, Africa, and the Pacific* (Oxford: Oxford University Press, 2003).

Newman, William R. and Principe, Lawrence M., *Alchemy Tried in the Fire: Starkey, Boyle, and the Fate of Helmontian Chymistry* (Chicago, University of Chicago Press, 2002).

Newman, William R., 'The Alchemical Sources of Robert Boyle's Corpuscular Philosophy', Annals of Science 53 (1996).

Newman, William R., *Promethean Ambitions: Alchemy and the Quest to Perfect Nature* (Chicago and London, University of Chicago Press, 2004).

Nicholson, Marjorie Hope ed. *Conway Letters: The Correspondence of Anne, Viscountess Conway, Henry More, and Their Friends, 1642-1684* (New Haven: Yale University Press, 1930).

Niebhur Niebuhr, Richard, *Radical Monotheism and Western Culture* (New York, Harper and Row, 1960).

Nock, Arthur Darby, *Early Gentile Christianity and its Hellenistic Background* (New York, Harper Torchbooks, 1964).

Norris, Richard A., Jr., ed. and trans., *The Christological Controversy* (Philadelphia: Fortress Press, 1980).

North, Douglass C. and Thomas, Robert Paul. *The Rise of the Western World: A New Economic History* (Cambridge, Cambridge University Press, 1973).

North, Douglass C. and Weingast, Barry R. "*Constitutions and Commitment: Evolution of Institutions Governing Public Choice,*" Journal of Economic History, 49 (1989)

North, John, *The Ambassadors' Secret: Holbein and the World of the Renaissance* (London, Phoenix, 2004).

North, Roger, *The Lives of the Norths*, Vol. II, ed. Augustus Jessopp (London: Gregg International Publishers Limited, 1969).

Nuovo, Victor, *Christianity, Antiquity, and Enlightenment: Interpretations of Locke* (New York, Springer, 2011).

O'Leary, Don, *Roman Catholicism and Modern Science: A History* (New York, Continuum, 2006).

Oberhelman, Steven M., ed., *The Oneirocriticon of Achmet: A Medieval Greek and Arabic Treatise on the Interpretation of Dreams* (Lubbock, TX: Texas Tech University Press, 1991).

Oberman, Hieko A., *Luther: Man between God and the Devil*, translated by Eileen Walliser-Schwarzbart, (New Haven, Yale University Press, 1989).

O'Brien, John J, *Samuel Hartlib's influence on Robert Boyle's scientific development*, Annals of Science, 1965, 21:1).

O'Connor, Daniel, *The Chaplains of the East India Company, 1601-1858* (London, Continuum, 2012).

Ogborn, Miles, *Indian Ink: Script and Print in the Making of English East India Company* (Chicago, University of Chicago Press, 2007).

Ogg, David, *England in the Reigns of James II and William III* (Oxford, Clarendon Press, 1955).

Oldridge, Daren Darren, *The Supernatural in Tudor and Stuart England* (New York, Routledge, 2016).

Olmstead, Justin Quinn ed., *Britain in the Islamic World: Imperial and Post-Imperial Connections* (London, Palgrave Macmillan, 2019).

Ophir, Adir and Shapin, Steven '*The Place of Knowledge. A Methodological Survey*', Science in Context, vol. 4, no. 1 (1991)

Ordahl, Kupperman Karen, *The Jamestown Project,* (London, Belknap Press, 2009).

Osler, M. J. and Farber, P. J., eds., *Religion, Science, and Worldview* (Cambridge, Cambridge University Press, 1985).

Osumi, T., *Printed Cottons of Asia: the Romance of Trade Textiles* (Tokyo, Charles E. Tuttle Company, 1963).

Outram, Dorinda, *The Enlightenment* (Cambridge, Cambridge University Press, 1995).

Owens, Joseph: "*Aquinas as Aristotelian Commentator*," in St. Thomas Aquinas (1274-1974). Commemorative Studies (Toronto: Pont. Ins!. Med. Stud., 1974).

Ozment, Steven, *The Age of Reform 1250-1550,* (London, Yale University Press, 1980).

P.C. Floud, 'The origins of English calico printing', Journal of the Society of Dyers and Colourists, 76 (1960).

Pagden, Anthony, *Lords of All the World: Ideologies of Empire in Spain, Britian, and*

France, C. 1500-1800 (New Haven: Yale University Press, 1995).

Pailin, David A., *Attitudes to Other Religions: Comparative Religion in Seventeenth and Eighteenth Century Britain* (Manchester, Manchester University Press, 1984).

Parker, Geoffrey, *The Military Revolution,* (Cambridge, Cambridge University Press, 1988).

Parker, Kim Ian, *Newton, Locke and the Trinity: Sir Isaac's comments on Locke's: A Paraphrase and Notes on the Epistle of St Paul to the Romans*, Scottish Journal of Theology / Volume 62 / Issue 01 / (February 2009).

Parkinson, G. H. R., (Ed.), *The Renaissance and the Seventeenth-century Rationalism* (Routledge, London, 1993).

Patrides, C. A., *Approaches to Paradise Lost: The York Tercentenary Lectures* (Toronto, University of Toronto, 1968).

Paxman, David B., " 'Adam in a Strange Country': Locke Language Theory and Travel Literature," Modern Philology, vol. 92, No. 4 (May, 1995).

Pearl, David, *A Textbook on Muslim Personal Law*, (London: Croom Helm, 1979).

Peck, Linda Levy, *Consuming splendor: Society and Culture in Seventeenth-Century England* (Cambridge, UK; New York: Cambridge University Press, 2005).

Perille, Laura, "A Mirror to Turke": "Turks" and the Making of Early Modern England", Ph. D. thesis submitted to the Department of History at Brown University Providence, Rhode Island, May 2015).

Peters, Edward, *Heresy and Authority in the Middle Ages* (London, University of Pennsylvania Press, 1980).

Peters, Edward, *Inquisition* (New York: Free Press, 1988).

Peters, Edward, *Torture* (New York: Basil Blackwell, 1985).

Pfizenmaier, Thomas C., *Was Isaac Newton an Arian?*, Journal of the History of Ideas, Vol. 58, No. 1 (Jan., 1997).

Pharr, Clyde, trans., *The Theodosian Code* (London, Oxford University Press, 1952).

Picciotto, Joanna, "*Implicit Faith and Reformations of Habit.*" JMEMS 46, no. 3 (2016).

Picirilli, Robert, *Grace, Faith, Free Will: Contrasting Views of Salvation* (Nashville, Randall House, 2002).

Pierce, Mary Lynn, *CONTROVERSY IN SEVENTEENTH-CENTURY ENGLISH COFFEEHOUSES: TRANSCULTURAL INTERACTIONS WITH AN ORIENTAL IMPORT* (Dissertation Submitted to the Faculty of the Department of History, the University of Arizona, 2015).

Pincus, Steve, "*Coffee Politicians Does Create: Coffeehouses and Restoration Political Culture*" (in Journal of Modern History, 6:4 (1995)).

Pinkham, Lucile, *William III and the Respectable Revolution: The Part Played by William of Orange in the Revolution of 1688* (Cambridge, Mass., Harvard University Press, 1954).

Plumb, J. H., *The Growth of Political Stability in England 1675–1725* (London, Macmillan, 1967).

Pocock, J. G. A., '*Contexts for the Study of James Harrington*/ II Pensiero Politico, 2 (1978).

Pocock, J. G. A., *The Machiavellian Moment: Florentine Political Thought and the Atlantic Republican Tradition* (Princeton, Princeton University Press, 2017).

Pocock, J. G. A., *Barbarism and Religion: The Enlightenments of Edward Gibbon,* 1737–1764, Cambridge, Cambridge University Press, (1999).

Poole, William, *Milton and the Idea of Fall* (Cambridge, Cambridge University Press, 2005).

Porter, Roy and M. Teich (eds.), *The Enlightenment in National Context,* Cambridge, Cambridge University Press, (1981).

Prasad, Beni, *History of Jahangir* (Allahabad, Indian Press, 1962).

Preudenthal Freudenthal, Gidion Gideon and McLaughlin, Peter eds., *The Social and Economic Roots of the Scientific Revolution: Texts by Borris Hessen and Henryk Grossmann,* (New York, Springer, 2009).

Principe, Lawrence, *Chymists and Chymistry: Studies in the History of Alchemy and Early Modern Chemistry* (Sagamore Beach, MA: Science History Publications, 2007).

Principe, Lawrence, *The Aspiring Adept: Robert Boyle and his Alchemical Quest* (Princeton: Princeton University Press, 1998).

Pugh, Martin, *Britain and Islam,* (New Haven, Yale University Press, 2019).

Purrington, Robert D., *The First Professional Scientist: Robert Hooke and the Royal Society of London* (Boston, Birkhauser, 2009).

Quantin, Jean-Louis, *The Church of England and Christian Antiquity: The Construction of a Confessional Identity in the 17th Century* (Oxford, Oxford University Press, 2009).

Rabb, T. K., *Jacobean Gentleman: Sir Edwin Sandys, 1561–1629* (Princeton, NJ: Princeton University Press, 1998).

Rabb, Theodore K. "*Puritanism and the Rise of Experimental Science in England*," , Cahiers d'Histoire Mondiale, VII (1962).

Rabb, Theodore K., *Enterprise and Empire: Merchant and Gentry Investment in the Expansion of England, 1575–1630* (Cambridge, MA: Harvard University Press, 1967).

Rachfahl, F., "*Kalvinismus und Kapitalismus,*" inj. Winckelmann, ed., Die Protestant Ethik II (Hamburg, 1972).

Rafiabadai, Hamid, Naseem and Kak, Aadil, Amin, *The Attitude of Islam Towards Science and Philosophy* (New Delhi, Sarup and Sons, 2003).

Rafiabadi, Hamid Naseem, *Emerging from Darkness: Ghazzali's Impact on the Western Philosophers* (New Delhi, Sarup & Sons, 2002).

Rahman, Fazlur, *Major Theme of the Quran* (Minneapolis, Bibliotheca Islamica, 1994).

Raj, *Relocating Modern Science: Circulation and the Construction of Knowledge in South Asia and Europe, 1650–1900* (New York, Palgrave, 2007).

Rajan, Raghuram G. and Zingales, Luigi, *Saving Capitalism from the Capitalists: Unleashing the Power of Financial Markets to Create Wealth and Spread Opportunity* (New York, Crown Business, 2003).

Rattansi, P. M., *"Paracelsus and the Puritan Revolution"*, Ambix, xi (1963).

Reedy, Gerard, *The Bible and Reason: Anglicans and Scripture in Late Seventeenth-Century England* (Philadelphia, University of Pennsylvania Press, 1985).

Rees, Evans Robert, *Pantheisticon: The Career of John Toland* (New York, Peter Lang, 1991).

Renard, John, *Islam and Christianity: Theological Themes in Comparative Perspective* (Berkeley, University of California Press, 2011).

Riello, Giorgio and Roy, Tirthankar, *How India Clothed the World: The World of South Asian Textiles, 1500–1850* (Leiden, Brills, 2009).

Rippin, Andrew, Muslims: *Their Religious Beliefs & Practices* (New York: Routledge, 1990).

Ritchie, Susan J., *Children of the Same God: The Historical Relationship between Unitarianism, Judaism, and Islam,* (Boston, Skinner House Books, 2014).

Robertson, H., *Aspects of the Rise of Economic Individualism: A Criticism of Max Weber and his School* (New York, Kelley and Millman, 1959).

Robertson, John ed., *A Union for Empire* (Cambridge, Cambridge University Press, 1995).

Robertson, John, *The Case for the Enlightenment: Scotland and Naples 1680-1760* (Cambridge, Cambridge University Press, 2005).

Robertson, Randy, *Censorship and Conflict in Seventeenth Century England: A Subtle Art of Division* (University Park, Pennsylvania State University Press, 2009).

Robertston, John, 'Hugh Trevor-Roper, Intellectual History and "The Religious Origins of the Enlightenment', English Historical Review, cxxiv, 511 (2009).

Robinson, Benedict S., *Islam and Early Modern English Literature: The Politics of Romance from Spenser to Milton* (New York: Palgrave Macmillan, 2007).

Robinson, Edward Forbes, *The Early History of Coffee Houses in England* (London, 1893).

Robinson, S., *A History of Dyed Textiles* (London, Studio Vista, 1969).

Rodinson, Maxine, *Europe and the Mystique of Islam* (London, I. B. Tauris, 2002).

Rosenthal, Franz, *Man Versus Society in Early Islam,* edited by Dimitri Gutas, (Leiden: Brill, 2015).

Ross, Richard P., *The Social and Economic Causes of the Revolution in the Mathematical Sciences in Mid-Seventeenth-Century England*, Journal of British Studies, Vol. 15, No. 1 (Autumn, 1975).

Rummel, Erika, (Ed.), *Biblical Humanism and Scholasticism in the Age of Erasmus* (Leiden, Brill, 2008).

Russell, Alexander, *The Natural History of Aleppo and Parts Adjacent*, Vol II (London: Gregg Publishing, 1969).

Russell, Conrad, *Unrevolutionary England, 1603-1642* (London, Hambledon Press, 1990).

Russell, G. A. (ed.), *The 'Arabick' Interest of the Natural Philosophers in Seventeenth-Century England* (Leiden, Brill, 1998)

Sachedina, Abdulaziz A., *The Just Ruler (al-Sultan al-'Adil) in Shi'ite Islam*, (Oxford, Oxford University Press, 1998).

Said, Edward, *Orientalism* (New York, Vintage, 1979).

Sajdi, Dana, *OTTOMAN TULIPS, OTTOMAN COFFEE: Leisure and Lifestyle in the Eighteenth Century* (London, New York: Tauris Academic Studies, 2007).

Saliba, George, *Islamic Science and the Making of European Renaissance* (London, MIT Press, 2007).

Samuelson, K., *Religion and Economic Action: The Protestant Ethic, the Rise of Capitalism and the Abuses of Scholarship* (Toronto, University of Tornoto Press, 1993).

Saurat, Denis, *Milton, Man and Thinker* (New York: AMS Press, 1975).

Scammell, G.V., *'European Exiles, Renegades and Outlaws and the Maritime Economy of Asia c.1500-1750'* in Modern Asian Studies, Vol. 26, No. 4 (1992).

Schaff, Philip, *Augustin: The Writings Against the Manichaeans and Against the Donatists* (New York: The Christian Literature Publishing Co., 1890).

Schmitt, Carl, *Political Theology: Four Chapters on the Concept of Sovereignty*, trans. George Schwab, (Chicago, University of Chicago Press, 2006).

Schmitt, Carl, *The Concept of the Political*, trans. George Schwab, (Chicago, University of Chicago Press, 2007).

Scholder, Klaus, *The Birth of Modem Critical Theology: Origins and Problems of Biblical Criticism at the Seventeenth Century*. John Bowden tr., (Philadelphia, Trinity Press, 1985).

Schroeder, John J., *"London and the New Model Army, 1647"*, The Historian, Vol. 19, No. 3 (May, 1957).

Schroeder, John J., *War Finance in London, 1642-1646* (Historian, 1959 Vol. 21; Iss. 4).

Schülting, Sabine, *Sabine Lucia Müller, and Ralf Hertel, Early Modern Encounters with the Islamic East: Performing Cultures* (Burlington: Ashgate, 2012).

Schulz, Zachary W., *THE ENGLISH IN THE LEVANT: COMMERCE, DIPLOMACY, AND THE ENGLISH NATION IN THE OTTOMAN EMPIRE, 1672-1691*, A Ph.D. (Dissertation Submitted to the Faculty of Purdue University, West Lafayette, Indiana, 2018).

Schwoerer, Lois G., *"William, Lord Russell: The Making of a Martyr, 1683–1983."* Journal of British Studies 24.1 (1985).

Schwoerer, Lois G., *Locke, Lockean Ideas, and the Glorious Revolution, Journal of the History of Ideas*, Vol. 51, No. 4 (Oct. - Dec., 1990)

Scott J., *Algernon Sidney and the Restoration Crises, 1677-1683*, (Cambridge, Cambridge University Press, 2002).

Scott, Jonathan, *England's Troubles: Seventeenth Century English Political Instability in European Context* (Cambridge, Cambridge University Press, 2004).

Servetus, Michael, *Christianismi restitutio* (Vienne en Dauphine: Balthazar Arnollett, 1553).

Servetus, Michael, *The Two Treatises of Servetus on the Trinity: On the Errors of the Trinity*, 7 books, (A.D. 1531); *Dialogues on the Trinity*, 2 books; *On the Righteousness of Christ's Kingdom*, 4 chapters, (A.D. 1532), trans. Earl Morse Wilbur (Cambridge, MA: Harvard University Press, 1932).

Setton, Kenneth, *Europe and the Levant in the Middle Age and the Renaissance* (London: Variorum Reprints, 1976).

Shagan, Ethan H., *The Birth of Modern Belief: Faith and Judgment from the Middle Ages to the Enlightenment* (Princeton, Princeton University Press, 2018).

Shah, Zulfiqar Ali, *A Study of Anthropomorphism and Transcendence in the Bible and Quran: The Concept of God in Judaic, Christian and Islamic Traditions,* (London, International Institute of Islamic Thought, 2012).

Shah, Zulfiqar Ali, *St. Thomas Aquinas and Muslim Thought,* (Swansea, Claritis Books, 2021). Shah, Zulfiqar Ali, Islam's Reformation of Christianity, (Swansea, Claritis Books, 2021).

Shannon, Hoff, *"Locke and the Nature of Political Authority"* (The Review of Politics, 2015, 77 (1)).

Shapin, Steven 'Placing the View from Nowhere: Historical and Sociological Problems in the Location of Science', Transactions of the Institute of British Geographers, vol. 23 (1998).

Shapin, Steven and Schaffer, Simon, *Leviathan and the Air-Pump: Hobbes, Boyle and the Experimental Life* (Princeton: Princeton University Press, 1985).

Shapin, Steven, *The Scientific Revolution* (Chicago & London, University of Chicago Press, 1996).

Shapiro, B. J. 'Latitudinarianism and science in seventeenth-century England', Past and Present, (1986).

Sharp, David, *Oliver Cromwell,* (Portsmouth, Heinemann, 2003).

Sheils, W. J. ed., *Persecution and Toleration. Studies in Church History*, 21, (Oxford, Blackwell, 1984).

Shrewsbury, J. F. D., *A History of Bubonic Plague in the British Isles* (Cambridge, Cambridge University Press, 1970).

Simmel, G., *The Philosophy of Money*, (New York, Routledge, 2011).

Sims, James H. and Ryken, Leland eds., *Milton and the Scriptural Tradition* (Columbia, University of Missouri Press, 1984).

Sinn, Simone and Sinaga, Martin L. eds., *Freedom and Responsibility, Christian and*

Muslim Explorations (Minneapolis, Luther University Press, 2010).

Sirota, Brent S. *The Trinitarian Crisis in Church and State: Religious Controversy and the Making of the Postrevolutionary Church of England, 1687–1702* (Journal of British Studies, 2013, 52).

Smith, David L., *The Stuart Parliaments, 1603–1689* (London: Arnold, 1999).

Smith, Pamela H. "*Science on the Move: Recent Trends in the History of Early Modern Science*." (Renaissance Quarterly, vol. 62, no. 2, 2009).

Smith, Pamela H. and Findlen, Paula eds., *Merchants and Marvels: Commerce, Science and Art in Early Modern Europe* (New York, Routledge, 2002).

Smylie, James H., *A Brief History of the Presbyterians* (Louisville, KY: Geneva Press, 1996).

Snobelen, Stephen D., *Isaac Newton, Heretic: the Strategies of a Nicodemite* (British journal for the history of science (BJHS), 1999, 32).

Sombart, W., *The Jews and Modern Capitalism* (New York, Martino Fine Books, 2015).

Sombart, W., *The Quintessence of Capitalism: A Study of the History and Psychology of the Modern Business Man* (New York, The Classics, 1967).

Sommerville, Johann P., 'The Royal Supremacy and Episcopacy "iure divino", 1603–1640' Journal of Ecclesiastical History, 34 (1984).

Sowerby, Scott, *Making Toleration: The Repealers and the Glorious Revolution*, (Cambridge, Mass., Harvard University Press, 2013).

Spellberg, Denise A., *Thomas Jefferson's Quran: Islam and the Founders*, (New York: Knopf, 2013).

Spellman, W. M., *John Locke and Problem of Depravity*, Oxford, Clarendon Press, 1988

Spurr, John (ed.), *Anthony Ashley Cooper, First Earl of Shaftesbury 1621–1683*, (Surrey, Ashgate, 2011).

Stam, Cornelius M, *Commentary on the Epistle of Roman*, (Steven Point, WI, Berean Literature Foundation, 1984).

Steve Pincus, *"Coffee Politicians Does Create"*: Coffeehouses and Restoration Political Culture, The Journal of Modern History, Vol. 67, No. 4 (Dec., 1995).

Steward Stewart, M. A. (ed.), *English Philosophy in the Age of Locke* (Oxford, Oxford University Press, 2000).

Stewart, Michael Alexander, *English Philosophy in the Age of Locke* (Oxford, Clarendon, 2000).

Stoll, Abraham Dylan, *Milton and Monotheism* (Doctoral dissertation submitted to Princeton University department of English, 2000).

Stoll, Abraham, *Milton and Monotheism* (Pittsburgh: Duquesne University Press, 2009).

Stone, Lawrence "*The Bourgeois Revolution of Seventeenth Century England Revisited*," Past and Present, 109 (1985).

Struve, Lynn A. (ed.) *The Qing Formation in World-Historical Time* (Cambridge, MA:

Harvard University Asia Center, 2004).

Subrahmanyam, Sanjay (ed.), *Merchants Network in the Early Modern World* (New York, Routledge, 2016).

Subrahmanyam, Sanjay, *Europe's India: Words, People, Empires 1500-1800* (London, Harvard University Press, 2017).

Subrahmanyam, Sanjay, *From the Tagus to the Ganges* (New Delhi: Oxford University Press, 2005).

Sugirtharajah, R. S. ed., *Wilderness: Essays in Honour of Frances Young* (London: Continuum, 2005).

Sullivan, Karen, *Truth and the Heretic. Crises of Knowledge in Medieval French Literature* (Chicago, University of Chicago Press, 2005).

Sumner, Charles, *White Slavery in the Barbary States* (Reseda, CA, Enhanced Media, 2017).

Sweetman, John, *The Oriental Obsession: Islamic Inspiration in British and American Art and Architecture 1500-1920* (Cambridge, Cambridge University Press, 1991).

Syfret, R. H. "*The Origins of the Royal Society*," Notes and Records of the Royal Society, 5 (1947-8).

Sylvia Brown ed., *Women, Gender and Radical Religion* (Leiden, Brill, 2007)

Tabbernee, William, *Fake Prophecy and Polluted Sacraments* (Boston, Brill, 2007).

Tagliaferri, Filomena Viviana, "Tolerance Re-Shaped in the Early-Modern Mediterranean Borderlands Travellers, Missionaries and Proto-Journalists (1683–1724), (New York, Routledge, 2018).

Talbot, Ann, "*The Great Ocean of Knowledge*", *The Influence of Travel Literature on the Work of John Locke* (Leiden, Brill, 2010).

Talbot, Michael, *British Ottoman Relations, 1661-1807: Commerce and Diplomatic Practice in Eighteenth Century Istanbul* (Woodbridge, Boydell Press, 2017).

Tawney, R. H., '*The Rise of the Gentry, 1558–1640,*" Economic History Review, 11 (1941).

Tawney, R., *Religion and the Rise of Capitalism* (New York, Routledge, 1998).

Taylor, Charles, *A Secular Age* (London, Belknap Press of Harvard University Press, 2007).

Taylor, Eva G. R., *Mathematical Practitioners of Tudor and Stuart England* (Cambridge, Cambridge University Press 1954).

Taylor, F. Sherwood, "*An Alchemical Work of Sir Isaac Newton*", in Ambix, Vol. 5, (1956).

Tchitcherov, A.I., *India: Changing Economic Structure in the Sixteenth to Eighteenth Centuries: Outline History of Crafts and Trade* (New Delhi, Manohar Publishers, 1998).

Thomas, D. O. ed., *Price: Political Writings* (Cambridge, Cambridge University Press, 1991).

Thomas, D. O., *Enlightenment and Dissent* (Aberystwyth, Cambrian Printers, 2000).

Thomas, David and Chesworth, John eds., *Muslim Christian Relations: A Biographical History*, v. 13, Western Europe, *1700-1800* (Leiden, Brills, 2019).

Thomas, David and John Chesworth eds, *Christian Muslim Relations, A Biographical*

History, vol. 8, (Leiden, Brill, 2016)

Thomas, Keith, *Religion and the Decline of Magic: Studies in Popular Beliefs in Sixteenth and Seventeenth Century England* (London, Penguin Books, 1991).

Thompson, Andrew, *The Oxford History of Protestant Dissenting Traditions*, Volume II: The Long Eighteenth Century c. 1689-c. 1828 (Oxford, Oxford University Press, 2018).

Thompson, Edward, *The Life of Charles Lord Metcalfe* (London, Faber and Faber, 1937).

Tillyard, E. M. W., *The Elizabethan World Picture* (New York, Routledge, 2017).

Tinniswood, Adrian, *Pirates of Barbary: Corsairs, Conquests and Captivity in the 17ᵗʰ Century Mediterranean* (New York, Riverhead Books, 2010).

Tolan, John V., *Faces of Muhammad: Western Perception of the Prophet of Islam from Middle Ages to Today* (Princeton, Princeton University Press, 2019).

Toland, John, *Nazarenus*, ed. Justin Champion, (Oxford: Voltaire Foundation, 1999).

Toland, John, *The Life of John Milton*. London: 1698. Reprinted in Early Lives of Milton. Helen Darbishire, ed. (London: Constable, 1932).

Toomer, G. J., *Eastern Wisdom and Learning: The Study of Arabic in Seventeenth-Century England* (Oxford, Clarendon Press, 1996).

Toomer, Gerald James, *Easterne Eastern Wisdom and Learning* (Oxford, Oxford University Press, 1996).

Torrell, Jean-Pierre, *Aquinas's Summa, Background, Structure and Reception*, translated by Benedict M.Guevin, (Washington D. C., The Catholic University of America Press, 2005).

Topinka, Robert J., *Islam, England, and Identity in the Early Modern Period: A Review of Recent Scholarship*, Mediterranean Studies, "https://www.jstor.org/stable/i40051739" Vol. 18 (2009).

Tracy, James D., *The Rise of Merchant Empires: Long Distance Trade in the Early Modern World 1350-1750* (Cambridge, Cambridge University Press, 1993).

Tracy, James D., *The Rise of Merchant Empires: Long Distance Trade in the Early Modern World 1350-1750* (Cambridge, Cambridge University Press, 1990).

Trevor-Roper Hugh, *History and the Enlightenment* (New Haven, Yale University Press, 2010).

Trevor-Roper, Hugh, *The Crisis of the Seventeenth Century: Religion, the Reformation and Social Change* (Indianapolis, Liberty Fund, 2001).

Trevelyan, G. M., *History of England* (London: Longmans, Green and Co., 1926).

Trevelyan, George M., *The English Revolution, 1688-89* Oxford, Oxford University Press, 1965).

Trevor-Roper, H, *The Rise of Christian Europe* (London, Thames and Hudson, 1965).

Trevor-Roper, Huge, *Archbishop Laud 1573-1645* (London, Macmillan Press, 1988).

Turnbull, G.H., *Samuel Hartlib: A Sketch of his Life and his Relations to J.A. Comenius* (Oxford, Oxford University Press, 1920); his Hartlib, Dury and Comenius: Gleanings from Hartlib's Papers, (Liverpool, University Press, 1947); his "*Samuel Hartlib's Influence on the Early History of the Royal Society*," Notes and Records of the Royal Society, 10 (1952-3).

Tyacke, Nicholas, *Anti-Calvinists: The Rise of English Arminianism, c.1590-1640* (Oxford, Clarendon Press, 1987).

Uyar, Mesut, and Erickson, Edward J.. *A Military History of the Ottomans: From Osman to Atatürk* (Wisconsin, Pleager Security International, 2009).

Vaughan, Virginia, Mason, *Performing Blackness on English Stages, 1500–1800* (Cambridge, Cambridge University Press, 2005).

Vermes, Geza, *Jesus the Jew: A Historian's Reading of the Gospels* (Minneapolis: Fortress Press, 1981).

Vernon, Richard (ed.), *Locke on Toleration* translated by Michael Silverthorne, (Cambridge, Cambridge University Press, 2010).

Vickers, Brian (ed.), *Occult and Scientific Mentalities in the Renaissance* (Cambridge, Cambridge University Press, 1984).

Vitkus, Daniel J. ed. *Piracy, Slavery, and Redemption: Barbary Captivity Narratives from Early Modern England.* (New York, Columbia University Press, 2001).

Vitkus, Daniel J., ed. *Three Turk Plays from Early Modern England* (Cambridge: Columbia University Press, 2000).

Vitkus, Daniel J., *Turning Turk: English Theater and the Multicultural Mediterranean, 1570-1630* (New York: Paigrave Palgrave, 2003).

Vlami, Despina, *Trading with the Ottomans: The Levant Company in the Middle East* (New York, I. B. Tauris, 2015).

Wainwright, Arthur, *A Paraphrase and Notes on the Epistles of St. Paul to the Galatians, 1 and 2 Corinthians, Romans, Ephesians* (Oxford, Clarendon Press, 1987).

Waite, Arthur E., *The Secret Tradition in Alchemy: its Development and Records* (London, Kegan Paul, 1926).

Wakefield, W. L., *Heresy, Crusade and Inquisition in Southern France, 1100–1250* (London, ACLS Books, 1974).

Wallace, Dewey D. "*Socinianism, Justification by Faith, and The Sources of John Locke's The Reasonableness of Christianity.*" Journal of the History of Ideas, vol. 45, no. 1, (1984).

Walker, Christopher J., *Islam and the West: The Dissonant Harmony of Civilizations,* (Stroud, Gloucestershire, History Press, (2013).

Christopher J. Walker, *Reason and Religion in Late Seventeenth-Century England: The Politics and Theology of Radical Dissent,* (London, I.B. Tauris, 2013).

Wallace, Robert, *Antitrinitarian Biography: or Sketches of the Lives and Writings of Dis-*

tinguished Antitrinitarians (London, E. T. Whitefield, 1850).

Walsh, John, Haydon, Colin and Taylor, Stephen eds., *The Church of England*, c. 1689 – c. 1833, (Cambridge: Cambridge University Press, 1993).

Walsham, Alexandra, *Charitable Hatred: Tolerance and Intolerance in England 1500-1700* (Manchester, Manchester University Press, 2006).

Warden, Blair, *God's Instruments: Political Conduct in the England of Oliver Cromwell* (Oxford, Oxford University Press, 2012).

Washbrook, David, "*From Comparative Sociology to Global History: Britain and India in the Pre-History of Modernity.*" Journal of the Economic and Social History of the Orient, vol. 40, no. 4, (1997).

Waters, David W., *The Art of Navigation in England in Elizabethan and Early Stuart Times*, (London, Hollis & Carter, 1958).

Watt, W. M., *Islamic Surveys: The Influence of Islam on Medieval Europe* (Edinburgh, Edinburgh University Press, 1972).

Watt, William M., *Early Islam: Collected Articles* (Edinburgh: Edinburgh University Press, 1990).

Watts, Michael R., *The Dissenters, vol. 2, The Expansion of Evangelical Nonconformity*, (Oxford: Oxford University Press, 1995).

Watts, Michael R., *The Dissenters, vol. 2, The Expansion of Evangelical Nonconformity* (Oxford: Oxford University Press, 1995).

Webb, Henry J., *Elizabethan Military Science: The Books and the Practice* (Madison, University of Wisconsin Press, 1965).

Weber, M., "*Anticritical Last Word on the Spirit of Capitalism,*" American Journal of Sociology, 83, v. 5, (1978).

Weber, Max M., *The Protestant Ethics and the Spirit of Capitalism*, trans. By Talcott Parsons, (London and New York, Routledge, 2005).

Webster, Charles, "*English Medical Reformers of the Puritan Revolution: A Background to the 'Society of Chymical Physitians'* ", Ambix, xiv (1967).

Webster, Charles, *The Great Instauration, Science, Medicine and Reform, 1626-1660* (London: Duckworth, 1975).

Webster, Charles, *The Great Instauration: Science, Medicine and Reform, 1626-1660*, (London, Peter Lang Publishing, 1974) and Webster, ed., *Samuel Hartlib and the Advancement of Learning* (London, Cambridge University Press, 1970).

Webster, Charles, *The Intellectual Revolution of the Seventeenth Century* (New York, Routledge, 1974).

Weeramantry, C. G., *Islamic Jurisprudence, An International Perspective* (London, Macmillan Press, 1988).

Wellhausen, J., *The Arab Kingdom and Its Fall*, translated by Margaret Graham Wier

(Calcutta, Calcutta University Press, 1927).

Westfall, Richard S., *Force in Newton's Physics. The Science of Dynamics in the Seventeenth Century*, (London: Macdonald; New York: American Elsevier, 1971).

Westfall, Richard S., *Science and Religion in Seventeenth-Century England*. (New Haven: Yale University Press, 1958).

Westfall, Robert S., *The Scientific Revolution in the 17th Century: The Construction of a New World View* (Oxford: Clarendon Press, 1992).

Westfall, S. Richard, *Never at Rest: The Life of Isaac Newton* (Cambridge: Cambridge University Press, 1994).

Whelan, Frederick G., *Enlightenment Political Thought and Non-Western Societies: Sultan and Savages,* (New York, Routledge, 2009).

White, Andrew Dickson, *A History of the Warfare of Science with Theology in Christendom*, 2 volumes, (Cambridge, Cambridge University Press, 2009).

White, Michael, *The Pope & the Heretic: The True Story of Giordano Bruno, the Man Who Dared to Defy the Roman Inquisition* (New York: William Morrow, 2002).

Wiker, Benjamin, *The Catholic Church & Science: Answering the Questions, Exposing the Myths,* (Charlotte, Tan Books, 2011).

Wilbur, Earl Morse, *A History of Unitarianism: In Transylvania, England and America Volume II* (Boston, Beacon Press, 1945).

Wilbur, Earl Morse, *Our Unitarian Heritage: An Introduction to the History of the Unitarian Movement* (Boston, Beacon Press, 1963).

Wiles, Maurice, *Archetypal Heresy: Arianism through the Centuries* (Oxford, Clarendon Press, 1996).

Wiley, Tatha, *Original Sin: Origins, Developments, Contemporary Meanings* (Paulist Press, New York & Mahwah, 2002).

William, Lamont, *Godly Rule: Politics and Religion, 1603–1660,* (New York, Macmillan, 1969).

Williams, George Huntson, *The Radical Reformation* (London, Weidenfeld & Nicolson, 1962)

Williams, Roger, *The Bloudy Tenent of Persecution [1644]*, ed. E. B. Underhill, (London, 1848).

Williams, Stephen and Friell, Gerard, *Theodosius, The Empire at Bay*, (London, Routledge, 1994).

Wilson, F. P., *The Plague in Shakespeare's London* (Oxford, Oxford University Press, 1963).

Winterbottom, Anna, *Hybrid Knowledge in the Early East India Company World* (London, Palgrave Macmillan, 2016).

Winterbottom, Anna, *Robert Knox, the East India Company and the Royal Society*, The

British Journal for the History of Science, Vol. 42, No. 4 (Dec., 2009).

Wolf, Eric, *Europe And The People Without History* (Berkeley, University of California Press, 2010).

Wolfson, H. A., *The Philosophy of the Kalam,* (Cambridge, Mass., Harvard University Press, 1976).

Woodhead, Christine, '*The Present Terrour of the World*'? *Contemporary Views of the Ottoman Empire c1600* (History, vol. 72, issue 234, 1987).

Worden, Blair, *God's Instruments: Political Conduct in the England of Oliver Cromwell* (Oxford, Oxford University Press, 2012).

Wren, Christopher, the Junior, '*Parentalia: or, Memoirs of the family of the Wrens*', viz. of Mathew Bishop, printed for T. Osborn; and R. Dodsley, (London, 1750).

Yates, Frances, *Giordano Bruno and the Hermetic Tradition* (Chicago, University of Chicago Press, 1964).

Yerby, George, *The Economic Causes of the English Civil War: Freedom of Trade and the English Revolution* (New York, Routledge, 2020).

Yoder, John Howard, *The Politics of Jesus* (Cambridge, William B. Eerdmans, 1994).

Young, B., *Religion and Enlightenment in Eighteenth-Century England*. Theological Debate from Locke to Burke (Oxford: Clarendon Press, 1998).

Yurdusev, A. Nuri et al., *Ottoman Diplomacy: Conventional or Unconventional?* (New York, Palgrave Macmillan, 2004).

Zagorin, Perez, *How the Idea of Religious Toleration Came to the West* (Princeton, Princeton University Press, 2006).

Zagorin, P., *Ways of Lying: Dissumulation, Persecution, and Conformity in Early Modern Europe,* (London, Harvard University Press, 1990).

Zakai. Avihu, *The Rise of Modern Science and the Decline of Theology as the 'Queen of Sciences' in the Early Modern Era*, Reformation & Renaissance Review 9.2 (2007).

Zanon, Irene, *The Alchemical Apocalypse of Isaac Newton* (Ph. D. dissertation submitted to Università Ca' Foscari Venezia, 2013).

Zonta, Mauro, *"Influence of Arabic and Islamic Philosophy on Judaic Thought"*, The Stanford Encyclopedia of Philosophy (Spring 2011 Edition).

Zonta, Mauro, *The Relationship of European Jewish Philosophy to Islamic and Christian Philosophies in the Late Middle Ages,* Jewish Studies Quarterly, Vol. 7, No. 2 (2000).

Zwartjes, Otto ed.,*Poetry, Politics and Polemics: Cultural Transfer Between the Iberian Peninsula and North Africa Atlanta* (Rodopi, 1996).

Index

Abd Allah, Ahmad bin, 293
Abd el-Ouahed ben Messaoud, King, 58
Abrahamic religions, 111
Abu Lughod, Janet, 352
Abu-Lughod, Janet, 46
Academy of Science, Paris, 193
Acemoglu, Daron, 140
Achmet, Book of Symbols, 218–19, 220
Adams, John, 278, 397
Addison, Lancelot, 161
Adelard of Bath, 36
Agha, Asan, 288
Aikenhead, Thomas, 282–3, 349
Albertus Magnus, 215
Albigenses, 56
alchemy, 207–18
Alciat, Paul, 458
Alcoran see Qu'ran
Aleppo, 157, 160, 161, 193, 223
Ali Abgali, Mohmmed ibn, 197
Ambrose of Milan, 85
American colonisation, 146, 155
Amin, Samir, 27, 352
Anabaptists, 237
Andrewes, Lancelot, 65
Andrews, Thomas, 227
Anglican Church, 119, 121–2, 136, 241–5;
    and Unitarianism, 459–63
Anglo-Ottoman alliance, 301
Anne, Queen, 255
Annet, Peter, 467
anthropomorphic shift, in religious belief,
    264–6
anti-nomianism, 108
anti-Trinitarianism: in 17th

century England, 67, 69–70; and
    Enlightenment, 268–9; European,
    115; and Isaac Newton, 411–14,
    431–3; Islamic, 95, 97–8, 101, 269–79,
    451; and Michael Servetus, 394; and
    Stephen Nye, 444–6 see also Unitarian
    Controversy
Aquinas, St Thomas, 33, 40–1, 215, 425,
    427–8
Arabic books, 208
Arabic language: borrowed words from,
    39; at Oxford and Cambridge, 193, 205;
    taught at Westminster school, 195–6,
    303
Arabic manuscripts: English collections
    of, 157–9, 187–91, 205; translations of,
    328, 344
Arabic studies, at Oxford and Cambridge,
    193
Arian controversy, 413–14
Arianism, 69, 84, 85, 91, 266, 307, 347,
    364, 369–70, 373, 373–5, 428–9, 443
Aristotle, 33, 169
Arius, 373–5, 413–14
Arminianism, 121, 137, 267, 376 see also
    General Baptists
Armstrong, Sir Thomas, 239
Ashcraft, Richard, 133, 304, 380
Athanasian Creed, 440
Athanasius, St, 413–14, 415
Aubert de Versé, Nöel, 453–4
Augustine, St, 82, 86–8
Augustinian school, 78–9, 122
Averroes see Ibn Rushd
Avicenna see Ibn Sina

'Awad, Luwis, 409
Ayloffe, John, 239

Bacon, Francis, 58, 138, 165, 172, 176, 207, 210, 215, 247, 290
Bacon, Roger, 215
Balling, Pieter, 389
Banks, Joseph, 177
Baptists, 229, 240
Barbary pirates, 147–9
Barbary States, 287–91
Bargrave, Robert, 167
Barker, Thomas, 148
Barnabas, Gospel of, 337–41
Barnardiston, Samuel, 253
Baron, Richard, 437, 438
Barrow, Isaac, 190, 196, 213, 411
Barton, Sir Edward, 275
Bauman, Michael, 401, 402, 405
Baxter, Richard, 23, 26, 145, 237
Bayle, Pierre, 323
Beale, John, 197–204
Beckingham, C. F., 166
Bedwell, William, 187, 188
Bellini, Gentile, *St Mark Preaching at Alexandria* (1504–07), 49–51
Belloc, Hilaire, 373
Belsham, Thomas, 473
Bendysh, Thomas, 167
Bentley, Jerry, 352
Ben-Zaken, Avner, 212
Berlin, Isaiah, 261
Berman, L. V., 427
Bernard, Edward, 194
Bernier, François, 164–5
Best, Paul, 132, 135, 257, 270, 399, 402, 404
Bethel, Slingsby, 238
Biandrata, Giorgio, 397
Bible, and salvation, 82
Bibliander, Theodore, 112
Biblical hermeneutics, 218–21
Bichitr (Mughal artist), 151
Biddle, John, 132, 135, 156, 228, 390, 399, 402, 404, 421, 442
Biddulph, William, 128, 246, 406
Birch, Jonathan C., 335
Birchwood, Matthew, 46, 68, 148, 292, 302, 350
Bishop, George, 324

Blasphemy Acts, 91
Blount, Charles, 270, 282, 312, 323–4, 421, 466
Blount, Henry, 128, 139, 165–6, 225, 246, 270, 283, 294, 323–5
Bodleian Library, Oxford, 158, 159, 205, 252
Boindin, Nicolas, 69, 278
Bonneval, Comte de, 287
Booth, Edward, 40
Bosworth, C. E., 326, 327
Boulainvilliers, Henri, Comte de, 69, 205, 278, 283
Boyle, Robert, 71, 172, 174, 176, 177, 182, 185, 194, 197, 206, 207, 209, 211, 214, 216, 251, 307, 319, 352
Brahe, Tycho, 181
Braudel, Fernand, 27, 225, 287, 291
Brehant, Louis de, 69, 278
Brenner, Robert, 140, 227
Brewster, David, 438
Bright, William, 374
Brodie, Alexander, 427
Brooke, John, 217
Brooke, Lord, 184
Brotton, Jerry, 44, 45, 48, 49, 50–1, 58, 352
Brown, Peter, 87
Bruno, Giordano, 61–2, 63, 69, 71, 175
Burckhardt, Jacob, 45
Burigny, Jean Levesque de, 69, 278
Burke, Edmund, 320
Burrell, David, 40
Burton, Jonathan, 68, 292–3
Bury, Arthur, 282, 327, 346, 356, 441; *The Naked Gospel* (1690), 446–8
Busby, Richard, 195–7, 303
Butterfield, Herbert, 170

Caliphate, 109, 110
Calvert, Thomas, 391, 458
Calvin, John, 26, 53, 55, 394, 396–7
Calvinism, 23, 26
Cambridge Platonists, 176, 182
Cambridge University, 193, 205; Lucasian Chair of mathematics, 187–8, 190–1
Capitulations, 146, 147, 149–52
Cappadocian school, 78–9
Carboni, Stefano, 351
Care, Henry, 325

Carey, Daniel, 165
Carlyle, Thomas, 296
Carré, Abbé, 160
Carter, Michael G., 42
Carthage, Council of, 82
Casola, Canon Pietro, 51
Cassem Alqiada Aga, 197
Cassirer, Ernst, 261
Castell, Edmund, 194, 195
Catharism, 56
Chambers, Richard, 227
Champion, Justin, 261, 270, 278, 309, 326,
    327, 331, 337, 340–1, 343–4, 347, 352,
    368, 376, 432, 439, 449, 452, 455
Chapple, Bartholomew, 406
Chardin, Jean, 221–2
Charles I, King, 120, 121, 122, 123–5, 126,
    129–30, 136–7, 142
Charles II, King, 116, 122, 156, 191,
    199–200, 216, 235, 236–40, 248, 251,
    252, 254, 294, 314, 453
Charles V, Holy Roman Emperor, 47–8, 57
Chénier, Louis de, 287
Chennell, Francis, 390
Cherbury, Edward Herbert, 1st Baron
    Herbert of, 400, 404, 421
Chew, S. C., 68, 292
Child, Sir Josiah, 153, 239
Chillingworth, William, 198, 369
chocolate, 247
Christian Apologists, 416–19
Christianity: central dogmas, 76–8; and
    Greco-Roman culture, 75–6, 80
Christian-Muslim marriage, 295
Christie, Archibald H., 351
Christological controversies, 84–5
Clarendon Code, 237
Clark, George N., 190, 439
Clarke, J. C. D., 259
Clarke, Samuel, 69, 437–8
Classen, Albrecht, 348
Claude, Jean, 273
Cochrane, Sir John, 239
coffee drinking, 230, 245–6
coffeehouses, Turkish, 70, 245–55, 293, 294
Coffey, John, 67, 69, 137
Cole, Juan, 284
Coleridge, Samuel Taylor, 314, 320
Coller, Ian, 286

Collet, Joseph, 192
Collins, Anthony, 331, 346, 356
Columbus, Christopher, 186
Comenius, Johann Amos, 55, 184, 215
Congregationalism, 135, 240
Constantine, Emperor, 84
Constantinople, 52
Constantinople, Council of (381), 429
Conventicle Act (1664), 237
converts, to Islam, 54–5, 113–14, 147,
    288–93, 458, 462
Conway, Anne, 161, 318, 320, 352
Conway, Edward, 2nd Viscount Conway,
    318–19, 344
Copernicus, Nicolas, 181, 182
Copland, Robert, 208
Corporation Act (1662), 467
Coryate, Thomas, 293
Cotterell, Charles, 453
Coudert, Allison P., 147, 213, 347
Counter-Reformation, 121
Covel, Dr John, 159, 271, 291, 411
Cowley, Abraham, 198
Cransto, Maurice, 304
Crell, Samuel, 347, 397, 436
Croix, Chevalier de la, 167
Cromwell, Oliver, 116, 127, 130, 137, 141,
    184, 188, 205, 228–9, 233, 235, 236
Cromwell, Thomas, 47
Crone, Patricia, 103
Crowe, Sir Sackville, 128
Crusades, 34
Currell, David, 406, 408
Cuse, Nicholas de, 112
Cyprian, St, 82

Dalrymple, William, 119, 152, 296
Danielson, Dennis, 405
d'Argenson, Marquis de, 278
Daubuz, Charles, 219
David, Ference, 308, 397
David, Francis, 393, 462
Davidson, Herbert, 40
Davis, John, 189
Davis, Ralph, 163
Davis, Robert C., 148, 287
De Keyser, 150
De Krey, Gary S., 235, 238
Declaration of Indulgence, 240

Dee, John, 216
Defoe, Daniel, 160, 231–2, 399
Deists, 69, 71, 91, 111, 175, 242, 243, 262,
    265–6, 268, 277, 323–5, 337, 466–8
democracy, and Islam, 107–12
Dennis, John, 400
Descartes, René, 212, 267
Diggers, 229
Dimmock, Matthew, 58, 68, 285, 292, 313,
    350
Dinteville, Jean de, 47, 48
Dissenters, 240, 249
divine right monarchy, 82–4, 108–9,
    119–20, 121, 123–5, 240
Dobbs, B. J. T., 209, 210, 211
Donatist heretics, 86
Drake, Roger, 153
Draper, John William, 93, 99, 100
Dryden, John, 238
Du Marsais, 69, 278
Dunn, John, 386
Dury, John, 212, 216
Dutch converts to Islam, 288–9
Dutch Republic, 126, 150

Eamon, William, 208
Early Turkey Company, 155
East India Company, 115, 116, 126, 129,
    146, 152–6, 161, 162–4, 177, 185, 192,
    221–2, 227, 244
Eaton, Richard, 230
Edleston, J., 431
Edward, Daniel, 246
Edwards, Jonathan, 347, 353, 366, 368,
    369, 377, 378, 438, 439, 458, 460
Edwards, Thomas, 175, 235
Eliot, Sir John, 148
Elizabeth I, Queen, 57–8, 59, 117–19, 290,
    294
Ellan, Ethan, 397
Elvin, M., 27
Empson, William, 401
England: 16th century, 225–6; in the 17th
    century, 117–20; encounters with
    Islam, 65–72, 138–40, 226–9, 290, 302;
    overseas trade, 126–31, 229–35
English Civil War, 67, 115–16, 120,
    129–30, 135, 138, 226–9
English Commonwealth, 129–30, 137, 141,

227, 229–35
English Reformation, 47
English Revolution: economic causes,
    140–4; and overseas trade, 144–7;
    religious roots, 137–40, 227–9
Enlightenment, as religious revolution,
    259–69
Enlightenment, English, and Islam, 112–16
enslavement: of Europeans by Muslims,
    147–9, 287–8; of Muslims in Europe
    and America, 290
Enyedi, George, 347
Epistle Dedicatory (1682), 452–9, 473
Eran, A., 427
Erasmus, 47, 55, 126
Erastianism, 89, 119, 157, 199
Esposito, John L., 111
Eugene of Savoy, Prince, 331
Eugene the Emir, 38
European Dark Ages, 31–2
Evelyn, John, 196, 197, 216, 221, 248
Exclusion Crisis, 245–6

Fabricius, Johan Albrecht, 335
Fakhry, Majid, 40, 427
Falkland, Lucius Cary, 2nd Viscount, 198,
    199
al-Farabi, Abu Nasr, 40, 41, 44, 210, 424,
    427
Feijoo, Benito Jeronimo, 299
Ferdinand I, Holy Roman Emperor, 57
Ferguson, Robert, 239, 369
Fifth Monarchists, 131, 229, 237
Filmer, Sir Robert, 142, 238
Finch, Sir John, 128, 150, 151, 161, 318,
    319–20, 344, 351, 352
Firmin, Thomas, 156, 224, 265, 440, 443,
    444
Fischer-Galati, Stephan A., 56, 57
Fisher, Samuel, 133
Fowke, John, 227
Fox, George, 325
Frampton, Robert, 159
Francis I, King of France, 47–8
Franco-Ottoman Alliance, 48, 276, 286
Frangipani, John, 47
Franklin, Benjamin, 278, 397
Frederick II (the Great) of Prussia, 38, 41,
    256, 260

Frederick V, Elector of the Palatinate, 59
Freke, William, 327, 346, 356, 442, 448–52
Fryer, John, 192
Fulgentius, St, 82
Fullwood, Francis, 459, 460

Galileo Galilei, 176, 181, 182
Games, Alison, 155
Garcia, Humberto, 46, 224, 240, 257, 278, 302, 320, 326, 350, 352, 354, 466
Gardiner, Samuel, 228
Garraway, Sir Henry, 155
Gelder, Maartje van, 288, 289–90
General Baptists, 131, 132, 134
Gerard of Cremona, 37
al-Ghazali, Abu Hamid, 40, 210, 354, 424, 427
Gibbon, Edward, 271, 451
Gildon, Charles, 323
Gillespie, Michael Allen, 394
Gilson, E., 40
Giochon, A. M., 40
Glanvill, Joseph, 209
Glorious Revolution (1689), 116, 234, 236, 241–2
Gnosticism, 213
Goffman, Daniel, 167
Goldie, Mark, 238, 240
Golius, Jacob, 390
Goodman, Godfrey, Bishop, 121, 138
Goodwin, John, 137
Goody, Jack, 30, 42, 43, 58, 225, 329, 352
Gordon, Alexander, 455
Graf, Tobias P., 292
Grassby, Richard, 156, 222
Great Tew Circle, 198, 326
Greaves, John, 157, 158, 187, 188, 194
Greengrass, Mark, 68
Greenham, Paul T., 220
Gregory of Nyssa, 85
Gresham, Sir Thomas, 186–7
Gresham College, 186–7, 188–91, 193
Griffel, Frank, 40
Grillmeier, Alois, 416–17
Grotius, Hugo, 199, 376
Guillaume, Alfred, 40
Gunpowder Plot (1605), 119

Habermas, Jurgen, 239

Haddu, Muhammad bin, 453
Haggatt, Bartholemew, 160
Hakluyt, Richard, 166, 187, 188
Hales, John, 198, 199, 369
Hall, M. B., 197
Hallet, Joseph, 438
Halley, Edmond, 172, 194, 195
Hammersley, Sir Hugh, 155
Hammond, Henry, 198
Hammond, Robert, 40
Handson, Ralph, 187
Hapsburg Empire, 47–8, 52–3, 55, 88–9
Harbourne, William, 58, 149–50
Harkness, Deborah E., 218
Harrington, James, 138, 141, 249–50, 253, 312, 325
Harris, James, 305
Harrison, Peter, 180, 215, 338
Hartlib, Samuel, 165, 182, 184–5, 194, 205–6, 210, 214, 215, 216
Harvey, S., 427
Harvey, Sir Daniel, 150
Haskins, Charles Homer, 35–7, 38, 39
Hastings, Warren, 160
Hawkins, William, 225
Haynes, Hopton, 437
Hayyan, Jabir bin, 218
Hazard, Paul, 204–5, 267, 273, 339
Hearne, Thomas, 435
Heber, Bishop Reginald, 295
Hedworth, Henry, 440
Hegel, G. W. F., 269
Helmont, John Baptist von, 181
Helwys, Thomas, 132
Henry, Philip, 196
Henry VIII, King, 47, 48, 286, 293
Herbert, Thomas, 247
Hereford, Henry, 202, 203
heresy, 84–6, 200
Hermann of Carinthia, 37
Hermeticism, 212–13
Hessen, Boris, 186, 190, 191
Hicks, Baptist, 304
hierarchies, medieval Christian, 32–4, 63–4, 80
Hill, Christopher, 142, 175, 186, 190, 217, 227, 236, 326, 405, 460
Hill, Nathaniel, 159
Hillar, Marian, 394

Hippolytus, 417
Historia Monotheistica, 218, 221, 278, 467, 469
Hobbes, Thomas, 111, 137, 138, 251, 325, 399; *Leviathan*, 321–2; natural religion, 312, 321–2, 324
Hobson, John, 45, 352
Hodgson, Marshall, 287
Hogarth, William, 248
Hohenheim, Theophrastus von *see* Paracelsus
Holbein, Hans, 47
Holbein, Hans, the Younger, *The Ambassadors* (1533), 47, 49
Holloway, James, 239
Holmyard, E. J., 211
Holt, P. M., 326
Holymard, E. J., 36
Hood, Thomas, 186
Hooke, Robert, 194, 196, 209, 251
Hoornbeck, Johannes, 390
Horsley, Samuel, 471–2
Hoskins, John, 221
Hottinger, Johann Jakob, 112, 390, 398
Houghton, John, 246
Howard, Deborah, 351
Howard, Sir Philip, 248
Hugh of Santalla, 37
Hughes, Peter, 394
Huguenots, 149, 240, 272–3
Hukluyt, Richard, 349
humanism, Islamic influence, 41–2
Hume, David, 254
Hungarian-Ottoman alliance, 302
Hungary, Protestantism in, 60–1
Hunneades, Hans, 190
Hunter, Michael, 165, 250
Huntington, Robert, 159, 271, 345
Hussian ibn Ali, 110
Hussites, 56
Hutton, Sarah, 318
Hyde, Thomas, 194, 198
Hyman, Arthur, 426

Ibn abi Dinar, 289
Ibn Haddu, Muhammad, 197
Ibn Jawziyyah, 106
Ibn Qasim al-Hajari, Ahamad, 293
Ibn Rushd (Averroes), 40, 41, 44, 424, 427

Ibn Shatir, 44
Ibn Sina (Avicenna), 40, 41, 44, 210, 215, 424, 425, 427
Ibn Tufayl, *Hayy bin Yaqzan*, 135, 182, 346, 352, 382
Ibrahim, Sultan, 127, 129
iconoclasm, 58–9
Iliffe, Rob, 217, 412, 413, 421
Inani, Muhammad, 406
Inati, Shams C., 424
Independents, 131, 238
Indian imports to England, 230–5
Indian Mutiny (1857), 469
Ingegno, Alfonso, 62
Inquisitions, 87, 88
Ireton, Henry, 138
Irving, James, 150
Islam: Christian conversions to, 54–5, 113–14, 147, 288–93, 458, 462; as Christian reformation, 93–101, 114–16; and democracy, 107–12; and English Enlightenment, 112–16; and human equality, 105–6; and human salvation, 101–5; and scientific revolution, 168–79; and Unitarian syncretism, 270–9; and Unitarianism, 457–8
Islamic "Golden Age", 35
Islamic Law *see* Shari'ah law
Islamic Republicanism, 469–74
Ismaïly, Sultan Moulay, 151, 295, 453
Israel, Jonathan, 89, 259, 262, 263, 278, 283, 299, 389, 390
Istanbul, population, 16th century, 225
Italian anti-Trinitarians, 115

Jacob, James A., 256, 325, 326, 327, 329, 337, 341, 344, 352
Jacob, Margarete, 260, 272, 312, 321, 322
Jahangir, Mughal Emperor, 150, 152
James I, King, 59, 118, 138, 142, 151, 290
James II, King, 116, 156, 238, 240–1, 314
Jamestown, Virginia, 119
Janissaries, 127
Jansenists, 268
Jardine, Lisa, 351
Jefferson, Thomas, 278, 283, 397
Jelles, Jarig, 389
Jerkins, Jae, 57, 58
Jesus Christ, 75

Jews, 127
Jha, Saumitra, 129
John of Seville, 37
Johnson, Simon, 140
Jolley, Nicholas, 368
Jonathan coffeehouse, 254
Jonson, Ben, 198
Juda, Joseph Ben, 427
Judaism, 426–7
Julian, Emperor, 84
Julius II, Pope, 52
Justin Martyr, 416
Justinian, Emperor, 88

Kadane, Matthew, 261
Kant, Immanuel, 181, 261
Karbala, battle of, 110
Katz, Victor J., 194
Kearney, H. F., 176
Keeble, N. H., 238
Kelley, Maurice, 402, 403
Kelly, J. N. D., 417
Kepler, Johannes, 176, 181, 182, 212
Ketton, Robert of, 394
Keynes, John Maynard, 425
al-Khwarizmi, Muhammad ibn Musa, 39
King James Bible (1611), 119
Kiraly, Bela K., 60
Knolles, Richard, 349–50, 406
Krstic, Tijana, 54
Kuhlmann, Qurinius, 55
Kuhn, Thomas S., 179

La Croze, M. V. de, 393
Lamont, William M., 229
Landes, David, 27
Lang, Thomas, 386
Langham, John, 227
Lannoy, Benjamin, 160
Larson, Martin A., 405
Lateran Council (1215), 52
Latitudarianism, 71, 175, 440, 452
Laud, Archbishop William, 122, 123–5,
    136–7, 142, 158, 205, 244
Laudian Canon, 390
Lawson, Philip, 129
Le Clerc, Jean, 397, 432
Leaman, Oliver, 426
Lecky, William, 259, 440

Leibniz, G. W., 368
Leslie, Charles, 347, 400, 459, 460, 463–4
L'Estrange, Sir Roger, 238, 381
Levant Company, 125, 126, 128–30, 146,
    156, 157, 162–4, 221–3, 227, 239, 244;
    chaplains, 157–9, 271, 345, 406
Levellers, 131, 132, 133, 135, 229
Levitin, Dmitri, 199, 201, 202, 203
Lilburne, John, 133
Limborch, Philipp van, 397
Lindsay, William, 154
Lithgow, William, 294
Lloyd's coffeehouse, 254
Locke, John: anti-Trinitarianism, 432;
    and Christ's pre-existence, 358–65;
    and coffeehouses, 251, 253; and
    Early Enlightenment, 299; influence
    of Pococke and Shaftesbury, 303–5;
    interest in alchemy, 207, 211, 215,
    216; and Islamic Christology, 373–9;
    Islamic influences on, 307–9, 345–7,
    350–4; and Islamic Minimalism,
    354–8; and merchant traders, 156;
    and Messianic Christianity, 366–73;
    and 'Muhammadan Christianity',
    469–71; and popular sovereignty,
    380–3; religious influences on, 133;
    and religious tolerance, 243–4, 327–8,
    383–8; and Socialism, 397; and travel
    literature, 347–50; as Turkish infidel,
    301–2; and Unitarianism, 69, 71, 278,
    283, 442, 443, 446; on wars of religion,
    120; at Westminster School, 196;
    Discourse on Minds, 357; *An Essay
    Concerning Human Understanding*,
    377; *Paraphrase*, 361–5; *Reasonableness
    of Christianity*, 355–7, 357, 361–2,
    366–7, 371, 372; *Third Letter*, 358; *Two
    Treatises of Government*, 238–9, 380
London, City of, 162–4
London merchant community, 232–4
Louis II, King of Hungary, 48
Louis XIV of France, 238, 239, 240
Louise de Savoie, 47
Lowe, Sir Thomas, 155
Lubieniecki, Stanislas, 393
Lucas, Henry, 190
Lucci, Diego, 336, 364–5
Ludheim, Rudolph de, 112

Luke, John, 345
Luther, Martin, 26, 53–4, 55–6, 58, 60, 99–100, 210
Lutheranism, 57

Macaulay, Thomas, 400
Mack, Rosamond, 351
Mackinnon, M. H., 26, 27
MacLean, Gerald, 46, 65, 68, 167, 248, 290, 350, 409
Maclean, Ian, 217
Madrid, Treaty of, 47
"Mahometan Christians", 339
Maimonides, Moses, 40, 425–7
Makdisi, George, 40, 42, 43
Malcolm, Sir Noel, Useful Enemies, 72
Mandelbrote, Scott, 421
Manuel, Frank, 412
Maracci, Louis, 112
Marrone, Steven P., 36
Marsh, Elizabeth, 150
Marshall, John, 126, 346, 347, 350, 355, 358, 362–3, 365, 369–70, 372–3, 383, 389, 442
Martin, David, 267
Marvell, Andrew, 121, 326, 440
Marx, Karl, 140
Mary II, Queen see William III and Mary II
Mason, Stephen F., 33, 191
Matar, Nabil, 65, 68, 148, 150–1, 290, 292, 295, 302, 307, 310, 326, 344, 350, 352, 453
mathematics, Arabic manuscripts, 195
Mather, James, 46
Maurice, Henry, 461
Mavroudi, Maria, 220
McAuliffe, Jane D., 351
McGinnis, Jon, 40
McJannet, Linda, 68, 69
McLachlan, H. John, 326, 389, 406
Mclean, Gerald, 46
Mede, Joseph, 182, 202, 206, 213, 218, 220
Meggitt, John, 393, 448, 453, 455, 458, 473
Mehmed II, Sultan, 50
Mehmed IV, Sultan, 55, 127, 301
Melius, Peter, 390
Merton, R. K., 172, 175, 185, 190, 191
Milton, John: anti-Catholicism, 132–3; anti-Trinitarianism, 399–400, 402–3; Christology, 400–3; on lay theologians, 137; member of the Rota Club, 250; and Middle Eastern Culture, 406–9; and Samuel Hartlib, 206; Scripturalism, 404–6; The Cabinet Council, 188; De Doctrina, 402, 403; Paradise Lost, 242–3, 400, 402, 408–9; Paradise Regained, 407; The Readie and Easie Way, 235
Mirabaud, Jean-Baptiste de, 69, 278
Modalism, 79
Moghul Empire, 49
Mohac, Battle of (1526), 48
Monophysites, 375
Monserrate, Fr Antonio, 225
Moore, Barrington, 140
More, Andrew, 406
More, Henry, 182, 212, 213, 219, 220, 318, 352, 400
More, Louis Trenchard, 418
Morgan, Thomas, 467
Moriscos, 149
Morley, George, 198
Morocco, 151
Morrill, John, 227
Mortimer, Sarah, 61, 201
Moryson, Mary, 304
Mugabetonians, 229
Mughal Empire, 117, 151–2, 154, 224–5
Muhammad, Prophet, 25, 41, 99–100, 109, 128, 285–6; as Machiavellian Prince, 323
'Muhammadan Christianity', 278, 300, 313–30, 341–4
Mulsow, Martin, 397
Murad III, Sultan, 57–8, 59
Murton, John, 132
Muslim converts, 288–93
Muslim pirates, 147–9
Mustafa, Grand Vizier Kara, 150–1
Mustafa I, Sultan, 127
Mustafa II, Sultan, 127

Nantes, Edict of, revocation of (1685), 240, 272
Napoleon Bonaparte, 278, 283–5
natural law, 320–2
natural philosophy, 180–5, 209–10
natural religion, 321–2, 324
natural theology, 180–5
Needham, Joseph, 27

Needham, Walter, 196
Neuser, Adam, 61, 199, 458
Neville, Henry, 238, 249
New Model Army, 226
Newbury, Colin, 154
Newton, Isaac: anti-Trinitarianism, 370, 411–14, 429–32; Biblicism, 412–14; commercial interests, 177; cosmology and mechanics, 182–3; and Early Enlightenment, 299; hererodoxy, 435–40; interest in alchemy, 207–10, 211–12, 215–16; Lucasian Chair of mathematics, 191; and 'Muhammadan Christianity', 469–71; and Nicean Christology, 428–35; and Primitive Christianity, 414–15; and *prisca sapientia*, 213, 217–18, 220; and Socianism, 397; and Unitarianism, 69, 71, 268, 422–8
Nicaea, Council of (325), 84
Nicole, Pierre, 370
Nieuwentijt, Bernard, 299
North, D. C., 140
North, Sir Dudley, 160–1, 163, 239, 305
Nuovo, Victor, 359–61
Nye, Stephen, 224, 282, 327, 346, 356, 359, 421, 440, 441–2, 443–6; *Brief History*, 442–3

Ochterlony, David, 295–6
Oldenburg, Henry, 164–5, 194, 197, 216, 251
Omar, Abdalla Mahumed, 464–5
opium, 247
"Oriental Obsession", 144, 164, 230, 245, 344
Orientalism, 222, 293
Origen, 82
original sin, 77–8, 81; Enlightenment rejection of, 261; Islamic rejection of, 95–7, 99–101; Locke's rejection of, 372, 377–8, 382
Orme, Robert, 154
Osborne, Francis, 138–9
Osman II, Sultan, 127
Othman (Caliph), 109
Ottoman Empire, 113–14, 225; French alliance, 48, 276; and the Hapsburg monarch, 52–3; heirs to Byzantine

Empire, 167–8; and the Protestant Reformation, 53–61; religious diversity in, 128; and Renaissance art, 49–50; "soft empire", 149–52
"Ottomanism", 167, 293–4
Outram, Dorinda, 255
Overton, Richard, 133, 134
Owen, John, 134
Oxford University, 187–8, 190, 193

Pagden, Anthony, 22
Paine, Thomas, 279, 325, 397
Palmer, Thomas, 164
Pangle, Thomas, 387
papacy, 34
Papillon, Thomas, 253
Paracelsus, 214
Parker, Geoffrey, 362
Parker, Henry, 138
Parmenian, bishop, 86
Paser, Matthias, 195, 303
Pasha, Ibrahim, 60
Paul, St, 82–3
Pavia, Battle of (1525), 47, 48
Paxman, David, 348
Pell, John, 187, 196, 197
Penington, Isaac, 226
Penn, William, 238
'People of the Book', 111
Pepys, Samuel, 192, 248, 250
Peter, Hugh, 121
Petty, William, 192, 247
philosophes, French, 257, 268
Pilkington, Sir Thomas, 305
Piquer, Andrés, 299
Pittion, J. B., 404
Plato of Tivoli, 37
Plelo, Comte de, 278
Plot, Robert, 187–8
Pocock, J. G. A., 259, 439–40
Pococke, Edward, 128, 135, 158, 187, 188, 194, 196, 246, 252, 256, 270, 303, 344, 352, 376, 406
Pope, Alexander, 248
Popish Plot (1678), 238
Popkin, Richard, 212, 219, 425
Postel, Guillaume, 344
predestination, 25–6
Presbyterians, 131, 135, 238

Price, Richard, 471
Prideaux, Edmond, 224, 341, 351
Prideaux, Humphrey, 357, 448, 461–2
Priestley, Joseph, 283, 397, 471–4
print media, distributed in coffeehouses, 254–5
prisca sapientia, 213, 217, 218, 220
prisca theologica, 213, 217, 220
Pritchett, Thomas, 406
Proast, Jonas, 386
Przypkowski, Samuel, 347, 397
Ptolemy's Almagest, 37
Pugh, Martin, 94, 99, 104–5, 288, 291, 292, 376
Purchas, Samuel, 349, 400, 406
Puritanism, 27, 66–7, 118, 119, 130, 131–7, 144, 175, 176, 193
Pyke, Isaac, 192
Pym, John, 126, 184, 191

Quakers, 135, 149, 229, 237, 240, 324–5
Quarles, Francis, 138
Quint, David, 408
Qu'ran, 94, 101, 103, 104–5, 108–9, 110, 111, 130, 137, 203, 274–5, 282, 286, 313, 340, 352, 382

Rabb, T. K., 179
Racovian Catechism, 137, 346, 390–1, 399–400, 462
Rahner, Karl, 79
Rais, Admiral Joseph, 288–9
Rais, Moerad (Jan Jansz), 289
Raj, Kapil, 168, 171
Rajan, Raghuram G., 140
Raleigh, Sir Walter, 138, 188
Ralph, James, 254
Ramsay, Chevalier de, 69, 278
Ranelagh, Katherine Boyle, Viscountess, 185, 197
Ranters, 137, 229
Rattansi, P. M., 190
Rauwolf, Leonhard, 127
Ravis, Christian, 189
al-Razi, Abu Bakr, 40, 44, 215
Reelant, Adriaan, 462
Reformation: Protestant, 53–61; Unitarian, 61–7
regicide, 127, 142

religious persecution, 84–6
religious tolerance, 126–8, 383–8
Renaissance: Italian, 44–6; medieval, 35–9
Renaissance Art, 47–50
Renan, E., 40, 425
Respublica Mosaica, 212–14, 218, 220–1
Restoration England, 236–41
Rieuwertsz, Jan, 389
Rightly Guided Caliphs, 109
Ritchie, S., 394
Robert of Chester, 37
Robertson, John, 90
Robinson, Henry, 156
Robinson, James, 140
Robson, Charles, 128, 159, 406
Rochester, John Wilmot, Earl of, 329
Roe, Sir Thomas, 146, 150, 151–2, 224, 308
Roger, King of Sicily, 38
Rogers, John, 402
Rosee, Pasqua, 246
Rosen, Lawrence, 102
Rosenthal, Franz, 102
Ross, Alexander, 252, 448
Ross, Richard, 193
Rota Club, 249–51
Rous, Francis, 184
Royal African Company, 192
Royal Society: and Arabic books/ manuscripts, 158–9, 208; and coffeehouses, 250–1; and Gresham College, 189, 191; and overseas trade, 172, 191–5, 221–2; and Samuel Hartlib, 185; and travel literature, 165; and Westminster School, 195–7
Ruar, Martin, 347
Rudolf of Bruges, 37
Russell, Alexander, 161
Russell, Conrad, 122
Russell, G. A., 303, 344, 352
Russell, Lord William, 234, 239
Russell, Patrick, 161
Russia Company, 144
Rycaut, Sir Paul, 160, 163, 167, 349
Rye House Plot (1683), 239

Sabians, 111
Safvid Empire, 49, 154
Said, Edward, *Orientalism*, 68, 222
Sale, George, 464

Saliba, George, 39
salvation: Christian, 81–2; Islamic, 101–5
Sand, Christopher, 347
Sanderson, John, 167
Sandys, George, 160, 167, 198, 199, 406
Scaliger, Joseph, 344
Schlichting, Jonas, 346
scholasticism, Islamic influence, 39–41
Scholder, Klaus, 398
Schroeder, John J., 226
science, modern: history of, 170–2; and the
    merchant community, 191–5
Scientific Revolution: and the Islamic world,
    168–79, 197; and overseas trade, 185–7
Scot, Michael, 38
Scott, Jonathan, 66–7, 120
Seekers, 229, 237
Selden, John, 138, 158, 205, 312, 325, 327,
    400, 403
Selve, Georges de, 47, 48
Servetus, Michael, 61–4, 69, 71, 175, 181,
    272, 275, 310, 393–8, 405
Setton, Kenneth, 56
's-Gravesande, Willem, 299
Shaftesbury, Earl of, 133, 172, 234, 235,
    237, 239, 243; and Arianism, 369–70;
    and coffeehouses, 253–4; influence
    on John Locke, 304; opposition to
    Catholicism, 304–5; and overseas trade,
    304; as Turkish infidel, 301–2
Shagan, Ethan H., 269
al-Shahrastani, Muhammad, 40
Shapin, Steven, 173, 192
Shapiro, Barbara J., 67–8
Shari'ah law, 106–7, 108, 110, 142
Shea, William R., 207
Sheldon, Gilbert, 198
Shelley, Percy Bysshe, 321
Sherman, Roland, 160
Sherwood Taylor, F., 207
shurah (rule by consultation), 106, 110
Sicily, Muslim rule in, 38, 41
Sidney, Algernon, 234, 238, 239, 326
Simon, Richard, 267, 335, 454
Siraj ud Daula, 153
Sirota, Brent S., 460
Sloane, Sir Hans, 208
Smaltz, Valantin, 346
Smith, Pamela H., 168, 178

Smythe, Sir Thomas, 59, 155, 186, 304
Snobelen, Stephan D., 217, 430, 431, 435, 436
Socinians, 135, 199, 389–98; and John
    Locke, 346–7
Socinus (Sozzini), Faustus, 389
Socinus, Faustus, 346
Sophia of Hanover, 331
Southwell, Robert, 247
Sozzini, Lelio Francesco Maria, 393
Spain, Muslim, 37
Spanish Armada (1588), 308
Spinoza, Baruch, 278, 389
spiritual alchemy, 210–12
Sprat, Thomas, Bishop, 175–6, 179, 215
Staehl, Peter, 251
Starkey, George, 216
Steele, Sir Richard, 196
Stillingfeet, Bishop Edward, 334, 367, 383,
    459, 462
Stoll, Abraham, 405
Strauss, Leo, 387
Stuart monarchy, overthrown, 255
Stubbe, Henry: and coffeehouses, 251–2,
    253; and Deism, 323–5; and English
    Civil Religion, 325–30; influence of
    Pococke and Shaftesbury, 303–5;
    influence on John Locke, 345–6;
    Islamic influences, 108, 111, 203,
    242–3, 307–9; and 'Muhammadan
    Christianity', 214, 278, 283–4, 469–71;
    on opium and chocolate, 247; quotes
    the Qu'ran, 282; radicalism, 255–7; and
    religious tolerance, 234, 327–8; and the
    Royal Society, 251; as Turkish infidel,
    301–2; at Westminster School, 196;
    *An Account of the Rise and Progress
    of Mahometanism*, 312, 313–20, 326,
    329–30, 345–6, 464
Stuijt, Simon Maartenszoon, 289
Suleiman the Magnificent, Sultan, 47, 48,
    52, 57, 60, 294
Sumner, Bishop Charles, 400
Supremacy, Act of, 117
Sweetman, John, 352

Tagliaferri, Filomena Viviana, 113
Talbot, Ann, 209, 347, 349
Tangier, 161
Tatian, 417

Tawney, R. H., 140
Taylor, Charles, 259, 264, 381, 383
Taylor, G. R., 190
"Teckelites", 301, 305, 308
Teckely, Count (Imre Tokoly), 301, 308
Temple, William, 344
Tenison, Thomas, Archbishop of
    Canterbury, 453–4, 459
Terry, Edward, 349
Test Act (1673), 467
Theodore of Antioch, 38
Theodosius, Emperor, 85, 429
Thevenot, Jean de, 167
Thirty Years' War, 59, 136, 174
Thomasius, 299
Tillotson, Archbishop John, 223–4, 265,
    369, 440, 460
Tindal, Matthew, 339, 346, 356, 467
Tinniswood, Adrian, 292
Tolan, John V., 284–5, 285, 344, 350, 351,
    352, 354, 394, 396, 397, 441, 462
Toland, John: and coffeehouses, 252;
    and the Gospel of Barnabas, 337–41;
    influence on John Locke, 346; and
    'Muhammadan Christianity', 213, 214,
    243, 283–4, 324, 339–44, 469–71; and
    natural law, 320; and New Testament
    Criticism, 335–6; politics and
    scholarship, 331–5; and Primitive
    Christianity, 336–7; *Amyntor: Or a
    Defence of Milton's Life* (1699), 335;
    Christianity not Mysterious (1696),
    333–5; *Nazarenus* (1718), 326, 331, 337
Toleration Act (1689), 467
Tombes, John, 134
Topinka, Robert J., 69
Transylvania, 60, 61, 115
travelogues, 164–8
Trevelyan, G. M., 440
Trevor-Roper, Hugh, 27, 332–3, 394
Trinitarian Controversy *see* Unitarian
    Controversy
Trinitarian theology, 32–4, 78, 79, 80, 81,
    90–1, 413–15, 429, 440
al-Tusi, Sadr, 195
Tyrrell, James, 238, 270, 347, 446

Ulema (religious scholars), 110
Umayyad caliphate, 110

Uniformity, Act of (1662), 117, 237
Unitarian Controversy, 442–3, 460
Unitarian Islamic syncretism, 270–1,
    278–9, 281–97, 309, 327, 342–4, 443,
    452, 473–4
Unitarianism, 34–5, 61–4, 69, 266–7,
    270–9, 277, 441–64
universities, medieval, Islamic model for,
    43–4
Ussher, James, Archbishop of Armagh,
    189, 194

Van Helmont, Francis Mercury, 319
Van Kley, D., 259
Vane, Sir Henry, 141, 234, 256, 319
Venice, and the Islamic world, 50–1
Vergennes, Comte de, 286–7
Verney, Edmund, 248
Verstagen, Richard, 58
Vienna, siege of (1529), 48, 52, 57
Virginia Company, 155
Vitkus, Daniel, 68, 166, 292
Vives, Joan Lluís, 112
vocabulary, of Arabic origin, 39
Volkel, John, 346
Voltaire, 260, 278, 398

Wadud, Amina, 106
Wainwright, Arthur, 371
Waldensians, 56
Waldron, Jeremy, 386
Waller, Edmund, 198
Wallis, John, 194, 195, 251
Walpole, Sir Robert, 120
Walwyn, William, 133–4
Warburton, William, 219
Ward, John, 288, 292
Watson, Foster, 190
Watt, W. Montgomery, 52
Watt, William, 153–4
Weber, Max, 23–7, 225
Weingast, Barry R., 140
Wellhausen, J., 108
Wesserstrom, Steven, 426
Westfall, R. S., 207, 209, 412
Westminster School, 195–6, 303
Wheelock, Abraham, 187, 199
Whiston, William, 212, 413, 437–8
Whitston, William, 397

Wilbur, Earl Morse, 403
Wildman, Major John, 133
Wiles, Maurice, 367, 370, 374, 413, 421, 437, 438
William III and Mary II, 116, 122, 241, 255, 334
Williams, Roger, 131, 132, 134, 319
Williamson, Sir Joseph, 192
Winstanley, Gerrard, 138
Winterbottom, Anne, 192
Wippel, John, 40
Wislon, Sir Thomas, 138
Wissowatius, Andreas, 347, 397
Wolf, Eric, 22, 27–8
Wolfe, Don M., 134
Wolff, Christian, 299
Wolzogen, John von, 347
Wood, Anthony, 329
Woodward, John, 190
Wooten, David, 366–7, 377, 387
Worthington, John, 352
Worthington, Samuel, 352
Wortley Montagu, Lady Mary, 320
Wotton, Sir Henry, 138, 198
Wren, Christopher, 196, 221, 251, 352
Wyche, Sir Peter, 129

Yahuda, Abraham Shalom, 425
Yates, Frances, 213, 217

Zagorin, Peter, 69, 126
Zápolya, King John Sigismund, 48, 301
Zenta, battle of (1697), 301
Zingales, Luigi, 140
Zuckert, Michael, 387
Zwingli, Huldrych, 53

Made in United States
North Haven, CT
16 November 2024

60386377R10407